THE EBBING OF EUROPEAN ASCENDANCY

THE EBBING OF EUROPEAN ASCENDANCY

An International History of the World 1914–1945

Sally Marks

Hodder Arnold

A MEMBER OF THE HODDER HEADLINE GROUP

First published in Great Britain in 2002 by
Hodder Education, part of Hachette Livre UK,
338 Euston Road, London NW1 3BH

www.hoddereducation.co.uk

© 2002 Sally Marks

British Library Cataloguing in Publication Data
A catalogue record for this book is available from the British Library

Library of Congress Cataloging-in-Publication Data
A catalog record for this book is available from the Library of Congress

ISBN 978 0 340 55566 8

6 7 8 9 10

Typeset in 10 on 12 pt Sabon by Cambrian Typesetters, Frimley, Surrey
Printed and bound in India by Replika Press Pvt. Ltd.

What do you think about this book? Or any other Hodder
Education title?
Please send your comments to the feedback section on
www.hoddereducation.co.uk

All the world's a stage
And all the men and women merely players:
They have their exits and their entrances,
And one man in his time plays many parts,
his acts being seven ages.

William Shakespeare
As You Like It, II, vii

CONTENTS

LIST OF MAPS

PREFACE

This survey of international history in the first half of the twentieth century addresses relations among states – and, on occasion, would-be states – and the factors affecting those relations and the power equation. It attempts to explain clearly what happened in international relations, why, and to what effect as it studies comparative power and how it shifted over fifty years, for comparative power is what matters most in international politics. The work examines which states had power and which did not – and what those with power did with it, often at the expense of those who lacked it. It addresses not only actual power but ebbing and potential power, touching on matters directly relevant to the international politics of the period or of a coming era – such as nationalism in colonies. In dealing with the interwar years, it seemed appropriate to use the historian's hindsight to focus on factors and events which would be significant for the post-war world – though these were not necessarily what was considered important by leaders at that time.

The book aims to provide a broad-brush global introduction to the international politics of the first half of the twentieth century, particularly 1914–45, for students, lovers of history, and other educated general readers, who can then go on to pursue what particularly interests them. It also aims to provide a larger world context for those focusing on a single continent, though some may be dismayed to discover that continent's placement in a fundamentally comparative global context where all is relative, at least in the power sense. A global approach has required a good many cross-references. If these do not suffice, readers should consult the index.

A survey of this nature is often criticized for its omissions – which are legion. If a 700-page text were feasible, most of these matters would be addressed. Indeed, many were included in initial drafts of chapters which often took longer to cut than to write, for preparing the manuscript became an exercise in compression, trying painfully to focus on what seemed most essential. Thus the book is merely a skeleton whose flesh must be supplied by more specialized works and/or professorial lectures.

In the circumstances, little space could be devoted to major historiographic controversies, and exceptions to generalizations could rarely be noted. It has also been necessary to accept that, China and Japan aside, in the period under discussion diplomatic activity was dominated by white men who gave little attention to cultural and social aspects of diplomacy, often ignored the role of propaganda, did not know or care what a non-governmental agency was (except for the Red Cross), and mostly assumed that women's role in international politics was confined to giving and attending soirées. Further, in addressing the shift of global power from

Europe westward to the United States and on toward the advent of a decol-onized world, I have found that a candid description of this progression sometimes collides with political correctness. While I have tried to accom-modate sensitivities wherever possible in these instances, I have consistently opted for the realities of power, as any honest international historian must.

It must be stressed that in using Shakespeare's seven ages of man to describe regions and individual countries, I am merely engaging in short-hand to help readers along and that *I am speaking only in terms of state power and broadly significant diplomatic activity, not in any other respect.* There is no intent to denigrate anybody. References to the baby Baltics indi-cate merely that, *as sovereign states*, if not in other senses, they were new, small, and weak. In saying that a political playbill would have listed African colonies as a flock of small children, I am merely noting that they were not independent and indicating how they were viewed at the time by those who held power, *not* suggesting childishness. Nor does indication that few Latin American states engaged in much diplomatic activity of global significance say anything whatever about that region's rich and varied culture and other desirable attributes.

In rendering names of people and places, the policy has been to use the most common English-language form of the era. Hence Adowa, not Adwa. Alternatives or later names are given in parentheses at first mention and not repeated unless that is absolutely necessary for clarity. As the book focuses on events before 1949, that holds true for Chinese names, which are rendered in traditional form with initial parenthetic Pinyin versions. With apologies to Canadians and Latin Americans, it has been necessary to use 'American' as an adjective and 'Americans' as a collective noun in regard to the United States and its citizens since there are no satisfactory short alter-natives.

This is a work of synthesis which owes a debt to hundreds of other works, many of which could not be acknowledged in the notes or bibliog-raphy. I apologize to those whose works had to be excluded because of space limitations. To avoid a lengthy and cumbersome scholarly apparatus, which is impractical in a survey, the notes are largely restricted to verbatim quotations. In a very selective bibliography, I stressed clarity and the most useful works even if they are not necessarily the most recent.

My heartiest thanks to Michael Jabara Carley, Xixiao Guo, Mary Karasch, Whitney Perkins, and Janice J. Terry, who read portions of the manuscript. I am immensely grateful for their copious comments, including those which I rejected – of course at my own risk. I am equally grateful to my friends in the historical profession who have sustained me through many travails and spurred me on. The book could not have been written without access to the facilities and services of the Rockefeller Library at Brown University, the Adams Library at Rhode Island College, and the Providence Public Library, both the central library and the Rochambeau branch.

Finally, I can scarcely find words to express my gratitude to Christopher Wheeler at Edward Arnold. His patience, encouragement, and unfailing support have been extraordinary, especially after chronic fatigue syndrome struck as I tackled the Russian Revolution and slowed my pace to a crawl, where it remained. There was never a word of reproach about slow, sometimes barely perceptible progress as the years slid by. Would that all editors were so helpful and understanding. Thank you, Christopher.

Prologue
EUROPE'S WORLD

Totus mundus agit histrionem.
[The whole world acts the actor.]

Motto, Proscenium Arch
Drury Lane Theatre, London
c. 1674

Above: Tsar Nicholas II of Russia and family with Queen Victoria of England and her son, later King Edward VII (Nicholas A. de Basily Collection, Hoover Institution.)

CHAPTER

1

DIPLOMACY AND THE STATE SYSTEM TO 1900

As the performers within a theatre are individual actors, the players on the world stage are sovereign states. Where domestic politics is a drama played out within a single state, international politics encompasses the relations and rivalries among independent nations. It is an unending struggle among a changing cast of characters for advantage and power or dominance.

The two possible relationships between sovereign states are war or peace. These are opposites but closely related. An old French proverb declares that 'peace is the daughter of war'; possibly the reverse is also true. As 'war is simply a continuation of political intercourse, with the addition of other means',[1] so peace is often war by other methods. Wars come in several varieties, chiefly small and large, limited and unlimited, but, except for civil or colonial clashes, always involve armed conflict between independent states. Definitions of peace are sadly negative, usually in terms of the absence of war, but peace has many gradations from armed truce or cold war through détente (reduction of tension) to rapprochement (harmonious relations) or entente (friendly understanding), formal alliance, and special relationship.

If two independent states are not shooting at each other, they will be talking to each other. The established form of international discourse is diplomacy, a term derived from the ancient Greek word diploma, meaning a folded document, especially as time passed one containing a solemn agreement between rulers. A diplomatist or diplomat is an individual authorized to negotiate on behalf of a sovereign state. Envoys (from the French, envoyé, one who is sent) represent a state in another country, protecting their state's interests, reporting on the other country, and promoting good relations, if such are desired.

Although diplomacy predates recorded history, Europe's diplomatic system, which became that of the world, arose along with the modern state system in the seventeenth and eighteenth centuries. It derived from Byzantine, papal, and Italian Renaissance practice, but was considerably developed by the French. As France became militarily and culturally dominant in the era of Louis XIV, French became the language of diplomacy and so remained until 1919, when English achieved parity. In a monarchic age, diplomacy was conducted by aristocrats representing one king at the court of another; it remained largely reserved to social elites through the first half of the twentieth century. And despite the prominence of female emissaries in very early history, modern diplomacy was an exclusively male preserve until after World War I.

Much diplomatic energy is devoted to negotiating, which is bargaining between countries. Since governments cannot easily retreat from their initial maximum demand in public, especially if they are responsible to parliaments, negotiation requires secrecy to succeed. The goal is usually to arrive at an agreement between or among states, though sometimes one state prefers to avoid coming to terms. If agreement is reached, it is embodied in a treaty or other international instrument. A treaty is the international equivalent of a contract between persons, and is binding in both domestic and international law.

When diplomats negotiate, they are pursuing the national interest or what is perceived as such by those who formulate policy. The national interest, sometimes called *raison d'état*, is what would be best for the state in question. As those who formulate policy are only mortal, they sometimes see only a narrow context, assume that what is will continue to be, confuse the short term with the long run, and mistake surface appearances for underlying realities; thus their policies do not always benefit the national interest. However, they *think* that is what they are pursuing.

The national interest is dictated primarily by geography, history, and economic needs, along with cultural assumptions and external conditions imposed by other players upon the world's stage. Safeguarding the state's independence, security, and integrity in territorial, political, and economic terms always comes first. Preserving freedom of action also matters. Diplomacy is used to strengthen the state in relation to others and to gain maximum national advantage without resort to force, preferably without causing much resentment. It is an alternative to war as a way of furthering the national interest and achieving policy goals. Diplomacy, whose weapon is words and which sometimes employs the threat of force, usually (but not always) seeks to preserve the peace, resolve issues between states, and reach agreement.

The diplomat employs a variety of tactics within a broad strategic plan toward policy goals which are largely dictated by the national interest. Some states have little policy beyond reacting to initiatives of others. Policies are sometimes driven by greed or temptation, especially that of weak neighbours, for nature abhors a vacuum in the international arena as in the physical world. Individual leaders, ideas and emotions, popular movements and domestic politics, attitudes toward the existing situation (or *status quo*), and the unexpected all affect policy to a degree, but only to a degree. Gradations of policy are limited by the fact that past history, geography, economic needs, and the external world usually do not change radically, and so the national interest does not change a great deal. Thus tactics toward goals are more likely to change than the goals themselves. Geography dictated that Britain be a naval power; Japan's lack of resources and arable land determined that it be a trading nation, importing food and raw materials, dependent upon its suppliers. And past history often generates assumptions and predilections, friendship or distrust, and progressive narrowing of options, thereby reducing a state's precious freedom of action.

How successfully a nation pursues its goals depends in part on domestic circumstances, luck, and the skill of both its leaders and its diplomats, but primarily upon the existing power configuration. Power is the primary and essential determinant in international politics, for power is what makes it possible to execute policy in competition with other states attempting to achieve their goals. What occurs on the world stage is usually a power struggle, whether in the form of a shooting war or the more veiled competition of diplomacy. As in wrestling matches, victory goes to the stronger and more skilful competitor.

Power comes in many forms, some of which have varied over time. Geography and climate can be an asset or a liability. Island nations, such as Japan and Britain, are difficult to invade. Russia has historically been impossible to conquer because it is so vast and General Winter has been such a faithful ally. Germany, however, has found being in the centre of a crowded continent with few natural boundaries a drawback. Switzerland is much smaller and equally in the centre of Europe but ringed by such high mountains as to be fairly secure. Population is significant in several senses. The sheer quantity, and the willingness to use it as cannon fodder, is relevant to power. The youth or age of a population and its birth-rate determine the size of future armies. In the twentieth century, as economic and military competition became more technologically complex, the skills of that population mattered. Its morale, nationalism, political stability and support to the regime became significant ingredients in a state's power.

The size, sophistication, and quality of a state's military establishment in terms of both troops and equipment contribute to national power. Economic strength is as important as military. Both basic resources and industrial might (including advanced technology) are forms of power, though possession of one without the other is limiting and creates vulnerability. Which resources matter most varies with time. Before the existence of civilian and military forms of automotive and air transport, coal mattered far more than oil. In the nineteenth and twentieth centuries, industrialization and technological innovation created dramatic power gaps between those possessed of superior weapons and the means to mass-produce them, and those dependent upon costly purchase or less sophisticated forms of military power.

Those who can afford advanced weaponry are better off than those who cannot. Money is an important form of power, and wealth can be used as a diplomatic weapon. Knowledge adds to strength, so a good intelligence service confers an advantage. Skilful propaganda can create influence and impressions, thus enhancing power and furthering policy. An ample food supply is an asset, as is anything creating self-sufficiency or assets to use against other nations. Dependency on others for anything essential is a drawback limiting a state's power. Colonies require defending and can be a burden, but the more desirable ones contribute to many of the components of power; strategic locations, such as those controlling the narrows between the world's oceans, confer an advantage. Unless it consists of undeveloped desert or impenetrable jungle, an empire may heighten power and can prop up an ageing, tiring imperial country.

Some states are stronger than others. That is a crucial fact, for power is always relative. What matters is not how much power a state has absolutely but how much it has in relation to other states. In describing the Peloponnesian wars of the fifth century BC, Thucydides remarked, 'What made war inevitable was the growth of Athenian power and the fear which this caused in Sparta.'[2] In relation to twentieth-century Uruguay or Thailand, Athenian power was slight, but it was comparatively threatening in its time and place.

Since power lies at the heart of international politics, those who lack it count for little. The role of small, weak states, unless mountainous or isolated, is usually to obey greater powers, especially those who will protect them from being swallowed by dangerous neighbours. At times, a small state possessed of a key commodity or a strategic location can command allies easily or, if endowed with sufficient nerve and skill, hold the great powers at bay or play them off against each other. Medium-sized states, especially if of the second or third rank, have more freedom of action. They often become regional powers, as the United States was in the nineteenth century and Japan in the twentieth. Regional powers are supporting players in the global theatre but prominent and strong enough to generate respect, fear, and often obedience from smaller neighbours.

The stars of the international drama are the great powers, whose interests are by definition global and whose reach often is as well. No great power is generously endowed with every element of power, but they all have much more than other states. Since power is relative, that suffices. At a given time, some will be ageing and satisfied, trying to preserve the *status quo* and retain what they hold. Others will be young and thrusting, seeking change and gain, a situation which tends to generate wars.

Although great powers are interested in everything and arrogate unto themselves the right to act anywhere or to make decisions affecting weaker states, they are usually reluctant to commit and use their power except in pursuit of their own national interest. Despite oratory to the contrary, altruism is rare in international politics. Various elements of power are employed in war and in peace to further the national interest and pursue policy goals, whether toward change or to counter it.

When the clash of goals between major states results in war, the outcome is likely to alter the power alignment, frequently adding to or subtracting from the ranks of great powers. The consequences and ramifications of such changes are so far-reaching that wars provide the punctuation marks of history. Since the power drive of lusty young states seems to be a fact of nature, keeping the peace is difficult unless the great powers are in rare agreement or precarious balance.

Fortunately, the interaction of the national self-interest of the several major states often produces the latter. Thus, the balance of power mechanism developed as the modern European state system emerged in the seventeenth century. Its goals were to preserve the independence and freedom of action of participants and to prevent domination of the European continent by one power or a group of powers. Preserving the peace was very secondary in an era when wars were small and did little damage. States combined against a threat of universal monarchy, as posed by Louis XIV, or divided into two competing blocs with smaller powers gravitating to the weaker side where they found greater freedom of action. The balance of power mechanism, a semi-automatic device figuratively resembling a see-saw, works best when there are a number of great powers and no ideological issue imposing rigid divisions among them.

* * *

So it was in the mid-seventeeth century when the five great powers of Britain, France, Austria, Prussia, and Russia emerged, all of them monarchic and aristocratic. So it remained two hundred years later. In the mid-nineteenth century, the five great powers were the same, still monarchic and aristocratic despite France's brief deviations into republics and despite gradations from British liberalism to tsarist autocracy. France and Austria, which had dominated the seventeenth century, were now tiring as Britain reached its prime, having led in introducing the significant new element of industrialization.

Fifty years later much had changed. Industrialization had marched across Europe from west to east (and across the New World in the opposite direction), transforming the continent and state economies and creating a world economy. The transportation and communications revolution wrought by the railway and telegraph along with technological innovation and mass production of more deadly weapons modernized warfare. Further, the legacy of the French Revolution and Napoleon had democratized and nationalized war, involving whole populations and economies. As nineteenth-century wars were generally brief, the full impact of the combined changes had not yet been appreciated.

Diplomacy was equally affected by the transformation of transportation and communications, together with technology and progressive political democratization. Earlier, the slowness of communication meant that an ambassador was largely cut off from his foreign ministry. In theory, this afforded him freedom of action; in practice, he often did nothing for fear of making a mistake. The telegraph meant he could report often and seek instructions; equally, the foreign minister could consult the ambassador. The telegraph and the typewriter meant that reports proliferated; foreign ministries and embassies swelled correspondingly. The advent of the penny press, thanks to new technology, and political involvement of the middle classes (and in some instances the masses) meant that foreign policy was no longer exclusively the preserve of foreign ministries, but increasingly affected by politics, public opinion, and other imponderables. Nonetheless, in a society which on the surface seemed still to enshrine the monarchic and aristocratic principles, diplomacy remained a career of the upper classes.

As the railway and telegraph shrank a small continent, there was a growing need for a co-operative approach to mutual problems. Even early in the nineteenth century, at the Congress of Vienna in 1814–15, the great powers who dominated it saw that it was in their interest to address common issues jointly, especially as they all wished to prevent a recurrence of Napoleon's attempt to become master of Europe. Thus they made notable contributions to international law, codifying the rules and ranks of diplomatic missions, establishing regulations governing international rivers, and creating an international commission to apply these to the Rhine. The great powers continued to meet thereafter in congresses to deal jointly with international concerns and crises. A growing divergence of interests between eastern and western powers soon brought the spectacular summits to an end, but the principle was continued intermittently throughout the nineteenth century in conferences of ambassadors meeting quietly, usually in London or Vienna, to address specific problems and by congresses again to the same end late in the century. The system, based upon certain tacit understandings and guidelines to ensure that no great power was either dominant or humiliated and that no great revolutions or major wars ravaged the continent, functioned on an erratic basis under the name of the Concert of Europe. This informal directory aimed at preserving the balance of power and the *status quo*, or, where necessary, at managing orderly change sanctioned by joint decision of the great powers.

The Crimean War was a departure from the system, but the treaty of Paris of 1856 furthered international law in several respects and applied the principles of Vienna to the Danube River. 1856 also brought creation of the Universal Telegraph Union as a permanent intergovernmental agency, followed in 1874 by the Universal Postal Union. Meanwhile in 1860 the Red Cross was founded as the first universally recognized non-governmental international organization. Others soon followed as the world became closer knit. At century's end, the Hague peace conferences of 1899 and

1907 further advanced the laws of war and peace. An internationalist spirit, typified by the Permanent Court of Arbitration, the International Association of Chambers of Commerce, and the International Law Association, developed along with a peace movement, but these remained relatively weak minority voices.

By 1900, there were important differences between the industrialized, democratizing west of Europe and the less advanced east. Yet the states and societies of Europe had much in common. Though France was reluctantly a republic, most were monarchic and aristocratic, and all were Christian. Further, the royal families and nobilities had intermarried heavily, a fact of some but declining diplomatic significance. This international elite and the educated classes across Europe shared a common cultural tradition and the French language. In the west, the emergent middle classes had gained prominence and power; everywhere, urban working classes were growing, organizing, and becoming restive. In the Second International, some labour groups were linked internationally. It was not yet clear whether ties of class would supersede those of nation, but everywhere in varying degree there was pressure from the bottom of the pyramid on the privileged top.

In the international arena, the Europe of 1900 was not that of 1850. There were now six great European powers, not five. The newest and least was Italy, united by a series of short wars. Lacking political stability, wealth, resources, arable land, and heavy industry, it was in truth more of a regional power but appreciably stronger than other European nations and thus admitted by courtesy to the concert of the mighty. The former weakest power was now the greatest on the continent as Prussia had swallowed the other German states (excluding Austria) to become the German Empire or Second Reich.* It is often said that when this occurred in 1871 the European state system suffered indigestion, which lingered until Germany was divided after World War II. Though the new German Empire remained militarily quiescent through the remainder of the century, a population explosion and industrial surge only accentuated the power imbalance caused by the creation of a state much stronger than the others at the centre of the continent. Practically speaking, the vaunted Prussian army was only enlarged by unification, and by 1900 the new Germany was building a major navy to challenge Britain's dominance of the seas.

Italy and Germany were unified (during a hiatus when the Concert of Europe did not function) at the expense of France and Austria, losers in the wars of unification. These dominant powers of the seventeenth century were now ageing and being overtaken by younger, more vigorous states. Defeat in the 1870 Franco-Prussian war meant that in 1871 France lost two provinces, Alsace and iron-bearing Lorraine, to the new Germany just as

---

* The First Reich was the Holy Roman Empire, the Second that of 1871, and the Third Hitler's regime from 1933 to 1945.

new processes made the mass production of steel economic. Thereafter, her industrial growth was slow and her population both stagnant and much smaller than that of the new Germany. Further, it was an older population and the birth-rate was low, portending more imbalance in the future. France was still a great power, possessing exportable wealth, industry, many colonies, and a large army and navy, but a power past her prime.

Austria, or the Habsburg Empire, was much weaker and had become Austria-Hungary, with both halves possessing a veto over major actions. Germans and Magyars became co-equal elites ruling an array of ethnic minorities which together constituted a majority. Driven out of its traditional spheres in central Europe and Italy, Austria's only remaining arena was the Balkan peninsula, where it competed for dominance and influence with Russia and what remained of the Turkish Ottoman Empire, which had been viewed throughout the nineteenth century as the Sick Man of Europe, propped up by the powers to avoid a war over the pieces if it collapsed. By 1900, the Habsburg Empire was increasingly seen as the new hospital patient. Both empires suffered from the same contagion: nationalism, which was pandemic in nineteenth-century Europe. Revolt of subject nationalities, which became squabbly independent Balkan states, had detached most of the Ottoman Empire's European realms. Now the Habsburg Empire's subject peoples were restive, often encouraged by other states, large and small. With a weak, under-equipped army, modest industry, no overseas domains, and a dissatisfied population, once-mighty Austria was becoming a regional power with an uncertain future.

To the east lay the Russian colossus, only half-awakened and half European, sprawling across the Eurasian landmass. It was industrializing at last, but on the whole still substituted its vast area and population for technology, skill, financial strength, and the other attributes of power which it lacked in quantity. Its decaying monarchic system and the pillars supporting it, especially the army and navy, were soon to be severely shaken by defeat and revolution in 1905. It possessed no empire but instead pressed steadily overland to acquire more territory or influence on several of its many borders, especially in the Balkans, south-west Asia, and Manchuria (Dong Bei), thereby clashing with Austria, Britain, and Japan.

At the other end of Europe and of the spectrum in most respects lay Great Britain, a power in its prime. Traditionally, it was a naval nation with a small army, accustomed to paying other powers to fight most of its battles on the continent. Historically, its parliamentary system and free press meant it was the most liberal of the great powers; it was also the most and earliest industrialized. It imported raw materials and food, and exported manufactured goods, capital, and 'invisible exports' (shipping, insurance, financial services), thereby relying heavily on world trade. Economically dominant and possessed of the ocean narrows, a global empire, and vast wealth, it had through the nineteenth century, as an island nation of but not in Europe, tended to play a lone and skilful hand, functioning as the fulcrum of the power balance and able to tip it as it pleased. However, as the century closed, Britain increasingly felt isolated and fretted about industrial and naval competition from Germany.

Thus Britain moved to repair relations with its eldest son. When the United States became a nation, it was probably a power of the third rank, but the first state outside Europe of concern to the great powers since ancient Carthage. A child of Europe, it accepted the European state system and its diplomatic norms without question, as did its younger sister republics to the south. In the thirty years after 1865, the United States spanned its continent and built its industry, largely preoccupied with these dramatic processes. It became a major industrial power but not one of decisive importance in world trade, since an immense domestic market absorbed most of a burgeoning production other than agricultural products. By the end of the nineteenth century, the United States was clearly at the top of the second rank despite accretions of power elsewhere, an important factor in both Atlantic and Pacific equations, and ready to move up to a major role on the world stage.

Despite its self-absorption, the United States had at mid-century played a key role in ending Japan's isolation from the rest of the world. Thereafter, the Japanese realized that unless they acquired power in European terms, they would be devoured. Not wishing to share China's fate as a target of occidental imperialism or to accept the humiliations imposed by tactless westerners who treated the 'little yellow men' as inferiors, Japan transformed itself with dramatic speed in thirty years, imitating the best European models: the German army, constitution, and industrial organization; the British navy, finance, and commerce; and French law, educational system, and social style. As 1900 approached, Japan, already known as the occidental of the orient, had reached the second rank in the hierarchy of nations and was clearly a regional power. Like the United States, it was ready to turn outward.

With an economy akin to Britain's, Japan imported raw materials and exported manufactured goods. Thus it was heavily engaged in the world economy. And by the end of the nineteenth century, there *was* a world economy, as economic activity had been nationalized by industrialization and new forms of transportation and communications, then progressively internationalized. From 1840 to 1870, an all-European economy developed, thanks in part to a liberal economic orthodoxy which decreed relatively free trade, with low tariffs and easy movement of goods and people, and economic internationalism in an era of rising political nationalism. New financial instruments and investment banks aided development, as did the gold standard. With major monies pegged to gold at fixed rates, currencies were stable and easily convertible at steady exchange rates, thus facilitating international trade.

Between 1870 and 1900, the European economy became global. The advent of steamships and marine cable networks played a role, as did American and Canadian transcontinental railways, the Calais to Constantinople line, the trans-Siberian railway, the Suez Canal and eventually the Panama Canal, completed in 1914 as the final key link in a world transportation system. So did the new prominence of Japan and the United States. A global demand for European goods was fostered by a vast migration between 1870 and 1914 out of overcrowded Europe, chiefly to the United States but also to Latin America, from European Russia to Siberia, and to the British Dominions, those 'white' elements of the Empire which, led by Canada in 1867, followed after 1900 by Australia, New Zealand, and South Africa, were granted self-government in purely domestic questions.

A world economy with a global market and uniform prices was also facilitated by the fact that London was the world's economic capital. Toward 1900, Britain's share of the global economy was shrinking, despite continued economic growth, because Germany, the United States, and Japan were claiming ever larger shares and because the disadvantages of having industrialized first were appearing, especially in the form of older equipment and less innovation than elsewhere. In this respect as in others, Britain's power continued to grow absolutely but declined relatively, thanks to new competition from younger economies with faster rates of growth. But Britain had long held a commanding economic lead. Thus it had unrivalled shipbuilding and shipping industries, dominated the carrying trade on the world's oceans, was the global commercial insurance centre, dominated telegraphy and marine cables, and provided the financial clearing-house which facilitated shipment of Honduran bananas to Sweden, American tobacco to Australia, British pots and pans to Calcutta, and French wines to Buenos Aires. Together with Paris, London supplied the loans, the export of capital, which fuelled economic development in eastern Europe and East Asia alike.

Another factor knitting the world together into a single economic and financial unit, which unfortunately underwent economic booms and depressions as a unit, was a renewed interest in empire, particularly in terms of actual possession and colonization rather than of trading posts and investment. The leading players, particularly France, had never abandoned the acquisition of empire altogether, but after 1870, and especially after 1885, the pace quickened dramatically, as the major powers, including Japan and the United States, competed to acquire colonies and protectorates in Africa and Asia, the Caribbean, the Middle East, and the Pacific island groups. The latecomers, notably Germany and especially Italy, had to settle for the leavings. As a consequence of what became a frenetic race, Europe came closer in thirty years to imposing servitude on the rest of the world than it had in the previous three hundred.

Occasionally, motives were economic, especially at first. Developed industrial economies demanded raw material and markets; they needed to export manufactured goods and capital, to invest profitably where fortunes could be made, and to import food for their urban masses. Other motives often mattered more. A wish to export surplus population sometimes came into play, as did psychological factors, such as France's need to salve a national ego bruised by the humiliation of 1871. Empires brought prestige and at least the appearance of much might. Developing power vacuums were a temptation as the major non-western and Spanish empires decayed. Strategic concerns played a large role: once Britain gained the Suez Canal and its direct route to India, it sought territories near the Canal to protect it. Balance of power considerations became important in the latter stages of the race, when European powers hastily grabbed chunks of African desert and jungle chiefly to keep them out of the hands of rivals.

As a result, Africa was swallowed up except for Liberia, effectively an American protectorate, and mountainous Ethiopia, where indigenous forces humiliated Italy at Adowa (Adwa) in 1896. In Asia, China, perhaps the world's oldest surviving empire, lost territory in the north and south, and in her cities suffered the indignity of having to accept 'treaty ports', extraterritorial foreign settlements existing by treaty outside the reach of Chinese law. China was the target of both direct annexation and indirect imperialism, which afforded Europeans influence and sometimes control while leaving indigenous rulers nominally in charge. This latter system, usually the result of excessive debt which led to occidental control of a state's finances and more, was used in dealing with the remnants of the Ottoman and Persian empires and to some degree in the Caribbean.

Not all imperial powers were European. In 1898, the United States stepped to centre stage and defeated Spain (Europe's only net loser), absorbing most of her Pacific and Caribbean islands, dominating the rest, and also annexing Hawaii. Thereafter, economic and strategic factors, plus the building of the Panama Canal, led Washington to turn the Caribbean into an American lake. Acquisition of the Philippines made the United States an Asiatic power, while commercial considerations caused it to participate in the complicated international politics of the China question.

Japan, too, demanded a share of the limelight and the booty. In 1895, it defeated China, gaining Taiwan (Formosa) and economic control of Korea (Chosen). It also took China's Liaotung (Liaodong) peninsula, but a Russian-led coalition of European continental powers forced it to disgorge this prize. Japan did not forget the humiliation, particularly Germany's peremptory tone. Russia sought Liaotung, including especially Port Arthur (Lüshun), to obtain a Pacific port which was ice-free all year round, and gained it briefly. But in the Russo-Japanese war of 1904–05, Japan decisively won not only the vast land battle of Mukden (Shenyang) but also the naval confrontation at Tshushima straits, and consequently absorbed

Russian rights in Liaotung and Manchuria, as well as taking half of Sakhalin and then Korea.

The European and European-derived powers were able to swallow the globe because there existed a large power gap between them and other areas, some not organized into states. The European countries had the administrative and economic systems, the masses of disciplined people, the wealth, technology, skills, and weapons to dominate. It is worth recalling that in the German language a distinction is made between *Kultur* (philosophy and the arts) and *Zivilisation* (technology). China sadly learned that its ancient and sophisticated culture did not suffice against the technologically advanced weaponry of Western civilization. African tribes who, unlike the Chinese, had not invented gunpowder were even more helpless against European firepower.

As European states sought colonies, at first there was plenty of room for them all. As more territory was swallowed up, however, the powers began to bump into each other, as Russia and Japan did in north-east Asia, Russia and Britain in Persia (Iran), Britain and France in Africa. This contributed to international tension, especially after Germany joined the race, and, as the world became a single strategic unit, European politics became world politics and strategy. The European great powers now had to think globally and consider the effect of their actions in one continent upon their interests in another. Thus international politics became more complicated.

So did international trade. It also became much larger. As demand for European products mounted in the non-Western world, global trade in manufactured goods doubled between 1900 and 1913, the majority of it carried in European ships. North and west Europe still accounted for over half the world's trade and produced the bulk of the manufactures despite the increasing importance of Japan and the United States. Colonial economies, geared to producing food and raw materials, were closely tied to what was usually but inaccurately called the mother country.

The accretion of power to the imperial overlords varied with the size, quantity and value of the acquisitions but was sometimes considerable. The British Empire, already vast in 1870, became 50 per cent larger, much of it strategically located. The French Empire, second in size to the British, gained much, especially in Africa. The United States, Japan, Germany, and even Italy gained an empire, though the Libyan desert was a liability and a drain on the new Italian kingdom. Despite the defeats of 1905, Russia managed to extend its influence elsewhere in Persia. And such small European states as Belgium, the Netherlands, Denmark, and Portugal gained or enlarged or at least retained an empire.

European domination of the world brought with it a degree of Europeanization, but only a degree. Western systems of economics, governance, and military organization were brought to subject areas along with aspects of Western culture. English and French became world languages;

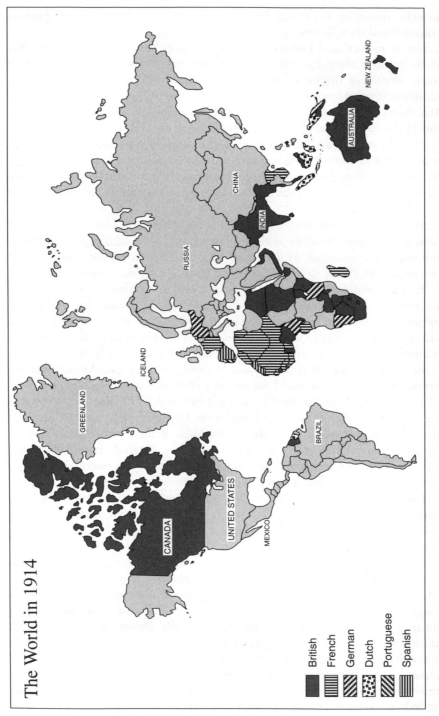

The World in 1914

■	British
☰	French
▨	German
▦	Dutch
▧	Portuguese
▥	Spanish

The World in 1914

missionaries spread Christianity both before and after the conquerors. Europeanization was always partial, especially where imperialism was indirect, and it was chiefly urban, varying according to the length and brutality of occupation, density of the indigenous population and strength of its culture, and degree of colonization. But by 1914, a veneer of Europeanization had spread across the globe, and the future leaders of Africa and Asia were being educated at Cambridge, the Sorbonne, Harvard, and Howard University in Washington.

Europeans thought the civilized world meant Europe and those countries which had inherited European culture, systems, traditions, and values. This view was not shared in Khartoum, Shanghai, and Amritsar. Europeanization was always countered by the hatred of subject peoples for arrogant overlords. In the eyes of indigenous populations, colonial status meant brutal and ruthless exploitation at worst, humiliation at best. Generally, their view of 'the blessings of civilization' brought (not always in any quantity) by Europeans and Americans in the form of schools, hospitals, railroads, and economic development was distinctly mixed.

To the colonies, Europeans exported modern conveniences, measles, institutions, and ideas, many of the latter brought by missionaries. In developing the economies in hopes of making the colonies profitable, creating administrative structures and schools, and training colonial armies to protect their holdings, European powers were providing their subject peoples with weapons which in time could be turned against the imperial overlords to end occidental hegemony. One of Europe's chief exports was ideas, most especially those of freedom, the rights of man, and above all nationalism. By 1900, these had taken root, including especially a nationalism which was sometimes already overtly anti-European. The Ethiopian victory at Adowa sent an electric thrill through Cairo. But Italy was known to be weak. However, when Japan's 'little yellow men' annihilated mighty Russia's imperial navy at Tshushima, Europeans were aghast with shock and cheers rang out in Indian cities, celebrating 'one for our side'. More importantly, Japan's triumph proved that non-Western peoples could master the West's strengths and use them to defeat the European powers, who were not impregnable after all.

But Japan alone borrowed from Europe in time to escape domination. The celebrations in Indian cities and Cairo coffeehouses expressed only hopes for the future. Meanwhile Europe ruled the world. It did so as if by natural right of inherent superiority, a view that subject peoples were not yet in a position to challenge openly. As Europe ruled the world, so, too, did Europe's upper classes rule the lower. In both instances, the ruled were restive and sometimes unruly.

Yet most of the turbulence was suppressible and suppressed. Much roiled and bubbled underneath, but on the surface there seemed to be a secure, settled order of things. Indeed, it was widely assumed that the international economy was so interlocking that a major war was improbable. Europe and America's newly rich industrial barons were incorporated into the old elites, often by marriage to impoverished aristocrats, but the era of privilege was at its peak, both within Europe and in relation to its empires. Europe possessed wealth, power, and stability. It was still economically dominant, though significantly the United States had already become the world's richest nation. Europe possessed great armies and navies and empires. Europe ruled the world, and the old elites ruled Europe, or at least reigned in style, as many of them had for centuries. When Edward VII of England died in 1910, his funeral was attended by nine kings, five heirs apparent, forty imperial or royal highnesses, seven queens, and flocks of minor German royalty. There was never another funeral like it, for the world it symbolized, Europe's world, was swept away by a single shot, which killed one of the heirs apparent, an event soon used to set off an explosion in the volatile Balkans. Five weeks later, the great European powers were in bloody collision, primarily in Europe but elsewhere as well. As they poured out wealth and lives, both European and colonial, against each other for more than four grim, blood-soaked years, this world which Europe had created became one of the casualties of the earth's first global war.

◆ Notes to Chapter 1

1. Carl von Clausewitz, *On War*, ed. and tr. by Michael Howard and Peter Paret, rev. edn (Princeton, NJ, PUP, 1984), p. 605.
2. Thucydides, *History of the Peloponnesian War*, tr. Rex Warner (Harmondsworth, Penguin, 1954), p. 49.

ACT I

EUROPE'S WAR

Mad world! Mad kings! Mad composition!
William Shakespeare, *King John*, II, i

CHAPTER

2

THE COMING OF THE FIRST WORLD WAR

There is little that historians debate more endlessly than causation, and certainly much ink has been expended in arguing the origins of World War I. In recent years, however, a degree of consensus has emerged, even among German scholars, that primary responsibility should be assigned to the Second Reich, though debate continues about German motives and intentions. It now seems clear that Germany's power, policies, actions, and diplomatic style provided a continual factor between its creation in 1870–71 and the great collision of 1914.

Germany's unification, coupled with its industrial and demographic growth, brought a young but very strong power to the centre of the European stage, hitherto a comparatively weak area. The power balance was at once implicitly altered. But Prince Otto von Bismarck, Chancellor of the new Germany until 1890, chose not to make this explicit in Europe or elsewhere. Preferring to build the Reich's institutions and industry, he restored the Concert of Europe, used it to settle quarrels threatening the peace and his new empire, and eschewed colonies.

Bismarck also tended to Germany's defences to protect its future. He had firm grasp of the inescapable geographic fact that it occupied the centre of the continent without defensible natural boundaries and had three great power neighbours. He knew his Reich was unlikely to triumph in a war against two of them. Hence the central task of Bismarck's diplomacy was to ensure that no two of these great powers combined against Germany. As France was unlikely to forgive its humiliating defeat in the Franco-Prussian war of 1870, this meant ensuring that Russia and Austria-Hungary remained at Germany's side despite their clashing interests in the Balkans. Through increasingly convoluted diplomacy, Bismarck managed this tricky task throughout his tenure, also adding Italy to Germany's allies.

By Bismarck's last years, however, keeping Russia and Austria in the same camp was becoming difficult and pressures were growing within the Reich to join the imperial race. Further, in a move predictive of future Berlin diplomacy, Bismarck tried to pressure Russia by refusing to list its bonds on the Berlin stock exchange. Like later German efforts to browbeat great powers, this had the opposite effect from that intended. Financial necessity and the decision of Bismarck's successors not to renew the Russian alliance sent St Petersburg into the arms of France. The latter, now in its Third Republic, had capital to export; Russia had the population for cannon fodder which France lacked; and both feared Germany's growing power. Austria and Italy remained tied to Germany by formal defensive treaties in the Triple Alliance or Triplice.

France and Russia also signed a defensive treaty in 1894. The impetus to further alliance-building came when Germany began to flex its new muscles and develop more. In 1897, the irrepressible young German Emperor (or Kaiser), Wilhelm II, announced that Germany was embarking on *Weltpolitik* or a world policy. Though initially aimed at China and colonies, this was always amorphous and undefined, an unfocused expansionism, but it often meant that when another power gained something, Germany demanded compensation. Then in 1898 in Damascus, Wilhelm declared himself the protector of the world's Muslims, most of whom were subjects of other European powers. Also in 1898, Germany, already the possessor of Europe's finest army, launched a major naval building programme, which alarmed London, and in 1899 it signed a contract with the Turkish government to build a railway from Berlin to Baghdad. Since railway construction offered many opportunities to acquire political and military as well as economic influence, the possibility now arose that Germany might displace Britain and France in the Ottoman Empire and thus in the Middle East.

Though Germany, chronically short of capital, offered financial participation in the railway to foreign powers, these moves were potentially or directly threatening to Britain, France, and Russia. Britain, offended by Berlin's vociferous support to South Africa's Boers as tension built toward the Boer war of 1899–1902, viewed Germany's *Weltpolitik* and naval programme as threats to its Empire and import-driven economy. Thus it reacted quickly in 1898 with the first of several overtures to Germany, all of which failed because Berlin was confident that Britain would never join its traditional enemies, France and Russia, and so Germany could wait to attain fully its steep terms for an arrangement and perhaps even an alliance against France and Russia.

After the initial failure to reach agreement, and with vital interests at stake, Britain hastened to solve its problems elsewhere so as to be free to face the new challenge. 'Splendid isolation' no longer seemed so attractive. In 1900, it conceded the future Panama Canal to the United States, moving toward a rapprochement of the English-speaking nations, and in 1902 it signed an alliance with Japan, which was initially directed partly against Russia. It also began to modernize the Royal Navy, which led to a naval race with Germany. Meanwhile, Britain's effort to acquire a north–south line of African colonies from Cairo to Capetown clashed with France's reach for an east–west string from the Red Sea to the Atlantic and had led in 1898 to a tense confrontation at Fashoda in the southern Sudan. Mindful of her own limited power and her burgeoning neighbour, France backed down. The confrontation cleared the air and led in time to the Anglo-French Entente Cordiale of 1904. This was not a formal treaty but rather merely the settlement of a series of colonial disputes, notably in North Africa, and an informal but historic willingness to be friends after five hundred years of hostility. Clearly, both states were responding to perceived threats from the new great power.

The Entente Cordiale had been negotiated but not yet signed when the Russo-Japanese war broke out, raising the possibility that Britain and France could be forced into war with each other by their respective allies. That did not happen, but the prospect occasioned further diplomacy, especially as France was eager to bring her two friends together. In addition, the destruction of the Russian fleet at Tshushima and the transfer of Russian attention after its defeat from east Asia to the Balkans made Russia seem less threatening to Britain whereas Berlin continued its blustering, browbeating diplomacy, notably during the first Moroccan crisis of 1904–05. Germany seemed to seek both domination of the European continent and parity with Britain elsewhere in the world and on the seas, thereby ensuring German pre-eminence, endangering British imperial lifelines, and negating London's long-standing policy of resisting the continental ascendance of any power. As a consequence, Germany now seemed the greater danger to Britain, who accordingly came to terms with Russia in 1907, ending long hostility and signing agreements about Tibet (Xi Zang), Persia, and Afghanistan. There now developed the Triple Entente (with Japan attached), an informal grouping of Britain, France, and Russia.

Although the old Concert was not quite moribund, all European powers of consequence were thus aligned in the two blocs, the Triple Alliance down the centre of Europe, and the Triple Entente on the edges. Germany saw the Entente policy of containment as encirclement, and its fears in this respect only increased 'the amalgam of insecurity and self-assertion in her make-up. . .'.[1] Thus its diplomacy became more bullying, which had the effect of driving Britain and France together, causing the Triple Entente to solidify. Both Germany's insistent claims and Russia's return from East Asia to compete with Austria in the Balkans contributed to growing conflict and tension between the two alignments.

*   *   *

Most of the conflicts concerned imperial matters although a European power struggle underlay them all. Part of the trouble was that the days when there were plenty of colonies available for everybody had passed, and as the powers bumped into each other, the latecomers were dissatisfied. Timing proved crucial to the imperial race; those who did not seize the moment encountered difficulties in doing later what other powers had done earlier. The latecomers were Germany, Japan, and Italy, impatient young-sters who remained dissatisfied, always seeking more until they went down to decisive defeat in World War II. But in the decade before the First World War, the collisions were not only in Africa and Asia, but also in the Balkans, as Russia turned to Austria's sole remaining sphere. Wherever confronta-tions occurred they brought with them the risk of a major conflagration, not merely a local conflict between two states, but a global struggle between two alignments of powers.

War among the major powers was avoided for a decade despite a series of crises, but only at the price of exhausting options and reducing flexibil-ity, thus rendering resolution more difficult for the future. Great powers, especially the more precarious ones, could not repeatedly accept defeat and humiliation and still remain great powers. Another option which several states exhausted was that of not supporting an ally. With Europe divided into two camps, both of which were arming briskly, retaining one's allies was vital. However, one can desert an ally only so often and still keep it as an ally. Equally, the need for allies meant that both crises and atonements for desertion tended to solidify the two rival alignments, further reducing flexibility.

During the decade before 1914 the Anglo-German naval competition continued, despite British efforts to come to terms, and crises, often entail-ing lack of support from allies or diplomatic defeat, were too numerous to recount briefly. Though all depleted the reservoirs of good will and elastic-ity, only a few were so serious that they brought the risk of a pan-European war. Nonetheless, the fact that Europe came to the brink of a great war five or six times in ten short years is indicative of the instability and tension which were mounting.

Part of the problem was that Europe's power system was increasingly out of balance. The Habsburg Empire was no longer really a great power, while France was fading in comparative terms. Russia's vast size did not fully compensate for technological and organizational weakness, especially after the regime was shaken by defeat and revolution in 1905, while at the other end of the continent, Britain's economic lead was less commanding than before. In the middle of Europe Germany was becoming comparatively something of a superpower, already dominant economically, especially in relation to its neighbours, and aspiring to a comparable political and world position. And this young, thrustingly ambitious Reich pursued a high-risk policy of confrontation which created or aggravated crises, contributing to ten years of international tension.

The first dramatic flashpoint arose when Berlin set off the first Moroccan crisis of 1905–06 in an unsuccessful effort to test and disrupt the new Entente Cordiale. Secondarily, Germany was not averse to gaining additional colonies or other compensation for acceding to France's consol-idation of her sphere of interest in Morocco, as had been agreed between

Paris and London in the Entente Cordiale. Paris had also gained the consent of Rome, which – unlike Berlin – had well established aspirations in the area. However, for Berlin, detaching Britain from France and humiliating the latter came first. Despite initial successes, Germany overreached itself and ended up with little, in part because Austria gave minimal support and Italy none. The United States mediated but did not endorse German claims. As the danger of war receded, Britain concluded that Germany was the greater threat. Thus it moved to détente with Russia and military talks with France, solidifying the Entente. Germany found itself isolated and concluded illogically that it must prop Austria up as a great power in order to have a major ally.

For this reason and because nightmares about encirclement made it feel dependent on its only reliable ally, Germany backed Austria-Hungary in the next truly dangerous crisis, which occurred in the Balkans. In 1897 Austria and Russia had agreed to end their Balkan rivalry; in 1908, an effort to extend their collaboration abruptly ended it. Negotiations had been in progress between their two foreign ministers toward Austrian support for Russian naval access to the Straits from the Black Sea to the Mediterranean (through the narrows known as the Bosporus and the Dardanelles) and toward Russian support to Austrian annexation of Bosnia-Herzegovina, Turkish territory which it already occupied and administered. But in 1908 the Young Turk revolution heralded reform in the Ottoman Empire, so the Austrian foreign minister invited his Russian counterpart to his castle and arrived at a vague oral agreement with no mention of a timetable. To Russian dismay, Austria promptly proclaimed the annexation of Bosnia-Herzegovina. St Petersburg had not lined up other powers toward Russian passage at the Straits; Britain and France were much opposed. Serbia was enraged at the annexation of an area which it coveted and which had a large Serbian population; it demanded part of Bosnia-Herzegovina as compensation. War seemed likely, but both Austria and Russia hesitated, mainly because their respective allies blamed them, provided no military support, and worked for a settlement. Mindful of the need to avoid Austrian humiliation, Germany proposed a formula which amounted to an Austrian victory. Russia, still weak after the lost war and the revolution of 1905, had to accept defeat and abandon Serbia, which also had to back down. The episode led to a greater German commitment to the Habsburg monarchy and to the idea of an Austrian attack on Serbia, as well as a more anti-Serbian policy in Vienna. The Entente also consolidated, for Russia clearly needed allies while Britain and France were ashamed of their lack of support.

Before the Balkans could explode again, Germany set off a second Moroccan crisis in 1911, trying again to browbeat France into submission. French activities in Morocco gave Berlin a pretext to demand that France transfer the vast French Congo (Congo) as the price of German acceptance of French control in Morocco. There was a war scare, for all Europe saw Germany as too aggressive in European terms and thought it also sought a continuous central African empire linking its east and west African colonies. Britain conveyed a warning through diplomatic channels, reinforced by a speech by David Lloyd George, then Chancellor of the Exchequer. Not even Austria backed Germany, which had thus to settle for a slice of the French Congo. For the nonce, the British concept of a balance of power had prevailed over Germany's drive toward European hegemony. But the crisis led to a fateful Anglo-French naval agreement whereby the French fleet would concentrate in the Mediterranean and the Royal Navy would cover France's North Sea coast, which effectively tied Britain more closely to France. Equally significantly for the future, Germany noted that Austria was not a reliable ally unless its own interests were engaged.

Also in 1911, Italy attacked the Turkish provinces of Libya (with prior consent of the powers) and seized the Dodecanese Islands, defeating the Ottoman Empire quickly, though the Libyans proved difficult to subdue. Because Turkey was thus preoccupied and seemed such easy meat, the Russian-sponsored Balkan League attacked in October 1912. Russia was pursuing the Straits, as always, but lost control of its clients. Within a month, Turkey was defeated and lost its European realms except Constantinople (Istanbul) and environs. The Sick Man of Europe had died, and a large war over the corpse seemed likely, but Austria and Russia both acted with restraint. The Concert of Europe, acting through a conference of ambassadors in London, patched together a peace, which did not last because Serbia was determined to gain an outlet to the sea while Austria and Italy equally intended to create an independent Albania in the same territory. However, Russia curbed Serbia sharply and forced its evacuation of the disputed districts.

In 1913, a second Balkan war occurred over the spoils of the first. Bulgaria, Austria's client, attacked Serbia, and was promptly defeated, partly because Germany and Italy kept Austria from substantial aid to Bulgaria. There was a new crisis over Albania, another Serbian refusal to evacuate the disputed territory, more negotiations in London toward what proved to be the Concert of Europe's last success, and an Austrian ultimatum to Serbia. Again lacking any Russian support, Serbia had to yield and Albania became an independent state.

Yet Serbia was for Russia an essential ally, both in nationalist terms if Russia was to retain leadership of the pan-Slav movement and pose as big brother to all the Slavs, and in strategic terms if Russia was to break the Austro-German barrier forming through the Balkans and gain access to the Mediterranean. Moreover, it was doubtful whether a precarious Russian regime could sustain any further defeats and humiliations. It had to promise Serbia that there would not be another desertion and even that Serbia's future lay in Hungarian territory. On the other hand, despite some benefits from an apparent victory, Austria-Hungary was weakened. It had not wanted the demise of European Turkey. Vienna was losing clients and its new one had been severely mauled. Serbia was now larger, partly because German support to Austria had been distinctly limited, but still without an outlet to the Adriatic and very angry. The Balkan wars did not set off a pan-European war because the great powers, especially Germany and Russia, were not yet ready, but many options were expended in keeping the peace.

The Balkan wars effectively removed Turkey from Europe. Thus, Austria and Russia and their respective clients confronted each other directly in the Balkans. As a result as well, the Balkan states shifted their attention from the Ottoman Empire to the Habsburg Empire, aiming to liberate subject brethren from Austrian rule. For these reasons, the third Balkan crisis proved to be catastrophic. From the viewpoint of the region's inhabitants, what eventuated in August 1914 was a third Balkan war. For the rest of Europe, it quickly became something else altogether.

In the chanceries of Europe, a major war was anticipated before long. Some leaders thought that sooner rather than later would be more advantageous for their countries. All assumed that a pan-European war would be short – for economic and technological reasons. But despite the decade of crises and mounting tension, the situation seemed more serene in 1914. In particular, Anglo-German relations appeared improved. The two countries had worked together at the conference of ambassadors in London in 1913 to prevent an Austro-Serbian war, though the German calculation and hope was that if war came, Russia would be blamed and Britain would remain neutral. But that was not public knowledge. However, the citizenry did know that there had not been a major European war for a hundred years; collisions between the great powers had been short and snappy, especially since mid-century, and the last one had occurred nearly 45 years before. A widespread assumption had developed that wars were something which occurred only overseas or in the backward Balkans among quarrelsome infant states. Even Anglo-German naval relations were now less tense, and in July of 1914 the two countries reached an agreement about the Berlin to Baghdad railway. For these and other reasons, the prospects for peace looked better than in the recent past as the spectacularly beautiful summer of 1914 opened.

*   *   *

The sunny calm was shattered on 28 June 1914 by the assassination of the heir to the Austrian throne and his wife in Sarajevo, the capital of Bosnia, by young Bosnian nationalists backed by Unification or Death,* a secret Serbian society in which key Serbian army officers were dominant. Their complicity is clear; members of the Serbian cabinet may have had partial

---

* Popularly known as the Black Hand.

foreknowledge as well. The chanceries of Europe anticipated an Austrian reaction directed against Serbia, whose involvement was widely assumed, but not a major war. However, the assassination led to the July crisis of 1914, culminating in World War I.

In Vienna, where those favouring war were dominant despite Hungarian hesitations, key leaders felt that Austria could not endure any more Serbian provocations. Its status as a great power, its traditional role in the Balkans, and its survival as a single multinational entity in an intensely nationalistic era seemed at stake. It was easy to blame Serbia for Habsburg failure to solve the nationality problem and, as against Piedmont-Sardinia in 1859, to seize the chance to put an end to a pest. War might solve both diplomatic and domestic problems and curb the appetite of other Balkan neighbours for Habsburg territory. But war against Serbia would entail the risk of war against Russia and perhaps its allies. Thus Vienna hastened to consult Berlin.

Powerful voices in the German capital also favoured war, again partly for domestic reasons, for an aggressive foreign policy had long been used to uphold conservative monarchism against democracy and to concoct a coalition against the Social Democratic party. There was real concern about Austria's survival as a great power and as an entity. Since the Entente was visibly peaceful, those urging war expected that it could be localized, embroiling Russia but probably not France or Britain, though the chancellor and other top leaders recognized from the outset that war against Serbia might lead to a world war.[2] Nonetheless, the German generals agreed with Bret Harte's axiom:

Blest is the man whose cause is just;
Thrice blest is he who gets his blow in fust.[3]

They thought the timing favourable, more so than in the future when Russia would be stronger. And military considerations were particularly important in view of their existing war plans.

When the Franco-Russian alliance had forced the German General Staff to face the prospect of a two-front war, it had devised the Schlieffen Plan, named for the army chief of staff who created it. This was and remained the German army's *only* detailed war plan. Its purpose was to avoid the two-front war by dealing separately with France and Russia, one at a time. The plan assumed Russia's mobilization would require some weeks because of the country's vast size and underdeveloped rail net. Germany would use those weeks to throw most of its army across the plains of Belgium (whose supposedly 'chocolate soldiers' were expected to melt at once) into northern France. There they would sweep the coast, seizing control of the Channel ports, push south, encircle Paris, and force the French army to surrender within six weeks. Then Germany would use its interior lines and excellent railways to ship its forces east to face Russia.

The plan rested on several assumptions and a tight timetable. But France was rearming and had instituted a three-year term of military service to compensate for demographic inferiority. Russia was not only building strategic railways at France's behest as the price of French loans but was also in the process of military revival, reorganizing and increasing its army after the defeats of 1905 and the humiliation of 1908–09. These factors could affect the Schlieffen Plan's prospects, and army leaders expected the military balance of power to shift against Germany within two years. Indeed, military and civilian leaders, together with the Kaiser, had debated a preventive war in December of 1912 and the spring of 1914 and the chief of the German staff, like his Austrian counterpart, strongly favoured war. As the debate was renewed after the Sarajevo assassination, on 2 July the Kaiser wrote, 'Now or never' in the margin of a document,[4] siding with the army against the diplomats. 'Now or never' quickly became the German watchword.

Thus when an Austrian official arrived in Berlin a few days later, both the Kaiser and the Chancellor, Theobald von Bethmann Hollweg, assured him of full German support for an Austrian war against Serbia, even if Russia should intervene, and urged immediate action.[5] With this 'blank cheque' in hand, the Austrian government drafted an ultimatum to Serbia. Thereafter a lull set in, partly because half the Austrian army was on harvest leave and partly because President Raymond Poincaré and Premier René Viviani of France were embarking upon a state visit to St Petersburg. Austria preferred to await their departure, so that they would be at sea when the crisis erupted, and Russia would be unable to consult the leaders of its essential ally.

One hour after the French leaders sailed from St Petersburg, the Austrian ultimatum, which Berlin had seen in advance, was presented in Belgrade at 6 p.m. on Thursday, 23 July. It carried a 48-hour deadline and was given to other governments and the press the next day, startling both public opinion and chanceries, which had been lulled by nearly a month of inactivity and ostentatious holidays by German leaders. The British foreign secretary termed the ultimatum 'the most formidable document I have ever seen addressed by one State to another that was independent'.[6] A week later, Europe was on the brink of a world war as the crisis suddenly moved with breathtaking speed and events outstripped the ability of leaders to control them.

Serbia mobilized its army on 25 July and just before the deadline presented a conciliatory and skilful reply, accepting most of the Austrian demands. Without bothering to read it carefully, the Austrian envoy broke diplomatic relations and within half an hour was on the train to Vienna. When Kaiser Wilhelm saw the Serbian response on the 28th, he said that 'every cause for war has vanished'.[7] But German officials, who had already urged Austria onward and rejected British efforts to revive the Concert of

Europe toward either mediation or a conference, delayed his moves toward conciliation. In fact, Austria declared war on Serbia on 28 July and proclaimed a partial military mobilization. Both its chief problem and its chief reason for war were encapsulated in its mobilization order, which was issued in 15 languages.[8]

Although German military leaders wanted war now, before the military balance of power shifted, it was not the same war that Austria wanted. The Habsburg Empire was intent on a local war against the Serbs, preferably without Russian involvement, and wished to concentrate the Austrian army against Serbia. Germany sought its own version of a local war, mainly versus Russia, and angled for a Habsburg troop commitment against the Russian army. By 28 July Germany had accepted the prospect of a continental war against France and Russia, but not a world war. Thereafter German efforts were bent to gaining the best position, keeping Britain neutral, and seeing to it that Russia would be blamed.

German thinking about British participation, which would entail a world war fought on and beyond the seas as well as in Europe, was erratic and contradictory. Germany did not want a world war and so convinced itself, off and on, that Britain would not fight. The generals, most of them eager for war at once, anticipated British participation but thought it unimportant. The diplomats anticipated it as well but thought it crucial and tried to prevent it. The politicians, who made the final decisions, exerted themselves to keep Britain neutral, and acting on the principle that what needs to happen in fact will, convinced themselves that British neutrality was likely.

Britain, upon whom the crisis had burst without warning, was on the brink of civil war in Ireland, which was one reason German leaders adduced for its probable neutrality. When news of the Austrian ultimatum arrived, on 24 July, London bent its energies toward delay, mediation, and trying to prevent even a local war – because any war was likely to spread and grow. The Cabinet remained divided and reluctant to make a military commitment, but nonetheless on 29 July London warned Berlin that British neutrality was unlikely. Thus far France had been largely a bystander, though backing all mediation efforts, as her leaders were absent until the 29th.* However, the French ambassador to Russia, acting on his own initiative, had urged Russian firmness and promised French support, ignoring instructions to caution St Petersburg.

Like Britain and France, Russia sought delay and to prevent war while lending cautious, partially restraining support to Serbia, far short of a blank cheque. But after many years of strong words and weak actions as well as

---

* Since radiotelegraphy was in its infancy, at sea Poincaré and Viviani received only brief garbled messages transmitted from the Eiffel Tower. Upon arrival in Stockholm, they learned the seriousness of the crisis, cancelled their other Scandinavian state visits, and arrived home on the evening of the 29th.

repeated desertions of Serbia, the council of ministers judged that a partial mobilization was necessary if Russia was not to lose great power status, leadership of the pan-Slav movement, and all authority and prestige in the Balkans. But it notified Germany that this would occur only against Austria and only if the latter invaded Serbia.

After this message had arrived in Berlin and after Austria had shelled Belgrade (which lay directly across the Danube from Habsburg territory) on 29 July, there ensued confusing struggles over military mobilization in both St Petersburg and Berlin. Amid French statements that no promises would be made and German demands to cease military preparations, Russian leaders engaged in a tug-of-war to push the tsar to partial or full mobilization. To a degree, Russia was prisoner of its military plans, though not as fatefully as Germany. The initial decision for partial mobilization had been made without realization that Russia had no plan to mobilize against Austria alone (as that had seemed so unlikely), that attempting to do without a plan would be chaotic in view of the organization of the Russian army and could even inhibit defensive action against Austria, and especially that partial mobilization would endanger a full mobilization and future offensive operations, should either be needed.[9] The pressure, especially from the generals, for a full mobilization was strong, but the tsar was reluctant. Finally, on 30 July he accepted a general mobilization to be proclaimed on the 31st.

In Berlin, the military leaders also sought immediate general mobilization, but Bethmann Hollweg delayed, seeking British neutrality and an opportunity to blame Russia. Finally, he agreed that if no word of Russian mobilization had arrived by noon on 31 July, Germany would proceed to full mobilization. Word arrived at 11.55 a.m., whereupon Germany sent an ultimative enquiry with an 18-hour deadline to France about whether it would remain neutral in a Russo-German war and an ultimatum to Russia, requiring suspension of all military measures within twelve hours. This was meant for rejection, as it was both politically and technically impossible, and Bethmann recognized that Russia did not intend war.[10] Beyond a lingering hope of British neutrality, his concern was to put Russia in the wrong and to rally German opinion for war.

Russia pointed out the impossibility of meeting the German demand but promised no provocative action. Germany and France proclaimed general mobilization virtually simultaneously on 1 August, Austria having done so the day before. France, however, carefully withdrew her forces 10 kilometres (6 miles) from the frontier to prevent incidents. Much has been made of the fact that Russia mobilized first, but the German mobilization was the crucial one. The Russian army could mobilize and sit indefinitely behind its frontiers, doing nothing, as could the Austrian and French armies, but because of the tight time constraints of the Schlieffen Plan, the German general mobilization constituted a decision for immediate continental war.

So it proved to be. Germany declared war on Russia on 1 August. That afternoon, it told France that if she chose neutrality, she must surrender her chief eastern border forts to guarantee it. Whether Germany meant to force French neutrality or a French declaration of war is in dispute. At any event, Viviani merely replied that 'France would act in accordance with her interests',[11] and proceeded to mobilization. The next day, in view of the existing Anglo-French agreement on naval dispositions, Britain notified France and Germany that it would not countenance hostile naval action against the French coast or in the English Channel, which constituted British home waters. Germany promised to refrain from such action. More importantly, the British cabinet decided that German violation of Belgium would force British intervention. Not only were all the great powers except Italy committed by the 1839 treaties creating Belgium to defend its independence, territorial integrity, and neutrality, but London had for centuries resisted any great power domination of the Low Countries facing Britain across the Channel.

That evening, 2 August, Germany delivered a 12-hour ultimatum to Brussels, demanding troop transit through Belgium in violation of the 1839 treaties. On 3 August Belgium rejected it, upholding her treaty commitment to defend her neutrality. Germany responded by declaring war on France, as effectively dictated by the Schlieffen Plan's tight timing, while the British Cabinet decided upon an ultimatum to Germany to honour Belgian neutrality. Also on the 3rd, Germany both gained and lost an ally. It achieved a treaty with Turkey, but Italy, whose allegiance to the Triple Alliance had long been doubtful, opted for neutrality, noting that Austria and Germany were the aggressors and thus the defensive Triple Alliance did not apply.

On 4 August, Germany invaded Belgium. The British ultimatum was to expire at midnight Berlin time, 11 p.m. London time. Earlier, Bethmann Hollweg indicated that Germany would not comply. Thus at 11 p.m. Britain issued its declaration of war against Germany, bringing the global conflict that Bethmann dreaded. Two days later, Austria-Hungary declared war on Russia, and on 12 August Britain and France declared war on the Habsburg Empire. Thus, Triple Entente and Dual Alliance (or Triplice minus Italy) collided in the First World War, during which the two blocs were renamed the Allies and the Central Powers.

When Bethmann Hollweg told the British ambassador on 4 August that Germany would not honour Belgian neutrality, he complained that 'just for a scrap of paper, Great Britain was going to make war on a kindred nation. . . .'.[12] That same day in addressing the Reichstag, he publicly acknowledged Germany's violation of the scrap of paper, but added, 'Necessity knows no law!'[13] Although this dictum was hardly the accepted criterion for the conduct of diplomatic relations among European states in peacetime, it became the norm in the course of a long and brutalizing war for supremacy and then survival.

*   *   *

In the intricate chain of events culminating in the Great War, there is ample room for allotting some degree of responsibility to all concerned. Everywhere in varying extent, there existed timidity, miscalculations, panic, and mediocre leaders. Indeed, most powers of the first rank were led by men of the second rank or worse. Each nation made mistakes, but some mistakes mattered far more than others. For example, we now know that Russia would have been wiser to delay its mobilization, but that would have had more effect on the historical debate than on events.

In addition, the actions of some countries mattered more than others in bringing on a world war. Those of Italy mattered little. In the July crisis, those of all three Triple Entente states were clearly largely reactive, not of themselves causative. Austria's actions played a substantial contributory role, and the Habsburg monarchy is usually assigned secondary responsibility for causing World War I, but only secondary, because Austria's actions were obviously contingent. It is beyond serious doubt that it would not have acted against Serbia or risked war with Russia without solid German support. Berlin not only gave that support and repeatedly urged Austria on but also decided upon war now and declared it against Russia and France without any direct provocation from either. A leading German scholar of the July crisis has concluded that 'the German Government opened Pandora's box in an act of sheer political and ideological despair'.[14]

One must ask what brought the European continent's strongest power to such despair and created a situation where it almost desperately opted to set off a continental war with the risk of world war. Some of the answers lie within German domestic politics and the psychological frame of reference of its leaders. Additional answers lie, as do the contributory errors from other powers, in broader aspects of the European scene in 1914.

For example, there were both men and nations which could ill afford to back down. Too often in the past, the Russian foreign minister, his Austrian counterpart, and the German Kaiser had all displayed timidity, hesitation, and reluctance to commit themselves to firm action. Kaiser Wilhelm in particular was determined to prove that he was not a coward, and, like the Russian foreign minister, he was rather unstable. Similarly, it was doubtful whether the Austrian and Russian regimes could survive major diplomatic defeats. Austria was internally so precarious and Russia had sustained so many recent humiliations that disintegration of the one and revolution in the other were real possibilities. This factor loomed large in the calculations of leaders in Vienna, St Petersburg, and Berlin. Paris concentrated more on retaining its Russian ally. Moreover, the intensity of public opinion in most countries made backing down almost impossible for weak regimes and politicians who wished to retain office. Under the circumstances, it was easy to hope that a strong stand would deter others and solve the problem.

The stronger great powers feared that their allies would cease to be great powers and, to varying degrees, felt a need to bolster them. There was also a widespread fear of losing an ally altogether. Both Britain and France had worried in past crises about losing Russia: France because she compensated for her own deficiencies with the Russian tie, Britain from fear of adding Russia to its enemies. Austria and Germany feared losing each other: Austria because its need was great, Germany from a sense of isolation. Both France and Germany worried that Russia and Austria would fight only if their own interests were involved. Each concluded that it was better for war to come on an issue where the ally's concerns were directly engaged.

Most states feared losing prestige and great power status. This was of intense concern to Austria and Russia, and in both instances was focused primarily on the Balkans, which impacted on domestic concerns and where the situation had changed so rapidly with the removal of Turkey. Yet dread of the results of backing down was widespread and extended even to Britain, master of the seas and of the world's greatest empire. On 31 July 1914, a senior British official argued for action by saying, 'The theory that England cannot engage in a big war means her abdication as an independent state. . . . A balance of power cannot be maintained by a State that is incapable of fighting and consequently carries no weight.'[15]

Threats to prestige, authority, and vital interests were almost universally perceived. Britain had long recognized a German challenge on and beyond the seas; the invasion of Belgium seemed to be striking at the British heartland. France, aside from other considerations, could hardly hand over her border forts without becoming a defenceless laughing stock. Russia felt its future in the Balkans and among the Slavs was at stake. Austria saw Serbia as a danger to its very existence, whereas Germany perceived a Russian threat and perhaps was as obsessed by Russia as Britain had been in the mid-nineteenth century and the United States would be in the mid-twentieth century. Clearly, some threats were more real and immediate than others, but leaders acted upon their perceptions, even if erroneous.

Nationalism, whether unifying or divisive, and imperialism contributed to the crises and tensions of the pre-war years, if they did not themselves directly cause the war. And certainly Austria-Hungary's ageing, archaic multinational empire, trying to maintain itself against mounting nationalist pressures, was a major contributing factor, as was the Austro-Russian rivalry among the infant national states of the Balkans. The pre-war arms race contributed to the international tension of the era but of itself was not a direct causal factor, despite the beliefs of a later generation, particularly of Americans.

More important, probably, was a widespread pseudo-Darwinian view of international politics, an assumption that it was a question of dog eat dog with the strongest and speediest dog surviving. Furthermore, crises had become the norm, so much so that some leaders expected war before long. Especially in Germany, there was a belief that war and Darwinian struggle were unavoidable, which perhaps explains the preoccupation with an assumed Russian threat and a fatalistic view that a Russo-German war was inevitable soon. Nowhere was there any awareness of what a war would be like; as a result there was scant caution about the dangers war would bring. The short war illusion was widespread and had contributed to the arms race on the assumption that the war would be fought with what equipment one had at the outset. The businessmen would see to it that the war was brief (if they did not prevent it altogether, as some believed, but not those determining national policies). Few in power had much appreciation of what the industrialization, nationalization, and democratization of war signified. Indeed, it was widely held that war was good and glorious and cleansing.

In some countries, military men and military plans played a considerable role. The military plans were rigid, too few in number, and had tight time-tables; the military men were wedded to them. The generals tended to be more eager for war than the civilian leaders; even where they were not, there was a fear that any delay in mobilization would be catastrophic. Initially there was often lack of co-ordination between civilian and military leaders, thanks to administrative inadequacy at the top, especially in Germany and Russia, and then tugs-of-war ensued, particularly to sway the autocrat. At a more fundamental level, appreciations in various countries of the military balance of power, then and as it would be in the future, clearly contributed to the pressures toward war.

The alliance system did not of itself cause any war, local, continental, or world. But it constituted a substantial reason why a local crisis became a world war, and partially explains why a murder in Bosnia caused Germany to invade Belgium and why that event in turn led to a world war, with Japan occupying Germany's Asian colonies. This is particularly true in view of the suddenness and speed of the crisis. Peace movements collapsed, and little time was left for diplomacy. Furthermore, previous crises had made the alliances more rigid. Europe had managed to edge past the abyss repeatedly in recent years, but only at the price of expending options and losing flexi-bility. Now governments felt they had few choices left.

Each power acted according to its perceived national interest. All the major powers felt threatened; the fact that all the older powers dedicated to the *status quo* were weakening, at least relatively, only increased the sense of danger. Austria, like Germany, felt deeply threatened at home, and Serbia seemed a menace to its survival. Russia felt much the same about the Austrian challenge in the Balkans. France feared Germany's move toward continental hegemony and Britain its demand for world parity. Germany already possessed military superiority, but sought naval as well; its power drive was unmistakable, but unfocused, all over the globe. As Britain and France perceived a German challenge to the European balance of power, the existing international system, and to British world predominance and the French Empire – a challenge which was becoming steadily less latent and more overt – their willingness to fight and their sense that this trend must be stopped grew. This too was a factor.

Clearly Germany's naval, colonial, and economic rivalry with Britain was not a precipitating cause of world war, for what Germany sought was war against Russia with Britain neutral. But the German challenge on and across the seas (far more than the Reich's economic growth) contributed to tension, the British tightening of the tie to France, growing hostility in England, and awareness that Germany, once regarded in a kindly light, could be a threat and a potential enemy. In British eyes, the threat materialized when Germany moved to dominate the continent, to destroy what remained of the balance of power to which Britain was dedicated, and into Belgium toward Antwerp, which Napoleon had once rightly termed a pistol pointed at the heart of England. Though the 1839 treaties regarding Belgium provided something of a much-needed moral cause, Britain, like France, acted in response to an explicit German threat to its security.

In the end, the debate always comes back to Germany. Clearly, Austria intended to start nothing without Germany at its side, and none of the Entente powers actively wanted a war in 1914. There was no Entente equivalent to Wilhelm's 'Now or never'. Thus, one must ask whether Germany wanted war in 1914, if so why, and what its reasons and motives were. Why did it encourage local war, accept continental war, and risk world war? The answers are contradictory, thanks to illogic, conflicts, and differing perceptions within Berlin's upper echelons, where policy-making was disorganized.

Some reasons for Germany's choice were purely domestic, such as the preoccupation with having a forceful foreign policy to rally support to the monarchy and against Social Democracy. There was also a swelling movement to claim *Mitteleuropa* as a right. The *Mitteleuropa* concept, which was at heart anti-Russian, entailed at a minimum German economic and cultural domination of central Europe. In the eyes of some, it meant political incorporation of the region, including sometimes in varying combinations Belgium, Holland, Luxembourg, northern France, Denmark, Switzerland, and the Ukraine and the Baltic coast of Russia, that is, domination of Europe. Furthermore, Germany had the power potentially to make such dreams a reality. It was the only continental power possessing the instruments to alter the European *status quo* substantially.

But any German expansion would immediately affect the power balance as well as its neighbours, who could be expected to react. From the days of Bismarck, however, Germany tended to assume that browbeating would gain its desiderata, though the record of failures against great powers gave no grounds for such faith. German leaders were more prone than those of other powers to assume that whatever needed to happen to ensure the success of their plans would occur, even if the indications were otherwise. This may be one reason why the German government tended, both before the Great War and during it, to take dangerous gambles.

Clearly, Germany was not going to be content with *Mitteleuropa*. It aimed as well at *Mittelafrika* and other overseas empire, along with the naval strength to guard it. Through a mixture of pride, nervous insecurity, and blindness to the attitudes and probable reactions of others, an assumption by some of its leaders that war was necessary to *Weltpolitik,* by others that blustering would suffice, Germany tried to force its way to the top of the world heap. This contributed to international tension, as did its late arrival on a crowded colonial scene.

Germany's policies and its style in trying to carry them out caused reactions from other powers. These reactions offer some partial explanation for the curious apprehensions which afflicted German foreign policy, which paralleled the dread of Social Democracy in domestic policy. Usually, there was little appreciation among Germany's leaders that their country's actions had any share in generating the situation which provoked the anxiety. For example, in 1887–90, Germany sent Russia into the arms of France and then complained fearfully of encirclement. This fear remained acute in 1914, though on the other hand German leaders understood that the Entente's intentions were peaceful, which is why they thought initially that war could be localized. There was fear of economic encirclement as well, an exaggerated response to a trend toward higher tariffs and to French investment in eastern Europe. There was a sense of isolation, which made Germany feel dependent on its sole reliable ally, and a corresponding fright that this ally would collapse or cease to be a great power. This led to an irrational view that one should bolster Austria at almost any price in order to have a great power ally, however precarious and costly it might be.

Above all, there was fear of Russia and belief that Russia had military plans and intentions directed against Germany. What led to this conviction is unclear. Germany was equally convinced that the military balance of power would shift away from it toward the Entente, and especially Russia, within two years. Though Russia was recovering militarily from extreme weakness, there was little basis for German concern, at least in the short run. Russian revival and military modernization were far from complete, its railways were shoddy at best, and tsarist leaders knew their empire was in no condition to launch an unnecessary and risky offensive campaign. But German fears were real if not rational, and there was a belief that the Russian wolfhound would soon destroy the Dobermann pinscher if the Dobermann did not first lunge at the wolfhound's throat. Germany acted on its perceptions, thinking it important to have a war in 1914 before the situation became disadvantageous. In so doing, it pursued the illusion of complete continental security at the expense of other great powers and, in seeking so much, risked losing everything.

War came when it did primarily because Germany opted for a war, if not necessarily for the war which eventuated. There has been a good deal of debate about why Germany did so and to what end. Was it largely a matter of miscalculation? Had there been a systematic two-year German plan for world conquest? Was Germany running a calculated risk, hoping to get its way without intent of war? Was the goal a preventive war, to deter future Russian aggression, or was Germany itself engaging in an opportunistic war of aggression?

The answers to these questions are a matter of opinion and the object of heated historical debate. Certainly there was miscalculation aplenty, and repeated gambles constituted calculated or miscalculated risks. It is perhaps begging the question to say that little German policy formulation was systematic, but, despite conferences debating war in December 1912 and thereafter, evidence for a conscious systematic two-year drive toward a world war depends heavily on interpretation and is hotly disputed. Clearly, Germany seized the opportunity for a war of aggression, but the question is why it thought it should.

Perhaps it is best to let German leaders speak for themselves. In February 1918 Bethmann Hollweg, who had been Chancellor in 1914, explained privately, 'Yes, my God, in a certain sense it was a preventive war. But when war was hanging above us, when it had to come in two years even more dangerously and more inescapably, and when the generals said, now it is still possible, without defeat, but not in two years time.'[16] And in August 1916, Bethmann's close aide and confidante, who himself propounded the theory of the calculated risk, explained that the purpose of the war was 'defence against present-day France, preventive war against the Russia of the future, struggle with Britain for world domination'.[17]

◆ **Notes to Chapter 2**

1. Modris Eksteins, *Rites of Spring: The Great War and the Birth of the Modern Age* (Boston, Houghton Mifflin, 1989), p. 87.
2. L. C. F. Turner, *Origins of the First World War* (New York, Norton, 1970), pp. 83–4.
3. Quoted in Joachim Remak, *The Origins of World War I, 1871–1914* (New York, Holt, Rinehart & Winston, 1967), p. 119.
4. Imanuel Geiss, *July 1914, The Outbreak of the First World War: Selected Documents* (New York, Norton, 1967), p. 64.
5. *Op. cit.*, pp. 76–80.
6. Zara S. Steiner, *Britain and the Origins of the First World War* (London, Macmillan, 1977), pp. 221–2.
7. Geiss, *July 1914*, p. 256.
8. Paul Kennedy, *The Rise and Fall of the Great Powers* (New York, Random House, 1987), p. 216.
9. D. C. B. Lieven, *Russia and the Origins of the First World War* (London, Macmillan, 1983), pp. 149–50.

10. V. R. Berghahn, *Germany and the Approach of War in 1914* (London, Macmillan, 1973), p. 207.
11. Geiss, *July 1914*, p. 345.
12. Sidney B. Fay, *The Origins of the World War*, 2nd edn (2 vols, New York, Macmillan, 1966) II, p. 545.
13. Remak, *Origins*, p. 130.
14. Geiss, *July 1914*, p. 372.
15. Steiner, *Britain and the Origins*, p. 228.
16. Imanuel Geiss, 'The Outbreak of the First World War and German War Aims', in Holger H. Herwig, ed., *The Outbreak of World War I: Causes and Responsibilities*, 5th edn (Lexington, MA, D. C. Heath, 1991), p. 107.
17. Fritz Fischer, *From Kaiserreich to Third Reich*, tr. Roger Fletcher (London, Allen & Unwin, 1986), pp. 54–5.

CHAPTER

3

THE FIRST WORLD WAR

The Great War, which rang down the curtain on an era and on Europe's world, did not conform to anyone's script. Most leaders had envisioned a brisk one-act drama coming to a swift climax in a decisive battle on land or sea and a triumphantly victorious denouement. Instead, what eventuated was a grim pageant of endless scenes and epic proportions which seemed to participants and audience alike as if it would never reach resolution.

The short war illusion was nearly universal. To the relief of statesmen, the masses put country before class and flocked to the colours, even in France where socialist leader Jean Jaurès was assassinated on 31 July. Almost everywhere patriotism greeted the opening scenes of the most nationalistic of all European wars; eager chants of '*Nach Paris*!'and '*A Berlin*!' and similar slogans elsewhere indicated that peoples of democracies and autocracies alike were willing to make war. The classes were as enthusiastic as the masses, perhaps more so. Upper-class youths initially saw the war as cleansing, ennobling, glorious, and joyous; thus they rushed to join the great adventure before it ended, no doubt by Christmas. The English poet Rupert Brooke, who would die in 1915 in the Aegean, wrote, 'I've never been quite so happy in my life, I think.'[1]

Just as individuals did not face up to death, so governments did not contemplate defeat. The great powers, with their accustomed hubris, all expected to win quickly. None had formulated any war aims except victory. They assumed that in a brief war the domestic, international, and imperial repercussions could easily be contained and controlled. As they did not anticipate a total war of entire economies and nationalities and thought existing stocks of munitions would suffice for a quick military campaign, governments took few economic, financial or industrial measures, and did not immediately proceed to mobilization of home fronts.

After two months, all assumptions were in ruins. Germany's Schlieffen Plan had failed: the Channel ports were not seized, Paris not encircled, the French armies not trapped, and France had not surrendered. Thus Germany faced the dread two-front war. Its Austrian ally fared no better. Belgrade had not fallen, let alone the rest of Serbia, and a Russian offensive at first spelled disaster on the eastern front. But the impossibility of resupplying

Russia and the grave inadequacy of its rail network meant a fatal lack of mobility and munitions, ensuring that such victories could not be exploited; its great offensive against Germany was soon halted. France still stood, but her military doctrine of the offensive was shattered; so were her northern industrial provinces, which had been occupied by Germany, as had most of Belgium. Offshore, Britain could not find a decisive victory against a German fleet which did not leave port; it was reluctantly girding itself and the Empire for an unwanted continental war. And the powers had largely exhausted their stocks of ammunition.

Further, they were trapped in a muddy impasse which lasted four years. Each side laid siege to the other, effectively trying to bridge the enemy's moat and reach its castle. Stalemate developed at sea and on the western front, where two lines of trenches ran from the Swiss border across northern France to the south Belgian coast. Artillery barrages and periodic efforts to break the battle-line brought appalling casualties (psychological as well as physical) but no substantial movement. The eastern front was more fluid, but greater mobility did not bring decision, only a different sort of stalemate, for Russian armies could and did defeat Habsburg ones, only to be repulsed by Germany, but never decisively. As each side mobilized all resources of population, money, and industry for total war, the jolly little *Blitzkrieg* or lightning war became a bloody, brutal fray of attrition with each bloc trying to mow the other down, strangle it economically, and bludgeon it into submission. Both sides learned what the industrialization and democratization of war meant. The combination of alliances and technology resulted in a larger, longer, more deadly war; munitions manufacture achieved miracles of mass production, while alliances could fight on when one ally suffered disaster, as France, Italy, and Austria did. Thus, the bloc with the most long-term assets had an edge, but not necessarily a decisive one assuring victory. The Allies had more such assets, actual and potential, which is why Germany took so many gambles, all of which failed, trying to win before it was too late. But both sides tried to break the impasse through costly military campaigns and diplomatic efforts to gain an advantage less bloodily.

*   *   *

The outbreak of a major European conflict (as World War I was in the first instance) abruptly altered international discourse, and not only in Europe. Though the eastern and western European fronts, together with the economic battle between German submarines and British blockade on the naval approaches to the European land mass, were decisive in determining the outcome, the existence of great colonial empires, and Japan's early involvement, ensured that the war was global from the outset. Indeed, the first months saw fighting in the South Pacific, at both ends of the African continent, and in the waters off the Falkland Islands. Hence the war affected most nations in one sense or another, particularly economically, as normal trading patterns were broken and both demand and supply shifted.

In the Pacific in particular, Japan took advantage of Western preoccupation with Europe to seize Germany's holdings on the Chinese mainland and its islands north of the equator and also to impose sweeping demands on China.* Revolt in 1911 had deposed the Manchu dynasty and created a Chinese republic, which then suffered 15 years of feeble short-lived governments, civil wars, and chaos. With little diplomatic aid from abroad, it could not resist Tokyo's demands effectively. Despite Japan's gains, however, Asia and most other non-European areas were essentially sideshows in the larger scheme of the Great War, though that was not necessarily apparent to those who suffered and died in the Middle East, Africa, and elsewhere.

In Europe, and eventually globally, the war's first change in diplomacy was severance of diplomatic relations between states at war with each other. But they continued to communicate through surreptitious trading links, neutral nations, or unofficial emissaries, especially ones carrying peace feelers. The tasks, focus, and subject-matter of diplomacy were much affected, but negotiations continued throughout, and the purpose of diplomacy had not changed. As always, but in new circumstances, diplomats sought the greatest national advantage.

For neutral states, this meant trying to avoid the vortex and remain neutral, though for some it meant selling oneself to the highest bidder. European neutrals struggled to ensure the arrival of essential food and raw materials through the British blockade and German sinkings. And neutrals took on new tasks, not only carrying messages between the belligerent blocs but also safeguarding the interests of one warring nation in the capital of another. In August 1914, the American legation† in Brussels helped German nationals to return home. Later, as economic war against civilian populations became total, the American envoy, with his Spanish and Dutch colleagues, earned the title of 'protecting minister' for efforts to keep the Belgians from starvation.

For the belligerents, diplomacy was much affected by the tide of battle; thus it was erratic and often contradictory, for policies and tactics shifted with the military outlook. Defeats induced thoughts of a compromise peace, but then initiatives were often postponed until a victory afforded a stronger bargaining position. Territorial promises were made to Allies, neutrals, and subject nationalities because of military exigencies of the moment, not from any considered policy planning. For example, Britain had long opposed the death of the Ottoman Empire and did not in the

---

* For details, see Chapter 10.
† Until after World War I, ambassadors resident at embassies were exchanged only between great powers. Lesser states sent and received ministers resident at legations.

Great War arrive at any plan to dismember it, but in 1915 it promised Ottoman territory to Italy, Russia, and Turkey's Arab subjects in order to gain and retain allies. Other commitments soon followed, for Britain had by its actions accepted destruction of the remnants of the Ottoman realm.

Diplomacy was complicated by the need to consider one's allies' aspirations or vital interests, particularly if their commitment to the fray seemed doubtful, as Russia's did at times. In this respect, the two coalitions were dissimilar. In both, there was a diversity of aims and of enemies, for neither bloc was monolithic even in its inner core, but diplomacy was simplified for the Central Powers because Germany was dominant. Though Austria pursued its own interests tenaciously, it was so heavily dependent on its partner, especially for munitions and military aid against Russia and ultimately for survival, that in the end it had to accept Berlin's dictation. Of all the great powers, Germany probably had the greatest freedom of decision, but one limited nonetheless by the need to ensure that the Habsburg monarchy did not collapse altogether.

The Allies, however, were led by three fairly equal powers, soon joined by Japan and Italy, both locally dominant. Whereas Japan had no interest in Europe and Russia gave France a free hand on Germany's western borderlands in return for concessions where it cared, on other issues coalition partners clashed over goals, as occurred between Italy and the nascent south Slav movement over the Adriatic coast, and between Italy and the Entente partners over a separate peace with Austria. There developed an understandable tendency to postpone divisive issues whenever possible, including any formal statement of war aims.

Both coalitions dickered to allocate war matériel, food, and other scarce resources, including money and military aid. Efforts to gain an ally's aid or to keep it in the war led to parleys over the spoils, with concomitant jockeying for post-war position vis-à-vis coalition partners, and instances when two Allied great powers would combine to impose an unpalatable decision on the third, as Britain and Russia did to France in 1915 over future tsarist control of Constantinople. Both sides progressively tended to co-ordinated military planning. By war's end, the Central Powers had a supreme military commander in the east, and the Allies had one in the west. After Serbia was overrun in late 1915, the Central Powers, now including Bulgaria and Turkey, had the advantage of contiguity. The Allies were so geographically far-flung (creating complex supply problems), so diverse, and eventually so numerous that they developed more systematic joint planning. They proceeded, after a 1915 conference to co-ordinate 1916's military offensives, to a Supreme War Council with a permanent military committee at Versailles; repeated economic, political, and organizational conferences in Paris; and a Marine Transport Council, a Council on War Purchases and Finance, and an array of committees to allocate scarce materials.

Diplomacy was much affected by domestic factors. The obvious example was Russia in 1917, but in most states a fragile domestic truce existed; its continuance was essential to military success, and thereby restricted concessions that could be made or war aims that could be announced. Domestic events in both Russia and Austria in 1917 impacted their own diplomacy and that of their allies. In the Habsburg monarchy, the nationalities issue, exacerbated by a war of nationalities, and progressively acute internal weakness, to the point where the survival of not only the regime but the country was at stake, made flexibility impossible and dictated a search for a compromise peace in 1917. Diplomacy was not only circumscribed by the politics of domestic coalitions but also by lack of unity within a country's governing circles. Co-equal Austrian and Hungarian cabinet ministers did not share the same goals. German leaders saw that peace with one foe would help to defeat the others but could not decide whether to approach France or Russia. Arriving at coherent national policies was complicated by disputes among politicians, among generals, and especially between generals and politicians. This last problem was a chronic factor in Germany until the onset of a virtual military dictatorship in 1917.

*   *   *

The military situation dominated virtually all diplomacy. Each power pursued its national interest, and each knew its interest was to break the impasse and win. As military efforts to this end did not succeed, diplomacy was enlisted early on. Since reducing the number of one's enemies was difficult, the alternative, often pursued simultaneously, was to increase the number of one's allies while preventing any increase to the foe. Thus, from the outset those neutrals which might be lured to join one bloc or the other received much attention from both coalitions. Generally, one bloc strove to keep a country neutral whereas the other tried to convert it to an ally.

The most powerful neutral was the United States. Though both sides took care not to offend it excessively, neither saw any prospect at the outset of enlisting it as an active ally. In Europe the neutrals receiving early attention were Italy and the Balkan states, for only Serbia and Montenegro were engaged from the start. Despite the quarrelsome nature and military weakness of these monarchies, each coalition sought the strongest possible Balkan bloc. In this troubled region, the legacy of the Balkan wars, which had generated deep hatreds along with aspirations to regain or retain territory, was a key factor, usually more important than the larger issues inherent in the war; equally a factor was the nearby presence of Russia, whose ambitions in the area were no secret. Beyond that, most Balkan states aspired to jump on the winning bandwagon at just the right moment, not so early that they would need to fight much, not so late that they would be unworthy of substantial reward. In this delicate timing they failed miserably.

The most forthright was Turkey. It was driven by fear of Russia and of partition by the Allies as well as hope that Germany could preserve the Ottoman Empire, for the main goal was survival. Russia tried to bribe Turkey to remain neutral, but Germany offered ships, large loans, and promises, territorial and otherwise, for active involvement. As Britain was courting Bulgaria and Greece, it opposed territorial cession to Turkey. The Reich also gained control of the Turkish navy as well as the army, already under German direction. The hesitations of a divided Turkish cabinet were overcome by a *fait accompli* when the German-led Turkish fleet engaged the Russian navy and shelled Odessa in late October 1914, causing the Entente to declare war.

Despite its weakness, Turkey was vital to Germany. It tied up Russian and British armies on its borders; the sultan proclaimed a *jihad* or holy war, which proved less effectual than anticipated. Above all, by closing the Straits Turkey prevented resupply of Russia. Tsarist armies were soon critically short of guns and ammunition, for Russian manufacture was insufficient and 95 per cent of all imports had been cut off,* a situation of crucial military import on the eastern front.

Like Turkey, Italy declared neutrality and talked to both sides. It sought true great power status, domination of the Adriatic, more colonies at Ottoman expense, and completion of unification by annexing *Italia irredenta*, Habsburg territory extending beyond ethnic Italian areas. Negotiations fluctuated as Russian ardour for Italian entry waned, that of Britain waxed, and Germany urged Austria to concede enough to keep Italy neutral. But Germany could not arrange Italian control of the Adriatic, and Austria, who at first hoped to stall until this short war ended, could not cede enough of its own domains to satisfy Italy without serious danger of dissolution.

The Allies had no problem in promising enemy territory. Their chief complication was the clash of Italian and south Slav (Yugoslav) aims on the Adriatic coast. As Russia had done nothing for Serbia militarily, it rendered diplomatic support for the long-sought goal of a sea outlet, but was induced partially to abandon this stance by the March 1915 Anglo-French promise of Constantinople. With that obstacle to alliance removed, Italy suddenly came to terms because it seemed that Russia might defeat Austria without Italian help and the Allied attack on Turkey at the Dardanelles implied that the Allies might win and then offer less from a strong position. Thus it signed the secret treaty of London, gaining large British loans, some ill-defined colonial areas, and most of Italy's Habsburg desiderata, on 26 April 1915.

---

* The Baltic was controlled by the German navy, barring use of St Petersburg (or Petrograd, as it was renamed), Archangel was icebound for more than half of each year, the port of Murmansk did not open until 1917, and Vladivostok was 8000 miles from the front by a single rail track.

It specified Italian entry in the war within thirty days. By then, the tide had shifted. Russia was in retreat, and at the Dardanelles the Gallipoli campaign was faring poorly. Thus Italy would have to earn her rewards. In fact, though she tied up Habsburg armies, her military contribution was scant; she was indifferent to the main struggle focused on German power and, the Austrian front aside, fought a separate war aimed to secure her Adriatic desires. Both this and the London treaty aggravated Italo–south Slav relations, causing a Serbian–south Slav rapprochement. Further, the treaty of London was the chief obstacle to peace between Austria and the Allies.

Austro-German gains against Russia and the failure of the Gallipoli campaign contributed, along with German loans and an ardent desire to undo the losses of the second Balkan war, to Bulgaria's decision to join the Central Powers. Both sides wooed and bribed it, though the reverses of 1915 and an inability to offer much led the Allies to aim at keeping Bulgaria neutral. In fact, Allied diplomacy only increased the price Germany and Austria had to pay for their new ally. In 1913, Bulgaria had lost territory to Serbia, Rumania, and Greece; the Central Powers promised it all back if Rumania and Greece joined the Allies. They made firm promises and generous loans, told Bulgaria it could keep what it conquered, and got Turkey to cede a border strip. The Allies could not offer Serbian territory after the London treaty prevented compensation elsewhere, nor could they promise Greek or Rumanian districts since they were courting both states. Thus Allied offers were limited and contingent. As the Bulgarian tsar and prime minister favoured Germany, Bulgaria reached agreement with the Central Powers in September 1915.

Bulgaria's significance lay in its location, permitting invasion of Serbia on two sides, as occurred in October. Bulgarian mobilization triggered a request from Greek Prime Minister Eleutherios Venizelos for an Allied landing at Salonika (Thessaloniki). Greece had close ties to Britain and France, its mentors since 1827, but was divided. King Constantine, whose wife was the Kaiser's sister, was royalist, neutralist, and inclined to Germany, whereas Venizelos was democratic, interventionist, expansionist, and oriented toward the Allies. He aspired to northern Epirus (southern Albania), Aegean islands, Smyrna (Izmir) in Anatolian Turkey, and control of the Adriatic's entrance. But primarily as a beneficiary of the Balkan wars, Greece feared Bulgarian revenge or shifts in the *status quo*. Initially, Greece stayed neutral, hoping Bulgaria would as well. After the Kaiser failed to browbeat his brother-in-law, the Central Powers sought only Greek neutrality. Britain sought an alliance, but when Venizelos invited the Anglo-French landing, the King dismissed him. Allied forces remained at Salonika without legal sanction. In October 1916, Venizelos established a provisional government there, which the Allies recognized. In June 1917, they forced the King's abdication; Venizelos returned to Athens and declared war.

The other available Balkan state, Rumania, also a beneficiary of the local wars, was influenced by its appetite and the tide of battle, which it mistimed. After its Hohenzollern king died in October 1914, bidding opened for its services. As most areas it coveted were Habsburg, the Central Powers could offer little except Russian Bessarabia and only enabled Rumania to gain more from the Allies. Its price was Transylvania, Bukovina, and the Banat. The Allies were willing but not winning militarily. But in June 1916 a Russian offensive suggested Russia might defeat Austria before Rumania could claim its reward. Thus it signed a military pact to attack Bulgaria in conjunction with an Allied offensive from Salonika. After some delay during which Russia's offensive stalled, Rumania declared war in August 1916, invaded Transylvania, and collapsed militarily. Bucharest fell in December, giving the Central Powers control of Rumanian wheat and oil. Their allies, though fewer in number, were more useful than those of the Entente.

*   *   *

The number of potential partners, especially European ones, was finite so, as the war continued without resolution, both sides turned to encouraging the aspirations of subject peoples restive under the rule of their enemies. Such groups could constitute additional allies, sometimes of genuine military significance. At the same time, they could weaken enemy regimes, inhibiting effective political control and perhaps fomenting revolution on a sizeable scale. Anything which might distract the enemy and pin down his regiments was worth trying.

The Central Powers were at a disadvantage not only because their own treatment of ethnic minorities had been repressive but also because they lacked any ideological appeal. The Allies, making the most of their defence of Belgium in terms of the rights of small states, called for freedom, a pleasingly vague term which could be interpreted variously as local autonomy, independence, or democracy. After the spring of 1917 brought the first Russian revolution and American entry into the war, Allied oratory about democracy became more pronounced.

Both sides found the Habsburg nationality question troublesome. It was difficult for the Central Powers to subvert subject peoples elsewhere when rights for ethnic groups in the multinational empire were blocked by Hungary. The Allies knew these peoples were ripe for disaffection and that emigré groups were encouraging it, but fomenting disintegration was not compatible with the hoped-for separate Austrian peace, so the Allies did little until early 1918, when military crisis on the western front led them to recognize Polish and Czech independence movements, hoping entire divisions of the ethnically organized Habsburg armies would defect.

Both blocs also struggled with the Polish question, for ethnic Poles were divided among Germany, Austria, and Russia. Neither bloc was agreed on the matter though each was willing to create some sort of Poland. Germany, who meant to control whatever state eventuated, proposed a puppet Poland in conquered Russian territory, as was proclaimed in November 1916; Austria resisted, fearing the precedent and the impact at home but could not prevail against Germany's greater power. Russia, which offered a Polish kingdom under the tsar, deemed Poland within its domain, a claim Britain and France did not seriously contest. After the tsar's abdication in March 1917, they began to talk to the Polish National Committee established in Paris in January.

The south Slav problem was even more awkward for the Allies. Despite support from British intellectuals, Allied reluctance to break up the Habsburg monarchy and Italian insistence on the treaty of London prevented an Allied commitment. Relations were tense between the Serbian government and the south Slav leaders, emigrés from Croatia and Slovenia with a sprinkling of Serbs, but in July 1917 they agreed in the Declaration of Corfu to create under the Serbian dynasty a future kingdom of the Serbs, Croats, and Slovenes. As Italy seemed briefly to soften, the Allies largely endorsed this plan at the end of the year.

Each side pursued the Muslim subjects of the other without heed to the consequences. Turkey's call for a *jihad* aimed at India, the Middle East, North Africa where it had some effect, and Russia's Muslim regions. Germany also fostered disaffection among India's Muslims. Britain focused on Turkey's Arab subjects with more success. In the McMahon pledge of 24 October 1915, Britain promised an Arab kingdom in return for a military revolt to ease Turkish pressure on Russia in the Caucasus and perhaps cause Germany to shift divisions from the western front. Thereafter in the Sykes–Picot agreement of 16 May 1916 Britain and France divided most of Turkey's Arab domains between themselves, later adding Italy to the scheme. Later still, first the French cautiously and then the British forthrightly in the Balfour Declaration of 2 November 1917 told the Zionist (Jewish nationalist) movement that they favoured a Jewish home in Palestine. These conflicting arrangements derived from the need to gain or retain support for the war effort.

For the rest, each bloc encouraged restive ethnic groups wherever they found them. From the outset, Russia capitalized on its role as patron of the Slavic peoples but encountered more fear than enthusiasm. Germany on the other hand tried to stir up the subject nationalities of Russia's western borderlands, but accomplished little until 1917. Thereafter, it made some headway with the Finns and Ukrainians. Meanwhile, it fostered Flemish nationalism against the Walloons of Belgium and aided Irish nationalists in Britain's backyard, both with modest success.

Promises to subject peoples as well as those to independent nations, also made to gain or retain allies or secure aid in time of crisis, led to formal written pledges by the Entente, many as secret treaties. There were treaties

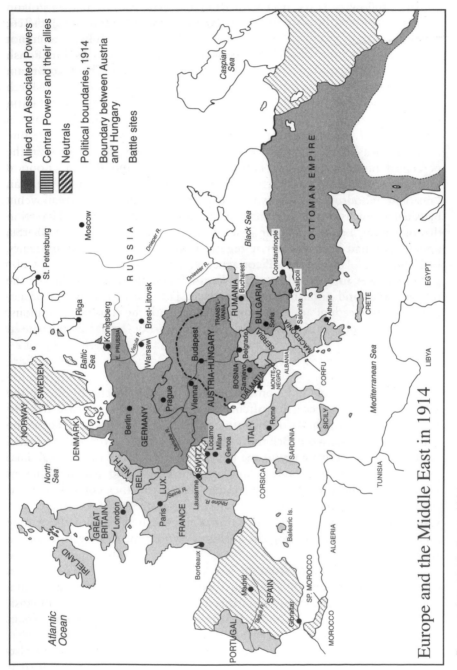

Europe and the Middle East in 1914

to bribe a state into joining the war, of which that of London with Italy was the first, followed by the pact with Rumania. There were treaties to gain more military aid, notably one with Japan where, in return for Japanese naval aid Britain promised in February 1917 to support Tokyo's retention of Germany's China leasehold and north Pacific islands. As Japan had seized these, this cost little; France and Italy followed suit. There were those commitments about the Levant. The Balfour Declaration about Palestine was published, but the McMahon pledge, the Sykes–Picot agreement carving up much of the Middle East, and the treaty of St Jean de Maurienne of 19 April 1917, adding Italy to the division of the booty, were not.

Britain was at the centre of these semi-conflicting pledges dictated by perceived military necessity; France signed many and Russia endorsed several. Washington was party to none;* upon its entry into the war, President Woodrow Wilson was told of most of the secret treaties but brushed them aside, noting that his nation was not bound. His long-distance rival, Lenin (Vladimir Ilyich Ulanov), shared his disgust. Britain and France had kept the tsarist regime informed of their commitments, including the blatant Sykes–Picot scheme, which Russia endorsed. Upon gaining power in November 1917, Lenin found the texts in the foreign ministry files and published them at once. The contrast of Allied propaganda about freedom and self-determination with the wholesale bandying about of peoples and territories was as starkly embarrassing as he intended.

*   *   *

Despite efforts to gain aid, some more fruitful than others, by the end of 1916 the failure of successive offensives on the eastern and western fronts meant that the war had frozen into deadlock. By now it had become a contest of wills between Britain and Germany, for their respective allies could not long survive without the key partner. However, Britain was a sea power and Germany a land power; despite attack and counterattack in Flanders and the struggle on and under the sea, neither could knock the other out. Blood and money continued to flow freely. Hence there were several serious efforts in 1917 to achieve a negotiated peace with some or all of the parties and to bring the curtain down on the deadliest drama the world had yet seen.

Peace feelers abounded from the war's first months until its last year, for dividing one's enemies or reducing their number was always attractive. Some were more substantial than others, but on the western front all failed until 1918. But in 1917 deadlock was only one factor pressing toward negotiation. In Vienna, a new emperor realized that survival of his dynasty and state was increasingly in doubt. After the first Russian revolution in

* The United States did approve the Balfour Declaration.

March,* moderate leadership was dominant across Europe for some months. And beyond the usual secret emissaries, Bethmann Hollweg, Wilson and the pope joined the procession of those trying to end the carnage.

Secret messengers tended to certain characteristics which contributed to their failure. Some had no authorization or only that of a single cabinet minister. Some were told only to listen but negotiated without a mandate. In their enthusiasm, fully empowered emissaries often offered too much and were disavowed. Wilson's confidant, Edward M. House,† who toured Europe early in 1916, made rash promises to Britain, leading Wilson to qualify the commitment. Many envoys were inexperienced and eager; they accentuated the positive and minimized the negative, misrepresenting each side's view to the other. Their efforts foundered on the rock of reality.

A power's willingness to negotiate increased when its military situation was poor. Thus it would ease its terms a bit, but not enough to tempt the enemy seriously. For example, France's first war aim after liberation was return of Alsace and Lorraine, the lost provinces of 1871; when Germany sought a separate French peace, it offered a sliver of Alsace-Lorraine, which hardly sufficed. Similarly, it failed to induce talks in the east by proposing to retain a bit less conquered Russian territory. And the urge to parley was tempered by an inclination to await 'the next victory', after which a stronger position generated new hope and less desire to negotiate at all.

Coming to terms was often impeded by a partner. Unlike Britain and France, Germany could not offer Russia Constantinople at Turkey's expense. Similarly, Britain and France yearned for a separate peace with Austria, with whom they had little quarrel, but Italy's insistence on the London treaty *in toto* rendered that improbable, a fact which they did not face. The Habsburg monarchy also wanted peace but could not satisfy Italy without its own disintegration. Austria endorsed restoration of Belgium and return of Alsace-Lorraine, about which it did not care as it did about Serbia, but had no prospect of persuading its senior partner on either issue. In the 1917 efforts toward a compromise general settlement, as opposed to a separate peace for certain powers, Belgium was the reef on which all efforts foundered, for its strategic location led the Allies to demand the pre-war *status quo* as a matter of vital interest to Britain and France, while Germany was determined to retain effective control.

---

* Until 1 February 1918, Russia used the Julian calendar, whose dates were 13 days behind those of the Gregorian calendar observed in the West. Thus the first Russian revolution occurred from 24 to 28 February, Russian style, or from 8 to 12 March, Western style. The second revolution took place on 24–25 October or, in Western terms, 6–7 November 1917. Western or Gregorian dating will be used throughout.

† Generally referred to as Colonel House, he was an honorary Texas colonel but held no such rank in the US Army.

Bethmann Hollweg began the procession of proposals in December 1916; he wanted American intercession and a way to counter demands by the German generals for unrestricted submarine warfare, whose impact he gauged more realistically than they. As the presidential election in November delayed Wilson, Bethmann took advantage of Rumania's recent defeat to ask on 12 December 1916 that belligerents declare their war aims. Though Bethmann hoped for a compromise peace, the Allies did not think his overture serious and rejected it on 30 December. This led to hardening of the German position and a final decision on 9 January 1917 for unrestricted submarine warfare.

The German initiative became entangled with that of Wilson, who on 18 December asked each side to state its terms. On 26 December the Central Powers agreed to negotiate but stated no terms. The Allies on 10 January 1917 in their first indication of war aims called for return of lost territories, reparation, national self-determination, and an international organization. Wilson sought German terms again and on 22 January declared 'it must be a peace without victory. . .'.[2] On 31 January he received a secret German note outlining expansionist terms and another announcing immediate resumption of unrestricted submarine warfare. That ended that.

The Allies were equally unmoved by peace without victory; Anatole France compared it to 'a town without a brothel'.[3] But they wanted fewer enemies, so they listened when in March 1917 the Austrian Emperor Karl sent his brother-in-law Prince Sixtus de Bourbon secretly to the French. Ostensibly Sixtus was exploring a comprehensive peace, but Karl had not consulted Germany and the proposed terms were unacceptable to it; the Allies understood that Karl sought a separate peace. Britain and France feared Russia would leave the war; if so, peace with Austria seemed the sole hope of victory. Karl forbade disclosure to Italy, but at the St Jean de Maurienne conference in April, broad hints led to an adamant Italian stand, dictated in part by the impossibility in Italian domestic politics of accepting after much bloodshed what could have been obtained in 1915 as the price of neutrality. Though Karl tried again, his feeler had failed.

Like Wilson, Pope Benedict XV had tried earlier to end the fray but hoped that now the time was ripe. Besides, he feared for the survival of Austria, Europe's greatest Catholic state. After consulting the Central Powers, he urged in a note published on 16 August 1917 an absence of indemnities, disarmament, Belgian independence, and negotiated solutions to territorial disputes. As Britain feared Russian defection, its reply of 23 August left the door ajar; with French assent, it focused on Belgium and noted that Germany had not issued terms in response to Wilson. The German reply (as the pope had advised) was general but said Belgium could not be evacuated until Britain left the continent; Germany hoped to use Belgium as a bargaining counter to gain a separate peace with Britain, a continental war, and victory. The American reply endorsed much of the pope's programme but refused to accept the word of Germany's present rulers; in the first distinction between the German people and their leaders, it all but invited revolution. The Allies were delighted and did not pursue matters further. The pope again sought a specific German commitment on Belgium but gained none. The only sequel was secret German overtures to Britain and France, which failed.

*   *   *

Before these overtures reached a predictable close, events began which led to the sole major separate peace and also determined the war's outcome. In March, the tsarist monarchy was overthrown. In April, the United States joined the Allies and raised their war to a moral cause; to 'make the world safe for democracy' was easier without the world's greatest autocrat as an ally. And in Russia before 1917 ended, Bolshevism came to power, enthroning an ideology hostile to those prevailing elsewhere. The ensuing competition between liberal capitalism and Communism complicated diplomacy, distorted the interwar European power balance, and influenced the world's history far longer.

The momentous events of 1917 in Petrograd showed which eastern regime would first collapse under the strains of war. The new Russian government assured the Allies that it would honour its commitments and publicly repeated Russia's claim to the Straits. But it soon was evident that the troops were more interested in returning home than in dying for Constantinople.

The military situation and socialist pressure to leave the war led to Russian overtures to Germany and secret negotiations between March and June. But German terms meant considerable loss of territory and no influence over a future Poland; thus the talks failed, and Germany did not capitalize on what proved to be its last opportunity for a favourable outcome. In July, Russia's final military offensive also quickly failed, and reverses set in. The Allies began to write Russia off in terms of any active military contribution but hoped it would remain in the war to tie up German divisions, for their circumstances were desperate despite the acquisition of the United States as an ally.

American entry into the war grew out of economic warfare at sea between Britain and Germany. This began in February 1915 when Germany declared the waters around the British Isles a war zone, where ships would be sunk on sight by German submarines. Britain countered with a blockade of sea approaches to Germany. The blockade was actual, not merely a paper decree, and thus according to international law, though Britain's contraband list became excessive. But submarines, whose safety and effect depended on submersion and surprise, could not conform to obsolete laws of warfare requiring warning and a wait for those aboard to take to lifeboats.

As in the Napoleonic wars, the United States was the chief neutral trader and thus soon entangled. The British seized cargoes and detained ships; that hurt American property and pride. German sinkings cost ships and lives, a far graver matter, to which was added inept German propaganda and clumsy spies who were caught. Wilson's sympathies were with Britain, and he demanded the largest possible interpretation of neutral rights, including that of American citizens to travel safely on liners flying belligerent flags. When these were sunk with loss of American lives, sharp protests and threats led Germany to suspend the Atlantic submarine campaign, thus effectively permitting unlimited American resupply of the Allies.

After the indecisive Anglo-German naval battle of Jutland on 31 May 1916, where the German navy failed to break out of the Baltic Sea into the Atlantic, pressures mounted in Germany for a return to submarine warfare. As the German High Command saw that its 1916 effort to bleed France into surrender at Verdun had failed and that a war of attrition took too long to win, the generals joined the chorus. When Bethmann's initiative failed to produce peace, they prevailed. On 31 January, Wilson was told that on 1 February shipping in the waters around Britain, France and Italy would be subject to sinking without warning.

The German generals knew the United States would enter the war but, in the largest of their gambles, hoped to win before American support arrived in force. They argued that Washington was already heavily engaged in every sense but the military one. In theory, as a neutral it traded with anybody. In practice, Britain had the financial ties, common language, and control of the seas in the absence of submarines. Geography and the Royal Navy cut Germany off from American trade; the United States was sending the Allies a stream of food, manufactures, munitions, and loans to pay for them. The American economy was now substantially bound up with the Allies, as were American sympathies; for these reasons, reinforced by historic ties, skilful Allied propaganda, and Wilson's predilection for Britain, an Allied victory was perceived to be in American national interest.

Berlin realized that but expected much from the submarine, which was supposed to bring Britain to heel in five months – and nearly did so. But by forcing the issue, Berlin tipped the balance against itself. It did not know how desperate the Allies were; nor did Washington. Morale, resources, and reserves of men were low. In February, the Allies were within weeks of being unable to make further American purchases.[4] The pre-war view that no one could afford a long war had been disproved; all nations sold assets abroad and borrowed wherever they could, including from their people. However, massive loans to the Allies from New York bankers had reached the limit of private lending capacity. Hindsight reveals that patience would have paid Berlin more dividends than the sinkings.

But when Germany made its decision in January 1917, it knew neither the situation on Wall Street nor what would soon occur in Petrograd. When submarine warfare resumed, American entry into the war was eased by two events. The first was the Zimmermann telegram from the German foreign minister proposing in January that Mexico join the fray and regain territories lost to the United States in 1848. The British intercepted it and, after protecting the secret of their ability to read German codes, provided it to Washington. Its publication on 1 March swung isolationist sections of the United States toward intervention. The second event was the March revolution in Russia.

That occurred while Wilson awaited sinkings. In mid-March several ships were sunk, most without warning, with some loss of American lives. Thus Wilson called Congress into session, and the United States declared war on Germany on 6 April 1917. But it remained an 'Associated Power' so it need not endorse Allied war aims or commitments and might negotiate separately with the enemy. As with Britain's earlier hopes,[5] Wilson thought the American role would be mostly economic and naval but would confer much influence at the peace conference and enable him to force the Allies to his war aims after the fighting ended.

Wilson underestimated his nation's military role. It was negligible in 1917 but in 1918 swelled to two million men. With all European powers drained, such an army, however inexperienced, became determining. Meanwhile, the Allies received American government loans immediately after American entry until the Armistice, which saved them from disaster. Further, Washington insisted upon naval convoys for merchantmen and contributed American warships to them, which reduced the submarine threat to manageable dimensions in the nick of time.

American entry prolonged the war and transformed it in broader ways. Though it was a close call in the spring of 1918, the United States tipped the balance and determined the outcome. Wilson's moralistic rhetoric raised the war to a cause, lending more oratory and credibility to talk of freedom for oppressed peoples. The Latin American countries, Liberia, Siam (Thailand), and China followed the United States into the war, often for economic reasons or to gain loans. And as the New World came to the rescue of the Old, the torch was passed from one generation to another and from one continent to another. It was no longer entirely Europe's war and it was rapidly ceasing to be Europe's world as power visibly shifted elsewhere. Russia's departure equally altered the war. Before American troops arrived in number, Russia's second revolution in November brought Bolshevism to power. Lenin at once urged a peace of no annexations and no indemnities and an end to hostilities to gain time to consolidate his regime. Disintegration of the remnants of the army spurred him on. Thus Russia accepted draconian terms in the treaty of Brest-Litovsk on 3 March 1918. Thereupon, Germany shifted a million men westward for its last great gamble, the Ludendorff offensive, which, like submarine warfare, aimed to win the war before the American army arrived in force.

*   *   *

The war now truly encompassed the globe in both its participants and its promises and claims. Each side had aspired to the colonies of the other from the outset, but three years of fighting had done much to refine war aims both in Europe and elsewhere. Through the 1917 negotiations, the great powers had avoided detailed statements of their aims, though much thought had been given to them. Despite domestic divisions, most powers knew their desiderata, and their allies understood as well.

War aims assumed victory and constituted the reward for struggle, sacrifice, and triumph. Each side had private war aims and eventually public ones as well, not necessarily the same. War aims were rarely as they were stated publicly, and they were stated as seldom and briefly as possible. Public war aims contained a propaganda element, as with the Entente emphasis on freedom, and until American entry, were often prettified to impress the United States. Thus Britain and France declared war on 'militarism' and endorsed a future international organization.

Statements of war aims were kept vague to avoid shattering fragile domestic truces and to preserve negotiating room, should a compromise peace eventuate. Such statements were postponed if possible to avoid distraction from the war effort, division among allies, and possible embarrassment if the tide of battle shifted. The question of war aims usually entailed jockeying for post-war position and negotiating for the spoils, and so diplomatic efforts were often directed more against one's allies than the enemy who, if defeated, could be forced to accept.

Most countries had maximum and minimum aims; ambitions grew with victory, shrank with defeat and despair. Even minimum aims were subject to revision, though mainly of detail. German domination of Belgium and Poland was central to every German plan but the schemes varied; however, the basic issue, like other powers' minimum aims, was not negotiable. Both sides preferred annexations overseas and indirect control (with exceptions) in Europe. In general, appetites grew as the war became more costly, thus requiring more gains to justify the sacrifices.

That was especially true of Germany, whose ambitions were large and formulated early. In September 1914 Germany developed a programme, criticized by some for its moderation, aimed at hegemony and total security in Europe for all time, with France destroyed as a great power and Russia shoved eastward; Germany would control the tsar's non-Russian borderlands. In the west, Belgium and France would cede much, including the Longwy-Briey iron fields; both would submit to economic subjection and France to a crippling indemnity. Luxembourg would be annexed, Belgium and Holland reduced to satellites, along with a Poland. Germany would dominate an economic *Mitteleuropa* stretching from the Atlantic to the new Russian border and gain a consolidated empire in *Mittelafrika*. Of these claims, Belgium was always the barrier to peace in the west and Poland in the east. With time and the collapse of Russia, the list came to include global naval bases, more indemnities, Mediterranean districts, dissolution of the Entente, annexation of Baltic regions, destruction of Britain's world power, a trade treaty ensuring control of the Russian market, and domination of Finland and the Ukraine.

Austria's goals were more modest. Foremost was return of conquered areas to regain geographic integrity. Though at the outset Austria forswore annexation of Serbian territory, it came to seek part or all of Serbia and Montenegro and domination of the rest, despite Hungary's objections to adding Slavs to the empire. Austria coveted much of Rumania, border rectifications against Italy, and an Albanian protectorate. Unlike Germany, it aspired to a Polish kingdom comprising Russian Poland and Austrian Galicia in personal union with the Austrian emperor.

Tsarist Russia on the other hand coveted German and Austrian Poland. In August 1914 it promised a united self-governing Poland under the tsar. Russia favoured the break-up of the Habsburg Empire with rewards for Serbia along the Adriatic coast, which impeded a separate peace with Austria nearly as much as the London treaty did. At Turkey's expense, Russia expected the Straits and Constantinople, Armenia, and Kurdistan. It sought reparations and maintenance of the Entente.

France, too, wanted to preserve the Entente and the power balance, though her primary goal was survival as an independent power. Return of Alsace-Lorraine, security against Germany in the Rhineland, and domination of Belgium were priorities, along with funds to rebuild the devastated areas; some coveted the Saar basin. Though Europe came first, France sought colonial booty in the Middle East and Africa, but her propagandistic demand for an end to 'Prussian militarism' revealed her real concern.

Britain, however, focused primarily on empire: its security and enlargement. It wished to take the German fleet and colonies and Turkish territory as well. Its dominions aspired to German possessions in south Africa and the south Pacific. In Europe, Britain wanted to restore Belgium, prevent German hegemony, and re-establish the classical balance of power. It accepted the idea of a league of nations without enthusiam and was more concerned about preserving its own great power status from assorted challengers, not least now the United States.

Unlike greater powers, Italy had ample time to decide her aims and gain commitments to them before she entered the war. Her goals, mainly territorial, were defined by the treaties of London and St Jean de Maurienne, to which she clung with limpet-like fixity. Japan's aims, on the other hand, were defined mainly by what she conquered in 1914. This meant Germany's leasehold on the Shantung (Shandong) peninsula and its Pacific islands north of the equator. Moreover, Japan intended to retain the concessions it wrested from China in 1915, take over China's market and rail construction, and gain a buffer state in Inner Mongolia.

As a group, the three great European Allies in 1914 agreed quickly not to make a separate peace, to contain German power, and to require restoration of Belgium. Beyond that this disparate lot was loath to go until their brief declaration of Allied war aims to Wilson in January 1917. Thereafter, the progressive democratization and departure of Russia simplified matters, whereas American entry altered the equation. With these events, the Allies could increasingly emphasize a crusade of democracies to achieve self-determination and the blessings of liberty for oppressed peoples, an ideological advantage which the Central Powers could not match. Where possible, however, they preferred to do so in imprecise slogans and high-flown rhetoric.

Though peace programmes derived in part from war aims, they encompassed other motives, both propagandistic and competitive, as became clear in December 1917 and January 1918. As the parleys at Brest-Litovsk opened on 22 December, the Bolsheviks proposed a peace based on self-determination for all peoples, including colonies, and without annexations or indemnities. On Christmas Day, the Central Powers accepted with key reservations, if the Allies did as well.

As the Allies had failed to agree on a programme, they answered separately. British Prime Minister David Lloyd George led off on 5 January 1918. Beyond responding to the message from Brest-Litovsk, he was trying to quell domestic opponents, counter war-weariness, encourage the German and Austrian opposition, seek a separate Austrian peace, and pre-empt Wilson, whose growing power vis-à-vis the European Allies he feared. With such an array of motives, the programme's chief feature was ambiguity. But under a lofty moral tone lay firmness about Britain's overseas goals and willingness to compromise at the expense of its European Allies. He endorsed an international organization, restoration of Belgium and other occupied territory, and Turkish retention of Constantinople, since the Bolsheviks had repudiated the Straits agreement. For the rest, there were vague but noncommital references to Poland, Alsace-Lorraine, Italian claims, and the rights of nationalities. The statement was striking for what it did not say or do.

It was overtaken by Wilson's more specific Fourteen Points of 8 January. In snappy slogans which made excellent propaganda, Wilson called for open diplomacy (a misleading attack on secret treaties), disarmament, free trade, freedom of the seas (the right of neutrals to trade or travel as they saw fit), a fair adjustment of colonial claims considering the interests of the populations, and a league of nations. To reply to the Bolshevik programme and the Christmas Declaration, to keep Russia in the war, and to encourage the anti-Bolshevik opposition, Wilson promised evacuation of all Russian territory and generous treatment. On other territorial questions, he made an important distinction. Wilson said Belgium 'must be' evacuated and restored; all else specified 'should be', deliberately less binding. All invaded territories should be evacuated and restored, Alsace-Lorraine returned, Poland established and, like Serbia, given access to the sea. Italy and Turkey should be granted an ethnic frontier, while Austria's nationalities should have a murky 'autonomous development', which preserved the option of a separate peace with the Habsburg monarchy.

While more specific than Lloyd George, Wilson had written a programme designed to encourage the downtrodden, appeal to idealists, foster opposition in Russia and in enemy states, further the war effort, and impose the American peace programme on the Allies. The Fourteen Points were admirably suited to these ends. But these propagandistic slogans were not designed as the negotiating basis for peace and were too imprecise to be the foundation for an armistice, much less peace treaties to follow. However, despite the imprecision and the impossibility of ethnic frontiers as specified in several points, the Fourteen Points became the basis for the armistice ending hostilities.

*   *   *

That event was closer than anybody realized. When Russia left the war in March 1918 and the Ludendorff offensive followed, American strength had not begun to tell on the western front. German forces again reached the Marne River near Paris, and the Allies became desperate, leading to hare-brained schemes, notably the dispatch of American forces to Siberia in response to frantic pleas. That helped not one whit, but in the west the Allies created a unified command (except Belgium and the United States) under Marshal Ferdinand Foch, American troops arrived to plug holes in the line, the Allies held grimly on while gradually recognizing the Czech and Polish independence movements which had military units, and the Ludendorff offensive was narrowly defeated. On 20–21 July Germany withdrew from the Marne.

By then, the French were counterattacking; Britain launched a devastating offensive in August; in September Foch loosed a general attack along the front. After four years of immobility, the line moved – eastward. Equally important, Germany had suffered over a million casualties since March, roughly the number of troops transferred westward from Russia, and could not replace the losses, but Americans were streaming across the Atlantic, 300 000 of them in July. At the end of September, German leaders agreed that an immediate armistice was necessary.

To that end, a new liberal government was installed under Prince Maximilian of Baden, who asked Wilson for an armistice, a cessation of hostilities implying nothing about victory or defeat, based on the Fourteen Points. Though preoccupied with congressional elections, Wilson negotiated alone for some weeks while his nervous Allies sought participation, fearing he might be too generous. In fact, Wilson was intent upon ensuring that Germany could not resume hostilities, as it had initially hoped to do. He largely invited the Kaiser's departure and implied that a democratic Germany would receive better treatment.

While negotiations proceeded, Germany's allies collapsed. Bulgaria sought an armistice on 26 September and received it on the 29th. A convention with Turkey, requested on 14 October, was signed on the 30th. By then, Wilson had told Austria-Hungary that autonomy for ethnic groups was no longer enough. Even so, on 25 October it sought a separate peace but broke into two pieces before an armistice with Austria took effect on 4 November. Rumania seized the moment to re-enter the war and invade Hungary; as the Habsburg armies had disintegrated on all fronts, there was no resistance and Rumania occupied and claimed the areas initially awarded it in the 1916 agreement upon its first disastrous entry into the war. In the armistice finally signed with Hungary on 13 November, this occupation was legitimized.

Meanwhile, Wilson sent House to Paris to consult the Allies about a German armistice. On Foch's insistence, military terms were stiff, requiring rapid withdrawal and Allied occupation of the Rhineland, Germany's westernmost region. House's chief concern (and that of Germany) was to tie the Allies to the Fourteen Points. Through an American interpretative document clarifying them (never officially given to Germany though it obtained a copy) and threats of a separate American peace, House achieved agreement subject to a British reservation on freedom of the seas and an interpretation that 'restoration' meant compensation for all damage done to civilians and their property by the Reich.

These terms arrived in Berlin just as German leaders were about to surrender altogether. They coolly parlayed a naval mutiny at Kiel and signs of urban unrest into a Bolshevik menace requiring easier military terms. Envoys were despatched to Foch's headquarters to receive them. Then, on 9 November in Berlin a republic was declared to prevent a revolution; a new cabinet took office, led by Germany's largest but utterly inexperienced party, the Social Democrats; old government and new demanded the departure of the Kaiser, who fled to Holland. Alas, the new government was saddled with responsibility for the deeds of its predecessors, including the mis-named Armistice of 11 November, in fact a surrender, which rang down the final curtain on more than four years of brutal bloodshed.

* * *

Leon Trotsky observed that 'War is the locomotive of history.'[6] To this dictum the First World War was no exception. Many trends were already in progress: the Romanov and Habsburg regimes were precarious, the Ottoman Empire moribund. France was declining; Britain's lead was shrinking; power had begun to shift out of Europe, notably to the United States and Japan. But the Great War accelerated these tendencies, along with domestic trends, often to democracy but not necessarily to stability as Communism became a terrifying new factor, while the war was viewed as liberation from the bourgeois world not only by the elite youth of both sides, many of whom died in Flanders, in 1914 but by the European left and right and overseas subject peoples.

The shift of power out of Europe was accelerated especially in economic terms. For four years, Europe had not only slaughtered its youth but also squandered its treasure, consuming its industrial resources and its accumulated wealth. As a result, it suffered a general impoverishment and economic decline not experienced elsewhere. War and blockade disrupted the existing web of relations; all Europe suffered, including the neutrals, but others benefited. American industry expanded to meet the wartime demand, India created a vast iron and steel complex, and textile industries sprang up in several states. Thus when European production regained pre-war levels in 1925, it was a pre-war share of a larger post-war pie, for the European segment shrank proportionally as that of others expanded. The stimulation of non-European trade and production meant that Europe's share declined permanently.

In several senses, there was a transfer of wealth to other continents. Germany was cut off from world trade by the blockade; Britain and France sold overseas assets, especially American ones, to pay for purchases. Most European powers lost markets overseas to Japan and the United States, which took over the lucrative carrying trade on the world's oceans from Britain while the world's financial centre shifted from London into the inexperienced hands of Wall Street.

The war caused a net loss of wealth worldwide despite gains outside Europe. Much of this came from damage to resources. French mines and railways were devastated; British mines and rails suffered in old age from four years without maintenance; the Russian economy had collapsed. Destruction was severe, especially in industrial areas, in northern France, Belgium, Poland, Serbia, and other areas where armies had rampaged. Battlefield damage was aggravated by the German policy of picking occupied areas clean and removing all assets: factories, farm equipment, tools, livestock, seed, and machinery. The spinning industry of northern France and Belgium had disappeared into Germany. In the economic sense, the victors, on whose soil the war had been fought, suffered far more than the losers.

Europe was also impoverished by its debts. Britain had reverted to its historic role as banker of its allies but that soon became a matter of arranging American loans for them. By 1918, the Allies owed Britain $7 milliard,* and Britain owed $4 milliard, mostly to the United States. Continental Allies also borrowed directly from the United States, who afforded $10 milliard in credits in all. Both lenders expected to be repaid. In addition, France made direct loans to Russia and the smaller Allies; the new Russia declined to honour tsarist debts to capitalists. Among the Central Powers,

---

* A milliard is an American billion, a British thousand million.

the smaller states borrowed from Austria, who in turn borrowed from Germany. Of the major belligerents, only the United States and Germany emerged without large foreign debts. But all powers which were substantially involved borrowed from their own people.

One consequence of the loans was that the United States became a creditor nation as well as a net exporter; since American politicians thought Europeans should pay their debts while running up new ones by buying more from the United States than they sold to it, the international economic system suffered. The pound was no longer the leading currency; belligerents, including the United States, abandoned the gold standard in practice. At war's end, currencies were floating, often in disorganized fashion, which further impeded a revival of trade at first.

The monetary system was acutely afflicted in other senses. Inflation was severe in Europe, as states had financed the war by modest tax increases, borrowing, and printing money. Increases in note circulation of 500 per cent to 1000 per cent across Europe were common, with concomitant currency depreciation. Economic dislocation and reconstruction costs ensured that inflation continued after the war and in several instances became hyper-inflation, rendering any stable fixation of parities between currencies difficult, thereby causing more dislocation. Wartime government intervention in economies continued, and the pre-war liberal laissez-faire economic system was a casualty of the war, severely if not fatally wounded. In many respects, the pre-war system based on Britain and the gold standard was no more.[7]

Europe's loss of economic primacy meant a decline in relative power, but it was not the only cost, immediate or long-term. There was also the loss of a generation. Roughly 8·5 million men were killed, 20 million wounded, with a high proportion of the natural future leaders killed early in the war. As a consequence, there was no normal transition of power in the interwar era. The old men were still running Europe in the 1930s, often too old to react well to new problems. While immeasurable, this sad fact was important.

More immediately, the war took a toll of Europe's political leadership and configuration. The Osman, Romanov, Hohenzollern, and Habsburg dynasts left the stage altogether; the Ottoman and Habsburg Empires departed the scene for good, while Russia was in the wings for some years. The United States had reached stardom, Germany had been reduced for the nonce to a secondary role. The stage was crowded with new young players, mostly European. The old drama of five great European powers had been transformed.

There were other costs, difficult to measure but affecting Europe's world power. Bills were coming due from Europe's children, those overseas empires which contributed so much to Allied victory in food, raw materials, and especially men. New Zealand sent overseas more than 40 per cent of its men eligible for military service. For the British Dominions, the reward would be independence in foreign policy, for India more self-government. Both had implications for British power. Similarly, two thirds of a million of France's colonial subjects served in Europe and became less docile thereafter. Arab nationalism had been roused. Europe's preoccupation led its subjects to press for liberation, not least because they heard and heeded Western calls for freedom and self-determination not intended for their ears.

The decisive role of Europe's children, including the United States, meant that the battle their parents fought to save the power balance in fact destroyed the classical balance based on five European powers. While the war outside Europe was mostly minor, the only real victors were non-European. Europe was no longer the centre of the world; it was in fact no longer Europe's world although, despite Japan's role, it remained predominantly the West's world. The long trend in which Europe dominated and influenced the rest of the world had seen its first reverse. Now the United States and semi-Asiatic Russia had a great effect on Europe, even if often from the wings,[8] as the advent of the Wilson–Lenin rivalry on the world stage encapsulated the shift away from Europe and its liberal capitalist creed. Certainly, the Armistice ushered in a new era – of American statecraft, spreading democracy, Communist challenges, lusty and often squalling infant nations, restive empires, uncharted economics, and a host of other problems impacting upon a very weary and diminished European continent.

◆ Notes to Chapter 3

1. Geoffrey Keynes, *Letters of Rupert Brooke* (New York, Harcourt, Brace & World, 1968), p. 662.
2. Patrick Devlin, *Too Proud to Fight: Woodrow Wilson's Neutrality* (London, OUP, 1974), p. 604.
3. Z. A. B. Zeman, *The Gentlemen Negotiators: A Diplomatic History of World War I* (New York, Macmillan, 1971), p. 194.
4. David Stevenson, *The First World War and International Politics* (New York, OUP, 1988), p. 76; Kathleen Burk, *Britain, America, and the Sinews of War, 1914–1918* (Boston, George Allen & Unwin, 1985), pp. 93–5.
5. J. M. Bourne, *Britain and the Great War, 1914–1918* (London, Edward Arnold, 1989), pp. 133–45.
6. *Op. cit.*, p. 191.
7. Gerd Hardach, *The First World War, 1914–1918* (Berkeley, University of California Press, 1977), p. xv.
8. Bernadotte E. Schmitt and Harold C. Vedeler, *The World in the Crucible, 1914–1919* (New York, Harper & Row, 1984), p. xvi.

CHAPTER

4

THE RUSSIAN REVOLUTION

Even before the curtain fell on the tragedy of World War I, the opening scenes of a new drama had played out. The latter was largely a result of the former. Two revolutions in Russia in rapid succession, both substantially a response to the strains war imposed on precarious Russian regimes, ushered in a new era, shattering the cultural unity of the great powers and altering both diplomatic practice and the power balance.

August 1914 created the conditions of this new drama by severely straining the creaky tsarist system and presenting insoluble problems for the international socialist movement which saw itself as the world's greatest force for peace. With five million members which it thought it could mobilize against militarism, the Second International* seemed substantial and was considered for the Nobel Peace Prize in 1913. Statesmen feared it could rally workers against patriotic defence of existing regimes. But when the European world order collapsed in 1914, the International disintegrated.

Like others, socialist leaders were overwhelmed by the sudden speed of the crisis. They thought there was time for a socialist congress in August. They assumed as well that war was impossible, Europe would edge past another crisis, and they could launch a peace offensive to ensure this. A week later Europe was at war. Anti-war demonstrations abruptly ceased as workers displayed both patriotism and fear of invasion, subjection, and the death of their nations. Only the parliamentary socialist parties of Russia and Serbia refused to endorse war credits to finance the war. Truces at home became the norm, and French socialists joined the Cabinet with their party's consent, the first ever to do so.† The illusion of the international solidarity of the working class lay in ruins.

So did the International, its unity split in two basic ways. There was division into the two wartime blocs with Franco-Belgian socialists unwilling to

---

* The First International (or International Workingmen's Association) lasted from 1864 to 1876. The Second International, created in 1889, was a federation of diverse socialist parties and groups with headquarters in Brussels.
† Emile Vandervelde, president of the International, became a minister of state and thus a member of Crown Councils in early August 1914 but did not join the Belgian Cabinet until January 1916. The British Labour party entered the government in May 1915.

meet their German brethren who, as they saw it, had voted for credits to invade them. In addition, there was a three-way split according to attitudes toward the war. On the right, patriotic socialists who backed their national war efforts formed the largest group. In the centre were anti-war socialists who refused to vote credits and sought to end the war within the framework of the Second International. On the left, a small element led by Lenin, who passed the war in Swiss exile, wished to break with the International and convert the war into a revolutionary struggle. As the leadership of the Second International could make no move without smashing the remaining façade of socialist unity, it did nothing.

Its paralysis led centre and left socialists to meet in September 1915 at Zimmerwald, Switzerland. Though Lenin's faction was a small minority, Zimmerwald provided the impetus toward a left-wing split from the Second International and later creation of the Third International. Its manifesto opposed the war and called for a peace based on self-determination without annexations or indemnities. Though published, this programme created little stir, but the ideas circulated and were adopted by the Russian left. At Kienthal in Switzerland in April 1916, the Zimmerwaldians met again to demand that socialist parties vote against war credits. Again, the majority rejected leaving the International, but the minority was stronger as Lenin prodded socialism leftward.

The March revolution generated enthusiasm and plans for an international socialist conference in Stockholm, with Russian socialist support. The oft-postponed conference never managed to meet though many labour and socialists groups reached Stockholm and conferred there in the summer and fall of 1917. The Zimmerwaldians met there separately in September before subsiding into the Bolshevik movement. However, the main conference, though supported by many socialist elements including the Second International, fell victim to the refusal of Allied governments to grant passports to delegates and to rapidly changing events in Russia.

*   *   *

Socialists were not alone in welcoming the first Russian revolution of 1917. Allied governments hoped the Russian war effort would be revitalized, especially as the provisional government assured them that Russia would honour its commitments and fight on. American entry into the war was eased by the end of tsarist autocracy, and the Allies gained a propaganda advantage which was quickly exploited as they declared themselves for 'freedom'.

But the situation in Petrograd was less straightforward than it seemed. In November 1916, Pavel Miliukov, who became the first foreign minister of the revolution, said 'you cannot fight an external war with a war going on inside the country'.[1] That proved to be the problem in 1917. The provisional government, dominated by liberals from the only political element committed to continuing the war, lacked authority. A soviet (council) of workers', soldiers', and peasants' deputies, initially led by moderate socialists but gradually moving to the left, controlled Petrograd's streets and garrison. Thus, 'responsibility without power confronted power without responsibility',[2] as the soviet kept shoving the government leftward.

The pattern emerged early on. In April, an all-Russian conference of soviets supported the government and the war but also endorsed the Petrograd soviet's formula for a peace based on self-determination without annexations or indemnities. The government adopted this in an ambiguous statement which also declared that Russia would honour its commitments to the Allies. But Miliukov, whose devotion to obtaining Russia's historic goal of the Straits was such that he was known as Pavel Dardenel'skii, reinterpreted it to imply that Russia was still committed to victory. There ensued a cabinet crisis, his removal, and a new government with a substantial socialist component which accepted the soviet's formula of an early peace without annexations.

Meanwhile Lenin arrived in Petrograd in mid-April. Berlin arranged his rail transit from Switzerland so he could add to the confusion and war-weariness in Russia. He campaigned for peace, bread, freedom, and land, further eroding the war's support. The Allies, on the other hand, tried to keep Russia in the war, brushing aside the new regime's effort to revise Allied war aims, variously offering and threatening to withhold loans, and sending delegations, especially of socialist ministers, to stiffen Russian resolve – all to little avail, as Petrograd was too preoccupied to pay much heed. After mid-summer, the Allies saw that little active fighting could be expected of Russia, but they still wanted it in the war to tie up German divisions which otherwise might be sent to the western front.

Russia remained in the war because its leaders wished to avoid defeat and separation from the Allies, but the summer was disastrous. Peace feelers to Germany yielded only humiliating terms; the Stockholm conference, which might pressure governments to an early peace, did not materialize; the last Russian military offensive on 1 July, launched to honour a commitment, halt military disintegration, and impress the Allies, stalled in a few days and turned into a rout as the army melted away. An abortive popular rising led to a new cabinet with a moderate socialist, Alexander Kerensky, as prime minister. Pacifism mounted as support for the war vanished; subject nationalities at the fringes of Russia's empire began to demand everything from cultural autonomy to full independence. What remained of the army voted with its feet as the regime approached complete collapse. German advances were limited only by Russia's inadequate railways and concern for the western front.

Kerensky was not the heroic superman such times required. As a Western witness said,

He made speeches. He made endless speeches. At one moment there was a possibility that the Germans would make a dash for Petrograd. Kerensky made speeches. The food shortage grew more serious, the winter was approaching and there was no fuel. Kerensky made speeches.[3]

In truth, he had little to work with except words.

September brought a badly organized attempt at a military coup. In early October the Bolsheviks* gained control of the Petrograd and Moscow soviets. At the end of the month, the Petrograd garrison withdrew its recognition of the provisional government, throwing its support to the soviet. Under the circumstances, Lenin's Bolsheviks were able to seize power in the capital a week later in a classic *coup d'état*. The Kerensky government collapsed like a pricked balloon.

*   *   *

Revolutions rarely play by the rules, for it is their purpose to alter them. That in Petrograd sought to overturn the world order. It rejected the values and practices of the existing state system and added an ideological component to international politics which distorted the balance of power mechanism for seventy years. There was no longer an agreed vocabulary, for Bolsheviks used words differently, and such terms as democracy and propaganda took on new meanings. For Bolsheviks, initially all capitalist regimes were enemies, and no basis of understanding was possible, as their ideological hatred was deep and they mounted a direct challenge to the nineteenth-century world system based on Europe's great powers and their joint assumptions.

Lenin, who starred in the first act of the new Russian drama, shared this hostility to a degree. In February 1918, he closed debate on whether to accept Allied aid against German attack by scribbling, 'Please add my vote in favour of taking 'tatoes and weapons from the bandits of Anglo-French imperialism.'[4] Lenin was a dedicated and ruthless Marxist revolutionary but also a realist, as his note indicated. His goals were fixed but his tactics flexible. When he lacked information, which was often during Bolshevism's early isolation, he relied on ideological formulations which led him astray, but when the facts became apparent, he accepted them and corrected course at once, not clinging to theoretical dicta in the teeth of the evidence.

For Lenin, protecting and furthering the revolution came first. He would lie to capitalist states and sign any treaty, with little intent of honouring it, to save his revolution. Marxist theory dictated a chain reaction of revolutions

---

* The term 'Bolshevik,' meaning 'majoritarian,' was given by Lenin to his left socialists in 1903 at a time when they were usually in the minority. After November 1917, the term Bolshevik came to mean Russian Communist.

across Europe, and Lenin did all possible to hasten it, not least to save Bolshevism. He and his first Foreign Commissar, Leon Trotsky, overestimated the imminence of world revolution, reading too much into strikes and food riots. Indeed, Trotsky said, 'What diplomatic work are we apt to have now? I will issue a few revolutionary proclamations to the peoples of the world and then shut up shop.'[5] He set up a Bureau of International Revolutionary Propaganda and a Press Bureau at once; conventional offices came later when he and Lenin learned from reality.

Despite his hopes of world revolution, Lenin knew Russia must have peace. He had a small party, no army except a Red Guard, and little control of the sprawling Russian Empire; after two weeks, Petrograd gained precarious mastery of the major cities in the central core but not yet of the outer areas of north, south, east and west. The imperial structure was disintegrating, and Lenin had promised peace so categorically that now he must provide it. Besides, there was no choice, for Russia could not continue the war, and most of the front had evaporated. Unlike his colleagues, Lenin saw that the peasants, 85 per cent of the people, would not accept the revolutionary war he had preached at Zimmerwald and that Russia could not fight without an army.

Accordingly, on 8 November 1917 a decree of peace was broadcast* to the world. It sought an immediate armistice and negotiation of a peace without annexations or indemnities, but these familiar terms were defined to require the abolition of colonies and involuntary past incorporations of one nationality by another, which would have destroyed the Habsburg Empire. The decree was addressed to both governments and peoples, and the latter were enlisted to pressure the former to peace. Indeed, Russia would 'help the peoples to take a hand'.[6] Further, Russia rejected secret diplomacy, announcing that it would publish the secret treaties concluded by prior regimes at once.

This first diplomatic act of the revolution encapsulated several strands of Bolshevik diplomacy. A propagandistic text and radio broadcast reflected the centrality of propaganda. Issuing secret treaties, an act embarrassing to Russia's supposed allies, abruptly rejected existing norms. Russia requested conventional diplomacy with governments but also appealed over the heads of cabinets to peoples, an act of interference in domestic affairs intended to pressure, and perhaps overthrow, regimes. From the outset, Russia wished to negotiate in conventional diplomatic fashion with existing governments and to do all possible to overturn them by propaganda, agitation, and revolution. This meant a two-pronged foreign policy employing co-existence

---

* Though some official and unofficial diplomatic agents remained in Russia until the summer of 1918, most early exchanges between the Soviet regime and the capitalist world occurred by radio. For the Allies, this method had the advantage of avoiding diplomatic recognition.

and subversion simultaneously. Since the initial goals were both peace and revolution, both tactics were used from the start.

When Trotsky gained entry to the Foreign Ministry, he sent the peace decree to the Allies. They ignored it, so on 26 November he asked the German High Command for an armistice. It had no idea who he was but was enchanted to see a second miracle of the House of Hohenzollern.* It seemed a miracle of the House of Habsburg as well, for Austria was frantic for food and peace before its Empire exploded. It is arguable which needed peace more, Russia or Austria.

Negotiations began at German headquarters at Brest-Litovsk on 2 December and continued sporadically for three months. The Russian delegation symbolically included a worker, a peasant, a soldier, a sailor, and a woman – who had assassinated a tsarist cabinet minister. The Bolsheviks pursued both diplomacy and propaganda, insisting on public negotiations with release of the transcripts. They missed no chance to distribute Bolshevik newspapers or further troop fraternization, and on trips to Brest-Litovsk they tossed propaganda leaflets to German soldiers from the train. As Russia sought both peace and revolution, it protracted the negotiations to gain maximum propaganda effect, buy time to strengthen Russia's revolution, and hasten others.

The negotiations were also prolonged by disputes within and among the parties. In Petrograd, many leaders wanted a revolutionary war; Lenin knew that peace was necessary or the revolution would be overthrown (as the troops made clear); and some hoped to temporize in the middle. There was tension between the German High Command, which wanted maximum annexation, and the foreign ministry, which preferred indirect imperialism in the east, with Kaiser Wilhelm wavering between. Austria, with a starving capital and no annexationist aims, pressed the German generals for haste.

The Entente was initially more uncertain than divided. Like most coalitions, it could agree only on what not to do. It would not join the talks or recognize the Bolshevik regime, dealing instead through unofficial agents. Britain and France arrived at a division of labour in south Russia to aid those anti-Bolshevik elements willing to fight on against Germany. Beyond that, the Allies did not know what to do and so did nothing, though Lloyd George and Wilson took care to issue statements of war aims based on self-determination and no annexations.

These were partly replies to Trotsky's appeals to Allied workers to force their regimes to join the talks. Though Lenin wanted World War I to continue to prevent combination of the two blocs against Bolshevism,

---

* The first occurred in 1762 during the Seven Years' War when the tsaritsa Elisabeth of Russia died and her successor Peter III, who was an admirer of Frederick II of Prussia, left the war just in time to save Prussia from disaster.

Trotsky tried to gain a propaganda edge and remove the stigma of a separate peace, hinting to the Allies that failure to join would cause repudiation of Russia's foreign debt, as occurred early in 1918 in a challenge to capitalist society. When Trotsky's appeals brought no response, he called for Europeans to rise against regimes and specifically for Austrians and Germans to rebel against their governments, with which he was negotiating.

These tactics did not derail negotiations because the German High Command wanted peace in order to transfer forces westward, which process began at once. Thus, an armistice was signed on 15 December 1917 based on the existing military line. It permitted troop fraternization, of which Russia made the most, and forbade German transfers westward beyond those already in progress. As orders had already been issued to shift one third of the forces west, this clause presented no impediment to the German army.

Treaty negotiations ensued. Trotsky consumed a month in pyrotechnic debate while the Germans quietly and separately dealt with a delegation from a new Ukrainian republic. Germany signed the war's first peace treaty on 9 February 1918 with this regime as it collapsed under onslaught from Red Guards. Since Austria needed its grain and the German army could and did prop it up again, Ukraine received favourable terms. The German generals expected then to force a rapid conclusion upon a Russia now deprived of its bread basket. However, Trotsky stupefied them on 10 February by stating that Russia was leaving the war but could not sign Germany's terms. His formula of 'no war, no peace' had been reluctantly accepted by Lenin, who did not have the votes to prevail, to avoid splitting the party leadership and on the understanding that if Germany marched, Trotsky would not oppose accepting its terms.

Germany marched, without military opposition, and neared Petrograd,* leading the government to move to Moscow in early March. Russia had already sued for peace but found the terms were now more severe. Trotsky left the Foreign Ministry to become War Commissar and was replaced by Georgi Chicherin, a former tsarist Foreign Ministry official who brought a more conventional approach to the Narkomindel (People's Commissariat of Foreign Affairs). Lenin threatened to resign as well and thus narrowly won agreement for signature, which took place at Brest-Litovsk on 3 March 1918 after the Russian envoys ostentatiously refused to read the final text to demonstrate that the treaty was a '*Diktat*', not a negotiated pact. Lenin won a bitter struggle in Moscow over ratification, consolidating his power in the process. In Germany, only the Independent Socialists, who had split off to the left of the Social Democrats in April 1917, opposed ratification.

* Renamed Leningrad in 1924. In 1991, it again became St Petersburg.

Germany's terms meant that Russia lost one fourth of its prewar European territory and 40 per cent of its European population, 25 per cent of its total population, one-third of its rail net, more than half its factories, a third of its agricultural land, and more than three quarters of its iron and coal supplies. There was territorial transfer to Finland, the Ukraine, and Turkey, as well as German-occupied areas, whose disposition was unspecified but out of Russian hands. The treaty legalized German seizure of Russian resources, gave the Reich access to Russian wheat and oil, and granted Germany control of the Russian market. Brest-Litovsk has long been a symbol of a draconian peace, but it deprived the Bolsheviks of a hope, not a reality. They did not control the detached areas, most of which were neither populated by Russians nor desirous of Russian rule, especially by Bolsheviks. Though the German army would not grant true self-determination, on paper the terms were consonant with the peace decree, and the frontier facing Poland and the Baltic area was more favourable to Russia than that of 1921 to 1939. As there were no direct indemnities, the chief hardship was loss of the Ukraine. Neither party seriously intended to honour the treaty.[7]

Germany had not detached Great Russian territory, but still, a year after Tsar Nicholas's abdication, it held a broad band from the Arctic Ocean to the Black Sea and 55 million inhabitants of the pre-war Russian Empire. Russia's border was that of the mid-sixteenth century, and by the two treaties of Brest-Litovsk and that of Bucharest of 7 May with a Rumania not only defeated but now isolated by Bolshevism, Germany had largely achieved *Mitteleuropa*. Yet the German armies kept marching. They entered Finland, conquered Ukraine and the Donetz coal basin, and penetrated the Caucasus. A million men were engaged, which may have affected the outcome on the western front.

Trotsky was organizing the Red Army, but it was no match for German troops. Moreover, it needed to face multiplying internal enemies and Allied interventions. Thus Lenin used the greed of German business to rein in the German army, offering economic concessions to halt the troops. His new envoy in Berlin, busily making the embassy a centre of subversion, remarked, 'If we entice the German financiers . . . then perhaps we might be able to hang heavy weights on the feet of these soldiers.'[8] As German diplomats thought another Russian regime might denounce Brest-Litovsk, they wished the Bolsheviks to retain power and so persuaded the Kaiser to negotiate. The supplementary treaties of 27 August 1918 imposed a Russian indemnity of six milliard marks ($1.5 milliard or £300 million) and 25 per cent of Baku's oil output in exchange for a vast German evacuation; a tacit agreement that Germany would not attack enabled Lenin to withdraw troops in the west for use against other enemies. Russia, whose economy had reached such collapse that it could not fulfill many specific clauses, did not expect to; it had bought time and stopped the German advance. In fact, Russia paid a little and Germany withdrew a little. These treaties, like those of Brest-Litovsk and Bucharest, lasted only until the Armistice in November.

*   *   *

In the West, the November revolution and the Brest-Litovsk treaty led to intense anti-Bolshevik feeling, particularly in France where the war was nearly lost. In its effect on world history, the Russian Revolution was surely a close competitor to the French Revolution, especially of the years 1793–94. Both brought to power in one of Europe's great states a set of political and social ideas then considered terrifyingly radical; thus both caused sharp reactions from other great powers, diplomatic crisis and war. But because Russia was so vast and remote, Europe was embroiled in World War I when Bolshevism arrived and exhausted thereafter, and the challenge posed by Bolshevism was not fully comprehended, the response of the powers was more diplomatic than military. Crisis in Russia generated civil wars in which the Allies dabbled rather than a new pan-European cataclysm.

All the Allies were hostile to Marxism, but until the Armistice, their primary concern was to keep some Russian elements in the war against Germany, not to overturn Bolshevism. However, the Russian scene was tangled in the extreme, occupied by numerous players operating at cross-purposes with a maximum of confusion and at times a minimum of information. On the vast Russian stage there developed a gigantic game of blind man's bluff, with many players often groping in the dark. The Bolsheviks were cut off from most of the world by ideology, geography, war and Allied blockade, and Lenin's fear of a pan-imperialist alliance. Allied telegrams took a month to reach London from some locations, were often inaccurate, and at best reported obsolete data; orders back were often impossible of execution or by the time they arrived had been overtaken by events. Allied junior officers and vice-consuls in some parts of Russia issued orders locally without knowledge of policy or the wider situation. Thus much occurred which was not in accord with fluctuating official policies.

After Brest-Litovsk, civil wars erupted, especially around the fringes, under leaders ranging from tsarist generals to agrarian socialists, as Lenin still controlled only the central core. Further, nationalities rebelled, mainly in Europe but also along the southern Muslim tier into central Asia; these groups were often in conflict with each other as well as with Bolshevik 'Reds' and anti-Bolshevik 'Whites' fighting for a unitary Russian empire. In Europe and the south, German troops lingered into 1919, fighting off and on until the Armistice for and against the Bolsheviks, for and against the Ukrainians. To this were added a Czech army trying to leave Russia and Allied interventions at the fringes. Initially, the Allies sought to turn various groups against Germany, but Bolshevik opposition and their own proclivities led to increasing support of the White movements against Bolshevism, especially after the Armistice.

Allied motives were as varied as the Russian scene. Some allies pursued economic or imperial advantages; Britain had strategic concerns regarding India; France had an eye to potential alliances with Russia and/or new states. Allied rivalries were a factor, as powers tried to block each other. In addition to anti-Bolshevism, there was undue alarm about the military potential of 1·5 million German and Austrian prisoners of war in Russia, concern about debt repayment, a tendency to view Bolsheviks as German puppets, and fear of a Russo-German combination leading to German domination of eastern Europe. Not surprisingly, the Allies were never able to proclaim clear aims and particularly could not choose between lending support to a unitary White Russia or to the separatist aspirations of nationalities. For this reason, as well as war-weariness and common sense, Western Allied opinion consistently opposed the interventions by Allied governments.

The Allies discovered that units within Russia often were not susceptible to their control. On occasion, loyalty was to the commander, not to the Allies or the anti-Bolshevik cause. Some units were fairly democratic with the troops deciding what they would fight for. Units were lightly armed and poorly financed; aside from tsarist generals, their leaders were not always experienced. They would push far into weakly defended areas, often by rail, to the limit of their capacities and supplies, occasioning optimism and policy shifts in Western capitals. But they basked in their triumph, seldom taking effective defensive precautions, until the foe gathered enough troops to counterattack, whereupon the line would lurch rapidly in the other direction.

Allied intervention was militarily minor; units were small and rarely fought the Bolsheviks except in skirmishes. They never threatened Bolshevism but gave it an opportunity to rally Russia against the invader as well as providing a distraction from economic chaos and domestic problems. Allied aid to the Whites was another matter, as money and military supplies kept White revolts alive, prolonging the civil wars. Otherwise, intervention accomplished little except to strengthen the Bolshevik belief that revolution was necessary to defeat an 'international imperialist conspiracy'.

In the turbulent Russian scene, one futile Allied move led to another, but initially World War I dictated intervention to protect stocks of military supplies from German seizure and to preserve or reconstitute the eastern front. At Archangel huge stocks had piled up as the Russian rail net collapsed. At Murmansk a moderate socialist soviet gained brief Bolshevik permission in March 1918 to co-operate with the Allies against an apparent German–Finnish military threat. Thus British forces offshore with token French units made the first Allied landings at Murmansk, then in August at Archangel. American troops followed, reluctantly sent under Allied pressure in a vain effort to avoid more foolish ventures, and survived a miserable

Russian winter before leaving in June 1919. Meanwhile, as the Bolsheviks sought control, the British propped up a puppet White government, World War I ended, the peace conference solved nothing in Russia, other White regimes collapsed, and an increasingly pointless operation was ended in October 1919.

Britain and France were equally active in the south. In December 1917 they agreed that Britain would aid anti-Bolshevik movements south and east of the Black Sea, France to the north of it. Accordingly, British forces moved briefly to oil-rich Baku to block Germany and Turkey and into Transcaspia against a potential German thrust into central Asia, staying a year after the Armistice to buttress separatist regimes. Further west, France backed a Volunteer Army under various commanders, notably General Anton Denikin, which (unlike other White forces) wanted to fight Germans. As these patriots sought a unitary Russia, they also fought Ukrainians and other separatists. Allied support continued after the armistice into 1920 in an anti-Bolshevist vein, particularly a French occupation of Odessa from December 1918 to April 1919.

In central Russia was situated the strongest military force east of the German armies, which Russian Reds and Whites and the Allies all aimed to use: the 70 000-man Czech Legion formed earlier from prisoners of war eager to fight the Central Powers in hopes of creating a Czech state. Now it wished to leave Russia via Siberia to fight on the western front, to which the Bolsheviks agreed. But they tried first to use, then to disarm it; clashes occurred amid conflicting reports and orders, after which an awkward Allied compromise decreed that half the Czechs reinforce the Allies in the north. The Legion, adrift in an uncertain sea, smelled a trap in disarmament and division, rebelled, and voted to fight its way as a single armed unit to Vladivostok. Soon it controlled the entire 4700 mile Asian length of the trans-Siberian railway. Though it tried to be neutral, its arrival in an urban railway station usually caused Bolshevik authority to evaporate. Thus its actions set off White revolts, adding to Russia's civil wars.

In June 1918, part of the Legion was asked to turn west as the vanguard of a new front against Germany on the Volga. It obliged, pleased at the prospect of fighting Germans, until Trotsky sent the Red Army against it in September with tacit German co-operation. But in July and August, the Czechs took one town after another, the Allies landed at Archangel, Denikin advanced from the south toward a junction with the Czechs, and hopes were high of an eventual link to White and Allied forces in Siberia. This pipedream collapsed but, before it did, it provided a vehicle for the Allies to gain a long-sought Japanese–American intervention in Siberia, which somehow was supposed to ease German pressure in France. Wilson rightly viewed this as unrealistic, but his refusals over six months when the western front was *in extremis* severely strained the Entente. Japan, with designs on Siberia, Manchuria, and the Chinese Eastern Railway, wished to land at Vladivostok, but not without American blessing and aid, which Wilson did not give. Finally in early July 1918, he consented to small American and Japanese landings, supposedly to rescue the Czechs, guard the 800 000 tons of military stores at Vladivostok, and render such aid to the Russians as they requested.

Wilson's motives were probably mixed. He may have had some sentimental attachment to the 'gallant Czechs', who also provided both an excuse for intervention and a way to limit it. He needed a gesture toward the frantic Allies as well as a device to curb Japan and protect the Open Door for American trade in northern China and Siberia. The American contingent was small and did little, though its engineers worked to keep ramshackle railways running. The American army took the last restive Czechs, who had long since refused co-operation with Reds or Whites in Siberia, out from Vladivostok and left in April 1920. The Japanese forces, which swelled to 70 000 and lingered until late 1922, were the last foreign contingents to leave Russia.

Aside from the Japanese, foreign military interventions ceased in 1920, as did effective White resistance. Both left a residue of ill will. Battles with Poland and in the Baltic region ended, and border delimitations began. Other separatist nationalities – Azeri, Armenian, Ukrainian – were subdued and re-incorporated. Lenin had finally gained effective control of most of Russia; he could now turn to reconstruction, Marxist transformation, and the problem of co-existence with a capitalist world which had tried and failed to overturn him.

*   *   *

Lenin responded to the Allied interventions with caution. He tried to 'manœuvre, withdraw, wait, and prepare',[9] since Bolshevism's weakness left little choice. When possible, he tried to postpone clashes, divide the Allies, and scare them with the threat of the German army. He shifted quickly as the situation changed, allying with the lesser evil against the immediate threat, always aware that today's enemy might become tomorrow's ally in a kaleidoscopic scene. As survival became the immediate goal, events pushed world revolution into the future. With Bolshevism in Russia at stake, Lenin employed expediency, calculation, power politics, and classical diplomacy where possible. In August 1918, when the tide ran strongly against Bolshevism and Lenin himself was attacked, massacres, the secret police, and the Red Army were turned against enemies, internal and external.

Lenin exploited traditional diplomacy when possible, but the opportunities were limited by overwhelming world hostility to Bolshevism, aggravated by nationalization of private property (including foreign concerns) in June 1918 and murder of the royal family in July. Therefore, for several years he made the most of para-diplomacy, using the Russian Red Cross

Society, an organization of consumer co-operatives, and such trade missions as other powers would receive. Negotiations over exchanges of hostages or prisoners of war were stretched to the utmost as he increasingly gave priority to co-existence.

In 1918, Lenin used Germany against the Allies, but from September on it was clear that the Central Powers were collapsing. At the November Armistice, Russia denounced the treaty of Brest-Litovsk, made unsuccessful overtures to the Entente, invaded the Ukraine, and began to hope again for revolutions in central Europe, especially Germany, though the new republic there rejected Bolshevik overtures. Viewing the world through ideological spectacles, Lenin again feared that the capitalist states would now combine against Bolshevism.

Lenin also intensified his long-distance rivalry with Wilson for popular support. With their competing peace programmes, both were messianic prophets, one a philosophic materialist, the other a Christian moralist, but neither brooking much argument about what was right. Both were anti-imperialist but in different senses. Though Wilson stood for reform and Lenin for revolution, both sought a reordering of international politics.[10]

*   *   *

One reason why Allied interventions in Russia lasted beyond any useful purpose was a desire to postpone action until the peace conference arrived at a common policy toward Bolshevism. However, the statesmen assembled in Paris were even more unsuccessful in this respect than in instituting Wilson's new diplomatic order. Though various expedients were tried, no common solution was achieved. Divisions within delegations were a factor, but the main problem was that the Big Three of the conference did not agree. They all fluctuated and evolved, but Georges Clemenceau of France wished initially to overturn Bolshevism, Lloyd George increasingly to do business with it, and Wilson to withdraw from Russia.

Though the Russian problem was addressed only intermittently and distractedly, fear of Bolshevism haunted the conference, which saw it as a fatal virus assaulting the structure of Western societies when their resistance was low. The peacemakers thought it urgent to settle east European borders before the infection swept westward. To do so seemed to require Russian co-operation, but who in Russia to co-operate with? There were so many regimes, and no Western power wished to confer diplomatic recognition on the Bolsheviks, who controlled the heartland. In Paris a Russian Political Conference represented the major White governments but, as the Allies did not wish to face Russian claims arising from the secret treaties, it never gained entry to the peace deliberations.

To evade this problem and that of recognition, the peace conference decided on 22 January 1919 to invite all Russian regimes to consult with the Allies. Since Clemenceau refused to have the Bolsheviks in Paris, the island of Prinkipo in the Sea of Marmara was chosen as a resort with ample hotels which the Bolsheviks could reach without crossing other states, where they might strew propaganda. An invitation, requiring a military truce as the sole condition for participation, was duly broadcast. Most separatist regimes accepted, as did Moscow, but without mention of a cease-fire, which fact later served as a pretext to claim the Bolsheviks had refused. The major White regimes declined, primarily because Denikin and Admiral Aleksandr Kolchak, now the dominant White leader in Siberia, were planning anti-Bolshevik offensives, Allied representatives put little pressure on them, and French agents encouraged refusal. In any event, it is difficult to see what such a disparate and discordant gathering could have achieved.

A new struggle developed in Paris between those who wished to intervene in Russia and those who sought accommodation with Bolshevism, with simultaneous proposals from both camps. In mid-February, Winston Churchill, British Secretary for War, pressed with French and Italian support for increased military intervention to create a grand coalition against Bolshevism. As Lloyd George and Wilson opposed this, a stalemate developed, during which an emissary was sent to Lenin. William Bullitt, a young American, arrived secretly in Moscow in mid-March on an unofficial American exploratory mission with informal British blessing. The inexperienced Bullitt negotiated alone with Lenin and Chicherin and within a week gained an agreement which traded Russian debt payment and economic concessions for an end to intervention and blockade. How long Lenin would have honoured such an arrangement is an open question.

By the time Bullitt returned to Paris on 25 March, Kolchak's briefly triumphant march to the Volga had begun, heartening interventionists, and Bela Kun's left-wing regime had taken control in Hungary, followed by a republic of soviets in Bavaria, frightening moderates into thoughts of slaying the revolutionary virus at the source of infection. Wilson, who was unwell and preoccupied with crisis over the German settlement, gave Bullitt's report little attention. Lloyd George, similarly engaged and under attack in Parliament for being too accommodating to Bolshevism, disavowed Bullitt. Thus, the Bullitt scheme fell by the wayside, and those who favoured an anti-communist crusade briefly had their day. But Wilson, Lloyd George, and Clemenceau, who would have to provide the money and troops, were all moving toward containment and did not approve ambitious schemes aimed at destroying Bolshevism and preventing the nightmare of a German–Bolshevik alliance.

As the pendulum swung back, Wilson's deputy, House, proposed to use food shipments to moderate Bolshevik behaviour. Using food as a diplomatic weapon could be made to appear altruistic while providing a non-military form of intervention. A scheme was approved by the great powers and eventually broadcast to Moscow. Since it required a unilateral

Bolshevik cease-fire and would have given the Allies control of Russian transportation facilities, food, and local government, Chicherin rejected it early in May, while indicating willingness to parley.

The Allies, divided within and among themselves, never stuck to any scheme for long. By May, Admiral Kolchak appeared to be consolidating political authority as the dominant White leader and his spring offensive was at high tide. The Allies had long sought a Russian government they could support. A considerable movement grew up to recognize Kolchak, but American relations with him in Siberia were poor, Kerensky lobbied in Paris against him, and Wilson, who distrusted him, preferred withdrawal. As a compromise, in late May Kolchak was offered aid in return for a promise of democracy, concessions to the nationalities, and assumption of tsarist debts. By the time the autocratic and unpopular admiral sent a text vaguely promising democracy to Paris in June, it was becoming evident even at a distance that his military effort was failing. The United States, which would have had to supply most of the aid, dropped the plan.

The statesmen disbanded without further attention to the Russian problem, whose implications they had not faced. Their approaches had been *ad hoc*, unrealistic, and short-term, not addressing the Bolshevik challenge to capitalist society. Harried statesmen coping with Germany's fate had little time to reflect. In their disunity, they never jointly faced the need to cut their losses and leave Russia, trading withdrawal for a Bolshevik amnesty to their White allies. So the embittering interventions lingered on, relations with Russia were not resolved, and the east European settlement was incomplete. The Versailles treaty abrogated that of Brest-Litovsk, reserved a Russian right to reparations, and obliged Germany to abandon all claims to and accept future Allied arrangements for districts within Russia's 1914 borders. Thus the peace conference's solution to the Russian problem proved to be procrastination, which was no solution at all.

* * *

As the peace conference met in Paris, invitations were broadcast from Moscow to left socialists for a rival conference to create a new International. Lenin wanted to combat Wilson's influence, block efforts to revive the Second International, exploit unrest elsewhere, and gain support of European workers against anti-Bolshevik moves their governments might undertake. Signs that revolutions might spread and interventions in Russia might grow were also factors, as was Lenin's longtime wish to leave the Second International and create his own.

Given Bolshevik isolation, most non-Russians who attended the founding congress in Moscow from 2 to 6 March 1919 were resident in Russia; thus Bolsheviks dominated. The world's only other communist parties were in Germany, Austria, and Hungary. On 4 March the assembly became the first congress of the Third or Communist International (or Comintern) and established a bureau of five members, including Lenin, Trotsky, and Gregory Zinoviev, who was elected chairman. A second congress with broader attendance was held in Moscow in July 1920. It approved 21 conditions for entry, designed to maintain the split of left socialists from the moderates and to ensure Leninist orthodoxy. One report declared that the Russian Communist Party was to be the model 'because of its iron discipline and its strict organization'.[11] Parties had to favour the revolutionary overthrow of capitalism and dictatorship of the proletariat, create underground cadres, and accept the International's decisions. Their programmes were to be dictated by local circumstances and Comintern resolutions and required Comintern approval, ensuring conformity to Bolshevik desires. They were to aid Soviet republics against counter-revolution.

With creation of the Comintern, the two prongs of Bolshevik foreign policy superficially diverged as the Russian government pursued diplomacy while the Comintern fostered revolution and issued propaganda. As the former came to pursue co-existence and sought diplomatic recognition by the capitalist world, its behaviour could be starchily bourgeois, while the Comintern attended to subversion and agitation in Europe and among Asian and African subject peoples. The Soviet government claimed ignorance of Comintern activities, but the divorce was only nominal. At first personnel shifted back and forth between the Narkomindel and the Comintern, both agents of Bolshevik foreign policy; Comintern agents were hidden on legation rosters, and diplomatic couriers routinely carried propaganda materials and funds to finance subversion of other regimes.

Socialist parties now had to choose between the Third International and what remained of the Second. In the strongest European parties, those of Britain, France, Germany, and Italy, the Third International's first congress aroused much enthusiasm and hope that it would be a more vigorous version of the Second International. After the second congress and the 21 conditions, the difference was clear. Thus left-wing groups split off, formed communist parties, and joined the Third International whereas most socialists did not. The communist parties remained small: on the whole, European workers were moderate socialists, not communists. Besides, the obligation to support political platforms geared to Russia's needs dictated programmes unattractive to local voters.

Efforts to reconstruct the Second International proved ineffectual. Poorly attended preliminary meetings passed resolutions pointedly endorsing democracy and condemning dictatorship, but never gained real support. The passions of war, socialist participation in governments, and the Leninist dictatorship had fractured international socialism, and several efforts to knit it together failed. Though the prewar unity of the socialist movement had perhaps been more apparent than real, it never recovered from the effects of war and revolution.

◆ Notes to Chapter 4

1. Harold Shukman, *Lenin and the Russian Revolution* (London, Longman, 1977 edn), p. 157.
2. George F. Kennan, *Russia and the West under Lenin and Stalin* (Boston, Little Brown, 1960), p. 20, quoting F. L. Schuman, *Russia since 1917* (New York, Knopf, 1957), p. 70.
3. W. Somerset Maugham, *Ashenden* (New York, Avon, 1969 edn), pp. 212–13.
4. Richard Pipes, *The Russian Revolution* (New York, Knopf, 1990), p. 591.
5. Richard K. Debo, *Revolution and Survival: The Foreign Policy of Soviet Russia, 1917–18* (Toronto, University of Toronto Press, 1979), p. 18.
6. For text, see John W. Wheeler-Bennett, *Brest-Litovsk, The Forgotten Peace: March 1918* (New York, Norton, 1971 edn), pp. 375–8.
7. Kennan, *Russia and the West*, pp. 41–2.
8. Debo, *Revolution and Survival*, p. 195.
9. *Op. cit.*, p. 263.
10. John M. Thompson, *Russia, Bolshevism, and the Versailles Peace* (Princeton, PUP, 1966), p. 11.
11. Julius Braunthal, *History of the International*, tr. John Clark (2 vols, New York, 1967), II, p. 171.

ACT II

THE WEST'S PEACE

What a beautiful fix we are now
in: peace has been declared.

Napoleon Bonaparte, 1802

CHAPTER

5

THE PARIS PEACE CONFERENCE AND THE VERSAILLES TREATY

The Paris peace conference of 1919 was an entr'acte between total war and comparative peace, a year-long scenario featuring the Wilson–Lenin rivalry. The contest was unequal, with one at centre stage and the other in the wings. Both wished to change the existing world order, one to reform it, the other to radically revise it. With the United States ascendant in November 1918 and Wilson in Paris, his more modest goal seemed feasible. But in the limelight Wilson's effort to reorder world politics was hampered by other star players plucking at him and pulling in various directions.

During the conference, whose task was to deal with the considerable detritus of World War I, the threat of Bolshevism was an ogre in the wings, never forgotten, occasionally sticking its nose on stage as Marxism seemed to menace Berlin, seized Bavaria briefly, and ruled for some months in Hungary. The peacemakers, who had come of age in the capitalist, liberal, less than fully democratic nineteenth century and who were influenced by its premises, feared Bolshevism, which they saw as a new virus potentially fatal to the world they knew. To save their world, a very broken and debilitated European world at a moment of great susceptibility to infection, speed was imperative in setting boundaries and restoring some sort of European state system.

The Bolshevik threat, which Russia tried to further, was only one reason for haste. Influenza also swept across Europe and North America, ultimately claiming 20 million lives; winter was coming on, and famine, as economic and often political chaos reigned east of the Rhine. Of the four eastern empires, that of the Habsburgs had shattered; that of the Romanovs was partly in Lenin's hands and partly in those of hostile forces, Russian and foreign; that of the Ottomans barely stood; and that of the Hohenzollerns was intact but in inexperienced socialist hands and hardly functioning, especially economically. Vast areas lacked boundaries, established governments, food, transportation networks to carry supplies to the starving, and currencies worthy of the name. And the European victors, who faced the vast challenge of putting this world in order, were exhausted.

Nobody and nothing was ready. The sudden collapse of the Central Powers had taken the victors by surprise. Some planning had been done in foreign ministries or special entities staffed largely by university scholars, but relatively little had been endorsed by political leaders, let alone by Allies. At the Armistice the victors had agreed on its terms and their interpretation of the Fourteen Points, deciding for instance that an 'impartial adjustment of all colonial claims'[1] would apply only to colonies of the losers, but progressed no further. A December meeting in London made some tentative decisions without American participation, as House was ill and Wilson preferred to await the peace conference, partly because his views on European issues were as yet unformed.

Wilson was at one with other Allied leaders in wanting to defer confrontation and hard decisions, but his delay mattered the most, for American power was at its peak at the Armistice and immediately thereafter. Overseas colonies had kept the Allies going, but in the end American military force had been decisive. 'The age of European domination of the world was beginning to close; the strength of the New World . . . [had been] . . . necessary to contain the most powerful nation of the Old.'[2] A prostrate continent desperately needed American loans, supplies, food, seed, and machinery. This spelled power for America, as did Britain's decision to move closer to the United States and away from France.

Yet Wilson's personal power was waning. Congressional elections at the Armistice repudiated him, returning a Republican majority to the Senate, which constitutionally must approve treaties – a fact Wilson ignored in choosing his delegation. His precedent-shattering decision to lead the delegation himself did not delay the conference, as nobody else was ready, but it further eroded his influence, especially as he was inexperienced in debate and negotiation. His first trip to Paris was not costly but his second was; he would have been wiser to remain in Washington. Saying no is easier from a distance, especially if one can command the heights. He was also bound to disappoint the conflicting hopes of the 'little people' who worshipped him frenziedly during a pre-conference tour of Allied capitals. Their brief adulation, however, strengthened his Calvinistic tendency to see himself as God's chosen instrument to right the world, thereby increasing his rigidity and decreasing his effectiveness.

Britain also had an election, overdue because of the war and held in an atmosphere of wartime hysteria and overheated oratory. Lloyd George did not speak of hanging the Kaiser and squeezing the German lemon until the pips squeaked, but others did. The result was a political situation and a House of Commons briefly requiring a hard line. One cabinet minister remarked, 'We are going into these negotiations with our mouths full of fine phrases and our brains seething with dark thoughts.'[3]

France, as yet unaware of a desertion already in progress as Britain pulled away from the continent toward empire and America, wisely deferred the electoral process, but it too was unready. Once Wilson ruled out neutral Switzerland as site of the conference, Paris could not be denied, but it was the battered capital of a war-torn country. Hotels needed for conference delegates were serving as military hospitals; they had to be evacuated, disinfected, and refurnished while unobtainable luxuries, such as milk, had to be found. As hosts, the French prepared a schema for the peace conference; since it listed the League of Nations last, Wilson dismissed it. Thus, even basic organizational planning remained undone.

Also left undone during the interval between the Armistice and the peace conference, and indeed during the main phase of the latter until late spring, was any effort to bring defeat home to the German people. The war had ended suddenly for them, too, without invasion or devastation of Reich soil, and with as little awareness as the Allies of the inability of the German army to continue. Few recognized or accepted defeat. Responding to the public mood, the new chancellor greeted the army, 'As you return unconquered from the field of battle, I salute you.'[4] The Allies assumed the Germans knew who won and who lost the war; they never faced up to the problem of a Germany which quickly reached the comforting conclusion that the result had been a draw and entered what one German termed 'the dreamland of the Armistice period'.[5] This view was facilitated by the misnomer 'Armistice', by a modest occupation limited to the Rhineland alone, and by six months of neglect as the Allies turned to peacemaking. Germans awaited a treaty of equals while in Paris the Allies wrote a peace of victors.

*   *   *

The Paris conference was the largest of those periodic gatherings to rearrange the map of Europe after great wars, such as had been held in 1648 and 1814–5, although it was the first whose reach extended far beyond Europe. Perhaps unfortunately, it did not build upon the work of the Congress of Vienna, which largely preserved Europe's peace for a century. Wilson forbade mention of the Viennese exemplar, condemning its preoccupation with the balance of power and arbitrary assignment of 'souls' wherever convenient to preserve it. Thus the power configuration was not discussed at Paris.

In several respects, however, Paris resembled Vienna. The great powers again dominated and constituted themselves a supreme court before which small states and other interested parties could plead. Just as it had been agreed at Vienna that France would be preserved largely intact as a great power, so it was accepted without discussion at Paris that Germany would not be divided. Again, the victors fell out over the issues, and Paris became one prolonged inter-Allied haggle. Perhaps, the opening weeks 'were no more than the Indian summer of the wartime alliance. . .'.[6] If so, in a misordering of seasons, frost arrived in April with the crisis of the conference when Italy withdrew and Wilson, Japan, and Belgium nearly did the same.

The size of the conference, which opened on 18 January 1919 at the French Foreign Ministry (Quai d'Orsay), was immense. There were more than a thousand official delegates and at least as many in supporting staff. In addition, eminences such as the Amir (Prince) Faisal of Arabia and Albert, King of the Belgians, arrived with their entourages to plead before the mighty. Also in Paris, though not officially part of the peace conference, were motley individuals and groups hoping to influence its course by private contacts: Zionists, Irish nationalists, the King of Montenegro (whose realm was being absorbed into Yugoslavia), two groups representing mostly American blacks, Russian diplomats from the defunct Kerensky regime, the Russian Political Conference of Whites, and Korean nationalists who hiked across the Eurasian land mass, arriving too late to plead for liberation. Any remaining hotel space was snatched up by a vast press corps, including practitioners of the latest news medium: newsreel photography.

Equally important was who was *not* there. Kings were conspicuous by their absence. The more powerful ones had lost their thrones; in an era of increasingly representative government, the remaining regnant monarchs left diplomacy to their delegations. None of the losers attended. Originally, a conference of victors was to be followed by a congress with the defeated powers, but the first stage took so long and agreement was so difficult that the second stage was abandoned. Memory of how Talleyrand had driven a wedge between victors at Vienna contributed to this decision. Russia was also excluded, though abortive efforts were made to deal with it. The neutrals did not participate, though some were summoned for consultation when issues affecting them arose. Most of the infant states rising from the ashes of the old were allowed delegations, but the Baltic republics and Finland were not, pending the outcome of the wars in Russia.

Twenty-seven nations,* the majority non-European, were represented at Paris; of these, three really counted. There were officially five great powers, but Japan's and Italy's interests were regional, and neither cared about much of the German treaty. The heart of the peace settlement was devised by three men, each dominant in his delegation and government. Arthur Balfour's comment on watching them settle the fate of Asia Minor with the aid of a young British diplomat, 'these three ignorant men . . . with a child to guide them'[7] could apply equally to many aspects of the European treaties.

Perhaps Clemenceau was clearest in his focus. This old man, the Tiger who had held France together and hung on until salvation arrived, had lived through two German invasions of his country and was determined to prevent a third. France was for the moment the great continental land power, but mainly for lack of another. Clemenceau knew she was fundamentally

* Plus the four British Dominions and India.

weakening and severely wounded, whereas a stronger Germany was barely scratched despite short-term political uncertainty. He wanted the return of Alsace and Lorraine, transfer of the Saar Basin, detachment of the Rhineland from Germany and creation there of a French-dominated buffer state. Financial reparation was imperative to repair the devastation of France's ten richest and most industrial provinces; a share in colonial booty was France's due, though this was secondary to ensuring security against Germany. He wanted German military might restricted, and favoured generosity to the new states on Germany's east, which he hoped to enlist as allies to replace Russia. What Clemenceau wished to impose on Germany was more rigorous than the Anglo-American ideal but as moderate as the French political scene could tolerate; despite all his immense prestige and power, Clemenceau had constant trouble with his right wing.

The mercurial Lloyd George was equally dominant in his delegation and equally sure of what he wanted, but less direct. He aimed to end German naval and imperial competition; when he gained that early on with informal allocation of German ships and colonies, he ceased to fear Germany and, true to British tradition, began to jettison the wartime ally. Of political necessity, he wanted a substantial share of reparations for Britain (though much less than did some members of his delegation, included in a patchwork of expedients aimed at solving a domestic political problem). He sought to consolidate the pre-eminent position in the Middle East that Britain had gained in the last month of the war. Above all, Lloyd George wanted to turn away from Europe to domestic problems and empire. Accordingly, he did not want to expend resources on enforcing the peace treaty. Thus he favoured including only what Germany would accept, so that enforcement would be unnecessary; but no French politician could sign a treaty confined to what Germany would genuinely accept and expect to survive in office.

Wilson, the other triumvir, sought almost nothing concrete. Beyond a self-enforcing treaty and favourable terms for American trade, his concerns were abstract. He wanted justice, democracy, and a new world order; he expected to arbitrate among the others and impose his view. The League of Nations and self-determination of peoples were his panaceas. But the one was weak whereas the other confused ethnicity with nationality and created new problems. Wilson knew little of foreign affairs; yet with faith in his rectitude, he intended to impose God's will, as he saw it, on the world.

These three leaders each had four other plenipotentiary delegates to assist them, as well as flocks of experts and junior diplomats, but each relied primarily on a chosen one or two: André Tardieu, Edward House, Philip Kerr, and the British delegation's secretary, Sir Maurice Hankey, whose reduction of chaos to order may have saved the conference. Leaders of small states had intermittent prominence, if not power: Eleutherios Venizelos of Greece charmed the Three, especially Lloyd George; the outspoken Paul Hymans of Belgium, *de facto* leader of the small states, infuriated them; William Hughes of Australia faced Wilson down over colonies; Jan Smuts of South Africa brought him to dubious decisions over reparations; Faisal fascinated the Ten but gained little.

With three men so dominant, not only their policies but also their prejudices played a role. Lloyd George detested all things Polish and fought to keep Poland as small as possible, as he had no intention of defending it against Germany. Clemenceau wanted a strong Poland to the east of Germany and as a buffer against communist infection. Wilson had a large Polish-American voting bloc to consider and a Polish expert who, as a recent convert to Catholicism, saw a powerful Poland as a bulwark against atheism. With such idiosyncracies added to the ethnic and geographic complexities, decision-making became an excruciating process.

None of this was apparent when the conference opened. The great powers understood that they would decide matters in secret. 'Open covenants of peace, openly arrived at' meant only that the resultant treaties would be published and submitted to parliaments. Most plenary sessions, which did little more than ratify great power decisions, were open to the press, but negotiations were not. Commissions were created on specific issues, such as the League of Nations, reparations, international labour legislation, and ports and waterways. These reported to a Council of Ten consisting of the delegation head and his deputy (normally the foreign minister) of each of the five powers.

As the great powers dominated the commissions, the small states had little to do; hence they had to be given the appearance of some activity. In addition, the Big Three showed a natural desire to feel each other out and to defer clashes on key issues, so the small states were allowed to plead their cases before the Ten, droning documents that had already been submitted. This led to formation of territorial commissions and finally a Central Territorial Committee to co-ordinate their findings which, like those of other commissions, were to go to the Ten for decision.

Thus few clauses of the peace treaty were settled in the first month, aside from the League of Nations Covenant. A hiatus followed as Wilson, Lloyd George, and Vittorio Orlando of Italy all went home to cope with legislative bodies, and Clemenceau was wounded by an assassin's bullet. Upon Wilson's return in mid-March, the Ten resumed, but the crisis of the conference was approaching as it dealt with contentious issues; and the Ten, consisting of about 60 people, was a cumbersome and leaky vessel. So the Big Three and Orlando constituted themselves the Council of Four, meeting privately at Wilson's house. This was chaotic until Hankey insinuated himself to record their decisions; even so, discussions hopped randomly from topic to topic. As the conference reached its crisis in April over German and Italian questions, the Italian delegation withdrew, reducing the Four temporarily to the Three. Meanwhile, the foreign ministers met as the Five to settle lesser issues.

The resultant Versailles treaty was presented to a German delegation on 7 May, after which the Four moved on to other matters and also reconsidered what they had wrought, as Lloyd George tried with small success to revise the treaty to Germany's benefit. After it had been signed – on 28 June 1919, on the fifth anniversary of Sarajevo in the Hall of Mirrors at Versailles, using the same table and pens as for the proclamation of the German Empire there in 1871 – the heads of governments departed, leaving lesser lights to draft the other treaties. Gradually, those with other European Central Powers were completed, copying much from the Versailles treaty, but when the conference closed on 21 January 1920, that with Turkey was far from finished.

*   *   *

When the conference opened in January 1919, Wilson insisted that the League of Nations Covenant be drafted first and that it constitute the first section of all peace treaties. He was probably correct in assuming it must be written first or not at all, but not in thinking that its inclusion in the treaties would ensure American Senate approval. He chaired the League of Nations Commission, meeting nightly so as not to delay the daytime droning sessions.

Of the Four, Wilson was the sole true believer in the League. Clemenceau was openly cynical, preferring more conventional guarantees of security. Orlando was not greatly interested. Lloyd George wished to continue the great power Concert of Europe with the United States and perhaps Japan added; beyond that he was not eager to go. He gave lip service to the League to placate British liberals, who tended to enthusiastic support, and to please Wilson in hope of further rapprochement and concrete benefits elsewhere. Lloyd George agreed with Australia's Hughes, who growled, 'Give him a League of Nations and he will give us all the rest. Good. He shall have his toy.'[8]

That being so, the French proposed a powerful League with a military force and general staff, aiming to perpetuate the wartime alliance and create a weapon against renewed German aggression. When faced with Anglo-Saxon opposition, they tried to amend the Anglo-American proposals to gain their ends, but without success. The Commission worked with a merger of British and American drafts, and the Anglo-American scheme was rammed through with relatively little change. Wilson laid a draft Covenant before the peace conference on 14 February.

It provided for an Assembly of all member states and a Council originally composed of the five great powers. An outburst by Hymans in the League Commission led to allocation of four temporary seats with three-year terms for small states chosen by the Assembly. Both bodies required unanimity in votes on substantive matters. There would be a Secretariat at League headquarters in Geneva and a Permanent Court of International

Justice, established in 1922 at The Hague. Membership in the League was confined to independent states, mostly Western, and the British Dominions, marking their progression toward independence in foreign affairs.

The Covenant required registration and publication of treaties, endorsed disarmament and provided for arbitration of disputes likely to cause a war. Should war nonetheless eventuate, the miscreant would be deemed to have committed an act of war against all League members, who would proceed at once to economic sanctions and be advised by the Council about possible military sanctions. Most famously, Article X specified that

> The Members of the League undertake to respect and preserve as against external aggression the territorial integrity and existing political independence of all Members of the League. In case of any such aggression or in case of any threat or danger of such aggression the Council shall advise upon the means by which this obligation shall be fulfilled.[9]

Much was made of this by American senators as an excuse to reject the treaty because allegedly the ability of the League to require military action would violate the Congressional prerogative to declare war under the American constitution. In fact, the unanimity requirement and great power seats on the Council ensured freedom of decision. However, this clause reinforced the new *status quo* despite provisions elsewhere for peaceful change.

In combining national sovereignty and collective security, the Covenant tried to square the circle. The result was collective security riddled with loopholes, for the great powers – which would have to provide this security – were much less enthusiastic than the potential small state beneficiaries. At best, collective security rested on precarious premises. It assumed that world opinion would be united, on the side of the angels, and effective in deterring potential aggressors, and that if moral suasion failed, men and nations would spill their blood and treasure in foreign fields that were of little concern to them.

This issue was not squarely faced, because any real solution would be inconsistent with national sovereignty, which was sacrosanct. Once the Covenant was completed, Wilson returned to Washington, where opposition to the League was mounting. His efforts to quell it boomeranged; thus, on his return he had to seek amendments to the Covenant to preserve any hope of American approval. These he obtained eventually by promising Britain to delay American naval construction. Thus the completed Covenant excluded a state's domestic questions from the League's purview, and included a right of withdrawal on two year's notice, the Monroe Doctrine and other regional arrangements, and a proviso that states need go to war only in accordance with their own constitutions.

The League of Nations came into being in 1920 as a sort of permanent international conference, affording opportunities for quiet diplomacy. It did splendid work in administering the plebiscites specified by the peace treaties and in supervising specialized international agencies, many of them pre-existing; it helped make the colonial settlement something less than blatant imperialism. Yet in its larger tasks it disappointed idealists. It could not, as Wilson hoped, remedy the deficiencies of the treaties and serve as a vehicle for peaceful change; he had not given it that authority. It could not fulfil its primary goal of preserving peace because it lacked power; the great states guarded their might, their prerogatives, and their problems unto themselves. The League was often paralysed by the unanimity requirement and lacked ability to cope with defiance by a great or even a regional power. As always, the task of compelling obedience rested with the great states, who had the military might. Yet, despite its weakness, the League of Nations proved a useful innovation which on occasion kept the peace. The disappointment was great mainly because hopes had been unrealistically high.

*   *   *

The Versailles treaty furthered international law in other ways as well, notably in regard to international rivers and in the Labour Charter, which created the International Labour Organisation and enunciated general principles, such as the eight-hour day, as aspirations. But for the great powers, these were secondary issues. As the Great War was fought over the German question, so too this question dominated the peace settlement. The crisis of the conference in April was not entirely over German issues, as Italy and Japan made themselves felt, but the Three cared most about Germany because of its potential to disturb Europe's peace again – a potential they did little to reduce – and clashed most bitterly over its fate. They all thought Europe's future peace depended on the German terms, but saw the solution variously, with Lloyd George urging leniency, Clemenceau advocating more rigour, and Wilson steering the middle course. Yet although they endlessly debated specific questions, they never discussed Germany's role in Europe, to which it was now to be confined after loss of all colonies, or the net effect of their terms. Germany's challenge to the existing balance of power had been a major cause of the war, but discussion of the power configuration was taboo. Thus, though it was never far from the minds of Clemenceau and Lloyd George, neither the power balance nor Germany's place in it was jointly debated.

Moreover, Germany's borders were handled piecemeal. Those not reserved for consideration by the Four were parcelled out to a Belgian and Danish Commission, a Czech Commission, and a Polish Commission. Some were settled without much Allied controversy. Alsace and Lorraine were returned to France while tiny border districts went to Belgium. A plebiscite promised in 1864 was held on the Danish border; the segment of Schleswig transferred as a result was the sole European territorial loss that Germany fully accepted. Finally, the Four easily agreed to ban *Anschluss* (union) of Austria and Germany. As both Germany and the Germanic rump Austria wished to merge, the decision violated Germany's interpretation of the principle of self-determination, which in fact Wilson had hedged with various caveats. But *Anschluss* would heighten Germany's economic, demographic, and political domination of the continent; it would surround the Czechs and place Germany on the Brenner Pass at the Italian border; it would also put the Reich on the Danube River, poised to dominate the Balkans. Thus allowing Germany to reverse the military verdict and gain victory via *Anschluss* was never an option.

For Germany's other borders, self-determination was a factor. France claimed the Saar Basin, partly to gain its coal mines, but the inhabitants were indisputably German. After a bitter battle, a way was found to give France the Saar mines without the Saarlanders. The mines were transferred outright, but the district was to be governed for 15 years by a commission under the League of Nations. Then the population would choose between Germany, France or the League as a permanent affiliation. If victorious, Germany would repurchase the mines.

The Rhineland was equally contentious, for its population was German, but geography dictated its centrality to France's security. If German troops remained west of the Rhine River on France's frontier, another invasion would be all too easy; if, on the other hand, Germany were pushed east of the Rhine and the French army were across it, treaty violations could be quickly punished and the infant eastern republics could be rescued from any German effort to dominate them or worse. France preferred a French-dominated Rhenish buffer state* together with a long occupation, Allied control of the Rhine bridges, and Allied bridge-heads to the east. Lloyd George resisted extended occupation or creation of a new Alsace-Lorraine in reverse; he wished to bring British troops home. To induce moderation and give France a sense of security, he proposed an Anglo-American guarantee of French soil; then in his famous Fontainebleau Memorandum he urged easier terms for Germany at the expense of its fearful neighbours. France resented being asked to bear the sacrifices and doubted that moderation would pacify Germany but faced Anglo-American opposition to detachment or long occupation of the Rhineland. In late April, during Lloyd George's absence in London, Wilson and Clemenceau reached agreement on the Anglo-American guarantee, a permanently demilitarized but still German Rhineland (with a demilitarized zone on the right or east bank of the river), and a phased Allied occupation of the left or west bank along the French and Belgian

---

* However, the Rhenish Republic proclaimed on 1 June 1919 was the doing of French army officers in the occupied Rhineland without Clemenceau's consent. He was outraged at the ill-timed, embarrassing and potentially costly (but brief) episode.

borders in 5-, 10-, and 15-year zones together with the key bridges and bridgeheads. If Germany fulfilled all treaty obligations, the Rhineland would be evacuated at once; if, however, she failed to pay reparations in full, as Clemenceau anticipated, the occupation could be prolonged or renewed. If fully maintained, these arrangements would constitute considerable security for France.

On Germany's eastern frontier, self-determination encountered both economic considerations and ethnically mixed populations, in part resulting from fairly recent German colonization in Polish areas. The rebirth of Poland arose from the collapse in the war of all three empires which partitioned it in the eighteenth century; none participated in the peace negotiations. Wilson had promised a Polish state of indisputably Polish populations and with secure access to the sea. But the populations were mixed on all sides on the flat defenceless plain and the only sensible route to the sea was along Poland's great artery, the Vistula River. Its Baltic port was Danzig (Gdansk), a thoroughly German city, and transferring territory along the Vistula would sever East Prussia from the rest of Germany.

The badly divided new Polish government claimed Poland's 1772 boundaries and more. The Polish Commission granted many of its wishes, but Lloyd George fought ferociously in late March and April to reduce Germany's territorial loss and the number of Germans to be included in the new Poland for fear that Germany would refuse to sign the treaty and in the hope of forestalling German irredentism. Poland was granted a corridor to the sea through territory over 60 per cent Polish, Germany was allowed rail transit across it, and Poland given economic rights in Danzig,* which was to be a free city under the League. Plebiscites were to be held in small border zones and (after Lloyd George returned to the fray in June) the important region of Upper Silesia. Aside from plebiscite zones, 260 square miles and three million people, the majority not German, were transferred to the new Poland,[10] whose eastern borders were left unsettled in the absence of Russia. This was probably as good a solution as was achievable, but Germany never accepted it, deeming indisputably Polish districts to be those with few Germans and displaying outrage at the detachment of East Prussia and the subjection of Germans to 'inferior' Slavic Poles.

Contention was not limited to territorial questions. The disarmament promised in the Fourteen Points was to begin in Germany, though the League of Nations was to prepare a general convention. Again, Lloyd George sought to minimize causes for German complaint. Further, he and Wilson, prisoners of the Anglo-Saxon tradition of no peacetime conscription, rejected France's preference for a sizeable German conscript army in favour of a volunteer professional army of 100 000 men on long-term enlistments. Germany was forbidden a general staff, heavy artillery, an air

---

* But tensions were such that Poland soon built its own port at Gdynia.

force, submarines, and battleships but allowed lesser vessels for coastal defence.*

Alleged war criminals were to be surrendered for trial by the victors (but in the end were not); the Kaiser was included at Lloyd George's insistence, though there was no reason to think the Dutch would relinquish him. German colonies would go to the victors, already in possession. Berlin was forbidden to discriminate against Allied trade, which was guaranteed five years of most-favoured nation treatment before Germany regained control of its tariff policy. To ease economic dislocations arising from territorial transfer, goods from Alsace-Lorraine were to enter Germany duty-free for five years and from Poland for three years.

*   *   *

The reparations clauses were among the most controversial of the treaty, both while they were being debated in 1919 and for a decade and more thereafter, for they had direct implications for the power balance. At the time of the Armistice France, the fundamentally weaker power, had huge domestic and foreign debts and an industrial heartland devastated by military and economic warfare as well as wholesale destruction and removals, while Germany was unscathed and without foreign debt. If vast reconstruction costs were added to French burdens while Germany escaped without financial penalty, France would be disastrously further weakened, the power balance would tip, and Germany would become the victor in the West. Thus, the prolonged reparations battle amounted to a continuation of the war by other means.

In the short run, Germany was in better financial and economic condition than any European victor, especially those on whose soil the war had been waged. All Allies wished to trade with Germany, but none wished to see it economically dominant. And the continental victors needed cash to rebuild their devastated areas; they and the British each sought maximum advantage. Thus reparation was a contentious topic among the Allies during the six months spent on the German treaty. Though difficult throughout, it contributed markedly to the crisis of the conference in April, to an ailing Wilson's threat to depart, and to a Belgian threat to do the same.

Most victors sought their war costs in full from Germany. As this was both impossible and a violation of the Armistice terms, Wilson held firm, and only Belgium, whose invasion contravened international law, gained war costs. But since Britain had little physical damage on which to base claims, Smuts persuaded him (when Lloyd George threatened to withdraw) to accept war widows' pensions and military separation allowances as civilian damages.

---

* The existing high seas fleet, interned at Scapa Flow in the Orkney Islands, was to be transferred to the victors, but German crews scuttled it on 21 June 1919.

This dubious decision appeared to increase Germany's liability. In fact, as the final figure in 1921 rested on an estimate of German capacity to pay, not the larger total of Allied claims, pensions and allowances did not expand the reparations pie but enlarged the British Empire's slice of it. The size of that slice remained undetermined in 1919, as the victors could not agree on allocation of reparations.

The size of the pie was also left unsettled at Paris, for agreement on the amount of German liability proved impossible, both within and between delegations. The French were split among those who wanted maximum reparations, those who preferred trade with Germany, and those who clung to a scheme rejected by the United States to continue wartime Allied economic arrangements. Clemenceau, like Wilson, preferred a moderate figure. In the British delegation, Lloyd George, backed by John Maynard Keynes, wished to ask as little as possible whereas the British delegates to the conference's Reparation Commission, chosen to solve political problems in the election atmosphere at home, produced the highest figures of all.* Wilson sought to verify claims** whereas Lloyd George and Clemenceau came to see the political utility of postponing decision, for any realistic figure was bound to prick the balloon of inflated expectations. Politicians had promised Germany would pay, but the experts knew its capacity to do so did not exceed 60 milliard gold marks,† far less than damage estimates. As passions faded, a more reasonable figure consonant with German capacity to pay might become politically feasible. Thus Germany was to make an interim payment, primarily to cover costs of the Allied occupation and food shipments,†† of 20 milliard gold marks, chiefly in goods, before 1 May 1921, when the total German liability was to be set. This postponement meant financial uncertainty for Germany and Europe, and gave Germany the undeniable propaganda advantage of being able to complain of having to sign a 'blank cheque'.

Allied political necessity was addressed by making Germany theoretically responsible in Article 231 of the treaty for all damage suffered by the Allies, but tempered by limiting actual liability in Article 232 to civilian damages, as defined in an annex. Germany, anticipating a war guilt clause, seized on Article 231 and fulminated in 1919 and long after about the injustice of being saddled with 'unilateral war guilt'. The Allies had intended the awkwardly worded Article 231, which says nothing about war guilt, unilateral or

* They were Hughes and the 'Heavenly Twins', Lords Cunliffe and Sumner, who were always together and at one in their astronomical estimates.
** The task proved so vast that in the end the US Army Engineers surveyed only Belgium.
† The gold mark existed as actual currency pre-war but not post-war, when it became merely an essential book-keeping device as inflation caused the paper mark to fluctuate sharply in value. There were four gold marks to the dollar and twenty to the pound.
†† Despite lack of German cooperation, the Allies provisioned Germany before starvation set in. The 'hunger blockade' was effective German propaganda, but food shipments were permitted.

otherwise, as a legal basis for reparations. Its American author, young John Foster Dulles, also hoped to use it to limit Germany's burden, but his wording, as later altered, had other implications which escaped all Allied experts.[11] Moreover, in the debate with Germany over the treaty before it was signed, Allied rhetoric verged on informal assignment of guilt for causing the war. Thus, as Lloyd George told Germany in March 1921, if Germany could clear herself of 'war guilt', the basis for reparations would collapse; therefore, Germany continued its campaign on this topic through the 1920s. Curiously, neither Austria nor Hungary followed its lead. To gain reparations wherever possible, the Allies assigned collective responsibility and inserted the equivalent of Article 231 in their peace treaties, but only Germany viewed it as a war guilt clause.

The victors agreed that reparation payments should be confined to one generation, or 30 years. Restitution was required of seized property, including art and archives, farm animals, securities, and cash balances of banks, while Germany would pay for a permanent Allied Reparations Commission to oversee accounts. It would be credited on reparations account for battlefield salvage and for state properties transferred, such as submarine cables, the Saar mines, and railways in areas awarded to Poland. Reparation was to be paid in cash and 'kind' or goods, primarily coal, timber, and chemical products. Payments were to be a first charge on German revenues and assets, a provision which in theory would prevent German extravagance while northern France languished in ruins.

*   *   *

When the last reparations clauses were settled, the Versailles treaty was rushed to the printer without anybody having read all 200 pages and 440 clauses. Upon its return, young Anglo-American idealists at Paris were appalled by what they saw as a peace of vengeance, not justice. Their view reinforced the German 'dreamland' belief that the war had resulted in a draw and that 'a just peace' meant the *status quo ante bellum* with rectifications to incorporate in the Reich all Germans in Austria, Hungary, Poland, the Czech borderlands, and the south Tyrol, that is, the interpretation of self-determination most favourable to them. The terms came as a shock to German opinion, if not to Berlin's shrewder politicians. In fact, the territorial terms were somewhat harsher than intended, for the various commissions had written maximum terms, anticipating a negotiation process with Germany which did not occur. Thus Germany lost 10 per cent of its population, 13 per cent of its territory, and 13.5 per cent of its economic potential but 75 per cent of its iron ore;[12] still it remained fundamentally Europe's greatest power politically, economically, and potentially militarily as well.

After presenting the treaty to Germany on 7 May, the Four turned to other matters, especially central and eastern Europe. On 29 May, Germany replied; its rebuttal of 443 pages contested nearly every clause. Lloyd George reacted by launching a drive to revise the treaty. He feared Germany would refuse to sign; further, the moderation he had always preferred was now politically feasible. In mid-April he had faced charges from an angry House of Commons that he was being too easy on Germany, but the political winds had shifted and wartime passions were fading; his cabinet and delegation now pressed him to soften the terms. His efforts gained little beyond additional plebiscite zones, especially in Upper Silesia, and alleviation of the Rhineland regime. Wilson felt sure the treaty was just whereas Clemenceau knew it was the least that French opinion would tolerate. The fragile interlocking structure of compromises had been so excruciatingly difficult to achieve that starting over was not feasible. Thus, after minor modification, Germany was given an ultimatum, the much advertised *Diktat*. After a cabinet crisis, it capitulated.

When Germany signed the treaty on 28 June 1919, diplomacy itself became theatre, carefully staged for the newsreel cameras. One elderly French diplomat wrote disgustedly to another,

> The papers are full of the future signing of the peace with the plan of the Hall of Mirrors at Versailles. Nothing else than this plan could indicate such a profound revolution in the customs of diplomacy. There are found a hundred seats and tables for the assistants and the plenipotentiaries, as well as that table on which the treaty will be placed, in a type of theater. They only lack music and ballet girls, dancing in step, to offer the pen to the plenipotentiaries for signing. Louis XIV liked ballets, but only as a diversion; he signed treaties in his study. Democracy is more theatrical than the great king.[13]

The ceremony was good theatre but inflicted a pointless and childish humiliation on Germany. In this it was emblematic of a treaty which imposed too many pinpricks but no real chains.[14] A French critic said it was 'too mild for its severity',[15] a view which has stood the test of time. The treaty was severe enough to outrage Germany but too weak to restrain it effectively. Though Germans resented the fact that it was not written on the basis that the war resulted in a draw, it equally was not written on the basis of the truly crushing defeat in progress at the time of the Armistice. The so-called 'draconian *Diktat*' did not impose extensive occupation, dismemberment, or denial of self-government. Germany was somewhat truncated but still Germany, and still potentially Europe's strongest power.

The greatest single difficulty with the treaty was Germany's refusal to accept it because it symbolized and embodied the defeat which Germany rejected. As compelling the strong is difficult, it is wise to ask of a great power what it will accept. This was especially true in 1919 with Russia offstage, not providing an eastern counterbalance. But what a power will accept is determined by its perception of its circumstances. In 1814 and 1815, France accepted moderate treaties; defeat had been brought home by the presence of the Russian army and tsar in Paris. In 1871, German armies paraded the Champs Elysées; France accepted and quickly fulfilled a punitive peace. The Versailles treaty was less moderate than those of 1814–15 but not as draconian as Germany claimed. But Allied armies were not parading the Unter den Linden in Berlin; German armies marched there, hailed by the chancellor as having 'returned unconquered' from battle. Thus there was little perception of defeat and no readiness to face it. For this, the victors bear responsibility.

In May 1919 after Germany received the treaty, Wilhelm Groener, perhaps the most realistic of its generals, stressed in a military report: 'One must really face up to the result of the past war. It is the defeat, the elimination of Germany as a European Great Power after the failure from the outset of its unconscious attempt . . . to compete with England for world rule.'[16] But no German or Allied leader said this to the German people. Thus they were enraged, and their leaders, being politicians like others elsewhere, told them what they wanted to hear and continued to feed their rage, which contributed much, in combination with French insecurity, to the bitter diplomacy of the next decade.

This treaty which Germans did not accept required their co-operation to be fulfilled, above all in its reparations clauses. Enforcement provisions were startlingly few. Those which existed were temporary, as with the Rhineland occupation, and required Allied unanimity which, to the extent it had ever existed, was fraying fast. Equally temporary were most restrictions on German power and freedom of action, which made France timorous and inflexible when it was soon asked to concede further to Germany. Pressure for concessions came primarily from Britain, which also did not accept the treaty. Chivalry to the fallen foe (mainly for balance of power reasons), traditional hostility to France, trade considerations, Lloyd George's determination to undo what he had wrought, and the success of Anglo-German propaganda in inducing a national sense of guilt over the treaty terms all contributed to relentless British revisionism, which largely succeeded. Thus Versailles crumbled. For this reason and because American withdrawal distorted all treaty mechanisms from the outset, the treaty never operated as intended. Facile judgements that it caused World War II fail to consider these facts.

In other respects, criticisms of the Versailles treaty arose from a striving for an impossible perfection. Some abandonment of self-determination was inescapable, not least for economic and defence reasons, as was some compromise and acceptance of political reality in victor countries. Germany was treated more gently than it had intended to treat its foes. The treaty was written in great haste and under intense pressure; one might enquire why it was not a great deal more imperfect. Yet the fact remained that

Wilson had come down off the mountaintop to play poker with more skilled players; their bluffs induced him to yield often, abandoning his vision and his principles. Compromises came quickly and ever more easily after he sat down at the table. His original vague soaring vision could never have been implemented in full, but Wilson the philosopher-king became just another horse-trading politician, agreeing to the trial of the Kaiser and to war widows' pensions to placate Lloyd George, detachment of the Saar to retain Clemenceau in power. In short, he became one more fallible mortal, unable to deliver anybody's notion of perfection, let alone everybody's.

The fact that expectations of Wilson had been so great was one reason why the British delegation and leaders became so disillusioned about the peace, so bitter and guilt-ridden. Another was fear that Germany would not accept, would not fulfil, would not let Britain turn away from Europe. Yet another was fear of France, especially of her army which initially was the strongest on the continent, and total misjudgement of the underlying power balance, a false assumption that France was strong and Germany weak, when in fact the reverse was true if one looked past the short run and the fragile bonds of Versailles. Germans worked on the British sense of fair play, claiming without cease that the treaty was unjust. They were echoed by Keynes, whose 1919 polemic, *The Economic Consequences of the Peace*, was brilliant and influential if not entirely accurate, owing much to his guilt as a pacifist at having served Britain's war effort and his passion for a German reparations expert. Keynes's views helped to shape a climate of opinion enabling Lloyd George to continue his campaign, launched at Paris in June 1919, for treaty revision and 'appeasement' of Germany. His efforts toward quiet *de facto* revision achieved much without meeting Germany's desire for dramatic renunciation and wholesale renegotiation involving Germany's participation as an equal.

Lloyd George's accomplishments only heightened French fears. French defenders of the treaty deemed it barely adequate if fully enforced. Clemenceau had accepted a Rhineland settlement unsatisfactory to French military opinion to gain the Anglo-American guarantee; when the United States failed to ratify the treaty, both the American guarantee and the contingent British one lapsed, leaving France empty-handed, yet continually pressed to make more sacrifices of its security to satisfy what soon approached an Anglo-German condominion. The collapse of one of Paris's most crucial compromises left France insecure and frightened, thereby aggravating interwar Europe's instability.

Germany and Britain both desired treaty revision before the treaty was signed and constantly thereafter. They were Europe's two strongest powers; thus the Versailles treaty's life expectancy was doubtful from the outset. Both felt the treaty placed too many restrictions on German power; France thought it put too few. The issue, as always, was Germany's potential European predominance, a problem which the Paris conference did not squarely address. The peace diminished German power somewhat but did not effectively harness it. Little thought was given to the fact that a wounded lion can be dangerous and less to the question of how to force that snarling lion to obey.

◆ Notes to Chapter 5

1. Point V, Fourteen Points of 8 January 1918.
2. J. M. Roberts, *Europe, 1880–1945*, 2nd edn (London, Longman, 1989), p. 302.
3. Edwin Montagu to A. J. Balfour, 20 December 1918, cited in A. Lentin, *Lloyd George, Woodrow Wilson, and the Guilt of Germany* (Baton Rouge, LA, Louisiana State University Press, 1985), p. 30.
4. Robert G. L. Waite, *Vanguard of Nazism* (New York, Norton, 1952), p. 7. See also Marc Ferro, *The Great War, 1914–1918*, tr. Nicole Stone (London, Routledge, 1973), p. 222.
5. Klaus Schwabe, 'Germany's Peace Aims,' quoting Ernst Troeltsch, in Manfred F. Boemeke, Gerald D. Feldman, and Elisabeth Glaser, *The Treaty of Versailles: A Reassessment after 75 Years* (Cambridge, CUP, 1998), p. 42.
6. Erik Goldstein, *Winning the Peace: British Diplomatic Strategy, Peace Planning, and the Paris Peace Conference* (Oxford, Clarendon Press, 1991), p. 111.
7. Alan Sharp, *The Versailles Settlement: Peacemaking in Paris* (London, Macmillan, 1991), p. 30.
8. Michael Dockrill and J. Douglas Goold, *Peace Without Promise: Britain and the Peace Conferences, 1919–1923* (Hamden, CT, Archon, 1981), p. 59.
9. Article X, Treaty of Versailles, signed 28 June 1919; for full annotated text, see United States, Department of State, *Papers Relating to the Foreign Relations of the United States: The Paris Peace Conference, 1919*, 13 vols (Washington, US Government Printing Office, 1942–7), XIII.
10. Sharp, *Versailles Settlement*, p. 122.
11. Sally Marks, 'Smoke and Mirrors', in Boemeke *et al.*, *Versailles Treaty*, pp. 342–3.
12. Gerd Hardach, *The First World War, 1914–1918* (Berkeley, University of California Press, 1977) p. 244; Sharp, *Versailles Settlement*, pp. 127–8.
13. Paul Cambon to Jules Cambon, 28 June 1919, cited in Keith Eubank, *Paul Cambon, Master Diplomatist* (Norman, OK, University of Oklahoma Press, 1960), p. 193.
14. Lentin, *Lloyd George*, p. 133.

15. Jacques Bainville in *Action Française*, 8 May 1919, as cited in Lentin, *op. cit.*, p. 132.
16. Andrew J. Crozier, *The Causes of the Second World War* (Oxford, Blackwell, 1997), p. 30, citing Marshall Lee and Wolfgang Michalka, *German Foreign Policy, 1917–1933* (Leamington Spa, Berg, 1987), i.

CHAPTER

6

THE EASTERN TREATIES, 1919–1923

After Germany had signed the Versailles treaty, the Four departed, leaving work on the other treaties to underlings. Fortunately, much could be carried over from the German treaty. The League of Nations Covenant appeared in all treaties, as did the Labour Charter and the work done at Paris to enlarge on Vienna's efforts to regulate international rivers. The basic principles of the disarmament and reparations clauses were also incorporated in the other treaties, though the details varied.

Much work was already done. The Ten had heard east European claims at the end of January and had set the experts to work on them. The Four had intervened, chiefly in Italian issues and in Hungary after Bela Kun's Communist regime took power in March. Generally, they made decisions in ignorance, with no clear scheme in mind and little power to enforce their decisions, for only Italy had many troops in the region. The Habsburg collapse had set off a scramble in November and December 1918, as eastern states, existing and new, sought Austro-Hungarian provinces and seized as much as possible. Since ultimata from Paris had little behind them, the treaties often registered what had happened. The conference did not break up the Habsburg Empire; it had already shattered and could not be glued together without use of massive force against resisting Allied peoples.

Of the great powers, France and Italy were clearest about their goals. France wanted strong new states as allies, buffers against the spread of Bolshevism, and barriers to German expansion eastward. Italy favoured territorial transfer at German expense as a precedent for her own grandiose claims but opposed French domination of south-eastern Europe and especially any concessions to Yugoslavia. Thus Italian generosity shrank as one moved southward. Italy also sought all territory accorded it in the London treaty and more, control of the Brenner pass on the Austrian frontier, and a prohibition of *Anschluss*. Britain and America both wanted stability and trade. Beyond that, Britain urged a Danubian economic federation, a sort of Habsburg system without the Habsburgs. For all four powers, Bolshevism was a factor, as it swept Hungary and Bavaria in March and seemed to threaten Berlin, Vienna, and perhaps Prague.

Wilson had committed the Allies to satisfaction of national aspirations where this was feasible without creating discord and (within reason) to self-determination of peoples, a right to choose one's nationality. He explicitly rejected Vienna's principle of legitimacy – the rights of hereditary rulers – and its bartering about of peoples; thereby he ratified the war's resolution of the century-long battle between legitimacy and nationality. Wilson assumed that language was the key to nationality and that choice would solve the difficulties inherent in the problem.

In practice, self-determination as he saw it met endless complications. Nationalities were so intermingled that an ethnic line was rarely possible. Even when it existed, ethnicity clashed with the imperatives of economics, transport, or defensible frontiers as language lines wandered across railways, rivers, and mountain ranges. Peasants often avoided choosing a nationality lest they become part of a downtrodden minority; in plebiscites to determine affiliation, minorities and majorities often voted their economic interest. Further, race and religion were as important as language in determining nationality, which, in east European eyes, was something one was born with, not something one could choose. In short, personal and political nationality were not necessarily the same.[1] These factors afforded endless pretexts for dispute; at Paris, the interested states, great powers or small, favoured and opposed self-determination as convenient, for only Wilson was a true believer.

*   *   *

The Four approved Austria and Hungary's borders before they departed. Austria, unlike other east European states, emerged with a homogeneous population but little else to celebrate except transfer of a Germanic district from Hungary. It renounced both *Anschluss* and the Habsburg monarchy. The severe territorial losses largely registered what had already transpired, especially in the last days of the war, as Galica went to Poland, the rich realms of Bohemia and Moravia to the new state of Czechoslovakia,* and other areas to Rumania and Yugoslavia.† Italy gained the Brenner frontier, the Trentino, and the Germanic south Tyrol, to which Wilson agreed for strategic reasons and from ignorance of its ethnic composition.

The economic and psychological dislocation was acute. Austria had been one of Europe's great powers, if an increasingly hollow one. Vienna had been capital of an empire, seat of an imperial court and a major army, as well as central Europe's financial centre; now emperor and empire were gone and the army limited to 30 000 volunteers. The great city with its well organized socialist working class was circled by an uneconomic Alpine

* Divided in 1993 into the Czech Republic and Slovakia.
† Titled the Kingdom of the Serbs, Croats, and Slovenes until 1929, but here called Yugoslavia throughout. In 1991, Croatia, Slovenia, Bosnia-Herzegovina, and Macedonia seceded and became independent states, leaving only Serbia and Montenegro within Yugoslavia.

Europe after World War I

hinterland of conservative Catholic peasants. The new republic was politically divided, dismayed by its demotion to small power status, and too impoverished to pay the reparations in the treaty of Saint-Germain-en-Laye of 10 September 1919.

The new Hungary was almost as ethnically homogeneous owing to even greater truncation, arising in part from the separate work of three commissions. Its treaty was delayed by Allied refusal to deal with Bela Kun's regime from March to August 1919 and by Hungarian protest. Thus, the treaty of Trianon was signed on 4 June 1920 and reluctantly approved by the Hungarian Parliament in November. Like Austria, Hungary renounced the Habsburgs and accepted arms limitations and reparations, of which it paid little. But the emotive issue was loss of territory.

At the Armistice, Rumania seized many Hungarian domains, ignoring the Four's demand for partial withdrawal; thus possession was a factor, as was Allied fear in the spring of 1919 that Bolshevism was spreading, though in fact Kun's advent largely resulted from Allied demands. Losses to Austria, Italy and Poland were modest, those to Czechoslovakia and Yugoslavia large, and those to Rumania vast, amounting alone to more than the size of the surviving Hungary. Loss of the Istrian peninsula and Fiume, disputed between Italy and Yugoslavia, meant a landlocked state.

Hungary lost two-thirds of its pre-war population and domains. What remained was economically viable, thanks to its fertile plains and concentration of industry around Budapest, but unreconciled to its losses. More than three million Magyars now lived outside Hungary, though mostly not as majority populations. Hungary did not accept their exclusion, and irredentism was constant in the interwar era. Its bitterness rivalled that of Germany, but Hungary was not a major power and so could not compel treaty revision. Besides, its army was limited to 35 000 volunteers whereas the combined forces of its chief heirs – Czechoslovakia, Rumania, and Yugoslavia – amounted to half a million men.

Bulgarian territorial losses were less severe but were greeted with equal bitterness by a much smaller state. For Bulgaria, its third Balkan war had been a disaster, and the costly struggle from 1912 to 1918 had achieved nothing. On the Yugoslav border, where Bulgaria invaded Serbia in 1915, ethnic and strategic considerations clashed, but Anglo-French desire to strengthen Yugoslav defences gave Yugoslavia some contested districts. Ethnically mixed western Thrace went eventually to Greece, ending Bulgaria's access to the Aegean Sea gained in the Balkan wars.

The treaty of Neuilly of 27 November 1919 limited the Bulgarian army to 20 000 volunteers. Return of farm animals was required as well as reparations. Unlike other treaties, that with Bulgaria set a fixed sum, $450 million or £90 million. This fairly modest-sounding sum has been estimated at a quarter of the national wealth.[2] Bulgaria paid about a third of it. The treaty left Bulgaria without minorities, aside from a long-integrated Turk-

ish one, but bitter and revisionist. There was constant trouble over Macedonia and Macedonians, whom Bulgaria saw as Bulgars, and irredentism
over Thrace and southern Dobruja. Further, Bulgarian losses in relative
terms far exceeded those in absolute terms, for it emerged much weaker in
relation to its neighbours as Greece initially increased 50 per cent, Rumania doubled, and Serbia, as Yugoslavia, tripled in size.

*   *   *

Such startling gains resulted from self-determination, the wartime secret
treaties, fortuitous circumstances, strategic concerns about Russia and
Germany, and the ancient tradition of awarding the spoils to the victors.
Poland, for example, had no secret treaties but was among the victors,
while the three powers occupying it since the eighteenth century were all
losers. It received both Austrian and German territory along with a sizeable
Germanic population but, above all, large portions of the old tsarist empire.
Just how much remained unclear, as its eastern boundary was not settled
during the Paris conference. Czechoslovakia was also on the winning side
and recognized as an ally by the end of the war. Its elongated inland territory, comprising Czechs, Slovaks, and Ruthenes came mostly from Austria
and Hungary and was economically well balanced. On the German border,
economic and strategic factors took precedence over strict ethnicity; thus
the historic frontier was followed, incorporating in the new state a large
Austro-German minority.

As new states emerged from the collapse of old great powers, following
the principle of self-determination where feasible, the pre-existing Allied
states gained as well, making the most not only of ethnicity but also of the
secret treaties by which they had been bribed to enter the war, using whatever claim seemed most likely to enlarge their territory. Rumania was the
most dramatic example of self-aggrandizement, doubling in size and acquir-
ing an array of ethnic minorities despite its miserable military record,
thanks to a secret treaty, speedy deployment against Hungary in November
1918 and again in 1919 against Kun, and disregard of Allied ultimata. In
addition, the territories it sought were those of the losers. Beyond that,
Rumania, like Poland, benefited from France's need for strong eastern allies
and the Allied desire to protect western Europe from the contagion of
Communism. Both became key elements of the *cordon sanitaire*, the string
of buffer states stretching from the Baltic to the Adriatic. Greece, too, benefited from the fact that its European aspirations were at the expense of the
losers as well as from Venizelos's ability to charm Lloyd George.

Yugoslavia was the southern bastion of the *cordon sanitaire*, and it also
aspired to Bulgarian and Habsburg territory. However, its north-eastern
aims clashed with Rumania's, leading to division of the Banat, and its
north-western claims, well-anchored in ethnic and economic factors,
clashed with Italian aspirations to dominate the Adriatic and thus generated

the most bitter fight at Paris of any east European boundary. The new Yugoslavia, a merger of Serbia, Montenegro, and large amounts of Austro-Hungarian territory, had been born partly from fear of Italian designs on the part of disparate Slavic peoples, who therefore rushed into the arms of Serbia. At Paris, it was the only new state in direct confrontation with one of the Four. It had American support and Anglo-French sympathy, but Italy had an army, the treaty of London, and great power status. The Four dealt directly with Italy's claims whereas those of Yugoslavia went to expert commissions.

The London treaty had promised Italy Trieste, the Istrian peninsula, and part of the Dalmatian coast – to which it had no ethnic claim. After the Armistice, it occupied these areas plus Fiume (Rijeka). At the peace conference, it demanded Fiume, whose population was predominantly Italian. However, this predominance was debatable because adding the suburb of Susak gave a Slavic majority, which only increased if the hinterland was included. Further, without Fiume Yugoslavia would have no viable commercial port.

The Four dealt with Italian claims in April as they wrestled with the most difficult German problems, and the Fiume question became part of the April crisis of the conference. Italy sought her 'natural frontiers', as defined by her, regardless of nationality except at Fiume where the claim was ethnic. Britain and France felt forced to honour the London treaty; Wilson was not so bound. He became overly embroiled, crawling around his sitting room floor examining maps of five proposed lines in the Istrian/Fiume area. His opposition to Italy's claim led the Italian delegation to withdraw from the conference and then to leave Paris on 24 April after Wilson had appealed over its head to the Italian people. His ill-advised, improper action was based on expectation of public Anglo-French support, which did not materialize, and on memories of his frenzied welcome in Rome. But the public temper had changed, especially when Italy's aspirations were at stake, and Wilson was now vilified. When Britain and France threatened to denounce the London treaty and leave Italy to make a separate peace, the delegation returned for presentation of the Versailles treaty to Germany. Thereafter negotiations resumed. Italy conceded most of Dalmatia and the possibility of Fiume as a free city with a future plebiscite, but the political repercussions drove Prime Minister Orlando from office before the matter was resolved. Fiume became part of the unfinished business of the peace conference.

For the rest, the new Yugoslavia, half the size of France, became a country of two alphabets, three religions, four languages, five nationalities, six republics, seven bordering states, and eight legal systems. Moreover, it possessed five rail nets with four track gauges, each with a different centre. And beyond the five nationalities were six large and six lesser minority groups.

*   *   *

Yugoslavia's ethnic diversity was unusually complex, but most central and eastern European states incorporated sizeable minorities as a result of inter-mingled populations and some inescapable attention to possession, economic necessity, and defensible frontiers. In some instances, the size of the minority group could have been reduced if ethnicity had taken prece-dence over all other factors, but such irrational procedure would not have eliminated the problem altogether. Nor would have smaller minorities meant reduced tensions or abandonment of continuing territorial aspirations. It would have been possible to design a Polish Corridor awarding Poland fewer Germans (and Germany more Poles) but, given Berlin's claims to any area with a 10 per cent German population and its determination to reunite east Prussia with the Reich, the 'bleeding border' would still have bled.

Wilson had qualified self-determination in terms of not creating injustice or new discord. It was obvious, however, even where no secret treaties complicated matters, that injustice to individuals was likely. The peace-makers took various steps to alleviate it. One was to write option clauses into all treaties whereby a person finding himself in a minority within the new boundary could accept that nationality and stay or renounce it and leave, retaining full property rights in either event.

Another device to mitigate injustice was to require special minority treaties with the Allies by the smaller east and central European states, including Austria and Hungary. As great powers, Germany and Italy were exempt though both contained ethnic minorities. As at the Congress of Vienna, the original concern was to protect Jewish communities from harassment or worse. East European Jews formed an ethnic minority, culturally, linguistically, and often geographically distinct; the first minority treaty, with Poland, guaranteed them Jewish schools and the Jewish Sabbath. But the minority treaties also included option clauses and full rights of citizenship for all inhabitants regardless of prior affiliation. States were required to promise religious, cultural, and linguistic freedom to minority nationalities, including the right of schools and courtroom appear-ances in their own language. These commitments were placed under League of Nations guarantee, and violations could be reported by any League member to the Council, which in theory could act as it saw fit.

These well-intentioned measures exacerbated the problems. When nationalities gained their own state after centuries of subjection, individual cases of injustice were inescapable, instances of tactlessness or cruelty common, and old ruling elites often outraged at being subjected to peoples they considered inferior. As a result, there were endless appeals to the League, of which other states made the most. Germany in particular assid-uously supported appeals from the German minority in Poland to bolster its case for territorial revision.

Minority problems were aggravated by the intense nationalism of new infant states where long-suppressed ethnic groups were dominant at last.

This nationalism exacerbated the region's economic problems as well and doomed Britain's hope of peace, stability, and a Danubian economic federation. The Habsburg Empire had been an excellent economic unit, if politically ramshackle in later years, and a federation to replace it would have made economic sense. But squalling infant states, squabbling over borders and ethnic minorities, would not co-operate. Czech steel in theory could be traded for Hungarian wheat; in political practice, it could not. Besides, nationalist pride dictated that Hungary possess its own steel industry. Thus the economic unit fragmented along political lines, causing much dislocation and hardship as various stages of one manufacturing process often ended up in three different countries. Further impoverishment was added to that caused by war.

*   *   *

Economic fragmentation is one ground on which the east European settlement has been criticized. But the peacemakers were not responsible for the break-up of the Habsburg Empire or for the failure of the successor states to co-operate economically. On occasion, they gave precedence to ethnicity, defensive borders, or treaty commitments, but it was clearly impossible to base borders on a single factor. The settlement is also criticized for the political fragmentation which occurred. The Allies had been as free as the Central Powers in promising the domains of their enemies, but that did not cause the collapse of the Habsburg Empire nor the nationalist pressures which could no longer be denied. Both were facts existing before the conference met and not reversible by it.

The settlement is also criticized for not following ethnic lines and for creating so many minorities. But ethnic borders were not feasible amid mixed populations, and economic and defence factors required consideration, as did possession and treaty commitments, however unfortunate. The frontiers were an uneasy compromise, devised in haste in view of disease, starvation, and the Bolshevik tide, between practicality and the secret treaties on one hand and the idealism of European socialism, Lenin's programme, and the Fourteen Points on the other. Though the Four rejected forced population exchanges, they reduced the number of people under regimes of differing nationality by 50 per cent. Still, 30 millions had minority status, some because they did not vote according to their language in plebiscites, but put other factors first. Nonetheless, the settlement created new irredenta; there was usually a neighbouring state of the same nationality as the minority to listen to the wails of its separated brethren and to make the most of them. Italy and Hungary did so, Germany as well. It was bordered by youthful states with large German minorities who were preoccupied by quarrels with each other. Revisionist states, of which Germany was the foremost, could and did capitalize on this situation to seek territorial revision.

The east European settlement was excruciatingly difficult to devise and easy to criticize. Interwar eastern Europe was not a great success, but one must ask how much of the difficulty was dictated by what came before or after and how much of it lay in the lap of the peacemakers, who were only mortal. One of them remarked, 'General Plunkett's solution of our eastern European difficulties is that we should put the whole area in charge of a genius. We have no genius's [sic] available.'[3]

*   *   *

The small states of eastern Europe were not alone in having large appetites. The great powers were also hungry for spoils, but their aspirations lay mainly outside Europe. They scrambled for overseas territory as the successor states had done for rocky Balkan terrain. Often the colonies were of doubtful value: the German overseas empire had produced a net economic loss and much less than 1 per cent of Germany's trade. Allied motives were primarily strategic, especially those of Britain, concerned about imperial communications and the route to India, and its Dominions, who feared other powers in nearby territory. In the Arab portions of the Ottoman Empire, motives were more mixed. Britain wanted to protect the Suez Canal and the approaches to India, but also had economic aims. Oil, now economically and militarily important in an era of increasing mechanization, was produced in Persia (Iran) and was suspected in Mesopotamia (Iraq). Beyond that, for some nations, including France and Italy, there was an element of national prestige and keeping up with the Joneses.

Not surprisingly, the disposition of German colonies was the first major topic addressed at Paris. The approximate division was quickly understood, but Wilson postponed formal allocation so the powers would not appear to rush to divide the spoils. Indeed, Allied appetites clashed with the anti-annexationist rhetoric of socialists, Bolsheviks, British liberals and Wilson's Fourteen Points, point 5 of which promised that 'the interests of the populations concerned must have equal weight' with the claims of the victors. A device to mask imperialism with apparent altruism was needed. Smuts devised the mandate system whereby Germany and Turkey ceded territories to the League of Nations, which allocated them to victors to administer on a mandate from the League as 'a sacred trust of civilization'. Mandates came in three categories, based on the 'stage of development' (mainly westernization) and other factors. A mandates, within sight of independence, were subject to 'administrative advice and assistance'[4] of a mandatory power, in whose choice the wishes of the population were supposed to play a major role – this last a nod to self-determination not honoured in practice. B mandates were governed directly by the mandatory power subject to freedom of religion and free trade for all other League members, annual reporting to the League, and bans on fortification, using indigenous troops outside their territory, and on slave, liquor, and arms traffic. C mandates, which were tantamount to annexation, omitted the provision for free trade; the area could be ruled as an integral part of the mandatory power, subject to its laws. Australia, New Zealand, South Africa, and Japan protested, seeking annexation. Lloyd George reassured Hughes that Australia, which restricted immigration to whites, could bar Japanese migrants from its mandates; he insisted that C mandates amounted to annexation and probably could be absorbed in time, as was generally expected, though in practice the mandate system worked more toward independence. France, whose survival in World War I depended in part on 665 000 colonial troops, was brought to agree by a proviso in her mandates that she could raise troops in case of general war.

Classification and assignment of mandates, which often preceded the rationale therefor, was affected by economic, security, and strategic concerns of Western powers. Wartime occupation and promises played a large role, and possession was crucial. Emotive factors entered in: Britain wanted German East Africa (Tanganyika or Tanzania) not only because it was on the water route to India but also to complete its north–south African axis and gain the route for the Cape to Cairo railway which, in fact, was never built. The German colonies were allocated first. Most African territories were B mandates, divided between Britain and France, with Belgium retaining a small but desirable area it had conquered. South-west Africa (Namibia) went to South Africa as a C mandate. The German Pacific islands were also C mandates, split along the equator, the northern ones going to Japan, the southerly ones to Australia and New Zealand. Turkish territories, A mandates all, were settled later, with Arab lands outside the Arabian peninsula ultimately divided between Britain and France. The United States declined a mandate for Armenia, a headache nobody wanted. As its independence could not be maintained, the region soon reverted to Turkey and Russia.

The colonial settlement is often criticized for putting a fig leaf on imperialism. That it did, and the British Empire, the largest in the world's history, reached its zenith in the interwar era, as did the French Empire, then second largest. Yet the peace ushered in both the peak of the imperial era and the start of its decline, and so denoted a baby step away from outright imperialism. For all its cynicism, the colonial settlement encompassed the view that indigenous peoples had some rights and should progress (however slowly) toward independence; thus it started a trend which began to reach culmination after another world war. As in other matters, scaling the summit meant starting downhill, and the last major upward surge of overseas imperialism brought with it ideas and mechanisms which would accelerate the descent to self-determination, an idea of itself pressing toward independence.

Most inhabitants of mandated territories wanted immediate independence, but mandates were not necessarily undesirable for areas where independence was not possible in view of the appetites of powers strong and close enough to swallow them. This was true of Armenia and Kurdistan (for whom autonomy or independence was abortively raised in the treaty of Sèvres), some African territories, and Pacific islands. Though Hughes sought maximum gains for Australia, it was not primarily imperialism which led Australia and New Zealand to seize and hold German islands south of the equator; it was fear of the rising power of Japan, whose sphere of influence was approaching too close to them.

*   *   *

The Paris peace conference marked Japan's debut in the councils of the mighty. While clearly the *ingénue* of the great powers, it took to its role as if born to stardom. Led by a former prime minister and a former foreign minister and staffed by ambassadors at Allied capitals, its delegation was courteous, diligent, and attentive, unlike nodding Westerners. On European issues of no concern to Japan, it backed its British ally often but not always, usually voting with any majority and abstaining if there was none. Like Italy, Japan was a regional power with no interest in much of the German treaty. For this reason and because the delegation was not led by a head of government, Japan did not take part in the Four except on East Asian and Pacific questions. However, it participated faithfully in the Ten, the Five, and the commissions. Japanese delegates knew that this represented the first inclusion of a non-Western and non-white state in a great power conclave; they sought to be and to be recognized as a great power in all respects.

Japan equally sought recognition of China as its sphere of interest. Given Russia's preoccupation and Germany's elimination from the area, it was now dominant regionally. Possessing the same imperial drive as other powers, Japan wanted to play on the Asian mainland in the twentieth century the role played there by European powers in the nineteenth century. But timing is significant in international politics; so is race. At Paris, Japan tenaciously pursued two issues. It sought a clause proclaiming racial equality in the League of Nations Covenant. It wished to retain Germany's north Pacific islands and concessions on China's Shantung peninsula, which it had seized in 1914. In its territorial claims, Japan combined possession with a strong legal case and could hardly be denied.

The Japanese proposal for a racial equality clause, however, aroused alarm in Australia and New Zealand, and on the west coasts of Canada and the United States, and, depending on wording, posed a potential problem for South Africa and the American South. Japan tried a variety of phrasings aimed directly at American restrictive legislation and the British Empire's principle of white supremacy. Nobody denied the justice of Japan's position, and Wilson showed some initial willingness to entertain a weakly worded clause, but Hughes was obdurate. In the end, even a weakly worded clause was blocked by an Anglo-American combine in the person of those

two leading idealists, Woodrow Wilson and Lord Robert Cecil, both prisoners of their constituencies.

On the territorial side, Britain was also embarrassed. In 1917, with
French support, it endorsed Japanese retention of the German colonies; it
did so to gain naval aid, in recognition that Japan would not be dislodged,
and in hope of confining Japan north of the equator. The United States had
not been told of this secret treaty, which interested it most. Like Britain and
the Dominions, it feared the growing power of Japan, which now had the
world's third largest navy. Unlike the British and American fleets, Japan's
was concentrated in one area and thus dominant there. Anglo-American
hostility to Japan stemmed from this fact, from racial bias, from the contiguity of Japanese-held territory to weakly defended British and American
colonies, and from fear that Japan would fortify its C mandates – as it did.
Wilson's unease was increased by the Japanese army in Siberia. Nonetheless, British and French hands were tied, and Wilson could not prevail
against three other great powers. Outright annexation was avoided, but
Japan received C mandates for the Caroline, Mariana, and Marshall island
groups.

However, Japan rejected a C mandate for its claims on the Chinese mainland, namely the Kiaochow-Tsingtao (Jiao-Zian and Qingdao) leasehold
and Germany's economic rights in the rest of Shantung. Beyond Anglo-
French endorsement, the Japanese claim was bolstered by reluctant Chinese
recognition in 1918. China's delegation reflected the divisions of civil war
but was united on the territorial issue. Wilson fought hard for China but at
a time when his position was weakened by reparations battles and Italy's
departure; if Japan also withdrew, as threatened, the conference could
collapse. Thus the Kiaochow lease and Shantung concessions were ceded
outright to Japan, who promised that sovereignty over Kiaochow would
revert to China at some unspecified date, which proved to be 1922. As a
result, China refused to sign the Versailles treaty. Like the United States, it
signed a separate peace with Germany in 1921.

*   *   *

Dividing the booty proved even trickier in the Ottoman Empire and delayed
the Turkish treaty. No area had been subject to more wartime promises,
chiefly British, than Turkey's Arab domains, with successive pledges to the
Arabs, French, and Zionists. Indeed, 'the British sold the same horse, or at
least parts of the same horse, twice'[5] – or thrice in the case of the Palestinian part. Much ink has been spent to prove that the various promises were
not in conflict,[6] but those left with hollow pledges were not convinced. In
August 1919, Balfour, who had issued the 1917 Declaration, remarked, 'In
fact, so far as Palestine is concerned, the powers have made no statement of
fact that is not admittedly wrong, and no declaration of policy which, at
least in the letter, they have not always intended to violate.'[7]

That was especially true of the last promise, which Lloyd George said superseded the rest. On 7 November 1918, Britain and France declared that they fought for 'the complete and definite emancipation of the peoples so long oppressed by the Turks and the establishment of national Governments and administrations deriving their authority from the initiative and free choice of the indigenous population.'[8] This declaration, which neither country intended to honour, aimed to counter the effect of Bolshevik publication of the 1916 Anglo-French Sykes–Picot agreement (which had divided much of the Middle East between Britain and France), impress Wilson, and reassure increasingly distrustful Arabs.

The various pledges had aimed to gain and retain allies to win the war. Little thought had been given to the possibility of having to honour them. The British, who doubted Arab capacity for self-government, did not expect the promised Arab state to materialize. If it did, it should be firmly within Britain's orbit and, as Colonial Secretary Lord Milner said, 'independent native rulers should have no foreign treaties except with us'.[9] In the circumstances, mandates became a useful device to bridge the abyss between Allied promises and Allied imperialism.

One reason why Lloyd George declared all promises superseded by the 7 November 1918 statement was that he wished to revise the Sykes–Picot scheme to Britain's benefit. At the war's end Britain dominated the region, had a million men there, and held all areas France wanted. British policy and the idiosyncracies of Lloyd George, who controlled it, thus assumed great importance. He was hostile to French aspirations and to Turkey, which he hoped to remove from Europe. He strongly favoured the Greece of Venizelos, which he erroneously thought could enforce the settlement on Britain's behalf. Beyond that, he sought to use the moment of military dominance to consolidate Britain's position in an area where it had strong commercial and especially strategic interests. As always, the overriding concern was India and the land and sea routes thereto; that meant the Suez Canal and Egypt, along with the Persian Gulf. Thus Britain wished to control the eastern end of the Mediterranean as well as the western and to make it an English lake. So Lloyd George hoped to retain Syria, awarded to France under the Sykes–Picot scheme, and Palestine, originally to be ruled jointly.

A further concern was oil. The Royal Navy had converted to oil before the war, and with mechanization of military and civilian vehicles, demand was skyrocketing. There had been acute shortages during the war; the United States, which then produced two-thirds of the world supply, had furnished 80 per cent of Allied needs after Russia withdrew. A serious shortfall was expected soon. But oil had been found in Persia in 1908; a successful strike in Mesopotamia was expected shortly. For this reason, Britain wanted Mosul province, which Sykes–Picot gave to France.

As France did not accept eviction from the Levant, where she had been building a pre-war sphere of influence in Syria and Lebanon, the history of the Middle Eastern settlement became a long Anglo-French haggle. Still, there was a large area of agreement. All Allies (and Turkish nationalists as well) assumed that Turkey should lose all non-Turkish areas. Britain and France agreed at heart that they should control the Middle East, an attitude which bode ill for Italian aims. And both worried about the effect on their millions of Muslim subjects if they treated the Sultan, the titular head of Islam, too harshly. Thus, in the treaty of Sèvres he kept his throne and, in the end, Constantinople.

*   *   *

In London on 1 December 1918, Lloyd George and Clemenceau reached informal, unwritten agreement to revise Sykes–Picot. Britain would gain Palestine and Mosul. In return, Clemenceau expected to hold what became Syria and Lebanon, acquire Cilicia in southern Anatolia with British diplomatic aid, receive a share in Mesopotamian oil, and gain support (which never materialized) at the peace conference on European issues, especially the Rhineland. They disagreed afterwards about what they had agreed and especially about Syria (then a vague geographic term generally encompassing Lebanon and Palestine) as Lloyd George tried to dislodge France from that area.

A year of bitterness showed Lloyd George the damage being done to Anglo-French relations. Facing the conflict between his policy and his promises to the French, he chose France. Thus, the eventual division of the booty followed the 1918 London plan. Earlier, however, Britain had installed Amir Faisal, son of the Sharif (religious-political leader) Husain of the holy city of Mecca, to whom the McMahon Pledge had been made, in Damascus and then abandoned him when they agreed that Syria should go to the French, who dislodged him. Britain soon gave him a throne in Iraq.

When Faisal came before the peace conference, he agreed to A mandates if the people of an area were willing and suggested sending an international expert commission to ascertain which mandatory power each area desired. Wilson was enthusiastic, and it was so agreed, though Britain and France were much opposed and, like Italy, never appointed members. Thus the King–Crane Commission was purely American. Though denigrated by those who found its recommendations uncomfortable, it did a good job of surveying opinion in the Middle East and Armenia. By the time it reported, Wilson had been felled by a stroke. As the Commission said that France was not wanted in Syria and judged the Balfour Declaration endorsing a Jewish 'national home' in Palestine a mistake, Britain and France buried the report.

Along the way as well, Italy had offended the other powers by an unauthorized landing at Adalia on Asian Turkey's Anatolian peninsula and had infuriated them over Fiume. When she withdrew from Paris, a landing at Smyrna, also in Anatolia, was expected. Italy had a claim in Anatolia under the 1915 London treaty and to Smyrna under the 1917 St Jean de Maurienne treaty, which Russia never ratified and which Britain and France thus deemed conveniently void. Lloyd George seized the moment of Italian absence to urge that Greece be authorized to occupy eastern Thrace in Europe and to make a nominally inter-Allied but essentially Greek pre-emptive landing at Smyrna, which had a Greek population. This was agreed just before Italy returned, and on 15 May 1919 Greece took Smyrna. Turkish bitterness about this most hated rival led to Turkish nationalist revival, a Greco-Turkish war, and revision of the treaty of Sèvres.

Before Sèvres could be revised, it had to be written, and that awaited Allied agreement. Washington was another cause of delay. First, it was unclear whether it would accept mandates for Constantinople and Armenia. Wilson's health became a factor after his September collapse. Soon American participation in even the German settlement became doubtful. The Senate's first rejection of the Versailles treaty in November implied there would be no American mandates.

By then, Britain had faced the damage to Anglo-French relations from the Middle Eastern wrangle and realized that it needed French co-operation in Europe if it was ever to calm that continent sufficiently to turn elsewhere. Besides, costs were mounting and the British army shrinking. Britain was over-extended and coping with too many imperial crises. Thus abandoning efforts to evict France from the Levant and retain Faisal in Syria, it agreed to honour the December 1918 scheme.

*   *   *

With that, the Turkish treaty could be written at a long Allied meeting in London in February and March 1920. Formal approval took place in April at another Allied conference in San Remo, Italy, without any consultation of Arabs or Turks. As the Sultan was a virtual prisoner in Constantinople, which was under Allied occupation, no difficulty was anticipated.

The treaty awarded Greece eastern Thrace, a number of Aegean islands, and effective control of a large Smyrna district in western Anatolia. Italy gained clear title to the Dodecanese islands seized before the war. Syria and Lebanon went as A mandates to France, Iraq and Palestine to Britain, with the Balfour Declaration promise of a Jewish 'national home' as an obligation. Transjordan* was part of the Palestine mandate but Britain excluded it from the area of Jewish settlement. Husain's second son, Abdullah, became its ruler whereas his younger brother Faisal was made king of Iraq to lend a façade of Arab administration to British control. No matter that the Iraqis had chosen Abdullah and the Syrians Faisal; not surprisingly, abortive Arab uprisings in Syria, Iraq, and Palestine ensued.

Sharif Husain became king of the Hejaz in the western Arabian penin-

---

* Renamed the Hashemite kingdom of Jordan in 1949 when it gained the west bank of the Jordan River.

sula. As this desert area was remote, inaccessible, and of no known value, the promised Arab kingdom was permitted to materialize. But Husain was under challenge by Ibn Saud* of the neighbouring Nejd, who ousted him in 1924. Meanwhile, the least developed Arab area became independent though more sophisticated regions were put under European Christian tutelage. In Anatolia, the great powers did not take territory, but a separate treaty recognized Italian and French areas of 'special interests' which amounted to faintly disguised spheres of influence. Another pact granted France 25 per cent of Iraqi oil.

In the area left to the Sultan, Turkish sovereignty was circumscribed. The Straits from the Black Sea to the Aegean were demilitarized and internationalized under great power dominance. European financial control, particularly of the Ottoman debt, was imposed, along with occupation costs, but reparations were waived. There were military restrictions and clauses to protect minorities stemming from past Turkish persecutions, especially of Armenians. Pre-war economic concessions to Europeans and the capitulations† continued, as did other Allied privileges.

Sèvres was a nineteenth-century European imperial treaty which ignored self-determination, dismissed Arab and Turkish nationalism, and reflected European great power politics, not reality on the ground. As Italy received no Anatolian territory, the terms of the treaty could not be enforced. The Allies could enforce their decisions in Europe, in the Arab areas, and on Anatolia's coastal fringes. Elsewhere they relied on Greece, ensconced at Smyrna, but much too weak for the task. When he received the treaty, the Sultan protested and stalled, but eventually he was forced to sign it in August 1920. But he delayed ratification, which never took place. The Sèvres treaty was in fact obsolete even before it was signed by a sultan whose control of the area remaining to him was purely nominal.

*   *   *

The Smyrna landing on 15 May 1919 had set off a Turkish nationalist rising four days later led by Mustapha Kemal, Turkish hero of Gallipoli. By autumn he controlled most portions of Anatolia not in Allied hands, including the supposedly independent Armenia and autonomous Kurdistan, and both France and Italy were eager to settle with him. Britain badly underestimated Kemal, thinking him a bandit and assuming that a powerless sultan could control him. In fact, he was skilled at exploiting Allied divisions, Russian isolation, and Western fear of Russia, with whom he soon came to terms.

Kemal and his deputy Ismet* drove Greek forces out of Smyrna and

---

* Properly known as Amir (later king) Abd al Aziz ibn (son of) Saud, but widely called Ibn Saud in the West.

† Special treaties, some from the sixteenth century, granting extraterritorial rights and privileges to nationals of 'capitulatory' powers, all European.

Anatolia in September 1922. Their pursuit to sweep the Greeks out of eastern Thrace as well led to a dangerous confrontation with British forces at Chanak in the Dardanelles. Lloyd George backed Greece to the last but was abandoned by France and Italy, his military commander, and the Conservative members of his coalition; he lost power in October to a Conservative cabinet. The Turkish question was reopened at once and addressed with the new nationalist government at Ankara, which deposed the Sultan on 1 November.

At the Lausanne conference, which met in two sessions from 20 November 1922 to 24 July 1923, the triumphant Turks saw themselves as victors while the great powers viewed them as a defeated foe and as lowly Orientals. Turkish policy was directed by Kemal and ably executed by Ismet, who used his deafness, lack of fluency in French, and tenacious ability to stall. With patience and determination that Turkey receive full equality as an independent sovereign state, he outlasted European leaders who had expected to dictate terms and who, after the Ruhr crisis burst upon Europe in January 1923, were eager to settle quickly. Turkey had certain advantages: it alone was willing to resume fighting. It received Russian and American support for various portions of the treaty. Much was gained by playing on Western fears that Turkey would shift to a Bolshevik orientation, though Ismet in the end placed Turkey between Russia and the West, avoiding dependence. More was obtained by capitalizing on renewed Russo-British rivalry in the region, obvious divisions among the Allies, and the patent eagerness of France and Italy to settle and gain economic concessions.

As a result, the treaty of Lausanne of 24 July 1923, revising the purely Turkish portions of Sèvres, was largely a Turkish triumph. Turkey regained eastern Thrace and retained Armenia and most of Kurdistan. It gained the presidency of the commission to oversee demilitarization of the Straits and the right to close them to belligerents if it was at war. Other military restrictions were ended, as were the capitulations, financial controls, and protected status for economic concessions. As Turkey promised to join the League of Nations, the minority clauses, which Turkey viewed as an excuse for Allied infringements on its sovereignty, were diluted. After a right of option, there was to be a forcible population exchange. This occurred from 1923 to 1925 and, though brutal in execution, eliminated Greek minorities in Turkey and the reverse.

The Grand National Assembly at Ankara ratified the Lausanne treaty on 23 August 1923, and the Allies withdrew from Constantinople[†] within six weeks. The Turkish capital officially moved to Ankara, and the Turkish republic was proclaimed; Kemal became president of a revitalized Turkey. The Lausanne treaty marked both Turkey's rebirth and its renunciation of

---

[*] When Turks took surnames in 1935, they became Kemal Ataturk and Ismet Inönü.
[†] Titled Istanbul (its Ottoman name) in 1930.

Ottoman imperialism. Aside from changes to the Straits convention, the treaty lasted, unlike others of the peace settlement. Its longevity owed much to its moderation and to the fact that it was negotiated, not imposed. Certainly it was the most successful of the major treaties.

The Lausanne treaty did not alter the decisions of Sèvres in Turkey's former Arab domains. Those boundaries and mandates remained, as did political volatility. Arabs thought the mandates in practice violated Allied promises, ignored self-determination, and prolonged imperialism; the Palestine mandate in particular was seen as betrayal. The upshot was anti-Western sentiment, Arab nationalism, and the Palestine conflict. Still, the fact that progress toward independence was much less than Arabs had hoped does not mean that no progress was made. These areas were A mandates, implying independence in the foreseeable future, not the annexed colonies to which Europe had aspired. However, European Allies had encouraged Arab nationalism in areas they intended to take for themselves. Mandates papered over the conflict for the nonce – but only for the nonce.

＊   ＊   ＊

By the time the Sèvres treaty was settled in April 1920, boundary commissions were going forth all over Europe to delimit frontiers with precision. Some were still at work when the Lausanne treaty took effect, for states haggled interminably over every hamlet and stream. Plebiscite commissions to supervise the votes called for by the treaties lasted nearly as long. Meanwhile, a sizeable administrative structure had been called into being by the peace treaties. The Paris peace conference itself closed in January 1920, when the Versailles treaty took effect, and was replaced by Supreme Councils, periodic meetings over the next five years of the European Allies in their capitals or pleasant resorts to complete or revise the treaties.

The Supreme Councils sat atop what might be called the peace structure. Lesser tasks were delegated to a Conference of Ambassadors, meeting in Paris. Also in Paris was an Allied Reparation Commission to deal with the ever more complicated payments of the losers to the victors. An Allied Rhineland High Commission oversaw Germany's occupied area. An Inter-Allied Military Committee at Versailles supervised disarmament commissions, which in turn monitored execution of the military clauses of the peace treaties. After the definitive American rejection of the Versailles treaty on 19 March 1920, the United States withdrew from one agency after another.

As these entities came into being, peace began to arrive in eastern Europe as well as the west. In the south, Italy and Yugoslavia agreed in November 1920 to partition the Istrian peninsula and establish Fiume as a free city. This arrangement lasted until Italy occupied it in 1923 and annexed it in 1924. More importantly, Bolshevik Russia accepted that no chain reaction of revolution would occur and settled for co-existence with the capitalist world, deciding in December 1919 to offer negotiations to the Allies individually or together. Its attempt to break out of isolation started with its immediate neighbours, with whom peace treaties were urgently necessary in order to establish frontiers.

After much hesitation, the Allies sanctioned independence for the Baltic states as anti-Bolshevik resistance was collapsing in Russia. In Western eyes, these states and Finland were to anchor the northern end of the *cordon sanitaire*. During 1920, Russia signed peace treaties with Estonia, Lithuania, Latvia, and Finland. Trade agreements with Britain and Germany soon followed, as did normalization of relations with Austria, Afghanistan, Iran and Turkey in 1921.

The problem of Poland also lingered into 1921. In December 1919, a Supreme Council proposed an ethnic Russo-Polish frontier, the 'Curzon Line', named after the British Foreign Secretary. This Russia accepted but Poland rejected. In April 1920 a Polish attack on the Ukraine launched the Russo-Polish war, seen by some as the last act of the Russian civil wars and by Bolsheviks as the last foreign intervention. Large but primitive armies without heavy armour or logistic support swept across the plains, conquering vast areas – until a counterattack pricked the bubble of control. Within two weeks, Poland seized Kiev, but by August the Red Army was at the gates of Warsaw. General Jósef Pilsudski saved Warsaw, effectively ending Soviet export of revolution westward, and counterattacked eastward, taking Minsk, the capital of Byelorussia (Belarus), in September. Lenin then accepted defeat, and negotiations began. The resultant treaty of Riga of 18 March 1921 put the frontier 150 miles east of the Curzon Line. The Soviet Union* saw this border roughly as Germany viewed the Polish Corridor, and hostility to Poland was something the two outcast states shared. Thus peace did not bring stability and good relations to the east any more than it did to the west.

*   *   *

Lack of stability is one of many grounds on which the Paris peace has been criticized. Yet, except in the Middle East, much of the instability was not inherent in the settlement but arose from what came later: in western Europe, the Anglo-French quarrel over whether to revise or uphold the Versailles treaty, in the east the refusal of new nations to co-operate with each other. Further, the settlement was substantially transformed within five years both by American withdrawal, which meant that the peace structure did not operate as intended, and by considerable revision of treaty terms.

---

* Or Union of Soviet Socialist Republics (USSR), created in December 1922 by attaching the Ukrainian, Belorussian, and Transcaucasian SSRs to the Russian Soviet Federated Socialist Republic. The federal structure was a sop to nationalities, but all was directed from Moscow. Until the Soviet Union's demise in December 1991, the terms Russia and USSR or Soviet Union were used interchangeably.

Although, almost inevitably, the wishes of no nationality had been met in full, only in the Middle East had they been massively disregarded. Moreover, the idea that those wishes should matter had been validated as a new and potent factor in international politics.

The conflicting claims of ethnicity, economics, and defensible frontiers forced some awkward compromises, as was bound to happen. Equally, the clash of great power appetites with the aspirations of non-Western peoples meant that the mandate system was less than it might have been – but also more than four great powers had hoped. Even as the British and French empires reached their greatest extent and Europe seemed to be astride the globe, the war and peace had loosed and accelerated forces which would weaken and ultimately end the West's grip.

Already the world's stage was much more crowded. There were many new states, chiefly European, but also in Arabia, and Britain's Dominions had clearly progressed well into adolescence, with adulthood in sight. Even more important, Japan had emerged as the first major non-Western player. As power shifted away from Europe, the real victors were the United States and Japan. Europe was no longer the sole star, the hub of the world. Its hegemony was evaporating even as Europeans assumed it would continue, for Europe's civil war primarily benefited non-European powers, who were not battered and bleeding and bankrupt.

World War I destroyed Europe's classical balance of power, which was effectively the world's balance. The peacemakers did little to replace it. Thanks to Wilson, they did not address the problem. As a group they seem to have had no concept of a new European or world state system. In matters economic, political, and territorial, they dealt with specific cases without regard to any vision of a broader picture beyond Wilson's panaceas – self-determination and the League of Nations. Thus they made no real effort to reconstruct and reintegrate a European or world system. This is perhaps the underlying reason why the peacemakers failed in their larger purpose: to establish a lasting peace.

They were only human; thus they were prisoners of their prejudices and of forces they did not understand, some of which they themselves had loosed, which would in time end the world they knew. For this reason, the peace settlement could not rise far above the assumptions of the pre-war era which had nurtured its authors. These were nationalistic, Eurocentric, liberal more than democratic, and imperialistic. They assumed white Western leadership, the superiority of western Europe to eastern Europe, and that of the West to the rest of the world, which was to be held in tutelage and guided slowly to the West's notion of civilization. Yet the peace based on these late nineteenth-century premises raised the curtain on the final acts of the long drama of European dominance.

◆ Notes to Chapter 6

1. See Alan Sharp, *The Versailles Settlement: Peace-making in Paris, 1919* (London, Macmillan, 1991), p. 132.
2. Barbara Jelavich, *History of the Balkans* (2 vols, Cambridge, CUP, 1983), II, p. 166.
3. A. J. Balfour, as quoted in Sharp, *Versailles Settlement*, p. 158.
4. Quotations from Article 22, Versailles treaty.
5. Michael Dockrill and J. Douglas Goold, *Peace Without Promise: Britain and the Peace Conferences, 1919–1923* (Hamden, CT, Archon, 1981), p. 141.
6. See Elie Kedourie, *In the Anglo-Arab Labyrinth: the McMahon–Husayn Correspondence and its Interpretations, 1914–1939* (Cambridge, CUP, 1976) and Peter M. Holt, *Egypt and the Fertile Crescent, 1516–1922: A Political History* (London, Cornell University Press, 1966), pp. 264–9.
7. Peter Mansfield, *The Ottoman Empire and its Successors* (New York, St Martin's Press, 1973), p. 50
8. David Stevenson, *The First World War and International Politics* (New York, OUP, 1988), p. 296.
9. Sharp, *Versailles Settlement*, p. 177.

ACT III

THE WEST'S WORLD

One half of the world must sweat and groan
that the other half may dream.

Henry Wadsworth Longfellow
Hyperion, I

CHAPTER

7

THE IMPERIAL FACTOR

The Paris peace conference was the last real colonial scramble, despite later lunges by dissatisfied powers. The preoccupation with overseas territories early and late at Paris represented both the classic view that 'to the victor belongs the spoils' and a renewed appreciation of the extent to which colonies were a factor in the balance of power. These attitudes, especially the latter, owed much to the war just past, in which colonies had aided the European Allies massively for the first time. In Europe, they remedied Anglo-French deficiencies in numbers, helping 'mother countries' to remain in the fray. They fought as well in the eastern Mediterranean, the Pacific, and Africa, releasing European forces for service on the western front. The costs were considerable, especially for semi-autonomous areas. Not all the broken bodies were European, nor all the war debts. Beyond troops, empires contributed essential commodities, such as Indian cotton and Canadian wheat.

Much was made of colonial solidarity with the metropole. To a degree, this existed in Britain's 'white' settler Dominions. Elsewhere, service was involuntary and often reluctant; strikes, riots, and small rebellions erupted in Ireland, among French Canadians and South African Afrikaners, in French West Africa, and among Muslim Indians in Singapore. Others were nearly as negative, but some scented an opportunity. France appointed Blaise Diagne of Senegal, the first black member of the French Chamber, as commissioner for recruitment; his real goal was to assure African soldiers 'the ransom for their political liberty in the future'.[1] Colonial troops were angry at being used but hopeful, as the war created imperial debts to colonies for which medals did not suffice. The relationship changed as the weakness and dependency of European powers was revealed. The war decreased European prestige, especially among those who served on the western front or in the post-war Rhineland occupation. Acquaintance with Western living standards bred discontent with impoverished peonage, and exposure to the seamy side of European life knocked white gods off their pedestals. Metropolitan control was not yet threatened; most colonial subjects did not demand independence, which did not seem possible, but their new attitudes had implications for the permanence of European control.

In general, Europeans tried to ignore these. Colonies were popular, thanks to their wartime contribution, but the attention of ordinary Europeans turned elsewhere. Governments, more acutely aware of the wartime contribution, saw the implications but tried to ignore them. Resolving to hold as much as possible for as long as possible, they proceeded on the assumption that the evil day when the vitally important colonies would not be freely available for use could be postponed indefinitely.

The importance of colonies lay in their role in the power equation. They added to European prestige and military potential and usually possessed economic or strategic value, or both. Though costly to rule and defend, they justified themselves in imperial eyes if they possessed fine harbours for naval bases or supplied essential commodities. At Paris, as earlier, colonies were sometimes claimed to prevent their acquisition by rival powers, but even that often rested on strategic motives. Generally, power, prestige, need of raw materials, and military and strategic factors were the reasons for seeking territory at Paris. As empire had been vital in the war, it was expected to remain similarly advantageous in the post-war power balance, and so it proved to be. It was overseas empire, the largest in the world's history (along with a temporary absence of east European competition), which made Britain the dominant European power of the 1920s. And it was empire, the world's second largest, which kept France precariously among the leading powers, delaying her descent into the supporting cast. But this key element in the power equation was starting to fray in the interwar era, along with European predominance.

Not all imperial powers were European. In terms of overseas territory, not domination of contiguous areas, in 1914 six major states, including the United States and Japan,* ruled a third of the globe, involving all oceanic areas and continents except Antarctica. Five smaller European states also had sizeable overseas holdings. After 1920, there was one less European imperial power, as Germany lost its colonies to the victors, but even more territory became colonial, as the Ottoman Empire's non-Turkish domains became A mandates in Anglo-French hands. Now 180 million Europeans governed more than 700 million overseas subjects. Further, the ranks of those ruling over others had been swelled by Australia, New Zealand, and (contiguously) South Africa. These were not exactly colonies holding colonies, but neither were they fully independent states.

Yet the era of colonial conquest was essentially over. The pre-war years had been the grand age of imperial acquisition. That of decolonization had not begun. For most Western imperial powers, the interwar years were a time of consolidation. They gained effective control of the interior of their colonies and subdued the inhabitants, often bloodily, sometimes with the

* For Japanese colonies, see Chapter 10.

new weapon of air power. Then they developed empire-wide or global corporations and built ports, roads, and railways to bring troops in and raw materials out. Most of these imperial states were satisfied powers, not seeking to expand further. Besides, the remaining pickings were slim, mostly areas unhealthy for white settlement or of little economic or strategic value.

*   *   *

The nature of empire did not change greatly in the interwar era, but its rationale and rhetoric did. In the Fourteen Points Wilson decreed that 'the interests of the populations concerned must have equal weight' with those of governments, but he did not specify who would determine the interests of 'the populations concerned'. Article 22 of the League Covenant stated that in mandates 'the well-being and development of such peoples form a sacred trust of civilization'. Now colonies were supposedly the concern of the international community, not just of the imperial power, and the ideology of imperialism shifted accordingly, becoming more paternalistic in theory, if not practice. The welfare of subject peoples was to take priority over the interests of the ruling power, and they should evolve toward eventual independence or voluntary integration into the imperial state. European governments usually took this to mean that if they provided minimally for the indigenes, they could take the raw materials they sought. Imperial rhetoric talked of advancing primitive peoples, assuming always that Europeans were advanced and others were not, but practices lagged far behind the rhetoric. Viewing the mandate system as a fig leaf on imperialism, Europeans treated mandates as colonies, stifling nationalism and not preparing the people for self-rule. Imperial control rested on a wide technology gap, especially militarily, and ruling powers meant to maintain it. Thus industry was discouraged and colonial education was low-level and vocational. In most colonies, technological and administrative jobs were reserved to agents of the imperial power.

The sole instrument of enforcement of the 'sacred trust of civilization' was feeble. The League had a permanent Mandates Commission to which mandatory powers submitted reports. However, its role was unobtrusive and advisory, its members often former colonial officials without political power from imperial states, its chief concern not to weaken the control of mandatory powers, and its oversight slight. It consistently refused to make on-the-spot enquiries; as subject peoples could petition the Commission only through the mandatory power, they rarely did so. Thus the imperial powers had their way. If indigenes now doubted inherent European superiority, their overlords did not. Western imperialists assumed white superiority, and most expected the civilizing mission, that convenient justification for their rule, to be well-nigh perpetual. They thought that Kipling's 'lesser breeds'[2] would be sufficiently 'developed' to stand alone only in a distant future, that those who had been independent did not want self-rule, and that colonies were immune to nationalism. Britain assumed economic development and gradual progress toward democracy would proceed together, whereas France saw its subjects as assimilating French culture and evolving toward citizenship. Both envisaged a long, slow process.

British and French socialists attacked imperial abuses of power, endorsed more rights for subject peoples, and favoured a paternalistic colonialism. Only Marxists as a group condemned imperialism – unless they were settlers. Liberals held that indigenes had a right of self-government, but not until they 'developed' sufficiently to avoid chaos or absolutism, conditions not unknown in Europe itself. Europeans assumed that their subjects merely wanted good administration, and that only they could provide the necessary security and progress. As protest within colonies became more common, European regimes became ingenious in devising ways to give their subjects the appearance of some role in governance without substantial power. A puppet indigenous ruler conceded the form while retaining the substance, as did appointment of a few local notables to consultative councils. To the rulers, such a patina of participation should suffice for the foreseeable future.

The ruled disagreed. An impatient post-war generation was not fooled by mere consultative councils. It knew the principle of evolution toward independence had been admitted and meant the eventual destruction of empires. The question was one of timing. The visible weakening of imperial overlords in Europe's civil war encouraged educated elites to press for greater speed, as did rhetoric about self-determination and Wilson's Fifth Point. The phenomenon of the King–Crane Commission actually seeking Arab opinion had its effect. Europe had also unwittingly exported nationalism, which subject peoples soon turned against Europeans, often focusing on ousting the foreigner, not on creating a nation, even if the colony consisted of a jumble of mutually hostile ethnic groups. The divergence between the assumptions of the rulers and those of the ruled widened considerably. Britons saw the post-war Egyptian political movement the Wafd as ultra-nationalistic, for it was openly discontent with British control. But in an Egyptian, Middle Eastern, or colonial context, its efforts toward self-rule seemed moderate. In English eyes the fact that Egypt, like India, had an ancient civilization and an educated elite (in Western terms) made little difference. Wogs were still Wogs.

Nevertheless, changes were coming, often but not always in response to revolt. In 1902 the United States granted Filipinos various rights, including a bicameral legislature whose lower house they elected. This first broad application of the democratic principle to non-white colonies evoked no imitation until after World War I, and then slowly, usually in response to the ricochet of rebellion from one area to another. Subject peoples closely watched the Irish struggle toward the Irish Free State in 1921; they noted revolt in Egypt in 1919 and in Iraq in 1920, followed by nominal independence for both. In

India, consultative councils were clearly too little too late, for demonstrations at Amritsar in 1919 provoked a British massacre. This in turn spawned the passive non-co-operation movement of Mohandas K. Gandhi, a devastating tactic for the weak to use against the strong, which was widely imitated. Nationalists silently cheered when the Rif War in Spanish Morocco, which soon inspired the Druse in Syria and the Sanusi in Libya, tied up Spain and then France for five years. In the Middle East, A mandates held out hope for the future. And in Asia, all eyes turned to Japan, despite its own imperialism, as the state which had escaped subjection. Upper-class Asian youth often studied in Japan unless they attended Oxford or the Sorbonne – where they learned ideologies and tactics to turn against their masters. Clearly, a new mood developed in many colonies after World War I. Given the variety of empire, every generalization has exceptions, but usually there was little organized drive for liberation. Still, the idea of working toward independence got a toehold in the more sophisticated colonies and gathered force, especially where youth had studied or served militarily in Europe. There were many small challenges to colonial rule and more protest, as the interwar period became an era of testing. Though most were easily suppressed, imperial responses were as varied as the challenges, for overlords lacked long-range goals.

Protest took many forms, starting with military resistance to conquest, followed often by guerrilla war. Then came forms of passive resistance, including inaction, polite delay, and symbolic challenges. Peasants and tribesmen often hid in the interior to escape imperial exactions. In the cities, strikes, demonstrations, and mass meetings became more common. Reform movements, nationalist groups, and political parties developed in some areas, as did associations of students, workers, and exiles abroad. Local uprisings and urban political activity led to repression which bred clandestine movements and also led nationalists to abandon reform in favour of calls for independence. The level and type of activity varied according to the sophistication of the leadership and the prospect of results. However, most of the nationalist ferment of the era was small-scale and easily controlled. Literary protest by small coastal and urban elites had more effect in the long run than the short but instilled racial pride and national consciousness. By and large, political progress was a vague ideal and independence seemed impossibly remote. Both rulers and ruled saw self-government as being in the distant future. With this the imperial powers were satisfied.

*   *   *

Not all imperial powers or would-be imperial powers were satisfied. The disaffected included both the losers and some victors of World War I. Among the defeated, Germany had lost its colonies, thanks to Allied appetites and convenient charges that it had failed in its civilizing mission. But Germany's imperial interests did not disappear. Colonial enthusiasts continued to agitate in the 1920s, mainly about the former German East Africa. In China, Germany used its lack of an empire to develop military and industrial ties, creating an informal partial economic sphere between 1928 and 1938. It also recaptured much of its pre-war role of training, advising, and equipping Latin American armies for some years. But German efforts overseas were small-scale and always secondary to liberating the Rhineland and regaining lost domains in Europe.

The Soviet Union was also among the dissatisfied losers. Historically, Russia's imperialism took the form of expansion on its many borders. A new ideology did not alter that goal, but despite dissatisfaction with the Baltic, Finnish, and Polish frontiers and an abortive effort to dominate Kemal's Turkey, the new regime was too preoccupied with imposing itself on the Soviet Union to accomplish much against neighbouring states. However, the Comintern denounced overseas imperialism and briefly fomented revolution in South Africa, India, and China. But Lenin decided in 1920 that colonial revolt must occur in two stages, with liberation before Communism; thus he decreed co-operation with bourgeois nationalist parties seeking independence. In the late 1920s, Russia abandoned this policy in order to foment revolts in China, India, Indochina, Syria, and North Africa – until the advent of Adolf Hitler in Germany dictated new coalitions with bourgeois groups to protect Russia against Hitler's intense anti-Communism. Marxist parties in colonies were tiny and often composed mostly of foreigners or ethnic minorities. They were too geared to Russia's needs and too industrially oriented to appeal to colonial masses, for they ignored peasants, local conditions, and the countryside. The Comintern largely disregarded black Africa and Latin America in favour of the Middle East and East Asia, areas of greater concern to the Soviet Union.

For Russian geopolitical reasons, the Comintern focused particularly on China, where it enjoyed its greatest success. The Russian-dominated Chinese Communist Party flourished in co-operation with Sun Yat-sen's (Sun Zhongshan) Kuomintang (Guomindong). But in 1927, Sun's successor, Chiang Kai-shek (Jiang Jieshi), expelled the Communists from the Kuomintang. Russian Communism had failed in China, but Marxism remained as Mao Tse-Tung (Mao Zedong) invented agrarian Communism and built a vast movement among the peasants of the interior.

Some victor powers were as dissatisfied in matters imperial as the losers. Italy was among these, for she failed to obtain the large Adriatic and Anatolian domains she sought. Aside from modest European gains and confirmation of pre-war conquests, she had to make do with what she had – without a single mandate. Chiefly what she had was Somaliland (Somalia) and Libya. In both, control was only coastal until military campaigns in the 1920s subdued the interior; then the Libyan tribes were reorganized by decree to suit imperial convenience. Italy colonized and Italianized, closing Muslim schools and transplanting overcrowded Italy's surplus population to Libya's few agriculturally viable areas at the expense of the Libyans; it found little other use for its arid colony except as a base for Benito Mussolini's empty dream of converting the Mediterranean into an Italian lake.

Japan gained more of value but was equally dissatisfied. Temporary possession of rich Shantung province and C mandates for Pacific islands were not enough for a frankly imperialist state with ambitions. Japan fortified its C mandates in violation of the League Covenant and wasted little rhetoric on the civilizing mission. Beyond its 1919 gains, it aimed to expand into China. Given that nation's vastness, Tokyo preferred (except in areas of special interest) to control through economic penetration and obedient puppet rulers, but did not achieve this on a large or permanent enough scale to satisfy it. Japan and Italy had been latecomers to the imperial race; both still wanted large empires. They soon reached for what remained and so contributed much to the mounting crises of the 1930s. But the conquest of Manchuria and then Ethiopia was condemned, not condoned, by other powers who had built their empires in the same fashion before World War I.

*   *   *

Of the smaller European imperial states, only Belgium fought in World War I and only she gained a mandate, Ruanda-Urundi (Rwanda and Burundi). There tribal chiefs retained much power, but in the contiguous Belgian Congo (Democratic Republic of Congo), Brussels ruled through the most docile chiefs or appointed new ones, trying to preserve the traditional social order. But economic development undermined this order, as towns emerged near copper mines and factories. Though organized like chieftancies, these communities were not tribal. Belgium took the civilizing mission seriously and aimed at good but very centralized governance with all initiative from Brussels, better living standards, and economic development. African agriculture and land-owning were encouraged, Africans trained to replace whites at technical levels, and senior urban educated Africans paid the same as whites.

Belgian rule rested on the state, large corporations, and Roman Catholic missionaries. All three were paternalistic. The clergy and the state provided Africa's most extensive elementary and vocational schooling, but secondary education was scant. Brussels wanted all to progress together so the few could not exploit the many and thus refused to create an elite. Its regulations decreed a healthy life; the corporations responded with food, clothing, medical and religious services, education, and social benefits, bragging, 'See how well we look after our cattle.'[3] Such paternalistic benevolence stifled protest, aside from prophetic religious sects with anti-white overtones, but equally stifled initiative, for the corporations and state saw Africans as large children.

The Dutch likewise saw their Indonesian subjects as large children. Holland ruled Caribbean islands and Dutch Guiana (Suriname), but the valuable Dutch East Indies (Indonesia) were what mattered. Here the Dutch combined direct and indirect rule, governing unobtrusively (except on Java) through local rulers whose states were kept as a bulwark against nationalism. But the fact that the Dutch welded separate peoples, religions, and traditions into one political unit fostered nationalism, as did a national council established in 1916. At first it was only advisory, then subject to the governor-general's veto, but it was partially elected, and Indonesians gained representation, though not on equal terms with the Chinese and especially the Dutch.

Holland launched the 'ethical policy' to further Indonesian welfare, but previous exploitation had sapped peasant initiative, and capitalism was causing villages and the social structure to disintegrate. Education remained sparse, especially above the primary level, though Dutch-language schools were permitted to prevent Malay becoming a force for nationalism and to counteract pan-Islamic tendencies. But in Dutch Indonesians read Rousseau, Locke, Mazzini, and Marx. As a result, the Islamic movement split into nationalist and Communist factions. In 1926, in defiance of the Comintern, the latter rebelled unsuccessfully. The next year Ahmed Sukarno founded the Indonesian National Party among those who had studied in Holland. Again, Holland imposed arrests, exile, and suppression. Nationalism was weak but growing, thanks to Islam, Western influence, heavier taxes, the effects of Dutch rule, and exploitation by Dutch corporations. The 'ethical policy' ignored reality, trying to improve indigenous conditions but also to give Western capitalism free rein. Its response to political ferment was uniformly negative; after the Dutch rejected Indonesian efforts at co-operation in the mid-1930s, the varied parties formed a united front, which hoped to co-operate with Holland against external threats. As the Dutch again refused, they soon reaped the results.

Not all European governance was repressive. Denmark sold the Virgin Islands in 1917 to the United States but in its other North American possession, Greenland, it administered a protectorate actually designed to protect, both militarily and culturally. Its location near shipping lanes and fishing grounds meant the vast but thinly populated island had little hope of independence. Denmark provided a comparatively very benevolent (but still resented) paternalism with some local legislative and judicial authority. Icelanders were more restive, despite home rule. In 1918 Iceland became a separate kingdom, united with Denmark only in the crown, some joint legislation with Icelandic consent, and the conduct of foreign affairs. Iceland indicated at once that it would use a clause enabling it to abrogate the arrangement in 1944, as it did.

The other smaller imperial powers were both Iberian and more typical in their approach. The once vast Spanish Empire had shrunk to the Canary Islands, small west African areas, and Spain's narrow coastal strip of

Morocco. This was mountainous, strategic, unprofitable, and difficult to subdue. An effort to do so in 1921 led to rout of the Spanish forces by Rif tribesmen under Abd-el-Krim and contributed to the 1923 coup and military regime in Spain. A Rif republic looked likely, but Abd-el-Krim invaded French territory and so brought a Franco-Spanish combined operation and defeat on himself. The army, which dominated the area, completed 'pacification' in 1927. Thereafter Spain ruled through local officials closely 'guided' by Spanish agents.

Portugal had more benevolent aims, which were frustrated by an equally weak and turbulent domestic scene. It retained toeholds on the west African, Indian and Chinese coasts, but its main colonies were Mozambique and Angola in southern Africa. These large symbols of past glories were poorly endowed, economically stagnant, and disease-ridden. The republic had an ideal vision of colonial governance, but good plans were rarely carried out, safeguards were seldom enforced, and Portugal did not escape the racism and paternalism of the era. 'Civilized persons', not all white, were Portuguese citizens under Lisbon's law; educated adult men had the vote and token representation in the Parliament. The other 99 per cent of the indigenes were wards of a paternalistic but ineffectual state, expected to pay taxes, be cheap labour, and farm as told. Portugal did not control the interior or educate more than 2 per cent of the Africans to literacy. In 1920 Lisbon delegated effective control of Angola and Mozambique to high commissioners with proconsular powers. The result was financial disaster, corruption, brutality, and forced labour. A 1925 scandal over slavery contributed to Portugal's 1926 military coup. The new regime restored financial order in the colonies and used authoritarian methods to achieve maximum economic gain. But it failed to solve the problem of white unemployment, which grew in the 1930s; the racism of this class worsened with the economy, giving rise to some nationalism and pan-African sentiment among the indigenous populations.

＊   ＊   ＊

Of the Allied great powers, the United States alone sought no new colonies at Paris. Only twenty years had passed since it had hesitantly gained an empire; the mandates it was offered, such as Armenia and Constantinople, were problems nobody wanted; and the areas which interested it were not on offer at the conference. Thus it remained above the territorial scramble. Besides, it was using a more informal imperialism. In Africa, Liberia had long been a virtual American protectorate. From 1926 on, it became more so as coastal repatriates descended from American slaves governed, but the Firestone Rubber Company and its financial arm ruled. Liberia barely escaped international control after a League inquiry into the export of slave labour. In Central America and the Caribbean, primary American interests because of the Panama Canal, military and financial intervention now led to one *de facto* protectorate after another. Elsewhere, American concern centred on areas seized in 1898. Of these, Hawaii had citizenship and full territorial government; Spanish-speaking Puerto Rico gained citizenship and local self-government, including an elected legislature.

The Philippines in the far Pacific were a special case. There, as in the Caribbean, the United States built hospitals, roads, and schools; it provided sanitation, health services, a fair judiciary, and engaged in land reform, buying monastic lands for Filipino peasants. The islands prospered in the American market, but those yearning for freedom viewed forcibly imposed benevolence with mixed emotions. In fact, Washington intended Filipino independence from the outset. By World War I, a sizeable majority of civil servants, most teachers, and all governors of Christian provinces were Filipino. In 1916, an elected Senate able to veto the governor-general's choice of department heads was granted and voting criteria were eased. Filipinos were largely running their own affairs.

In the 1930s Philippine eagerness for self-rule ebbed as Japan seemed a threat, but the prospect of independence grew as a result and because of economic depression. American isolationists thought the Asian commitment risky and economic rivals wanted the islands outside the American tariff zone, so a 1933 law with barriers to Filipino trade and immigration specified early independence. Filipinos requested dominion status in an American commonwealth on the 1931 British model.* But Congress insisted in 1934, so a transitional Filipino Commonwealth was created. The 1934 act specified formal independence in a decade or so. Despite the considerable interruption of World War II, that took place on schedule on 4 July 1946 as the first post-war liberation of non-white peoples. Progression to equality was an American tradition, though leading here to independence rather than statehood. Britain did much the same in the 'white' Dominions, but the American example found no interwar imitators in non-white colonies.

*   *   *

Britain and France, who held the lion's share of colonies, did not think of planning for their independence until just before World War II. Britain vaguely intended that non-white areas follow the pattern of the white settler colonies – eventually. For the nonce, they were deemed very unready, and Britain alone would decide the stages of that distant evolution. Meanwhile, colonial governors ranked 'only just below the deity'.[4] The British Empire reached its zenith in the interwar era with more than a quarter of the world's land area and population. It amounted to about 90 million square miles (233 million km²) and 500 million souls, of whom nearly three-fourths were Indian. At the other extreme, Tristan da Cunha and Pitcairn

---

* See below, p. 140.

Island each had about a hundred inhabitants. Equally, Canada had almost four million square miles (over 10 million km^2), Gibraltar 2.3 (6 km^2). This disparate jumble contained more Muslims than any Muslim potentate ruled as well as 300 million Hindus.

In fact, Britain was overextended and past its imperial prime. It had spent its treasure – in North America, and the Royal Navy's manpower shrank by a third between 1914 and 1931. Rapid post-war demobilization meant Britain could not suppress trouble in several places at once, so concessions were sometimes unavoidable; lack of money aggravated weakness. As the late 1930s showed, Britain no longer had the resources to defend the whole. The Singapore base illustrates the problem. Britain decided in 1921 to build it because Japan potentially could render Hongkong (Hong Kong) untenable. By 1930 lack of funds had prevented much construction. When the Japanese threat became real in the late 1930s, only determined howls from Britain's most romantic imperialists prevented abandonment of the base in order to concentrate on the European danger to the Empire's heartland.

This sprawling Empire, centred on land and sea routes to India and China, was ramshackle in its arrangements. Some colonies were valuable, but 'many of them were frankly nuisances, burdens on the economy, handicapped children at best'.[5] Even these usually had strategic value. Governance varied but, beyond the autonomous Dominions, included the viceroyalty of India, crown colonies ruled by the Colonial Office, protectorates with nominal native rulers, condominiums of joint rule with another power, Chinese treaty ports, and mandates. Most of these were less regulated from the capital than were the colonies of other powers. The godly governor had much latitude in a decentralized system. Beneath him, young men from Britain's public schools* often oversaw districts larger than European states. Segregation was the norm, and officials had little to do with indigenes. Britain had taken its Empire into a European war in 1914 without consulting any part of it. The Empire had responded, English-speaking settler colonies loyally, with relatively little protest elsewhere. At war's end the Empire, except for Ireland, seemed to be in satisfactory condition from London's viewpoint. Soon, however, revolution broke out in Egypt and Iraq, Iran refused to ratify a treaty imposed on it, and Afghanistan invaded India, where also the massacre occurred at Amritsar.

*   *   *

At first, however, Britain's oldest colony was the primary worry. A bill to grant Ireland home rule passed Parliament in 1914 over protest from Ulster (the six northern Protestant, pro-British counties), but it was shelved during the war. Ireland was quiet until fears of conscription set off the abortive

* In American parlance, private schools.

Easter Rebellion in 1916. This had little support until the English executed the leaders, creating martyrs to a nationalist cause.

A brutal Anglo-Irish war occurred from mid-1919 until a mid-1921 truce marked the start of the Empire's dissolution. Talks in London led in a December 1921 treaty to Dominion status as the Irish Free State, excluding Ulster. When the previously illegal Irish Parliament accepted less than full independence, civil war erupted until mid-1923. Ulster remained part of Britain with a Parliament at Belfast, but the Irish Free State joined the League of Nations and Imperial Conferences and became the first Dominion to open a legation, in 1924 in Washington. A reluctant Dominion, in the 1930s it gradually snipped ties to the crown and renamed itself Eire. It was neutral on Britain's doorstep in World War II, withdrew from the Commonwealth in 1948, and proclaimed independence in 1949.

British troops left Ireland in 1922. Britain could then turn its attention to other imperial issues. Palestine, a veritable Pandora's box of ills, was the most pressing and remained so. But other areas from India to Iraq presented more problems than Britain had foreseen. Nationalism had reached Malta and the Middle East. The West Indies were in economic decline and suffered from more than one kind of racial discrimination, as did Cyprus and Ceylon (Sri Lanka). India and Ceylon sought self-rule, and Ceylon seemed on its way as it gained universal suffrage in 1931, but Britain conceded more form than substance in the interwar era, granting too little too late.

It did the same, only more so, in the vast Indian subcontinent, the famous jewel in the crown whose departure therefrom was unthinkable to Britons, if not to Indians. In 1901, as Viceroy, Lord Curzon said that if Britain lost India it would 'drop straightaway to a third-rate power'.[6] That remained the prevailing wisdom forty years later. In the interim, British rule was arrogant and autocratic; even as World War II began, Britons assumed self-government was generations away.

That had long since ceased to be true. Like the British, Indians understood the economic and military importance of their contribution in World War I. A million and a half Indians had served, a million in Europe. They returned knowing how European farmers lived; astonished to be treated as equals, not coolies, by the French; and thirsting for freedom. They took pride in India's ancient civilization and had an Oxford-educated elite eager to lead. The two religions co-operated as the Muslim League and the Hindu-dominated Indian National Congress* jointly sought reforms. The Easter Rebellion, Russian Revolution, and Wilson's statements only deepened the desire for self-rule.

In 1917 Britain promised a larger share in administration and progress by stages to 'responsible government', which Indians took to mean Dominion status. As Britain intended to determine the stages, thirty painful

* In the Indian context, Congress means a political party, not a legislative body.

years ensued. Britain imposed reforms in 1919–21 providing local self-government and some provincial autonomy, though under a 'dyarchy' system reserving key functions to the crown. Nationally, a bicameral legislature was partially elected by a tiny electorate, but the viceroy retained control. Congress refused to join in the elections. Yet Indianization of the civil service proceeded gradually. India joined Imperial Conferences, breaking the colour barrier, and the British Empire delegation to the peace conference; its delegates (the Indian Secretary and a maharajah) signed the Versailles treaty. India also joined the League as its only non-self-governing member, but Britain chose the Indian delegates, who had little policy independence.

Clearly, the 1919 reforms lacked substance. Disappointment led to the Amritsar riots. When most Britons defended the massacre, in which at least 379 Indians died, Gandhi launched his non-violent non-co-operation campaign and a boycott of British goods and institutions. Repeated arrests and jail terms increased his popularity. He transformed Congress, which he dominated, from an elite group to a mass movement, for he had the support of rich and poor, both urban and rural, including the Muslims at first. Britain was flummoxed by the tiny half-clad man in his *dhoti*.

As concessions were few, the situation worsened. In 1927 Britain announced a commission with no Indian members to study new reforms. In 1928 Congress and the Muslim League split; the religious issue thereafter complicated and poisoned all reform efforts. In 1929 Congress called for independence, launching a civil disobedience campaign backed by the entire country. In April 1930 Gandhi's march to the sea, where he seized a lump of salt in defiance of the government's monopoly and heavy salt tax, symbolized the nation's mass rejection of Britain. London partially imposed new reforms in 1935–37, detaching Burma (Myanmar) from India with much self-rule. In India, separate Muslim and Hindu provinces with full autonomy were created, inadvertently paving the way for post-war division; nationally, the suffrage was widened somewhat and an intricate dyarchy planned. But this met so much opposition from Indian princes, Congress, the Muslim League, and imperial diehards led by Winston Churchill that it never took effect.

In 1939, the viceroy informed Indians that they were at war, as in 1914. Congress was furious; its provincial ministries resigned, and a new campaign of non-violent non-co-operation began. Two million Indians served, making a vital contribution especially to the defence of Egypt and Iraq. Though most Indians supported the West, some saw Japanese triumphs in 1941–42 as Asian victories against white oppressors. By then it was clear that Indian independence was coming in some form. The war widened the Muslim–Hindu divide, leading the Muslim League to seek a separate Muslim state. In 1939, Britain offered Dominion status in a vague future, essentially the pledge of 1917. Congress spurned this and a later

British wartime proposal, both for the future. Gandhi supposedly termed offers of post-war concessions 'a post-dated cheque on a bank that was failing';[7] he launched a 'Quit India' campaign. This slogan caught on and was often hurled at Britons. Even Churchill saw that independence was coming but refused to act during the wartime emergency. India's urgency increased as Britain was defeated in Europe and Asia, for Indians wished to seize upon British vulnerability. But Britain's control held until the war's end; then it reaped the whirlwind.

*　　*　　*

India was never a Dominion. Among this elite group who enjoyed self-rule save for defence, foreign affairs, and a right of judicial appeal to London, Britain's oldest overseas colony was the newest and initially smallest member. But Newfoundland neither signed the Versailles treaty nor entered the League of Nations. In 1934 bankruptcy arising from her crushing war debts led her to end Dominion status. A British commission governed until she became a Canadian province in 1949.

In the imperial family, Canada, oldest and geographically the largest Dominion, was the assertive eldest son, pressing for more adult freedoms and seeking its own envoy in Washington to deal with Canada's American problem, which Canadians liken to sleeping next to a restless elephant. Canada was the only Dominion abutting a great power, and its policies were shaped by this fact and by internal splits between east and west and English and French Canadians, adding to an identity crisis. Part English, part French, and part American in some respects, Canada was not yet mature enough to see that it was entirely Canadian.

Canada's nationalist aspirations emerged at the Paris peace conference, where it led the fight for separate Dominion signature of the Versailles treaty and seats in the League of Nations. These were symbols of a new international status despite Canadian dislike of Article X for collective action against aggression, not least in terms of tackling the United States if it again invaded Mexico. Canada insisted as well on a Dominion right of election to the League Council, itself becoming the first to sit there in 1927 when informal regional allocation guaranteed a Dominion seat. A small Department of External Affairs existed pre-war but expanded post-war. Its first legation was created in Washington in 1927, followed by others elsewhere. Meanwhile, Canada urged greater Dominion independence, eschewed mandates, and shared American isolationism, its delegate to Geneva remarking that Canada lived 'in a fire-proof house far from inflammable materials' with no need of the insurance European states sought.[8] It also successfully fought renewal of the Anglo-Japanese alliance, which conceivably could force an Anglo-Canadian war against the United States, and opposed the League's abortive Draft Treaty of Mutual Assistance and Geneva Protocol for similar reasons. Increasingly Canada went its own

way, particularly in American issues, though good Anglo-American relations were its paramount concern. However, by 1930 American investment
in Canada had overtaken British; thus, Canada moved somewhat closer to
Britain for protection against economic absorption. But it continued to
assert its own identity and to press successfully for a readjustment of imperial relations.

The other Dominions were newer and less nationalistic.The little daughter of the imperial family, timid New Zealand, preferred to cling to her
father, but ethnicity, economics, and geography dictated many common
attitudes with adolescent Australia. Both were psychologically dependent
on Britain; indeed, until 1940, both settler colonies thought they *were*
British despite their aboriginal populations. Both relied on export to
Britain, on whom they depended for security. Neither sought its own
foreign policy until 1940 demonstrated that their safety depended on the
United States.

In World War I, they made their first overseas forays, contributing troops
to Britain and, at its request, conquering Germany's south Pacific islands.
These they intended to hold, preferably to annex with Japanese immigration barred. At the peace conference they fought together for what became
their C mandates and against a racial equality clause in the Covenant. Later
they jointly opposed the Draft Treaty of Mutual Assistance, for it committed states to act only on their own continent, and so nobody would aid
them. Neither wanted greater independence; Australia ratified the 1931
Statute of Westminster granting it only in 1942 and New Zealand in 1947.

In the 1930s, both saw events through British eyes. Japan was the only
potential threat; they were intensely relieved when it went north into
Manchuria. The Singapore base, under fitful construction until partial
completion in 1938, represented security. By 1937, they were anxious, but
Britain said a fleet could reach Singapore in 70 days. Somehow, they were
reassured, though there were another 4400 miles to Australia and 6000 to
New Zealand, and Britain did not have a spare fleet to send to the Pacific.
Until 1940, they were ostrich-like about Japan on the strength of assurances
which Britain doubted it could fulfil. The shock was great when Churchill
told them in mid-1940 that Britain could not cope with East Asia on top of
Europe and said they must rely on the United States. They grew up quickly
and began to work together.

For most of the interwar era, New Zealand was the more timid one,
content to leave foreign policy to papa, never seeking consultation. London
remained the centre of her world, and she wishfully saw the Pacific as a
British lake. At Paris she followed Australia's more assertive lead on
mandates and racial issues; she did not seek her League seat. Thereafter she
lost interest in the outside world. Though concerned that Japan's industrial
and population pressures could lead to aggression, she left the problem to
Britain and rested on the Royal Navy, which had few other reasons to fight

in the Pacific. After 1935 and the Labour party's rise to power, there was more concern about Japan, less confidence in British promises, nascent nationalism with some restiveness, and a new awareness of the United States. Anxiety led to requests for British assurances and vain efforts toward League sanctions against Japan's invasion of China in 1937. But as crises mounted in the Pacific in 1939, she fell back on her father, while seeking closer co-operation with Australia.

Interwar Australia was typically adolescent, assertive one day, seeking shelter the next. Thus its policies fell between those of Canada and New Zealand. It wanted Britain's protection but did not want to be dragged into its wars. At Paris it followed Canada's lead as brash Billy Hughes ignored his cabinet's objections and demanded separate treaty signature and a League seat. He hoped for a weak League, resisting both the Covenant's Article X and racial equality, battling as well for war costs. Thereafter Australia subsided, and its foreign policy 'was almost indiscernible'.[9] Hughes did not support Canadian and South African efforts for more autonomy at the 1921 Imperial Conference. After the 1921–22 Washington conference seemed to bring peace to the Pacific, Australia felt secure and became more isolationist, not learning that it must pursue its own interests and resisting Dominion autonomy, a separate external affairs ministry, and requests from other states for an Australian envoy. Events between 1935 and 1941 forced it to have a foreign policy as isolation and leaving all to Britain became impossible. Unlike New Zealand, Australia, more northerly and more exposed, favoured appeasing Japan; otherwise it trusted to British promises, and rushed to declare war at once in 1939.

The same could not be said of South Africa. Large, wealthy, and strategic, it shared some Canadian and some Australian views but was influenced by its own distinctive location and problems. South Africa had even more complex linguistic and racial mixes than Canada but, having conquered South-west Africa at British request, it shared Hughes's stand on mandates and racial matters. Smuts was prominent at Paris regarding the Covenant, League seats for the Dominions, reparations, and the mandate system. On Dominion autonomy and envoys abroad, South Africa followed Canada. Both had large white non-British populations and wanted clearcut Dominion status; Smuts contributed much to the eventual compromise of 1926 and 1931. He loosened the ties of empire but, as the most British-oriented South African leader, he also worried about imperial unity.

In 1935, most South African peoples, including the Bantus, supported League sanctions against Italy's invasion of Ethiopia. Then white unity ceased as Afrikaner nationalism grew and became increasingly pro-German. The government stated in May 1936 that South Africa would enter a war only if it were in its own interest and only with the consent of its Parliament. The Nationalist leader favoured appeasement whereas Smuts would follow Britain into war. Had that come in 1938, South Africa would have remained neutral. Thereafter, it learned that Germany aimed to regain its South-west African mandate and Tanganyika. Even so, when war came to Europe in 1939, the South African cabinet, Parliament, and electorate were utterly divided.

*   *   *

That problem had not arisen in 1914 when Britain took the Empire into war without consultation, but as the Dominions' military contribution swelled, they pressed for a voice. At first, Britons debated policy only among themselves, maintaining a united front before the children. Canada challenged the lack of information without result until Lloyd George in 1917 created the Imperial War Cabinet in which Dominion prime ministers sat from time to time. This became the British Empire Delegation at the peace conference, where the Dominions acted both on their own and as part of a great power. In 1917 the Dominions also asked for a post-war definition of Dominion status and a readjustment of relations allowing them to act as autonomous nations within a self-governing empire, with an 'adequate voice' and 'continuous consultation' in foreign policy for themselves and India.[10] A debate ensued over the future, with some support for a federal union, which Canada resisted. After the war, the idea of an imperial federation was abandoned, but that of a common foreign policy lingered until 1922. Otherwise, only the name Commonwealth survived.

The peace conference was the formal diplomatic debut of the Dominions and India. They made the most of it and emerged with international recognition despite grumbling by some about six British seats in the League. Not only did they sign the treaty separately, but it was agreed that each must ratify it as well and that Britain would do so only afterwards. As some Dominions had misgivings about Britain's proposed guarantee of France, they were excluded unless they specifically adhered. This formula quickly became the norm. Britain could no longer speak for all British subjects; an accession clause or formal agreement was required. The right of legation and to conclude treaties without British countersignature quickly followed.

The 1921 Imperial Conference tried to maintain a common foreign policy. Regarding the Japanese alliance, the Dominions wanted a voice but no commitments; beyond that they disagreed but ultimately accepted British policy. At the Washington conference of 1921–22 the British Empire Delegation functioned one last time. The limitation on British naval forces agreed there included the Dominion navies, but they signed and ratified separately. Then they went their separate ways, for there was no consultative mechanism, and no Dominion wanted a peacetime defence burden for future aid to Britain.

The 1922 Chanak crisis when Britain nearly went to war with Turkey further sapped imperial unity. Lloyd George sought troops and published his appeal at once. New Zealand's prime minister sighed, 'I had hoped that the Empire would have recovered from the last war before being called upon to take part in another', but agreed in three minutes and raised recruits at once. The aboriginal Maoris chimed in, 'I will go. Be brave, O father.'[11] However, South Africa and Canada stalled. Canada's prime minister was enraged to hear of the matter from the press hours before the official telegram arrived and said it must go to his Parliament, whereas Smuts carefully continued his tour of Zululand. Dominion confidence in London was dealt a severe blow, and questions arose about British power. A common foreign policy did not survive.

Thereafter, the Dominions attended some European conferences but not others. In 1925 the Locarno treaties, again guaranteeing France against German attack, exempted the Dominions and India unless they acceded, which none did. British and Dominion policies were divorcing, but the legal situation remained murky. At the 1926 Imperial Conference, Canada, Ireland, and South Africa sought clarity. The Conference declared that the Dominions 'are autonomous communities within the British Empire, equal in status, in no way subordinate one to another in any aspect of their domestic or external affairs, though united by a common allegiance to the Crown, and freely associated as members of the British Commonwealth of Nations.'[12] The monarch's title was duly changed, and Britain now concluded treaties as His Majesty's Government *in* the United Kingdom. The Dominions exchanged high commissioners with London and each other, dealing government to government as sovereign nations do, but the 1926 formula did not have the force of law. Thus the Dominion parliaments asked the Imperial or British Parliament to remove existing restrictions and recognize their equality legally. This was done by the Statute of Westminster of 1931. The British monarch acquired six new crowns as the king of each Dominion and was obliged to accept the advice of the prime minister of each regarding that Dominion. The monarch could even be at war with him- or herself.[*]

The Commonwealth was based in part on a united white 'European' front against 'the natives'. In addition, two events preserved some economic unity as the Empire divided politically. When Britain took the pound off the gold standard in 1931, the entire Commonwealth except Canada adopted the pound sterling, not gold, as its monetary standard. With some small nations, they constituted the sterling bloc, with a virtual common currency for foreign exchange purposes. Equally in 1932, high American tariffs led Canada to convene the Ottawa conference which produced a series of bilateral agreements for tariff reductions among Commonwealth members. This system of imperial preference led to an increase in inter-imperial trade.

The Statute of Westminster was the proudest achievement of Britain's dreary interwar years. British leaders rejoiced in it and were reluctant to do

---

[*] And was during the 1947 Indian–Pakistani war.

anything which might endanger the new Commonwealth. Thus the Dominions affected Britain's foreign policy, especially in 1938. They had little interest in Europe, though only there could the Empire's heart be directly threatened. In the late 1930s, the one policy on which they all agreed was appeasement of Germany. This was not the primary reason why Prime Minister Neville Chamberlain chose appeasement, but it made other policies unattractive. London's solicitude found its reward in Dominion loyalty in World War II.

*   *   *

France's empire was equally vital to her great power status and defence. It too sprawled across the globe and varied in its arrangements, though France, like Britain, often preferred to rule inexpensively through indigenous rulers. But interwar France developed nothing like the British Commonwealth, mainly because its assumptions about evolutionary progress were different and no colony had a settler majority. In addition to A and B mandates, the French Empire included colonies and protectorates, one condominium, and one overseas semi-metropolitan area; these were governed by three Paris ministries and five colonial services, but well-connected settler businessmen had much influence in Paris and affected policy. Decentralization was the norm, however, and colonial administrators had great power. French colonial agents, unlike their British counterparts, lacked prestige and were in bad odour between the wars. Pre-war agents had often deserved their poor reputation, but 1912 reforms in recruiting and training brought improvement. By the mid-1930s, most administrators were able, and a few from Senegal, French Guiana, or the West Indies were black, but by then the *status quo* had crystallized into stagnation and doctrinal immobility. France, unlike Britain, transferred agents rapidly from colony to colony, which meant they had little contact with the peoples they ruled.

World War I revealed French dependence on her Empire for men and matériel, and on the Royal Navy to bring both to Europe; the 1922 Washington Conference decisions meant that France remained unable to reach most of her colonies in wartime. Nonetheless, post-war Colonial Minister Albert Sarraut recognized the moral debt to the Empire and believed France's future was tied to the welfare of the colonies; he drew up plans, never enacted, for education, health, economic development, and good governance. In the mid-1930s, the socialist Popular Front sought reforms but also failed. Sarraut's hope of gradual representative government never went beyond advisory councils instituted in 1919–20. These had a limited advisory role on economic and financial topics only. Indigenes were always in the minority, chosen by the French except occasionally in cities, and required to deliberate separately. The councils were not a vehicle for popular expression or real political activity. France's heavy hand was reinforced by insistence that the colonies pay for themselves. Most did so by onerous taxes, forced labour, and draconian quotas to increase production of cash crops, but little money remained for health services, schools, and public works.

French colonial doctrine wavered between assimilation, turning indigenes into overseas Frenchmen, and association, governance through local rulers with due regard to traditional societies. France never decided between the two, often pursuing both at once. Both were more the stuff of Parisian rhetoric than consistent guidelines in the colonies. Actual practice amounted to 'much subjection, very little autonomy, a touch of assimilation'[13] to maintain the *status quo* indefinitely.

Associationism, the French form of indirect rule through local potentates and institutions, began in Indochina, then spread to Africa. Its intent was to respect local societies and help them 'evolve', but France lacked enthusiasm for indigenous culture, and associationism was often seen only as a tactic on the road to eventual assimilation. France assumed more powers, supplanting local regimes; its rule became less indirect. It destroyed all but the shell of old structures but did not replace them, especially not with liberty, equality, and fraternity.

These blessings were to be conferred by assimilation – some day. The civilizing mission would lead to the *évolué* or 'developed man', an imitation Frenchman living in a colonial copy of France. Some became so evolved that they were more at home in Paris, where they enjoyed full rights, than in their birthplace. But assimilation was always for the few, and token representation in the French Chamber was given only to the oldest colonies, for it was dangerous to allow citizenship except on an individual basis; if representation were widely granted, the sheer numbers would swamp the French political system. This factor alone mitigated against extensive assimilation. So did French practice. Colonial subjects were to gain the blessings of French culture, and white settlers, French or otherwise, did. But in 1939, 85 per cent of Indochinese children had no schooling and 90 per cent of Algerian Muslim children did without. This record was no worse than that of some other European powers, but it reveals that the colonies were a school neither for civilization nor for French culture. Paris thought educating a local elite in French and often in France would co-opt them, breeding loyalty and minor officials. But if educated, they tended to denounce French rule – in good French. Those who studied in Paris lived as poor students in working-class districts, absorbing socialism and Communism, as happened with Ho Chi Minh (Nguyen Tat Thanh)* of Vietnam and later Pol Pot (Saloth Sar) of Cambodia. If they returned home with degrees, few suitable jobs were open to them. Others served in Europe during and after World War I; they returned with European values, resisting the traditional social

* Also known as Nguyen Ai Quoc and by a variety of other pseudonyms.

order. France responded neither to them nor to educated elites who sought assimilation or independence. In most areas, nationalism was an undercurrent in the interwar era, particularly at first, but a budding challenge, which France ignored. Heretofore educated Africans and some Asians had seen colonial rule as a factor for progress; now younger elites viewed France as its chief impediment.

*   *   *

One area where nationalism was overt was Indochina, composed of Laos, Cambodia, and the three Vietnamese provinces of Tonkin, Annam, and Cochin China. The last was a colony, the rest protectorates. Mountainous Laos and thinly populated Cambodia were buffers against the British to protect Vietnam, France's richest possession. Its Annamese inhabitants had an advanced Chinese culture which, along with greater exposure to the French, made them the most hostile to French rule.

France used both association and assimilation in Indochina, ruling through the kings of Annam, Laos, and Cambodia. But by 1925 indigenous power was eliminated, and French officials closely supervised their Asian counterparts. Advisory councils were introduced as window-dressing. These did not satisfy the educated classes, who wanted reforms but learned that French rhetoric about 'cultural association' and the glorious tradition of 1789 meant no concession of any self-government. When white settlers blocked such reforms as the governors-general were willing to grant, taxes increased, promises were broken, and even the most loyal Vietnamese associations were banned, moderates who had accepted French culture turned elsewhere.

France also cultivated the elites, educating them in French schools.That led to a burst of nationalism among those who did not wish to be imitation Frenchmen, so Paris ordered a larger dose of French culture, founding the University of Hanoi, which promptly became a nationalist centre. As France could not imagine that anybody might not want to share in its splendid culture, it encouraged study in Paris. There the young learned technology was the basis of power and mastered Western ideologies. Upon their return to underemployment and discrimination, they turned these ideologies against their masters in an independence movement.

Vietnamese nationalism was born of the Japanese victory over Russia in 1904–05 among Vietnamese students in Japan. Formative influences included Wilsonian self-determination, the Russian Revolution, Marxist ideology, the example of the British Dominions, and the Chinese Revolution of 1911 as the doctrines of the revolutionary Kuomintang filtered southward from Canton (Guangzhou) to Hanoi. The National Party of Vietnam (VNQDD) was founded in 1927 on the Kuomintang model to seek a republic, but nationalism soon revolved around Ho Chi Minh, who studied and worked in Paris, Moscow, and Canton, a centre for Chinese nationalism and Communism. In 1930, he founded the Indochinese Communist Party among Vietnamese dissidents in Hongkong. Ho was a dedicated Marxist but above all a Vietnamese nationalist.

1930 was a turning point for Vietnamese nationalism. Salt and alcohol monopolies, heavy taxes, industrial and agricultural exploitation of labour, near slavery on plantations, and the contracting world economy all led to disturbances. There was an abortive military mutiny organized by the VNQDD, piracy against large landowners in Cochin China, peasant revolts and hunger marches in Tonkin, along with strikes, demonstrations and local risings organized by the new Communist Party. Significantly, the masses participated. Those favouring co-operation with France were isolated, and the nationalist movement swelled, with moderates in Cochin China advocating gradual progress to Dominion status. France responded repressively, suspending all political groups, executing hundreds and driving the Communists underground. Ho fled a death sentence into exile. But Communism spread underground, creating friendly associations and trade unions. Nonetheless, it lacked mass support in the 1930s. The French harassed it but did not destroy it or the nationalism which arose from repression. Preoccupied with the growing Japanese threat and the German menace at home, France made no concessions. By 1939, its control rested only on force; if that were destroyed, as it was in World War II, there would be nothing to fall back on.

*　　*　　*

The other area of overriding concern to France was the Maghrib* in north Africa across the Mediterranean from France. Aside from Libya, it consisted of Algeria, Morocco, Tunisia, and the French-dominated international zone of Tangier. France had annexed Algeria and governed it under the Interior Ministry; Morocco and Tunisia were protectorates under the Foreign Affairs Ministry. All three had inland zones under military control where population was sparse and French control slight for some years. Despite similar problems throughout the region, there was no co-ordination.

Everywhere the influential settler class or *colons*, an elite who had little contact with the Muslim majority, blocked reform. All *colons* of whatever origin were French citizens under French law and courts. They seized the best land, weakening the tribes and creating tenant farmers or a dispossessed landless class who drifted to the cities. *Colons* were distinguished from indigenes not by race, which was not always obvious, but by religion. The overwhelmingly Muslim and mainly Arabic-speaking indigenes were a mixture of mountain Berbers and coastal Arabs. An Islamic revival hastened rejection of imperial overlords, especially as a perceived threat to

---

* An Arabic term meaning the west or north-west Africa.

Islam occurred in each area in 1930. In their personal status, Muslims were subject to Islamic law and law courts. Educated North Africans could apply for naturalization as French citizens if they abandoned Muslim status, which meant a virtual desertion of religion and culture few were prepared to accept.

The area was of such importance to France that her Middle Eastern policies were often decided with an eye to repercussions in North Africa, especially since troops from the Maghrib were used to suppress Levantine rebellions. France kept a quarter of her army in the Maghrib after World War I and invested heavily economically there. Introduction of modern hygiene caused a huge population increase leading to underemployment and shantytowns, which bred discontent. As there was a pro-French évolué element, France underestimated the developing nationalist challenge, which was fuelled by wartime service and expectation of reward. In any event, interwar French governments were too weak to push through reforms unpopular in France and among the colons.

In Tunisia, the French kept the bey (ruler) but reduced him to issuing French edicts; a French-dominated Grand Council had limited budgetary power. Here as elsewhere, land seizures were an issue. The first Resident-General of Morocco, Marshal Louis Lyautey, ruled gently until 1925, favouring association and protection of native traditions as well as creation of an elite and economic development; thereafter French civil servants took charge, preparing decrees for the sultan to sign. Nationalism, which arose from Islam, was tied to Lyautey's departure, Abd-el-Krim's revolt, and more direct French rule. Algeria had the most direct French rule of all; the north, which had a million French settlers by 1930, was governed as part of metropolitan France, though subject to decrees by the French president and the governor-general. It had political representation in Paris, but only French citizens could vote. Protest over sending troops to France in World War I led to repeated reform efforts, but colons blocked all but a few token measures.

A moderate reform movement in Tunisia before World War I centred on the Destour (constitution) party. In 1934, Habib Bourguiba split from Destour and founded the Neo-Destour Party, advocating universal suffrage, independence by stages, and alliance with France. Repression soon made it the sole voice of Tunisian nationalism. In Morocco, on the other hand, nationalism developed after 1930 but lacked cohesiveness and a leader, though Sultan Mohammed V became its symbol. Algerian nationalists, at first mostly évolués, were also divided, chiefly over retaining Muslim status. Middle-class intellectuals like Ferhat Abbas wanted to be Algerian, Muslim, and French. Simultaneously in the 1920s, religious reformers argued that Algeria was a separate nation to be rallied by Islam. In 1931 they created the Ulama party which was anti-Western, against assimilation, and for uniting Arabs and Berbers in an Islamic community. After colons blocked Popular Front efforts to grant some of the reforms jointly urged by Ulama and *évolué* groups, in 1937 Messali Hadj, leader of the Algerian proletariat in Paris, founded the Parti populaire algérien, favouring independence, which spread quickly. In a progression soon followed elsewhere, even moderate nationalists and traditionalist Muslims now sought an Algerian republic in federation with France.

In the Maghrib, there were signs by the late 1930s, which French administrators and settlers ignored, that the *status quo* could not be maintained indefinitely. Nationalism was not as advanced as in the Middle East, but considerable ferment existed. Assimilation had been so very gradual that it had failed. The *colons* had privileges and social position, but the indigenes had the numbers in their favour and knew it. Aside from a small group of *évolués*, the gulf between the two elements had not narrowed. As the French commentator Raymond Aron remarked,

> The Europeans did not understand and did not want to understand the authentic nature of the traditional culture. As the dominant minority, they feared that they would be swamped by the majority if they accorded the vanquished the civic equality which the latter had long demanded.[14]

The fears of the settlers were real but blinded them to North African yearnings: 'Not to be known as a "salarab" (dirty Arab), to be at home in one's own country, to have equality before the law, to have absolutely equal opportunities for education, and even for literacy – these were the telling slogans of nationalist independence movements.'[15]

*   *   *

With local variations, these were colonial aspirations everywhere, not only in the Maghrib but throughout the French Empire and the colonies of most European states. At the start of the interwar era and for some even at the end, the existing state of affairs seemed permanent to both ruler and ruled. Indeed, the 1930s brought added subjections in Manchuria and Ethiopia, but at the same time they brought growing realization on the part of some European overlords, especially on the eve of World War II, that colonies could not continue forever.

Meanwhile, the Statute of Westminster had been a key change, if only for whites. Others were not far behind. The Indian reforms of the 1930s, though disappointing to impatient nationalists, admitted the concept and fact of a larger Indian role in governance. In a sense, this had already occurred, and it was an open question whether the British ruled India or the native bureaucracy under them did, just as in Africa it was unclear whether the district commissioner or his interpreter governed.[16] But such power was veiled and undemocratic; the 1934 American law for the Philippines was more forthright and far-reaching. In an era when each advance had an impact elsewhere, these were significant events, as was the French Popular Front's reform effort, however abortive.

The interwar period was the hiatus between the great Scramble and the nationalist era, the time in the brief century of imperial domination from the mid-1870s to the mid-1970s (when the United States left Vietnam) afforded to European powers to organize and develop their empires as they wished, for control was now complete and resistance not yet a major threat. Most did so only modestly beyond 'divide and conquer' tactics and maintenance of the *status quo*. They were constrained by belief that colonies should be self-supporting, by lack of interest (especially of the populace), and by war debts and other pressing claims on national exchequers. For imperial overlords colonies had fewer advantages than anticipated. Many were unprofitable, especially without heavy capital investment, which was seldom made. Still, they were of strategic use and provided reservoirs of men. They were also of psychological value, making Belgium more important and appearing to compensate France and Portugal for their decline in power in Europe. For some European states, overseas colonies seemed the only way to maintain their position in Europe's power rivalry.

For subject peoples, the disadvantages of colonial status generally outweighed the advantages, but there were some advantages as well, often unintended by European rulers. It is unlikely that much of Africa and Asia could have long remained outside an expanding world economy, and while most subject peoples would have preferred independence, that was rarely a practical possibility. The situation in 1898 when the United States took the Philippines with German and British fleets offshore awaiting the American decision as well as Spain eager to regain the islands and Japan to claim them was unusually dramatic, but otherwise typical of imperial appetites; this is why the race in Africa before 1900 was called the Scramble. Ethiopia, geographically the Switzerland of Africa, was saved by its terrain and by Italian ineptitude. In the interwar era, Liberia, even with American support, had great difficulty in maintaining its borders against European encroachment. In short, for many if not most areas, independence was not a viable option, as their technological weakness and European power rivalries doomed them to colonial status. Perhaps one should criticize European overlords less for seizing areas which some Western country was bound to rule than for doing so little to prepare the colonies to rule themselves.

That said, what did the inhabitants gain from becoming subject peoples? Though intended primarily for the profit of the rulers, imperialism left a legacy of ports, roads, railroads, and public buildings, some splendid or at least grandiose. There were schools and health facilities, however inadequate. Systematic attacks on epidemic diseases largely conquered plague, yellow fever, smallpox, and sleeping-sickness (though white man's diseases and old pestilences were spread by new trade routes). If force was a factor in colonial rule, so were peace and continuity, as colonialism ended tribal wars and outright slavery, bringing a sometimes heavy-handed order in a pax Europa. Imperialism also brought a common language to large areas, superimposing Western tongues on the 800 languages of India and the 700 tongues of Africa. In theory, the common language could perhaps have been Arabic, Hindi, Hausa, and Swahili (Kiswahili), though not without bloodshed. In fact, world languages eased entry into world trade, access to Western technology, and obtaining the Western education needed to gain and maintain independence.

Both the pax Europa and the Western languages fostered trade and prosperity, though unevenly. Colonies gained sound, stable, convertible currencies, some entering the money economy for the first time; this, along with the trading patterns of their masters, brought them into the world economic system. They gained access to Western capital, though never enough of it. Nonetheless, there was some economic development, especially of mines, though industry was rarely encouraged. Imperialism brought modernization (for better or worse), urbanization, mobility, communications, an infrastructure, and new classes, including an urban proletariat and a literate urban middle class, both powerful later on. For a very few, there was the best education Europe had to offer in its leading universities and, for fewer still, lower- or middle-level government posts which provided a little training toward independence. However, imperialism was not a school for self-government. Circumstances varied, with British Asia gaining a bit more preparation than Africa. Nonetheless, except in the Philippines, tutelary powers usually only began crash courses in governance at one minute before midnight after any hope of a gradual transition was clearly gone.

In the Congo and the Philippines, literacy and public health measures were widespread. In a few west African areas, notably the Gold Coast (Ghana), colonial status brought real prosperity. In India, it bred a democratic tradition and in the interwar era the basis for an outstanding diplomatic corps. In the majority of colonies, however, for the ruled the plus side of the ledger was depressingly scant compared to the humiliations and restrictions of subjection.

*   *   *

One unintended effect of imperial rule was detribalization. In Africa, this phenomenon developed not only from undercutting the powers of the traditional chiefs but from the creation of new cities and large mines to which workers of various tribes flocked from all over the colony, living together outside any tribal organization. In Asia, reducing the power of local princes had a similar effect. As old loyalties waned and tribalism declined, nationalism grew. It was furthered by literacy, experience in world trade, exposure to European ideologies and, for some, European education, rebellion in other subject areas, and the arrival of modern communications, including newspapers and radios.

Nationalism arrived earlier in some places than others and developed more rapidly in certain colonies. In 1914, independence seemed inconceivable in most areas, and in the 1920s only timid reforms were sought, but by 1939 nationalism was highly developed in the Middle East and growing in south-east Asia and North Africa, though not yet into mass movements. Nationalism came later to sub-Saharan Africa, but a spirit of resistance had begun to develop though change seemed distant. In the most docile colonies, there were campaigns of complaints against abuses by the ruling power. These rallied peoples who were seeking dignity and an end to forced labour, arbitrary taxes, and harassment. The nationalistic urge to create a new state was stronger where the heritage of an ancient civilization was evident, as in the Middle East, India, and Indochina. Where there was also an educated class to lead, as in Egypt, India, and Vietnam, nationalism became intense. Asianism and pan-Islamic solidarity were emerging, both directed against Western imperial intruders, but more often the original goal was not independence but autonomy and some form of real association. Frustration at the refusal of substantial reforms then drove moderates to greater demands, as did World War II, which provided an opportunity and a demonstration of imperial weakness. Ferhat Abbas, who so wanted to be French, in 1936 denied the existence of an Algerian nation, but a decade later he was leading it in hope of federation with France and in another decade he had declared for independence. At that, he was slower than most.

European leaders understood how important colonies were in the power configuration. That is one reason why they would not dilute imperial control. Colonies played a key role in World War II before they stormed on stage, demanding independence, and caused the imperial system to disintegrate altogether. But in retrospect, it is clear that in the 1920s and 1930s colonies, which were so vital to European predominance, were a wasting asset and one which European imperial states continued to waste prodigally with little thought to the future. Thus they hastened a process they wished to delay, numbering the days when one could speak of the West's world and laying the basis for the post-war deluge.

◆ Notes to Chapter 7

1. Raymond F. Betts, *Uncertain Dimensions: Western Overseas Empires in the Twentieth Century* (Minneapolis, University of Minnesota Press, 1985), p. 42.
2. Rudyard Kipling, 'Recessional' (1897).
3. Ruth Slade, *The Belgian Congo* (London, OUP, 1961 edn), p. 4.
4. Edward Grierson, *The Death of the Imperial Dream* (New York, Doubleday, 1972), p. 279.

5. *Op. cit.*, p. 276.
6. Denis Judd and Peter Slinn, *The Evolution of the Modern Commonwealth, 1902–80* (London, Macmillan, 1982), p. 52.
7. Stanley Wolpert, *A New History of India* (New York, OUP, 1989), p. 334. See also Peter Calvocoressi, Guy Wint, and John Pritchard, *Total War*, 2nd revised edn (New York, Pantheon, 1989), pp. 1022–3.
8. C. P. Stacey, *Canada and the Age of Conflict* (2 vols, Toronto, Macmillan and University of Toronto Press, 1981), II, p. 61.
9. Peter G. Edwards, *Prime Ministers and Diplomats: the Making of Australian Foreign Policy* (Melbourne, OUP, 1983), p. 66.
10. Frank H. Underhill, *The British Commonwealth* (Durham, NC, Duke University Press, 1956), pp. 52–3.
11. Grierson, *Imperial Dream*, p. 195 for both quotations.
12. Kenneth C. Wheare, *The Statute of Westminster* (Oxford, OUP, 1933), p. 2.
13. Henri Grimal, *Decolonization*, tr. Stephan De Vos (Boulder, CO, Westview, 1978), p. 60.
14. Betts, *Uncertain Dimensions*, p. 7, quoting Aron preface to Pierre Bourdieu, *The Algerians*, trans. Alan C. M. Ross (Boston, Beacon Press, 1962).
15. Richard M. Brace, *Morocco, Algeria, Tunisia* (Englewood Cliffs, NJ, Prentice-Hall, 1964), p. 46.
16. D. A. Low, *Lion Rampant: Essays in the Study of British Imperialism* (London, Frank Cass, 1973), pp. 24–5.

CHAPTER

SUB-SAHARAN AFRICA

In 1939, a British Colonial Office official declared, '. . . in Africa we can be sure that we have unlimited time in which to work.'[1] The previous year, the Labour Colonial Secretary Malcolm MacDonald proclaimed, 'It may take generations, or even centuries for the peoples in some parts of the Colonial Empire to achieve self-government. But it is a major part of our policy, even among the most backward peoples of Africa, to teach them and to encourage them always to be able to stand a little more on their own feet.'[2] Africa's other colonial powers shared their views. The far-sighted knew that imperial domain could not last indefinitely in India and Indochina, Egypt and Algeria, but black Africa was another matter. Though centre stage pre-war and in the background during the war, this area was now in the wings, a political backwater. No part of sub-Saharan Africa other than Ethiopia (Abyssinia) and South Africa was considered an actor on the world's stage. Liberia might be given a walk-on role, and any political playbill would have listed the colonies as a flock of children. But children grow steadily and sometimes in spurts toward adulthood, whether their seniors notice or not.

The Sahara desert was the great divide. The Maghrib and Egypt were of the Mediterranean world, but south of the Sahara lay black Africa, whose peoples Europeans saw as large, mentally inferior children. Except in South Africa and the eastern highlands, there were no white settlements of size, only sprinklings of European administrators. For the indigenes, the colonial era was a brief period in Africa's long history but one of major if uneven impact, integrating Africa into modernity.

There was no doubt about the basis of imperial rule. As British poet Hillaire Belloc said:

> Whatever happens we have got
> The Maxim gun* and they have not.[3]

Imperial powers aimed to rule cheaply and to make their colonies self-supporting, if not profitable. That dictated indirect rule using native chiefs,

* An early machine gun.

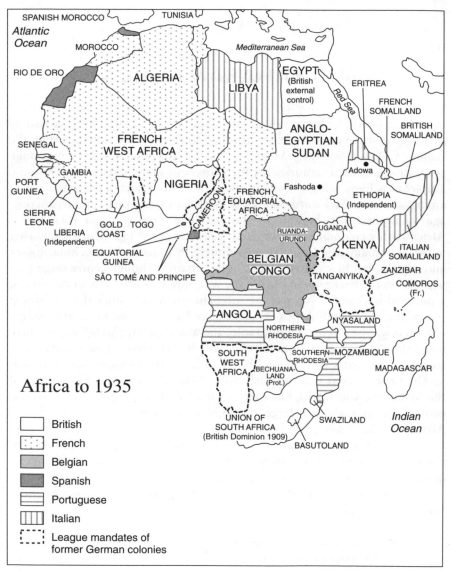

Africa to 1935

☐	British
▦	French
▨	Belgian
▨	Spanish
▤	Portuguese
▥	Italian
⌐ ⌐	League mandates of former German colonies

Africa to 1935

though turning them into civil servants eroded their authority, and relying on cheap African labour to provide clerks and build roads, ports, railways, and public buildings for administrative or extractive purposes. But few Africans saw any reason to work long hours at strenuous manual labour in the hot sun for minimal pay. Thus they were seen as lazy, though a Congo governor noted, 'what we must overcome in order to lead the Black to work is not so much his laziness as it is his distaste for *our* work, his indifference to *our* wage system.'[4]

European overlords met this problem by taxation and forced annual labour on public works. In a regime medieval by European standards, such serfdom was easy to rationalize. Lord Leverhulme argued in 1924: 'The African native will be happier, produce the best, and live under the larger conditions of prosperity, when his labour is directed and organized by his white brother who has all these million years start ahead of him.'[5] The African was not convinced, especially that he would receive much of the promised prosperity. As compulsory labour could not become year-round slavery without outcries in Europe but the colonies must be self-supporting, indigenes were forced into the money economy by taxation. This provided revenue and obliged Africans to earn money to pay their taxes. Taxation was usually by head and by hut, not by income; if unemployed, one still had to pay, even in hard times such as the 1930s. Taxation was central to the system; the Golden Rule of colonial administrators was, 'Thou shalt collect thy tax, thou shalt not worry thy government.'[6]

As frugal administration was so vital, imperial overlords, especially British ones, were thin on the ground. In World War I, armies supporting them were often shifted elsewhere, forcing a few concessions to the indigenes. Post-war armies, in any event mostly African, reverted to normal strength, but Europeans were no more numerous. A few whites ruled through 'native authorities' and semi-educated, ill-paid African underlings. In Nigeria in 1930, 20 million Africans were ruled by 431 Britons, including 80 officers to direct 14,000 African police. In the interior, the lone district officer was 'King of the Bush' in his vast domain. Thus imperial rule rested on bluster. Britain's colonial service came from Oxbridge and the public schools as 'It was logical to employ men who had been brought up to regard themselves as natural rulers because holding down Africa was largely a matter of bluff.'[7] Lord Lugard, father of indirect rule, argued that if one white were to rule thousands of blacks, he needed self-confidence and a sense of superiority more than capability.[8]

The pressure for self-sufficiency meant that economic policies were extractive, not developmental. Funds for real development were rarely supplied by governments or private sources, who saw African ventures as risky. Rulers discouraged processing and manufacturing, preferring mining and single cash crops. Areas without resources were neglected. The mines, however, became vast enterprises, attracting Africans from all over a colony and neighbouring colonies, creating concentrations of men without their families (except in the Congo). Plantations also emerged in areas with many white settlers. The only climates suited to white settlement were at the northern and southern ends of Africa and on the spine of cool highlands running north from South Africa toward Ethiopia. Here plantation agriculture and the settler economy took priority in the 1920s at the expense of the indigenes. As African farmers proved more efficient, in the 1930s the priority reversed.

The imperial system was largely unplanned and haphazard. It also was profoundly racist, especially in settler areas. But there was a clear racial barrier everywhere, with whites in charge and well paid, blacks under them and ill paid, sometimes for the same work. Whites gained educations, health services, and social privileges rarely available to blacks. In British and Belgian colonies, the colour bar was absolute. France and Portugal were more flexible about race relations, partly owing to the doctrine of assimilation, though only to a degree and only for a few. But the dual judicial system existing everywhere was more severe in their colonies, where the hated *indigénat* prevailed. This empowered administrators to fine or jail Africans for up to 15 (later five) days at will for minor infractions and served as an effective weapon of social control.

The scarcity of Europeans and the need for economy dictated some education for Africans. Missionaries provided many of the primary schools. Africans were trained as priests, primary school teachers, artisans, veterinarians' aides, and doctors' assistants. In cities, those with schooling became clerks for governments or European traders, entering a new middle class. An urban elite developed, whose goals clashed with those of traditional chiefs. Whites preferred the old elite, though their policies weakened it, not the *évolués* who urged reforms. They also favoured the 'unspoiled, bush African' as easier to handle, though their rule left him less unspoiled and amenable.

*   *   *

Nationalism developed slowly in areas where conquest came late, just before World War I, and where colonies were artificial creations corresponding to nothing in the African past. Elsewhere, a common cultural identity, history, and language preceded nationalism. Often resistance and then nationalism had to be created out of heterogeneous peoples of varying languages and cultures within European-imposed boundaries.[9] But European rule and economic exploitation in time generated new social structures and resistance.

It is a truism that in Africa imperialism destroyed the old social, cultural, and political systems without replacing them. Like most truisms, this is simplistic but not entirely untrue. European rule weakened the chiefs and ethnic society. Christianity and a money economy eroded traditional family

life. Huge mines worked by men without families damaged the social structure, village life, and tribes. Urban concentrations of blacks developed
outside ethnic life. A new proletariat arose at mines, a rural proletariat at
plantations, a new urban working class plus a new middle class and usually
a small new elite. As these elements grew, so did organizations within them.
The web of relationships among overlords came to have its mirror image in
networks among Africans in Africa and elsewhere. Thus, not only rebellion
ricocheted from one colony to another; ideas, tactics, and key personnel did
as well. These networks began in coastal towns where Africans with long
exposure to whites turned European methods against their rulers.

Education forged both elites and networks among them. France and
Britain established a few boarding schools for boys from wide areas for
secondary education. France imposed a Parisian curriculum complete with
'liberty, equality, and fraternity'; Britain taught Abraham Lincoln's
Gettysburg Address for the beauty of its prose, but young Africans read
about, 'government of the people, by the people, for the people'.[10]
Graduates of these schools formed influential associations, as did those
with advanced training; a Graduates' General Congress emerged. To gain a
university degree meant years of exile in Europe or North America, but
formal and informal associations of African and West Indian students
developed in London and Paris, providing cross-fertilization.

At home, young Africans, better educated than their elders, formed organizations which became political, as did cultural groups. Where political
parties and black trade unions were allowed, they sprang up, along with
African newspapers. Like schools and youth groups, unions trained future
leaders. The growing number of African government clerks formed societies. Moreover, imperial armies trained future leaders as Africans became
non-commissioned officers and, in the French army, junior commissioned
officers. Nigeria had women's groups which rioted in 1929 and 1930;
usually the lot of women was worsened by imperialism. Gradually, African
organizations moved inland as farmers found they could unify around their
economic interest. These groups and others resisted European rule in many
ways. World War I encouraged resistance, especially in Muslim areas, and
delayed European control of the interior, but overt military resistance ended
in the 1920s. Thereafter Africans hid, fled to the bush or across the border,
evaded taxes, and did minimal work. As they learned the white man's ways,
petitions, delegations, strikes, boycotts, and riots became common, as did
use of the pulpit, press, radio, and international congresses. Elites led the
way, usually seeking reform to end abuses and grant equal rights within the
imperial system.

Religion was less dominated by educated elites. Islam, anti-colonial and
often nationalistic, provided unity in some areas against Christian rulers.
Anti-European Christian sects sprang up, reacting to missionary paternalism, creating something Africans could run themselves (including schools

sometimes), and playing a key role in early nationalism. The Watch Tower or Kitiwala, based on Jehovah's Witnesses but much altered, preached 'Africa for the Africans' in central Africa as did messianic religions with millenarian prophets and an emancipatory anti-colonial ideology.These externalized hostility, created a sense of unity and ethnic identity, and became political movements offering hope of liberation when political groups were banned. Despite mass followings, they often lacked organization and so did not cause serious unrest.

*   *   *

Interwar African resistance and nationalism were not seriously destabilizing but caused imperial concern and repression. Europeans tried to isolate blacks from the outside world but failed. African nationalism gained much in ideology, tactics, expertise, and inspiration from events elsewhere and the aid of non-Africans, often of African descent. The first strong anti-imperial influence was Indian, not least because of the substantial Indian minority in eastern and South Africa. Also, Mohandas Gandhi launched his first civil disobedience campaign against racist regulations in 1906 among the Indians of South Africa before taking this tactic to India. Thereafter, India's struggles usually benefited Africa later on. Several future African leaders were disciples of Gandhi, and the battle for non-white self-rule was largely fought out in India, as Africans closely watched. India's impact increased when many Africans served there in World War II, and India's independence thereafter facilitated that of the Gold Coast.

Lenin was less influential than Gandhi. His 1917 anti-imperial statements had some effect, but he was preoccupied elsewhere. He hoped Africa could attain Marxism without a capitalist stage and at first encouraged African groups. As imperial control tightened, these faded, and Lenin's views changed. He came to rely on the leaders of European Communist parties and a few radicals or New World Pan-Africans. But in 1927, the Comintern held a congress in Brussels which attracted 180 delegates from four continents and formed a League against Imperialism and for National Independence, whose name was more imposing than its activities. In Africa, Marxism made small inroads among urban workers but influenced some future leaders.

World War I affected Africa, causing economic hardships, flu epidemics, and Muslim resistance, but *évolués* often gained better jobs as whites left. The impact on troops who served elsewhere was great. Africans were astonished to see whites fighting each other and learned that Europeans were not supermen; they were even told to kill enemy whites. They returned with a new assertiveness. Travel to Europe and North America always had a profound effect. Self-determination and Wilson's Fourteen Points were not meant to apply to Africa, but Africans took heart anyway. League declarations about development of colonized peoples, rarely enacted, also bred impatience.

The Irish revolt had wide influence as a great power newly victorious in the Great War was humbled by a colony on its doorstep. Egypt's nominal independence in 1922 raised hopes while Rif victories in Spanish Morocco from 1921 to 1924 bred pride and taught guerrilla techniques. The war built ties between Anglophone and Francophone colonies, as did new Islamic movements and pan-Arabism, spread by traders; all this furthered networks and incipient proto-nationalism. A modest trend grew until in the late 1930s the Senegalese Léopold Senghor and West Indian Aimé Cesaire as students in Paris created the *négritude* movement, which stood the European stereotype of Africans on its head. So-called African faults were virtues, contrasting the warm, emotional, generous African culture with Western civilization's cold intellectualism. To be black and African was a privilege, not a stigma, and Africans would be both distinctive and equal. Though not initially political and never deep-rooted in British areas, *négritude*'s long-term implications were profound.

Earlier, Africa was influenced by three New World blacks. The first of these was Booker T. Washington, founder of Tuskegee Institute in Alabama, which stressed agricultural and vocational education. In 1912, he held an International Conference on the Negro at Tuskegee, attracting many Africans and setting a precedent for the future. World War I and then Washington's death prevented a planned second conference. His educational philosophy, stressing the art of the possible in the here and now, was popular in Africa with both rulers and the ruled.

The other New World emissaries wanted to enlarge what was possible quickly, and thus were unpopular with Africa's rulers. Marcus Garvey formed the Universal Negro Improvement Association in 1914 in Jamaica and moved it to New York in 1916. It swelled as he stressed 'Africa for the Africans' and 'Back to Africa', creating the Black Star Line to repatriate New World blacks to Liberia, which declined the honour. He preached driving whites out of Africa, gave blacks in two worlds pride, enthusiasm, and spirit, and helped to create the myth of universal black unity. Garvey, whose stated goals included, 'To assist in civilizing the backward tribes of Africa',[11] stirred African nationalism as he 'promised a Negro nation in the African homeland'.[12] He never visited Africa but much influenced pan-Africanism and west Africans who visited the United States. After he was jailed for tax fraud and deported in 1925, his movement fell apart.

Garvey's rival was W. E. B. DuBois, an American of West Indian descent. Well-connected and well-educated (including a Harvard doctorate), DuBois was intellectual rather than emotional and strove to sway elites, not to create a mass movement. He did not call the first small Pan-African Congress in London in 1900, but DuBois largely created the pan-African movement, partly in response to Garvey, and dominated it for nearly 50 years, though it outgrew him. Pan-Africanism, which developed simultaneously in the

New World, Africa, and Europe, saw Africans and African-Americans as a single people with Africa as their homeland. Stressing 'Africa for the Africans', cultural unity, political independence, and the 'redemption of Africa', it pressed for African political unity, though not on Garvey's terms.[13] DuBois initiated the second Pan-African Congress in Paris in 1919 during the peace conference to urge self-determination in Africa. Congresses were held in 1921 sequentially in London, Brussels, and Paris, seeking a black seat on the League of Nations Mandates Commission; in London and Lisbon in 1923; and in New York in 1927. Cross-fertilization was intense as African, American, and West Indian blacks attended along with those living in Europe. A hiatus then ensued with the movement less prominent, but it continued to influence young Africans who studied in Europe, and especially North America, who led later independence movements.

*　　*　　*

Garveyism, pan-Africanism, and other isms influenced the coastal colonies of west Africa, an area more politically mature and rich in organizations than elsewhere. It had a long urban tradition and a peasant agriculture geared to export which fared better than European planters ignorant of local conditions. These were the oldest colonies, well predating the Scramble, and here indigenes had a few rights. Thus, this region had early political organizations; long contact with Europe and its education led to professional classes and societies, which engaged in lively local politics. Numerous lawyers had the skills to address land titles, taxes, and constitutional rights. The area expected reforms to reward its wartime monetary and military effort, but imperial powers combined with chieftains against urban elites. Britain paid the chiefs better and gave them more status than France did though it had less interest in the area. Aside from the Maghrib, most of France's African empire sprawled across the west in a cohesive unit. Britain, with colonies all over Africa, had four scattered ones in the west but lost real interest in them after the Suez Canal became the route to India, though they had twice the population and several times the wealth of the much larger French area. Neither power engaged in energetic economic activity in west Africa, though French colonies, unlike British ones, relied on France's market and were important to its economy. France and Britain also split Germany's two west African colonies, with France taking the lion's share of Togo and the Cameroons.* Each attached its mandates administratively to neighbouring colonies; neither gained much economically. The British saw each colony as a separate entity; France, like Portugal, viewed colonies as overseas provinces and engaged in more direct rule. The

---

* Since 1961, Cameroon, comprised of the French Cameroons and part of the British Cameroons. The remainder joined Nigeria.

contiguous French colonies, unlike the British, were regionally grouped. Thus political parties in British colonies were territorial, French ones inter-territorial. The latter were offshoots of French parties, but British colonies followed the Gandhian model. The absence of a tie to British parties simplified and speeded the journey to independence. In the short run, however, interwar west Africa seemed on the surface economically and politically stagnant.

In French West Africa, Senegal was the key colony and much the oldest, with its capital, Saint-Louis, settled in 1659. The 80 000 *originaires* born in the four communes (towns)* gained citizenship and the vote without loss of Muslim status in 1848; they elected black Africa's only deputy to the French Chamber. An assembly of *originaires* in 1920 became the Colonial Council of all Senegal with limited budgetary powers. As the new members were chiefs on French salaries, this was not real progress. Senegal had the one elite school in west French Africa to train government clerks. It also had legal unions, strikes, the most industry of France's tropical colonies, restive war veterans who gained a few privileges along with socialist ideas, creoles, a professional class, and lively politics.

Neighbouring French colonies were offshoots from Senegal, and shared authoritarian governance, but without curfews, pass laws, or segregated toilets. Of these seven colonies, Dahomey (Benin) had a large Western-educated elite, a black press, a Garveyite political leader devoted to the France of 1789, and strikes of dockers and peasants in 1923. Elsewhere, there was no right of assembly or of free speech. The eight colonies,** covering 4 633 985 km^2 (1 788 718 square miles), comprised the federation of French West Africa (Afrique Occidentale Française or AOF), to which the French Togo mandate was attached. Governors of each colony reported to a governor-general at Dakar, the AOF capital, who in turn reported to the Colonial Ministry in Paris.

The four other French colonies in the west† (2 510 000 km^2 or 968 869 square miles) made up the federation of French Equatorial Africa (AEF), with its capital at Brazzaville and the French Cameroons attached. Its system copied that of AOF though population was sparse and abuses of power far greater. In both federations, consultative advisory councils met a few days each year. They could not oppose, only delay, and were composed of key whites and a few blacks, at first appointed and usually chiefs, then elected on a narrow franchise. AEF consisted of vast commercial estates with forced labour and harsh practices. A prophet preaching anti-European passive resistance sparked sub-Saharan Africa's largest interwar (and only

* Saint-Louis, Gorée (an island now incorporated in Dakar), Rufisque, and Dakar, now the capital.
** Including Mauritania, French Sudan (Mali), Upper Volta (Burkina Faso), Niger, Guinea, and the Ivory Coast.
† Gabon, Middle or French Congo, Ubangi-Shari (Central African Republic), and Chad.

major rural) revolt from 1927 to 1932 in Ubangi-Shari and parts of Middle Congo and French Cameroons. French repression was cruelly effective but did lasting economic harm to an already impoverished area.

In both federations, assimilation and naturalization were possible if one met stringent requirements and abandoned Muslim status. Between the wars in densely populated AOF, only about 2000 outside the four towns did so and came under French law. All others were under the *indigénat* though in time veterans, chiefs, and *évolués* were exempted. Elites were moderate and reformist, though a few were Communist. Some city councils were elected on a limited franchise which did not satisfy them. Trade unions developed in the 1930s and were legalized in 1937 by the Popular Front, which otherwise could not agree on reforms. Strikes had been common since World War I, voicing economic grievances and political demands which the middle class supported.

AOF was heavily Muslim; for political reasons, France backed Islamic leaders at the expense of animist societies. She also supported peasant farming and land ownership though some plantations existed, but peasants were pressed into growing cash crops. Despite an array of taxes, AOF was prosperous, especially on the coast. Its African producers (unlike whites) were little affected by the 1930s Depression since France was protectionist and absorbed Africa's produce. But a new stress on export production and plantations, along with increased taxes, brought social changes. By 1939, AOF seemed stagnant but had developed the preconditions for rapid change.

These were not perceived by France, for whom imperial might was a substitute for continental power and a way to maintain status in Europe. Colonies were a source of troops and grandeur; the empire was proof of France's continued greatness. As the 1930s wore on and European tensions worsened, she eyed Africa's strategic utility. Meanwhile, talk of the 'mission civilisatrice' continued without creation of many civilizing institutions. For Britain, colonies also obscured decline though it felt less need to prove greatness and talked a better theory of imperial governance as a school for eventual self-rule. But an acute British observer remarked,

> I so often think of that improving fable of the kind-hearted she-elephant who, while walking out one day, inadvertently trod upon a partridge and killed it, and observing near at hand the bird's nest full of callow fledglings, dropped a tear, and saying, 'I have the feelings of a mother myself', sat down on the brood. This is precisely what England . . . is doing in West Africa. She destroys the guarding institutions, drops a tear and sits upon the brood with motherly intentions; and pesky warm sitting she finds it.[14]

Britain's policy was to 'hasten slowly'.[15]

This was particularly true governmentally. Each colony was ruled separately, though they shared a currency and the West African Frontier Force. Each was divided into a coastal colony and an interior protectorate. Each had a Legislative Council, consisting of senior British officials and a few non-Europeans. No Africans were permitted on Executive Councils before World War II. Riots in 1919 all over Sierra Leone led Britain in the early 1920s to initiate national frameworks in artificial states. Nigeria, Sierra Leone, and the Gold Coast (but not Gambia) gained constitutions with some blacks on Legislative Councils, mainly appointed chiefs but also a few members elected by a limited coastal franchise. Freedom of the press, assembly, and association resulted, leading to political parties and other organizations, all pushing for more self-rule and in the 1930s more power to new younger elites at the expense of the chiefs. Here the seeds of future nationalist parties were sown.

Among the key instruments of nationalism were the 1920 National Congress of British West Africa, representing all four colonies, and its London adjunct, the West African Student Union, which soon accepted anyone of African descent. Both were pan-African, influenced by Garvey but inspired by the Indian National Congress and self-determination. Led by intellectuals from west Africa's two elite schools and British or American universities, the Congress sought eventual self-rule as a federated dominion, traditional land rights, more and higher education, and senior civil service posts. As this elite was barred from governance, it became more nationalistic, particularly the youth groups which dominated in the 1930s. They also included urban masses and the hinterland, moving politically for the first time into the interior which, with increasing primary education, was becoming politically aware though under indirect rule it lacked ways to express its views. These youth groups worked within each colony, not regionally. But there were no mass movements, no radical methods, and no assimilation as the British emphatically wished to have no 'dark-skinned Englishmen'.[16]

Britain saw chiefs as agents of production for non-African merchant capitalists. Alienation of land to Europeans was banned, as was forced labour, but pressures, including taxation, existed toward labour 'contributions' and cash crop farming. Farmers' groups emerged to resist the chiefs and merchants, resulting in a 1937 Gold Coast cocoa hold-up, which was almost 100 per cent effective in keeping crops off the market for seven months until prices rose. As rural primary school graduates drifted to the towns, they found no jobs. They joined new unions legalized in the 1930s or political groups, which after World War II linked coastal elites and peasants into mass nationalist movements.

*   *   *

The white settler colonies of southern Africa imposed the harshest conditions on indigenes. In Angola and Mozambique, most blacks lived under the *indigenato* with few rights; the 1930s brought passbooks to restrict and control blacks, and stricter labour laws.* They were no better off in British Africa's settler colonies, where whites wanted immediate self-rule. The Union of South Africa already had this in most domestic respects. In 1923, the 33 000 Britons of Southern Rhodesia (Zimbabwe) gained it when the British South Africa Company ended its rule, Britain declined to take over and, to avoid Afrikaner domination, the whites refused to join the Union of South Africa. For the same reason, South Africa's three enclaves successfully fought to remain British protectorates.

In southern Africa a large European element drove economic growth, particularly in industrialized South Africa, of which the other areas were economic satellites. The region was ethnically complex with a big urban proletariat, both black and white, and in South Africa both an Indian minority and a 'coloured' class of mixed race. Blacks became mere labourers and lost their land, especially good land, as they were restricted to barren rural reserves and urban ghettos and forced to work for whites, losing self-sufficiency. Whites struggled to control minerals, services, land, and jobs as black competition and nationalism developed. The economic system, especially the mines, relied on nearly a million migrant workers annually. Areas exporting labour suffered social disorganization and dependence on employing colonies, namely South Africa and Southern Rhodesia: '. . . the migrant labour system was one of the most highly regulated forms of interterritorial relations'.[17] Miners, virtually imprisoned for their contract's duration, went back and forth between village and compound. They developed a common culture, but constant migration delayed the emergence of class and national awareness. They undertook this life, which damaged marriage, family, tribe, and ancestral spirits, to gain money for taxes, goods, or a bride. Whites found the system cheaper than slavery as they did not support the aged, the ill, or families, who eked out an existence in the reserves.

Barriers to black progress were much higher than in the west, but an intelligentsia developed and slowly led the way to political identity and nationalism. Extreme racial bias meant this elite was closer to the masses than elsewhere. Resistance, sometimes united, emerged among Africans, Asians, coloureds, and liberal whites, mostly British. These groups had international ties and were often influenced by world events, above all in the Union of South Africa. Here World War I reinforced nationalism among Afrikaners, who saw themselves as a persecuted Calvinist elect; their religion reinforced discrimination against blacks, whose economic, social, and racial situation worsened as their aspirations grew. Whites and coloureds served in the war; blacks were used as labourers in France and were much affected by life in a country without a colour bar.

---

* For details of the Portuguese colonies, see Chapter 7.

Strikes erupted from 1918 to 1920 against inequities where white miners earned nine times the wages of blacks[18] without the heavy taxes imposed on the latter. These were quelled, but the Industrial and Commercial Union (ICU) of Africans and coloureds founded in 1919 grew to 100 000 members before 1930 laws and internal fragmentation largely destroyed it. The smaller African National Congress (ANC), formed in 1912 and black Africa's oldest political organization, initially covered all of southern Africa. A middle-class group influenced by Gandhi and linked to the chiefs, it feared violence, was disinclined to lead the masses, and became confined to the Union, with ties to movements elsewhere as well as to the main coloured and Indian groups. Widely imitated all over central and southern Africa and a part of the pan-African movement from 1919 on, the ANC in 1926 called the first Non-European Convention of black, coloured, and Indian groups. Then its moderation brought a decline until the mid-1930s, when new repression revived it despite lack of agreement on a programme beyond opposition to the pass laws. Even so, in 1938 it had only 4000 members.

The ICU and ANC had branches in Southern Rhodesia, where they faced similar problems: entrenched white urban workers and rural bourgeois, gold mines, an intensely segregationist society with a tiny number of black voters. Africans protested loss of their land, but the white settlers won: a 1930 Land Apportionment Act to ensure physical separation of the races froze Africans on crowded reserves. Meanwhile, the Union could govern South-west Africa, its C Mandate, as part of South Africa. Resistance was suppressed, and the plight of the blacks worsened as they were merely labour or on semi-desert reserves, worse off than in the Union. The Mandates Commission asked questions but had no right to visit. Afrikaner farmers bought up arable land with government aid, and South Africans took over the diamond mines. In the mandate and at home, the Union government tried to mobilize African labour and keep it cheap in the mines, cities and countryside to create migrant labour and ensure helpers for Afrikaner farmers. The 1913 Natives Land Act imposed three months of compulsory labour for landlords and banned black land purchase outside the reserves but despite white efforts to keep blacks on them, by the 1930s a segregated urban black population existed.

All over southern Africa, racial discrimination and the land issue united blacks, but protest was diverse and disorganized. Elites and masses had not merged, but black organizations existed, as did an urban industrial base. Acute segregation had the potential for broad politicization and creation of mass movements. In short, the preconditions for rapid change existed. But so did white settlers in quantity, and their determination ensured that change was a long time in coming.

*   *   *

South Africa's migrant labour system led to the spread of ideas. That was true of central Africa as well. This ill-defined area, which shared some characteristics of south and east Africa, included Northern Rhodesia (Zambia), Nyasaland (Malawi), and the Belgian Congo.* Remote and landlocked except for the Congo's tiny Atlantic outlet, it was disease-ridden and lacked much white population. It suffered from poor communications, as the rivers were only partly navigable, infertile soil in many areas, and erratic rainfall, but it was rich in minerals, especially copper. Mining companies dominated economically. Conditions in the mines were not bad, but black miners were poorly paid compared to whites. Economic development was done by private companies.

The area was rural, with towns few and small. Africans retained village ties while living in towns or the Copper Belt; Indians were urban. Pass laws prevailed, as did the demand for migrant labour. Except in the Congo, rulers tried to deny Africans alternatives to wage labour, chiefly by taxation and limiting access to land; thus, the rural economy declined. World War I conscription and requisitions caused economic distress and a high death rate for porters used elsewhere in Africa. Price inflation struck and the hut tax doubled; the death rate soared from infestations of the tsetse fly, bubonic plague, and influenza. In 1915 an uprising in Nyasaland, set off by a preacher's protests against taxes and conscription, began the struggle between Africans and settlers.

The first voluntary associations emerged, initially in Nyasaland, where missionary elementary education was good, to seek African rights in a reformed colonial system. They did not aim at self-rule but reform, equal opportunity, redress of grievances, an end to settler encroachments, and status for themselves. Like tribal organizations, graduates' associations, and groups of évolués, they were middle-class elites. They were patient (not least because they depended on whites for jobs), constitutional, and unsuccessful, but their protests prepared the future. British central Africa was a neglected area, lacking any secondary education. African squatters and renters were taxed heavily to force them to work for whites. Supposedly, Britain switched in the 1930s from direct to indirect rule outside the cities, but district commissioners yielded little authority and chiefs were unprepared. Africans saw little change; however, they faced a constant threat of federation with Southern Rhodesia, which the latter wanted, as did influential central African settlers. As British Protected Persons, not British subjects, Africans were barred from the administrative level of the civil service and any political activity except locally. Settler agitation for federation roused fears among migrants who had seen Southern Rhodesia's racial policies. Supported by British liberals, they convinced London, which decreed in 1930 and 1939 that African interests should be paramount.

* For details of the Belgian Congo, see Chapter 7.

In Nyasaland, the dearth of whites and Asians opened skilled jobs to Africans. White settlers seized land only in the Shire Highlands, and from 1919 on Britain favoured peasant agriculture though providing no roads or services. In the late 1930s Britain both encouraged migratory labour and banned further alienation of African land. Northern Rhodesia also had few white settlers, but in the 1920s they controlled a waning economy, seeking a settler state, seizing good land, crowding blacks onto reserves, and banning sale of 'white' land. In the 1930s the Copper Belt boomed, bringing migratory labour, low black wages, strikes over the pay differential, and whites with South African biases. Here as elsewhere in the interior, the colour bar, lack of opportunity and land, and religious prophets roused political consciousness.

*   *   *

Unlike southern and central Africa, eastern Africa was so diverse as to defy most generalizations. There was the large French island of Madagascar (Malagasy Republic), the small British island of Zanzibar (now part of Tanzania), and the three mainland regions of Kenya, Uganda, and Tanganyika, all British after World War I. The mainland, which had a *lingua franca* in Swahili, suffered from wartime fighting in and around German East Africa (Tanganyika). Indians outnumbered whites; they were urban and lived by their own labour, neither hiring nor competing with Africans; in Kenya and Uganda they fought with small success for equal, not token, representation on Legislative Councils. The coasts and islands had a significant Arab element. Politically, the region was two generations behind west Africa, though there were illegal and legal meetings, secret drills in the forests, and schismatic churches and prophets. Improvement associations and commercial groups protested administrators and European-appointed chiefs. Generally the members of these groups came from a new elite, seeking political rights and economic opportunity. Often ethnic in organization, they had little following in most places, were not nationalist, and sought reforms within the existing system.

The three British mainland colonies shared some British policies, such as trusteeship for the Africans. This meant more protection than development, but included improved education. In the 1920s priority went to European agriculture and ensuring its labour supply; as peasant farming proved more economical, the priority reversed. Britain tolerated African associations if their focus was worker welfare, not politics. More ambitious groups found their leaders arrested. Little nationalism emerged; most Africans did not yet see themselves as belonging to a Kenyan or Ugandan or Tanganyikan nation. The three colonies were also yoked by the determination of some ardent imperialists in Britain to weld them into a white dominion. Though some settlers favoured this scheme, some resisted, along with Indians, Africans, British liberals, and missionaries. The federation idea did not die easily and kept the area politically unsettled through the interwar years, especially as the three colonies began to co-operate in the 1930s. This area also contained the healthy 'white highlands' and so had numerous settlers, especially in Kenya where the British crown took the uplands in 1901 and allotted much of them to whites. They were closed to Indians and Africans, who were forced onto crowded, inferior reserves. However, in 1923 London declared African interests should be paramount over those of immigrant races; this was aimed against Indians but blocked settler efforts toward white self-rule and federation.

Uganda and Tanganyika were spared large settler classes, but in Uganda Britain's treaty with the Kingdom of Buganda (whose sovereignty London eroded) constituted a state within the colony whereas Tanganyika was much affected by its status as a mandate and former German colony, wartime devastation, loss of Ruanda-Urundi, and lack of English-speaking Africans. In much of Uganda, British rule was indirect and ineffectual, Indians blocked black entry into middle-class jobs, and indigenous associations were usually timid. British officials were very sparse, so Buganda and other kingdoms spared Africans the worse abuses, but Tanganyika had forced labour and a tax system which created migratory labour and an urban proletariat. Partly as a result, by the late 1930s nationalist groups emerged. By then, Adolf Hitler ruled Germany and wanted the colony back. German settlers began to plan a return. As British settlement and investment declined, the East African federal plan revived to bar German absorption. London was evasive about the future, giving the issue little priority until the 1938 Munich crisis in Europe showed that it must face the problem in Tanganyika to defend British east Africa.

Like Tanganyika, Madagascar suffered in the war. Economic problems continued, as did a choice between a tax or paid forced labour, but France supported Malagasy farming since it produced at half the cost of white agriculture. Some Africans gained land, forming a rural middle class. As the chiefs were weak and the education level fairly high, France used Malagasies as civil servants in jobs reserved to Frenchmen elsewhere. In 1924, the educated well-to-do bourgeoisie gained Economic and Financial Delegations on the Algerian model, with the French section dominant. French policy stressed skills, schools, and health services, but the feudally-minded *colons* thought the Malagasies were 'almost hopelessly inferior and incapable of being civilized'.[19]

That attitude contributed to the failure of the 'civilizing mission', as did wartime and post-war service in Europe. Vy Vato Sakelika (VVS) was founded in 1913 by those looking to the example of late nineteenth-century Japan. Nationalism was furthered by a socialist school teacher named Ralaimongo, a war veteran who had studied in Paris. He sought equal rights, application of French law, and an end to segregation and land seizure, hoping Madagascar could be a French department with full citizenship. Some businessmen, some Europeans, and part of VVS supported him, as did religious sects. Meanwhile, VVS tried to inspire the peasants to Gandhian passive resistance. A large demonstration for citizenship and an end to the *indigénat* set off militancy in 1929, but Ralaimongo was interned and his movement went underground. The press and unions renewed political demands after the Popular Front legalized the latter. By 1935 VVS urged independence, and overtly nationalist newspapers appeared, though the Depression curtailed business support and protest from those who feared loss of jobs. Even so, by 1939 most educated Malagasies wanted independence.

*　　*　　*

To the north-east lies the Horn of Africa between Kenya and Egypt. A region of nomadic herders scattered among six territories, it developed Somali and Sudanese national heroes in the battle against subjection lasting to 1920. Thereafter peasants were quiescent, herders disaffected about taxes and controlled by force, and urban areas dominant as towns grew into trade centres. Settlers and educated elites were few owing to lack of schools and Muslim hostility to Christian missionaries. Europeans tried to switch economies to cash crops for export with uneven success. Traditional rulers were usually co-opted, and nationalism was born mainly of events between 1935 and 1945.

The Sudan was technically an Anglo-Egyptian condominium. Egyptians staffed the army and civil service under British control until 1924 and after 1936. Sudan contained two distinct nationalities. The north was Arabic and Muslim, with ties to Egypt and a small educated elite. The tribal south was largely Nilotic and animist or Christian, with 80 languages. Until 1924, Britain favoured the north. Economy cuts and a new governor, Sir Lee Stack, along with ties to Egyptian nationalism, led to a revolt in 1923 and 1924 before and after Stack was murdered in Cairo by Egyptian nationalists. Resistance came from new 'young' associations, graduates' clubs and military cadets. Sudanese leaders were arrested and Egyptians expelled; a period of dormancy ensued. Britain turned southward with a policy of isolation to prevent northern and Egyptian influences, driving the two halves of Sudan further apart. In the mid-1930s, it switched to 'nation-building', letting Egyptian officials return, strengthening the sheiks, and creating an educated class for administrative use. British concessions aimed at quelling nationalism and weakening its leaders led to demands for more.

At the other end of the Horn were the Somalis, a distinct nationality scattered among five territories (including Ethiopia) from Kenya to the Red Sea's entrance, including French, British,* and Italian Somaliland. They were mainly nomadic Islamic herders though more urbanized than much of

---

* British and Italian Somaliland merged in 1960 as Somalia.

Africa; their culture, language, and institutions varied little, and they wanted unification, not division. They had no history of centralized rule, only clans, but the struggle against subjection bred nationalism; interwar uprisings occurred against France and Italy. European rulers played clans off against each other but fostered nationalism in the domain of other European powers. Taxes and forced labour heightened hostility, as did antagonism to Christianity. Only tiny French Somaliland (Republic of Djibouti) prospered, but the railway from Addis Ababa to Djibouti, linking Ethiopia to the sea, and the busy port with many Europeans meant Western influences. For all these reasons, 'young' associations developed among the small elites to articulate grievances and promote political consciousness. In 1935 a Somali National League of 'Young' Associations emerged; it was pan-Somali from the outset. No such political consciousness appeared in Eritrea on the Red Sea, where governance worsened in the Fascist era as Italy built up the area to invade Ethiopia.

*   *   *

The interior of the Horn was landlocked, mountainous Ethiopia, Africa's sole truly independent state, never a colony, and the only one which had defeated a European power. It was mainly Christian, the only non-Arab, non-Muslim state in North Africa, but it identified until 1935 with the Middle East, not Africa. Haile Selassie ruled Ethiopia from 1916, first as regent, then from 1930 as emperor. His country contained 70 languages and many nationalities with powerful feudal lords. The modernizers struggled against the traditionalists, with Haile Selassie mediating but leaning toward the modernizers. Ethiopia's first constitution in 1931 aimed to curb the feudal lords. Haile Selassie banned the slave trade, agreed to suppress slavery, and arranged for its gradual eradication.

In December 1934 at Wal Wal in Ethiopia, forces from Italian Somaliland clashed with an Ethiopian patrol. Italy's dictator, Benito Mussolini, seized the moment to launch his planned conquest of Ethiopia and, after a long diplomatic crisis, invaded from Eritrea on 3 October 1935.* The ensuing war was the last campaign in the conquest of Africa, a clash of two very old civilizations, and one of modern European imperialism's final flings.[20] Italy said it was only doing what other powers had done elsewhere in Africa. But it was doing so much later, after a new code of behaviour had arisen and against a League member which was modernizing on its own. Upon Ethiopia's appeal, the League Assembly condemned Italy as the aggressor, but it was dominated by Britain and France, whose alarm about Hitler made them loath to offend Mussolini. Thus, despite some bluster, he was allowed to proceed. Ethiopian forces were at best ill-equipped, at worst armed with spears and bravery, but they made the war

* For the diplomacy of the Ethiopian crisis, see Chapter 15.

costly for Italy, before she prevailed on 7 May 1936; Haile Selassie rode the French railway to exile. Ethiopia then learned what being African meant. Italy's five-year rule provided roads, irrigation, hospitals, schools, agricultural stations, and other benefits at the price of killing governmental and intellectual leaders and the humiliation of subjection. Resistance never ceased.

The Ethiopian war far transcended its local significance. For Europeans, it was one of several major crises leading to World War II; for Africans and their descendants elsewhere, it was much more. Ethiopia was of great symbolic importance, the last bulwark of African political freedom, the 'promised land', the black Zion, especially for New World and South African blacks. It was the object of semi-religious Garveyite cults and the Garveyite African national anthem, which began:

Ethiopia, thou land of our fathers,
Thou land where the gods loved to be . . .[21]

Significantly Ethiopia had everything Africans were told they lacked: an ancient monarchy, a history dating from before Biblical times, a Christian church from the era of the Apostles, independence, victory over a European power, international recognition, and League membership. Thus the invasion and the perceived Anglo-French 'betrayal' galvanized African thinking.

Pan-Africanism revived and radicalized, particularly when Italy justified conquest by alleging Ethiopian racial inferiority and savagery. The west African press reacted sharply and pan-Africanism spread eastward across the continent, which united on this issue, as did blacks elsewhere. Kwame Nkrumah, the future leader of Ghana, was a student passing through London when he heard of the invasion; he walked the streets with tears running down his cheeks. His dedication to pan-Africanism, which he later led, was much stimulated. The West African Students' Union in London became anti-imperial, and the largely cultural Francophone *négritude* movement moved to politcal solidarity with other groups. In brief, the invasion of Ethiopia jolted African political consciousness a giant step forward.

*   *   *

It is easy to exaggerate the political ferment in interwar Africa, which in most areas at most times seemed stagnant on the surface. Discontent was rife, but its organization was embryonic. Even in North Africa, long part of the Mediterranean world, nationalists could cause intermittent trouble but could not yet make colonies ungovernable. South of the Sahara, even in west Africa there were no calls for independence before World War II. Demands came for reform, but elites rarely reached out to the peasantry or the new urban masses. In 1939, the colonial system seemed entrenched indefinitely, which is one reason why little was done to prepare Africans to govern.

The interwar era was both the golden age of colonialism and the formative period of African nationalism, as imperial policies gave impetus to the
latter. In retrospect, '20th-century African nationalism is indeed the child of
European colonialism, be it within or outside wedlock.'[22] Under a relatively
stable surface, Africa was seething, as political awareness grew.
Nationalism had not yet erupted, but national characteristics were developing in the patchwork of states created by imperialism. Africans, whose
horizons widened considerably between the two wars, now realized they
belonged to a nation and also to Africa and the black race. They developed
pride in their heritage and some knowledge of its history and culture. With
this had come European concepts of political rights and budding black
activism. Clearly, a catalyst might have dramatic effects, especially as
empires rested more on the illusion of power than on its reality.

In Africa, there were three catalysts in 15 years. The first was the
Depression. Its effects were uneven, but acute in west Africa as agricultural
export prices dropped to half or a third of previous levels, and revenues
from export taxes fell accordingly, as did African purchasing power, rural
and urban. As the white man's confidence was sapped by a devastating
phenomenon he could not handle, so was his rule in Africa, which rested so
much on self-assurance. Probably more important, however, was the spread
of anti-colonial discontent, especially in hard-hit rural areas, and impatience.

The second catalyst was the invasion of Ethiopia, and the third was
World War II, in which Africans had a large role. The new educated elite,
the improving advanced schools, the multiplying associations and their
greater politicization all meant Africa's 'large children' had been quietly
growing. When Mussolini moved Ethiopia to centre front of the world's
stage, the shock led to rapid maturation. World War II generated several
more spurts of growth. As a result, after the decade 1935–45, Africa was
less willing 'to tolerate its own humiliation'[23] and more prepared to call
Europe's bluff.

The signs had long existed though Europeans ignored them. Perhaps the
most pungent declaration of African views came in a 1931 editorial from
the supposedly docile Portuguese colonies:

> We are fed up to the teeth.
>> Fed up with supporting you, with suffering the terrible conse-
>> quences of your follies, your demands, with the squandering misuse
>> of your authority.
>> We can no longer stand the pernicious effects of your political and
>> administrative decisions.
>> We are no longer willing to make greater and greater useless sacri-
>> fices . . .
> Enough.[24]

Such outspokenness posed the question, crucial to the global power equation, of how long the world's second largest continent could be held in thraldom by coastal portions of the second smallest.

◆ Notes to Chapter 8

1. Margery Perham, *The Colonial Reckoning* (New York, Knopf, 1962), p. 141.
2. Henry S. Wilson, *The Imperial Experience in Sub-Saharan Africa* (Minneapolis, University of Minnesota Press, 1977), p. 290.
3. Perham, *Colonial Reckoning*, p. 32.
4. Raymond F. Betts, *Uncertain Dimensions: Western Overseas Empires in the Twentieth Century* (Minneapolis, University of Minnesota Press, 1985), p. 71.
5. Roland Oliver and Anthony Atmore, *Africa since 1800*, 2nd edn (Cambridge, CUP, 1972), p. 163.
6. Robert Henssler, 'British Rule in Africa', in Prosser Gifford and Wm Roger Louis, eds, *France and Britain in Africa* (New Haven, YUP, 1971), p. 588.
7. Andrew Roberts, 'The Imperial Mind', in Andrew Roberts, ed., *The Cambridge History of Africa*, VII (Cambridge, CUP, 1986), p. 49.
8. J. F. A. Ajayi and Michael Crowder, 'West Africa, 1919–1939', in J. F. A. Ajayi and Michael Crowder, eds, *History of West Africa* (2 vols, New York, Columbia University Press, 1973), II, p. 538.
9. On this key point, see B. O. Oloruntimehin, 'African Politics and Nationalism, 1919–35', in A. Adu Boahen, ed., *Africa under Colonial Domination, 1880–1935* (London, Heinemann, and Paris, UNESCO, 1985), *General History of Africa* (8 vols), VII, pp. 565–8.
10. Ndabaningi Sithole, *African Nationalism*, 2nd edn (London, OUP, 1968), p. 91.
11. P. Olisanwuche Esedebe, *Pan-Africanism*, 2nd edn (Washington, Howard University Press, 1994), p. 58.
12. Hans Kohn and Wallace Sokolsky, *African Nationalism in the Twentieth Century* (Princeton, NJ, D. van Nostrand, 1965), p. 22, quoting Edmund Cromer, *Black Moses* (1955).
13. Imanuel Geiss, *The Pan-African Movement*, tr. Ann Keep (New York, Africana Publishing Co., 1974), pp. 3–4.
14. The traveller Mary Kingsley, quoted in Edward Grierson, *The Death of the Imperial Dream* (New York, Doubleday, 1972), p. 276.
15. K. W. J. Post, 'British Policy and Representative Government in West Africa, 1920 to 1951', in L. H. Gann and Peter Duignan, *Colonialism in Africa*, 5 vols (Cambridge, CUP, 1969–75), II, p. 34.

16. A. Adu Boahen, *Topics in West African History* (London, Longman, 1966), p. 151.
17. David Chanaiwa, 'Southern Africa since 1945', in Ali A. Mazrui, ed., *Africa since 1935* (Oxford, Heinemann, Paris, UNESCO, Berkeley, University of California Press, 1993), *General History of Africa* (8 vols), VIII, p. 254.
18. A. P. Walshe and Andrew Roberts, 'Southern Africa', in Roberts, ed., *Cambridge History*, VII, p. 551.
19. George J. Moutafakis, 'The Colonial Heritage of East Africa', in Stanley Diamond and Fred G. Burke, eds, *The Transformation of East Africa* (New York, Basic Books, 1966), p. 49.
20. Ali A. Masrui, 'Toward the Year 2000', in Masrui, ed., *Africa since 1935*, p. 905.
21. Esedebe, *Pan-Africanism*, p. 59.
22. Alan Paton, Cry, *the Beloved Country* (London, Jonathan Cape, 1948), pp. 36–7.
23. Majhemout Diop *et al.*, 'Tropical and Equatorial Africa under French, Portuguese, and Spanish Domination, 1935–1945', in Mazrui, ed., *Africa since 1935*, p. 74.
24. *O Brado Africano*, 27 February, 1931, quoted in A. B. Davidson, A. Isaacman, and R. Pélissier, 'Politics and Nationalism in Central and Southern Africa, 1919–35', in Boahen, ed., *Africa under Colonial Domination*, p. 710.

CHAPTER

9

THE MIDDLE EAST

If most of Africa remained offstage during the interwar era, the Middle East did not. This region, whose very name is Eurocentric,[*] was not only where the first scenes of the world's history had originally been played but also where three continents met. Thus it had always been crisscrossed by vital trade routes, to which the Suez Canal and key railways were added before World War I. Both its geographic proximity to Russia, which had become the Soviet Union, and the start of oil production in Persia (Iran) in 1908 made the region even more strategic.

However, until petroleum became crucial in the 1930s, the area's most precious resource was water. Aside from Egypt's Nile Valley and the Fertile Crescent, an arable northerly strip blessed with rain and rivers stretching from the Mediterranean to Iran, the region was arid, and population was sparse. Under the Turks, Cairo, Damascus, and Beirut remained thriving cities, but Baghdad had become a faded provincial capital. Amman, Riyadh, and Abu Dhabi were little more than dusty villages. Many of the people were Bedouin (nomads) herding their flocks from oasis to oasis. By 1914 the twentieth century had reached the cities but not the villages and desert; the transformation of the Middle East was just starting as suspected oil reserves, Zionist claims, and new strategic concerns multiplied Western interest.

For centuries, the Ottoman Empire had ruled a vast Islamic entity, but by 1914 unity was fraying as Turkey lost control on the fringes. Then in World War I the Ottoman Empire collapsed. In 1920, Britain and France carved up the Middle East as arbitrarily as they had parcelled out Africa before 1914 and with equal disregard of ethnic factors. Most of these boundaries lasted, though not without border skirmishes. As African jungles delayed exact delimitation, so did Middle Eastern deserts – until Western oil firms needed to know the extent of their concessions.

In Africa, European rule was overt; in the Middle East, French rule was as well, but Britain created kingdoms to save money, erect an indigenous façade, and honour promises to Arabs a bit. Independence was more nominal than

---

[*] South-west Asia and Egypt would be more precise.

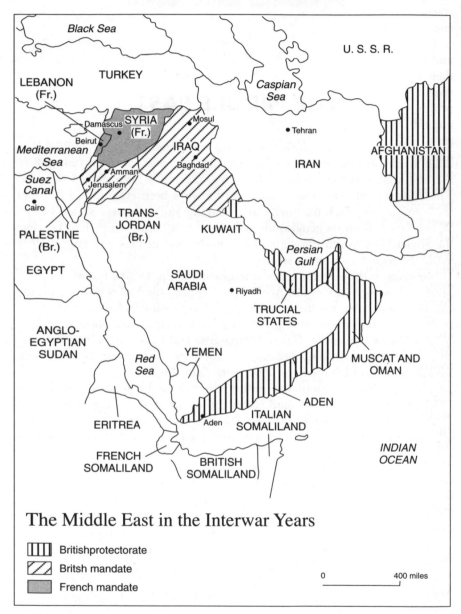

The Middle East in the Interwar Years

Britishprotectorate
Britsh mandate
French mandate

0   400 miles

The interwar Middle East

real. Both disguised and direct European rule faced mass urban and rural resistance, for the region was a generation ahead of Africa in nationalism, starting the interwar era as vocally anti-imperial as west Africa was at the end of it.

Before 1914, three Arab nationalist groups emerged among army officers and educated youth. Fostered by the Young Turks' initial liberalism and then by their extreme Turkification, they were tiny, but World War I sparked a mass movement. The war was a sideshow here militarily but had profound effects, bringing economic hardship, especially food shortages and inflation, as well as conscription of men and animals. Iran (a non-Arab state) was occupied, Iraq a battle zone, and Egypt a major military headquarters. One result of close acquaintance with British forces was that prewar admiration of allegedly liberal Britain turned to dislike, which deepened into hatred later under British rule. When Iran's oil production became substantial and oil deposits were suspected in Mosul province (eventually in Iraq), the area grew more important to technologically advanced Western powers, as petroleum products became crucial in a war which introduced tanks and airplanes and used submarines widely; this was one reason for Allied promises of everything from 'autonomous development' to full independence, notably the Anglo-French Declaration of 7 November 1918.*

To all this was added the Arab Revolt. The Hashemite family of Sharif Husain led it, but Syrian and Iraqi officers flocked to the cause of a united Arab kingdom, sweeping out of the Arabian peninsula across the Levant in concert with British troops. They led the entry into Damascus and briefly installed Faisal there as king. A national awakening ensued as wartime Britain supported Arab nationalism. By 1919, it was a mass movement, impatient, eager, and seeking immediate independence. Imperialists gravely underestimated its force and then either denied it or temporized without conceding much. Despite its promises, Britain, which had military control in 1918, never intended an independent kingdom except in the remote Arabian desert. The peace treaty provided that, for Husain became King of the Hejaz, but the dreamt-of unity faded in a new European-imposed fragmentation. As expectations were disappointed, hostility resulted among peoples who then had much in common and relatively little to divide them.

Aside from Mount Lebanon's Christians, the area was mainly Muslim. Despite many sects, most were Sunni or Shiite. Except in Iran, Sunnis dominated. Islam was a unifying factor, and the world's oldest university, al-Azhar in Cairo, was the centre of Koranic studies, drawing students from elsewhere who exchanged ideas. Turkey, Iran, and Afghanistan were not Arabic and shared neither that language nor a past as subject peoples of the Ottoman Empire but were all Muslim.

* For text of the operative clause, see p. 112 above.

The remainder of the Middle East was Arab, united by geography, language, culture, ideas, and the Ottoman past. The first generation of leaders often had been educated in Constantinople and had begun their careers in the Ottoman civil or military service. The next generation was more apt to attend the American University of Beirut, which in an era of increasing secularization became the new meeting place and training ground of the nationalist elite.

The region was divided by urban–tribal rivalries, clan feuds, struggles between monarchists and republicans as well as between pro- and anti-British factions, royal and national feuds, and the gap between elites and the poor. Political parties were often groupings around a charismatic leader rather than stable ongoing entities. Moreover, artificial new states with imposed Western governing systems lacked cohesion and national loyalty. Finally, Arabs were divided by the peace. Greater Syria became four states, none of them attached to Iraq or Arabia. The pan-Arab concept did not die, as Arab nationalism turned against the Western imperialists who now dominated instead of Turkey, but nationalism emerged within the new states, further dividing the area. It was young, rambunctious, and impatient but already had mass support, both urban and rural.

The interwar era brought secularization and modernization, imposed in the mandates by Britain and France. Elsewhere, it occurred by choice with Turkey as a widely imitated model, an independent secular Moslem state bent on westernizing. Religious leaders and traditionalists protested, seeing education for women, electricity and automobiles as infidel influences. Even without such resistance and rivalry between secular and religious nationalism, the clash of old and new cultures brought some destabilization. But most rulers chose modernization, despite risk to their regimes, to acquire the tools to gain and maintain independence from the West.

Arab leaders knew their rule was more nominal than actual. Saudi Arabia was the most youthful and most independent state. The others were old enough to be rebellious and sullen but not mature enough to be patient and to understand other viewpoints or the art of the possible, so the Middle East seethed with barely repressed unrest. Nationalists circumvented and thwarted Britain and France while avoiding overt challenges and taking advantage of Anglo-French dissension. Britain and sometimes France managed to co-opt some elites who wanted stability. This brought a degree of calm to the 1920s, but the next generation, often American-educated and full of ideas about liberty, was less docile. Europeans did not see how hostile Arab nationalism was, nor that the pan-Arab cause was reviving as a unifying factor with Britain, France, and Zionism in Palestine providing common foes.

*   *   *

As the area became more hostile to its European overlords, it became more important to them, thanks to oil. Neither Britain nor France nor their vast empires possessed known petroleum deposits, and both needed a secure supply of what was becoming the life's blood of industrial and military machines. Italy, Germany, and most other European nations also lacked petroleum, whereas the United States, which in 1919–20 produced 82 per cent of the world's oil supply, worried about exhausting its reserves. Interest increased accordingly. Cordell Hull, American Secretary of State in the 1930s, noted that 'in many conferences . . . the atmosphere and smell of oil was almost stifling'.[1]

A remarkable percentage of the world's oil was discovered in the inter-war era, and production tripled, but so did demand. For governments, supplies for air, land, and sea forces were vital. In industry, compression engines used oil for machinery and locomotives. Westerners began to consume oil for buses, trucks, home heating, and automobiles. By 1939, Middle Eastern production was about 6 per cent of the enlarged total, but its reserves were known or suspected. Large-scale exploitation in Saudi Arabia, Kuwait, Qatar, and the Trucial States (United Arab Emirates) was delayed by World War II, but by 1939 the significance of the area's oil was clear.

In 1914, however, the only proven oil was in Iran, where production by the British-controlled Anglo-Persian (Anglo-Iranian) Oil Company had begun. Britain's World War I Mesopotamian campaign was launched to protect the oil supply, the refinery at Abadan, and Basra's port facilities. In 1920, Iran produced 1 per cent of the world's oil, lagging far behind Russia, Mexico, Venezuela, Rumania, and the Dutch East Indies. Britain claimed and finally gained Mosul province for Iraq because of its prospective oil. In the mid-1920s rich fields were found; production began, and pipelines to Palestine and Lebanon were built in the early 1930s. The Turkish (later Iraq) Petroleum Company tried but failed to maintain a united European front against an American consortium. In 1928 all participants signed the Red Line Agreement that they would only seek oil together in Anatolia, Iraq, and the Arabian peninsula, excluding Kuwait.

Only Iran and Iraq achieved large-scale interwar production. At first, oil firms operated in isolated enclaves and had little effect on local life. Gradually their influence broadened as they hired some indigenous techni-cians and engineers. Oil contracts often saved rulers from financial distress, but their effect on the general population was narrow, for royalties were usually only about 15 per cent and went to governments only, reinforcing rulers. As revenues declined in the Depression, the Shah (king) of Iran achieved the first renegotiation upward.

The Red Line Agreement was a barrier to further exploration, but in time American firms not party to it took the lead. Qatar, Kuwait, Bahrain, and the Trucial States were protectorates where British consent to any concession was necessary, but American pressure achieved one for Standard Oil of California (SOCAL) in Bahrain and a joint Anglo-American venture in Kuwait. In 1932, SOCAL found oil on the Arab side of the Persian Gulf on Bahrain, a few miles offshore. Oil was not struck in Kuwait until 1938, but its ruler and those of other amirates were saved from bankruptcy by exploration fees after the Depression and Japanese cultured pearls had devastated their pearling industry.

Meanwhile, Ibn Saud, who had conquered most of the Arabian peninsula, lacked water and also money as the Depression reduced fees from pilgrimages to Mecca, so he hired an American expert to prospect for water and minerals. The upshot was an oil strike in 1938. SOCAL offered more money than Iraq Petroleum. Besides, the United States had no imperialist record in the Middle East and not even a legation in Riyadh. Thus SOCAL gained the concession. Production and a pipeline to the coast at Dhahran began but were largely shut down by World War II.

* * *

Ibn Saud was not alone in preferring countries without imperial interests in the region. Indigenous rulers sought to deal with states whose involvement was slight and to use them against nations which threatened their independence, for every Middle Eastern country was under the direct or indirect control of a great power or pressured by one or more. Usually that meant a preference for Germany or the United States. American interests were cultural and economic. Protestant missionaries, schools and colleges, archaeological institutes, and philanthropic foundations had long been active. American belief in its mission to reform or modernize other societies led to a focus on relief work for war victims (notably Armenian refugees), engineering, modern farming, hygiene, and health, including a key medical school at the American University of Beirut. Arabs admired the United States for its good works, modern products, political indifference to the region, Wilsonian decrees about self-determination, anti-imperial rhetoric, and democratic and republican government. It preached the 'Open Door' which meant opportunity for American firms. Its concern was oil; though self-sufficient, the United States, as the first automotive society, consumed 70 per cent of the world's supply in 1925. The State Department backed American firms seeking access to Middle Eastern fields during the 1920s scare about depleting American reserves – but not to the point of real clashes with Britain. Thereafter, private enterprise usually preceded government activity.

Historically, Washington had avoided the Eastern Question. After Wilson's brief foray into it at Paris, government and people emphatically wished to revert to tradition, hoping to safeguard good works and good business without political or military price. The State Department especially tried to skirt the Palestine problem. In practice, self-determination proved to be for 'mature' nations of eastern Europe, and since the children could not be left undirected, mandates were approved if they did not bar

American economic activity. The United States deferred to Britain's longer and greater knowledge of the region, playing the part of its understudy[2] and unwittingly preparing for its post-war role. Despite strategic indifference and a desire to avoid entanglement, oil increasingly mattered. Thus American interest in the Middle East grew as its role on the world stage enlarged.

Unlike the United States, Germany was active in the region before 1914. In the war, Germany tried, despite its ties to Turkey, to use the area against Britain and thus encouraged revolt. Post-war, the Weimar Republic was eliminated from the Middle East. It reaped the benefits of being weaker and non-imperialistic in terms of trade, expert advisers, and student exchanges but lacked surplus funds for overseas investment and could not afford collisions with great powers, especially Britain. Later, when Adolf Hitler became German Chancellor in 1933, Arab leaders misread him and hoped to use him against Britain and France, though most, other than the Mufti (religious leader) of Jerusalem, Haj Amin al Husaini, lacked Nazi sympathies. Hitler initially rejected their overtures, leaving the Mediterranean to Italy. He favoured Jewish migration to Palestine, which pleased neither Britain nor Arabs, and pursued a contradictory policy in the region, giving it low priority. From 1936 to 1938, he focused on non-Arab states, training the Afghan army, developing economic ties to Turkey, and trying to keep Iran out of Russia's orbit. Thereafter German policy was dictated by European crises; Hitler tried to distract Britain and France from these by shipping arms to several Middle Eastern states and supporting Arab nationalists, especially in Palestine.

Distrust of Italy was greater. Though weaker, it was closer, and its ambitions were clear. Turkey was particularly nervous: Italy's hope of a sphere in Anatolia had been dashed at Paris but had not died – and it held the Dodecanese Islands off the coast. Mussolini's talk of a new Roman Empire and of the Mediterranean as an Italian lake upset coastal states, though the mandates were unlikely targets. At first Mussolini was cautious, pursuing commercial, cultural, and religious ties and making anti-imperial statements. But in the 1930s he tried to be all things to all people, supporting and opposing Zionism and imperialism, leading to Arab, Turkish, and Zionist distrust. He beamed propaganda from Radio Bari, with little effect since broadcasts were in literary Arabic, not popular dialects, and in an era when radios required electrical wiring, few existed in the Arab world. After conquering Ethiopia, Mussolini developed ambitions in Egypt and Arabia, areas Hitler allotted to him, but by then he was too militarily embroiled in the Spanish Civil War to act.

Much of the time, Russia also was too preoccupied to pursue a forceful policy, though its long-standing interests in the area had not changed. Priority went to domestic matters, then to economic ties and diplomatic recognition. The focus was European, and the Soviet Union was not a true great power in the 1920s, but the Middle East was of strategic concern as a potential invasion route into Russia and because it was so tied to the West. Indeed, the Russian Revolution in part had given Britain the opportunity to conquer the region. The Soviet Union tried to replace military might with ideological force, but to little effect.

Most important to Russia were Turkey, Iran, and Afghanistan, neighbours all. It signed treaties with each in the 1920s, partly to counter British influence. Early on, Russia backed Turkish and Persian nationalism but without lasting influence. In Iran, it made border incursions when opportunity permitted in the early 1920s but gained nothing approaching the prewar sphere of influence. Russia recognized Saudi Arabia out of hostility to the Hashemite monarchies of Iraq and Transjordan but gave little attention to the Arab world. Lenin's successor, Josef Stalin (Iosif Vissarionovich Dzhugashvili), knew the limits of his power and was preoccupied with Europe.

*   *   *

The states which mattered were Britain and France. They made the territorial decisions, reserving most of the area to themselves and allowing none to other nations. Since both were *status quo* powers, the 1920s enjoyed an illusory stability. In fact, Arab nationalism seethed in the wings while Anglo-French rivalry was intense backstage. The Middle East poisoned Anglo-French relations as much as the German problem did. True friendship (as opposed to a marriage of convenience) is rare among nations, especially great powers, whose natural state is one of open or veiled rivalry. The 15-year Anglo-French Entente had not overcome centuries of enmity; competition resumed when the last shot was fired on the western front. France assumed a right to dominate the Levant, owing to its long interest and economic, cultural and religious position as protector of Christian sites, but Britain had possession and in December 1918 used it to revise the Sykes–Picot arrangement in its favour, shrinking French claims. Britain won the battle for regional predominance because of its military presence and because France was exhausted and preoccupied with the potential German threat.

In reality, neither power had much time for the Middle Eastern children. They were busy with their own marital problems, other troublesome children, and German efforts to disrupt their marriage. Despite their mutual hostility, they had much in common, including arrogance, tactlessness, and faith in their own superiority. In 1923, the historian Arnold Toynbee wrote, 'We do not primarily think of Turkey as the home of fellow human beings.'[3] The same held for Syria, Afghanistan, and Yemen. Race, colour, and religion were now forces in world politics as white supremacy became a unifying factor. Britain and France had small comprehension of Arab aspirations and assumptions; both were distracted by domestic problems, events elsewhere, power politics, and their own imperial concerns.

The mandates gave the mandatory state a privileged position, as did the treaties whereby Britain conferred nominal independence. Both powers introduced artificial state systems resting on armies and collaborators. Though superficially impressive, the regimes were not solid and lacked real ties to the people, especially in the French mandate of Syria and Lebanon, where French rule was direct, able but undemocratic, and French ambitions undisguised. A great power since the first days of the European state system, France was now a fading dowager, propped up by her empire but unwilling to face the ravages of time and World War I. Her pre-war imperial mentality lingered; she thought of 'French rights', and though she provided infrastructure, an administrative system, and modernization, she did not contemplate Arab rights. France was deeply earnest about her 'mission civilisatrice' and thought that Levantine admiration for French culture and an attachment by Maronite Catholics of Mount Lebanon to their Christian protectors meant that everyone in greater Syria wanted French rule. In fact, Muslims were hostile, but France believed in a 'Syria' which did not exist, grateful for and devoted to French culture. In India Britain faced reality after World War II at five minutes to midnight, but in the Levant France shut her ears and let the clock chime. She was shocked to find the children would *not* go to bed – and were old enough to stay up late.

Frequent disciplinary problems were seen as Britain's fault. France could not believe Muslim Arabs rejected French rule; she was badly scarred first by British failure to honour the 1918 promises which had led to French concessions over Mosul and Palestine, and then by the year-long struggle to attain what remained to her under Sykes–Picot. The result was an almost pathological distrust of British machinations, which rarely existed but which served to explain unrest. For the rest, France focused on protecting Christians and preventing a British monopoly in the Middle East.

She succeeded in this last goal only because Britain chose to give way, at Arab expense, to salvage Anglo-French relations. By the time Russia returned to an active role, Britain was firmly installed as paramount regional power. The interwar era brought no real challenges from any major state. Frequent difficulties led to improvised, shifting policies, but the problems arose from the ambiguities and contradictions of wartime promises which Britain did not expect to have to honour, from European considerations, and from struggles between London and the (British) Government of India, which played a role in Middle Eastern policy and wanted to do nothing which might rouse India's Muslims.

Unlike France, Britain disguised its ambitions in oratory and promises, opting for a modernized indirect rule on a national basis and improvising control by mandate or treaty. It backed local moderates, not realizing that they too were nationalists, and benefited from Arab quarrels after the dream of unity was foiled. Local elites were trained as officials to save money and to prepare for eventual independence. The object was long-term British control of economic, military, and foreign policy, but without subsidy or much military protection. Treaties made the countries *look* independent and evaded League oversight but safeguarded British goals.

They provided a cheap version of indirect rule, necessitated by British impoverishment and public hostility to paying the costs of empire, as well as a sop to Arab nationalism. London used force against early protests, implying it would always do so. This became a bluff as its eastern forces melted away in 1919's rapid demobilization. By 1922, the entire British army amounted to 200 000 men and could not cope with simultaneous challenges occurring in Ireland, India, and the Middle East, along with a near war with Turkey.[4] Thus partial retreats were necessary, but Britain pretended the gap between commitments and resources did not exist as it found that the Royal Air Force (RAF) could police the desert cheaply. Yet the underlying weakness remained, as the Ethiopian crisis showed. Italy was too weak and too much disliked in the region to be a serious challenge, but, even so, Britain could not stop her and would not press her – from lack of power.

*   *   *

In the Arabian peninsula, Britain let Husain be King of the Hejaz and then, when relations became strained, allowed Ibn Saud of the Nejd to swallow that kingdom in 1924 en route to a decade of conquest of most of the peninsula. The Kingdom of Saudi Arabia was proclaimed in 1932, marking the first unification of the Arabian peninsula in over 1000 years. The puritan, anti-modern Wahhabi Muslim sect's fanatical warrior corps, the Ikhwan (Brethren), spearheaded Saudi conquest, but the Ikhwan were difficult to control and rebelled in 1930. Ibn Saud crushed them but then needed an army, and money to finance it. That led to the SOCAL contract. Earlier, Ibn Saud's expansionism and Ikhwan zeal caused border clashes with neighbouring states, especially the Hashemite rivals in Iraq and Transjordan. Britain insisted on border delimitations in 1922–23 with both states and Kuwait, creating two neutral zones for areas used by nomadic tribes. Most powers other than the indifferent United States soon recognized Saudi Arabia, but it was not a League member. From 1930 on, Ibn Saud sought entry, which Britain repeatedly blocked, preferring a free hand.

Ibn Saud wanted an Arab balance of power and opposed any Hashemite combination, fearing revenge for his Hejaz conquest. As Britain controlled the peninsula's four corners (Aden, Oman, Kuwait, and Aqaba in Transjordan), he never sharply opposed London, working within the confines of its hegemony. But Britain did not object to American interest. The 1931 visit of a prominent American entrepreneur, resulting in the SOCAL contract, led the Foreign Office to remark:

Everybody knows that Arabs are incompetent, improvident, conceited, penurious, and generally difficult to deal with. Everybody also knows that American prospectors in unpromising and unexplored regions are apt to be interested adventurers.[5]

Oil had a sharp impact. Border delimitations and special arrangements for the neutral zones were necessary, and nomads were initially bewildered by technology. Governance was medieval in the European sense. Ibn Saud ruled personally and through his family, few of whom then knew the outside world. Government was minimal, and the tribes were raised when armies were needed. Some administration developed after 1925, using foreigners, but finance remained chaotic. Only fiscal extremity led to allowing entry to the infidel. In 1938 after oil revenues began, annual government income rose to $7 million. One cause of fiscal distress was clashes with Yemen, the peninsula's other independent state. As both coveted the same area, trouble was constant, resulting in two wars, both won by Saudi Arabia, which in 1934, at British instance, granted Yemen a generous peace. Thereafter Saudi relations with the Hashemites improved owing to fear of Turkey and Iran and joint concern about the Ethiopian crisis and Palestine. In 1936 Ibn Saud signed with Iraq a treaty of Arab brotherhood, to which Yemen adhered. By then, he was involved in the pan-Arab movement and the Palestine issue, cautiously trying to mediate.

On the broader diplomatic scene, Ibn Saud saw Italy's conquest of Ethiopia as a British defeat. He looked to Germany from 1937 on, seeking arms. Hitler responded slowly, and the 1938 Munich crisis cooled Arab ardour, but formal diplomatic relations in February 1939 were welcome to avoid being squeezed by Britain and Italy. However, diplomatic relations with the United States in June 1939 provided a new counterbalance to Britain and helped end the flirtation with Germany.

Difficulties continued with Yemen because Imam (religious leader) Yahya, who ruled from 1904 to 1948 without ever seeing the sea or leaving the country, hoped to reverse his 1934 defeat. He was conservative and autocratic, trying to isolate Yemen, which became independent in 1918, from outsiders and change. Lacking oil, he succeeded. Despite trade and Italian aid, Yemen was largely closed to foreigners. Trouble was constant on Yemen's other border with the Aden protectorate, for Yahya coveted the port of Aden, 'the eye of Yemen',[6] but the RAF ejected him from the protectorate. His search for anti-British allies led to a flirtation with the Axis but little else.

Aden (now part of Yemen) consisted of a large protectorate and a small colony governed from India until 1937, when it became a crown colony. The protectorate shielded the colony, which was valued for its port, oil refinery, and military base. Inhabited by Arabs in autocratic shaikhdoms (tribal entities) bound to take British 'advice', it lay on sea and air routes to

India. To the east was Muscat and Oman (now Oman), a British-protected agricultural and trading area. It had closer ties to India than to the Persian Gulf, for only its tip lay on the Gulf, the rest abutting the Gulf of Oman, but it controlled the Straits of Hormuz, the narrow entrance to the Persian Gulf and thus to Iran's oil riches.

Well into the twentieth century, the Government of India held British responsibility for the Persian Gulf except Iran. On the Arab side were most of the peninsula's few good ports, generally British-controlled. The Gulf was strategic for the route to India. It became more so as a shipping lane for oil and a refuelling area for flights from Europe to Asia and Australia. Britain's exclusive treaties with the shaikhs (tribal leaders) along the west coast isolated them from the Arab world until the oil companies arrived in the 1930s. The Trucial States, so called from the Perpetual Truce of 1853 which Britain negotiated among them to end piracy, consisted of seven tiny quarrelsome shaikhdoms, one on the Gulf of Oman and the rest on the Persian Gulf. Little more than primitive seaside villages, they were all protectorates. Britain focused on the route to India, not oil, and a commercial airfield was built in the 1930s. Japan showed economic interest in the area and was popular as a symbol of eastern liberation from the West. Exploratory oil leases saved the shaikhs from ruin after the pearling collapse, though development came only after World War II. In the Qatar peninsula immediately to the north, a primitive Wahhabi area, the situation was much the same.

The most modern British-protected shaikhdoms were Bahrain and Kuwait. Bahrain consisted of oil-bearing islands off the Saudi coast. Unlike elsewhere, British interference in internal affairs was direct and frequent, not least because an RAF base was established there in 1924 and a naval base in 1935. In the 1920s, Kuwait lost two-thirds of its territory in British-inspired border demarcations. Britain guaranteed independence to what remained, but Kuwait, whose port capital city was a trading centre, suffered from a Saudi economic blockade in the 1920s. Beyond Britain, Kuwait's survival depended on Iraqi–Saudi rivalry. When Iraq threatened in the 1930s, Ibn Saud suddenly became Kuwait's protector. Arid and dependent on pearling, Kuwait was impoverished until oil was struck in 1938, in what proved to be the Middle East's largest field.

*   *   *

Across the Red Sea from Saudi Arabia was Egypt, in Africa and strategically located on the Mediterranean and by the Suez Canal, the main route to Australasia. It was densely populated, agricultural, Arabic, and at least 90 per cent Muslim, the rest mostly Coptic Christians. Its location had meant repeated conquests and infusions of foreign culture and ideas, which since 1800 were chiefly Anglo-French. After World War I, Western ideas clashed with Western rule.

Before 1914 Egypt was nominally within the Ottoman Empire, but Britain ruled. Thus pre-war Egyptian nationalism was aimed at Britain, not Turkey, and separate from the pan-Arab movement. Britain ignored Egyptian nationalists, seeing them as 'unruly children in need of strong parental guidance'[7] and assuming that Egypt would not attain self-rule for centuries to come. Europeans dominated commerce and finance, though a Western-educated elite was emerging. Egypt was not a colony, but then and thereafter it suffered most of the penalties of being one.

World War I brought a protectorate and British-chosen nominal rulers. Egypt was technically neutral but under martial law and occupied by half a million British soldiers. Its forces fought the Turks with heavy losses. Forced contributions and recruitment of troops and labour, requisition of animals and forage, crop allocations, skyrocketing prices and food shortages, as well as a heavy financial burden led to urban and rural discontent and dangerous volatility, which Britain ignored.

Britain talked in wartime of 'progress toward self-government'.[8] Egyptians took seriously Wilson's statements about self-determination and felt they qualified owing to Egypt's large size, sophisticated financial system, and educated elite. Britain had no policy, deferring decision until after the war, but issued the November 1918 Anglo-French Declaration promising independence to former Ottoman territories. That led to an Egyptian delegation (Wafd) led by Saad Zaghlul on 13 November 1918 to the British High Commissioner asking to present Egyptian views in London. This was refused, as was a trip to the peace conference. Zaghlul, an experienced politician and brilliant orator, claimed to speak for the nation – and largely did, as he harnessed rural and urban discontent and had support from Muslims, Copts, and, at first, the Sultan. The Wafd became a vast movement as the voice of Egypt, with a role and a struggle comparable to India's Congress.

In March 1919 Zaghlul was arrested and exiled. Revolt swept all areas and classes, both sexes and religions. General Sir Edmund Allenby regained control in a month – after Zaghlul was released and allowed to visit Paris, where Britain ensured that he was ignored. Unrest continued through 1919, leading Allenby to decide the protectorate must end, in which he eventually prevailed. Britain hoped to replace the protectorate with a treaty but, as Zaghlul demanded full independence, no other politician could accept the offered half-loaf. Thus, after exiling Zaghlul again, Britain declared Egypt's independence unilaterally on 28 February 1922. It aimed to conserve and mask British control, define its interests, and restrict use of its power to them. It reserved the security of imperial communications, protection of minorities and foreign interests, defence of Egypt, and the Sudan; Britain would control foreign policy. The Egyptian government did not accept the declaration. It was free to do right but not wrong, and Britain would judge which was which, able to interfere at will.[9]

The Sultan became King Fuad I and was forced by Britain to a liberal constitution with a parliamentary regime on the Belgian model, though with more power to the monarch. The Wafd won all free elections under the 1923 constitution, the first in 1924 by 90 per cent. Zaghlul became Prime Minister but was weakened by Allenby's crackdown after the 1924 murder of Sir Lee Stack, for which the Wafd was blamed owing to its agitation over the Sudan. Between 1922 and 1936, negotiations took place on the four reserved questions, but the issues which doomed Zaghlul's first efforts in 1920, full independence and the Sudan, remained the sticking points. The Sudan, where the White and Blue Niles joined, controlled the vital waters. Both states had economic and strategic concerns as well; neither gave way. Britain could not get an agreement with the Wafd – or without it.

London kept power by placing British officials in key ministries but could not create a moderate party because it never conceded enough to get a treaty through Egypt's parliament. It gave too little too late, saw those who sought more as demagogues, and was patronizing at best. A triangular power struggle developed among King, Wafd, and British High Commissioner, with Britain often backing the King against the Wafd though he suspended the constitution repeatedly. After Zaghlul's death in 1927, his successors were weaker, and a period of 'surly calm' ensued.[10] Egyptians were preoccupied with their own struggle and, though anti-Zionist, lacked a strong Arabic consciousness as yet. In 1936 the young Farouk became king. He looked promising at first but 'showed himself to be decreasingly interested in either reform or responsibility'.[11]

The Ethiopian crisis sparked change. Egypt and the Sudan were wedged between Italy in Libya and in Ethiopia-Eritrea. Britain feared an Italian pincers movement and needed to pacify a vital base. The weakened Wafd knew Egypt must rely on Britain for defence and feared if war came, it would again be treated as a colony. Ethiopia led to Egyptian unity, making possible a Wafd approach to Britain. Thus a treaty in August 1936 provided an alliance, specified gradual British withdrawal to the Sinai and Canal Zone with a right of reoccupation in time of war or tension and RAF access to Egyptian air space, and required a friendly Egyptian foreign policy. Gradual army and police control and fiscal freedom were ceded with a minority voice in the Canal administration. London arranged an end to capitulations (treaties granting special European privileges) and Egypt's League entry in 1937 but retained the Canal and the Sudan. Egypt had gone from half a loaf to three-fourths but still lacked the most important quarter.

The 1936 treaty led to new opposition from students and the Muslim Brotherhood, a religious and increasingly political movement seeking an Islamic state; it attracted those losing out to westernization. The Brotherhood had a paramilitary unit and swelled during World War II, as did Young Egypt, a Fascist movement. The treaty prevented revolt but did not generate pro-British sympathies. Egypt broke relations with Germany in 1939 but did not declare war, seeking concessions as its price. The King, government, and upper classes were as pro-Axis as the 1936 treaty would permit, and a British show of force in 1942 was required to gain full co-operation, but Britain managed to maintain the 'surly calm' through the wartime emergency.

*   *   *

To the north, Britain's concern was not Italy but Russia, against which it hoped to use the Northern Tier of three non-Arab states as buffers. The Soviet Union had equally extensive aims if fewer means. Turkey, Iran, and Afghanistan all strove for a free hand against encroachments from both. The strongest, Turkey succeeded best, but once foreign troops left and independence was secure, each focused on domestic problems and sought a Russo-British power balance. Germany played a role as well but did not wish to cross either great power in the 1920s.

After a minor Russo-British clash in 1920, both accepted the Northern Tier as a buffer zone. In the new regime's first diplomatic successes, the Soviet Union gained treaties with all three – and then gradually more friendly treaties. After trying to crack the whip, Britain eased up, gaining regional stability at no cost and ending Communist and pan-Islamic agitation, to its benefit in India and the Arab world. Regional stability declined in the 1930s, as Stalin and Hitler competed in the area.

Growing tension, especially between Britain and Russia, led Turkey to seek a regional pact. In July 1937 the three states and Iraq signed the first Middle Eastern security treaty at Saadabad, the Shah's summer palace. It provided for peace and consultation among the four and a pressure group for a regional seat on the League Council. But the four were not all hostile to the same power, and their community of interest collapsed quickly. Though all were neutral in 1939, World War II ended the pact.

As the westernmost and most independent state, Turkey led in modernization and secularization. Kemal's 'foreign policy was based not on expansion but on retraction of frontiers'.[12] He insisted on the national domain which (aside from a rebellious Kurdish minority) was mostly Turkish-speaking, but no more. He used Russia and France against Britain to gain the Lausanne treaty; then relations with Britain improved, as did those with Greece after the population exchange. Kemal pursued Mosul until the 1926 League award to Britain, and gained Alexandretta (Hatay) province with a mixed population and a needed Mediterranean port from Syria in 1939 by taking diplomatic advantage of France's preoccupation with Germany. Otherwise, he eschewed territorial gain, saying, 'Let us recognize our own limits'.[13]

Kemal knew the Sick Man of Europe needed long convalescence, so he focused on national revival, modernization and secularism, renouncing pan-Islam. To protect the Straits from Russia, he sought good relations with the nearest great sea power, Britain, but also with the nearest great land power, the Soviet Union, whom Turkey feared. Relations with Russia fluctuated though Kemal worked to keep them smooth despite his dislike of Communism. He was horrified by Hitler and ensured that Germany's role in Turkish economic growth did not lead to domination. Stalin he respected, so he was vigilant but obliging about trade agreements without political commitment. He scorned Mussolini but feared his imperialism, using the Ethiopian crisis and patient diplomacy to obtain a free hand in the Straits in 1936. Seeking regional treaties to counterbalance the great powers, Kemal gained a shaky Balkan Entente in 1934 and the Saadabad Pact of 1937. His successor, Ismet Inönü, continued his pro-British policy.

Turkey was a model for Iran, once the latter had loosened the British grip. In the war, Russia and Britain occupied their respective spheres, but Russian withdrawal after the 1917 revolution led to anarchy in the north and a temporary British free hand. Iran was bankrupt, chaotic, and terrified of Communism; Britain was the sole stable element but increasingly resented, especially as British garrisons did not bring justice or reform. London's chief concern was Persian oil; it tried to legalize its hegemony by a 1919 treaty imposing a virtual protectorate, which Iran's parliament never ratified. Feeling ran high, especially as Britain failed to defend the north from Soviet incursions and a 1921 Russo-Irani pact formalizing earlier Soviet renunciation of tsarist privileges looked more generous than it was. Russia soon resumed its historic drive for a warm water port on the Persian Gulf, hoping too that Iran could be the route to revolution in Asia, especially India. As Britain withdrew its forces in favour of more subtle control, Iranian independence rested on rivalry between the two.

In February 1921 a military coup brought Reza Khan (chief) to power. In 1925 he took the world's oldest throne and became Reza Shah of the new Pahlevi dynasty. He reorganized the army, basis of his regime, using it to suppress tribal revolts and the Kurds and to centralize power at the expense of provinces and tribes as well as of Britain and Russia. In part he imitated Kemal, though Kemal had a political party and the intelligentsia's support, but Reza had neither; he ignored opinion, enriched himself, and was more brutal. Despite reforms financed by oil revenues, he was not a reformer but an absolute dictator. He forced more drastic change than Kemal in a less modern state, with often superficial results. Reza lacked an ideology but favoured statism, rapid modernization, and the ending of clerical power. As Persian nationalism rested in part on its distinctive Shiite religion and its resistance to Sunni neighbours, he failed in the latter. Compulsory military service controlled and helped unify the nation, for conscripts were taught reading, trades, and the Persian language, if necessary, and village youth were often urbanized. Iran was more independent and cohesive though less free.

Foreign advisers were American or German, never Russian or British. Reza tried to attract American oil firms to northern Iran, but Britain could block viable outlets, and the State Department ignored the area. Thus, as third power support was needed, German influence revived in the mid-1920s. Russia tried economic warfare, for it was north Iran's only trade outlet, but Reza built a railway to the south, established a trade monopoly with severe controls, and moved closer to Germany. In the Nazi era, economic penetration became political, then military. Iran was so pro-Nazi that in August 1941 Britain and Russia, allies once more, occupied it again, forcing Reza's abdication.

To the east lay landlocked Afghanistan, strategically located on trade routes and wedged between Russia and India. It too tried to emulate Turkey and to use Germany as a third force against Britain and Russia, pursuing a policy of 'defensive isolationism' to 1919 then 'defensive neutralism' until Britain left the region in 1947.[14] Before World War I, a defensive alliance with Britain afforded London's guarantee of Afghanistan's territorial integrity in return for a British right to advise on foreign policy. Afghanistan, which remained neutral in World War I on London's advice, thought it had an alliance of equals, but Britain saw a quasi-protectorate which it planned to strengthen post-war to protect India. However, 1919 brought an absolute monarch, Amanullah, who sought to retain his throne and his state's soil and freedom. He declared independence in April, rejecting dependency on Britain, and invaded India, setting off the third Afghan war. Indecisive fighting lasted a month but only in December 1921 did London reluctantly recognize Afghanistan's full independence.

Amanullah established relations with neighbouring states and with European powers, trying to balance between Britain and Russia and between France and Germany, which became economically dominant. He was a secular nationalist and a progressive reformer despite his ignorance of the world. He pushed too fast, flouting Islamic law and tradition; the result was rebellions, his ouster, and civil war. His successors reformed more slowly with the same foreign policy. In the 1930s, they feared Soviet economic penetration and possible attack, were affected by India's struggle for independence as they subsidized border tribes traditionally allied to Afghanistan against British efforts to control them, and became a market for Japan, whose successful dealings with the West they admired. The balancing act was so delicate that Afghanistan did not enter the League while Britain was a member and Russia not; it joined only after the Soviet Union did. It was alarmed by the Ethiopian crisis as it too was landlocked and dependent on arms transit across neighbours. Afghanistan decided Germany could provide a strong army and great power protection. It later sought alternatives, but the United States was uninterested and the Saadabad Pact of no military use. Afghan leaders stuck with Germany until it failed to aid a 1941 Iraqi rebellion and then remained neutral throughout the war.

*   *   *

As circumstances of members of the Northern Tier indicated, in the Middle East degrees of independence varied. No state was legally a colony and all mandates were class A with independence supposedly in sight. But mandates were a new system, giving Britain and France wide powers over peoples who had expected independence and who saw mandates as disguised imperialism. In the French mandate of Syria and Lebanon, this was largely true. Paris would have preferred a colony in its area of linguistic and cultural dominance, where it had a large economic and educational investment and had held a religious protectorate over Christians and Catholic sites since the seventeenth century. France wanted to control a centre of Arab and Muslim opinion, remain a Mediterranean power equal to Britain and Italy, protect routes to Indochina, and in the 1930s safeguard the pipeline from Iraq to Tripoli, which provided much of its oil. These aims required British co-operation, for France lacked a naval base east of Tunis.

France expected to be welcomed, overestimating its own acceptability and underestimating Arab nationalism, which grew during wartime repression, famine, and service in Faisal's army. The Levant* was a trade centre between the Mediterranean, India, and East Asia as well as for the Syrian and Arabian interiors. With armies, traders, and migrations constantly traversing it, coastal areas had become well educated and cosmopolitan. Arab nationalism was most intense in Syria and Lebanon, which expected independence in 1918. Imposition of the mandate led to a sense of grievance, but with frustration of the pan-Arab dream, greater Syria, and even Syrian-Lebanese unity, a more parochial Syrian and to a degree Lebanese nationalism developed. Solid political parties and strong leaders were lacking, however, since Turkey had executed many in 1915 and most of the rest passed the interwar years in opposition. France viewed Arab nationalism as an infectious disease, threatening North Africa, and partitioned her mandate partly to contain it. She favoured association, not assimilation, and used her Moroccan system as a guide despite its inappropriateness to a sophisticated area. Paris, whose rule rested on minorities and puppets, aimed to curb Arab nationalism, strengthen pro-French elements, and reinforce Lebanon against the interior. She resisted anything which might weaken her, aid Britain, or affect North Africa, whose manpower would be vital in any future war.

The mandate required an organic law within three years, but this was not achieved since what nationalists would accept did not suit Paris and vice versa. France kept the Ottoman system of autonomy to sects, favouring Christians and pro-French mountain minorities and stressing distinctness and separation, not similarities and unity. Both states had a melange of Christian and Muslim sects, on which politics was based. Paris could argue

---

* The eastern end of the Mediterranean, especially Syria, Lebanon, and Palestine.

that protecting minorities fulfilled the mandate, but her policy of confessional fragmentation exceeded the usual 'divide and rule'.

Though assaulting nationalism, the French tutelary system produced some of the nation building the League intended; it provided facilities and, with gaps, preconditions for a modern society, but linking the currencies to the depreciating French franc proved disastrous, partition hurt economically, concessions went to French firms, and some senior officials were inept. France treated Arabs with contempt, offended them by use of African troops, and had a heavy-handed bureaucracy. She retained maximum power, stressing good governance, not self-government.

In the 1930s, the Mandates Commission pressed for indigenous regimes to prepare for independence, the Levant was unsettled by the Ethiopian war, and the Popular Front leftist coalition took office in Paris in 1936. It negotiated pacts with Syria and Lebanon, ratified by both, for a three-year transition, alliance, League entry, and fewer French troops. Following the British example in Iraq and Egypt, they were to replace the mandates with virtual protectorates. But the Popular Front fell, and the French army and the Chamber of Deputies' worry about air routes, the oil pipeline, and North Africa grew. Revision to meet these concerns only angered Arab nationalists. Nothing was settled when World War II brought French defeat and the Nazi-dominated Vichy regime. On 8 June 1941, Britain and token Free French forces invaded to pre-empt Axis use, completing conquest in a month. France proclaimed the mandate's end and independence, declaring it formally in the autumn, but ruled as if nothing had changed, delaying a settlement amid strikes and riots. Britain, seeking wartime stability, pressed for changes – pressure seen by France as 'machinations'. As Allied diplomatic protests to Paris swelled, support of Lebanese Maronite Christians for French rule evaporated, and France bombarded the Syrian capital, Damascus, in May 1945; Britain, with greater forces on the ground, confined French troops to barracks and forced evacuation in 1946.

From first to last, Syrian opposition to French rule was especially heated. Syria was the cradle of Arab nationalism with an educated elite, Damascus a cultural and political centre. Unrest was the norm; French rule was seen as illegitimate for it had ousted Faisal by force. Inconsistent French policies affected by events elsewhere added to instability, as did lack of contact with Syrians as Paris tried to rule through figureheads. The Druse, a mountainous Islamic sect, rebelled in July 1925 against reforms violating their traditions. The 'Great Revolt' widened but did not become national. Even so, France bombarded Damascus and did not suppress the last rebels until 1927.

Attempts thereafter to achieve a constitution failed, so France imposed one in 1930, requiring French consent to all government decisions, but unrest caused suspensions. Syrian nationalism was not revolutionary but evolutionary; its *évolué* leaders favoured the local political *status quo*, which they dominated. Originally pan-Arab, the movement gradually narrowed to Syrian independence, slowly accepting Lebanese separation. The Syrian National Party grew as nationalism became more cohesive and radical, entailing mass movements, youth groups, and the middle class, and seeking social change. Tension mounted in the late 1930s as a general strike occurred, France failed to ratify the Popular Front's pacts for transition to somewhat more independence, and France conceded Alexandretta to Turkey. She reverted to direct rule to quell violence.

Lebanon was somewhat less anti-French for French ties were long and strong. Links to the Arab hinterland were weak as Lebanon's trade and ties were to the Mediterranean and Europe; it saw itself both as the western-most Arab state and as the eastern frontier of Christendom. The educational level was high, and pre-war nationalism had been Christian before it became Arab. The war had strengthened Lebanese separatism in some areas, resting on past autonomy, French ties, and fear of Muslim domination. This was particularly true of Mount Lebanon, an inland area with a Maronite Christian majority, a Druse minority, and no important cities. But in August 1920 France proclaimed Greater Lebanon, tripling its area by adding Beirut, other port cities, the Biqa Valley, and southern districts, all chiefly Muslim. Thus Lebanon was 'born schizophrenic'.[15] The religious mix became intricate, with Maronites the largest Christian sect, Sunnis the biggest Muslim group with a large Shiite minority, an array of smaller sects, and a bare Christian majority overall at first, though Muslims had a higher birth-rate. France retained the tradition of confessional representation in the 1926 constitution, which left the Lebanese government free to do exactly as Paris wished. Sectarian allocation of offices emerged with a Maronite president, a Sunni prime minister, Shiite head of the Chamber, and Greek Orthodox and Druse cabinet seats. Politics were sectarian and squabbly with ecclesiastics actively involved. Lebanese Christian and Muslim youth groups with paramilitary units pressed in the 1930s for independence, but the nationalists were divided over whether Lebanon should unite with Syria. However, by the French departure in 1946, the Lebanese state had been accepted, thanks to the growing role of Beirut, opposition to the mandate, the fact that the president and each deputy represented the whole country, and a twenty-year history of common political life. Lebanon became a founder member of the Arab League, signalling its choice to be an Arab state.

* * *

The innumerable links among the segments of greater Syria did not cease to exist in 1920. Indeed, unity was furthered by pan-Arabism and by common opposition to both European rule and Zionism, especially as Syria backed the Palestinian movement, whose leaders often fled to Beirut. Nonetheless, the area remained divided between French and British overlords.

Britain avoided France's most egregious errors owing to its need to economize and to placate Arabs. Thus Britain pulled the strings offstage, not in full view. Its dispositions were made at the Cairo conference of March 1921, attended by 36 Britons and two Arabs. Here it split the Palestinian mandate into two parts, one an Arab amirate, and created a kingdom in Iraq under Faisal. As in Egypt, it aimed to ensure its interests by nominal independence, with unequal treaties. The Cairo decisions arose from a costly 1920 Iraqi revolt sparked by creation of the mandate, unpopular wartime British practices, and the November 1918 Anglo-French Declaration. Thus at Cairo Britain retrenched with fewer British troops and officials, and security entrusted to the RAF. As Iraqis opposed the mandate, Britain agreed to a treaty which brought only cosmetic changes.

The 1922 treaty, ratified at virtual British gunpoint in 1924, was the prototype for all Anglo-Arab treaties. Each revision, including minor ones in the 1920s, gave the Arabs more as empire eroded. The 1922 treaty veiled the mandate; fewer Britons 'advised' Iraqi officials and the king, who had to obey. An organic law balanced king and a partially elected parliament, with an edge to the king but a cabinet responsible to parliament. Dissatisfaction remained acute, and a new treaty gave Iraq independence and League entry in 1932 despite disapproval from Iraqi nationalists, British imperialists, and France. An ambassador replaced the high commissioner, and British forces withdrew, except from two air bases and a military mission to train the Iraqi army; in wartime Britain retained a right of transit and use of all facilities, for it undertook defence of Iraq. A 25-year alliance required consultation on foreign policy. Britain safeguarded the route to India and its oil supply while ending the mandate. British hegemony continued as did resentment of it.

Until 1932, Iraqis focused on ending the mandate, seeing independence as a panacea for all ills, which it was not. Problems were legion. Iraq was an artificial British merger of three provinces with arbitrary boundaries under constant challenge and alien institutions which did not take root. Britain vacillated, unconcerned until oil was struck in 1927, and did little to develop, educate, or modernize the country. Politics were erratic and corrupt, and the dynasty tarred by the British link; Iraq was ruled by men, not laws, with a triangular balance of power involving the king, the British, and Sunni Arab politicians. The country was agriculturally productive but lacked roads, though eventual oil revenue created an infrastructure to unite the country. Divisions existed among tribes, between tribes and towns, between rich and poor. Shiites dominated the marshy south, linguistically distinct Kurds the mountainous north. A sizeable Sunni minority in the central region and cities held social and political control.

Only Faisal could manage this unstable array. He learned much from 1918 to 1920, including the impotence of small nations and the folly of confronting a great power, but he nibbled away at British authority by a policy of 'take and ask',[16] noting that 'Complete independence is never given; it is always taken.'[17] A son of the desert, he understood the tribes, linking them to the regime. A realist, he knew how to handle Britain, whose protection Iraq needed. Faisal restrained extreme nationalists, resolved border disputes with Saudi Arabia, held factionalism and anti-British feeling within bounds, and attained a precarious stability in a country without cohesion. He was the sole mediator, unifying force, and symbol of the nation.

Faisal died in 1933. His son Ghazi favoured the army and nationalists. Both stability and British influence declined as revolts and army control mounted. In 1939 Ghazi died in an auto crash, leaving a small son. Meanwhile, in October 1936 came the first of many military coups, setting a dangerous precedent for the Middle East. This first coup by young officers, intellectuals, and leftist reformers hoped in vain to imitate Turkey's military-based regime. Conservative army officers dominated the last pre-war years. The Palestine issue caused intense anti-British and pan-Arab feeling. Officers ignorant of diplomacy hoped Iraq could be an Arab Prussia, uniting Arabs in a Baghdad-led confederation. Many had been German-trained before 1914; uninterested in ideology, they renewed old ties, which German cultural and radio propaganda reinforced. Iraq became the only actively pro-German Arab state, though the officers were not Nazi sympathizers. The Mufti of Jerusalem, who was one, arrived in October 1939 and stoked anti-British sentiment.

Iraq refused to declare war on the Axis unless London pledged Palestinian Arab independence. It made overtures, of which Britain knew, to Germany and Italy, who seemed to be winning. In April 1941 a pro-German coup led to British attack and a thirty-day war in May. The Iraqi army fell apart, the RAF was effective, and Hitler was too preoccupied with plans to invade Russia to help. Britain imposed martial law, military occupation, and a pro-British regime for the duration of the war.

In contrast to Iraq, the other new Hashemite dynasty began the era with more drama than it ended it. After Faisal's 1920 expulsion from Syria, his older brother Abdullah, who lacked a role, moved north from the Hejaz, claiming he would march on Damascus to restore Faisal but eyeing British reactions. He reached Amman at the time of the Cairo conference, leading Britain to declare him Amir of Transjordan if he forswore attack on Syria. Transjordan remained part of the Palestine mandate, which Abdullah accepted, but was governed separately and exempted from application of the Balfour Declaration. Abdullah's new, largely desert domain, which became the most lasting Hashemite realm, was an area nobody wanted and which Britain had been too busy to organize. It was arid, very poor, and with few natural resources. Population was scant but socially cohesive; the new capital, Amman, was a mere village in 1921. Abdullah, whose rule there was personal and financially chaotic, was wily, extravagant, and disorganized. Both Britain and Transjordan's nationalists soon realized that he appeared more compliant than he was and came to distrust him. Britain ousted the nationalists and took charge in 1924, using Abdullah's 'independent government' as another Arab façade. Essential subsidies, ultimata, and British command of the Arab Legion curbed Abdullah, who became more docile after Husain's fall in 1924. Britons were few in Amman but close by in Jerusalem. A 1928 constitution and treaty on the Iraqi model gave Britain all it wished. Britain set the borders, which lasted, to suit it and turned Transjordan, which served as a land corridor from the oil fields to the Mediterranean, into a centre of British influence and military bases. When Saudi forces pressed on the border, the amirate became important to Britain as a buffer against Ibn Saud and Wahhabi ideology.

Abdullah, whose dependence ensured that he was closer to Britain than other Arab leaders, was frankly expansionist. He hoped to gain Syria or greater Syria, reconquer the Hejaz, and rule Iraq after Faisal's death; he would unite Transjordan with any neighbour – under him. He aspired to be the Bismarck of an Arab Prussia, but his ties to Britain isolated him from Arab masses, who distrusted his claim to be a pan-Arab leader. Moreover, he signed a land option with the Jewish Agency in Jerusalem which hoped to annex Transjordan to Palestine or to relocate Palestinian Arabs there. This earned him Palestinian Arab distrust and aggravated his poor relations with the Mufti. As the Palestinian problem became acute from April 1936 on, Abdullah sought to gain from it. He alone of Arab leaders endorsed a British proposal to partition Palestine, attaching the Arab portion to Transjordan. As his self-interest was obvious, he became a 'political leper',[18] turning British officials against partition to prevent his profit. Abdullah hoped to be the Husain of World War II, absorbing the rest of greater Syria, but Britain blocked that. He lacked a following, but the war strengthened him by eliminating or weakening rivals, including Iraqi leaders and the Mufti. During the May 1941 Iraqi war, Abdullah aided Britain, and the Arab Legion was used in Iraq against an Arab state as well as in Syria against France. As the war ended, his dreams of greater Syria lingered and he was poised to meddle anew in Palestine.

*   *   *

Long before, Palestine had become the area's most divisive and unifying factor, greatest drama, and worst running sore. 'Palestine, as a modern geographic and political unit, was the creation of World War I and the peace settlement',[19] as were its borders. It was the 'twice promised land'[20] to which both Palestinian Arabs and Zionists had substantial claims. A British officer noted in 1919 that the 'Peace Conference has laid two eggs, Jewish Nationalism and Arab Nationalism; these are going to grow up into two troublesome chickens.'[21] As both had already hatched, the troublesome chickens came speedily to roost in Palestine, clashing explosively with British imperialism.

The Zionist claim rested on the Balfour Declaration for a Jewish national home, a concept hitherto unknown in international law but sanctioned by the mandate.[22] Palestine was occupied by Arabs whose existence early Zionists, both Jewish and Gentile, largely ignored.[23] They equally ignored the existing Jewish minority, at most 10 per cent at war's end, who were mainly non-Zionist, Oriental, and religious, not political.[24] Variously, Zionists, notably key British leaders, thought Arabs would be pleased by an infusion of Jewish technology and capital, not realizing they would react sharply to what came with these blessings and underestimating Palestinian Arab nationalism. Zionists and Arabs were consistent in their conflicting goals. Zionists, then a small minority of European and world Jewry,[25] pursued the unspoken aim of a Jewish state in Palestine and to that end Jewish immigration and land purchase. In direct opposition, Arabs sought an end to the mandate affirming the Balfour Declaration and an independent state with a government responsible to a representative council. Britain wavered between the two, reacting to the greater pressure of the moment.

London wanted the mandate to block France, provide a reserve base if Egypt became untenable, and protect the Suez canal and imperial communications, roles which the Arab-Zionist clash prevented. Optimistic Britons ignored Arab nationalism, despite uprisings in 1920 and 1921, and saw the Jews of Palestine as a settler colony, like the whites in Kenya.[26] Then Britain enunciated 'equality of obligation', trying to be fair but enraging the Arab majority and the Zionist minority. Assurances to Arabs that their fears of a Jewish state were unfounded did not reassure them and outraged Zionists, who fought any limit on Jewish immigration. When the situation worsened, British leaders closed their eyes, believed what they wanted to believe (partly because of intense Zionist-generated political pressure), and hoped to muddle through to some Arab–Zionist accommodation. As Arab unrest mounted, Britain feared that if it abandoned the Zionists, it would lose the mandate, chaos would set in, and France or Turkey would seize the area. In the 1930s, vacillation led to loss of control requiring military reinforcement. At this stage, as World War II threatened, Palestine, with an oil pipeline, an excellent harbour at Haifa, an airport, and a naval base, was well worth holding.

Like the British, Zionist leaders failed to foresee problems with the Arabs, whose pre-war relations with Palestinian Jews were good, and underestimated their nationalism,[27] hoping they would migrate elsewhere. Zionists were united, purposeful, and tightly organized, steadfast in goals but flexible in tactics. Their leader, Chaim Weizmann, was a skilled diplomat, subtle, and aware that the unpalatable probably need not be accepted for long. He lived in London, had entreé to cabinet ministers, and knew the importance of connections, the press, and manipulating public and parliamentary opinion. Zionists, overwhelmingly European, knew how to pressure European politicians and American leaders as well. The pattern was set by the Balfour Declaration, whose drafters included not only Weizmann and Lord Rothschild of the Zionist organization but also Louis Brandeis, American Supreme Court justice and close adviser to Woodrow Wilson.[28] Similarly, the text of the mandate was subject to heavy Zionist lobbying.[29]

By contrast, the prior experience of the Palestine Arabs as subject peoples of the Ottoman Empire did not equip them to manoeuvre in Western great power diplomacy and politics. They had demographic numbers on their side but little else. They were new to negotiation, tactically weak, disorganized, and unaware of the power of parliamentary and public opinion. They saw Zionist colonization as European imperialism[30] and as a barrier to the self-rule promised by wartime declarations. They were irritatingly rejectionist, denying the validity of the mandate and everything under it because accepting it meant accepting the Jewish national home. Thus they refused limited self-rule (which Zionists also rejected because they would be a minority) and an Arab Agency to match the quasi-governmental Jewish Agency specified by the mandate. Though mostly Sunni and predominantly agricultural, unlike the urban Jews, Palestinian Arabs and their Middle Eastern supporters were divided by national and familial rivalries, Palestinian politics, and the Abdullah factor. In the 1930s the Mufti, an intense anti-Zionist filled with moral and religious fervour, became dominant. By then, Arabs had learned that refusal to co-operate gained concessions but doubted British promises would be honoured. These promises began before the mandate took effect on 1 July 1920 and became frequent as Palestinians feared their land would become a Jewish state. That was always the issue, together with the means Zionists used to this end: Jewish immigration, Zionist land acquisition and arms smuggling to settlers to defend the land and to fight Arabs. Land sales, often by Syrian and Lebanese landlords who now needed passports and visas to visit their property, were a modest part of total acreage but represented much of the arable land.[31] On land bought by the Jewish National Fund, Arab tenants or labour and resale to non-Jews were banned.

Tensions fluctuated with Jewish immigration. A few years in the late 1920s were peaceful, leading to British and Arab optimism, but incidents mounted from 1929 on. Britain sent a Royal Commission to examine the situation. Like its successors, it argued that Arab anxiety needed to be addressed; a White Paper did so but was soon reversed by Zionist pressure in London. That became a pattern. From 1932 on, Jewish immigration soared; London doubled the quotas twice, and migration multiplied twentyfold from 1931 to 1935. Some was caused by Hitler's virulent anti-Semitism in Germany and reluctance of Western nations to accept German Jewish refugees, but more was from eastern Europe and Asian areas,[32] the migrants attracted during the Depression to Palestine's prosperous citrus groves, Arab and Jewish alike. Thereafter, as the European Jewish tragedy deepened and welcoming havens were few, illegal immigration swelled, regardless of the quotas, as did Arab resistance.

In April 1936 the Palestinian Arab Revolt erupted in a general strike. A peasant rising at first, it aimed at the Zionists, then at Britain, and lasted fitfully for three years, often in open warfare. The Palestinian parties united under the Mufti in the Arab Higher Committee, which Britain outlawed in October 1937, making martyrs of its fleeing leaders. The rebels created paralysis, especially after the 1937 partition plan, forcing Britain to send troops and to retreat from partition, which everyone except Abdullah rejected. The triangular struggle of the 1930s only intensified Arab and Zionist nationalism. The 1936 Revolt also marked the Arab debut on the world stage as it became a wider Arab cause, and Middle Eastern leaders intervened diplomatically. With British connivance, four monarchs (Farouk was not allowed to join) mediated an end to the general strike in 1936. As the 1937 partition plan renewed and worsened hostilities in Palestine, they did not restrain pro-Palestinian agitation among their subjects. Egypt and Iraq protested the plan to Britain and the League. Though poorly organized, Arab leaders learned to use menaces. As Hitler encouraged resistance from 1938 on and inflamed it by radio propaganda, they threatened an Arab–Axis alliance.

For the first time, the international situation favoured the Arab cause. World War II was approaching. Given Hitler's anti-Semitism, Britain could count on Jews, who lacked an alternative, but needed to pacify Arabs, still 70 per cent of Palestine's population. It could ill afford to offend the entire Middle East plus the Muslims of India or to have a large force tied down in Palestine; with oil, communications, and the defence of the Empire at stake, Britain shifted course enough to ensure Arab neutrality in World War II. After a last failed try at accommodation at a London conference with various Arab and Jewish elements, it issued a new White Paper sharply restricting Jewish immigration and promising future independence, effectively an Arab state. The Mufti rejected this solution, for he doubted Britain would honour it under Zionist pressure. To Zionists, who felt betrayed, the White Paper meant the end of co-operation with Britain and of the Weizmann era.

In World War II, both sides suspended the battle with London – for the duration only. Illegal immigration, arms smuggling, and arms theft soared as Zionists prepared in Palestine for a new struggle once the war was over. Elsewhere, they were united, better organized and led than Arabs. As Britain's sway in the Middle East waned, their focus shifted to the United States, where the 1942 Biltmore Conference in New York of the World Zionist Organization passed leadership to David Ben-Gurion, and called for the first time for open immigration and creation of the Jewish state in Palestine.[33]

*　　*　　*

The Palestine problem was a catalyst for pan-Arabism. The doctrine of Arab unity had faded as territorial nationalism grew, but the 1930s brought revival. Islam played a role because it was an integral part of Arab culture, but Christians participated as well. A pan-Arab congress in 1931 achieved only emotional solidarity but one in 1934 mediated the Saudi–Yemeni war, while another in 1937 denounced the Palestine partition plan. By then, there were Saudi treaties with Iraq and Egypt, and Arab states had entered the diplomacy of the Palestine issue, itself unifying for them.

The immediate pre-war years and the war saw a competition for Arab leadership. Hitherto, Egypt had stood aloof from pan-Arabism, for it was preoccupied and viewed as an African state. But from 1939 on, its interest grew as both Wafd and King Farouk saw that Egypt could lead the movement. From 1941 on, Britain, hoping for stability and an end to Arab rivalries, urged Arab co-operation but insisted that Arabs, not Britons, must lead. Most educated Arabs were suspicious of the idea's British origins and the prospect of Egypt's leadership, but Saudi–Iraqi rivalry left no alternative.

Conveniently, France was no longer a factor. Egyptian–Iraqi planning led in May 1945 to the League of Arab States, whose original members were Egypt, Iraq, Saudi Arabia, Transjordan, Syria, Lebanon, and Yemen. Its seat was Cairo and its secretary-general Egyptian; it had a council and committees, but sovereignty of its members was undiminished. Abdullah called it 'seven heads thrust in a sack'.[34] At once the Franco-Syrian issue arose, but as the great powers in the new United Nations supported Syria, the League did not have to face France alone. It urged Libyan independence and engaged in social development, but soon became an anti-Zionist bloc because this was the one political issue on which all members could agree, at least at a basic level.

Despite its limitations and Middle Eastern rivalries, the Arab League was one of many reasons why the region's role on the world stage was expanding rapidly. Its existence signalled that members of the Middle Eastern family were growing toward adulthood. The interwar interlude of West European imperialism gave these youths infrastructure, better living conditions, world languages, modern technology, a little political freedom, Western ideas, and, above all, mass national movements. An established elite, a location on the Mediterranean and trade routes, and the model of Turkey, which bested the great powers and forced a grudging respect, all contributed to maturation, as had World War I and its aftermath. Nowhere did the problems stem more directly from wartime promises and pronouncements and a peace settlement which did not substantially fulfil them.

World War II largely completed what World War I began. The days of European control were numbered – and it was not a large number. This war ended France's imperial role as well as British dominance and brought greater American involvement. A new imperialism was in the wings, that of a historically anti-imperial power, but its imperialism was one of technology, money, and more indirect military might, involving neither occupation, bases, nor administrative control. Nonetheless, the growing American stake in Middle Eastern oil and thus in the area meant that the United States became more active there and correspondingly less liked. An equally indirect revived Russian imperialism arose to counterbalance, causing rivalry by proxy through client states.

It was oil more than anything else which catapulted the Middle East into a key role. Though not yet developed in the interwar era, the region's reserves were known; oil production was growing and clearly would grow faster in the post-war era to slake the world's thirst. It was evident that the worthless sandy domains of desert nobodies in fact contained untold wealth of immense economic and military significance. That alone sufficed to alter the power equation dramatically.

These newly wealthy states and their less fortunate neighbours were becoming genuinely independent and engaging in diplomatic activity on their own and together in the Arab League, inspired by their individual interests, pan-Arab nationalism, and the suppurating Palestinian sore, which World War II worsened. These factors, along with the end of European dominance and the world's increasing demand for oil, ensured that the Middle East would emerge from the background into the spotlight with an important *ingénue* role in the world's continuing historical drama.

◆ Notes to Chapter 9

1. Edward W. Chester, *United States Oil Policy and Diplomacy* (Westport, CT, Greenwood, 1983), p. 6.
2. Barry Rubin, 'America as Junior Partner,' in Uriel Dann, ed., *The Great Powers in the Middle East, 1919–1939* (New York, Holmes & Meier, 1988), p. 239.
3. Phillip Darby, *Three Faces of Imperialism: British and American Approaches to Asia and Africa, 1870–1970* (New Haven, CT, YUP, 1987), p. 90.
4. Bernard Porter, *The Lion's Share: A Short History of British Imperialism, 1850–1970* (London, Longman, 1975) p. 251.
5. Clive Leatherdale, *Britain and Saudi Arabia, 1925–1939* (London, Frank Cass, 1983), p. 195.
6. Manfred W. Wenner, *Modern Yemen, 1918–1966* (Baltimore, Johns Hopkins, 1967), p. 148.
7. Janice J. Terry, *The Wafd, 1919–1952* (London, Third World Centre, 1982), p. 9.
8. John Marlowe, *A History of Modern Egypt and Anglo-Egyptian Relations, 1800–1956*, 2nd edn (Hamden, CT, Archon, 1965), p. 217.

9. Elizabeth Monroe, *Britain's Moment in the Middle East, 1914–1971* (Baltimore, Johns Hopkins University Press, 1981), p. 72.
10. *Op. cit.*, p. 76.
11. I. William Zartman, *Government and Politics in Northern Africa* (New York, Praeger, 1963), p. 103.
12. J. P. D. Balfour (Baron Kinross), *Atatürk: A Biography of Mustafa Kemal* (New York, William Morrow, 1965), p. 3.
13. *Op. cit.*, p. 520.
14. Ludwig W. Adamec, *Afghanistan's Foreign Affairs* (Tucson, AZ, University of Arizona Press, 1974), p. 2.
15. William L. Cleveland, *A History of the Modern Middle East* (Boulder, CO, Westview, 1994), p. 209, quoting Michael C. Hudson, *The Precarious Republic* (New York, 1968), p. 37.
16. James Morris, *The Hashemite Kings* (New York, Pantheon, 1959), p. 77.
17. Majid Khadduri, *Independent Iraq, 1932–1958*, 2nd edn (London, OUP, 1960), p. 4.
18. Mary C. Wilson, *King Abdullah, Britain, and the Making of Jordan* (London, OUP, 1987), p. 123.
19. Jacob C. Hurewitz, *The Struggle for Palestine* (New York, Norton, 1950), p. 17.
20. Isaiah Friedman, *The Question of Palestine, 1914–1918*, 2nd edn (New Brunswick, NJ, Transaction, 1992). lxii.
21. D. Edward Knox, *The Making of a New Eastern Question* (Washington, Catholic University of America Press, 1981), p. 125.
22. Hurewitz, *Struggle*, p. 19; Knox, *Eastern Question*, p. 153.
23. Avi Shlaim, *Collusion across the Jordan* (New York, Columbia University Press, 1988), p. 13.
24. Janice J. Terry, 'Israel's Policy toward the Arab States', in Ibrahim Abu-Lughod, ed., *The Transformation of Palestine* (Evanston, IL, Northwestern University Press, 1971), pp. 338–9.
25. David Fromkin, *A Peace to End All Peace: Creating the Modern Middle East, 1914–1922* (New York, Holt, 1989), p. 294.
26. Porter, *Lion's Share*, p. 276.
27. Walter Laqueur, *A History of Zionism* (New York, Holt Rinehart & Winston, 1972), pp. 209, 247.
28. W. T. Mallison, Jr, 'The Balfour Declaration', in Abu-Lughod, *Transformation*, pp. 80–1; Friedmann, *Question*, p. 315.
29. Laqueur, *Zionism*, p. 451.
30. Hurewitz, *Struggle*, p. 37.
31. Shlaim, *Collusion*, p. 5.
32. Hurewitz, Struggle, p. 27; Christopher Sykes, *Crossroads to Israel* (Bloomington, IN, University of Indiana Press, 1973 edn), p. 136.
33. Shlaim, *Collusion*, p. 72.
34. Wilson, *King Abdullah*, p. 145.

CHAPTER

10

EAST ASIA

The Asian act of the interwar imperial drama was especially intricate, an unstable mixture whose climax was a series of sharp explosions leading to war. But even in the opening scenes during the 1920s, the players were numerous, varied, and in greater conflict than they superficially seemed. Asia was an area of empires, not nation states, and much of it remained in colonial status, although not always to European overlords. Thus nationalism, spurred by the Russo-Japanese war, World War I, Wilson's pronouncements, Marxism, and post-war events in Egypt, became the dominant theme in most subject territories.

The largest of all continents was in some ways the most diverse. In the family of nations, Asian and western Pacific political entities encompassed most of the ages of man, particularly the younger ones. There were colonies at the political level of East Africa, others as actively agitated as the Middle East or more so, one lonely example of progressive colonialism as well as 'white' Dominions, and at the far end of the spectrum undeveloped (or unspoiled) tropical island groups in Oceania. The area included a few precariously independent smallish states, together with a very large Sick Man of Asia, subject to indirect imperialism as debilitating as that which had afflicted the pre-war Ottoman Empire, but its revolutionary movement and leader provided a model for others.

Asia was a 'backward area' in which the powers competed, but it possessed its own rising great power which joined hungrily in the rivalry and also provided an inspiring example to subject peoples elsewhere in Asia. Not surprisingly, Asianism developed, stressing Asia for the Asians, upon which Japan capitalized. Growing hostility, both religious and political, to foreign rule and to rapid change from traditional ways, a decline in indigenous living standards as imperialists enriched themselves, and an educated elite receptive to nationalist and revolutionary ideas and impatient for positions of power added to a volatile mix. The interplay of these elements gave Asian history a convoluted plot line, exploding eventually into the climax of war and revolution.

*　　　*　　　*

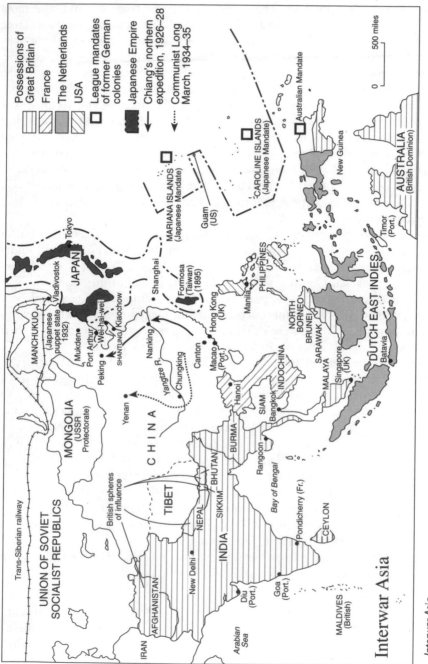

Interwar Asia

Nowhere was nationalism more directly energized by Japan's 1905 victory over Russia than in Asia. That was particularly true of India, the most populous of all colonies and perhaps the most restless. Here, a large educated elite spoke English and absorbed Wilsonian rhetoric about self-determination. The sub-continent seethed as it struggled toward self-rule, fighting not only for itself but in part for other subject peoples of Asia, the Middle East, and elsewhere. India breached the British Empire's colour bar by its wartime entry into the Imperial War Conference and its post-war participation in the Paris peace conference and the League of Nations, but it was preoccupied by its own struggle.* To the extent that it had a foreign policy, it was that of the Government of India, which presided over the world's largest Muslim state and so was more sensitive than London to Islamic opinion both in south Asia and in the Persian Gulf, where it had jurisdiction in British protectorates. It had similar jurisdiction on India's northern border.

Here three potentially strategic Himalayan kingdoms formed a buffer between India and Tibet, isolated by mountains and malarial forests, undeveloped and largely closed to foreigners. The largest, Nepal, was independent but provided Gurkhas to the British and Indian armies in World War I; the smallest, Sikkim, was part of the British Empire but semi-independent; Bhutan also was semi-independent but lacked much central government. In truth, all three were British protectorates, subject to advice in their external affairs by a British Resident sent from New Delhi.

The Government of India also watched Tibet. Like Outer Mongolia to the north on the Russo-Chinese border, its people were of Mongolian stock and its government long dominated by Buddhist lamas. Both states had been tributary vassals recognizing Chinese suzerainty, but China's civil and foreign wars from 1911 to 1949 gave them independence. Remote Outer Mongolia, cut off from China by the Gobi desert and the Altai mountains, turned to Russia before and after the 1917 revolution. After involvement in Russian and Chinese civil wars, it set aside its depraved and drunken (but holy) Living Buddha and in 1921 became Bolshevik Russia's first lasting satellite, proclaiming the Mongolian People's Republic in 1924. Inner Mongolia (so-called because it was closer to Peking†) remained part of China but subject to Japanese penetration.

Tibet also sought a patron but turned to Britain. In 1912 the Dalai Lama (religious–political leader) declared Tibetan independence but was in fact prepared to accept Chinese suzerainty (which Britain had recognized in 1906) with extensive Tibetan autonomy. An agreement to this end was arranged under British auspices but never ratified by China, which

* For details, see Chapter 7
† Called Peiping 1928-49. In 1949, 'Peking' was restored but became Beijing in the Pinyin style of romanization of Chinese names. Here Peking will be used throughout.

demanded full control in spite of its inability to impose that. Thus, despite intermittent Chinese military and diplomatic efforts, Tibet enjoyed *de facto* independence with occasional gentle British guidance from New Delhi during the interwar years.

British colonies on more southerly Indian borders were less isolated and so more directly affected by India's nationalist ferment. Fertile, gem-rich Ceylon was particularly influenced by events on the sub-continent directly to its north, but in Ceylon divisions were not only religious, as in India's Hindu–Muslim split, but also ethnic between Buddhist Singhalese and Hindu Tamils, plus a significant Muslim minority. Late in 1918 a Ceylon National Congress imitated the Indian example. It railed against Britain's few small concessions in 1920 and again in 1924. By then, Tamils had withdrawn from the Congress, ahead of similar Muslim action later in India. Events to the north continued to play a role, but Ceylon was more peaceful and co-operative and in the interwar years sought self-government within the Empire, not independence. Partly for these reasons, Britain decided to train it for self-rule and, to avoid oligarchy, issued a 1931 constitution with universal suffrage (the first anywhere in Asia) and semi-responsible government. This satisfied nobody, but the Singhalese hastened to prove their fitness to govern. As Tamils soon joined in, Ceylon remained largely peaceful and co-operative, with the ethnic divide papered over until after a smooth post-war transition to Dominion status and then independence.

On the mainland, Burma was spared serious ethnic and political divisions but was equally influenced by India, of which it was a province. Nationalism, stemming initially from the Russo-Japanese war, became bitterly anti-colonial, militant, and widespread when Burma was excluded from the reforms of the 1919 Government of India Act. In response, in 1923 Britain included Burma in India's dyarchy system and gave it seats in the new Indian legislature, which was not what Burmans wanted. Influenced by Gandhi, they agreed on seeking home rule but not on how to gain it. By 1931, they divided over whether to separate from India, with some fearing that separation would mean slower progress toward self-rule. By then as well, economic unrest had contributed to traditionalist rural political revolt supporting independence. Britain decided on separation, finally achieved in 1937, and gradual progress toward responsible self-government. But events in India continued to have an effect, and when Britain in 1939 refused to promise post-war independence, Burma welcomed the Japanese as liberators, only to find they were not. At war's end, Britain's new popularity was shattered by a tactless governor. His actions, together with the war's vast economic disruption, generated disorders until independence in 1948.

To the east of Burma lay South-east Asia's only interwar formally independent state. Prosperous Western-dominated Siam was spared colonial status so it could serve as a buffer between British Burma and French

Indochina, which was experiencing its own growing nationalist ferment.* It joined the wartime Allies, the peace conference, and the League, using these opportunities to end most restrictions on its jurisdiction over tariffs and foreigners by 1926, all by 1939. Siam was an absolute but usually modernizing monarchy until 1932, thereafter a constitutional kingdom. The change aimed at democratization but led to military domination. In the 1930s, Siam's foreign policy centred on protecting independence, furthering trade, and promoting Thai interests elsewhere in South-east Asia; to counter Britain and France on its borders, it increasingly favoured Japan. By 1939, a younger, more conservative military element was in control, semi-Fascist, more sympathetic to Japan, nationalist, and territorially ambitious. In World War II, this regime overreached greedily. Wartime Japanese occupation reversed popular attitudes and generated a resistance movement.

South of Siam, peninsular Malaya (Malaysia), South-east Asia's remaining mainland colony, had little national consciousness, for it was recently contrived and lacked ethnic, linguistic, educational, religious, or administrative unity. Muslim Malays, unassimilated Chinese, and Indians, Tamil and otherwise, mixed in a prosperous economy devoted to trade, rubber, and tin. Three geographically discrete straits settlements, including the island of Singapore (now independent) with a Chinese majority, formed a crown colony in which indigenous rulers, in treaty relations with Britain, were semi-self-governing. There were four Federated Malay States where Britain ruled indirectly through sultans, though British Residents held real power, and five heavily Malay but very diverse Unfederated Malay States, protectorates subject to British advice but less direct influence. The Chinese revolution and the pan-Islamic movement aggravated existing divisions. The Chinese of Malaya were Chinese nationalists, anti-British in the 1920s, anti-Japanese in the 1930s. The Depression led to some Islamic peasant rebellions with nationalist overtones, some left-wing anti-British Indonesian nationalism, and some Comintern-led Marxism – primarily among the Chinese. Nationalism among Malays, chiefly of a right-wing elite, was anchored in Islam and influenced by the Young Turks, Ataturk, and an Islamic reform movement in Cairo. It grew slowly but in the late 1930s achieved peninsula-wide political associations.

The numerous island groups of South-east Asia and the western Pacific, large and small, were directly or indirectly dominated by some imperial power. Of the largest single islands, north Borneo consisted of three British protectorates and eastern New Guinea of an Australian territory and mandate; the remainder of both were parts of the Dutch East Indies, where Indonesians engaged in an increasingly bitter struggle comparable to that of the Indochinese against France on the mainland. At the other political extreme, New Zealand was content as a British Dominion whereas the

---

* For details, see Chapter 7.

Philippines accepted rapid self-governance and a firm promise of independence.*

The other Asian colonies of note were northerly and ruled by Japan, the only non-Western imperial power. In 1895 after defeating China, it took Taiwan (which it called Formosa), off the China coast. The original aboriginal Indonesian inhabitants hated the Chinese and the Japanese equally. Like other imperial overlords, Japan brought law and order and development but also discrimination in education and employment, economic exploitation, Japanization, and heavy Japanese immigration as well as authoritarian rule, tight social control, and omnipresent Japanese police. Taiwan's standard of living was second only to that of Japan in East Asia; for this reason and because joining the chaos of interwar China was unattractive, the old tie to China waned. Still, Japan was resented, and a student organization advocating self-determination emerged in 1920 in the age of Wilsonian idealism. Japan liberalized governance somewhat, and a variety of nationalist, peasant, and Communist movements developed, which it quelled effectively. Prosperity and Japan's firm hand ensured that no organized national movement took root.

Japanese rule was equally firm in Korea, a rugged isolated peninsula historically dependent on China, which Japan forcibly made a protectorate in 1905 and annexed in 1910, though armed resistance lasted until 1920. Meanwhile, Japan blocked a Korean attempt to gain a hearing at the Paris peace conference. It was, however, taken by surprise on 1 March 1919 by an explosion of nationalism led by educated elites, who were both influenced by Wilson's views and resentful of Japan's egalitarian oppression and land seizures for immigrants. The unarmed uprising was widespread for two months before the Japanese army suppressed it. Thereafter Japan eased its oppressive regime and launched the 'cultural policy' of tutoring Korea for distant independence, but retained a large army, a vast corps of Japanese civil servants, and ubiquitous police – as on Taiwan. Even so, nationalist, socialist, and Communist groups developed both within Korea and in Korean communities in China, Siberia, Manchuria, and the United States. These lacked leaders, cohesion, and ideological unity, and were usually short-lived. Those in Korea were suppressed by Japan despite guerrilla movements, those abroad defeated by their weaknesses and terrorist acts in the 1930s. In the peninsula, Japan created a fine transportation and communications system, tried unsuccessfully to Japanize, and in the 1930s forced a disruptive, exploitative hothouse industrialization. From 1937 on, Korea was a military depot dominated by the Japanese army in a totalitarian system. The fractured independence movements survived, awaiting a major war to provide a liberation which in fact brought a new division.

* On the Dutch East Indies, New Zealand, Australia, and the Philippines, see Chapter 7.

Meanwhile, despite Japan's vigorous efforts, Korea and Taiwan could not satisfy its acute need for raw materials and for outlets for manufactured goods and excess population. Thus it practised an extensive informal imperialism in northern China, which it saw as its sphere of influence and a vital national interest. After the Russo-Japanese war, Japan had inherited Russia's economic and military rights in Manchuria, a base on which it continued to build. From World War I it gained Germany's concessions in Shantung province, retaining the economic ones. In addition, Japan engaged in economic penetration of Inner Mongolia and increasingly of other northern Chinese provinces. As long as Japanese imperialism remained economic, Western powers raised no objections, tacitly accepting Japan's sphere. When it turned to military conquest on the Chinese mainland in the 1930s, they delivered diplomatic protests but took no action.

*   *   *

Japan itself was the newest and first non-Western member of the great power club, though more a regional power. In the late nineteenth century it suffered some of the servitudes imposed in Asia by Westerners but rid itself of them by 1900. During the Meiji era (1868–1912), Japan modernized rapidly, absorbing Darwinian ideas of survival of the fittest in national terms and joining the West to defeat it in time. But cabinet, prime minister, diet and political parties were all weak. In the 1920s, prime ministers were chosen by the few surviving Genro, moderate elder statesmen from the Meiji era, in the 1930s by the military. In theory, the Emperor was absolute as well as divine, but he acted on the advice of responsible officials. Decisions were reached by consensus of key elements, including court officials, without debate or individual responsibility – so those whose views lost out could 'save face'. In Western terms, that meant avoiding humiliation but with stronger connotations and even more importance than in the West. The army and navy reported directly to the Emperor, not to the Cabinet, and the war and navy ministers had to be senior officers, who could bring a cabinet down if their military colleagues rejected a policy. As no cabinet could long survive defying the military, the army and navy held a virtual veto.

The Emperor was supposedly supreme in foreign affairs though advised by the Privy Council. The Foreign Ministry was politically weak, though somewhat less so in the 1920s, and foreign ministers were usually career diplomats with little political influence. Major decisions were often endorsed by imperial conferences and issued as imperial edicts, making them difficult to change and rendering Japanese diplomacy inflexible. In general, the Foreign Ministry favoured moderation, international co-operation, and concern for the views of other powers, whereas the military had a narrower field of vision and a more aggressive policy.

Between 1894 and 1918 Japan fought three territorially profitable wars, becoming an East Asian power, then a Pacific power, and finally a world power, at least officially. It became both the champion of Asia against Europe and a partner in the mostly European club of 'civilized' powers. World War I, which was its first involvement in European issues, was pleasant from the Japanese viewpoint: inexpensive and profitable, as no other power was active in the Pacific area. Like Italy, Japan entered the war for what it could gain, moving into the East Asian power vacuum created by the war and the Chinese and Russian revolutions. Its seizure of Germany's islands north of the Equator marked the first step on Japan's long march south. Russian preoccupation elsewhere facilitated consolidation in Manchuria and Inner Mongolia.

Japan also took advantage of chaos in China and the distraction of European powers to issue the 21 Demands to Peking in 1915. These included prolongation of existing leases in Manchuria, sweeping economic concessions, and clauses (dropped after criticism from the United States and the Genro) amounting to a protectorate, with Japanese dominance of the administration and police. As the United States did not act and European powers could not, Japan gained what it most wanted by threats of force. Chinese opinion and that of its Anglo-American supporters was outraged, but the British Foreign Secretary termed the Japanese demands moderate and comparable to what any overpopulated Western power would have done.[1] Japan continued to press for tutelage over China, especially in 1917 and 1918, with some justification in terms of the attitude of other great powers. In 1917, to gain much needed naval aid, Britain, France and Italy recognized Japan's principal interests in China and endorsed its 1914 conquests. In 1917 as well, the ambiguous Japanese–American Lansing-Ishii agreement murkily recognized Japan's special interests in China, especially in contiguous areas. The United States interpreted this to mean only economic interests and only in contiguous areas; Japan did not.

Like the 21 Demands, the Siberian intervention damaged Japan's international reputation and increased American suspicion of Japanese aims. Japan saw the disintegration of a European society, one it had always feared, and acted militarily on a scale ten times what the United States had proposed. But the venture was costly, very unpopular at home and abroad, and gained Japan nothing. It fared better at Paris, Japan's first major multilateral peace conference, gaining legal control of territory it already held and great power status, if not recognition of racial equality. However, it remained unenthusiastic about the League of Nations.

World War I also benefited Japan economically. Like the United States, it moved into the oceanic carrying trade vacated by belligerent European powers. As they withdrew from Asian markets, Japan's exports trebled, it became a creditor nation, and its foreign exchange and gold holdings soared. Allied war contracts spurred a dramatic and diversified industrialization, laying a basis for the Japanese economy for the rest of the century as mechanization spread from textiles to shipbuilding, iron and steel production, and coal mining, and from small workshops to vast factories. The economic surge brought urbanization, more liberal and democratic tendencies, and price inflation, as the cost of rice tripled. The boom ended with a jolt in 1920.

Though the 1920s were something of a liberal interlude in Japan, the strains of rapid modernization brought a conservative reactionary movement. Led by junior army officers of modest rural origins and anchored in peasant poverty, it favoured an aggressive foreign policy, and at home was super-patriotic, conservative, and devoted to the Emperor, whose wishes it presumed to know better than he did. Called the Shōwa Restoration because it rose early in Emperor Hirohito's reign[*] and wished to restore old ways, it opposed individualism, modernity, democracy, internationalism, the Occident, and the *status quo*. The Shōwa Restoration imitated the samurai[†] tradition, which equated compromise and concession with submission and defeat and which rejected discussion in favour of direct action. It took a hierarchical view of international relations, juxtaposing pride and humiliation, superior and inferior, and master and disciple. Samurai quixotically believed in risking their 'lives on one spectacular charge against the enemy' and preferred the death of Japan to surrender to Western domination.[2] The Shōwa Restoration of a younger generation of humble birth aimed at forcibly replacing the Western-dominated world order with a new Japanese-led system organized according to traditional Japanese values. Centred in proliferating secret ultra-nationalist and military societies, it was an undercurrent in the 1920s but throve on economic Depression and the reaction against internationalism in the 1930s.

The societal division was reflected in Japan's diplomacy as two factions struggled to control policy, the westernizing modernizing element, generally centred in the civilian leadership, and the conservative reaction, led by the military. Two Japanese leaders of the 1920s encapsulated this dichotomy, representing the present and the future.[3] Although Baron Tanaka Giichi died in 1929 and Baron Shidehara Kijūrō lived to be Prime Minister after 1945, Shidehara represented the present of the 1920s and Tanaka the future of the 1930s and early 1940s. Shidehara was a career diplomat, austere and urbane, rational and cosmopolitan, Western-oriented and non-political, both a pragmatist and a liberal idealist. He knew that Japanese prosperity depended on commerce, particularly with Britain, the United States, and China, and he pursued a strongly economic diplomacy focused on trade, industry, and markets. He favoured international co-operation, especially with Western democracies, negotiations, and compromise. As Foreign Minister from 1924 to 1927 and 1929 to 1932, he tried to stay out of

[*] He became Emperor in 1926 and took the reign name of Shōwa, meaning Era of Radiant Peace.
[†] The old military officer class.

Chinese politics, exercise patience, and use an economic approach to protect Japan's rights, largely respecting Chinese sovereignty and territorial integrity but seeking an economic conquest there.

Tanaka, a genial career soldier, represented the samurai verities and the coming shift from modernism to traditionalism. His anti-Western views stressed the Way of the Warrior and the Imperial Way. His 'autonomous diplomacy' as Prime Minister and Foreign Minister from 1927 to 1929 aimed at making Japan Lord of East Asia and perhaps then spreading its Imperial Way globally. His policy was intuitive and initially indifferent to economics. It was interventionist in China, three times sending troops to Shantung (which had reverted to China) and assuming that force would induce the Chinese to drop anti-Japanese measures. Instead, boycotts of Japanese goods spread, other countries gained at Japan's expense, and he was forced to revise his policy. Tanaka, who shared the samurai concern with 'face', saw China and Japan as being in the same family, which Japan headed. China was the inferior younger brother who must not 'humiliate' Japan, a naughty child whom the elder brother must chastise. His tenure left a legacy of Chinese hostility to Japan.

As national interests, not individuals, dictate the fundamentals of a country's foreign policy, the difference between Shidehara and Tanaka was less acute than it seemed, more a matter of degree, style, and methods. Some underlying aims were similar as both sought strategic raw materials overseas, feared the spread of Bolshevism, and tried to protect Japan's interests in China, including Manchuria and Inner Mongolia. Both focused on security as well as Japan's standing in the world. Shidehara saw diplomacy as negotiation and compromise while Tanaka viewed it as confrontation, but Tanaka twice curbed the army and ultimately altered his policy. Nonetheless, he anticipated war against Britain and the United States, wanted a garrison state, and sought to make Japan a great military power. He saw the international conferences, law, and agreements Shidehara preferred as tools of Western domination, and regarded Shidehara's policy of co-operation as subservience, relying instead on military power to challenge the West. Their policies toward China also differed, partly because Shidehara's first tenure predated truly strident Chinese nationalism in response to Tanaka. In his second term, he had little success against it or against equally strident Japanese nationalism.

There were also significant differences between Western policies in China and those of Japan, particularly in the Tanaka years. Japan had difficulty in taking China seriously. Western powers also despaired at China's disunity, but, with no vital interests at stake, sought a stable unified China with which to trade. Japan, with much more direct interests, tended to exploit the chaos, often using large loans to control China by bribes. All Japanese leaders wanted at least a trade empire there, whether achieved by negotiation or by force. Some sought more.

Japan's standing in the community of nations mattered to its civilian leaders. It was still seeking true great power status and the security thereof, wanting to be a great power and to act like one. At the same time Japan wanted to represent Asian peoples in world politics and be their champion. By its example and teaching, it urged an Asian consciousness but, as time passed, countered it by trying to be Asia's overlord. Japan sought in East Asia the hegemony that the United States held in Latin America and point-edly referred to an Asian Monroe Doctrine. When other powers protested its effort to dominate Asia, Japan saw a double standard and racism. This was true in part, but also a new code of behaviour had arrived after World War I. Criticism of Japan's 1931 seizure of Manchuria was no greater than that at Italy's conquest of Ethiopia. Japan had arrived at the imperial feast too late and, like Italy, felt unfairly criticized for trying to swallow the left-overs.

Japan had been remote from World War I and did not recognize that it was a great divide which had changed ideas of appropriate great power behaviour and imperialism. Japan had not absorbed the evolution in think-ing, at least about outward forms, and did not understand the new world order, practising the old diplomacy in the age of the new. Shidehara, Japan's leading liberal internationalist, called the League of Nations 'an extremely annoying thing for Japan'.[4] His French and British counterparts probably agreed but were too wise to say so. Above all, world standards had changed, especially regarding imperialism. The United States, China, and Russia were anti-imperial states, while Britain and France, with their huge empires, were now sated and frowned on further conquest. Western powers preferred that Japan's imperialism be economic.

Economic imperialism is admirable when conducted by one's own coun-try, deplorable when accomplished by a competitor. After World War I, the United States saw Japan as a rival in China. American interest in East Asia was sporadic, its attention elsewhere, and largely focused on trade. Its ideas had contributed to the upheavals taking place in Asia, but its policy was dedicated to the *status quo* there. Though the United States opposed further imperial inroads, self-determination was for Europe. It and Japan had become Pacific powers at the same time, and their respective navies eyed each other warily after World War I. By 1921, Tokyo feared the United States in the western Pacific, and the United States saw Japan 'as the inevitable enemy of the next war'.[5] Nonetheless, despite tension over Japan's Siberian venture, relations in the 1920s were fairly good, and the United States accepted Tokyo's Monroe Doctrine for East Asia within limits short of direct attack on China or the sacrosanct Open Door policy dating from 1899, which other powers endorsed, to ensure equal commercial opportuni-ties to citizens of all states trading in China, despite spheres of influence.

The greatest problem in Japanese–American relations stemmed from racial fears on the American west coast of the 'Yellow Peril' of Japanese immigration. Domestic political imperatives led to clauses in a 1924 American immigration law barring all Asians as 'undesirable aliens'. Japan was deeply offended at replacement of existing restrictive practices, which it had honoured, and at being classed with other Asians, to which it felt superior. Had Japan received a quota on the same basis as European countries, fewer than 150 Japanese would have entered the United States each year.[6] But racial hysteria in California caused Japan to lose face and to turn to pan-Asianism.

Like the United States, Britain wanted peace and quiet in Asia, especially as it now lacked the naval strength to fight there. By and large, it engaged in a veiled retreat, holding as much as possible but ceding secondary privileges to preserve trade, and trying to protect its position in India. Concern over Bolshevism was one reason among many to seek good relations with Japan, a former protégé but now a rival, especially in China. It hoped that Anglo-American pressure could restrain Japan there, but that shaky entente proved inadequate to the task. However, Britain's concern was trade and it showed little hostility to Japan until Tokyo's overt moves southward at the end of the interwar era.

Japan was dismayed in 1921 when Britain chose to end the Anglo-Japanese alliance, which it saw partly as protection against Russia. Anglo-Japanese co-operation against Bolshevik efforts in China in fact continued into the mid-1920s, a time when Tokyo feared Russia and Russo-Chinese agreement, especially if aimed at it. All Japanese leaders, liberal or conservative, feared Communism and a possible Soviet thrust to regain former Russian interests in Manchuria, where it had rivalled Japan. They could not decide whether the new situation created by the 1917 revolution was an opportunity or a threat, for Russia was temporarily weakened but potentially more dangerous. Some argued for an enlarged empire on the mainland to defend Japan against Russia. If Americans saw a 'Yellow Peril,' Japanese saw a 'White Peril' in Russia and worried constantly about the one power in the region capable of threatening their homeland.

* * *

Japan was small and strong, China large and weak. It had historically dominated Asia but was now the weary oldster facing an ambitious youth, as well as the encroachments of greedy but more mature occidental powers. It was not a colony but endured much of the misery of one, and in the interwar era was less a state than a culture and a geographic expression. Sun Yat-sen, key leader of its early revolution, declared, 'Whose semi-colony is China? China is the colony of every nation that has made treaties with her, and the treaty-making nations are her masters. China is not the colony of one nation but of all, and we are not the slaves of one country but of all.'[7]

China was spared formal colonial status by its sheer size. Britain, which arrived first and gained the lion's share of concessions, wanted to exploit

China, not rule any large part of it, and so avoided the burdens of administration by informal imperialism which was cheaper and which gave it in the nineteenth century a huge non-colonial empire in Persia, Siam, Turkey, and China. Here the system rested on unequal treaties which provided special privileges first to Britain and then to other powers. These privileges included treaty ports with extraterritorial districts for foreigners (not subject to Chinese law and not open to Chinese without proper credentials), foreign troops, and a Western-controlled tariff yielding only 5 per cent to China to prevent protectionism. As the system expanded to include the United States and France, Germany to 1914, and Japan after 1895, it was agreed that any concession one power extorted from China should be granted to all.

The treaty system, starting with five ports, existed from 1842 until 1943. Initially, China, which failed to foresee the potential impairment of its sovereignty, welcomed the segregation and self-rule of foreigners, so they would not contaminate the Chinese. The world's oldest civilization had a hierarchic Sinocentric view of the family of nations, which held that the Chinese and those under its cultural influence were civilized whereas others were 'barbarians'. Those in peripheral areas under its domination were to acknowledge the suzerainty of the emperor, kowtow to him, and pay financial tribute as an admission fee to the privileges of Chinese culture.

From 1842 on, the Chinese tribute system of unequal treaties was replaced by the new Western one. Vassals such as Burma, the Indochinese states, and Korea were seized by other powers. China was no longer the centre and arbiter, but rather the central target of the Western and then Japanese imperial drive in East Asia. Chinese attitudes remained Sinocentric in terms of moral and cultural superiority, but the treaty system grew until there were more than 80 treaty ports, some inland on rivers or at railheads. Foreign warships patrolled the Yangtze (Chang Jiang) and other rivers, and foreign powers could send more troops at will. In Shanghai, China's largest metropolis, half the city, including most of the commercial district, was foreign-controlled; the extraterritorial International Settlement had its own law courts, post office, police, armed forces, and Municipal Council elected by British, French, American, and Japanese residents. Like the adjacent French concession, it was closed to most Chinese. By 1930, war and revolutions also added to Shanghai's 3 000 000 Chinese, 30 000 Japanese and an intense anti-Japanese movement, 25 000 White Russian refugees, the headquarters of the Chinese Communist Party, and the Far Eastern Bureau of the Comintern, as China became a political as well as an economic prize.[8]

But the primary and enduring impetus for the treaty system was economic, as Western powers and Japan chased the myth of the China trade. Merchants were mesmerized by the potential market among China's millions. Indeed, its population swelled between 1920 and 1939 from 300 to 450 million as that of the United States grew from 105 to 125 million. But exporters forgot that China was self-sufficient culturally and economically, not needing or much wanting Western goods. Further, few of those millions had appreciable purchasing power and fewer still were accessible by China's scant railways. The interwar China market was stagnant, and unending civil war ensured that it remained so.

Though the China market always disappointed, it generated the unequal treaties which Chinese leaders blamed for all China's ills. The treaty system, with its balance of imperial powers, elimination of competition among them, and sharing of privileges, frustrated China's historic policy of 'setting one barbarian against another'[9] to keep them from joining against it. Not surprisingly, imperial inroads generated anti-foreign feeling by 1900. By then as well, China had abandoned its Sinocentric tradition and wished to be a member of the international system. It participated in pre-war international conferences but was not an equal member of the family of nations because its relationships with other members were governed by unequal treaties. Worse yet, by 1914 its modest government income was fully mortgaged to pay off foreign loans and indemnities arising from anti-foreign outbursts. And after the 1911 revolution, China entered into civil wars, often two or three at once, with the result that it often had no effective government or several.

Unlike Japan, China did not enjoy World War I. The absence of European competition brought some industrial development, but much of it was Japanese-financed and controlled and directed to Japan's needs. Japan also seized the moment, using a combination of enticement, coercion, and *faits accomplis*. Not only did it impose the 21 Demands, but it also provided massive loans, partly to keep China's civil wars going. In return China surrendered rights and gave written consent to continued Japanese possession of former German rights in Shantung province. Other powers, preoccupied in Europe, wanted to pacify Japan and so discouraged strong Chinese reactions. World War I altered the existing balance of power among the imperial nations within China as Japan moved in, replacing Britain as the state with the greatest stake in China. Germany's departure and Russia's preoccupation only reinforced Japan's position.

China declared war in 1917, becoming an Associated Power like the United States, in order to gain loans, prestige, and a voice at the peace conference. A delegation of the two main factions of the moment arrived in Paris with exaggerated hopes, thinking self-determination meant full sovereignty, territorial integrity, and equality. As reality set in, the delegates focused on Shantung but gained only an oral Japanese pledge to the Big Three in China's absence to restore full Chinese sovereignty over Shantung in the future, retaining only economic rights. Wilson has been much criticized for not accomplishing the impossible, but faced with British, French, and Italian formal wartime promises to Japan, China's prior written consent, Japan's physical possession in Shantung, Italian departure from the conference, and Belgian and Japanese threats to do the same, he had to yield. Because of the resultant uproar in China, it did not sign the Versailles treaty but rather a separate pact in May 1921, whereby Germany renounced all rights in China. It rejected direct negotiations with Japan, seeking as always to internationalize its problems[10] and in this instance to gain the aid of other powers against Japanese imperialism.

Events at Paris led to the first of many explosions of nationalist sentiment which affected Chinese policy since leaders seeking control could not ignore them. When word of the Shantung settlement reached China on 4 May 1919, 5000 students in Peking erupted into demonstrations, marking the onset of intense nationalism. The movement spread rapidly, encompassing a merchant strike and a boycott of Japanese goods, and lasted over a year. Contributing to its longevity were the Russian Revolution, with its anti-imperial creed, Japan's wartime efforts to reduce China to a virtual colony, and Dr Sun Yat-sen's existing 'rights recovery' campaign against the unequal treaties. The primary target was Japan, which alone seemed to seek control of China's core, though traditional hostility to Britain lingered.

By this time, China lacked any effective central government and continued without one until the late 1920s. Foreign powers recognized whatever faction controlled Peking even if it controlled little else. Regional governments came and went as civil wars waxed and waned. Fairly constant factors in the turbulent mix included the various factions of the Kuomintang (KMT) – the National People's Party or Nationalists – based on Sun's three principles of nationalism, democracy, and mild socialism, with one faction stressing the first and another the last. There were regional warlords, provincial gentry who conscripted peasant armies. Until 1926, Russian Marxism and the Comintern were influential; thereafter the small Chinese Communist Party (CCP) played a role. In the chaos, internal developments dictated diplomacy, and nationalism was the sole unifying factor as factions competed in the campaign against the unequal treaties. Bloody clashes with foreign troops in 1925 and again in 1927 in treaty ports intensified nationalist sentiment and led to more demonstrations and boycotts, especially of British and Japanese goods.

Clearly, Western and Japanese imperialism gave birth to Chinese nationalism. Its first dominant figure was Dr Sun Yat-sen. The most Westernized of early revolutionaries, he led a movement of elites but in 1923 entered a marriage of convenience with the Comintern and the tiny Communist Party of students and intellectuals. Marxism seemed dynamic, and hostile to China's oppressors. Russia needed an ally against the West, Japan, and White Russians whereas Sun's KMT hoped to use Russia against the West and to gain Russian aid and experience. Soviet advisers reorganized the Kuomintang, teaching the techniques of revolution and propaganda, providing money and arms. But Leninist doctrine was too Western to take root in China.

Sun died in 1925. Out of the infighting came a new leader. Like Japan, China had two men who typified its present and future, though in different ideological contexts and time frames. For two decades after 1925, the present was Chiang Kai-shek. Astute and ruthless, a product of the gentry and a military education in Japan, he was the first commandant of the Kuomintang's new military academy, whose graduates provided the core of his political and military support. In 1925, he became commander of the KMT armies; later, despite many rivals and brief exits from power, he came to dominate the movement. In 1926–27, he purged it of Communism, expelled Soviet advisers, and eliminated the CCP from the party. Thereafter German influence replaced Russian, reorganizing KMT armies and providing advice from 1928 to 1938, when Hitler ended the tie. An increasingly conservative Chiang turned the Kuomintang toward the right.

Soviet Marxism had failed in China (partly because Russia's China policy became embroiled in its own Stalin–Trotsky rivalry[*]), but Chinese Communism had not, though wounded by its expulsion from the KMT and destruction of urban trade unions. The young man of the future, Mao Tse-tung, took his tiny group inland to the mountains of Kiangsi (Jiangxi) province, abandoned the proletarian model, and refocused Chinese Communism on the peasants, who constituted 80 per cent of the population. Mao was intensely nationalistic, fusing national and class issues and seeking national revival along with recovery of lost territory and rights, but he also offered the peasants hope. He wisely focused on a few widely hated foes: foreign imperialists, feudal landlords, and capitalists enriched by ties to officialdom. CCP leaders lived simply without corruption, robbed the rich to aid the poor, instituted agrarian reforms, provided immediate benefits, and offered the illusion of self-determination for the masses, with whom they never lost touch. Mao promised democracy and a social revolution to overturn the exploitative class, rarely mentioning socialism.

The bourgeois Kuomintang, based on the educated classes, army officers, warlords, and unloved landlords, offered neither hope nor reforms to the masses. Such reforms as were decreed could not be enforced; there were good long-term plans but few immediate measures and talk of a future which never came, as the KMT lived from crisis to crisis. Mao's programme of national revival was agrarian Marxist whereas Chiang's stressed unification, restoration of national grandeur and lost territories, ending the unequal treaties, and recognition of China as a great power. This provided little for the masses, with whom the KMT lost contact as its reforming zeal evaporated.

Chiang was determined to unify China. In 1926, he launched the Northern Expedition, conquering south China in two months and moving

---

* Lenin's death in 1924 led to a power struggle, won by Stalin in 1927.

north. Unification was nominally completed by capture of Peking in June 1928, but warlords still ruled much territory, including Manchuria, in uneasy coalitions with the KMT government, which remained at Nanking (Nanjing). Unification strengthened Chiang's dominance of the Kuomintang; continuing internal and external threats made him the essential strong leader. The new Nationalist regime gained foreign recognition and concessions. China had its strongest government since 1911, despite corruption, but one too preoccupied by domestic and foreign challenges to satisfy the revolutionary urge.

Chiang continued to clash with former allies, but his main domestic concern was Mao's Communists in south central China. From 1931 to 1933, Chiang tried to exterminate them but failed. A new effort in 1933–34 led them to the Long March, which trudged more than 6000 miles in a year and then on to Yenan (Yan'an) in the remote mountain borderlands of north Shensi (Shaanxi) province at the end of 1936. Chiang steadfastly refused any deal with the CCP until forced to it by others. He remained more interested in suppressing the Communist challenge to his control than in fighting foreign foes.

Other powers had only marginal influence on China's domestic struggle. The Western imperial states wanted a united, stable non-Communist China with which to trade, and so they welcomed Chiang's successes. Japan, which intrigued with various factions, preferred a weak China, as did the Soviet Union after its expulsion in 1926. Early on, Russia had renounced its privileges under tsarist treaties – which in any event it was too weak to enforce, and Sino-Russian relations were soon on an equal basis. After 1926, Soviet diplomats maintained relations with whoever held Peking while the Comintern fomented revolution. In the 1930s the Comintern tried to keep the Kuomintang from attacking the Communist Party and Japan from attacking the Soviet Union. Thus it now wanted a united Chinese front against Japan.

For Japan, as for Russia, China was a direct and vital interest. Until the 1930s, Japan concentrated on the Chinese economy, imitating the British informal empire, though more harshly and intensely. By 1930, Japanese outnumbered all other foreigners combined in China. They often served as a conduit to transmit Western culture, technology, and ideas – as filtered through Japanese perceptions – but contributed little to modernization. Japan's attitude toward China was partly pan-Asiatic, with a desire to lead China and others in resistance to Western imperialism, but arrogance, insensitive patronizing, and humiliation of the Chinese bred a hostile reaction. Though Japan was of a Sinic culture and respected China's past, it was openly derisive of its present circumstances. Above all, Japan was sure that what it chose to do was best for China.

Anglo-Saxons sometimes thought that as well, though usually less openly. Britain and the United States were content with the *status quo* improved only by a united China. London was grudging about concessions and frustrated. Winston Churchill, who as Colonial Secretary in the early 1920s was responsible for the crown colony of Hongkong, complained, 'Punishing China is like flogging a jelly fish.'[11] The United States on the other hand, moralistic and at heart anti-imperial, though happy to enjoy the fruits of earlier British imperialism, pressed for steps to end the unequal treaties – though it was not the defender of China it was reputed to be. By 1928, it had assumed Britain's old role as the principal Western power in China though American missionaries, merchants, and schools were more active than Washington, which was not greatly interested. It tried to avoid confrontation there with Japan and Russia, opposed new encroachments on Chinese territory or sovereignty, wanted its share in the present and future China market, and held its treaty rights while advocating reduction.

*   *   *

The United States and Britain also took the initiative to preserve the Open Door in China, solve the Shantung question, and create a new regime for the western Pacific area. However, the Washington conference of 1921–22 was primarily designed to end a budding naval building race which Britain and Japan could not afford and the American Congress opposed. The United States hoped also to extract Japan from Siberia and north Sakhalin, ease tensions created by the immigration issue, and aid China. Japan was reluctant, knowing it would have to concede some gains, but it needed American loans. Britain was eager to settle China's problems without loss of prestige impacting on its position in India, and to turn its attention to Ireland. And both the United States and Canada wanted the Anglo-Japanese alliance ended.

After much hesitation, Britain bowed to North American pressure and chose the United States over Japan. The expiring alliance was replaced by an innocuous Four Power Pact including France to avoid isolating Japan and to lessen the dangers of cutting it loose, but the pact merely called for consultation if problems arose, not for action. It was now easier for China to play the powers against each other, though at first it was too divided to do so, but Japan felt excluded. Its leaders had not spotted the shift in the power balance heralding American dominance. A disgusted Japanese diplomat remarked, 'We have discarded whisky and accepted water.'[12]

The heart of the Washington settlement was the naval treaty, which established a ten-year naval building holiday, set limits on tonnage and size of guns for battleships and aircraft carriers, and established a 5:5:3:1.75:1.75 ratio for the number of these large vessels (capital ships) permitted respectively to Britain, the United States, Japan, France, and Italy. Shidehara, then ambassador in Washington, murmured, 'Rolls Royce, Rolls Royce, Ford.'[13] Though Japan gained dominance of the western Pacific, the only region which interested it, both white Western dictation and the lack of formal equality rankled. In addition, new fortifications or bases were banned on islands west of Hawaii and north of Singapore, aside from Japan's home islands. Despite its far-flung empire, France was reduced to humiliating parity with Italy, but retained the right to build the smaller vessels it wanted most.* Britain's European naval hegemony was assured, as was Japan's in the western Pacific. This, plus the fortification ban, assured the safety of Japan itself and rendered unlikely any American military effort to block Japan in China. Japan had hoped for more, but American ability to read Japanese diplomatic codes revealed how far the United States could press.

China also was disappointed, for it sought equal status and an end to special privileges, but it misplayed a weak hand and gained only the Nine Power treaty, which was for signatories a self-denying ordinance with no enforcement clauses, banning future encroachments but not addressing existing ones. The powers thought China should reform before the unequal treaties were revised, and they assumed a long tutelage. Signatories paid lip service to Chinese sovereignty, independence, and ,territorial and administrative integrity; enshrined the Open Door; and promised not to seek special privileges to the disadvantage of any friendly state or its citizens. This last was meant to bar spheres of influence, freeze the *status quo* and brake future Japanese expansion in China, but Japan, on the basis of informal American assurances, interpreted it as tacit recognition of Japan's special position in south Manchuria and eastern Inner Mongolia.

Japan had kept Siberia, northern Sakhalin, and Shantung off the agenda but in parallel negotiations agreed to evacuate all three, retaining only private property in Shantung. Britain promised to return Weihaiwei (Weihai), also in Shantung, but only did so in 1930. In addition, Japan cancelled 17 of the 21 Demands of 1915; the settlement on 4 February 1922 was China's first treaty since 1839 in which it gained rather than lost rights. The Washington conference left China in semi-colonial status, as the powers did not wish to grant it full sovereignty, but it eased tension between Japan and the United States and launched 15 years of mutual naval limitation. Whether it created a 'Washington system' of multinational consultation and co-operation for regional stability to replace the old Asian balance of power so battered by the Chinese and Russian revolutions, Germany's defeat, and Japan's new prominence is a matter of dispute. In fact, the powers were slow to honour promises to China and quick to abandon formal multinational consultation.

---

* The ratio, arising from an Anglo-American assault on the French position, preserved France's naval weakness and inability to reach much of its empire in wartime but maintained its ability to operate against Italy in the Mediterranean.

However, they did hold two meetings in Peking in 1925–26 to address the Chinese tariff and the question of extraterritoriality, as promised in Washington. The tariff conference ended abruptly when the Chinese 'government' was overthrown, but its draft report resulted in grant of tariff autonomy to China as of 1 January 1929. The commission on extraterritoriality opposed abolition until China completed judicial reforms, which were impossible in the existing chaos, with no national judicial system. Though the report brought no change, it implied a future end to extraterritoriality after reform. In fact, between 1921 and 1931, ten states concluded treaties with China without extraterritoriality, and others indicated willingness to end it if all powers did so.

The Chinese 'rights recovery' movement to end the unequal treaties made steady progress until 1931, when Japanese aggression gave China and Western powers a reason to retain Western concessions there. Chinese actions and attitudes contributed to erosion of the treaty port system. Bloody clashes in 1925 and 1927 at foreign concessions caused the Chinese Communist Party's membership to swell from 900 to 20 000,[14] increased anti-British nationalism, and led many Chinese to conclude that Westerners really were barbarians.[15] Each faction tried to outdo others in demanding the end of unequal treaties and provoking resistance. The United States favoured loosening the system, Britain was ambivalent but needed an end to boycotts which hurt its trade, and Japan was reluctantly amenable in the Shidehara years. Some cessions to China arose from fear of Soviet imperialism, desire to block Japan, and Chiang's military success. Thus Britain relinquished several concessions, and other powers did as well. In the interwar era, the number of leased areas steadily shrank, though foreign powers still stationed troops and warships in China. Nonetheless, the treaty system was crumbling.

So was Shidehara's control of Japanese foreign policy. In 1927, his refusal to let Japanese units join a Western bombardment of Nanking during a clash there meant such loss of face that the unit commander committed suicide and military leaders in Tokyo worked for Shidehara's downfall. When Tanaka sent troops to Shantung in 1928 for a small war with China, Shidehara's patient efforts were undone as Japan began to replace Britain as the primary target of Chinese nationalism. In addition, Chiang's Northern Expedition increasingly formed a potential barrier to Japanese expansion. Tokyo wished to deal with him, provided he co-operated with Japanese policies, which he did not. From 1928 on, Sino-Japanese relations were tense.

By 1927 as well, Japan sensed an impending clash with the United States, despite its dependence on the American market, which took 40 per cent of its exports. Japan was slow to see that the United States, now the most influential power in China, opposed the old imperialism, though wanting to retain its benefits. By the end of the 1920s American diplomacy had become more active, seeking a strong man to pull China together and thus trying to strengthen Chiang. Beyond Japanese–American disagreements over China lay continuing tension about naval questions as Japan built heavy cruisers, not covered by the Washington treaty, and the United States did not.

In Geneva in 1927, an ill-prepared conference tried to arrive at limits for cruisers and auxiliary ships. The conference was complicated by lack of agreed yardsticks, the absence of France and Italy (who could affect the European balance of naval power), and disagreements of the three powers present each with the other two. Japan, which was in financial crisis and could not afford a naval race, tried to mediate between Britain and the United States, but the conference failed. Thereafter a struggle occurred within naval circles in Japan which marked the divide between its relatively internationalist diplomacy of the 1920s and its more militant future.

After careful preparation and the arrival of new leaders less scarred by the past in all three principal countries, the five major naval powers tried again in London in 1930. They extended the holiday on capital ship construction to 1936, agreed to scrap some ships, and limited the use and size of submarines. The main dispute was over retaining the existing ratio (5:3 or 10:6) in all categories or ceding Japan 10:7 in heavy cruisers. What was at stake was whether Japan would be secure in its home islands or whether the United States could mount a naval offensive in Japanese waters. American leaders rightly assumed that Japan, again facing financial problems, would have to bow to an Anglo-American united front but did not realize how precarious its Cabinet was. The final arrangement was a virtual 10:7 under the appearance of 10:6 for the duration of the treaty (to 1936) as Washington agreed to defer construction of three ships. Tokyo thought its hegemony in the western Pacific was weakened; Japanese bitterness had the effect of undermining the 1922 Washington settlement, which constituted the basic international law for the Pacific area.

There ensued a five-month battle in Japan over ratification, since naval leaders claimed the Cabinet's approval of the treaty violated the Emperor's right of supreme command and their own control of military issues. As a bitter political and constitutional battle loomed, a split among the admirals and the deftness of the prime minister of the moment saved the treaty, but at a high price. He was shot in the first of many attacks on politicians and died a lingering death; several admirals resigned; the moderates, civilian and naval, were severely weakened and support swelled for military control of military matters; the Diet was excluded from foreign policy; and political unrest grew. Approval of another naval limitation treaty was unlikely. In fact, the 1930 treaty was the last success of Japan's liberal internationalists as ultra-nationalist sentiment triumphed.

Indeed, 1931 saw the first effort at an army coup, the first effort to assassinate the finance minister (who was killed in 1932), and movement of extremists into key positions in the army in Manchuria and Tokyo. By then, Japan was deep in economic depression. Suffering was acute in rural areas, stronghold of conservative ultra-nationalists, and led to agitation from the right, the left being in prison. Discipline in the army was deteriorating as junior officers intrigued with civilian extremists, formed secret societies, and pressed their more moderate superiors for an aggressive policy independent of the Cabinet. A new generation was taking over; younger field grade officers dominated the military bureaucracy and the Kwantung (Guantong, Kantō) army in Manchuria, which was becoming autonomous for neither the civilians nor the military in Tokyo could control it.

Manchuria, which had been part of China since 1644 but not under its effective control in recent years, was both Japan's frontier with Russian Communism and its 'special interest'. But in March 1931, an American diplomat noted that 'Manchuria is becoming more Chinese every day . . .'.[16] That was the difficulty from Japan's viewpoint. Chiang and his Manchurian warlord ally were seeking real control of the region, whose people were mainly Chinese despite Japanese and Korean settlers. China viewed it as part of China and as a buffer against Russian or Japanese invasion. Tokyo also saw it as a buffer against the Soviets but not as part of China. As the KMT ignored existing unequal agreements, challenged Japanese port facilities and control of the South Manchurian Railway, refused consent to Japanese development, demanded return of existing concessions, and spread anti-Japanese propaganda, the Kwantung army became enraged, saw the matter as a face question, and decided to act, lest Shidehara negotiate with China over the railway. On 18 September 1931, without orders from Tokyo but with tacit consent of a few General Staff officers, the Kwantung army contrived an explosion on the railway as an excuse to seize Mukden. In the absence of resistance which neither Chiang nor the local warlord could offer, it soon overran the region, dealing a body blow to the 1922 Washington treaty system.

As Shidehara tried to undo or limit the coup, Western leaders tried to aid him and thus were slow to condemn Japan's conquest of Manchuria. But the Kwantung army ignored orders from Tokyo, and the Cabinet soon lost hope of controlling the situation, especially since the conquest was immensely popular in Japan. Only the Emperor and his advisers, business leaders, and the Cabinet stood apart from nearly universal applause, including that of pro-Western liberals. As China refused to negotiate from a position of weakness and took the matter to the League of Nations, the Cabinet resigned. The long diplomatic crisis which ensued* signalled the end of Japan's co-operation with the West. The curtain fell on Shidehara and his internationalist diplomacy, on primarily economic penetration of China, on the attempt at party government in Tokyo, and on Japan's effort to integrate itself into the occidental world system. When the curtain rose again on Asia, the next act of the drama brought one scene of crisis after another.

---

* For the diplomacy of the Manchurian crisis, see Chapter 15.

◆ **Notes to Chapter 10**

1. Kajima Morinosuke, *The Emergence of Japan as a World Power* (Tokyo, Tuttle, 1968), p. 66; Malcolm D. Kennedy, *The Estrangement of Great Britain and Japan, 1917–35* (Berkeley, University of California Press, 1969), p. 42.
2. Bamba Nobuya, *Japanese Diplomacy in a Dilemma* (Vancouver, University of British Columbia Press, 1972), p. 369.
3. Much has been written about both Shidehara and Tanaka, but Bamba (*op. cit.*) elaborates the juxtaposition in detail.
4. Sydney Gifford, *Japan among the Powers, 1890–1990* (New Haven, YUP, 1994), p. 57.
5. *Ibid.*, p. 59.
6. Robert A. Scalapino, 'The United States and Japan', in Willard L. Thorp, ed., *The United States and the Far East*, 2nd edn (Englewood Cliffs, NJ, Prentice Hall, 1962), p. 23.
7. Richard W. Van Alstyne, *The United States and East Asia* (New York, Norton, 1973), p. 116.
8. F. W. Deakin and G. R. Storry, *The Case of Richard Sorge* (New York, Harper & Row, 1966), p. 79; Parks Coble, *Facing Japan: Chinese Politics and Japanese Imperialism, 1931–1937* (Cambridge, MA, HUP, 1991), p. 39.
9. Kennedy, *Estrangement*, p. 90.
10. For a later period, this concept is elaborated in Sun You-li, *China and the Origins of the Pacific War, 1931–1941* (New York, St Martin's Press, 1993).
11. Wm Roger Louis, 'Hong Kong: The Critical Phase, 1945–1949', *The American Historical Review*, CII (1997), p. 1076.
12. Richard Storry, *Japan and the Decline of the West in Asia, 1894–1943* (London, Macmillan, 1979), p. 125.
13. Thomas A. Bailey, *The American Pageant*, 3rd edn (Boston, D. C. Heath, 1966), p. 771.
14. Werner Levi, *Modern China's Foreign Policy* (Minneapolis, University of Minnesota Press, 1953), p. 182.
15. *Op. cit.*, pp. 191–2.
16. Warren I. Cohen, *America's Response to China*, 3rd edn (New York, Columbia University Press, 1990), p. 125.

LATIN AMERICA

The remaining Western-dominated area was Western itself in most respects, though unassimilated indigenous societies survived. Latin America, stretching from the United States's southern border through the Caribbean and Central America to South America's southernmost tip, consisted of a sprinkling of British, French, Dutch, and American possessions and twenty sovereign republics. The latter displayed a mixture of independence and dependence, especially after the United States largely displaced European influence during World War I. In general, the degree of dependence decreased with distance from Washington. Thus the ABC powers of Argentina, Brazil, and Chile and some other southerly nations were genuinely sovereign whereas the states of the Caribbean basin were subject to direct American interference until the 1930s. However, even in the wings Washington's presence was powerful.

It seems odd that an entire region could disappear from the world stage for a generation or more, but Latin America very nearly did. Though they had been independent for a century and had solidly established cultures and institutions as well as sophisticated, highly educated elites, none of the states were great powers or centres of heavy industry, nor had any of them spent their independent years in geographic proximity to the European powers which had long dominated the world. Thus, in the sense of comparative global power and world diplomacy, if not others, the larger, more mature of the twenty republics were still evolving, still students off at university learning the adult world and making cameo appearances at holidays. Their smaller sisters scampered on stage from time to time for spankings by a clucking United States to mounting Latin protest against such heavy-handed discipline. Other states were largely content to remain offstage, unseen and unheard more often than not, pursuing relatively little foreign policy.

This less than fully amplified region, diplomatically speaking, was twice the size of Europe, 8 million square miles (over 20 million km^2), much of it in the southern hemisphere, geographically distant from the world's centres of power and not heavily involved in most of the leading international issues of the era, but it shared the nationalism and anti-imperialism of

Africa, Asia, and the Middle East. The fact that in Latin America the states were independent only deepened resentment at foreign meddling, mostly by the United States. The region's population in 1939 was about 125 million, nearly half in the vast state of Brazil. Not all of Latin American was Latin or Hispanic. In South America, the three Guianas, British (Guyana), Dutch, and French, wedged on the Atlantic coast between Venezuela and Brazil, each officially spoke the colonial power's tongue, as did Caribbean islands of these nations and the United States, British Honduras (Belize), and the American leasehold of the Panama Canal Zone. Between the wars, Latin America received much immigration from Europe and Japan, often unassimilated in separate settlements. For the rest, Haiti was Francophone, and Brazil spoke Portuguese. Everywhere else, Spanish dominated, though American Indian languages were numerous.

The racial mix was equally varied, consisting of white, black (originally slaves), American Indian, and mixtures. Where indigenous cultures were highly developed, early Spanish rulers co-opted the Indians; elsewhere disease destroyed many, and greater resistance brought higher casualties of conquest. Thus the distribution was uneven. The region had a caste system but no formal colour bar. As a result, mestizos (white/Indian), mulattos (black/white), and zambos (black/Indian) were common. Haiti was mostly black, Uruguay mostly white, Bolivia mainly Indian, Honduras mostly mestizo. In general, whites were on top, blacks at the bottom of the caste system. Everywhere, the lightest skins ruled, in Haiti mulattos, in Bolivia and elsewhere a small white elite.

Most of Latin America had the remnants of an oligarchic society, made up mostly of small elites, tiny middle classes, and the masses, chiefly rural until the late 1930s. Elites consisted usually of land-holding 'old' families, the military bureaucracy (in which ambitious young men of middle-class origins could rise), and sometimes the hierarchy of the Roman Catholic Church. Colonial vestiges remained in vast estates and debt peonage, a form of servitude. Illiteracy was high, the standard of living low for most. Some countries were very poor, others prosperous.

North and South America shared an anti-colonial heritage; in theory they also had similar political institutions and ideologies, but the practice was very different. Latin America had little tradition of two-party democracy. An alliance of landowners and army officers often dominated. The region tended to constitutions which articulated democratic ideals but which were seldom honoured, personalist politics around a strong man called a *caudillo*, and military coups which changed the leadership but little else. Politics frequently were dominated by coups, *caudillos*, and *continuismo* (remaining in office beyond the expiry of one's term). Despite the appurtenances of democracy, electorates were small, elections rigged, and the opposition excluded. The politically important armies were trained by foreign advisers, often German or Italian. Many countries were politically and financially unstable, overly dependent on customs revenues for state income and heavily in debt, frequently owing in part to rash lending policies of New York bankers.

Financial dependence on foreign capital, especially British and American, was the norm. Britain was the old economically dominant power, the United States the new, moving in as London had to liquidate assets to pay for World War I and gradually reaching primacy in the 1920s. Some states were not extensively developed beyond primary economic activity: farming of one or two cash crops, ranching, forestry, and extractive activities. Despite climatic differences and local variations, including some prosperous states, this pattern prevailed widely, creating heavy reliance on imported manufactured goods, first from Europe, especially Britain, then from the United States. Industry tended to be light, for interwar Latin America lacked significant production of steel or heavy machinery.* In the 1930s economic nationalism and the Depression led to more import-substitution manufacturing to reduce dependence on costly imports as world market prices of agricultural exports plummeted.

Latin America suffered in the Depression, for of the less industrialized areas, it was the most integrated in the world economy. Already in the 1920s, some prices had declined owing to synthetic substitutes. A sharp new drop in 1928–30 as demand fell meant that Latin American states could not pay creditors, especially as new investment ceased. Defaults on loans became common, imports were curtailed, and nationalism surged, along with some Fascism,† an urban proletariat, labour unions, and a somewhat larger middle class. Hard times brought internal instability and conflicts with neighbouring states. Above all, they brought economic nationalism and a desire to curb foreign corporations. Earlier economic liberalism had led to foreign economic domination, which in turn led to pressures for industrialization, public enterprises, and some expropriations of foreign firms – all forms of nationalism aimed at greater economic independence.

Though foreign corporations dominated agriculture in some areas, they concentrated in the extractive industries. Mining, which employed relatively few but generated great wealth, mainly centred on Mexico's varied minerals and South America's copper, tin, and nitrates. Oil was a major new factor. Though only Mexico and later Venezuela were important in the world market, Peru also exported and several states could supply some or all of their domestic needs. World War I proved that oil was strategic, and briefly supplies were short. High prices in the 1920s led to rapid development, chiefly by large British and American firms, above all in Venezuela but also in Mexico. In the 1920s these firms enjoyed some government

---

* In 1939 Luxembourg produced 6.5 times as much steel as all Latin America.
† A right-wing authoritarian system created by Benito Mussolini in Italy after 1922.

support as they vied for control; both the rivalry and the government backing waned over time, in Washington especially with the New Deal's advent in 1933. Oil companies wanted political stability and so preferred to deal with *caudillos*; they also enjoyed highly favourable contracts, which in the 1930s gave rise to pressures for renegotiation as world conditions and Venezuela's rapid development led to an oil glut, low prices, and stronger forms of economic nationalism. Already in 1922, Argentina created the world's first state oil company to exploit part of its reserves. In March 1937, landlocked Bolivia, which had oil but no way to export it, without warning seized Standard Oil's holdings, which were of little value. Fearing to drive Bolivia into the arms of Nazi Germany, Washington admitted the right of expropriation and opted for quiet negotiation, which eventually produced token compensation. However, Bolivia's action provided the precedent for Mexico's more controversial and significant expropriation a year later.

*   *   *

Despite their dependence on foreign corporations and world trade, many Latin American states engaged in relatively little diplomatic activity of real global import. Most diplomatic ties were with Britain and the United States, the old dominant power and the new, or with Europe's Latin states and Germany. Latin American states had few links with each other, and little trade with neighbours, as shipping routes and economic ties were chiefly to Europe or North America. Relations with neighbours were often poor, thanks to boundary disputes over uncharted areas and the tendency of ousted leaders to reside nearby in hopes of return. Such diplomacy as existed often chiefly concerned trade, tariffs, and economic concessions. In general, Latin America early in the century was superficially but not substantially integrated into the world political system.

Until then, most of its states were not seen as equal by Europe's powers. Only Brazil and Mexico were invited to the first Hague Conference in 1899; in 1907, all were invited to the second, and most attended, but a Colombian delegate noted, 'the attitude of the Great Powers toward them resembled that of parents of the old régime: children at the international table should be "seen and not heard . . ." '.[1] Their tendency to sign treaties but rarely ratify them added to the world's disregard, as did geographic isolation. However, the changes wrought by World War I forced Latin America to face the world's power politics and accelerated its maturation in international diplomacy.

The war was felt in Latin America within a week as commercial and financial links to Europe were abruptly severed, causing trade disruption and financial crisis. The region was largely a bystander in the war, but much affected. Elites strongly favoured the Allies, for Britain was their historic bulwark and some already depended on the United States. Brazil and seven circum-Caribbean* states, largely Washington-dominated, declared war after the American entry, and five others severed relations with Germany. Only Brazil and Cuba made a modest military contribution. However, Latin America provided vital raw materials and food and so prospered after its initial distress. Economic nationalism began because the region's dependence was so evident, but profits were used in only a few states to diversify and industrialize.

The war accelerated Britain's decline as the leading economic force in Latin America and sharply increased American capital export and trade. However, the United States could not fully absorb the British role because it competed directly with Latin America as a producer of some agricultural and extractive products and, after the war, imposed protective tariffs. In general, the war led to replacement of the pre-war British-dominated world economy by a new one of less coherence. Further, the new dominant power was closer at hand and prone to intervene.

Eleven Latin American states attended the Paris peace conference and signed the Versailles treaty; all of these save Ecuador ratified it and became charter members of the League of Nations. Six more were invited to become original members. The other four joined later, some much later. Thus all Latin American states were members of the League at one time or another, though not all at once, for some departed before others arrived. Still, at a time when non-European members were few, the so-called Latin American bloc, which in fact did not act in concert or co-ordinate policy, made the League less European and more of a world organization.

The Latin American states, who had hoped in vain that the League would provide a counterpoise to the United States, disliked the addition of the Monroe Doctrine to the Covenant. Argentina departed for years over this issue. Though members tried to use the League to air grievances against Washington, Geneva pursued a hands-off policy in the western hemisphere, for the United States was not a member and little could be accomplished without its co-operation. The League rarely intervened in the region and deferred to any American desire to mediate. Latin America participated in the Permanent Court of International Justice, with Brazil and Cuba providing distinguished jurists, and held one of the non-permanent seats on the League Council from the outset, with Brazil as the first occupant. When that country made an unsuccessful bid for a permanent seat in 1926, no great power and no Latin American state supported it, the latter because they wished to maintain the equality of all states in the region. However, the 1926 reorganization of the Council gave Latin America three non-permanent seats which, from 1927 on, were chosen and rotated by an informal Latin American caucus.

Co-operation and attendance at Geneva was very sporadic, and dues were rarely paid. After Costa Rica withdrew for financial reasons and

---

* A term covering the islands, Central America, and Colombia and Venezuela.

Brazil did as well after its failed bid, half the population of Latin America was not represented at Geneva. As other states withdrew or stayed home, half the states were soon unrepresented. The difficulty was that the League addressed so little that was of interest to the region. There was a widespread recognition that purely American problems were to be settled in the New World in the existing Pan-American Union.[*]

Though some Latin American states lost interest in the League, they retained links to Europe, trying to use various nations as counterpoises to Washington. In South America, Britain and Germany reaped the advantages of greater distance and lesser involvement that the United States enjoyed in the Middle East and China. Though Britain was no longer dominant, except in Argentina, its influence was strong in Brazil, it retained an economic and financial role, and it held an important share of Mexican oil. A number of states retained ties to Europe's Latin countries, and in the 1930s Fascist movements in several states imitated those of Italy, Portugal, and Spain. Links to Germany were extensive, as both immigration and hire of German officers as military advisers resumed in South America after 1918, along with German economic acquisitions in Central America and the Caribbean. Especially in the Nazi era, the Reich capitalized on existing German settlements in South America; engaged in an economic offensive to gain food, raw materials, and trade treaties; and dominated civil aviation in some South American states near the Panama Canal. Its success stemmed from energetic efforts and Latin American hostility to the United States. This campaign slackened in the late 1930s as Germany focused on rearmament, but Washington saw a vast strategic scheme to gain client states at *yanqui* expense as a European war loomed and reacted sharply, displacing Germany where possible.

*   *   *

Latin America did not fear Europe, for World War I eliminated the last threat of European military intervention, but it could not dismiss its North American neighbour, for that war also established that the Americas were now Washington's sphere of influence. The war had spread its economic influence beyond the Caribbean, long its primary concern, and even beyond the Amazon River, heretofore deemed the outer boundary of American interest, as Washington entered into rivalry with London in a partially successful effort to take over the prior British role. As a result, fear, distrust, and suspicion of Washington deepened throughout Latin America, though no intervention after 1903 aimed at permanent control and Wilson formally renounced territorial acquisition in 1913. Many *yanqui* leaders cared more about profit than domination, but they did not wish non-Americans to control what they saw as the 'soft underbelly' of the United States. As the financial policies of some Latin American states provided occasions for

[*] See below, p. 232.

intervention, Washington assumed a parental relationship to what it viewed as Shakespeare's 'mewling infants' and 'whining school-boys'.[2]

In this, the United States was acting as a typical hegemonic power despite its non-colonial policy. Great powers customarily treat the highly educated, middle-aged representatives of weaker states as if they were small children, which invariably offends. American policy in Latin America was no exception. In the Caribbean, it bore striking similarities in some respects to that of Britain in the Persian Gulf, though American control, by Washington's choice, was much briefer. Nonetheless, its interventions generated as much bitter nationalist resentment, especially among sophisticated elites, throughout Latin America as did British policy in the Middle East. In general, the United States sought to maintain its hegemony and, in particular, to limit the British role and, in the 1930s, to eliminate German influence, especially in aviation.

Initially, Washington's policy had rested on the Monroe Doctrine, a unilateral American statement in 1823 that the New World was closed to further European colonization. Until World War I, the threat of European intervention was real, for politics and finances in the Caribbean basin were chaotic, causing defaults on debts to European creditors. In 1902–03, Britain, Germany, and Italy blockaded Venezuela, causing an American policy of intervening itself if European powers were likely to do so. In addition, construction of the Panama Canal led the United States to regard the Caribbean waters approaching it as a vital interest, where order and stability were needed, much as Britain viewed the eastern Mediterranean for similar reasons. Thus, between 1898 and 1920 the United States Marine Corps landed twenty times in the circum-Caribbean area. As a result, at the peak of Europe's imperialist Scramble, these small republics were spared becoming colonies though temporarily they were less than independent. Then and thereafter, there was relatively little correlation between American business interests and Marine landings.

Political and financial instability continued during and after World War I. Woodrow Wilson tried (his early Mexican policy aside) to avoid new interventions and reduce existing ones, which after the war conflicted with his message of self-determination, but keeping order in an area vital to the United States required intervention in Washington's eyes. Wilson also attempted to interpret the Monroe Doctrine as a joint policy of the region, though neither suspicious Latin Americans nor his Republican successor agreed. He declared in 1913, 'I am going to teach the South American republics to elect good men!',[3] in which the former professor failed. Wilson instituted a policy of *de jure* recognition, refusing to recognize unconstitutional governments unless confirmed by a free but not necessarily fair election. This well-intended but awkward policy aimed at ending endemic revolutions and furthering stable democracy but led to legal tangles and perpetuation of despotic regimes with Washington's support.

American interventions before, during, and after World War I ultimately failed, generating harsh criticism at home and abroad. Though the interventions were limited in area, all Latin America resented them. In the 1920s, Washington's policy for the region was formulated *in vacuo* without thought to Latin American wishes and reactions. Yet some landings occurred at the request of legally constituted authorities for good reasons and bad, reducing bloodshed and turmoil, and some circum-Caribbean regimes could not maintain order, much less solvency, in an era when government debts were meant to be paid. Though American business often profited, some effort was made to restrict exploitation. Administrators provided honest, stable governance and fiscal responsibility – until the Marines left, but seldom longer. Washington preferred stability to democracy, though it wanted the appearance of legality. While administering a country, it rarely insisted on fair elections, pressed social reform, or fostered economic progress. It replaced corrupt armies with well-trained police – who promptly seized political control. Its efforts increased irresponsibility as local leaders assumed Washington would solve their problems. All in all, opposition to the intervention policy swelled through the 1920s in Latin America and in the United States. Its most lasting legacy was Latin American hostility and distrust.

In the early 1920s, Secretary of State Charles Evans Hughes saw himself as a peacemaker and big brother to settle disputes among the small fry, as nobody else would. Latin American states, who wanted equality despite the power differential, found his condescending policy offensive. They sought to use the pan-American movement, dating from 1889, to undermine Yankee predominance. Its chief features were the Pan-American Union, established in Washington in 1890,* and inter-American conferences of foreign ministers meeting in one capital or another every few years. It was associated with 'Yankee imperialism' and dominated by the United States, which for some years after World War I kept political issues out of Pan-American meetings, thereby neutralizing Latin efforts to restrain it. Until 1936, the conferences dealt only with inter-American relations. The vacuum in which Washington created its Latin American policy was such that no connection was made to relations with the rest of the world.

By the late 1920s Republican leaders decided the use of force in the circum-Caribbean area was costly, ineffective in promoting democracy, and against American interests. Retreating gradually from a failed policy, they returned to *de facto* recognition of any regime in control, liquidated military interventions, and talked of a Good Neighbour policy, laying the basis for a new policy, with Republican claims of paternity. But Latin America was not satisfied, for Washington still claimed a right to intervene and had not signed a legally binding pledge to renounce intervention forever.

* Incorporated in the Organization of American States in 1948.

That was left to President Franklin Delano Roosevelt, his Secretary of State Cordell Hull, and FDR's friend Sumner Welles, who dominated the State Department's Latin American policy through most of the 1920s, all of the 1930s, and the early 1940s. Roosevelt himself was a charismatic personalist leader, a warm *caudillo* prepared to stretch American constitutional practice, and as he said, a juggler, willing to mislead to gain his ends. His predecessor called him a 'chameleon on plaid'.[4] Though disdainful of small countries and not much interested in Latin America, he was discreet, diplomatic, and generous, preserving Latin American dignity and trying to isolate the Americas from European events. He and Hull focused on Latin America in part because their efforts to play an active role in Europe and Asia met with rebuffs.

In his first inaugural address on 4 March 1933, Roosevelt spoke of a Good Neighbour policy in general terms. A month later at the Pan-American Union he applied the term specifically to Latin America, and in December Hull signed a pledge at the Montevideo inter-American conference that 'No state has the right to intervene in the internal or external affairs of another.'[5] Hull also offered Reciprocal Trade Agreements to circumvent high American tariffs. Latin Americans were delighted but wary, wondering if this policy would last and seeking aid as well.

The Good Neighbour policy was unilateral but ill-defined. Its key elements were renouncing intervention and ending the guardian/ward relationship. In return, FDR hoped to retain political influence and economic domination in the Caribbean basin. Beyond that, he aimed to integrate South America, Central America, and the Caribbean into one Washington-led bloc. He quickly ended the protectorates in Cuba and Panama and the occupation of Haiti, accepting Caribbean dictators as providing stability and safeguarding American economic interests. Though non-intervention was defined in a narrow military sense at first, Washington gradually eliminated most sources of hostility and provided the desired economic aid. Thus governmental relations improved though public opinion remained hostile and Latin American nationalism increased in the 1930s. There was no master plan and the Good Neighbour policy simply grew, spurred by world events. The public aspect received attention, as state visits became frequent, legations were upgraded to embassies, and an Office of Inter-American Affairs in the State Department launched Washington into cultural relations and exchanges, partly because Germany and Italy were doing so. Economic aid increased, and the United States financed some industrial development. But Latin Americans resisted Washington's view that if the United States treated a country well, it should reciprocally treat American citizens and corporations similarly.

Latin American states tried to broaden non-intervention to non-interference. Their efforts had some success, thanks to world events. An American historian has written, 'we were . . . no better neighbors than we had to be'.[6]

Certainly, the policy was defined to fit the occasion. But the international threats of the 1930s led Washington to be a better neighbour than it intended as FDR worried from late 1935 on about apparent German efforts to create Latin American client states. It soon seemed more important to please Latin American governments than to support American corporations against them, and the Good Neighbour policy became a security policy.

From 1936 on, when Roosevelt requested and attended a special inter-American conference in Buenos Aires, he tried to use the Pan-American system as a security structure for an integrated hemispheric defence, initially seeking a common neutral front if war broke out in Europe. Because Hitler was causing Latin Americans to reassess their opinion of the United States and because Washington accepted without reservation a new protocol on non-intervention, he largely succeeded. Henceforth the Pan-American system of 21 sovereign states was the world's only regional security system (brief groupings in Europe aside) until creation of the Arab League in 1945. It owed as much to the Good Neighbour policy as to external threats.

At Buenos Aires, where he began the process of Pan-Americanizing the Monroe Doctrine by suggesting it become multilateral, FDR gained a Declaration of Solidarity and a Consultative Pact to use if the hemisphere's peace were threatened but without any machinery therefor. In 1938 in Lima, procedural arrangements were added, though on a non-binding basis, as Argentina, the last bastion of British economic influence and intense anti-American sentiment, baulked at all proposals. But these arrangements sufficed. In 1939, American economic aid was enlarged to gain security co-operation, and the reciprocity principle was evoked for hemispheric defence. As war approached, co-operation increased, for the Good Neighbour policy and economic ties predisposed most Latin American states to accept Washington's leadership in World War II.

*　　*　　*

United States dominance was greatest among the small states of the Caribbean basin, and larger, more distant South American countries had more policy independence, a prerogative exercised vigorously by Argentina through World War II as it made the most of its southern position on a long, narrowing continent. This continent was dominated by its geography, especially the great mountains and the vast river systems. The towering Andes, the world's longest and second highest mountain chain, formed South America's spine, slicing it into two separate but unequal segments, a narrow western sliver and a broad eastern lion's share of the continent. Andean countries were effectively divided into two discrete pieces, scarcely connected at all before commercial aviation began to facilitate communication in the 1930s. Thus, not only for South America's two landlocked nations but also for the interior of Pacific states, access to one of the continent's large river systems was a matter of economic life or death.

Latin America

✗ Territorial dispute

✶ Major war

Latin America

The continent was drained by three great rivers, each with major tributaries and all emptying into the Atlantic. The Orinoco in the north was the smallest and least used. The mighty Amazon, the world's second longest river, was Brazil's great artery, while in the south the Paraguay–Paraná–Plata system was nearly as long. Ocean-going vessels could traverse the Amazon 2300 miles (3700 km) to Iquitos, Peru, providing that region's only sea outlet, and the Paraná–Plata system for 2000 miles (3220 km). Thus ill-defined boundaries in uncharted interior regions caused clashes between states if access to a navigable river system was at stake.

There were many uncharted areas for, upon independence in the 1820s, borders were set along colonial administrative lines, which lacked precision in the interior. Vast nearly unpopulated stretches of mountains, deserts, and tropical rainforests were impediments to travel and communication. Railways were few, especially across borders. Population centred in prime agricultural areas and cities, some large and cosmopolitan, where European influence was strong, though waning in the interwar era. Economic links were to the United States, Britain, and Germany in varying proportions, whereas France, Spain, and Portugal retained some cultural influence as Yankee culture increasingly penetrated. All South American republics remained Catholic and Iberian.

The largest of them, the world's fifth state in area, was Brazil, the only South American republic not Spanish in language. It had ten neighbours, abutted all other South American states except Chile and Ecuador, and provided arteries to the sea for many of them. An ambitious, well endowed nation, it became strategic as modern communications narrowed the world, for its hump was only 1900 miles (3060 km) across the Atlantic from Africa's western bulge. Most of its people were white, black, or mulatto, the whites including German and Italian settlers, and – after restrictive American legislation in 1924 – Japanese immigrants. Its fully developed foreign policy was oriented to Europe. There were large sophisticated cities, of which Rio de Janeiro was still the capital and São Paulo the economic centre, and a larger urban middle class than elsewhere, along with fairly diversified industries, none American-controlled despite much investment. The vast Amazon basin was no longer profitable as its natural rubber succumbed to blight and competition from synthetics and south-east Asia. Brazil depended heavily on export of coffee, whose price plummeted in the Depression, but it recovered quickly.

In the 1920s the oligarchy's control faded and collapsed when a 1930 coup brought Getúlio Vargas to power until 1945. In 1937 he became dictator of his semi-Fascist *Estado Novo* (new state) organized corporatively on a European model by interest groups, co-opting key elements. However, as in Mussolini's Italy, corporatism was more rhetorical than actual. Militarist, middle-class, and authoritarian, the *Estado Novo* challenged the power of the agricultural elite. The 1930s saw Nazi propaganda which the regime restricted. Vargas, who was motivated by love of power and Brazil's interests as he saw them, handled the Depression well and promoted more industrialization. His flexible foreign policy capitalized upon German-American rivalry for Brazil's support, seeking advantage from both sides and coping with pressures from domestic adherents of each. Vargas seemed Fascistic and some senior generals favoured Germany, but he opted for the United States, entering World War II in January 1942.

*   *   *

To Brazil's south-west lay the geographically remote Southern Cone of Uruguay, Argentina, and Chile. The three states were not a unit but shared temperate climate, low Indian populations, high literacy, more industry and a larger middle class than many states, and corporatism as a means to contain social revolution. They displayed strong nationalism but weak national unity. As they were more linked to Europe and the United States than to each other, they suffered in the Depression, though Argentina as a producer of diverse foods fared better.

As the richest and most industrialized state of Latin America, Argentina saw itself as an 'antipodean counterweight to the United States', but it peaked economically and diplomatically in 1914, when war cut off heavy European immigration and trade, and then entered 'a fitful decline',[7] its hopes of leading Latin America disappointed by Brazil and the United States. The country, whose land mass equalled continental Europe without Russia, had regular elections from 1916 to 1930, when the landed oligarchy, whose wealth lay in ranching on vast estates with sharecroppers, returned to power at the expense of the middle class. The army and rigged elections maintained this conservative regime until 1943 when a military coup brought in a more pro-Fascist system. Urban areas were politically weaker and the remote south isolated and ignored.

In some respects Argentina was a dependent colonial society, exporting beef and wheat, importing manufactured goods, and imitating Europe culturally. Its diplomatic relations with Europe were close, those with Washington strained at best. Its main economic ties were to Britain and Germany, though it imported from the United States. One reason for poor relations with the latter was that Argentina could not export there, for its goods competed with American beef, wheat, and oil. High American tariffs after 1922 and especially 1930 aggravated matters, as did a partial ban on Argentine beef in 1926 because of foot and mouth disease (and to appease American ranchers). Argentines also resented Standard Oil of New Jersey's (SONJ) role in the private sector of Argentina's oil industry. Governments were hostile to Washington and to the pan-American movement, which they saw as an American tool to dominate the region. Only heavy pressure pushed Argentina to declare war on Germany in 1945.

The smallest member of the ABC entente established in 1915 for the pacific settlement of disputes was Chile. Border disputes with Argentina meant it usually sided with Brazil in issues between the two. A Pacific state, it was condemned by the Andes to a long narrow configuration with the central areas dominant. In Latin America's context, it was mid-sized but waning, though it felt superior to its non-white Andean neighbours. World War I, in which Chile was neutral, sped its decline and its switch from British to American domination. A mountainous mining country of extreme wealth and poverty, it relied heavily on world trade. Copper provided half its exports, nitrates another 30 per cent. A post-war nitrates glut and cheaper synthetics hurt, as did the Depression, which the League of Nations deemed more severe in Chile than anywhere else. As American loans ended and exports in 1932 were 12 per cent in value of 1929,[8] Chileans blamed Wall Street and Washington's 1930 Hawley-Smoot tariff for their misery. Intense economic nationalism led to resentment and disdain, refusal of concessions or a most favoured nation trade pact, and treating the American copper firms as virtual hostages until the European market evaporated in 1939.

Interwar Chilean politics were unstable, including everything from a pro-Nazi party to a Popular Front of Communists, Socialists and centrist Radicals which held brief office in the 1930s. The old elite was weakening, the middle class small but growing and dominant in the army, which ruled from 1927 to 1931 and then left politics. The next 18 months saw nine governments as the Depression contributed to instability. The varied regimes of the 1930s did little for the peasants, more for the middle class, but a movement for greater economic self-sufficiency developed, along with lingering fears of American intervention well into the 1930s.

On the other hand, tiny Uruguay, South America's smallest independent state, did not fear Yankees, trusting to distance. Trapped between two strong neighbours which concerned it more, it played Brazil and Argentina off against each other to survive. A ranching nation exporting beef, lamb, and wool, Uruguay had little unity until shortly before World War I when a strong leader replaced regional *caudillos* with a divided executive; a political *modus vivendi* based on consent of opposing groups lasted until 1933. Peaceful, prosperous, socially progressive Uruguay accepted with aplomb Washington's replacement of London as the hegemonic economic power, but the miseries of the Depression led to a police coup and a mildly authoritarian regime. Uruguay favoured the Allies in both wars and supported the pan-American system, in which it was active.

Landlocked Paraguay to the north was neither part of the Southern Cone nor classed as an Andean state, though it faced some of the transportation problems of the latter despite being on key rivers. A bilingual mix of Spanish, Indian, and mestizo, its politics ran to personalist leaders in a fluid situation as the old elite waned and political strife set in. A sizeable German minority existed, as in the Southern Cone, and the army was pro-German. In the 1930s, German agents played on resentment of Yankee imperialism. However, Paraguay was a poor country with varied agriculture and limited exports since it consumed much of its own produce. The peasants were self-sufficient; thus, the effects of the Depression were limited to the few cities. For Paraguay, the crisis of the 1930s was not economic but military, as it fought the Chaco War with Bolivia.

*   *   *

That was true as well for Bolivia, the southernmost Andean state. These mountainous countries with isolated interiors were traditionalist, corporative, and heavily Indian, with a ruling white elite endangered by the Depression of the 1930s. World War I brought economic and some social dislocation, increasing dependence on the United States, especially for loans which created mounting debt. In the Depression, debt payments ceased, loans became a political issue as did SONJ, and American firms became hostages to threats of nationalization. As the world situation worsened, Washington avoided retaliation and issued new loans.

Some of the most irresponsible Wall Street loans of the 1920s went to Bolivia, including one for whose service it pledged 80 per cent of its total tax revenues.[9] A rural agricultural and mining country which lost its access to the Pacific in 1883 and still hoped to regain it, Bolivia is twice the size of France but in 1929 its population was only 2.5 million and it had fewer than 1200 autos.[10] A tiny electorate of Spanish-speakers dominated. Haciendas (estates) and Indian villages ensured a local supply of food and wool, but minerals, silver and especially tin, provided most of Bolivia's export earnings. In the early 1930s, profits dropped until Bolivia joined a cartel with other tin producers to raise prices. As debt mounted and earnings plunged, the oligarchic regime frayed, social problems developed, and American control of taxation arising from the debt became an issue, as did SONJ, which would not develop its holdings without an export outlet. The Chaco War ruined Bolivia financially and destroyed the political system, bringing it near disintegration.

World War I also brought dislocation and post-war Yankee investment to Peru, but it protected American investments, causing rising debt and concern in the 1930s about Yankee involvement in its affairs. Peru had a narrow fertile coastal desert with rivers, three Andean ranges with haciendas and Indian villages, and an isolated interior jungle. Coastal elites linked to the military ruled in a system of factions, personalist politics, a tiny electorate, and *caudillos*, but by 1930 the system was fraying as labour, students, Indians, and a middle class emerged, along with a growing Japanese minority. From 1919 to 1930 a pro-American dictatorship governed, and SONJ gained control of Peru's oil. Other exports, chiefly cotton, minerals, and sugar, were usually locally controlled but susceptible

to world market fluctuations. A 1930 coup led to instability, military dictatorship, and the rise of APRA (Allianza Popular Revolucionaria
Americana), founded by Victor Haya de la Torre, a student leader influenced by the Mexican revolution. He opposed foreign control, favoured
both traditionalism and reform, and seemed leftist to contemporaries,
arousing hostility at home, in neighbouring countries where APRA's influence spread, and in Washington. Outlawed in the 1930s, APRA sought
nationalization of land and industry, Latin American economic unity, and
eventual political unification.

The governing elites pursued a pro-American policy in hopes of large
diplomatic rewards in Peru's quarrels with neighbours but were perpetually
disappointed, which affected foreign policy. Peru was the continent's fourth
power and occasionally joined the other three in an ABCP combination to
settle disputes. Peru itself had border problems with all five of its neighbours, and was on poor terms with all but Brazil. Three of the four major
diplomatic/military crises of interwar South America entailed Peru's borders
with other states.

One of these was equatorial Ecuador, which suffered as the cacao market
shrank owing to African competition and disease. Other agriculture was diversified and mainly tropical. A smallish, impoverished country, its debt problems
were so severe that it was placed on the State Department's black list and thus
gained few new investments. Its interwar history was marked by urban unrest,
caudillos – civilian and military, and sporadic fraudulent elections.

Colombia and Venezuela are both Andean and Caribbean states.
Colombia, like Ecuador astride the Equator and mostly mestizo, is a Pacific
nation as well. Until an airline eased communication slightly in 1932, its
geographic problems were severe, for it consisted of a Pacific plain, the
Western Cordillera (mountain ridges), two large rivers on either side of the
Andes, the Eastern Cordillera, and an eastern plain, plus a dense interior
jungle. Mostly rural, it had high and low areas and thus hot and cold
climates and a varied agriculture, but population concentrated in the
healthier areas of the Andes and Caribbean coast. The chief exports were
coffee, bananas, and oil. As elsewhere, the United States displaced Britain
economically, and debt mounted, but exports rose in the 1930s as urban
states needed food even in a Depression.

Government was skeletal, resting on a tiny oligarchy and a small army,
whose prestige suffered after war with Peru. The existing political system
deteriorated as the lower classes entered politics. The old elites held no lasting resentment about Washington's role in Panama's revolution of 1903,
but a mild nationalist reaction developed against American economic and
diplomatic dominance, generating a successful effort to diversify export
markets. However, the United Fruit Company (UFCO), used to being a law
unto itself in Central America, attempted to evade Colombian law and was
threatened with expropriation.

Venezuela, astride the Orinoco River system, also concentrated its sparse mestizo population in coastal and Andean areas. Initially coffee was the main export, but as oil production soared in the 1920s, making Venezuela the world's second producer and leading exporter by 1928, agriculture was neglected. A single *caudillo*, Juan Vicente Gómez, ruled from 1908 to 1935 with American blessing, issuing oil concessions to British and American firms. They were unprepared for his death and reluctant to change as Venezuela sought a larger share of the profits. The world situation, Venezuelan patience, and State Department efforts (urging oil firms to build schools and hospitals and pressing for concessions) led to a 1943 law which set Venezuela's share at 16.66% (a doubling in some instances) and confirmed the concessions. By then, the national debt was retired, and oil provided over half the government revenues, but Venezuela still lacked political parties for fear of political strife. When Gómez died, the Cabinet selected his minister of war as the new *caudillo* who in turn chose *his* minister of war as his successor. The nation prospered and avoided serious disputes with its neighbours or other powers.

*   *   *

Relations among South American states tended to be prickly, causing many minor and four major interwar disputes, three entailing hostilities. Only the first, the Tacna–Arica question between Peru and Chile but also involving Bolivia, was settled without resort to force. An 1883 treaty called for a plebiscite, never held, in these two small desert provinces between the Andes and the Pacific which could be farmed with irrigation and in Arica possessed the only good port for about 300 miles (483 km) in each direction. Peru's concern was return of lost territories, Bolivia's regaining access to the sea. Both sought League intervention in 1920; when it refused, they agreed that Washington should decide on a plebiscite. In 1925 it called for one, pleasing Chile as the area was Chileanized. But the American generals sent to run it did not let Chile rig the vote, so it obstructed until Washington abandoned the plebiscite in 1926. Further American efforts failed, but Chilean and Peruvian delegates negotiated on a boat trip to the sixth Pan-American Conference in Havana in 1928, achieving a 1929 treaty which gave Tacna to Peru and Arica to Chile, with Peruvian port facilities in Arica Bay. It forbade ceding territory or building international railways across the area, dooming Bolivia's drive to the sea.* Peru's dismay at League refusal to act and Washington's impartiality led to lingering anti-American sentiment.

The only dispute not involving Peru was the bloody Chaco War between Bolivia and Paraguay with 100 000 casualties. It brought the first League involvement in Latin America, the first instance of one League member

---

* Until 1993, when Peru granted Bolivia port facilities further north and duty-free access by road to La Paz.

declaring war on another, the first League sanctions, and in the end the last League action in the region, all over the Chaco Boreal, a sizeable but uninviting wilderness of 150 000 square miles (390 000 km²), primarily Paraguayan but with ill-defined borders. Both impoverished, landlocked states wanted it, Paraguay to settle its growing population, Bolivia after its defeat in the Tacna–Arica question to gain a port on the Paraguay River leading to the Atlantic. Gradual Bolivian encroachments accelerated after oil was found nearby in Bolivia in the 1920s. Skirmishes led to incidents in 1928 and 1930, which the League tried to settle, though it then characteristically deferred to an inter-American committee. War broke out in earnest in mid-1932. Bolivia was stronger and expected to win, but its German-trained Andean troops were unaccustomed to low altitude, tropical diseases, heat, and humidity, whereas Paraguay's small army fought on home ground with much Argentinian aid. Paraguay held out, counterattacked, and in 1935 surged into Bolivia close to its oil fields but could not take them or destroy the Bolivian army. As both sides were financially and militarily exhausted, pressure by the ABC states, Uruguay and the United States gained a truce in June 1935. In the interim, the League, the ABCP states, and the inter-American committee had all tried and failed to end the conflict. Paraguay declared war on Bolivia; the League, the United States and Brazil embargoed arms to both sides, which did not stop brisk traffic by neighbours; after Paraguay announced its withdrawal from the League in 1935, the embargo was lifted on Bolivia, and Paraguay was sanctioned for violating the Covenant, though the sanctions never entered force. Then the League, preoccupied with European crises, deferred to the American states.

Tension between Argentina and the United States, Chile, and Bolivia complicated matters. Washington wanted the war ended, preferably without real problems with Argentina. Thus the three-year peace conference was held in Buenos Aires under Argentine leadership. The final treaty in 1938 gave Paraguay most but not all of what it held, and Bolivia gave up its claim to the Paraguay River. The settlement, which lasted, aroused bitter nationalism among young Bolivian army officers. To placate them and to obtain an asset so oil concessions could be used to gain allies at the peace conference, Bolivia had already in 1937 nationalized SONJ's holdings.

The other military clashes were much smaller but not insignificant. In 1932 as the Chaco War began, Peruvian troops seized the Leticia quadrilateral from Colombia. This empty little territory jutting south from Colombia proper, with Leticia the chief village and port, had little strategic value but made the country an Amazonian state despite Leticia's lack of surface transit to the rest of Colombia, which had gained it by a 1922 treaty. Peru acknowledged the treaty but sought to renegotiate it to gain the river port for trade and was astonished when Colombia sent a naval expedition from the Caribbean to the Amazon (where by a 1928 treaty Brazil was obliged to grant free navigation) and inwards to Peruvian waters.

Reluctant to fight, Colombia delayed but eventually began to regain territory, so a Peruvian flotilla set forth for the Panama Canal and the same route despite the difficulty of military operations by river in a remote area.

Washington had just completed its role in the Tacna–Arica dispute, was trying to stop the Chaco War, and was involved in two other border disputes, but everyone expected it to act. It had no interest and was impartial, to Peru's dismay. Brazil, Britain, and the League also tried to settle the matter. As FDR's inaugural approached, Washington's interest waned and it accepted League action with American and Brazilian envoys attached to the League committee. Geneva's efforts to find a face-saving way for Peru to back down were aided by assassination of that state's president; his successor, who knew Peru's military situation was deteriorating, was a friend of the president-elect of Colombia, whom he invited to Lima. Thus the League of Nations took over Leticia in June 1933 in the name of Colombia, hoisting both the Colombian flag and a League flag designed for the occasion. As Peruvian troops withdrew, Colombian police entered. Though the League possessed only the village for a year, this was the world's first international peace-keeping operation. A vaguely worded but lasting settlement was reached in 1934; as the League representatives left, Colombian troops remained.

The other crisis also involved Peru and the Amazon – or the Marañón River, as the Amazon was called above Iquitos. The area had been contested over a century with Ecuador, which was determined to be an Amazonian state. Despite efforts by Brazil, Argentina, and the United States, the Peruvian army attacked in mid-1941, scooping up much uninhabited wilderness against a weak Ecuadorean army, whose best forces were kept in the capital to prop an unpopular regime, and seizing an Ecuadorean province to ensure that Peru could dictate terms. After it gained its strategic goals, the ABC powers and the United States achieved an armistice in October. Pearl Harbor in December lent urgency and led Washington to encourage Brazil to find a solution during the Rio de Janeiro conference of January 1942. As Peru was in possession, it gained most of the disputed area, including the river frontage. Ecuador ratified the treaty, but border demarcation was not completed, and it continued to insist it was an Amazonian state.*

*   *   *

In South America, the American role, while important, was confined to the economic and diplomatic spheres. The small nations of Central America

---

* In 1995 a month-long border war led to creation of a demilitarized zone but not to agreement on the border. In 1998 both states accepted binding demarcation by the ABC powers and the United States. Peru retained its conquests, but Ecuador gained access to the Amazon.

and the Caribbean were subject to more direct interference. In the Caribbean, the United States owned Puerto Rico and the Virgin Islands and had effective control much of the time of the Dominican Republic, Haiti, and Cuba, encompassing most of the larger Caribbean islands and all key sea passages guarding the approaches to the Panama Canal, unquestionably a vital interest in Washington's eyes. The sea was not entirely an American lake, for most of the islands were held by European nations, but after World War I they accepted that it was an American sphere of influence.

The United States was a bossy but unsuccessful tutor whose bayonets did not instil democracy. Its security and strategic concerns came first, followed by economic interests. It sought order and stability to prevent an improbable European military intervention and to foster American trade. When the choice seemed to be dictatorship or chaos, it opted for dictatorship, however dubious, if it was pro-*yanqui*, in the circum-Caribbean area, which was its main Latin American concern. It saw this area as a single region, for which it had a single policy.

Caribbean leaders learned to gear themselves to that policy, to manipulate it, and to play to American opinion. However, coups, *caudillos*, and *continuismo* were the norm, along with debt, disorder, and corrupt elections. Washington's weapons included arms supply or embargo as well as non-recognition, which blocked essential loans and thus toppled regimes, sometimes causing rather than curing instability. American bankers were heavily but sometimes reluctantly involved at Washington's request, for when the Marines landed, the United States controlled customs, collected taxes, and reformed finances as well as running elections and training police.

That was largely true in Cuba though the intervention there from 1919 to 1933, unlike earlier ones, was not military. Cuba was an American protectorate whose foreign and financial policies were restricted by the Platt Amendment of 1901, which provided for an American naval base and permitted intervention to maintain Cuban independence and a regime protective of life, liberty, and property – a clause offering ample scope to Yankee interventionists. Their efforts reinforced the *status quo* in an era of change, undermined Cuban capacity to govern as meaningful Cuban direction of affairs became scant, and generated nationalist resentment of tutelage.

Economic trends reinforced anti-American feeling. Cuba prospered in World War I, but sugar prices collapsed in 1920–21 and declined again after 1925, owing to over-production. American firms bought up sugar mills and land at the expense of the rural middle class and investment soared in the era of maximum American interference in the early 1920s. In the Depression, prices for sugar and tobacco nosedived in the United States, Cuban sugar production dropped 60 per cent, and then the 1930 Hawley-Smoot tariff aggravated matters, halving Cuban sugar's share in the

American market and causing worse unemployment. The result was more anti-Americanism, increasing unrest, and hostility to an unpopular *caudillo* afflicted with *continuismo*.

When Roosevelt took office, Cuba was on the brink of revolution. He wanted trade revival for domestic reasons and used Cuba as the first testing ground of the Good Neighbour policy. He meddled, sending Welles to Havana, but refused military intervention, using non-recognition and economic pressure as tools. The result was short-term upheaval, long-term stability under a pro-American *caudillo*, and no real solution. Fulgencio Batista, whom Welles endorsed, installed his own regime with a puppet president in 1934 at the start of a lengthy reign (with one break) until the 1959 revolution. Washington recognized this regime at once and abrogated the Platt Amendment except for the leased naval base at Guantánamo Bay.

The other large Caribbean island, Hispaniola, lay between Cuba and Puerto Rico in a key position, able to block access to the Panama Canal and American ports on the Gulf of Mexico. Its western third was Haiti, the remainder the Dominican Republic, which was subject to American fiscal intervention from 1905 on because it defaulted on European debts. A Dominican revolt in 1916 led to Marine landings and then an American military government until 1924, with financial controls to 1941. This brought little change in the country's political habits and contributed to a 1930 coup bringing to power the American trained police chief, General Rafael Trujillo, a more lasting (to 1961) and totalitarian *caudillo* than most, of whom FDR, who honoured him with a White House visit, remarked, 'Yes, he is an s.o.b., but he's our s.o.b.'[11]

The other half of Hispaniola was the New World's poorest country, the least educated and developed, with a Frenchified elite and a dense population increasingly stressing its African heritage. It too defaulted on a large debt to European creditors, causing a sharp reaction. Since Washington did not want Haiti to become a pawn in World War I and it was in chaos and civil war, the Marines landed in 1915 just before British and French warships arrived. As Haiti was strategically located, they stayed 19 years, accommodated by puppet presidents to avoid military government. Resistance continued until 1920, suppressed at the cost of at least 3000 lives. Other forms of protest ensued as Americans ran finances, the police, and sanitation. In 1915, the American admiral in charge reported to Washington, 'Next Thursday ... unless otherwise directed, I will permit [the Haitian] Congress to elect a president.'[12]

As Haiti became a virtual protectorate, American racism intensified hostility, for white administrators resented the Haitian bourgeoisie and treated blacks cruelly. Atrocity charges against the Marines led to a Senate inquiry and dispatch of a high commissioner, a southern segregationist not sympathetic to ideas foreshadowing *négritude*. His rule was efficient, but Americans gained much land, driving peasants off and hiring former owners at low wages. In an impoverished agricultural nation, the Depression only aggravated anti-Americanism. Partly for that reason, a phased withdrawal began which FDR completed in 1934, ending the protectorate.

* * *

Similar American policies in Central America had similar effects. The isthmus consisted of six small republics, of which Panama was often not considered Central American because of its past affiliation with Colombia. UFCO* was sometimes termed the sixth Central American state, for it, smaller fruit companies which it eventually absorbed, and oil firms had much local power as well as often shaping Washington's policy. Aside from Hispanic Costa Rica and a black element in Panama, the region was chiefly Indian and mestizo, though a coffee-growing white elite dominated some states economically and politically until 1930.

Heavily agricultural, each state produced one or two cash crops, mainly bananas and coffee. As American investment more than doubled in the 1920s, Yankee firms usually controlled those crops and their American market as well as mining concessions. Since Central America was integrated into the world market, it suffered greatly from the Depression when coffee and banana prices collapsed. The agricultural system was often nearly feudal, with Indian peonage. Modest middle classes and urban proletariats developed but little industry. Elite regimes were politically stagnant, neither democratic nor very despotic except toward the Indians. The Depression eroded their political power, leading most states to embrace military regimes and Fascist tendencies.

The Central American republics aspired to a regional system, which Washington nominally supported while contributing to the demise of the Central American Court of Justice in 1918. In 1923 the United States dictated a new system with a powerless tribunal, a promise of non-interference in each other's affairs, and non-recognition of revolutionary regimes until confirmed by free election. However, Washington's non-recognition policy was seen as interference, so Central America reverted to *de facto* recognition in 1934. From 1903 on, Washington's chief concern was security for the Panama Canal. It intervened freely, financially, and militarily to ensure stable pro-American regimes. This costly policy produced no lasting results and generated hostility. Thus, from the late 1920s on, the United States gradually shifted to a non-military policy, training local forces to keep order, which contributed to the advent of military rulers, and from 1934 on, signing Reciprocal Trade Agreements. As a consequence, trade grew even in the 1930s and relations improved, though distrust lingered.

* Later renamed Chiquita Brands.

In Central America, Panama was unique owing to its recent independence in 1903, evident American midwifery at its birth, and the 10-mile-(16-km-) wide Canal Zone, leased to the United States in perpetuity,* which bisected it. Panama's two largest cities were geographically but not administratively part of the Zone, where the United States had virtual sovereignty in a system based on China's treaty ports. Panama was a *de facto* protectorate, less independent than 'an annex of the Canal Zone'.[13] By a 1903 treaty, Washington was responsible for the Zone's defence and could intervene in Panama City and Colon to maintain order if it felt Panama could not. Until 1925, it did so from time to time and sent troops into Panamanian territory from 1918 to 1920. Though blatant intervention subsided, in 1927 a Panamanian diplomat wrote, 'When you hit a rock with an egg, the egg breaks. Or when you hit an egg with a rock, the egg breaks. The United States is the rock. Panama is the egg. In either case, the egg breaks.'[14]

Tiny Panama had a small mixed population. Washington, which imposed racial segregation in the Zone, dealt with the elites, preferring English-speaking whites or near whites. It wanted stability but faced corruption, coups, chaos and squalid poverty, contrasting with the tidy Zone where commissaries prospered at the expense of local merchants. As the American political role waned, investment increased, especially by UFCO, which dominated the banana trade. Panama was united in opposition to the 1903 treaty, the commissaries, and its exclusion from Canal profits. It lost no opportunity to denounce its unequal status to the League and the International Labour Organization. In 1936, FDR agreed to a new treaty which ended the protectorate, provided a larger annuity, gave Panama charge of the Canal's defence, and ended the right of intervention, though, because of European crises, the Senate insisted on a rider authorizing intervention in an emergency. Relations improved, partly because the United States tolerated any regime not endangering its interests, but popular Panamanian hostility grew. Further, the Canal was approaching obsolescence because its locks were too narrow and it lacked any defence against air attack. None was installed in World War II because Panama did not cooperate until late on.

Costa Rica, Honduras, and Guatemala were all UFCO-dominated, though they produced coffee as well as bananas. Relatively prosperous Costa Rica, with sparse population and an agrarian middle class, avoided both *continuismo* and military rule under personalist, paternalistic *caudillos* elected from the elite. Rural Guatemala, with wealthy elites and impoverished peons, had long-term UFCO-backed *caudillos* ruling by *continuismo,* as did Honduras, the hemisphere's poorest mainland state,

---

* A 1977 treaty specified gradual reversion of the Zone to Panama, with completion and tranfer of the canal on 31 December 1999.

where military rule was the norm. There, a civil war led to a Marine landing in 1924 until Welles arranged a solution in 1925.

In densely populated El Salvador, UFCO's role was financial, as there were no bananas, but excellent coffee in which the economy was concentrated. El Salvador had great extremes of wealth and poverty, for a few families had controlled all good land since 1600. An American observer noted, 'There appears to be nothing between these high-priced cars and the oxcart with its barefoot attendant.'[15] Until the 1930 price collapse, El Salvador had the strongest economy of the region. It had long avoided coups, but the oligarchy controlled elections until 1931, when discontent with worsening conditions led to rebellions, including a planned mass upheaval of starving Indian peasants led by Trotskyite Agustín Farabundo Martí. Discovery of the plot led to his execution in 1932 and set off army massacres, especially of Indians. Thereafter, the victorious generals ruled to 1945, but the landowners retained economic and social control.

El Salvador was the smallest, Nicaragua the largest and poorest per capita of Central American states. As the only site for a second canal, it was strategic and thus under American financial supervision from 1911 to 1924 and subjected to Marine landings from 1909 to 1910, again from 1912 to 1925 becoming a virtual protectorate, and yet again from 1926 to 1933. Nicaraguan sovereignty was in doubt, dependence reinforced by export, chiefly to the United States. Marine administration was efficient but supported the minority Conservatives against the majority Liberals; state revenues went to servicing debt and reorganizing the military, not to economic development. At particular issue was the Bryan-Chamorro treaty, ratified in 1916, which granted the United States base and canal rights in perpetuity for a trifling sum and which originally included interventionist clauses. Though the Senate deleted these, Costa Rica and El Salvador brought a case against the treaty to the Central American Court of Justice and won. Washington and Managua ignored the decision, speeding the Court's demise.

Civil war broke out upon Marine withdrawal in 1925. As Mexico encouraged the rebels, it became a convenient scapegoat in the United States when a new Marine landing in late 1926 evoked American protest. In 1927, Washington negotiated a truce, promising to run fair elections, train a police force (the Guardia Nacional) to maintain order, and leave. This it did, shifting policy in response to American opinion and not foreseeing the Guardia's political potential.

One Nicaraguan who did not accept the 1927 truce was the charismatic Augusto César Sandino, a non-Communist revolutionary army officer with a sweeping social programme, who sought to end elite exploitation of the masses and American control. Immensely popular, he conducted an intermittent insurgency, vowing to fight until the last Marine left and notifying one officer, 'I remain your most obedient servant, who ardently desires to put you in a handsome tomb with beautiful bouquets of flowers.'[16] After the Marines withdrew in January 1933, he laid down his arms but was soon murdered on orders of the Guardia chief, Anastasio Somoza.

Washington's decision to withdraw the Marines was speeded not only by criticism and cost but by a failed policy and realization that condemnation of Japan in Manchuria was awkward while Marines chased Sandino in Nicaragua. Ultimately, intervention led to the Somoza family dynasty from 1936 to the 1979 revolution. To Latin American dismay, FDR invited its founder to the White House in 1939, terming him another Washington-owned s.o.b., though Somoza, like Trujillo, manipulated Washington skilfully to his own ends. In Nicaragua, as elsewhere in the Caribbean basin, stability and a pro-American stance mattered most.

*　　*　　*

Mexico had long seen Central America, which it ruled in 1822–23, as its historic sphere of influence. Roughly three times all Central America in area and population, it was the only Latin state to share a past war and a 2000-mile (3200-km) border with the hemisphere's dominant power. Its leaders were wont to sigh, 'Poor Mexico, so far from God and so close to the United States.'[17] It suffered from American intervention, notably Wilson's view that 'My ideal is an orderly and righteous government in Mexico.'[18] Propriety aside, that was unattainable in an era of turbulence and civil war. A 1910 reform movement spiralled into the New World's first real social revolution, in part against economic and cultural penetration by foreigners, and led to bloody violence from 1910 to 1924 and at least 1.5 million deaths, 10 per cent of the population.

External factors influenced the course of the revolution, though they did not determine its outcome. Other powers viewed it as Bolshevik, and Mexico was long unable to gain loans or service its debt. World War I affected the situation, particularly in German efforts to spark a Mexican–American war, and influenced Washington's policy as well. Mexico was not asked to join the League of Nations until late 1923 and did so only in 1931. Its interest in Nicaragua alarmed the United States and Central America. In general, continental European states left the convoluted Mexican problem to Washington after World War I, so that for some years Mexico's relations with the world were determined by those with the United States. Of necessity, its earlier internationalism was overtaken by tension with its northern neighbour.

Washington wanted order, stability, and protection of American lives and extensive properties. Circumstances in Mexico, Wilson's tangled non-recognition policy, and Washington's paternalism, indicated by Wilson's Secretary of the Interior's view that Mexicans were 'naughty children who are expecting all the rights and privileges of grown-ups',[19] defeated American hopes. The United States mounted two major futile punitive expeditions in 1914 and 1916–17 before its attention shifted to World War I. The war, with Mexican oil production soaring 600 per cent in six years, and stabilization of Mexico in the 1920s into moderate rule by authoritarian leaders, who chose their successors and in 1929 created a one-party state, eased tension and led to the first of periodic partial Mexican–American settlements.

American envoys played a role as well, meddling heavily among factions early on. In 1927 the financier Dwight Morrow replaced an ambassador so lofty that he would not negotiate with mestizos and announced, 'I know what I can do for the Mexicans. I can *like* them.'[20] He embraced them wholeheartedly and resolved much. A decade late, FDR's Good Neighbour emissary, Josephus Daniels, took the same approach with the same productive results. Both had instructions to avoid strife, but in between relations were bumpy at best.

A constant issue in Mexican–American relations was the Mexican constitution and interpretations thereof. In force early in 1917 before the Russian Revolution, it was then the most radical in the world and shocked foreign investors. Article 27 restricted the right of foreigners to acquire real estate and permitted expropriation of both rural property and the subsoil rights of foreign oil companies. Mexico was the world's main oil exporter, and 98 per cent of the oil was foreign owned, chiefly by American and British firms. Thus the oil companies took immediate alarm. In general, Britain followed Washington's lead on recognition and debt questions, but the oil firms were rivals, and London took a feistier line, causing severance of diplomatic relations in 1938.

For twenty years after 1917, Mexican regimes and Supreme Court rulings accommodated the oil companies without altering Article 27 or abandoning a 1918 decree that all oil deposits belonged to the nation regardless of prior rights. Oil had become the symbol of Mexican economic nationalism. In 1926 Mexican–American relations became dangerous over oil and Nicaragua but, from 1927 on, Washington – if not the oil firms – gradually came to terms with the Mexican revolution in an era of relative calm engineered by Morrow.

In 1934 Mexican President Lazaro Cárdenas created a mass movement and renewed reform. Oil workers unionized and struck, seeking a higher minimum wage. When foreign oil firms ignored a Mexican Supreme Court ruling in the workers' favour, Cárdenas expropriated oil holdings in 1938 rather than surrender to foreign firms. Thereafter oil profits went to Mexican development, not abroad. Though Washington joined London in diplomatic protest, partly from fear of setting a precedent for other nations, FDR conceded Mexico's right to expropriate and Cárdenas accepted the oil firms' right to compensation. For the United States, if not Britain, the issue was now how much and how soon. Washington backed the oil firms briefly, using economic pressure, but decided that security had priority over commercial interests. Constrained in part by the Good Neighbour policy, it ruled out force, ultimata, or economic coercion, and sought accommodation, especially as Mexico sold oil to Germany. In 1940, a small oil company broke ranks and settled, speeding a comprehensive settlement in 1942, largely on Mexican terms.

The 1938 crisis was the peak of Mexican revolutionary nationalism, which ebbed a bit thereafter. Its success owed much to the world situation, FDR's fears of instability or a Fascist regime, his desire for an inter-American alliance, and the fact that Brazil and Mexico were key to his hemispheric defence policy. As crises mounted in Europe, Washington wanted Mexican co-operation in Pacific defence and wished to avoid a hostile southern border. In those crises, Mexican policy was consistent, seeking sanctions against Italy in Ethiopia and both Italy and Germany in the Spanish Civil War, supplying the Republican government in Spain and taking Spanish refugees, opposing the Austro-German *Anschluss*, seeking League measures against Japan in China, denouncing dictators, and conducting its own foreign policy until World War II, when it co-operated in hemispheric defence. But in 1943 a Mexican diplomat voiced the concern of all Latin America in saying, 'We see the United States advancing as a giant, fighting nobly for our ideals, but in the degree that the giant grows, its shadow falls on us, and we are frightened.'[21]

*   *   *

This power disparity had long been Latin America's concern and so remained. Most of the hemisphere was precariously united in World War II, thanks to the Good Neighbour policy, Washington's efforts to pacify the region about the past, economic aid, and FDR's tactic of giving Latin America a share of the profits and of the decisions in inter-American questions. The 1936 consultative pact led to inter-American conferences as war came, and to the 1940 Act of Havana to ensure that the Axis could not absorb existing New World colonies. The war brought economic dislocation, which the United States tried to alleviate, but profit for some. However, Washington decided that Latin American economies should be geared to its own needs for the duration, which both stressed extraction over development and made the region more dependent on the United States, despite some new industries. The power differential and the fears it generated remained.

Nonetheless, World War II brought a degree of diplomatic maturation, as elsewhere. Though its role was mainly economic rather than military, Latin America was growing into international politics, and by the end of 1941, the region as a whole had moved onto the edge of the world stage, ready to join the extras before the audience, if not yet seeking much of a speaking part. Some of the smaller states were still very dependent, others too shy, but Mexico had developed a distinct diplomatic personality and Argentina had become a late adolescent rebel whereas Brazil accepted the role of older brother of the brood, taking on some responsibility in the American family as war threatened the New World and preoccupied the paterfamilias.

◆ **Notes to Chapter 11**

1. Clarence H. Haring, 'Latin America Comes of Age', in L. S. Rowe *et al.*, *Latin America in World Affairs, 1914-1940* (Philadelphia, University of Pennsylvania Press, 1941), p. 7.
2. William Shakespeare, *As You Like It*, II, vii.
3. Thomas A. Bailey, *A Diplomatic History of the American People*, 10th edn (Englewood Cliffs, NJ, Prentice Hall, 1980), p. 555.
4. Fredrick B. Pike, *FDR's Good Neighbor Policy* (Austin, TX, University of Texas Press, 1995), p. 138. See also pp. 139–59.
5. Donald M. Dozer, *Are We Good Neighbors? Three Decades of Inter-American Relations, 1930–1960* (Gainesville, FL, University of Florida Press, 1960), p. 19.
6. Pike, *FDR's Good Neighbor Policy*, xi.
7. David Rock, 'Argentina in 1914', in Leslie Bethell, ed., *Cambridge History of Latin America* (11 vols, New York, CUP, 1984–95), V, p. 394; David Rock, 'Introduction,' in Rock, ed., *Argentina in the Twentieth Century* (Pittsburgh, PA, University of Pittsburgh Press, 1975), p. 1.
8. Paul Drake, 'Chile, 1930–58,' in Bethell, ed., *Cambridge History*, VIII, p. 275.
9. Derek H. Aldcroft, *From Versailles to Wall Street, 1919–1929* (Berkeley, CA, University of California Press, 1977), pp. 259–60.
10. Laurence Whitehead, 'Bolivia since 1930', in Bethell, ed. *Cambridge History*, VIII, p. 513.
11. Hugh M. Hamill, 'Introduction,' in Hamill, ed., *Caudillos: Dictators in Spanish America* (Norman, OK, University of Oklahoma Press, 1992), p. 10.
12. Bailey, *Diplomatic History*, p. 553.
13. Michael L. Conniff, 'Panama since 1903', in Bethell, ed., *Cambridge History*, VII, p. 610.
14. Michael L. Conniff, *Panama and the United States: The Forced Alliance* (Athens, GA, University of Georgia Press, 1992), p. 3.
15. Walter LaFeber, *Inevitable Revolutions: The United States in Central America* (New York, Norton, 1983), p. 71.
16. James Dunkerley, *Power in the Isthmus: A Political History of Modern Central America* (London, Verso, 1988), p. 55.

17. Richard Goff, Walter Moss, Janice Terry, Jiu-hwa Upshur, *The Twentieth Century: A Brief Global History*, 5th edn (Boston, McGraw Hill, 1998), p. 184.
18. Bailey, *Diplomatic History*, p. 555.
19. Linda B. Hall, *Oil, Banks, and Politics: The United States and Post-revolutionary Mexico, 1917–1924* (Austin, TX, University of Texas Press, 1995), p. 18.
20. Bailey, *Diplomatic History*, p. 680.
21. J. Lloyd Mecham, *The United States and Inter-American Security, 1889–1960* (Austin, TX, University of Texas Press, 1961), p. 258.

CHAPTER

12

THE UNITED STATES

If the United States seemed an overbearing, potentially threatening bully to its weaker southern neighbours, in the world's great power league it seemed infuriatingly adolescent to its more mature European counterparts, which had been dominant for centuries and which were experienced and sophisticated in statecraft. The American tendency to act maturely, if not necessarily wisely, one day while reverting to childish irresponsibility the next was not easy for older powers to deal with even as they had to accept a non-European member in the big boys' club for the first time in modern history. This new great power, which had erupted onto the world stage so swiftly, also had a strong moral streak, wanted (unlike most imperial states) to be liked and approved of, and had an inferiority complex vis-à-vis Europe, ensuring a prickly relationship.

Despite its substantial European heritage, the United States was different, a muscular, gawky young giant which had shot up almost overnight, intelligent but inexperienced, overly optimistic, and inconsistent. It was non-European and proud of it, anti-imperial despite 1898 and its Caribbean and Chinese policies, and a satisfied state territorially by 1900. It had a distinctive, if often delusive, self-image and unlike European states, was not preoccupied with power for, as a result of its previous history, it did not fully recognize power's role in effecting policy.

The United States had had the inestimable advantage of growing up in isolation, sheltered by vast seas, comparatively weak neighbours, and Britain's Royal Navy. With such a cloistered youth, it was slow to mature, especially internationally. In the nineteenth century, it did not have to pay the costs of its foreign policy, as geography, Britain, and diplomacy sufficed. Traditions of free security and of isolation developed, especially as security usually meant non-intervention. In the twentieth century, as the United States moved toward the responsibilities of a great power, tradition tugged in the opposite direction, making for an erratic course as technology narrowed the oceans and the Royal Navy no longer provided an adequate shield.

Before 1895 the United States was something of a hemispheric power. In 1898, it burst to the front of the world stage, taking the role of juvenile second lead. Thereafter its transformation was startlingly swift, unnerving both itself and Europe as the corn-fed young giant developed some of the strongest muscles in the world and flexed them uncertainly, not sure what to do with them, for it catapulted too fast to stardom and was bashfully dismayed to find itself at centre stage and in the spotlight, a position with which it was not yet comfortable. A nostalgic yearning to abandon the world stage for a simpler role overcame it often.

The United States fought no overseas wars until 1898 and assiduously avoided European entanglements until 1917. In 1885 its navy was negligible, ranking below Chile's; twenty years later, it was the world's third navy, and soon the second. As its economic strength grew, the United States became a Pacific power, dominated the Caribbean, and began gingerly to participate in European conferences. It was now a power of some note, though chiefly economically; World War I completed the process of turning it into a great power as it projected its strength overseas, sent two million men to France in an abrupt departure from its past, and equally untraditionally played a major role in the peace settlement. It was idealistic and thought itself unfailingly so, as well as distrustful of what it saw as corrupt, morally tainted elder European nations.

No nation had come so far so fast – in a mere two decades – nor had become so rich so quickly. Americans thought the United States unlike other powers and in some respects it was. Its sudden emergence as the first modern non-European great power forced adjustments in both the New World and the Old. American national wealth more than doubled during World War I and then doubled again in the 1920s. The United States was the world's leading industrial nation by 1920 and became decisive economically and financially as its expansion continued. It was the world's leading exporter and second importer after Britain. It had simultaneous agricultural, industrial, and capital surpluses, which had never happened before anywhere. Unlike other major powers, the United States of itself was both very large and very efficient. As it poured forth food, automobiles, new appliances, machinery, and oil, and the rest of the world relied on American capital for reconstruction or development, by 1925 the United States had nearly half the world's income. But prosperity was patchy, as railways, textiles, and coal were depressed, agricultural surpluses developed once Europe regained full productive capacity in 1925, over-production was not fully solved by instalment purchase, and risky speculation in partially unpaid-for stocks became common. Meanwhile, Americanization of the world began as the United States exported radios, telephones, jazz, films, industrial techniques, and autos and sent forth missionaries, philanthropic and educational institutions, and business groups such as Rotary International. Some states, France above all, tried to resist in hopes of safeguarding their own economic and cultural identities. American mass culture was especially popular in

Europe in the 1920s, but organized cultural diplomacy followed slowly in the 1930s, mainly in Latin America.

*   *   *

In the early twentieth century, other great nations sought to exert their strength globally. A majority of Americans, who had not really learned to think internationally, seemed to consider power immoral. The United States had much potential political might but was reluctant to use it or to take responsibility in world affairs. When it did, domestic opposition developed in an era of narrow nationalism. As American expansion had been chiefly continental and largely in isolation, the interests of most Americans remained parochial. World War I changed the country's role, but popular perceptions had not caught up with reality. Though overseas markets were necessary to dispose of agricultural surpluses, farmers whose land lay as far as 1500 miles (2400 km) from every coast did not yet think in such terms. Thus, with notable exceptions among businessmen, government leaders, and coastal intelligentsia, Americans saw the great departure of 1917 (as well as the imperialism of 1898) as an aberration and, by 1920, turned inward to domestic preoccupations. The United States became a reluctant, sometimes inattentive, great power.

Domestic politics, and especially the domestic mood, played a considerable role in setting foreign policy, but the differences between the two main parties in this respect were more in tone, nuance, tactics, and personality than in substance. Underlying policies showed little change. Presidents could, if they chose, personally control foreign policy without reference to their cabinets, including the secretary of state, but they could not ignore the Congress, as Wilson demonstrated. The entire political leadership was intensely anti-Communist, orchestrating a Red Scare in 1919, devoted (including labour) to capitalism, concerned to maintain prosperity, anti-Asiatic, and eager for economic expansion overseas, not least to ease social pressures arising from domestic racial and religious tensions and from the clash between the urban Jazz Age of the Roaring Twenties and the intensely religious conservatism of small towns and rural areas.

Certain aspects of the American past shaped American foreign policy from Wilson to Roosevelt. The distinctive anti-monarchic origins of the United States as the first country deliberately to create a governmental system based on the philosophical doctrine of the innate rights of man, led late eighteenth-century European intellectuals to consider the new nation coterminous with the area of freedom, and twentieth-century Americans to think it still was. The first president's Farewell Address in 1796 urged avoidance of European rivalries and permanent alliances – sensible advice to a small remote nation, but as the United States became a great power, free hands and avoiding 'entangling alliances' were Holy Writ. The Monroe Doctrine of 1823 reiterated American refusal to involve itself in European wars and declared the New World closed to further European colonization, contributing to maintenance of Latin American independence and preparing future American hegemony. In 1893, historian Frederick Jackson Turner argued that the frontier and its availability of free land had had a formative effect in American history, providing an opportunity for social mobility and thus a safety valve for domestic social pressures. Leaders of the 1920s of both parties, all familiar with the Turner thesis, held that the United States, after the frontier closed in 1890, had moved to expand overseas, first territorially in 1898, and then economically, finding its new frontier in the world market and its safety valve in the resultant prosperity. Finally, the Open Door note of 1899 enunciated a policy for China, soon applied globally, that American businessmen should be entitled to compete on an equal basis with those of other states. After World War I, this came to imply creating a system where American businessmen would replace Britons as managers of the world economy.

*   *   *

Though trying to delay that process, Britain was startled by the speed with which American might grew in World War I – and assessed it more realistically than Americans did, for Yankees on the whole were hostile to the balance of power as an immoral European concept and did not view the world in such terms. Few Americans realized the extent to which power had shifted in World War I or considered the responsibilities of a great power, especially since the United States in the 1920s did not seek a larger role on the world stage, except economically. After 1921, it made no effort to emulate Britain's overwhelming pre-war naval dominance and chose not to build to authorized quotas under the era's naval agreements.

As Britain knew, power was shifting from it to the United States – peacefully but inexorably – for Britain had spent its treasure in World War I, chiefly in North America. In 1921 after some hesitation, it chose the United States over Japan and France, hoping in a startling reversal of the past that the American navy could help defend the British Empire. Britain and the United States were dominant between 1918 and 1933. Britain had the real estate (25 per cent of the globe's land surface) and the world's leading trading bloc, the United States the money; both had naval strength, comparatively speaking. Their dominance arose from formal and informal empire; the economic, naval, and especially financial might of both as Britain remained a major lender; a degree of commonality of viewpoint; and a temporary lack of competition. The United States was a rising young power, Britain a much older one, past its prime, often competing in China, Latin America, and the Middle East. Two countries of common political traditions and language, but not always common interests, dominated the globe though both had small armies.

In the 1920s, American military might, like that of Britain, dropped considerably – but not to pre-war levels, and the wartime organization was retained. The United States possessed a modern army, navy, and diplomatic service, all of recent vintage. However, Republican presidents between 1921 and 1933 were reluctant, except in Central America and the Caribbean, to use force, which opinion opposed, and Charles Evans Hughes, Secretary of State from 1921 to 1925, failed to link power with policy. In any event, it was politically impossible to increase American military force or to join alliances to further his goals. Thus a gap often developed between political settlements the United States arranged or accepted and the military means to ensure them.

As a great power, the United States was supposedly interested in everything everywhere, but in fact it was not. Its interests and policies were lopsided, its activities largely confined to the Americas and Europe, with a limited interest in China and a wary eye on the Japanese navy. There was little interest in South-east Asia or Africa, except Liberia, and only late and fairly modest concern with the Middle East. Even where interest was strong, the national mood restricted action. There was wide agreement on economic expansion and hegemony in Latin America but little support for other adventures. Most Americans, in accord with their tradition, saw no need for involvement in Europe and no benefit from it.

The 1920s saw an isolationism of the spirit and national mood, if not of policy, an emotional rejection of entanglement and alliances. The isolationist impulse was reinforced by the fact that the United States, unlike other powers, could largely maintain prosperity on the basis of its own resources and market with relatively little recourse to international trade. Though the country contained active isolationists and committed internationalists, most Americans were indifferent to foreign affairs beyond an instinctive rejection of much involvement. Thus American political oratory was isolationist but its actions, though carefully circumscribed, were not. Hughes, who did not favour isolationism, conducted as active a foreign policy as circumstances permitted. But a national reluctance to use power, to limit freedom of action, to make commitments, especially to participate in Europe, dictated reliance on *ad hoc* agreements with other states and commitments limited to consultation, evading any obligation for enforcement or sanctions, as collective security implied. Washington wished to remain involved in world affairs but to avoid war, so it chose not to intervene in most areas, evaded commitments which might lead to war, and pursued an independent internationalism, often by indirect or unofficial means.

Rejection of the Versailles treaty did not greatly affect the American role, for the United States remained more involved in world affairs than ever before in peacetime – but its previous peacetime experience had not been as a great power with a major role in shaping a global peace settlement. It sought greater economic and cultural ties, but was extremely cautious about political ones. Policy was more unilateral than isolationist as it sought full control over its own destiny, an increasingly unlikely prospect in the twentieth-century world.

Though naive in this respect, the United States was conservative beyond its years as a great power in its devotion to stability, the *status quo*, property rights, and the rule of law, and its allergy to radical change, especially social revolutionary upheavals. Businessmen seeking profit abroad and a powerful peace movement influenced these views. When twentieth-century revolutions expropriated foreign property in nationalist reaction against foreign economic domination, as in Russia and Mexico, Washington often became legalistic, trying to play by established rules, which revolutions seek to overthrow. As a territorially satisfied and economically ambitious nation, the United States valued order and permanence, often above democracy, and on the whole opposed force, vigorous diplomacy, and the balance of power, which are the primary ways to deter aggressors. No major aggressors appeared until the 1930s, but the existing tradition constricted the American response when the challenges came.

Having rejected the balance of power and the League's Wilsonian system of collective security based on a concert of many powers, Washington needed other methods to ensure the peace and stability it craved. Wilson had taught a foolish reliance on world opinion to deter aggression, and that view lingered. In addition, Hughes, who set the pattern for the Republican era, favoured the rule of international law, the *status quo*, arbitration and conciliation, and gradual or moderate change arrived at by consent or consensus. Hughes emphasized order rather than power – not recognizing that power is necessary to ensure order, diplomatic accommodation, and rules based on reason that civilized states would supposedly accept as obligatory despite selfish national interests. This policy accorded with his inclinations and those of the American people as well as his political circumstances, if not with the harsh reality of power politics, and worked passably in an era lacking major military challenges to the *status quo*.

In its inexperience, Washington believed it could bolster international stability without commitments, alliances, or projection of its strength, and American opinion erroneously thought the world accepted its creed of peaceful change by consensus, not realizing that relative peace survived because the dissatisfied states temporarily lacked power. Thus Washington pursued a 'utopian internationalism'[1] with little policy but much drift, assuming democracies were invariably peace-loving and 'moral force' could replace the Old World's way. Thinking the preoccupation with power 'a European vice',[2] Americans attributed their own security to geography and virtue.

* * *

Virtue was something most Americans felt sure that their nation possessed far more than other states, especially those of 'decadent' Europe. The

United States was an idealistic country which saw itself as it at times aspired to be, not as it was. The American self-image stressed innocence and virtue with frequent reference to 'a virgin continent'[3] and a desire to preserve that supposed innocence through neutrality. Like the French, Americans thought their way was best and wanted to sweep others into it, but for the United States, superiority was moral and constitutional more than cultural. It saw itself as a model for and as the primary exponent of liberty and democracy. This creed of superiority led to a certain moral imperialism and a tiresome complacency and preachiness. Belief in American exceptionalism and virtue became so ingrained that some American historians have been dismayed to discover that their nation often displayed the same single-minded selfishness as other powers, pursuing economic profit, spheres of interest, strategic advantage, and exclusion of other states. This conviction of moral superiority appeared in Wilson and Hughes, as well as in the remark of a midwestern senator that it was the United States's 'divinely ordained mission to develop and exercise, by friendship with all and partnership with none, a moral influence circling the globe'.[4] A French historian drily noted, 'The American people have the virtue of always confusing their cause with the great cause of mankind',[5] and Wilson, the ultimate exponent of this view, declared, 'I hope we shall never forget that we created this nation, not to serve ourselves, but to serve mankind.'[6]

It is not surprising that Americans convinced themselves, if not others, that it was their duty to bring the blessings of liberty to less fortunate, moral, or 'civilized' peoples. Evangelism played a role along with a Protestant sense of responsibility for the disadvantaged, as did three deeply held but contradictory concepts. There was a strong missionary spirit, religious and secular, embodied in a zeal to help other peoples but with implications of cultural imperialism. Americans also believed in self-determination, that each society should establish its own goals and means to them. But they were convinced that other societies could only better themselves by copying the American approach, contrary to self-determination; this caused resentment elsewhere and fears of losing economic, political, or psychological independence. Americans were so sure what was good for the United States was good for other societies that they sometimes tried to impose their system of government elsewhere, ignoring both hostility and local traditions in a one-size-fits-all approach encapsulated in a midwestern senator's boast, 'With God's help, we will lift Shanghai up and up, ever up, until it is just like Kansas City.'[7]

Given American premises and beliefs, an era of fulsome oratory, and elections every two years to Congress and every four to the presidency, it is not surprising that during the interwar years American diplomacy relied more on maxims and declarations of principle than on active policies. Diplomats everywhere continued to pursue national self-interest, but in an era of greater democracy, propaganda, and public awareness of foreign affairs (if still not consistent attention in the United States), they were curbed by their political masters, who employed platitudes and misdirection to satisfy the masses and the parliamentarians. In the United States, as elsewhere, there was a good deal of drift, of not facing problems, and of reliance on simplistic slogans stressing American virtue. Pronouncements of lofty principles often served as a convenient substitute for policy, as in the doctrine of non-recognition, first devised by Wilson in 1913 to deal with Mexican revolutionary governments, which he felt must be elected to gain formal American diplomatic recognition, but applied in the Caribbean and in reaction to Japan's 21 Demands upon China in 1915 and its conquest of Manchuria in 1932.* In Asia, non-recognition had no effect on events but satisfied the American sense of virtue without committing the United States to action.

Belief in American virtue included intense devotion to peace. In a strong peace movement during the 1920s, isolationists and internationalists disagreed on how to achieve it, but all strongly favoured peace, as did government leaders, without exception. Republicans led a sizeable minority of Americans in rejecting the League as entangling, or sometimes as a tool of Anglo-French imperialism, and the State Department did not answer League communications until 1923. Then informal co-operation began. By 1925 Washington posted official observers in Geneva and took part in all of the League's disarmament conferences and most of its economic and social conferences. Meanwhile, the question arose of American participation in the Permanent Court of International Justice, which most Americans favoured. Though the World Court had no enforcement power or compulsory jurisdiction, Congress rejected membership unless the United States was effectively exempted from its jurisdiction, creating an impasse which was never resolved.

Americans, including key senators, also strongly favoured disarmament, hoping to substitute economic means for military. After the United States built more naval vessels than the rest of the world combined in the first three post-Armistice years, raising the prospect of a naval race with Britain and Japan, pressures for naval disarmament became irresistible, leading to the 1921–22 Washington naval conference.† As a consequence, the 1920s became the only decade of arms reduction until the 1980s. The American peace movement, which played a role in achieving real naval disarmament, saw the Washington arrangements as a victory over power politics and a step toward a new world order. However, the Senate approved the Four Power treaty calling for consultation at threats to the Pacific *status quo* only with a reservation, stressing that there was no commitment or obligation to any defence, whereas the other two treaties contradictorily imposed the

* See Chapters 11, 10, and 15.
† See Chapter 10.

paper chains of the Open Door on Japan in China while giving it naval dominance of the western Pacific. The supposed collective system for the Pacific solved little beyond naval quotas and fostered an illusory sense of security and real peace.

So did the other main contribution of the peace movement, American and European, the Kellogg–Briand pact of 1928, which arose from French Foreign Minister Aristide Briand's effort to lure the United States back into Europe by outlawing war between the two nations. To avoid any appearance of an alliance, Secretary of State Frank Kellogg insisted that the pact be multilateral. With cameras recording the event for cinema newsreels, a number of states (eventually virtually all) signed a treaty renouncing war as an instrument of national policy but permitting self-defence against aggression. It did not address the causes of war, provide machinery to settle disputes, or deal with enforcement. Franklin Roosevelt, not yet president, rightly said, 'It does not contribute in any way to settling matters of international controversy.'[8] Members, if not leaders, of peace movements thought outlawing war was a real solution, though governments knew better, including the State Department. American internationalists and isolationists alike approved because there was no commitment to action. The Kellogg–Briand pact satisfied American moral idealism, committed the United States to moral sanctions (which rarely succeed), and perhaps was a step away from true neutrality toward collective security. On the broader world stage, it contributed to the gradually growing view that war was immoral.

＊　　＊　　＊

If war was immoral, profit was not, and most Americans were as committed to its pursuit as to peace. Politicians of both parties, businessmen, labour unions, and public opinion held that the world market was the new frontier and that economic expansion abroad was essential to ensure full employment, absorb agricultural and industrial surpluses, and create a greater prosperity to ease social pressures. Wilson hoped to curb the role of big business at home but strongly favoured overseas trade and the Open Door for, if competition were open to all, the United States could dominate. Characteristically, he hoped to use American economic strength, which he fully recognized, to do good, but economic might did not mean political leverage. Republican leaders equally recognized an era of economic interdependence, sought the lion's share for the United States, and hoped for a world economic order based on co-operation. Less concerned to curb large corporations, they promoted American business interests abroad, but chiefly to gain access to strategic materials, such as Middle Eastern oil and Liberian rubber. There was no sustained economic policy, but in general the United States sought international co-operation. If American firms were excluded, Washington exerted itself to gain an Open Door.

The startling American expansion occurred in a stagnant world economy and amounted to a dramatic challenge to Europe's centuries-old economic dominance, especially in the western hemisphere, including Canada. Significantly, American imports from Europe dropped as growth centred on Latin America and East Asia. The United States had become a creditor nation, owed money by others rather than owing, enjoyed a favourable trade balance, exporting more than it imported, and possessed surplus capital to lend abroad. Americans thought their economic dominance would lead to peace, not realizing that their policies were far more nationalist than internationalist. In the 1920s, the United States set small immigration quotas, especially for south-east Europeans, which intensified population pressures in eastern Europe and restricted immigrant remittances to the 'old country'; it enacted high tariffs as a barrier to foreign products; and it insisted that European nations repay with interest their war and post-Armistice debts, though it was difficult to do so without earning dollars by selling goods in the United States.

As a result, the prosperity which all Americans deemed essential depended primarily on American loans abroad, though growing American tourism contributed some dollars, chiefly to Europe. Loans of surplus American capital sometimes aimed at ensuring stability in an era of revolutionary impulses, but also enabled others to purchase American agricultural and industrial surpluses, reconstruct war-torn areas, develop economically unsophisticated regions, indulge in luxuries, and service their American debts when the threat of an end to loans forced debt settlements. Though the loans were invariably private, not governmental, Washington used loans or their refusal as a political tool in Mexico, Central America, the Soviet Union, and west-central Europe as its role, often informal, in the international lending of private capital grew. Much of the world shifted from Europe to the United States as a source of funds, creating an interlocking global economy based on the continuance of American loans. Though the diplomacy of the dollar dominated the 1920s financially, it was conducted mostly by Wall Street bankers. They decided who got the money, not Washington, and they co-operated with government policy only when it suited their interests to do so. The State Department hoped for loans to China, but bankers shunned its turmoil, preferring Japan's stability. Washington and Wall Street never arrived at a lasting consensus, and neither wished to accept the responsibilities of a world financial leader.

In 1928 American lenders switched to investment in the booming New York stock market, depriving foreigners of the means to buy American agricultural and industrial surpluses. Hard times arrived on the farm and in the factory, but overly optimistic lenders and borrowers became reckless. Bankers floated bonds for risky loans at high interest rates which attracted an eager American public. On 24 October 1929, the overheated American stock market collapsed, thanks to continuing productive surpluses, inadequate purchasing power as wages lagged, and buying on margin, which meant using half-paid-for stock to purchase more stock, piling up a paper fortune (which might shrink rapidly) but also a large fixed debt payable on demand. The situation was aggravated by an undervalued dollar, a shaky unregulated banking system, a Federal Reserve Board lacking both power and courage, and a precarious corporate structure, including vast paper pyramids of holding companies which collapsed when one firm failed and pulled the rest down. President Herbert Hoover pursued traditional policies, reluctant to intervene heavily in the economy, and Congress raised the tariff in 1930, causing retaliation by other nations which contributed to a 50 per cent drop in American exports, creating a great glut with pitifully low prices. Tourism largely ceased, as did lending to foreign governments; overseas investment ended and funds were recalled; those dollars still abroad were committed to fixed obligations such as debt service, and none remained to buy American goods. The economic premises of the 1920s lay in tatters and the world in economic depression.

*　　*　　*

The Depression which economically dominated the 1930s fundamentally affected American foreign policy, initially reinforcing isolationism, but it had relatively little effect as to empire. The Open Door remained an American creed throughout, and in imperial policy Democrats in the 1930s largely continued what Republicans had begun in the late 1920s. Both were anti-colonial, leading to an 'imperial anticolonialsm'[9] that was paternalistic and controlling, with the usual American gap between rhetoric and actuality. The United States possessed both informal and formal empire, but called its colonies territories in the tradition of its westward development, implying eventual statehood, which Alaska and Hawaii gained after World War II.

The United States thought it was anti-imperialist, not recognizing that it had always been expansionist, if not always territorially annexationist, and showed only modest toleration for the expansionism of others. It accepted the British Empire, formal and informal, because after 1920 it was complete, the United States displaced it in large part in Latin America, and American firms gained their share of Middle Eastern oil. French investment in eastern Europe was no threat to American interests. But Japanese expansion, similar to that of Britain in the nineteenth century, was in mid-stride. In East Asia, Washington largely accepted past Japanese acquisitions, military and economic, but thought that in 1922 it had created a *status quo* to be defended, not disturbed, especially by a power whose expansion threatened existing and potential American interests.

Americans engaged in an imperialism of idealism, sometimes misplaced. This was primarily secular, though infused with the Protestant ideals which then dominated the nation. Missionaries and American schools taught

American values but usually from a posture of moral and ideological superiority. Moreover, the American firms whose role was dominant did both bad and good in many areas. There were undoubted economic depredations but also creation of public health services, schools, and housing, and development of both communications and economic resources which then became valuable. Unlike the missionaries, American businessmen and their allies in Washington rested on the doctrine of the Open Door. Quickly after World War I, they moved from the view that the United States should get a fair share of the China market to the belief that American economic might should dominate the underdeveloped areas of the world. Among their cardinal principles were capitalism, making the world safe for American business, a Darwinian interpretation of the Protestant ethic, and a dedication to informal empire. The expanded concept of the Open Door implied that the United States rejected military action and the balance of power, but thought it could win world domination economically, without wars.

American imperialism was most intense in Latin America, where the United States was the hegemonic power, and deeply affected relations with that region.* American opinion and Washington believed American interests were those of Latin America, which they were not and could not be. With cultural blindness and deafness to the protests of others, the United States thought it was being altruistic, promoting inter-American understanding, imposing good government, and exporting superior Anglo-Saxon values – often at bayonet point, as it assumed it had special rights and behaved as hegemonic powers usually do.

It sought stability, democracy or the appearance thereof, prosperity, profit, and pro-American policies. To a degree, Washington and major firms created an informal alliance to control and develop the region. Though skyrocketing American investment was the work of private corporations and bankers, Washington had a hand in it, exempting export firms from existing anti-trust laws and aiding access to strategic materials as commercial and security interests coincided. Latin America was a key supplier of raw materials for American industry, and Washington wished to assure supplies of Chilean nitrates and copper as well as Mexican and Venezuelan oil, in the late 1930s urging concessions by American firms to ensure supplies. By then, as commercial aviation became significant in Latin America, Washington supported Pan American Airways against German competition to ensure that Americans controlled the hemisphere's air spaces. Washington also struggled with Mexico's nationalistic social and political upheaval, eventually coming to terms as World War II threatened American security.

The United States was attempting to disengage militarily as well. Anti-imperial American opinion opposed the use of force; all Latin America

---

* For details, see Chapter 11.

condemned Washington's policy; and in the Caribbean and Central America, anti-Americanism was acute. A less blatantly imperial policy was needed. From 1921 on, Republican leaders sought ways to withdraw while maintaining dominance, not tolerating other powers except for a reduced British presence. They gradually liquidated much of the Caribbean empire, and Democrat Franklin Roosevelt completed the task in 1934, when withdrawal from Haiti meant that no American troops remained on Latin American soil. The Good Neighbour policy, born of both parties, was designed to maintain hegemony without force or hostility, placate Latin America and American opinion, continue the dominance of Yankee corporations, and, in the late 1930s, protect American security against foreign threats.

In more distant East Asia and the western Pacific, where the United States lacked any prospect of hegemony, its role was more restrained. In 1922, it achieved pacification and a regional security system without teeth, thereby starting naval disarmament and ending the Anglo-Japanese alliance at little cost but creating a gap between the political settlement and the military means to ensure it, as well as formal internationalization of the American Open Door policy in China. Japan accepted the 1922 system partly because Wall Street was the only source of the loans that it would need to finance a war. Thereafter, the United States, which had both economic interests in China and a sentimental attachment owing to the influence of missionaries and 'China hands', saw itself as standing determinedly by the Open Door as defender of China's territorial integrity. Despite troops in Shanghai and gunboats on the Yangtze River, it did not think it participated in exploitation. Though Washington was legalistic about American rights when facing revolutionary nationalism directed against foreign encroachments on Chinese sovereignty, American observers were enthusiastic about Chinese acceptance of the need to modernize and eager to westernize and 'civilize' the world's oldest civilization. As China saw the United States as the most distant and least dangerous imperial power, its anti-foreign activity was directed against Japan and Britain. The United States assumed this apparent friendliness was permanent.

Actually, American interest in China was relatively slight, and there was little policy beyond the Open Door. The presumed potential of the China market was tempting, but exports to China in the 1920s were always below 3 per cent of the American total, and the United States did three times as much trade with Japan. The American role was also circumscribed by public opinion's refusal to tolerate force. It accepted guns and gunboats on a small scale if unnoticeable and unused. Businessmen urged their retention, but American opinion demanded peaceful solutions, limiting policy choices and dictating a relative non-interference. In the late 1920s, the United States accepted concessions to Chinese nationalism, as missionaries urged. Business interests opposed waiving treaty rights, but when Washington belatedly addressed the issue, it saw that concessions were unavoidable if the powers would not use force to preserve the *status quo*. American pronouncements, especially moral ones, raised Chinese hopes beyond early realization, but the United States became China's chief friend as its relations with Britain, Russia, and Japan worsened.* Generalissimo Chiang Kai-Shek's links to the prominent westernized Soong family, conversion to Christianity, and American-educated advisers contributed to closer ties and to a growing American desire to help China, both in general and against Japan in particular.

Chiang had long foreseen a clash between the United States and Japan and sought to benefit from it as the two nations became rivals in China and the western Pacific. Tension also arose from American immigration and racial policy, especially the National Origins Act of 1924 barring Japanese. Nonetheless, the 1920s represented primarily a decade of co-operation despite American dislike of Japanese expansion which, as Tokyo noted, imitated the Monroe Doctrine. In the 1920s, both countries stressed economic diplomacy. The United States was Japan's chief source of capital and its best customer; Wall Street bankers largely financed Japanese imperialism in China, sometimes indirectly, contrary to Washington's policy. As the 1920s progressed, Japanese activities in China intensified, as did Tokyo's open dissatisfaction with naval disarmament. Washington was complacent, trusting in Shidehara, Japan's most internationalist leader. Not anticipating a clash and preoccupied with the spreading Depression, the State Department was taken by surprise when the Japanese army set off the Manchurian crisis in 1931.

*   *   *

The United States was not complacent about Europe, which offered no scope for imperial adventure except economic and cultural penetration. The American approach was traditional here, resting on fear of involvement in Europe's future wars and the Wilsonian belief that the balance of power was evil, immoral, and ineffective since it did not prevent war. At the Paris peace conference, Wilson saw himself as a progressive reformer fighting European 'bosses' who, in his eyes, did not represent their peoples.[10] Like him, other Americans wished to 'avoid or redeem the Old World'.[11] In an attitude typical of American thinking in this era, Hughes thought that the United States participated in European affairs for commercial and humanitarian reasons, particularly to help Europe, not from its own economic and security interests.

This participation was more extensive than it superficially seemed, especially in exports of popular culture and industrial techniques. Though these

* On Sino-Japanese questions, see Chapter 10.

non-governmental inroads were pronounced, in European questions Washington was much less isolationist and irresponsible than it appeared to be but used indirect means of diplomatic intervention to evade Congressional and public fear of entanglement. Thus the United States played a key role in post-war European stabilization, a primarily political question resting on major financial settlements. Wall Street bankers chosen and briefed by the State Department devised these, ostensibly as private citizens who could be disavowed.* This use of non-governmental personnel satisfied American opinion and eluded Congress, special interests, and other governments.

Other questions included lending policy, war debt settlements, tariffs, cartels, relations with the League of Nations, and peace initiatives, such as the Kellogg–Briand pact. As the leading consumer of metals and other primary materials, the United States fought, with little success, the metals cartels devised by European producers in the late 1920s. By then, the State Department knew that excessive lending to Europe, especially Germany, was becoming dangerous but, despite some informal warnings, ducked the problem for political reasons. Lending continued apace, often short-term loans for long-term projects, a dangerous gamble that no economic crisis would lead to recall of the loans. Throughout, American high tariffs impeded loan repayment.

Britain did not contract massive new loans and was the first country to come to terms on war debts, impelled partly by its desire for closer relations with the United States, but the Anglo-American relationship did not deepen appreciably in the interwar years. British leaders saw the United States as a potential asset to Britain and hoped for political and economic ties, but Washington evaded commitment. However, a certain community of views developed, despite American denial of the power balance which preoccupied Britain. By 1925, American officials depended on British interpretations of technical financial questions plaguing Europe. In addition, both countries favoured moderate revision of the Versailles treaty on the false assumption that this would placate Germany and pacify Europe so both could turn their attention elsewhere.

France had to live on the European continent next to Germany and thus had different views. Sympathy for it lingered, especially among Wall Street's most prominent bankers, but American officials echoed their British counterparts in erroneously thinking that a crumbling France was too strong, both militarily, and in the late 1920s and early 1930s, financially. At the 1922 Washington conference, at American instigation France's capital ship quota was held to the modest level of Mediterranean Italy. Thereafter Anglo-American pressure for reduction of France's decaying army was frequent.

* For details, see Chapter 13.

Unlike France, the United States and Britain did not fear Germany nor make it a top priority. However, Germany seemed key to European stability and prosperity, both desirable. Thus Washington assured France that German prosperity was the best hope for French security, ignoring the implications, and focused primarily on Germany in its indirect effort through American bankers to revive Europe economically, chiefly by loans, so that it could buy American goods. At first, there was concern about possible revolution in Germany, a fear carefully fanned by Weimar officials to gain concessions, as was the later Anglo-American belief that Germany should be bolstered as the primary barrier to Bolshevism.

In the United States Bolshevists were regarded with contempt, not, as in Europe, with fear; the Communist Party, which was committed to overthrow of the existing constitutional regime and followed the Russian diplomatic line, was unpopular. The Moscow regime, seeing the United States as the most distant and thus least dangerous imperial power, campaigned for trade, development aid and recognition in return for economic concessions, but its expropriation of foreign property, repudiation of foreign private and governmental debts, and then radical social philosophy precluded diplomatic recognition in the Republican years. Though the peace movement, some businessmen and a few senators favoured recognition, a diverse array of pressure groups and business organizations prevented it until the Depression. In 1921, however, the United States led the humanitarian aid against the Russian famine, which saved millions of lives and possibly the regime, though Washington's intent was to dispose of agricultural surpluses, enlarge American influence, do good, and perhaps save Russia from Bolshevism.

1921 signalled a temporary Russian accommodation with the West born of economic necessity. As Britain and Germany were eager to deal, American investors scrambled to get ahead of Europeans, make a profit, and perhaps convert Russia to capitalism. Moscow maintained a trading office in New York to arrange deals with American firms, which often provided short-term (and then longer-term) credits to facilitate purchases. American sales to Russia grew steadily from 1923 on, until by 1930 the United States had a quarter of the Soviet import market and a fourth of all investment in Russia. In addition, the Ford Motor Company built 85 per cent of Soviet trucks. Meanwhile, Moscow abandoned economic concessions in favour of lucrative short-term technical assistance contracts. American engineers and agricultural and steel experts poured in, and Washington did nothing to bar the technology transfer. Its policy had quietly become more flexible despite a rigid official stance. Washington aided businessmen in Russia, as elsewhere, and Moscow gained the trade, expertise, and financing it wanted. But formal diplomatic recognition remained excluded until the Depression's frantic search for markets and the advent of pragmatic Franklin Roosevelt altered the equation in 1933.

As debts were a barrier to formal relations with the Soviet Union, they were also the most nettlesome issue between west European nations and the United States. New nations had modest post-Armistice debts, so 13 European nations owed money to Washington, but the main issue was the large debts of Western wartime belligerents. These, especially France, argued that they had paid in blood, so Washington should forgive the debts and pay its share in money. The American Congress and people felt that debts should be repaid with interest; Congress intervened directly, creating a World War Foreign Debt Commission with strict rules, including a bar on loans to countries which did not come to terms about repayment. That induced European debtor states to face the situation and American administrations to find indirect ways to ease their burden.

European debts to the United States government exceeded $10 milliard, a vast sum in those days, contracted at 5 per cent interest. It was politically impossible to cancel, scale down, or link them – as Britain and France wished – to German payment of reparations for wartime damage done. The debt burden hurt European reconstruction and thus American prosperity, as Washington realized, but any forthright solution would cause a tax increase, so indirection was employed. Thus the United States devised the sort of financial legerdemain used with German reparations to achieve disguised partial cancellation, settlements based on ability to pay, and eventually a tacit linkage to reparations. Britain, which could afford to pay, gained a 62-year payment period, which became the norm, and a somewhat lower interest rate amounting to a modest debt cancellation. Later settlements with poorer debtors entailed much lower interest rates (thus more cancellation) and small payments in the early years, implying debt reduction when political circumstances permitted. The last of these was only ratified by France in 1929. With few exceptions, debt payments did not survive the next three years of economic upheaval.

＊　　＊　　＊

Much else did not survive the next several years as many of the premises of American policy were shattered by the Great Depression. The Roaring Twenties had been in and for the United States a relatively carefree time when most things went its way at relatively little cost, and many assumed they always would. In retrospect, it is clear that, in spite of a startlingly easy course, the gawky young giant was more mature than it seemed at first glance and growing, however indirectly, into its responsibilities, despite lingering backward yearnings for its golden sheltered youth. However, its world collapsed at the end of the decade, administering sobering shocks. These led initially to retreat from the world stage and turning inward, but as the 1930s progressed, world crises, Depression, and the mushrooming threat of major war forced the United States increasingly to prepare for its future role as the new world power astride the globe.

◆ **Notes to Chapter 12**

1. Norman A. Graebner, *America as a World Power* (Wilmington, DE, Scholarly Resources, 1984), p. 22.
2. Betty Glad, *Charles Evans Hughes and the Illusions of Innocence* (Urbana, IL, University of Illinois Press, 1966), p. 321.
3. Lloyd Ambrosius, *Woodrow Wilson and the American Diplomatic Tradition* (Cambridge, CUP, 1987), p. 9.
4. Senator Albert J. Beveridge of Indiana, as quoted by Graebner, *World Power*, p. 3.
5. Jean-Baptiste Duroselle, *From Wilson to Roosevelt* (Cambridge, MA, HUP, 1963), p. 427.
6. Lloyd C. Gardner, *A Covenant with Power* (Oxford, OUP, 1984), p. 3.
7. Senator Kenneth Wherry of Nebraska in 1940, as quoted in Sally Marks, *The Illusion of Peace* (London, Macmillan, 1976), p. 27.
8. Quoted in Foster Rhea Dulles, *America's Rise to World Power, 1898–1954* (New York, Harper, 1955), p. 160.
9. William Appleman Williams, *The Tragedy of American Diplomacy* (New York, Dell, 1962 edn), p. 17.
10. Robert Dallek, *The American Style of Foreign Policy* (New York, Knopf, 1983), p. 87.
11. Ambrosius, *Wilson*, p. 9.

CHAPTER

13

EUROPE IN THE 1920S

The United States was Europe's brawniest son, one whose manners often led the parental powers to cluck with disapproval even as they relied on his muscular arms and deep pockets. When Austria-Hungary fell out of the great power ranks, events forced the others to admit the United States, the first modern non-European member, as its replacement. Though dismayed at such an untoward event, their attitude remained essentially parental toward what they viewed as a newly grown European offspring. The fact that the United States had little interest in much of their continent enabled them to pretend that less had changed than in fact had.

It is the role of great powers to decide matters and of lesser states to attend and accept (though occasionally circumstances enable a small state with strong nerves to refuse). The European great powers had made the key decisions for centuries, set the rules, and dominated their known world for most of its historical drama, especially in recent decades. In their eyes, Europe was what mattered. It still ruled much of the world, Britain alone 25 per cent of it, but it had been weakened by the intense bloodletting, physical, financial, and economic, of its own recent civil war. The costs were so high that one can ask whether the European victors really won.

Largely as a result, the interwar era was a period of transition away from a Europe-centred world. Already the global economy was no longer Europe-centred, for in 1920 the continent's industrial production was no more than half that of 1913 and the United States had become the leading industrial nation, the only great non-European industrial power.[1] A long European preponderance based on material resources at home and abroad, physical energy, and intellectual inventiveness was fading after four years of mutual destruction and exhaustion. Power was moving out of Europe though in appearance it, especially Britain and France, seemed still to rule the world – and continued to act as if it did.

Of the European belligerents, Britain and Germany were comparatively fortunate, for they sustained little physical damage. Other industrial states recovered by the late 1920s, but the interim was painful. Trade recovered as well, though to a smaller share of the world's economic pie, and monetary stability was finally achieved after catastrophic inflations in several states. But Europe never regained economic dominance. It was deeply impoverished by World War I, but remained second only to the United States in wealth, industrial strength, and capital accumulation, especially after 1925. Collectively, Europe far exceeded its American counterpart in empire, naval strength, and armies though, like the United States, it was heavily disarmed. Thus the interwar years were an era when the West, primarily Britain, France, and the United States, but also other European economic and imperial powers, dominated the globe.

In Europe itself, the period showed a few consistent characteristics. Wealth and living standards were highest in the north and west, declining to the south and east. Fear of Communism was rampant everywhere. So was nationalism. The global trend toward liberation of subject peoples began in Europe between 1918 and 1921, though those who drew the maps had no idea that self-determination would be contagious elsewhere. In Europe, the war-generated collapse of empires made possible the fulfilment of nineteenth-century nationalist aspirations and the creation of new independent states. The Habsburg and Ottoman Empires were gone for good, though Hungary remained intensely revisionist despite lack of power to accomplish change, but Germany and Russia were only in temporary eclipse. Since most east European states were created or enlarged at the expense of these old empires, they remained precarious and fearful of future Soviet or German revisionism. Though nationalism was the dominant European political creed of the era, the fragmentation of Europe not only reduced minority problems by 50 per cent but also created economic and political problems, aggravated by the fact that in many of these states economic and political links conflicted rather than running parallel.

Europe had many small new nations, most of them beset by inexperience, economic difficulties, and recalcitrant minorities, often of former overlords. It was not easy for a young nation trying to grow up quickly in a crowded continent amid hostile neighbours and demanding great powers. In a 1932 fictional work, one explained:

> We are only a little country. A little new country. You must not be surprised if sometimes we do not seem to do things so well as you big countries who have been big countries for so long. You big countries do not know what it is like to be a little country. We are not used to being even a little country yet.[2]

Location often determined whether small states had a peaceful life. Few of the youngest were fortunate in this respect. Not all powers were equal in size, might, or involvement in the drama, and some European states mattered far more than others, even if not necessarily great powers. Europe's peninsular configuration with further peninsulas attached meant that there was a periphery and a core. The periphery – consisting of aged enfeebled old powers, small states, and a few infants – intruded into matters of high drama only rarely, whereas the great stars and their conflicts were to be found in the core, along with some important supporting players.

*   *   *

On the periphery, the Nordic region encompassed every variety of lesser state. Finland owed its birth to Russia's 1917 revolutions and its borders to direct negotiation in 1920 with a weakened Marxist pariah state which remained dissatisfied with a frontier close to Petrograd (Leningrad). After a brief civil war, largely a class conflict, Finland found unity in intense nationalism and anti-Russian feeling. However, its inexperienced leaders neither faced geographic reality nor accepted that Russia remained a great power; they vainly sought both outside aid and security against the Soviet colossus. At the end of the 1920s, its foreign minister announced a policy of 'splendid isolation', which solved nothing.[3]

Similarly, the baby Baltic states, barely learning to walk, were spared infanticide when Bolshevism survived in Russia; they also achieved eastern frontiers by direct negotiation. Their foreign ministers met annually through 1925, but by then their interests had diverged. Latvia and Estonia had sizeable Russian minorities and borders with the Soviet Union but none with Germany. They had close relations with each other and with Berlin, staying out of Lithuania's quarrels, especially after it seized German Memel (Klaipeda) in 1923, causing lasting anger in a powerful neighbour. Lithuania lost its Russian frontier when in 1920 Poland seized Vilna (Wilno, Vilnius), the historic capital but a mainly Polish and Jewish city, along with a long border slice, but it abutted Poland and Germany. It was shrilly nationalistic, and contacts with Poland were sparse as Lithuania closed the border, rejected diplomatic relations, and declared it was in a state of war, despite the economic cost. Berlin and especially Moscow made the most of this, trying to widen the breach and to use Lithuania as a weapon against Poland.

The Allies saw the Baltic republics as part of the *cordon sanitaire*, that string of east European states designed to protect Europe from Bolshevik infection. Berlin saw them as a region for economic penetration, Moscow as an area essential to Soviet security. All three states suffered from loss of the Russian market for their industry and became more agrarian, but as Weimar's aims were limited to economic dominance, it helped to maintain independence from Russia, as did a modicum of British involvement. Germany and Britain hoped for a transit trade through Latvia and Estonia to the Soviet Union, but the Russian market proved a disappointment, and trade dropped steadily. Equally, all schemes for a regional security system failed, partly because the three Scandinavian states rejected them..

These peaceful northern monarchies also had periodic meetings of foreign ministers or kings, and agreed to arbitrate disputes with each other.

Each strongly favoured the League of Nations and worked for its success; they developed a common League policy and by 1923, as a bloc, gained a non-permanent Council seat. They wished to remain neutral, opposed military sanctions and disliked economic ones, and thought they were safe on Europe's northern rim. Though Sweden was occasionally tempted, Norway and Denmark opposed all regional schemes.

Sweden, once a great power, was now a neutral old man, actively engaged in solving the disputes of others and peacefully accepting an unfavourable League decision awarding the Swedish-populated Åland Islands to Finland. Little Denmark was equally neutral and a supporter of disarmament. It gained a modest bit of territory from Germany as a result of the Versailles treaty and carefully sought no more, anxious not to offend a powerful neighbour whose resurgence it foresaw. It doubted the efficacy of collective security but reluctantly relied on it, abandoning a long history of total neutrality. Norway, independent only since 1905, had the advantage of an Atlantic position and thus put its faith in Britain's Royal Navy. It had serious economic problems but no major diplomatic disputes, and took pride in Fridtjof Nansen's service to the League as its high commissioner to repatriate prisoners of war, in settling refugees from the Russian revolutions, and in directing the Greco-Turkish population exchange.

Like Scandinavia, the Iberian peninsula was geographically remote from centre stage. Once a great power, Spain was now a feeble old woman with many infirmities. It remained neutral in World War I, but by 1919 was descending into political chaos. This led to a coup, a dictatorship with royal consent until 1930, more unrest, the king's departure in 1931, and then an unstable republic. It was too distracted by its internal divisions to have much foreign policy but, with decisive French aid, ended the embarrassing war against the Rifs in North Africa in 1926. It also withdrew from the League temporarily when refused a permanent seat on the Council. Its conservative regimes enjoyed good relations with Fascist Italy and the Vatican until 1931.

Portugal, once an important seafaring nation and still a colonial power, participated in World War I in France and Africa, though it could ill afford to do so. Resulting economic problems, political chaos and financial crisis led to a military coup in 1926. More financial crisis brought the dictatorship of Dr António de Oliveira Salazar and stability at the price of severity. The regime was and long remained very conservative, anti-parliamentarian, patriotic, intensely anti-Marxist, and pro-Fascist in its relative isolation, protected from Europe by Spain.

*　　*　　*

Isolation was a luxury most of eastern Europe did not enjoy. The successor states to the defeated empires were crowded together, usually abutted an unfriendly great power, and were 'frail and mutually hostile'.[4] In the 1920s

Russian and German exhaustion gave the area a respite from major crises of which it did not make the most, for the war and peace aggravated conflicts among nationalities. Victors were often greedy, losers resentful, preventing regional solidarity as states competed economically and made claims on each other. No state would aid another against a great power or unless its own interests were directly at stake. Efforts to consolidate the peace settlement were weak and limited: the Little Entente of Hungary's neighbours was directed solely against Magyar revisionism, the Balkan Entente of 1934 only against Bulgaria.

Eastern Europe was poor, underdeveloped, agricultural, weather-dependent, and stagnant. A new 1921 American immigration law with quotas favouring north-west Europe ended the flow of excess population to New York, resulting in rural overpopulation and the carving of holdings into ever smaller plots. These were so uneconomic in the absence of thorough agricultural reforms that Argentine and American wheat soon dominated the west European market. The collapse of empires disrupted manufacturing and trade patterns, but nationalism prevented economic co-operation, resulting in wasteful duplication. When suffering peasants radicalized to the right and small urban proletariats to the left, most states succumbed in time to static authoritarianism.

The eastern states were meant to form the *cordon sanitaire* to protect the West from Bolshevism, but their existence as buffers facilitated Russo-German collaboration. Though France allied with the *status quo* states, the beneficiaries of the peace settlement, against Germany and Russia, the Western great powers took little responsibility for what they had wrought. Even France, the most involved, lent money at high rates, erected protective tariffs against eastern agricultural products, and limited its investment (which was carried out by private firms at government request) to French-owned firms seeking quick profits, not to development of indigenous industry or creation of enduring economic links.

East European states had few friends and too many enemies. Each had one great power foe, Poland two. They were generally acquisitive, as were hostile smaller neighbours from whom territory had been gained or to whom land had been lost in the peace settlement. Regimes feared Communism, especially after the 1919 Hungarian revolution, and equally feared the Soviet Union, which none recognized until the 1930s. The region was almost universally anti-Semitic and ultra-nationalist, and most states were afflicted with internal enemies as well as foreign ones.

The peace treaties reduced the problem of ethnic minorities but could not eliminate it in view of mixed populations, economic and strategic factors, and enlargement of some *cordon sanitaire* states as bulwarks against Bolshevism. Thus minorities became a political factor among and within states. As they often consisted of the former ruling nationality and of the landlord and business classes, they faced retribution, including land expropriation. The problem was acute in states which gained the most territory: Poland, Yugoslavia, and Rumania. These treated minorities more harshly and were more dishonest than others in reporting minority population statistics, but most states discriminated sharply against Jews and Gypsies, each culturally and linguistically distinct, unassimilated, and lacking a kin state to assist them. Support to other minorities by neighbouring states, with appeals to the League, created internal unrest and diplomatic tension. Composite states had an additional problem: Serbs so dominated Yugoslavia and Czechs Czechoslovakia that Croats and Slovaks felt and acted like minorities struggling for autonomy, further weakening national unity.

It has been said that 'The people of the Balkans ... have too much history for their own good.'[5] None has more than Greece in both ancient and modern terms, and it had the distinction of being a victor which lost more than it gained, owing to its defeat by Turkey in 1922. After 2500 years, it was expelled from Anatolia and had to accept as the only alternative to genocidal slaughter the world's first compulsory population exchange, which dumped 1.3 million Anatolian Greeks on a pre-war population of 4.3 million. This effectively bankrupted Greece, a poor agricultural country of rocky hills. Its politics were unstable as parties, like those elsewhere in the region, tended to be shifting factions around an individual, not stable entities. Relations were poor with Italy, which gained territory at Greek expense, and with Bulgaria, which lost territory to Greece. Though involved in two of the crises of the 1920s, Greece primarily licked its wounds.

So did Bulgaria. Despite its territorial losses and reparations, Bulgaria enjoyed most of the attributes of a progressive modern state except stable politics. These were turbulent, violent, and tended to extremes, both left-wing and ethnic, involving Macedonians whom Bulgaria viewed as Bulgars. Relations with all neighbours were hostile as Bulgaria was intensely revisionist, especially coveting all of Macedonia but lacking the strength to improve its frontiers.

Even more powerless was tiny Albania, created only in 1913, Europe's sole state with a Muslim majority. It was ethnically homogeneous though many Albanians lived in Greece and Yugoslavia, but divided into the clans of a mountainous north and the peasant villages of an agrarian south. A clan chief named Ahmed Zogu became president in 1925 and King Zog I in 1928. He discovered that since the great powers had recognized Albania as an Italian sphere, he could not maintain independence by playing them off against each other. There was only one, and it intended to dominate. Italy was also the sole source of development capital, but required a treaty in 1926 in response to Yugoslav meddling and another in 1927 implicitly against Greece and Yugoslavia. When in 1931 Zog failed to renew the first treaty, Italy ended the subsidy.

Albania's large neighbour, Yugoslavia, was the most complicated of the new states.* Politics were very unstable, and the Serbian government system was ineffective in a state five times the size of pre-war Serbia. A royal dictatorship in 1929 aimed at unity, but led instead to Croat terrorism, encouraged by Italy and Hungary, both of which had territorial aspirations. Italy obtained Fiume in the end but hoped for far more, whereas Hungary sought to regain all territorial losses. Yugoslavia's foreign policy rested precariously on the Little Entente and France.

So did that of Rumania. Both were *status quo* powers and got on well, though they did not have the same enemies other than Hungary. As a key *cordon sanitaire* state, Rumania more than doubled in size and had serious minority problems, especially with Hungarians. Magyars were feared politically, Jews economically, and the old core of the state dominated, seeing even very old minorities as foreigners. King Carol was excluded by law from the throne in 1926, chiefly because of his flamboyant mistress, but returned in 1930 to rule for a decade.

*   *   *

Not all small states were on the periphery. Some found themselves in the core where they could not escape great power rivalries. Holland and Belgium were effectively wedged between Germany, Britain, and France and of concern to all three. The Netherlands, once a major maritime and commercial power but now a shrewd little old lady, long experienced in statecraft, knew exactly how to treat great powers to gain her ends, deploying her economic, technical, and financial assets with inconspicuous skill and never pestering the mighty. Though she leaned toward Germany, with whom she had close financial ties, she recovered swiftly from the international opprobrium initially heaped on her for refusing to surrender the ex-Kaiser in his long exile.

Belgium, created in the 1830s, had a sheltered childhood as a compulsorily neutral state guaranteed by the great powers. As a result, her diplomacy had been chiefly economic, and adulthood was delayed. War and peace forced rapid maturation, and Versailles treaty provisions catapulted Belgium to the centre of her great power neighbours' triangular battles over the 'German question', for she was the only small state with large reparations claims and a role in the Rhineland occupation. Belgian leaders adjusted quickly to this transformation, but few developed the instinctive delicacy of their Dutch counterparts in dealing with great powers. As the historic and recent invasion route between France and Germany, Belgium tried to rest for security on her two faithful guarantors, Britain and France, who disagreed about her, as about all else. Luxembourg, tiny but industrially and strategically important, entered

---

* For details of the east European peace settlement, including Yugoslavia's origins and complexities, see Chapter 6.

into reluctant economic union with Belgium but, unlike its partner, clung to permanent neutrality.

Czechoslovakia and Poland, also victor states, were larger and stronger than Belgium, but brand new and perhaps even more exposed, especially Poland. They were at odds from the outset, though both feared Germany. They clashed over the border district of Teschen (Cieszyn, Těšín), a Polish-populated industrial area containing coal and rail nets needed by Czechoslovakia, most of which it gained in 1920 at the price of enduring Polish bitterness. Each state wished to lead an alliance system including the other in a subordinate position. Beyond that, they were unlike in social structure, temperament, diplomatic style, and enemies, aside from Germany.

Poland was born into a temporary power vacuum created by the collapse of three empires and was an awkward merger of parts of all three, which had differing economic and political patterns. It spent the interwar years quarrelling dangerously with all its neighbours, despite its exposed position without defensible boundaries astride the north European plain between Russia and Germany. These two, who shared a mutual hostility to and contempt for the new state, used the German, Ukrainian and Belorussian minorities (as well as Lithuania) to cause trouble. Poland resented its minority treaty, whose existence it blamed on its large Jewish population; after complaints to the League about Polonization, especially by Berlin, it stopped co-operating with Geneva about minorities in 1934. It was geographically precarious, economically in deep crisis from 1923 to 1926, and politically divided until a 1926 coup launched the semi-dictatorship of Marshal Pilsudski, hero of the 1920 Russian war. He and the gentry who ran the state were dedicated to Poland's independence but more romantic than realistic about its predicament. As they knew, their nation was Weimar's first target, but Russia was hostile, too, so they conducted an excitable and 'acrobatic' foreign policy to little avail.[6] They counted on salvation from the West, but Britain was cool from the outset and France, Poland's anchor, proved inadequate. Both thought Poland's eastern frontier, achieved by force of arms, too generous and a source of future difficulty. By 1925, both anticipated and accepted future German acquisition of Poland's famous Corridor to the sea.

Czechoslovakia, the westernmost Slavic state, was territorially satisfied and possessed a balanced economy containing 80 per cent of the Habsburg Empire's industry as well as fertile farmlands, a stolid bourgeois society based on a large middle class, and east central Europe's only enduring democracy. But it also had three uneasy ill-unified components in the rich dominant Czech lands of Bohemia and Moravia, impoverished Slovakia, and Ruthenia. Beyond that were minorities, especially a large Austro-German one in the mountainous industrial borderlands, which resented being deposed from ruler to ruled. In time Germanic political parties began to co-operate and entered the government in 1925, but relations with Berlin were strained, while Hungary and Poland coveted Czech territory. The army and arms industry were excellent, but the state had little confidence in its assets and felt dependent on the West, especially France. The seemingly perpetual and ubiquitous Foreign Minister, Edvard Beneš, substituted involvement for influence, prominence at Geneva for power, becoming well known and much disliked. He joined in the Little Entente with Rumania and Yugoslavia against Hungary in response to Bela Kun's brief Marxist regime and two failed efforts in 1921 of the last Habsburg ruler to return as king of Hungary. The three foreign ministers met annually, but their countries had little in common beyond hostility to Hungary. As this system was otherwise useless, Czechoslovakia felt isolated and insecure.

Europe's core also contained studiously neutral little Alpine Switzerland and two severely truncated losers, Austria and Hungary. Clemenceau said, 'Austria, that is what is left over.'[7] It accepted its territorial loss but not demotion to being a second Switzerland. Psychological dislocation was acute, and Austrians yearned for the forbidden *Anschluss* so as once again to be a part of a great power. The ideological divide between socialist Vienna and the conservative hinterland deepened, with private right-wing armies united by 1927 into the Heimwehr, a growing political force. The old economic patterns were gone with the lost areas, especially as successor states erected tariff walls; economic decline and hyperinflation ensued. The League supervised financial reconstruction in 1922 with great power loans (and a proviso that Austria must not raise the *Anschluss* issue for twenty years), but more international loans were needed to keep Austria afloat financially, despite greater prosperity in the late 1920s and good relations with Czechoslovakia and Italy. Interwar Austria might have been viable with more imagination and less fear of being small, but in fact it barely hobbled along on the crutches of international finance.

Hungary, non-Slavic amid Slavic neighbours, was viable and homogeneous but utterly unforgiving of its territorial losses. Despite large losses to Rumania, it especially resented smaller ones to Czechoslovakia, seeing that state as the key to the post-war system and hoping it could divide it, but Ruthenes and Slovaks hated Magyars more than Czechs. All Magyars rejected the treaty of Trianon, but consolidation was required before even faint hope of revisionism existed. Hungary remained a monarchy with Admiral Mikós Horthy as regent, entered the League in 1922, underwent League financial reconstruction in 1924, and gradually emerged from isolation in the 1920s arriving at a *modus vivendi* with its neighbours. But powerless revisionism remained, along with constant intrigues with Italy against the *status quo* and the neighbours.

＊   ＊   ＊

The ability to preserve or change that *status quo* rested mainly with the great powers. Only they could maintain the peace and the peace settlement, but the majority of them opposed the latter, which is one reason why the former proved unstable. Another was that in the effective absence of the United States and the Soviet Union most of the time, only one power was at first truly great, and it wished to turn its attention elsewhere. The peace settlement did not reflect the true continental power balance, especially as the United States and Britain largely withdrew; thus upholding it required an active and continuing effort, which only one major power, France, now less than genuinely great, was willing to make. As the policies of the authors of the peace clashed and more major powers favoured revision than the *status quo*, the post-war settlement unravelled.

Though power gradually shifted, policy goals of the great states rarely changed much as cabinets came and went. Political changes brought new approaches, personal styles, emphases, and tactics, but the bureaucracies advising political leaders and the national interests dictating goals remained stable. However, though the principles on which the powers operated seldom changed sharply, interpretations of them sometimes did, owing to individual idiosyncracies and human error. Britain never abandoned its traditional commitment to a continental balance of power but misread it badly in the 1920s. Both the Weimar Republic and Hitler incorporated aspects of Wilhelmine diplomacy but interpreted them differently from their predecessors and each other. Nonetheless, as national interests or perceptions thereof were largely dictated by external conditions, geography, past history and tradition, economic factors, and widely held assumptions, policy goals most often varied only slightly and slowly.

Russia was briefly an exception. Soviet revisionism extended beyond the peace settlement, and encompassed both traditional Russian goals and at first the revolutionary imperatives of its new Marxist ideology. But for much of the interwar era, Russia's role in Europe was peripheral, in the wings or making brief cameo appearances. The new Soviet Union was a primitive giant, at first sorely lacking in sinews and suffering the effects of a raging fever. Domestic consolidation took priority, and Russia, unrecognized diplomatically except by its neighbours, was rarely seen or heard in Europe in the early 1920s as it embarked on the New Economic Policy, a temporary partial compromise with capitalism. Lenin set Soviet foreign policy and opted early for realism, a course confirmed when revolution in Germany late in 1923 failed, but some hope of broader revolution lingered into 1924, when Lenin died. Stalin was also a realist, a Russian nationalist as well as a Marxist. Knowing world revolution was not imminent, he chose co-existence and 'socialism in one country'. Westerners reacted with cautious detente and intransigence, often simultaneously, tempted by the illusory promise of the underdeveloped Russian market but dismayed by Soviet revolutionary imperialism as the Comintern[*] gained control of some

---

[*] On the Comintern, see Chapter 4.

liberation movements in their empires. Stalin pursued trade with the West until in 1928 Russia turned inward to rapid industrialization, forced collectivization of agriculture, and military build-up.

At first the new Marxist state (which produced the world's first modern women diplomats, including the first female head of mission) was isolated by choice and by capitalist quarantine. It had few diplomatic weapons to deploy in its implicit and explicit rejection of the traditional great powers and their assumptions. In seeking to destroy their balance of power system, Russia used diplomacy, propaganda, revolutionary activity, and via the Comintern intervention in the internal affairs of other states, especially labour movements, but it soon shifted to more conventional diplomacy, trying to end its isolation and using traditional balance of power tactics. Through the 1920s it imagined plots of capitalist states against it when none existed. Stalin especially feared aggression or domination of the continent by France, whose aims and strength he overestimated, as did others. He saw the era as a truce between wars; recognizing Russia's weakness, he hoped to keep it neutral until the capitalist powers were exhausted and Soviet intervention could be decisive. But first Russia needed to break out of isolation. The initial moves under Lenin were toward Turkey, another revolutionary regime viewed with hostility by Western powers, and then toward the other pariah, the Weimar Republic, which was both a barrier against Western aggression and an essential bridge to the West and to the trade agreements Russia badly needed.

Germany, centrally located, half again as populous as France with triple its crude steel production in 1921[8] and Europe's strongest industrial power, was a muscular, glowering youngish man locked in detention for the moment, somewhat bloodied but in no way bowed. The Weimar Republic imposed a veneer of democracy but left unchanged the traditional power bases: army, bureaucracy, industrialists, judiciary, eastern agrarian magnates, and universities. Imperial aims remained unchanged as well, though defeat halted expansion and forced revision of the timetable to avoid antagonizing too many powers at once. Though moderates prevailed at first, elites were revisionist, refusing to accept 1918's military verdict and the new Europe. Some aimed at full control of Germany and Austria without treaty restrictions, then continental domination, and ultimately global power, a scenario which not only assumed eventual war with Britain and the United States but also ignored the fact that the balance of power mechanism invariably reacted against attempts at continental domination by a single state. The republic was rent by social divisions, and a strongly revisionist foreign policy was the one thing on which most Germans agreed. Moreover, the few genuinely democratic politicians of an unloved democracy, damned as 'November criminals' because they signed the Armistice their predecessors had sought, felt obliged to prove their patriotism by one revisionist claim after another. As the Versailles treaty left German power largely intact if temporarily restricted, their task was far from hopeless for a technologically sophisticated industrial state with a vigorous young population and a high birth-rate. Gustav Stresemann, Foreign Minister from 1923 to 1929, achieved much by peaceful, indirect, and especially economic means, but not a dramatic reversal of the humiliation of the 'Versailles *Diktat*' which many – and then more and more – craved, until Hitler obliged them.

Since the Allies fought World War I to prevent German domination of Europe, not to destroy Germany, and since they needed a barrier to Bolshevism, the Weimar Republic remained a great power even if temporarily shorn of some of the appurtenances thereof. Though in absolute terms it was weaker than before the war, relatively it was stronger as the United States, Britain, and Russia all partly withdrew from Europe, France had been enervated, and its other neighbours were small and weak. From the outset, Germany used its economic vigour, minorities in neighbouring countries, the opportunities offered by Russia, propaganda and stubborn non-co-operation along with a fairly successful campaign to divide Britain and France to improve its position, undo the Versailles treaty, and gain greater power. After 1925, American capital investment, expiry and revision of treaty clauses, systematic economic penetration of eastern Europe, and surreptitious rearmament added more strength. But since Germany, unlike other major states, lay at the centre of Europe, it could expand as its might grew only at the expense of its fearful neighbours. Hence the 'German question' of how to contain its power peacefully.[9]

Unlike Germany and Russia, Italy was among the victors, but she was equally dissatisfied with the peace settlement, which did not meet her large expectations. The *ingénue* of the European great states, the youngest and weakest, she flirted with them all and perpetually scrambled to keep up, as she had more pulchritude than power. Italy was not really a member of the club, a 'great power' by courtesy but lacking the wherewithal in population, resources, industrial strength, and military might. She tried to sell herself to the highest bidder – or all bidders at once, but her long coastline exposed to naval bombardment inclined her often toward Britain, the Mediterranean's dominant naval power. Politics were unstable until Benito Mussolini became Prime Minister late in 1922, consolidating a dictatorship in the late 1920s. This he called Fascist, but he was slow to define the system, which was authoritarian but comparatively mild, perhaps because it lacked much ideology. Mussolini invented the corporative state, organized by economic activities, but pursued it only far enough to gain firm control. He was a bombastic little man, forever glorifying war, but his instrument was only a slender maiden, so he confined himself to minor escapades to gain glory cheaply. Italy sought to dominate the Adriatic Sea and, under Mussolini, also the Mediterranean. It intrigued with Hungary, especially at Yugoslav expense, dominated Albania, and propped Austria as a weak Alpine neighbour and a buffer against Germany. Mussolini wanted German reparations, particularly coal, but otherwise accepted Berlin's revisionism, provided it was at the expense of France with whom relations were strained, especially with regard to North Africa and anti-Fascist refugees on French soil.

Other great powers held Italy in contempt, and Britain was no exception. This bluff and powerful middle-aged gentleman was a bit less muscular than in the past, but trying not to think about that, especially as the loss of muscle was concealed by a greater reach than ever before as the empire reached its zenith. Britain emerged from the war physically unscathed despite much expense and loss of life, but lost the carrying trade on the world's oceans, the global financial centre, the Latin American market, and part of the Asian market to the United States. Two years after the Armistice, its army had shrunk to a tenth of its wartime level, leaving only 370 000 troops to police a quarter of the globe – and even fewer a year later. It was effectively disarmed on land, and only the Royal Air Force kept order cheaply and held the Empire. Britain was overextended and afflicted with debt and persistent economic problems, especially ageing industries that were facing younger, cheaper rivals. Though it seemed a big winner of the war, its strong position arose in part from temporary eclipse of other powers; besides, American and Japanese strength was growing. Since relative power is what matters in international politics – and aeroplanes were narrowing the defensive barrier of the English Channel, Europe's apparent greatest power was less secure than it seemed. As always, west European countries facing the Channel, from which Britain could be attacked, were deemed a vital interest; the rest of the continent was not.

Britain traditionally repudiated alliances at war's end and reconciled with the defeated foe, resuming a free hand. The Versailles treaty yoked Britain to France, preventing open repudiation, but Lloyd George zigzagged toward the middle, where London always wished to be. He and his successors wanted Europe stabilized without substantial British intervention, partly so that Britain could attend to economic recession at home and empire abroad; thus they evaded continental commitments and actions. They pursued a Russian policy of trade and containment and chose an Atlantic policy of co-operation with the United States, whom they saw as difficult but essential – and no threat to Britain or its empire. Traditional hostility to France quickly revived, along with a desire for reconciliation with the German 'underdog'. British politicians mistook the very short-term continental power balance for the underlying reality and thus believed France was too strong and Germany too weak. Some therefore wanted to build Germany up against a supposed French predominance. Britain was weary and ardently wished to avoid any repetition of the ordeal of World War I. Thus, though some British officials concurred in France's strategic assessment of probable future German continental domination unless the treaty was maintained, they knew Britain lacked the power and political will to enforce it, so they turned a blind eye, temporized, and engaged in appeasement. They did what was easiest, which soon was seen as 'moral' and 'wise' as Britain came to believe its own propaganda and that of Weimar, taking German statements at face value to escape continental embroilment.

Only France was prepared to engage in consistent (if far from complete) enforcement of a treaty she deemed barely adequate, but she was an ageing, fading dowager, trying to hide her exhaustion under a brave layer of rouge which did not fully conceal a fundamental loss of vitality in the bloodletting just past. She was haunted by her horrendous casualties and by a demographic nightmare, for the severe wartime drop in the birth-rate of an ageing population portended a small army in the late 1930s. Her industrial core required long, costly reconstruction. Her parliamentary system, like that of Weimar, was unloved and unstable, with frequent cabinet changes, and, like Germany, she was abnormally preoccupied with foreign policy in the post-war years. Her leaders knew France had not won the war but had merely hung on by her fingernails until rescued; they understood how weak France was, and their policies, which others termed imperialistic, arose from fear. They tended to be legalistic and rigid, clinging to the Versailles treaty as the barrier to German resurgence. The combination of legalism and inattention to propaganda by most leaders was a public relations disaster. France, which had been a great power for centuries, was seen as dominant on the continent, and very briefly she was, but only from a temporary lack of competition, which evaporated as Germany revived and Soviet Russia developed a competent army. In addition, French military superiority melted as the term of service was progressively cut from three years to one, budgets were slashed, and obsolescent equipment was not replaced. France was too weak militarily, economically, financially, and demographically to maintain the *status quo* single-handedly, especially as the artificial advantages of the treaty designed to compensate her for Germany's greater inherent strength lapsed or were cancelled one by one.

As the vital pre-war Russian alliance was politically impossible with a Marxist state, France compensated by pacts or military schemes with Germany's neighbours, starting with Belgium – where she hoped to fight the next war, sparing French soil. Next came Poland, seen initially as an asset to Germany's east more than a liability, and then between 1924 and 1927 all three Little Entente countries, starting with Czechoslovakia. This system was more impressive on paper than in practice and disintegrated when danger approached. It lacked cohesion, much serious French leadership, or effective economic reinforcement, for ruthless French economic imperialism was short-sighted. At heart, French leaders knew it would not suffice and that they were overextended militarily in Europe, with too many commitments to defend other countries. The eastern alliances lost credibility from

1926 on when France adopted a defensive military stance to protect only its own borders. Throughout, Paris sought but did not find security against German revival, trying to lean on a Britain which feared the French army, submarines, and air force (the only one then within bombing range of England), and which kept trying to loosen its ties to France. The fundamental problem, however, was pointed out in 1921 by a wise old French diplomat to a junior colleague: 'Young man, remember this: in the immediate future the difficulty will be to slide France reasonably smoothly into the ranks of the second-rate powers to which she belongs.'[10]

*　　*　　*

There was one additional new member of the cast, the League of Nations, whose role seemed unclear and in fact was created extemporaneously as it edged onto the diplomatic stage only to be shoved aside by the star players.* Though partly an agent of its Western great power parents, it was almost an orphan child, as Washington disowned it and London and Paris often maintained only a distant relationship, providing lip service for the sake of public opinion. As the great power members were mostly European, so were its focus and issues, its location in Geneva, its languages, and most officials in its Secretariat. Though France had hoped to make the League a real instrument to preserve the *status quo*, London's view, as expressed by a Canadian statesman, was that it should be 'an international round table but not an international War Office'.[11] Like other powers, Britain had no objection to delay and discussion – but not of its own vital interests. As state sovereignty remained intact, there was no way to ensure co-operation or obedience, and great powers circumvented Geneva, deciding great matters elsewhere among themselves. Still, the League provided a forum to air grievances and procedures for settling disputes, which worked when the states involved were willing and were neither great powers nor their clients. It also affected diplomatic methods as foreign ministers regularly attended annual Assembly meetings and quarterly Council meetings, getting acquainted with their counterparts and engaging in quiet diplomacy over dinner or in hotel suites. But major issues were settled in Geneva's hotel rooms, not in the Assembly or Council halls. The League failed to meet unrealistic popular expectations, proving unable to act when even a regional power defied it, but as long as state sovereignty exists without significant restriction, what an international agency can achieve is limited.

Britain, France, and Italy disliked the spotlight of Geneva and the universal commitment of collective security, preferring other Versailles treaty agencies they had created, which they controlled, and in which they could settle matters offstage among themselves, quietly if contentiously. Most agencies existed to carry out the peace treaties, and included a small power

---

* On the origins, structure, and fundamental problems of the League, see Chapter 5.

or two, always Belgium on German questions, but they were essentially tools of their great power creators. The Conference of Ambassadors in Paris, which supervised boundary commissions to engage in precise delimitation, was to carry out unfinished business of the peace conference. The Reparation Commission, also in Paris, dealt with payments in cash and kind from the losers to the victors, focusing on Germany as the only loser with much wealth. The Inter-Allied Military Control Commission (IMCC) and its naval and air counterparts tried with limited success to enforce the disarmament clauses of the treaties, primarily against a resistant Germany.

There was also an extra-treaty institution in which the most crucial decisions were made. The Supreme Council, a continuation of the Big Four of the peace conference, began to meet intermittently before the Versailles treaty took effect on 10 January 1920 and continued until the Locarno conference in late 1925. Though Japanese delegates and American observers attended at first, participants were Britain, France, Italy, and usually Belgium, since Germany was almost always on the agenda. After the Weimar Republic was admitted to the inner circle at Locarno, meetings continued from 1926 on in Geneva hotel rooms during quarterly sessions of the League Council, and became known as 'Locarno tea parties'. These were sharply criticized by smaller powers, who recognized that the real decisions were being made away from the well-lit public stage of the League.

The great powers had revived the nineteenth-century Concert of Europe in modern form and were engaging in secret diplomacy to settle matters themselves with the habitual arrogance of great powers. Their agenda was almost entirely European. Though they ruled much of the globe, and Britain kept hoping to give its empire undivided attention, continental concerns were parochial and traditional. European states cared chiefly about the Old World's power equation and rivalries which, in their eyes, were what mattered, not other power struggles in Palestine, China, or on Peru's borders. Even the quarrelsome Balkans seemed backward and tiresome, the United States also irritating but fairly easy to ignore much of the time, though not in financial questions. European great powers concentrated primarily upon each other and their neighbours.

They did so in changed circumstances, for secret diplomacy was somewhat less secret than in the past. The war and unstable peace aroused and maintained popular interest in international politics. Quiet meetings in Geneva and Supreme Councils were subject to intense press scrutiny, not only from newspapermen but also radio reporters and photographers filming for newsreels that were shown weekly in cinemas. The media reporter saw what was visible on stage, not the more important exchanges behind the scenes, and thus propaganda became an effective new instrument of diplomacy. Campaigns were orchestrated, especially by Germany and Britain; not only electorates but also politicians came to believe oft-repeated assertions by their own government and sometimes others. These became 'facts', whether true or not. Anglo-German propaganda skills contributed to the unravelling of the Versailles treaty even as it was first being implemented.

*   *   *

Initially Supreme Councils wrote the treaty of Sèvres, last of the original peace treaties, and began the complex task of implementing the Versailles treaty. Soon, however, the ongoing tension between French insecurity and German determination to break the treaty meant that debate narrowed mainly to disarmament and reparations, issues directly affecting Germany's military and economic power, especially in relation to France. As Berlin resisted on both fronts, Allied meetings in their capitals or in resorts, sometimes with German officials, were frequent and stormy as London resisted treaty enforcement. It thought it had more to gain from trade with Weimar than reparations, quailed before Berlin's threat of an export drive to British detriment to pay for them, and opposed asking anything of Germany which it might refuse lest action on the continent result. France, enjoying some support from Belgium and Italy and recognizing the power implications if it had to pay war debts and immense reconstruction costs whereas Germany paid nothing, held out for substantial reparation to pay for part of the damage done. Failing that, Germany would be the victor in 'the continuation of war by other means'[12] – which was a fundamental power struggle, not just a haggle over the technicalities of reparations.

Many plans were devised, each with a lower total than the one before and each designed to look as if the total would be far larger than it was. All parties agreed on this sleight of hand, if nothing else, for the reason that continental victors had promised their electorates vast sums and Weimar politicians were making political capital out of the supposed immensity of reparations, a chorus Britain soon joined. In May 1921, the victors patched together the London Schedule of Payments which required 50 milliard gold marks ($12.5 milliard or US billion, £2.5 milliard or thousand million) over 36 years under the appearance of 132 milliard gold marks in a misleading scheme of payments in cash and kind. This plan was probably within Germany's capacity to pay, had it seen any reason to do so. Under threat of seizure of its industrial heartland, the Ruhr Basin next to the Belgian and British Rhineland occupation zones, Germany bowed for the moment.

In the summer of 1921, Germany made the first cash payment of one milliard gold marks, mostly in borrowed monies, but gained the required foreign currencies by abruptly dumping paper marks on the market to buy them. The increased supply caused the paper mark to depreciate sharply in value. Then and thereafter, Germany blamed the existence of reparations for the progressive collapse of the paper mark and concomitant price inflation as each mark bought less, though after the first milliard, little cash was paid. It is unlikely that something which mostly did not happen could be a significant cause. Inflation arose primarily from printing money to accommodate a variety of domestic and foreign policy aims, including hope of reducing reparations. After the first milliard, Germany began to demand relief on cash payments; by then, defaults on coal quotas were routine and problems were arising on timber deliveries. More Supreme Councils only produced Allied impasse as Britain and France each blocked the other. Neither could gain a clearcut victory, though most plans gave France the form but Britain, and thus Germany, the substance.

In these circumstances, Lloyd George tried to shift the focus to opening up the Russian market, hoping reparations would pale into insignificance in the anticipated torrent of profits from the Russian trade. Thus a six-week conference was held at Genoa in the spring of 1922, involving most European nations, including the Marxist state in its diplomatic debut. Russia needed aid and trade to counter its famine arising from war and civil war, but its seizure of foreign properties and repudiation of tsarist debts to vast numbers of Western bondholders were problems which proved insoluble. The conference produced only a dramatic surprise: on Easter Sunday, the Russian and German delegations stole off to the nearby seaside resort of Rapallo and signed a treaty conferring recognition and cancelling all claims, including reparations.

The Rapallo treaty was an anti-Polish pact as well as a victory of the 'Easterners' in the German Foreign Ministry and army over those who preferred co-operation with the West. It led to trade and Russian recruitment of German industrial specialists as well as small but significant military collaboration and some joint installations in Russia. The Bolsheviks gained much-needed instruction in modern military technology, tactics, and techniques; with rearmament in mind, Germany tested tanks, trained pilots, and experimented with poison gases far beyond the purview of the IMCC. This mutually beneficial arrangement lasted throughout the Weimar era.

After Genoa failed, reparations returned to the fore. Though the London Schedule was suspended before Genoa for the rest of 1922 and Germany was making only token cash payments, it sought a long cessation of payment. France feared that once stopped, reparations would never resume, and urged seizure of a valuable asset, such as German state forests, to ensure otherwise. As 1923 approached, something had to be done or the London Schedule would regain force, but there was no agreement on what to do. A British proposal to collect only enough reparations to pay war debts to the United States, designed to embarrass Washington into debt reduction, failed. Though its economy remained Europe's strongest despite mounting financial chaos, Germany slid into hyperinflation in the autumn, alarming even those leaders who hoped to use mark depreciation to force reparations reduction. Allied meetings achieved only deadlock. In January 1923, Britain tried to take control of the reparations issue with a scheme politically ruinous to the leaders of continental victors, whereas Berlin made few significant concessions or financial reforms. Thus on the basis of timber and coal defaults declared by the Reparation Commission over British protest, France, with Belgian and Italian support, encircled the Ruhr and seized Essen within it to force Germany to honour the Versailles treaty. Britain disapproved but allowed rail access to the Ruhr across its Rhineland zone. Berlin ended coal shipments and called for passive resistance, paying Ruhr workers not to work and industrialists the profits they otherwise would have made. As tax rates were abnormally low, tax collection inadequate, and budget deficits chronic, money was printed night and day in ever larger denominations to finance payments at the cost of galloping hyperinflation.

France's premier, Raymond Poincaré, had not foreseen resistance, but he knew the treaty and France's so-called victory in the war were at stake, so he sent more troops, isolated the Ruhr, and hung grimly on, determined to avoid defeat in an extension of World War I. Though he never cut off shipments from Germany of the food and money sustaining the resistance and in fact created soup kitchens for the poor, France received a very bad press, which it did little to counter. In August 1923, Stresemann became German Chancellor and realized resistance could not be sustained or financed through the winter. He called it off in late September and with immense skill set about minimizing the damage to Germany. Briefly, the Reich nearly broke up, with abortive revolutions of both the Communist left and extreme right, including Adolf Hitler, but German unity held, and Stresemann, with remarkable ease in desperate circumstances, replaced the worthless marks at a rate of a trillion (British billion) old marks for one new one. Germany's public debt, including its war debt, was reduced in value to less than US 1¢ by this exchange,[13] and the great industrial concerns emerged similarly debt free, but the long-term cost was high, for the middle classes lost their savings, investments, war bonds, pensions, and often their salaries, valuables, property, and social status – and as a result became sharply radicalized to the right.

Meanwhile, London responded in the autumn of 1923 to Stresemann's appeals and approached Washington about a new reparations scheme. As Italy and Belgium joined in, France was isolated and had to accept an inquiry leading to a new plan. Since Washington's separate peace with Germany forbade involvement with Versailles treaty agencies without Congressional consent, American participants, chosen and briefed by the State Department, officially functioned as private citizens. Two committees set to work at the start of 1924. The resultant Dawes Plan, named after the American chairman, was reluctantly accepted by all powers for lack of any other. Its implementation, amounting to revision of the Versailles treaty, was arranged at a conference in London in the summer of 1924, initially among the Allies, then with Germany. France, which had slid into financial crisis, was brought to heel by British pressure, Stresemann's skill, and American bankers, whose political terms for financial aid were stiff. Thus France had to give up her instruments of compulsion and failed to gain a German trade treaty before five-year Versailles treaty economic clauses would expire in January 1925. Germany gained a large loan to cover the first year's token reparations payment, which would then gradually increase. All understood that when payments became onerous four years hence, Germany would seek new revision.

The Dawes Plan was not the only result of the year-long 1923 crisis. In January, Lithuania took advantage of the onset of the Ruhr occupation to seize Memel from Germany, gaining a good port. In August, as the Ruhr crisis approached its climax and France needed to keep Italy at its side, the Italian chief of a boundary commission delimiting the Greco-Albanian frontier was murdered on Greek soil, probably by Albanian bandits. Mussolini promptly bombarded and briefly seized the strategic Greek isle of Corfu at the entrance to the Adriatic. Greece, reeling from the influx of Anatolian refugees, appealed to the League. Mussolini preferred the Conference of Ambassadors, parent of the boundary commission, where Italy and France could outvote Britain. Small League members tried and failed to maintain League jurisdiction, overridden by the great powers. The League's first major failure revealed that it could not discipline a regional power which had tacit great power support. Their instrument, the Conference of Ambassadors, fined Greece, whose culpability was never proved. Mussolini had planned to retain Corfu but British threats of naval action led him to take the profit and evacuate, partly to ease his final seizure of Fiume in September. Mussolini aspired as well to lead the West into diplomatic recognition of the Soviet Union, but Britain's first Labour government anticipated him early in 1924. Others soon followed.

*   *   *

For France, 1924 was a year of disaster as the victory in the Ruhr was swiftly undone, but she salvaged from the London conference a British commitment seriously to inspect German disarmament. Since the first Rhineland (Cologne) zone was scheduled for evacuation on 10 January 1925 if Germany were in treaty compliance, with the reparations settlement the issue narrowed to disarmament. IMCC inspections demonstrated significant default, and evacuation was postponed. This situation presented Stresemann with a problem, as did a proposal for an Anglo-French-Belgian alliance. He wished to block that and gain evacuation of Cologne without further disarmament or inspections. His solution, the offer of a Rhineland pact, succeeded for several reasons. Britain also wanted to evacuate Cologne and end disarmament inspections; its Cabinet was divided over the proposed alliance. Further, it had vetoed the League scheme for a Draft Treaty of Mutual Assistance against aggressors, and the new Conservative government was about to reject the more limited Geneva Protocol, linking security, disarmament and compulsory arbitration, to which the Dominions objected. It found a limited regional system far preferable. Paris disliked the scheme, for it placed Germany on an equal basis with France and made Britain the arbiter of both while at the same time not applying to Germany's eastern borders. However, French officials dared not reject the long-sought British guarantee lest it never be offered again.

Thus in the absence of other schemes, the Rhineland pact moved forward through a long summer of negotiation by the three leaders who would dominate the diplomacy of the late 1920s: Stresemann, Austen Chamberlain of Britain, and Aristide Briand of France. Germany and France as well as Germany and Belgium would affirm the permanence of their existing frontiers and the inviolability of the Rhineland demilitarized zone, forswearing war against each other. Berlin could not be brought to any written affirmation of its eastern borders but agreed to limited arbitration treaties with Poland and Czechoslovakia, to whom France also gave new treaties as a consolation prize, since aid against German attack was still narrowly permitted. It was understood that the IMCC would not haggle, Cologne would be evacuated, and Germany would enter the League with a permanent Council seat but without obligation to participate in sanctions – this last allegedly because of its disarmament and exposed position but actually to mollify its Soviet ally which feared a Western bloc potentially turned against Bolshevism.

A conference in the small Swiss town of Locarno in October 1925 resolved the final problems. Mussolini had dithered all summer, not wanting any responsibility north of the Alps, but he found the prestige irresistible and at the last minute attended, joining Britain as co-guarantor of the Franco-Belgian and German commitments on the Rhenish frontier. The outward appearance at Locarno was studied amiability, including a hilarious press luncheon where German and Allied diplomats dined together for the first time, but behind closed doors, bargaining was bitter and tense, especially by France and her unhappy eastern allies. Nonetheless, the conference ended with a carefully staged ceremony of brotherhood accompanied by church bells and fireworks. The clear intent was to freeze the Franco-German and Belgo-German frontiers forever, affording France security, ending contention, and bringing peace in the West. However, treaties may be interpreted in many ways; a few days later, Stresemann seized upon a German-induced ambiguity in the text of the Rhineland pact and tried unsuccessfully to repurchase districts lost in the Versailles treaty to Belgium in an attempt to begin territorial revision in the west at the weakest point facing him. Though still pleading poverty, Germany could find funds for what it really wanted.

Locarno changed little, neither French fear nor German revisionism, and under a veneer of greater civility, relations remained strained. The public image of the conference, however, led to much talk of the 'spirit of Locarno', which meant different things to the several participants. Stresemann saw a platform from which to gain further treaty revision, which he expected sooner than it came, for Chamberlain, unlike most British leaders, was devoted to France in general and Briand in particular. Stresemann always had a list of concessions to Germany he said were needed to bring real peace to Europe; as he fought for the immediate goal, he added new items to his lengthening list. Meanwhile, he knew he could not use military force, which Weimar lacked in any event, so he patiently used other means to build German strength, especially creation of economically dependent client states, toward the goal of domination of east central and south-eastern Europe.

Briand understood Stresemann's goals and did all possible to slow the process of strengthening Germany mainly at French expense; he knew France was too weak to stop German resurgence altogether, and for him accepting it slowly was the price of the precious British guarantee. He hoped Germany's voluntary affirmation of its western frontier was valuable but feared it might not be, and understood, as did Poland and Czechoslovakia, that the lack of any affirmation in the east cast doubt on the validity and permanence of their borders with Germany. At heart for France, Locarno signified defeat and acceptance of British policy domination. Shortly thereafter, it assumed a defensive posture and in 1927 began constructing the Maginot Line of fortifications along the German border. However, what Briand had gained was only a militarily inoperable paper guarantee, for Britain, with no troops to spare, made military arrangements with nobody. Chamberlain, the sole true believer of Locarno, thought he had made peace. He also thought he had reorganized Europe with Britain holding the balance from, as he said, 'a semi-detached position'.[14] Indeed, until the balance tipped further, a largely disarmed Britain was briefly decisive.

Mussolini was never infused with the Locarno spirit. In 1926 and 1927, he imposed treaties on Albania and engaged in revisionist intrigues, especially with Hungary and against Yugoslavia. But he did not resist the main currents of European diplomacy and in 1929 even resolved Italy's long impasse with the Vatican, dating from its absorption of the Papal States in 1870, and negotiated an accord creating the world's smallest state, that of Vatican City, in the heart of Rome. Russia was alarmed by Locarno, seeing the Western offer of German League entry as likely to create a bloc for an anti-Soviet crusade. Stresemann provided a new treaty of Berlin in 1926 to calm unfounded fears. However, Russia sought trade agreements and Western technicians, and began to appear occasionally at conferences in Geneva.

One reason why the post-Locarno years were the best of the interwar era was that all major revisionist powers – Germany, Italy, the Soviet Union, and Japan – were fairly co-operative diplomatically with the *status quo*

Western powers most of the time; thus tension abated somewhat. Another was economic improvement as most west European countries except Britain reached 1913 levels, despite persistent high unemployment. Prosperity was uneven and rarely shared in eastern or Mediterranean states. In 1926 a steel cartel to limit production among major European producers in order to raise prices* was seen as a sign of a new co-operative spirit arising from Locarno, but in fact it was signed on Berlin's terms, as was the eventual Franco-German trade treaty in 1927. Before that, just after Locarno, the League Council stopped a small Greco-Bulgarian shooting war, thanks to forceful Anglo-French action. The great powers were decisive, but the League took the credit and engaged in much self-congratulation.

Though the Locarno pacts were signed in December 1925 and Cologne evacuated in January 1926, the treaties would not take formal effect until Germany entered the League. Its entry and permanent Council seat were not controversial, but several other claimants demanded permanent seats as well, causing difficulty and delay. Spain left the League temporarily and Brazil definitively over the question, which was resolved by increasing the number of non-permanent seats. With that settled, Germany entered the League in September 1926. Membership of Europe's strongest revisionist power in this *status quo* organization changed it considerably, especially as Stresemann quickly used the Council seat to support complaints of German minorities in Poland. Even before that, on the heels of German entry, Briand and Stresemann stole away for a private lunch together at a country inn at Thoiry near Geneva. Hailed as another sign of the spirit of Locarno, it was in fact great power secret diplomacy. They discussed a startling proposal whereby Germany would take advantage of French, Belgian, and Polish financial distress to buy its way out of much of the Versailles treaty. In the end, the scheme met with too many objections, and the currencies concerned were restored by conventional means.

Thereafter, Briand and Stresemann met often in Geneva hotel rooms during League sessions, either alone or at Locarno tea parties. These replaced Supreme Councils, as progressive dismantlement of the peace treaty meant fewer occasions where Berlin demanded and the Entente had to answer in unison, and they became a vital part of the diplomacy of the late 1920s, as Germany became a full member of the revised European Concert. Despite concentration on the German question, Locarno tea parties were far-ranging and dealt with many European problems, leaving the League Council to address 'such weighty matters as the appointment of the governing body of the International Cinematographic Institute at Rome'.[15]

*   *   *

---

* The United States produced half the world's steel but consumed its output; thus it was not a factor in export markets.

The optimism – in public at least – of 1925 and 1926 could not be sustained, as real peace stubbornly refused to jell. Despite improvement, economic problems continued, including slow growth, overpopulation, a smaller share of world trade, and Japanese and American competition in world markets. In late 1925 and 1926, Germany used its economic vigour toward political goals in an 18-month tariff war against Poland to force territorial revision. This failed when the 1926 British coal strike boosted Polish coal export permanently, enabling currency stabilization to accompany Pilsudski's political stabilization.[16] Efforts to create an organization in the east to match the Locarno structure in the west met with small success. A World Economic Conference in Geneva of fifty nations under League auspices in 1927 accomplished little. Efforts to extend disarmament to the victors, as promised in the peace treaties, made scant progress, as preliminary work on land disarmament begun in Geneva in 1925 inched along and a 1927 naval conference failed, though another in 1930 did better at a high price.* In addition, Moscow, which saw efforts toward pacification as hostile moves directed toward it, underwent a war scare in 1927, following assassination of its envoy in Warsaw and severance of diplomatic relations by Britain until 1929 because of interference in its internal affairs (especially the 1926 General Strike) and China holdings. The war scare arose from Moscow's idiosyncratic vision, not from reality, and a special Locarno tea party charged Stresemann to reassure Russia which, by now, needed Germany as a bridge westward far more than Weimar needed its Russian partner.

That became obvious when Germany but not the Soviet Union was invited to participate in the signing ceremonies for the Kellogg–Briand pact in August 1928.† An ailing Stresemann came for the ceremony, the first German foreign minister received in Paris since 1870, murmuring about the need for *Anschluss* as he pressed for early evacuation of the Rhineland. His immediate concern was promptly addressed. At Geneva in September, the powers promised to consider the matter along with a 'final' reparations plan and, at Briand's insistence, a scheme for verification of Rhenish demilitarization. France realized that as the occupation aged, its value as a bargaining counter was declining; thus, though the franc was finally restored, Briand sought to trade a shrinking asset for guaranteed cash, in which he largely failed. Early in 1929 a committee under Owen D. Young, American chief author of the Dawes Plan, drew up a new plan reducing German reparations and making them payable over 59 years to match Allied war debt settlements with the United States, but with significantly low payments in the first decade. The gulf between French and German views of the latter's capacity was papered over by making a third of each

---

* For details, see Chapter 10.
† Russia and a number of other states were allowed to adhere later. See also Chapter 12.

annuity unconditional and the remainder conditional, postponable in circumstances of economic or monetary distress. The Reparation Commission, much reduced by the Dawes Plan, would be abolished, along with Dawes Plan agencies. Instead, a Bank for International Settlements in Basle, Switzerland, would collect and distribute reparations as well as providing a badly needed mechanism for co-operation among governmental central banks, such as the Bank of England.*

Germany deemed this reduction inadequate since reparations were not cancelled altogether but reluctantly accepted it to avoid the higher Dawes annuities and to gain political advantages. At The Hague in August 1929 the powers gathered for a 'Conference on the Final Liquidation of the War', meaning the post-war peace settlement. At it, Britain's new Labour government demanded and gained a larger share of the dwindling reparations receipts. Meanwhile, as Stresemann added return of Germany's former colonies and the Polish Corridor to his lengthening list of treaty revisions, he got what he wanted most: reduction of verification to meaninglessness and evacuation of the second and third Rhineland zones by 30 June 1930, as Britain insisted.

By the time Stresemann achieved this considerable reward for accepting a reparations reduction smaller than Germany desired, the diplomatic agenda required the presence of the participants in Geneva. There at League meetings Briand issued a dramatic call for European economic union. It was agreed that he should provide particulars to governments and that the matter would be debated at Geneva a year hence. Once again, Moscow, with whom London had renewed diplomatic relations, saw a potential anti-Soviet cartel, but most League members were reasonably receptive, not least because of a growing awareness that some sort of co-operation was needed to compete with the American economic powerhouse.

In early October, Stresemann died at the age of 51, essentially of overwork, leaving an ageing Briand as the sole survivor in power of the Locarno triumvirate. In his last years, Stresemann had worried about evaporation of the middle in German politics, a shift to the right, and the growth of impatient clamorous nationalism which threatened his policy of piecemeal treaty revision. Others were alarmed not only at these ominous signs but at German indebtedness. In the late 1920s, Germany borrowed far more than it paid out in reparations, often to avoid unpopular taxes or for non-essential projects such as football stadia, and dangerously used short-term loans for such long-term projects. However, the powers provided reparations relief, as planned, though a German campaign against the Young Plan culminated in a referendum in December 1929 in which nearly six million voters opposed it, not enough to overturn ratification but sufficient to raise questions about future

---

* In the decentralized American banking system, the Federal Reserve Bank of New York assumes the functions of a central – or government – banker in international questions.

German good faith, upon which the Plan depended, and to indicate that it was seen as a humiliation, not a victory. Despite the implications, a second Hague conference in January 1930 completed the settlement. The reparations clauses of the Versailles treaty were cancelled, to be replaced by the new scheme, which was quietly made retroactive to the previous September, and formal provision was made for the Rhineland evacuation.

That occurred on 30 June 1930. The next day, Berlin issued a sharply nationalistic proclamation conspicuously omitting any mention of Stresemann, author of the early evacuation. The event was significant, and not only for Franco-German relations, for the strategic balance was altered. Where French and Allied armies had held not only the Rhineland but bridgeheads to the east of it, poised to strike into Germany if it attacked Poland, they had now retired behind their own frontiers, unable to act swiftly. Though still demilitarized, the Rhineland was now entirely German, forming a buffer between the West and the heart of the Reich.

The import of this situation did not escape France. When Briand's plan for economic union was circulated, it said little about economics but tried to freeze the political *status quo* and to enmesh Germany in as many pan-European constraints as possible, since the old ones of the Versailles treaty were gone. The plan was under discussion in Geneva when a German Reichstag election occurred on 14 September 1930 in which the National Socialist German Workers Party (NSDAP – Nazi) of Adolf Hitler came from almost nowhere to become the second largest party. The Rhineland evacuation had loosed the chains restraining German nationalism; it exploded in the programmes of all 24 political parties.[17] Since the Nazis, who offered little positive agenda, were the most nationalistic and the most hostile to the Versailles treaty as well as 'a catch-all party of protest',[18] they were most in tune with the national temper. Their attitude did not herald European co-operation, so the League quietly interred Briand's plan in a committee.

*   *   *

The 1930 German election decisively altered the diplomatic scenery. Chancellor Heinrich Brüning embarked on a more aggressive policy, partly to counter Hitler; Western powers made concessions, recognizing that one cause of the startling Nazi emergence was dissatisfaction with the *status quo*. The 1929 New York stock market crash had relatively little to do with it; German industrial workers, who were suffering recession but not yet Depression, voted for their usual parties, though some switched from moderate socialists to Communists. The Weimar Republic was already mortally ill, as the parties of the middle had declined sharply, politics veered to extremes, and Brüning had for months ruled by decree, using the emergency powers of elderly President Paul von Hindenburg under Article 48 of the constitution. Hitler, who excelled at propaganda, ran a splashy campaign using radio, newsreels, and aeroplanes skilfully. His support came mostly from rural areas, small towns, and the middle classes, especially the lower middle classes (such as artisans, shopkeepers, and small farmers) so traumatized by the hyperinflation of 1923. Like Hitler, they now opposed not only socialists and Communists but also capitalists, Jews, the Versailles treaty, the Weimar Republic, and modernity, which had damaged their economic and social standing long before the economic downturn began.[19]

Though the economic Depression spreading from Wall Street did not cause the German electoral returns and they in turn did not cause the Depression, the sudden emergence of the Nazi Party sped the Depression's arrival in central Europe and aggravated its effects there and, by chain reaction, elsewhere. The German economy had become addicted to foreign investment, which had already slackened. Now foreign investors, along with German Jews and liberals, took alarm at Nazi success and shifted their funds elsewhere. Within three months, more than a third of the foreign capital in Germany fled, and no new investments replaced the old. As short-term loans were recalled, major projects collapsed, adding to unemployment. By early 1931, Germany was in serious economic crisis, which soon spread through central Europe. Faced with the twin problems of aggressive revisionism in Germany and widening economic distress, Europe's leaders, accustomed to concentrating on their own continent, found that they were forced to turn their attention, however distractedly, to the world scene as their preoccupations were complicated by repercussions of the crash in the United States, whose deep pockets had sprung holes, and crisis in Manchuria as East Asia suddenly thrust itself to centre stage.

◆ Notes to Chapter 13

1. Gerd Hardach, *The First World War, 1914–1918* (Berkeley, University of California Press, 1977), p. 250.
2. Anthony Powell, *Venusberg* (New York, Periscope-Halliday, 1952), as quoted in David G. Kirby, *Finland in the Twentieth Century* (Minneapolis, University of Minnesota Press, 1979), vi.
3. *Ibid.*, p. 114.
4. Joseph Rothschild, *East Central Europe between the Two World Wars* (Seattle, University of Washington Press, 1974), p. 5. See his brilliant introductory chapter to which this passage owes a good deal.
5. Strobe Talbott, *Time* (1 June 1992), p. 74.
6. Rothschild, *East Central Europe*, p. 34.
7. Barbara Jelavich, *Modern Austria: Empire and Republic, 1815–1986* (Cambridge, CUP, 1987), p. 172.
8. Paul Kennedy, *The Realities behind Diplomacy* (London, George Allen & Unwin, 1981), p. 265.

9. See Fritz Fischer, *From Kaiserreich to Third Reich*, tr. Roger Fletcher (London, Allen & Unwin, 1986), pp. 83–98; Michael Laffan, 'Weimar and Versailles: German Foreign Policy, 1919–33', pp. 83–8, 97–8 in Laffan, ed., *The Burden of German History, 1914–1945* (London, Methuen, 1988), as well as Imanuel Geiss's penetrating essay, 'The Weimar Republic between the Second and the Third Reich: Continuity and Discontinuity in the German Question', pp. 56–80 in the same volume; see also relevant portions of two useful surveys, Volker Berghahn, *Modern Germany*, 2nd edn (Cambridge, CUP, 1987), and Helmut Heiber, *The Weimar Republic*, tr. W. E. Yuill (Oxford, Blackwell, 1993 edn).

10. Nicole Jordan, *The Popular Front and Central Europe* (New York, CUP, 1992), p. 5.

11. Frank H. Underhill, *The British Commonwealth* (Durham, NC, Duke University Press, 1956), p. 61.

12. The phrase of a German official. Karl-Heinz Harbeck, ed., *Das Kabinett Cuno*. Akten der Reichskanzlei, Weimarer Republik (Boppard am Rhein, Harald Boldt, 1968), p. 192.

13. Stephen Carls, *Louis Loucheur and the Shaping of Modern France* (Baton Rouge, LA, Louisiana State University Press, 1993), p. 9.

14. Jon Jacobson, *When the Soviet Union Entered World Politics* (Berkeley, University of California Press, 1994), p. 167.

15. David Dutton, *Austen Chamberlain: Gentleman in Politics* (New Brunswick, NJ, Transaction, 1985), p. 261.

16. Robert Mark Spaulding, 'The Political Economy of German Frontiers, 1918, 1945, 1990', in Christian Baechler and Carole Fink, eds, *The Establishment of European Frontiers after the Two World Wars* (Bern, Harold Lang, 1996), pp. 233–8.

17. Zara Steiner, 'The League of Nations and the Quest for Security', in R. Ahmann *et al.*, eds, *The Quest for Stability: Problems of West European Security, 1918–1937* (New York, Oxford University Press, 1993), p. 54.

18. Hans Mommsen, 'The Breakthrough of the National Socialists as a Mass Movement in the Late Weimar Republic', in Laffan, ed., *The Burden of German History*, p. 106.

19. See the analyses in Berghahn, *Modern Germany*, p. 113, and in Mommsen, 'The Breakthrough,' in Laffan, *The Burden of German History*, pp. 103–15.

THE WORLD'S CRISES

So runs the world away

William Shakespeare
Hamlet, III, ii

Previous page: Time cover 6th January 1936 of Haile Selassie of Ethiopia (TimePix)

CHAPTER

14

THE GREAT DEPRESSION

The Great Depression which crept and lurched across the world stage was unprecedented in global severity, mainly because national economies had become so interconnected, thanks to the gold monetary standard, far-flung empires, intricate patterns of international trade, and massive financial investment abroad by the United States, Britain and, to a lesser degree, France. Thus financial crises in London or New York had immediate repercussions in Asia and elsewhere. Financial catastrophe had political repercussions as well, and the 1930s were dominated by domestic instability, economic depression and diplomatic or military crises which culminated in world war. The Depression did not of itself cause war in Europe or Asia, but misery exacerbated emotional sores, contributed to aggressive right-wing nationalism, often urging revision of frontiers, and generated social unrest, leading some regimes to provide distraction by forceful foreign policies which heightened international tensions. In addition for some states, rearmament, which is uneconomic in terms of generating wealth, proved an effective antidote to depression as it not only created a military arsenal but also provided jobs and thus purchasing power to help revive an ailing economy. But in the democracies severe economic distress often meant preoccupation with domestic problems and passivity in the face of foreign dangers.

There is much disagreement about the causes and timing of the Depression. Britain, Japan, and eastern Europe did not participate in the boom of the late 1920s. Latin American exporters of agricultural and mineral commodities were suffering in 1928. In North America, agriculture and coal were ailing and something of a business depression already existed, despite the speculative bubble on Wall Street, before prices fell 50 per cent on the New York Stock Exchange on Black Thursday, 24 October 1929, followed by an even blacker Tuesday on 29 October. Thereafter the Depression arrived by fits and starts in different places at different times and with varying severity. Some countries recovered before France seriously felt the pinch. It was among the last to suffer, but even in other industrial countries of Europe and North America (what economists call the centre – as opposed to the economic periphery of less developed nations), there was no immediate descent into depression. Temporary economic upturns generated false hopes that the worst was past in the first part of 1930 and again early in 1931, delaying effective remedies. But by the end of 1931 misery was almost universal, with a nearly complete collapse of international trade and commodity prices. A stunned world faced an economic catastrophe of hitherto unimagined proportions. In the centre, questions were asked about whether Western civilization could survive, and in many regions of the periphery, similar questions were briefly posed about non-Western civilizations as well.

The causes of Wall Street's crash were domestic* but had international ramifications, particularly as Washington's policies aggravated the situation, as did those of European powers. Since the United States was the world's chief producer of goods, lender, and investor in development, its economic ailments had global effects. In the late 1920s a flood of rash foreign loans by American bankers created debt addiction to the point where some states borrowed to pay the interest on previous loans. When American investment capital switched to higher yields on Wall Street in 1928 and 1929, those nations were hard pressed to service their debts and could not buy American exports of food and manufactured goods, deepening the malaise in the United States and causing loan recalls which made matters worse. Similarly, high American tariffs in the 1920s impeded earning of dollars by other exporters, and the sharply higher 1930 tariff both aggravated that problem, further inhibiting purchase of American goods abroad, and led to foreign tariff retaliation, which clogged international trade.The world market was a modest part of the vast United States economy, but American actions, stemming in part from inexperience and reluctance to accept the role of international financial leader, sharply affected world capital flows and the international commodity trade. Policies of government and bankers often boomeranged, and the United States to a degree dragged the world down with it, as chain reactions set in.

However, Americans had no monopoly on human error and irresponsibility, and some problems were common to many countries. France was no more eager to serve as financial leader when Britain was forced to abdicate its traditional role in 1931, and there was no international co-ordination of monetary stability. Economic nationalism existed everywhere, especially as world trade dropped 40 per cent in value in 1929–30. Most governments had little control over the economy. Fragile, unregulated banking systems with weak or non-existent central banks were common, and corporate structures precarious. There were basic economic maladjustments arising from World War I and the peace settlement; currencies were poorly aligned, straining the international financial system; and gold backing for some European currencies was weak.

* See Chapter 12.

In addition, the problem of over-production was global, especially since wages – and thus purchasing power – lagged at the centre, a problem only postponed by instalment purchase. Too much steel and too many newfangled appliances were produced, but the problem was most severe, even before 1929, regarding primary commodities, notably metals and cotton (both for slowing manufacture), rubber for automobile tyres, and food. Oversupply meant that prices of coffee, tea, and sugar sagged even before spreading depression caused all commodity prices to nosedive. Simultaneous global bumper crops of rice and wheat between 1928 and 1932 created huge surpluses. Moreover, the 1914 opening of the Panama Canal, which led Japan to become a major maritime nation, generated excess shipping capacity.

The world's monetary system contributed to the severity of the Depression. After the disruptions of war and post-war, by 1930 most major states and many smaller ones had returned to the gold standard. As colonies generally used the metropole's currency or one pegged to it, a high percentage of the world's trading nations were directly or indirectly tied to the gold standard. Their currencies were freely convertible on demand to gold at a fixed rate. It was the British pound and the American dollar's respective gold rates which dictated that £1 equalled $4.86. Most countries maintained reserves to back their paper currency in gold, dollars, and pounds. Thus anything altering the value of any of those three commodities affected their financial reserves. The system produced stability but also rigidity and ensured that crisis in one financial centre would at once be felt everywhere. In addition, when export earnings sank as volume and prices plummeted, many states had to export gold to service their debts, which were fixed in gold, and to purchase essential imports. Their currencies were strong compared to those of countries not on the gold standard, and thus their export goods were expensive, for it took many units of a weak currency to buy them. To counter the export advantage of states with weak currencies, whose exchange rates meant that countries with strong currencies could in effect buy cheaply, nations on the gold standard tried to deflate or lower their prices to a competitive level. As depression and lack of demand pushed world prices downward, these states tried to squeeze their prices even lower, at the expense of wages and therefore purchasing power, in order to compete. Thus government policies aggravated the downward trend of the global business cycle.

There were two basic government responses to the Depression, often tried in sequence. Both usually entailed new governmental intervention in the economy in opposition to the prevailing liberal economic orthodoxy. Although Australia, New Zealand, and several Latin American states abandoned tradition and the gold standard early on, most countries initially tried to honour the existing rules, which decreed that debts should be paid, budgets should balance, and governmental deficits were a sin. In addition, some states thought abandonment of the gold standard would be immoral.

Countries which had experienced severe inflations did not dare to abandon deflation for reflation, raising prices and enlarging the money supply, for that could lead to renewed inflation – and did in China. Those so constrained included Germany, several east European states, France and Belgium to a degree, and several Latin American countries influenced by late nineteenth-century inflations or one in post-revolutionary Mexico.

Initially, most countries tried to retain the gold standard and the existing value of their currencies, but their exports were uncompetitive, requiring severe deflation and a gold drain to finance imports and service debts. When gold reserves ran out, they were forced off gold. Their effort meanwhile to balance budgets meant slashing government spending, reducing its payrolls, disarming, and ending public works, which increased the unemployment arising from inability to sell at home and abroad. Aspects of deflation such as high interest rates, exchange controls, and squeezing prices caused bankruptcies, all aggravating the downward economic cycle.

Sooner or later, most nations were obliged to abandon traditional policies in favour of the counter-cyclical tactics associated with British economist John Maynard Keynes. Few of the world's statesmen were consciously Keynesian; they were merely desperate. They abandoned gold and devalued their currency from lack of gold or to gain price advantages for the export drives which many attempted. Debt default was common. The economic pump-priming Keynes urged, financed by government budget deficits in order to give people jobs and purchasing power so that the economic circulatory system could function again, was combined with easy credit to help business. Extensive public works, especially road building for the new automotive age, provided jobs until private firms could do so. In some countries, rearmament for either aggressive or defensive reasons helped solve unemployment and gave people money to buy goods. Previously heretical deficit financing of economic activity generally aided recovery, though these countries, like others, aimed at economic self-sufficiency (autarky), raised tariffs, imposed import quotas, and engaged in other forms of economic nationalism, which clogged the world trade system as every country sought its own benefit regardless of the general welfare.

How long a country clung to gold was one factor affecting how much it suffered. Its financial policies, degree of dependence on foreign trade, export commodities (some being more in demand than others), and extent of reliance on the collapsed American market all mattered, as did exterior factors and local problems, such as weather and agricultural disease. China's foreign trade dropped sharply, but only the treaty ports suffered much, for external foreign trade was minor in China's economy. Since France was less dependent on foreign trade than much of Europe and had ample gold, the Depression arrived there late, as other countries were starting to revive. Indeed, France and five other European 'gold bloc' states clung to gold until 1935 and 1936. The closed Soviet command economy was of itself largely impervious to market forces, but the global price collapse meant that Russia had to export twice as much wheat to pay for machinery imports to industrialize under its Five Year Plan. Agrarian east European states, which were sharply affected by Weimar's woes, also had to double exports to service debts and pay for imported manufactures, but their usual Western market states both withdrew credits and restricted imports. The result was starvation, political radicalization to the right, and barter arrangements.

Though states of the periphery exporting primary products contributed to the great glut which largely set off the price collapse, problems and policies of the centre were often determining – and exacerbating, especially those of Britain and the United States. North America was undoubtedly the epicentre in terms of prolonged severity of what seemed to be an immense global economic earthquake. Canada's economic ties to the United States caused it to suffer, though the Commonwealth tariff preference achieved at Ottawa in 1932* provided some relief. Its powerful neighbour, however, which in 1929 accounted for 40 per cent of the world's industrial production, suffered the longest depression of any state, about a dozen years, finding its cure finally in World War II. This affected its trading partners, especially in Latin America.

*   *   *

In the short term, however, while hope still remained that an acute economic contraction was ending, Europe did its share to send the world into deep depression. The series of events which destroyed all doubt began with the September 1930 German election** and ensuing flight of foreign capital, including demands for repayment of short-term loans. By early 1931, Germany was in severe financial crisis which set off a chain reaction culminating in panic and global repercussions. In 1931, depression truly arrived in most of Europe, forcing it, the United States, and the rest of the world to shed illusions about a speedy upturn.

Germany's banking crisis led to severe deflation, not devaluation of the currency, because the recent inflation and the Young Plan barred a reflationary, expansionist policy. The Cabinet put ending reparations and an aggressive foreign policy to counter the Nazi threat first, despite the cost of soaring unemployment. Deflation, loan recalls, and a gold drain meant that gold cover for the mark was near its legal minimum under the Young Plan before a new crisis struck, for the situation worsened in the spring as announcement in March 1931 of a proposed Austro-German customs union† led to more loan recalls. It also aggravated problems in Austria, long

---

* See Chapter 7.
** See Chapter 13.
† See Chapter 15.

precarious financially, where the dominant bank absorbed a failing bank and failed in turn in May. Without international co-operation, which France refused unless the politically significant customs union proposal was withdrawn, Austria could not save it, though 70 per cent of Austrian industry and about half its banking depended on it. With its failure, large Anglo-American loans to it evaporated, but Britain, the centre for capital flows to central and south-eastern Europe, made its last effort to function as the world's financial leader and rushed to Austria's rescue with new loans, which exacerbated London's difficulties without alleviating financial crisis all over east central Europe.

An immediate 'run' on German banks occurred as investors and speculators withdrew funds, converting them into safer currencies. In early June, Germany declared itself unable to pay reparations. As the run continued and the prospect of a banking collapse endangered many American banks still heavily invested in Germany, Herbert Hoover proposed a one-year moratorium* on all inter-governmental debts to salvage private non-governmental loans as well as banks in Western Europe and the United States. Frenzied negotiation followed. Hoover was the first American president to rely on the telephone; he and Secretary of State Henry Stimson splurged on the costly transatlantic line as Stimson testily remarked, 'I cannot be disturbed when I am trying to prevent Europe from going bankrupt tomorrow.'[1] Thus the moratorium took effect on 6 July but did not stop the run or prevent failure of a large German bank. Britain could no longer help, and France would not without political conditions regarding Weimar's foreign and military policy. As a 'bank holiday', closing the banks briefly, did not stem the tide – which could destroy the Reichsbank, a debt of nearly $2.5 milliard to American citizens, and the entire financial structure of central and eastern Europe, where bank runs were also occurring – an international conference on 20 July froze all foreign credits in Germany. A German participant, noting the collapse of confidence in the existing credit system and abandonment of long-established rules, remarked, 'These disturbances will extend to other areas and I fear that those who experience this will see things of which today none has any idea. Even the actors who will be called to play in the drama today still know nothing of it.'[2]

His words proved prophetic. The immediate effect was a severe run on the Bank of England, especially by those needing gold to pay debts, reducing the Bank's inadequate gold cover to the minimum. Washington and Paris provided credits, which melted quickly without stemming the tide. Bank closures in the United States mounted, as the flight from the pound aggravated American problems and caused further German bankruptcies. For London, £70 million was frozen in Germany, more lost in Austria or frozen in eastern Europe, where severe exchange controls had been

---

* A legally sanctioned temporary cessation of debt service and repayment.

imposed, and all confidence in the pound, one of the world's two reserve currencies, evaporated as speculators rushed to convert sterling holdings to gold. The crisis forced Britain to form a 'national' cabinet and abandon the gold standard on 21 September. The pound was allowed to float and effectively devalued, soon sinking about 30 per cent from $4.86 to $3.25. The value of the reserves of countries holding sterling shrank accordingly.

Britain was the first major power to abandon gold, ending the pound's role as a reserve currency, shattering the world's monetary system, and revealing London's incapacity to lead and lend further. The implications were profound, particularly as many countries had linked their currency to the pound. Twenty-five other countries soon followed Britain off gold, chiefly European states, Commonwealth members, and key British trading partners. In 1932, more followed. But in September 1931, events in London at once reverberated in Tokyo, where world market contractions had brought depression early in 1930. When the pound toppled, Japan, Asia's chief trading power, suffered speculative bank runs for both financial and political reasons, causing it to abandon gold in December and devalue the yen.

By that time trade restrictions were spreading as each nation took refuge in economic nationalism. Tariffs rose, along with import quotas, prohibitions and restrictive licensing, and trade wars developed. By late 1932, European trade sank to less than 40 per cent of its 1929 level, which hurt the rest of the world, for the centre was not buying the products of the periphery. Lacking new loans or export earnings, several east European countries defaulted on debts in 1932. Meanwhile, July brought the *de facto* end of reparations and December the beginning of the end of war debt payments,* for Britain sought readjustment whereas Poland and France defaulted, though Paris could have paid despite growing distress in the gold bloc. As the gold countries began a late depression, others, notably Britain, showed faint signs of revival, though for most European countries the depths and the first upturns came in 1933.

As Europe started to revive, the United States was hitting rock bottom. Hoover, who blamed weak European banks for the crisis, was hesitant, traditionalist, and reluctant about heavy government intervention in the economy. Thus he did too little too late while American investment abroad declined 68 per cent, leaving most countries only enough foreign exchange for debt service but none to buy American goods. After he lost the November 1932 election, the American economy ground to a halt during the five months before Franklin Roosevelt was inaugurated in March 1933.† By then, unemployment had reached 25 per cent, bankruptcies were the norm, the stock market had sunk again, and bank failures and holidays

* Except for Finland, these ended in 1933.
† Thereafter inaugurals were moved up to January.

on a local basis were so widespread that some states had no functioning banks.

FDR was a pragmatist, willing to pursue anything that worked. Some of his contradictory policies helped. In his famous Hundred Days, he focused on the domestic emergency, creating jobs, providing direct relief, restoring credibility to the banking system, and on 20 April 1933 taking the United States off gold – despite an ample supply – to gain an export advantage. This led to new devaluations elsewhere, particularly in the western hemisphere. The dollar floated, then stabilized at 59 per cent of its former value; the price of gold rose from $20 to $35 an ounce.

Roosevelt soon confirmed his economic nationalism. When a purely European conference devised a disguised end to reparations in July 1932, it called for a World Economic Conference in London a year later to tackle the crisis internationally. Before it met, FDR forced removal of most relevant issues from the agenda. A British diplomat noted, 'discussion of war-debts, reparations and tariffs might be difficult at the World Conference. We could present *Hamlet* without the Prince of Denmark, Ophelia, and Polonius; it would be shorter. So would the conference.'[3] Afterwards, another observed with little exaggeration that the conference's only 'outstanding achievement was the establishment of the largest bar the world has ever seen, at which the delegates had opportunity to sample the world's national beverages.'[4] Though 65 countries participated, prospects were scant even before FDR bluntly rejected a brief temporary stabilization of currency exchange rates, making it clear that he put American recovery first. Major European conferences and any American role in world affairs ended for the time being.

Neither Roosevelt nor anybody else acted as global leader, as Washington largely ignored the world, though the United States established diplomatic relations with Russia late in 1933 for export reasons. In June 1934 Secretary of State Cordell Hull achieved Congressional approval for Reciprocal Trade Agreements to mitigate the high tariffs, especially for western hemisphere nations. These helped, but very slowly. Other government policies failed to aid agriculture, were declared unconstitutional, or complicated matters. So did a strong peace movement, fear of entanglement in another war, widespread belief that arms manufacturers caused wars, and a 1935 Neutrality Act which forbade sale of arms to belligerents, reversing a tradition of selling to both sides. Thus no rearmament stimulated the economy. In addition, after some economic improvement in 1936, government policies contributed to a sharp 1937–38 recession. In Europe, rearmament cushioned the downturn, but the periphery suffered from the American contraction.

* * *

Much of the periphery had suffered early on from cutbacks in American lending to Africa, Asia, Oceania, and then Latin America, as well as decreased American import. Prices of the primary agricultural and mineral exports, on which many developing areas relied, collapsed especially quickly and sharply. These areas were affected by wars, weather, policies of colonial masters and of major powers, and the degree of international demand for their products as well as the extent of their integration into world trade and their own policies. Countries or colonies with a heavy export concentration in one or two primary commodities suffered, especially since international restrictive schemes to curb over-production of rubber, tin, tea, and sugar were not always effective; those with more varied economies did better, as did regions of subsistence peasant agriculture. Those exporting gold benefited from its rise in price. In general, imports were cheaper, but shortages of foreign exchange led to import substitution industry and agriculture, often subsistence. Road construction and other public works laid the basis for future economic development.

As empires were integrated into the world economy, they were immediately affected. However, colonies often benefited from a formal or informal imperial preference as metropoles bought from colonies to save foreign exchange. Local processing of raw materials was encouraged to save costly shipping, as was greater self-sufficiency so colonies would be less vulnerable in a future war. Moreover, European powers seeking to conserve military forces at home wanted law and order in their overseas domains and so hastened to provide jobs for poor whites and urban blacks to avoid trouble. This fostered colonial industry, especially in areas where labour was very cheap.

Latin America had few sizeable colonies but was especially integrated in world trade, had economies dependent on one or two primary commodities, and was particularly affected by economic trends in the United States. Policy autonomy depended in part on the degree of reliance on the American market as well as size and distance from the United States. Decisions of several circum-Caribbean states were constrained by formal or informal use of the dollar as currency along with the local one, control of export crops such as bananas by American firms, and American occupation or financial control. However, despite some early departures from gold by financially independent states, most of Latin America was much harder hit than Asia because of its greater integration into world trade and closeness to the United States. Sharp trade drops in price and volume, big capital outflows, exchange controls, and debt servicing problems were the norm, as many states suffered from British, American, and German trade restrictions.

Britain switched much meat purchase from Latin America to Australia and New Zealand and, by threats of shifting the remainder, extracted preferential treatment from Argentina. The United States left Brazil free to engage in pump-priming and import substitution. Its government bought, stockpiled, and destroyed coffee, which accounted for over half of Brazil's exports, to the benefit of Colombian and Indonesian competitors.

Colombia's varied economy, which included gold export, slumped relatively mildly. Chile's exports dropped precipitously as importing countries. consumed existing stockpiles; as these were exhausted and the international situation became threatening, demand for strategic metals soared, and Chile revived quickly. Cuba was less fortunate; it lacked full fiscal and political freedom or any national bank and relied chiefly on sugar export, most of which went to the United States, where a 1934 law restricted import of Cuban sugar to benefit Hawaii, Puerto Rico, and the Philippines.

Debt default or deferral, leading to later cancellations, helped cushion Latin America, as did American droughts, and an influx of refugee capital from Europe in the mid and late 1930s. Though little other private capital arrived, governments in Britain, the United States, and Germany provided export credits tied to purchase of their goods. As political instability became the norm, civil war and war over the Chaco and Leticia* increased government expenditure.

Almost everywhere, political and economic instability weakened the landowning exporting oligarchy. New nationalistic populist regimes favoured autarky, import substitution manufacturing to reduce unemployment, and state intervention in the economy. They tended to be authoritarian, sometimes military, but financial institutions, industry and roads developed, as the role of the state expanded and governments pursued expansionist policies and economic controls. Some upturns started in 1932 as the United States sank downward. Thereafter, Latin America on the whole enjoyed a vigorous recovery until 1937, when the American recession struck it, but by then, the world situation generated demand for strategic metals and American aid for development efforts.

In general, Asia suffered less than Latin America and had a less dramatic recovery, except in Japan and its overseas territories, though Asia also tended to long-term agricultural over-production to offset low prices, saw rural areas switch to new crops or non-agricultural activities, and felt the 1937 recession. As Asia's most industrial and trade-dependent nation, Japan was crucial. The world price collapse produced severe misery in 1930 as exports declined, wages were cut, and gold drained out; the public blamed the politicians. The large silk industry died, overtaken by synthetics and war by the time recovery arrived. Acute agricultural distress in arch-conservative rural areas led to right-wing nationalist agitation, especially in the army which was drawn mainly from peasant and small landowner classes. As Japanese saw high tariff barriers rising everywhere and worried about obtaining future raw materials and markets, superpatriotic movements swelled. When the 1931 gold drain led to curtailment of the military budget, an abortive army coup ensued, followed by progressive militarization of Japanese foreign policy despite a shift in economic tactics.

* See Chapter 11.

Even in 1930, massive public works began, but the decline continued as central Europe collapsed in 1931. As unrest mounted, Japan devalued the yen almost 40 per cent in December and proceeded to spend its way out of the Depression. Cheap cotton, synthetic textiles, and light industry were developed, taking advantage of low labour costs as peasants sought added income, and also penetrating Asian and African markets. Massive deficit financing focused on rearmament, especially naval, until military expenditure exceeded half the national budget. Democracy was a casualty, but Japan was the first Asian state to recover. Its overseas territories benefited as well from Tokyo's expansionist, developmental, and military policies. Development was always geared to Japan's needs, but both rice production and industry grew rapidly after 1931 in Taiwan and Korea, and Manchuria boomed, thanks to Japanese investment after conquest. The benefits went mainly to Japanese owners and migrants, but heavy industry and mining became markedly larger, providing jobs and recovery as exports to Japan swelled.

China was on the losing end of Japan's policies. As its international trade was small, China's chief problems were war in 1931, civil war, and more war in 1937, again with Japan. It also suffered from an American law to raise the price of silver for the benefit of western silver-producing American states. The higher world price generated a flood of silver out of China. In 1935, it was forced off its silver monetary standard to a paper currency, of which it printed too much, causing hyperinflation to which big deficits and war contributed.

India suffered from prolonged orthodox deflationary policies imposed by its British masters, who clung to an overvalued currency. Though India did not depend heavily on the world market, it was now fully involved in the international economy. Exports suffered; the economy was otherwise stagnant, although imperial preference aided Indian industry, which Britain had intended to delay. The cotton industry spread, as did import substitution activities. Agriculture was little affected and food was cheap, though peasants lacked credit and purchasing power. But after Britain left gold, it insisted, despite intense protest by Indian nationalists, on maintaining the old pound/rupee exchange rate. Slashed government expenditures, price deflation, and increased taxes caused bankruptcies and more nationalist protest.

Misery was greater in South-east Asia. As it chiefly produced food and raw materials for the world market, it was devastated as prices of primary goods tumbled and state revenues were roughly halved. Governments, mostly imperial, and private firms were slow to react, not recognizing the severity of the crisis. When they did, they slashed costs, which often meant removal of expensive Western officials to the unintended benefit of indigenous employees, repatriated Indian and Chinese workers, and in the trade-dependent Dutch East Indies insisted on orthodox deflation, which aggravated the situation. A degree of alleviation was provided by international restrictive schemes for rubber and sugar, Philippine access to the American market until the mid-1930s, and French aid to Indochinese rubber. Some diversification occurred along with widespread bankruptcies. Japan's export drive seized the Indonesian market from Europeans until quotas were imposed. France also restricted Japanese goods, as did Britain to maintain imperial preference in its several colonies in the region.

In Africa as well, imperial preference brought benefits for British colonies, including some industrialization, savings of foreign exchange, and a boom in the Rhodesian Copper Belt. French colonies enjoyed a similar but less formal preference. The effects of the Depression varied greatly, though both agricultural over-production and suffering from the 1937 recession were widespread. West African rubber regions and agricultural exporters were greatly afflicted, though peasant subsistence farmers were not. Central Africa benefited from some industrialization and Eritrea from the Italian military build-up. In South Africa, diamonds did badly, but the nation otherwise prospered, thanks to a varied economy and the increased value of its gold exports when the dollar devalued. In Africa in general, as elsewhere, when European overlords signally failed to cope with economic crisis, their authority eroded.

The effects of the Depression were uneven in the Middle East even in oil countries, depending upon how developed they were. Demand for oil did not decline greatly though auto manufacture in the centre slowed, but prices dropped. Iran, the most established producer, saw its revenues decline sharply and renegotiated its contract. Iraq, a new producer, prospered under imperial preference. When pearling failed in Persian Gulf amirates, oil exploration fees compensated. As rearmament generated new demand in the developed nations, output increased and oil states did well. Elsewhere, world contractions led to some debt default or delay and sharply increased east European migration to Palestine.

*   *   *

In general, the periphery led the recovery, but signs of upturn were beginning in Europe by 1932, usually as a result of the same expansionary policies akin to Japan's. Sweden employed very successful counter-cyclical fiscal and monetary policies. Other west European countries came to do the same, some sooner, the gold bloc later. However, even in the West, recovery was limited and fragmented in 1934 and 1935. Trade tended to be bilateral, there was no international co-operation but rather more restrictions, and many countries relied on home demand, not export, to spark recovery. Monetary expansion despite fears of inflation, government intervention, and new industries all played a role. From late 1936 on, increased rearmament expenditures contributed to further improvement in Russia, Germany, and the West.

Widespread rearmament was a response to newly aggressive policies on the part of Hitler, who took power in Germany in January 1933,* and whose rearmament had become overt. At first he concentrated on job creation, enlarging existing programmes and creating new ones. Deficit financing provided massive public works, especially roads, which had military utility. A national labour service, paramilitary formations, and conscription in March 1935 solved unemployment, as did heavy military expenditure from 1936 on. Seeking autarky for military reasons but lacking sufficient raw materials and food, Hitler encouraged development of synthetics and launched an innovative trade policy in central and south-eastern Europe which led to Nazi domination of the region. Widespread loss of markets, loans, and creditworthiness owing to debt default left these states frantic to export agricultural and mineral products in order to import manufactures. Germany bought their produce under bilateral agreements which forced their earnings into blocked accounts which could be spent only for German products, not always of their choosing.

Germany was not distracted by an empire. Britain and France were, and both focused on imperial trade, leaving Germany free to exploit eastern Europe where both had long been interested. Neither linked political and economic policy, as Germany did throughout the interwar era. Britain overlooked the implications for the balance of power as Germany moved east and south, whereas France failed to defend her alliances and the eastern *status quo*, which Britain disliked in any event. Both were preoccupied at home and cut defence expenditure in the early 1930s just as Germany and Japan rearmed.

Britain revived quickly after 1931, thanks to an expansionist monetary policy, a shift to focus on the home market with an emphasis on manufacture of new products, and cheaper food owing to imperial preference. But the need to protect and foster this recovery dictated very slow rearmament in the mid-1930s and refusal to shift scarce skilled workers from reviving industries to defence contracts. By the end of 1934, Britain had reached its precarious pre-Depression economic level. By then, France was suffering from its devotion to gold and from severe political division. The downward trend continued, reinforcing French self-preoccupation, until France left gold in 1936. Other gold states followed. Limited recoveries ensued, boosted by rearmament which eased the 1937 recession.

Britain and France emerged from the 1930s with their world financial role much diminished and their grip on empire somewhat reduced even before war arrived because colonial economic diversification meant less dependence. In addition, Europe's economic role in Latin America declined sharply and permanently, aside from brief Nazi inroads. At the time, many thought the Depression heralded the decline of the West and especially of its economic leadership. That proved not to be, but leadership shifted

* See Chapter 15.

further west across the Atlantic as the United States finally revived and accepted its responsibilities.

The Depression destroyed the world's monetary system without replacing it, caused the disintegration of world trade, hampered it further by protectionism and economic nationalism, and increased government roles in the economy almost everywhere. Political and diplomatic results were equally severe. The Depression sharply frayed what remained of the post-World War I treaty structure and led to loss of faith in political solutions to international questions, thereby damaging world peace. The economic diplomacy of the 1920s in Asia ended as Japan and the United States in their different ways lost faith in internationalism. Preoccupation with the Depression meant fewer diplomatic initiatives from London, Washington, and Paris, as leaders worried but did little because of economic disaster, fear of war, and disarmament. All three states deemed peace essential, even at a high strategic price. Thus the 1930s were marked by a timid, reactive stance by the Western powers despite the fact that economic misery had aggravated most other problems and created situations which could be – and soon were – easily exploited.

The Depression spawned violence and political turbulence to varying degrees in such diverse locations as the ABC powers of Latin America, Australia, Japan, and Bulgaria. It gave birth to extreme political movements, mostly right-wing, and calls for authoritarian leaders to cope with the crisis. Democracy and parliamentarianism, which seemed so ineffectual, were more deeply discredited in some countries than others. They died in Germany and Japan, as the economic crisis contributed to the advent of Hitler and of the Japanese military regime. Through the dreary decade of the 1930s, depression, dictatorships, and diplomatic crises interacted, reinforcing and aggravating each other as international tension mounted in a dramatic crescendo.

◆ Notes to Chapter 14

1. Robert H. Ferrell, *American Diplomacy in the Great Depression* (New Haven, CT, YUP, 1957), p. 113.
2. Harold James, 'Innovation and conservation in economic recovery: the alleged "Nazi recovery" of the 1930s', in W. R. Garside, ed., *Capitalism in Crisis* (New York, St Martin's Press, 1993), p. 92.
3. Sir Robert Vansittart, *The Mist Procession* (London, Hutchinson, 1958), p. 465.
4. Patricia Clavin, *The Failure of Economic Diplomacy* (New York, St Martin's Press, 1996), p. 3.

CHAPTER

15

CHALLENGES OF THE DISSATISFIED, 1931–1937

In the 1930s, the spotlight of world diplomacy continued to focus on Germany and Japan but cast them in a new, harsher light. The first major crisis of 1931 – a German one – did more than most others to trigger the chain reaction into global depression and, unlike later European crises, it came with no warning. On 21 March Germany and Austria abruptly announced plans for a customs union. This was not the *Anschluss* banned by the peace treaties but a long stride of strategic significance toward it, as well as a violation of the 1922 Geneva Protocol for Austrian financial reconstruction and the first overt act toward renewed German imperialism.[1] Diplomatic reaction was sharp, and in early April France imposed political conditions for an Austrian loan, including postponement of the customs union proposal. This contributed to the failure on 11 May of Austria's leading bank, which in turn caused Austria to abandon the proposal and financial panic to spread throughout central Europe. The customs union plan was dead (and interred by a narrow decision of the Permanent Court of International Justice in September that it violated the 1922 Protocol) but Germany had plunged into financial chaos and demanded reparations relief. France, which by now had the strongest continental currency, insisted in return on political concessions regarding the customs union, Germany's technically legal naval building programme, and its army budget, which was nearly triple that of Britain. Berlin refused all concession, partly to forestall Hitler's growing political power, partly to end or reduce reparations. Impasse and swelling financial emergency led to the Hoover Moratorium too late to stem central European financial catastrophe and the dismal chain of events culminating in Britain's departure from gold on 21 September as Japan's Kwantung army overran Manchuria. These events in turn drove Japan off gold in December, rocking Asia economically in the midst of political/military crisis.

The juxtaposition of financial crisis in London and the Kwantung army's unauthorized 18 September seizure of Mukden would be typical of the years to come and explains in part why conquest of Manchuria was so immensely popular in Japan and why other powers did so little. The

Manchurian episode came as less than a complete surprise to Japan's military and civilian leaders, but European and American statesmen had been too preoccupied to heed the warning signs. Though Japanese actions in 1931–32 created a crisis of global proportions, they had little effect on European events. However, they revealed the League of Nations' futility in an emergency and the weakness of the Western democracies, all disarmed and distracted, as was the Soviet Union – the other power directly affected by Japan's seizure of Manchuria. The Depression loomed over every crisis of the 1930s, affecting all diplomacy and, along with disarmament, dictating the weak responses and reluctance to act so apparent as Japan conquered Manchuria.

After the clash at Mukden had provided an excuse to the Kwantung army, its conquest was swift, for it encountered no opposition. Throughout the Kwantung army drove events, which army leaders in Tokyo then approved – as eventually did the government, while restraining direct challenges to other powers, notably Russia with its long Siberian border with Manchuria. The young officers of the Kwantung army, who were oblivious to international implications, were seeking a heroic future and security. In their eyes, national survival required Japanese control of Manchuria, Inner Mongolia, and much of China. Their anti-Western pan-Asianism sought Sino-Japanese co-operation against the West at the same time as they hoped to dominate China. In Tokyo, there was genuine fear of losing control of the Kwantung army.

In China, Chiang's Nationalist regime was too precarious and preoccupied with enemies at home to offer resistance in Manchuria. From the outset, it saw the situation as the prelude to a Japanese-American war which would save China. Thus it avoided clashes and appealed to the League and the United States. The League Council sought American aid. Briefly Washington co-operated despite resentment at League 'nagging' and Stimson's determination not to let 'under any circumstances anybody to deposit that baby in our lap'.[2] Of economic necessity, Washington wanted peace, as did London. In December, the League settled upon a European and American investigative commission with Chinese and Japanese assessors attached under Britain's Lord Lytton. As its trip across the Atlantic, the United States, and the Pacific took until February 1932, the Japanese army marched on.

Its timing had been excellent. The powers were disarmed and preoccupied. The Soviet Union, in the throes of the first Five Year Plan and forced agricultural collectivization, was too weak to protect its ill-defined Manchurian border, so it opted for passivity. But it promptly reinforced its tiny Asian army, created an air force and navy there, sent colonists, and began double-tracking the trans-Siberian railway. In 1932, it signed non-aggression pacts with the Baltic states, Poland, and France for protection in the west, and renewed relations with China. Meanwhile it deplored Japanese imperialism but noted that it differed little from that of the West.

Indeed, the United States had recently sent troops into Nicaragua, Haiti, the Dominican Republic and Panama, a fact which somewhat tempered Stimson's moralism. The more cautious Hoover feared that economic sanctions would have no effect on the Kwantung army but would lead to war. The Depression, disarmament, fear of war, the coming 1932 presidential election, and the fact that Japan bought four times as many American goods as China were all factors in a confused American policy. In January 1932, after Japanese forces seized the last Chinese administrative centre in Manchuria, Stimson fell back for lack of an alternative upon non-recognition of the fruits of aggression, a policy which the United States had used with equal futility in 1915 to counter Japan's 21 Demands upon China. For two months, Stimson's statement remained the only official condemnation of Japanese actions by any state.

Washington, London, and Paris tended to view relatively westernized Japan as a defender of occidental interests against chaos and Communism in China. Few leaders saw a real threat to the West. They recognized a challenge to the League and collective security, but governments took these less seriously than public opinion did. A major military force, which none had, would be necessary for effective action. All were absorbed in economic and financial problems, and European states, especially France, had security concerns closer to home.

Like France, Britain was not a Pacific power; its nearest fleet was based at Malta. Its new National Government was coping with the departure from gold, a naval mutiny, tension in India, and the problem of what to do about reparations when the Hoover Moratorium ended. It would not take a strong line unless the United States would fight Japan and bear most of the burden, which it clearly would not. London was cautious, pragmatic, and eager for good relations with Tokyo so it could focus on the German problem. A few leaders knew it could not rearm to face Germany and also build up the Royal Navy against Japan, but all parties resisted ending East Asian commitments. Thus work resumed on the Singapore base in 1932 in response to the Manchurian crisis, and the standing rule that no war was to be expected in the next ten years was jettisoned, allowing the military to plan but not to spend. Meanwhile, as British opinion favoured disarmament, the League, and collective security (meaning the force of world opinion and, if need be, economic sanctions), London backed the League and organized the Lytton Commission.

Before it arrived and on the heels of Stimson's non-recognition declaration, a Sino-Japanese clash on 28 January 1932 at Shanghai led to fighting on the edge of the International Settlement. This upset Western powers more than Manchuria, for their citizens and economic investments were at risk. Japanese leaders in Tokyo, military and civilian, were dismayed and sought to extricate themselves. The United States sent military forces, protests, and bluffing threats, while Europe did nothing. British good offices brought a truce on 3 March 1932.

Six days later, the Kwantung army proclaimed the puppet state of Manchukuo (Manzhouguo). Tokyo delayed formal recognition until September in deference to the recently arrived Lytton Commission. In Geneva, the League adopted non-recognition at British request but otherwise awaited the Lytton Report in the autumn. The Report criticized Chinese disorder and nationalism, but recommended without regard to the *de facto* situation that Manchuria return to Chinese sovereignty and administration with Japanese economic rights. The Council passed the problem to the Assembly.

Before the latter could act, the Kwantung army seized the Chinese province of Jehol (Rehe),* whose location was strategic for Siberia, Outer and Inner Mongolia, and key passes into north China near Peking. In response, the Assembly adopted most of the Lytton Report with only Japan dissenting. After 17 months, it in effect arrived at a reprimand without sanctions.[3] On 27 March 1933, Japan withdrew from the League, the first major power to do so, but retained its island mandates. This signalled an end to international co-operation and deference to the West in favour of mainland expansion. In May Japan achieved a truce with China, bringing it to the Great Wall, ensuring its influence beyond, and preparing future incursions.

Japan had alienated every power interested in Asia, and could not risk fighting them all. Besides, the army and navy disagreed over the next goal; the army preferred to focus on Russia or north China, the navy to move against South-east Asia. Thus a pause. However, the Manchurian conquest revealed the military's primacy in policy formulation, constituted an overt challenge to the West, and was a milestone in the decline of Western influence in Asia.[4] Internationalism was discredited in Japan but also elsewhere, as the United States briefly tried and failed to preserve the internationalist structure of the 1920s and as the Manchurian debâcle spotlighted the League's inherent weakness, especially when proponents of disarmament issued the loudest calls for action. In March 1932, a Finnish delegate asked, 'Is the League really a live force and does it constitute a real guarantee?'[5] As always, it did not, and any hope of action rested on great powers whose means and will were limited. Mussolini's contempt for Geneva grew, as did that of Hitler, who took office before the Manchurian episode ended. Authoritarian states now saw war, not peace, as noble and desirable; peace was passive, weak, and dull in the eyes of those who dominated Italy and Japan and, then especially, Germany.

Under the circumstances, the long-heralded World Disarmament Conference, which opened in Geneva on 2 February 1932, was utterly

---

* No longer a province, since divided between Hebei and Liaoning.

mistimed. It was popular with opinion in Western democracies, where peace movements, belief that armaments caused war, and pressures for disarmament were strong, but unloved by governments, who expected little, especially as no key questions had been settled. By mid-1932, when a separate conference at Lausanne arranged a disguised end to reparations, the disarmament conference was moribund. Germany, whose rearmament started in the late 1920s, demanded equality, France security. These were not compatible since Germany was fundamentally stronger. Washington quaintly urged disarmament to gain security whereas Moscow alone, for domestic and propaganda reasons, advocated total disarmament. The fearful French were widely painted as militarists, for Germany said it wanted a change of status, not of its level of arms. But Winston Churchill, eyeing the swelling Nazi ranks, rebutted, 'these bands of sturdy Teutonic youths marching along the streets and roads of Germany – are not looking for status. They are looking for weapons.'[6]

Britain sought to mediate between France and Germany, pressuring Paris for concessions to Berlin. In March 1933, after Weimar had left the conference once, Britain proposed and France accepted doubling the German army and conscription, but in vain, for Hitler was now Weimar's last chancellor. In October, he withdrew Germany from the conference and the League. The conference was beyond hope of revival, but no democratic power wanted the blame for ending it, so it dragged on, finally fading away early in 1935. As that year ended, a last futile naval disarmament conference met. Japan sought parity in all classes of ships, giving it overwhelming dominance in the western Pacific; Britain and the United States, whose fleets were well below treaty limits, refused. Washington sought a 20 per cent reduction in all classes, which London and Tokyo rejected. Thus all limits on naval construction expired in 1936; Japan began building at once. Meanwhile the lingering World Disarmament Conference delayed rearmament in the disarmed English and French-speaking democracies.

*   *   *

By the time even ardent pacifists accepted that the World Disarmament Conference was dead, Hitler and Roosevelt had reached power nearly simultaneously in two countries severely impacted by the Depression. At heart FDR was an internationalist and sympathetic to China and the Western democracies, not their opponents, but at first he focused on the economic emergency, letting foreign policy drift, except as to Latin America. Hitler seemed to be doing the same but was not. He, too, worked to provide jobs, but he was systematically gutting the Weimar constitution, gaining full control of the instruments of power in Germany, and preparing the military weapons for an aggressive foreign policy. Until these goals were achieved, his stance seemed fairly moderate, but a French diplomat noted, 'In reality in Germany they have never spoken of peace in a more warlike tone.'[7]

In fact, after four days in power, Hitler told his generals that if France had real statesmen, she would attack at once and not let Germany rearm. Meanwhile he spoke the language of peace, leading some Western leaders to hope that responsibility would tame the Nazis and that their foreign policy was traditional in methods and aims. His early moves sought to break the Versailles treaty's remaining fetters as a prerequisite to much larger goals. Unlike Weimar politicians, he had no interest in Germany's 1914 borders, and war was his preferred instrument of policy from the outset. Of Europe's leaders, only he wanted war there, though Mussolini blustered; Europe's peoples, including Germans, were equally pacifistic.

Nonetheless, Hitler was immensely popular in Germany at first, for its citizens were as unclear as foreign statesmen about where he was leading them. A psychologically bruised nation needed a scapegoat; Hitler gave them the Jew while also stoking nationalist fires. His political strength derived from those who had suffered most from modernization, defeat, and the 1923 inflation. It drew on 'a sense of historic grievance and of the nation as misunderstood victim – a national self-pity zealously husbanded, nurtured, and sustained'.[8] Plebiscites in the first years endorsed his foreign policy moves by votes of well over 90 per cent. Even so, Hitler never trusted his people, for he believed the German army's myth that it had been stabbed in the back by the home front in World War I; thus, until forced by necessity in 1943, he imposed few heavy burdens on truly Germanic civilians while creating a police state to ensure obedience.

Though Hitler lied fluently when necessary, he was sincere in his core beliefs, which focused upon race and space, meaning arable land. He saw a hierarchy of races with Germans at the top as the pure master race, Jews and blacks (largely absent from Europe) at the bottom, 'subhuman' Slavs almost as despicable. The races or nationalities engaged in a Social Darwinian struggle for *Lebensraum* (living space or farmland), which Germany would find in Russia, expelling or exterminating most of the inhabitants. As a nationalistic, militaristic dictator, Hitler opposed democracy, socialism, and Communism – all too egalitarian – as well as pacifism and internationalism. His ideology combined with a hardheaded approach to power politics. He sought military might, autarky, and a free hand to conquer Europe, for in the struggle between peoples for land, strong races should expand at the expense of the weak. Thus Germany's population and territory should expand continuously. Though Hitler's goals were fixed, he was flexible and opportunistic about how he reached them, improvising freely.

To a degree, Hitler planned in stages, focusing initially on full restoration of Germany's great power standing and domination of central Europe. These goals required rearmament and autarky, creating economic and financial problems only solvable by war or by abandoning his aims. Autarky caused a trade shift to the Balkans and increased domination there to gain minerals, oil, and food; an effort to penetrate Latin America; and development of synthetic oil and rubber. The need for time to rearm dictated temporary abandonment of Alsace-Lorraine, the south Tyrol, colonies, and the German minority in Poland. It also meant weakening France to avenge the 1918 defeat and humiliate the land of *égalité*, remilitarizing the Rhineland, enlisting Poland as an obedient satellite, and perhaps persuading Britain to a temporary arrangement of convenience allocating Europe to Hitler and overseas empire to Britain.

Longer-range goals, especially after London and Warsaw failed to cooperate, were full continental hegemony by military defeat of France and conquest of *Lebensraum* in Russia. Once those aims neared achievement, Hitler turned to plans for overseas expansion and to war against Britain and the United States. He had paid little heed to powers outside Europe at first, but in the Old World Hitler dictated events through most of the 1930s. He acted and others reacted. The instability of the 1930s arose from the imperialist pressures of the have-not dissatisfied states – Japan, Italy, and especially Germany – and the gradual resistance of the satisfied powers plus the Soviet Union, which was not satisfied but saw itself threatened in both Europe and Asia.

That resistance came slowly, as no great power was prepared to act to prevent German rearmament. For this, Hitler used existing plans but greatly expanded their speed and scope, always imposing the final word in policy disputes. He consistently preferred bilateral treaties to multilateral as easier to break when the time came, pursued annexationist imperialist policies, and aimed at short small wars so as not to strain Germany's limited resources or tax the home front. With great skill, he capitalized on the West's fear of war and love of peace, knowing that the democracies he so scorned rarely engaged in preventive wars because they cost lives.

*   *   *

One reason for Hitler's success was that few statesmen studied his extraordinarily frank creed, *Mein Kampf* (My Struggle), published in 1925–26. One who did was Maxim Litvinov, Soviet Foreign Minister since 1930, who understood that Hitler intended to defeat France and then conquer Russia. Litvinov briefed Stalin, who heeded him. Like other leaders, they wanted to avoid war and, like most, they assumed that if war came, it would be a long struggle of equal sides. Russia should remain neutral until the decisive moment, but in the interim it should, like other powers, seek to avoid isolation. Thus in the 1930s Russia edged onto the diplomatic stage and gradually into the great power circle, joining the League in September 1934. Stalin saw all capitalist states as hostile and sought to divide them while keeping Russia's options open. Thus he made overtures to Berlin after Hitler quickly ended the Rapallo tie; these aimed at co-existence, turning Germany against the West, and security against the Japanese threat. At the same time Litvinov became an apostle of collective security and supported the League as the Comintern shifted to defence of democracy against Fascism; Stalin courted French and Spanish Popular Front left-centre cabinets in the mid-1930s, co-operating with democratic political parties for the first time, and pursued alliances with France and Czechoslovakia.

Though Stalin distrusted Britain, some of whose leaders hoped Hitler would save Europe from Communism, these ideologically antithetical states showed striking similarities of policy. Both sought deals with a reasonable Hitler who did not exist; both distrusted France and overestimated its power; both were overextended, militarily weak, and desperate to avoid war. They sold space (generally not their own) for time as long as possible; along with France, each tried to divert Hitler to somewhere else; each wanted allies but feared military ties as leading to war; they were passive early on, giving Germany time to rearm. Both based policy decisions on their view of the national interest.

Britain's mostly Francophobe leaders defined that interest narrowly; they knew their security frontier lay on the Rhine and assumed France would be there when needed, but they blamed Paris through much of the 1930s for inadequate concessions to Nazi rearmament. London, which for so long had seen France as too strong, did not ask whether maintaining French power was a British interest and undermined it, forgetting that power is relative and that every German gain meant a French loss. Britain blamed alliances for World War I and its own costly involvement; it did not wish to take sides, for British and Dominion opinion feared alliances would drag Britain into a new war. Though London was never willing to give Hitler the free hand he sought in Europe, it partially accepted his view of what British policy should be; its 'appeasement' or pacification, which began in 1919, now meant concessions to Hitler to persuade him to renounce change by force, though the Cabinet early recognized Germany as the main potential enemy. This was particularly true of Neville Chamberlain, who dominated British foreign policy through much of the 1930s, and who stubbornly insisted that Hitler was moderate. He thought German grievances should be rectified, and until 1938 British opinion largely agreed, partly to gain time to rearm. Thus Chamberlain doggedly tried to lure Hitler back into the League, achieved a naval pact with Germany, and, reflecting the national fear of air attack and belief that 'the bomber will always get through', vainly sought an air pact while trying to arrange territorial transfers to Germany before Hitler could conquer the areas in question.

Chamberlain's policy was born both of his deep hatred of war and of necessity arising from Britain's weakness. As he understood, his nation suffered from acute imperial overreach.[9] Since die-hard imperialists and all parties frustrated his desire to abandon the Singapore base and write off East Asia, he faced major threats in the sprawling Asian empire from Japan as well as in Europe from Germany plus the danger that Italy might cut

Britain's imperial lifeline through the Mediterranean and the Suez Canal. With a minuscule army, an air force needing expansion and modernization, and two fleets in the north Atlantic and Mediterranean to do at least three jobs, he temporized and did whatever seemed necessary to avoid a war which he knew would shatter Britain's Empire and end its great power status. However, he never reconsidered.

Britain began cautious rearmament in 1935, but most funds were allocated to the fleet and air force, leaving almost no army to aid France. Home defence and empire came first and second, with Europe a poor third. The Empire was global and remained the world's largest trading bloc; it was vital to Britain's precarious economy. London remained over-optimistic about the China market and so vainly tried to stem Chinese nationalism and Japanese imperialism. Because of its weakness and dangers elsewhere, it sought rapprochement with Japan in hopes of checking Tokyo and retaining south China as a British sphere. As Japan was acutely aware of its economic dependence on the United States and unsure what power was its primary enemy, this policy briefly looked more successful than it was. But from 1935 on, Japanese incursions into north China and Inner Mongolia increased. At the same time, Hitler began to abandon Germany's military ties with the Kuomintang and edge toward Tokyo. In November 1936, Germany and Japan signed an anodyne Anti-Comintern Pact without military clauses, though no Communist party still existed in either state. While perhaps 'an international kiss on the cheek',[10] it both aimed at the Soviet Union and signalled loosening Japanese ties to London and Washington.

China tried to move closer to the United States for protection, but American policy, like that of Britain, avoided conflict with Japan. It reacted passively to the Amō doctrine of April 1934, staking out China as Japan's sphere and opposing foreign technical, financial, or military aid there. The Manchurian crisis and the Depression led Washington to be less internationalist, to accept that world order was weakened, and to seek peace with Japan. It joined London in protesting Japanese incursions into north China in 1935–36 but took no action. By then, FDR was more inclined to a diplomatic role in Europe, which he knew well, but found he had underestimated the isolationist impulse reinforced by economic crisis, the peace movement, and those who believed that bankers and munitions-makers were 'merchants of death' responsible for dragging the United States into World War I, and who therefore demanded a ban on loans and an arms embargo. These pressures led to prohibiting loans to states defaulting on war debts and a series of Neutrality Acts from 1935 to 1937 barring sale of war material or loans to any belligerent; in 1937 these were applied to civil wars, but arms could be purchased for cash if carried in the buyer's ships.* FDR was

---

* In 1939 two months after the European war began, the arms embargo was repealed. This benefited the Allies, who controlled the Atlantic.

a master politician and expert at the art of the possible, with an army of 135 000 and a navy not only below treaty limits but also smaller than Japan's; he faced economic crisis, domestic political battles, a 1936 presidential election, and public sentiment fearful of any risk of war, so he inched cautiously. Americans wished to immunize themselves from world events and escape involvement. Racism, ethnic pressures, economic self-absorption and fear that Europe would somehow drop the 'baby' in its lap all meant that the United States turned inward, in some respects more so as world peace disintegrated. Nonetheless, relations with Nazi Germany deteriorated owing to its anti-Semitism, militarism, anti-Christian connotations, and efforts in Latin America. After the last naval conference failed in 1936, FDR sought to rebuild the American fleet and journeyed 7000 miles to Buenos Aires on a battleship to attend a conference he had requested to improve pan-American relations and initiate a New World defensive bloc. Europe, however, had to wait.

Curiously, this did not disturb that continent's most needy major power. France was so focused on Europe that it sought allies only there. It was pacifist and polarized, especially after February 1934 riots showed the strength of the conservative and Fascist right, raising the spectre of civil war. France was entering the lean years when low birth-rates during World War I meant a small army. Delayed Depression and deflationary policies left no funds for arms, only for the Maginot Line, that massive string of border forts behind which the French army would protect France alone. In 1935 France spent much more on propping wheat prices to combat rural poverty than on national defence.[11] The defensive military stance plus the evaporating mirage of French power as one diplomatic defeat followed another caused virtual collapse of the eastern alliances, which Paris did relatively little to preserve. It and its eastern allies, as well as Germany, all understood French weakness and dependence on a reluctant Britain, if others did not. One foreign minister, Louis Barthou, was an exception to the pattern of passivity. Knowing that allies saved France in World War I, that they were now gone, and that Britain refused an alliance, he energetically cultivated Italy, eastern alliances, an eastern Locarno, and a Russian tie. After his death, the Russian treaty was achieved in 1935, with both parties hoping to turn Hitler elsewhere but neither truly committed. His successor preferred to come to terms with Berlin. In general, France was terrified of war, weakened by years of British pressure, less than vigorous in defending its vital interests, and dependent on an aloof Britain which it assumed would be at its side when needed.

France also pursued Italy with some consistency. Its attractions were that it was not strong enough to destroy European peace, but, having rearmed first, it had a substantial army and air force in being, its fleet could free the French navy for duty against Germany, and it was the chief barrier to *Anschluss*. Mussolini was impulsive and erratic; his policy fluctuated accordingly. He had designs on Ethiopia but was unable to subdue the Libyan Sanusi until 1932. Thereafter, he preferred peace in Europe, where his goals were limited, and worried that *Anschluss* would place German troops on his northern border. Diplomatic disappointments in 1933 and 1934 along with Hitler's rise to a greater Fascist dictatorship than his own led Mussolini to feel overshadowed, though Berlin, Paris, and London courted him. France achieved an agreement in January 1935 which Mussolini thought meant tacit consent to his ambitions in Africa. However, Anglo-French efforts to make deals with him met the same problem as their efforts and Russia's for deals with Hitler: the two dictators wanted war (Mussolini on a small scale and outside Europe), not deals.

Clearly, the monopoly of power of the Western satisfied powers, which had anchored peace in the 1920s, was now gone. Britain and France were at best half-hearted about the *status quo* and international order, especially Britain, which now accepted drastic change if not made by force. It trusted to the RAF and Royal Navy, France to the Maginot Line. France still wanted security, Britain disengagement, but neither pursued effective policies toward their goals as the dissatisfied powers became more decisive. Democratic states were handicapped by public opinion's love of peace and fear of war, military and financial frailty, the effects of overselling disarmament, Depression, fear of Communism, and belief that Fascist dictators behaved rationally. Of the democracies, Britain, France, and the United States, were determining. Their policies in the 1930s were born of weakness but often led to greater weakness. That is clearer now than it was at the time. Diplomacy often fails because those who conduct it are only human and miscalculate, or duck problems. The frequent Western failures of the 1930s arose from weakness, refusal to face ugly truths, and repeated miscalculations as leaders desperately sought moderation and compromise where no inclination to either existed.

*　　*　　*

Hitler's foreign policy in fact began with moderation while he pursued rearmament and autarky. In 1933, he gained a concordat with the Vatican, which gave his regime an aura of respectability. In 1934, he signed a non-aggression treaty with Poland and eyed Austria, whose desire for *Anschluss* waned when Hitler took power. In July, an abortive coup in Vienna by Austrian Nazis was suppressed by Austrian troops and police. As international reaction was sharp, Hitler disavowed involvement. In January 1935, the plebiscite in the Saar Basin, specified in the Versailles treaty after 15 years of League rule, led to Hitler's only legal territorial gain when over 90 per cent of the population chose reunion with Germany. The League ran a model plebiscite, but Nazi claims that they would know how individuals voted, together with pressure from pro-German Catholic clergy, contributed to the lopsided outcome. As the Saar was the last advantage to be gained from the Versailles treaty, Germany could now proceed with less restraint.

Indeed, when Britain announced rearmament in March 1935 as the disarmament conference ended, Germany, whose army was already nearly triple the treaty limit, unilaterally denounced the Versailles treaty's disarmament clauses, declared it had an air force, and introduced conscription for a 36-division army. Hitler ignored the diplomatic protests, proceeding apace when the Russo-French treaty in May provided an excuse to claim encirclement, whereas London dismissed the implications of German actions. It wanted to rearm as cheaply as possible and to avoid both difficult decisions and commitment to Paris. In January, it rejected staff talks with France or any reaffirmation of its Locarno commitment to the Rhineland demilitarized zone, though agreeing to joint Anglo-French talks with Germany on arms questions. Despite that, when Hitler offered a bilateral naval treaty, London rushed to sign in June, authorizing German naval construction of surface vessels to 35 per cent of Britain's level and to 100 per cent for submarines. In violation thereof, Hitler quietly proceeded with construction of battleships and aircraft carriers for eventual use against Britain and the United States.[12] In signing the 1935 naval pact, Britain had, without consulting or informing France in advance, repudiated the Versailles treaty's naval clauses, giving Berlin control of the Baltic, but had also ended the threat of an Anglo-German naval race and simplified the Royal Navy's task of coping with Germany and Japan. French leaders were furious but dared not confront London, though their anger affected the Ethiopian crisis already brewing.

Meanwhile in April, British, French, and Italian leaders met at Stresa in Italy. They condemned German renunciation of disarmament and introduction of conscription, but did nothing about either; in a declaration defending the *status quo* and 'the peace of Europe', they reaffirmed the Locarno treaty and the need for Austrian independence. British officials vaguely warned Mussolini off Ethiopia, but he knew from a spy in the British embassy in Rome that London did not consider Ethiopia a vital interest, and he thought his careful insertion of the words 'of Europe' into the declaration about peace without objection from Britain and France amounted to a green light for the invasion he had long planned in Africa.

The Ethiopian crisis had been brewing since December 1934 when a clash between Italian and Ethiopian forces at a complex of wells at Wal Wal in Ethiopia at its conjuncture with British and Italian Somaliland gave Mussolini the pretext he sought to avenge Italy's defeat by Ethiopia in 1896 and to link Eritrea and Italian Somaliland, thereby dominating the Horn of Africa. A quick nineteenth-century colonial war, what others had done before, would bring empire, glory, virility, prominence on the international stage, along with distraction from economic problems at home, and enable him to return to Europe before Germany could move against Austria.

Britain and France had long deemed Ethiopia an Italian sphere and his plans were known well in advance, so Mussolini anticipated no difficulties. He did not realize that most European states, which found the League useful at times and had to consider public support for it, did not wish to see it tested or humiliated after its Manchurian failure. Also, his war was to occur in the twentieth century, after rules for imperialism had changed, was large-scale and modern with tactics considered shocking, and not only violated the League Covenant but was directed against a League member. No amount of Italian propaganda about 'barbarism' and a 'civilizing mission' could escape those facts.

In Ethiopia, Africa's one ancient Christian kingdom, Emperor Haile Selassie I was attempting to centralize and reform a feudal state. He had curtailed but not yet eliminated slavery, a fact of which Italy made much. He perhaps trusted excessively in the sanctity of contracts and the League, to which he applied for arbitration after Wal Wal. When the Italian invasion came, it reverberated across Africa* and beyond, attracting volunteers from many states, especially American blacks including pilots, who heeded Langston Hughes's call:

All you colored peoples,
Be a man at last,
Say to Mussolini—
No! You shall not pass.[13]

Beyond its importance to Africa, the Ethiopian war was a major European crisis; that mattered far more to France and Britain, though failure to oppose Mussolini would mean unrest in their empires. France needed Italy, the only power showing much opposition to Hitler, to counter him in Austria and the Rhineland, and preferred Italy in Ethiopia (with a façade of independence and France retaining the Djibouti–Addis Ababa railway) to Italy perhaps in Yugoslavia. In January 1935 Premier Pierre Laval gained a murky tacit agreement giving Italy a free economic hand – and possibly more – in Ethiopia in return for resistance to *Anschluss*. A military pact followed, enabling France to shift 17 divisions northward from the Italian border. Fear of Hitler and reluctance to choose between Italy and Britain led France to resist opposition to Mussolini.

Some British leaders were grateful for the French stand but could not say so. They too wished to preserve Austria and gain an Italian alliance; they did not oppose Italian aims, only war. An Italian feeler in January 1935 went unanswered, so Mussolini took silence as consent. In fact, Britain soon pressed Ethiopia for concessions, not facing Mussolini's determination to have a war. In June a Peace Ballot organized by the League of Nations

* For the African reaction, see Chapter 8.

Union showed overwhelming popular endorsement of League economic sanctions against aggressors and large support for military sanctions. With an election in the offing, eventually held in November after all parties campaigned contradictorily for disarmament and collective security, opinion mattered. Thus Foreign Secretary Sir Samuel Hoare affirmed Britain's support for collective security in Geneva in September, hoping the League would cover Britain's true policy of sacrificing much of Ethiopia to gain an Italian alliance. The Cabinet thought sanctions futile but wanted the League, not Britain, to say so. To an extent, it hid behind French foot-dragging. Indeed, when London sought an assurance of military support if the Italian air force attacked the Royal Navy, Paris, still smarting over the Anglo-German naval pact, was slow to provide that. As policy became more contradictory, Britain shifted its Mediterranean fleet eastward despite grave implications for Asian imperial defence if ships were lost and, to prevent this, promised Italy it would take no serious steps.

The crisis unfolded slowly, affording ample time to develop and co-ordinate policy, for after Stresa Mussolini's preparations were unmistakable. But Britain and France tried to straddle the dilemma of needing both Italy and the League. Neither wished to drive Mussolini into Hitler's arms or to destroy its own moral position vis-à-vis domestic opinion and colonial indigenes. Each convinced itself first that Mussolini would negotiate after he won a few battles and then that the war would be long, allowing time for diplomacy and economic sanctions to work. Both opposed a wider war, and each hoped the other would lead. Somehow the League, the anti-German bloc of Stresa, and national honour should be preserved – cheaply. Thus they sought a compromise whereby Ethiopia would gain a little and give much to pacify Mussolini, and the League's face would be saved. The impossibility of achieving both, together with the clash between French pragmatism and the idealism of British opinion, ensured that neither goal was attained.

On 3 October 1935, Italy attacked Ethiopia from Eritrea without provocation or the customary declaration of war. The Vatican blessed the 'civilizing mission', and Mussolini reached the peak of his popularity in Italy. Initial Italian advances were slow, not the *Blitzkrieg* (lightning war) Mussolini wanted, but terror bombings of cities and use of poison gas speeded progress, as eventually did mutilation of Ethiopian troops. The League Assembly declared Italy in violation of the Covenant, with Italy opposing and dependent Austria and Hungary abstaining. In a British bluff, limited economic sanctions were voted in November without a date or formal requirement for application, which was uneven. The hope was to nudge Mussolini to negotiation or arbitration by making a presumably long war costly and thus to stop him inexpensively before war spread to Europe. The chief effect, aside from offending him and driving him toward Hitler, was economic disaster in eastern Europe, about which Britain and France did nothing. Germany rescued these states, gaining economic and gradual political domination to the extent that by 1939 70 per cent of Bulgaria's exports went to Germany.[14] In the interim, Hitler encouraged Italy's African venture to distract it from Europe and gain an ally, while supplying Ethiopia with arms to prolong the crisis.

Oil, essential to Italy's modern military machine, was not embargoed, partly because Mussolini said oil sanctions meant war, and both Britain and France feared he meant it. An oil embargo would require at least three months to bite – *if* the United States, which still produced over half the world's oil, did not increase exports to Italy. Thus American policy was crucial, giving Britain and France an excuse of which they made full use. Roosevelt invoked the Neutrality Act at once, embargoing arms sales to both sides in a gesture toward American black voters, for only Italy had funds to buy. Since he lacked legal authority to ban oil shipments, FDR called for a 'moral embargo'; oil shipments to Italy promptly tripled. Given that fact and Italy's stockpiles, oil sanctions were much less of an issue than they seemed, but they became the test of League determination. Thus domestic and Dominion opinion finally drove Britain to seek oil sanctions, which were imposed in March 1936 in a costly futile gesture as Ethiopian resistance collapsed.

Long before that, shortly after fighting began, British and French experts began to explore what Laval called 'rearranging the map of Ethiopia'.[15] Once the British election was safely past and London was freer to pressure Ethiopia, these efforts culminated on 8 December 1935 in the Hoare–Laval plan, approved by both cabinets, to give Italy direct or indirect control of the lion's share of Ethiopia, awarding Ethiopia a seaport and allowing it to retain what *The Times* called 'a corridor for camels' to the port.[16] Ethiopia was not consulted, only partly because there was no telephone connection to Addis Ababa. French foes of the plan leaked it at once to the Paris press. The ensuing uproar in Britain over a reward for aggression, contradicting London's support of League sanctions, was so great that neither Italy nor Ethiopia was obliged to reject the plan. Hoare was sacrificed quickly; Laval lingered another month.

During this uproar, lightly armed Ethiopian units attacked Italian armour and planes with some initial success but eventual disaster. In February 1936 the tide turned and by April, when the rains which might mire armour in mud came, Ethiopian forces were routed. On 2 May Haile Selassie fled, on 5 May Addis Ababa fell, and on 9 May Victor Emmanuel III of Italy was proclaimed Emperor of Ethiopia. Though resistance never ceased, in the next five years Italy created a costly infrastructure for settlers who never came. Mussolini sought League recognition of his empire and expulsion of Ethiopia but gained neither. A Rumanian delegate remarked, 'The Italians want us to eat dung. So be it. We shall eat it. But they also want us to say that it tastes good. That is too much.'[17] Thus Haile Selassie addressed the Assembly on 30 June, stressing that collective security and the League's existence were at stake, which was true but sadly irrelevant. Sanctions were sheepishly lifted on 15 July, and the League, which Italy left in 1937, was ignored thereafter by major powers.

Though relieved to escape war, Britain and France had lost Ethiopia, Italy (including the French military pact), the League, and more. Small states feared to be the next Ethiopia and mourned the League, about which Britain and France did nothing, letting their creature decline as they did. Their interests were damaged, as they now faced Italian hostility in the Mediterranean, and their relationship strained, with French Anglophobia mounting. With limited capacity to aid Ethiopia militarily, they put self-preservation first but tried to satisfy both Mussolini and the League's supporters. Their equivocation sacrificed Italian support against Germany and encouraged both dictators toward greater boldness as they concluded that Britain and France would take no risks. In early 1936 Italy found itself isolated except for German friendliness. Mussolini began to waver on Austria; events, including the belated oil sanctions, drove him toward Germany for lack of an alternative. In July he reached agreement with Germany on Austria and in December he proclaimed the Rome–Berlin Axis, not an alliance but a step toward one. He hoped he had obtained a Balkan sphere; Hitler knew gaining Italy meant that preventive action against Germany was improbable and that he could move south-east.

*   *   *

The Ethiopian crisis chiefly benefited Germany, which gained an Italian ally, domination soon in eastern and south-eastern Europe, and time for re-armament while attention focused on Italy. In addition, Hitler took advantage in March 1936 of Anglo-French preoccupation with Ethiopia to send his army into the demilitarized Rhineland zone on the Franco-Belgian border. Rhenish demilitarization was crucial to French security and Europe's strategic balance. It also prevented an improbable new French incursion, protected France and the Low Countries from Germany, and barred German aggression in the east, for Western powers could invade it in reply.

European leaders knew Hitler meant to remilitarize the zone soon. France was deep in Depression, nearly bankrupt, and its weak caretaker Cabinet faced an election in six weeks. On 6 March, Belgium nominally renounced its military tie to France to gain parliamentary consent to rearmament; thus France's northern frontier was open and its plan to fight the next war in Belgium in doubt. After years of slashed budgets, the French army was a skeleton force with World War I equipment, able to control the colonies and man the border forts until mass mobilization, but little more.[18] In 1933 it had abandoned long-standing plans for a Rhenish offensive, which Germany knew and the French Cabinet learned belatedly, but before the March 1936 Rhineland crisis. The generals said action required a politically undesirable mass mobilization. The Cabinet knew that Rhenish remilitarization would mean losing the eastern allies but worried more about losing Britain. Pressure on London, which clearly would not act, might jeopardize what remained of the Anglo-French Entente and drive Britain to new deals with Germany. London's refusal to resist gave the French Cabinet, which had no intention of acting alone, a convenient excuse. Thus France sought British support for appearances' sake and angled for a renewed guarantee in return for doing nothing.

When on 3 March Paris sought reaffirmation of Britain's Locarno commitment against violation of the Rhenish zone, London was aghast, knowing neither power could engage in military action as both were just starting to rearm and most of the Royal Navy was in the Mediterranean facing Italy. Thus it aimed to evade its Locarno obligations and seek agreement with Germany, which it feared to provoke. In January 1935 the Cabinet had decided that the zone was not a vital British interest, despite Locarno and the zone's importance to France, Britain's chief bulwark on the continent. As fearful of air attack as France was of land invasion, and equally needing to buy time, the Cabinet hoped weakness would be read as good will and that it could trade ceding the zone for a German air pact, return to the League, and renunciation of territorial change by force in Europe. A clash with Germany might set off Italian or Japanese action against the Empire. The Dominions, especially Canada and South Africa, much opposed action, and home opinion did not object to Germans moving into 'their own back yard'. Cabinet, Parliament, and people deeply feared war and saw France as the barrier to reconciliation with Germany; nobody thought this the moment to stop Hitler. Chamberlain saw French ties to eastern Europe as an impediment to agreement, for he hoped to appease Hitler at the expense of Germany's neighbours there, and he feared that any economic sanctions would prevent negotiations to this end, which he hoped could remove German grievances in an orderly way. Knowing that, Hitler did not wait.

He wished to avail himself of Anglo-French preoccupation and to distract Germans from economic problems caused by full employment and rapid rearmament. He knew neither Poland nor Italy would act; Mussolini was delighted that attention was shifting elsewhere. The Foreign Ministry worked to sway France's eastern allies and League Council members, causing ambiguous reactions later in the east, abstentions by Latin America's two Council members, and a public joint refusal by the Scandinavian states of economic sanctions, which nobody proposed. Meanwhile, Hitler readied his army to enter the Rhineland, which 22 000 militarized police had infiltrated since 1934, and ordered a fighting withdrawal in the unlikely event of French action.

On Saturday morning, 7 March 1936, when the British Cabinet had scattered for the weekend to country estates and thus could not meet quickly, Hitler denounced the Locarno treaties, saying French ratification of the Russo-French pact violated Locarno but not testing this claim by established Locarno procedures. Within three hours, the German army marched. British protests without action against this use of force for Versailles treaty revision did not disturb Hitler. The French Cabinet, fearing a gold drain and virtual bankruptcy, both of which occurred, and an end to budding economic revival, reaffirmed its refusal to act unless Britain did. Any danger of that disappeared when its prime minister said Britain could not run even a 1 per cent risk of war.[19] Accordingly, French leaders concentrated on gaining a guarantee and staff talks.

They met with the British in London, as did the remaining Locarno powers and the League Council in special session. The Council condemned Germany's actions but did nothing. Widespread fear of Communism in Europe and Latin America was a secondary factor aiding Germany; when Litvinov pressed for a collective League effort for the future, he gained no support. To gain what one cabinet minister termed 'peace with as little dishonour as possible',[20] Britain unsuccessfully sought German conciliatory moves to facilitate negotiations. Hitler did as he pleased in the Rhineland, starting slowly to build fortifications in the summer. He also launched a 'peace offensive' with a flurry of proposals, none serious, to distract and consume time. Britain so wanted accommodation with Germany that it pursued these fruitlessly for a year; France was sceptical, but the new centre-moderate left Popular Front cabinet resulting from May elections was so anxious to gain a full British alliance that it made a genuine effort. London avoided a defensive treaty with France but conceded staff talks, which it gutted – while revealing its acute military weakness – and on 19 March an extension of the Locarno guarantee without its cumbersome procedures or military aid because Britain was too weak. Even these moves were grudging, because Cabinet and opinion, including the left, saw no threat and aimed to curb France. As Hitler dodged, and Britain refused to admit that conciliation had failed lest it then have to commit itself to France against Germany, the crisis subsided in a torrent of talk.

Britain's inability to fight meant loss of a bargaining counter and strategic position as well as weakening its only real ally, whose psychological and strategic surrender signified a partially self-inflicted defeat. Western weakness and desire for peace undermined peace, as Hitler became more aggressive, inclined to risks, and willing to threaten force.[21] Once Germany fortified the Rhineland, even a rearmed France could not rescue its eastern allies, especially after Belgium reverted to full neutrality in October, effectively shielding the Ruhr. The Little Entente knew this and that Hitler could now move east. Hitler had won at no cost, closing an open flank and altering the strategic situation in his favour as the military balance tipped.

It is often said that the Rhineland crisis was the last good opportunity to stop Hitler without war. One historian has suggested, however, that it was a chance to stop him *with* war, for Hitler intended to fight.[22] Even that assertion is debatable, for one must ask: stop him with what? Germany had begun rearmament first. Though the German army was still weak, power is relative, and it was stronger than the armies of France and Britain, for Anglo-French rearmament was just starting. The French army was in pitiable condition while that of Britain barely existed; neither air force had modern equipment. Under such circumstances, one cannot be sanguine about the outcome of a military action which British and French leaders did not dare to contemplate.

*   *   *

While Europe fruitlessly debated Hitler's proposals, its next major crisis arrived, again as less than a surprise, when Spain took centre stage. Its 1931 republic had veered from a left-wing government to the right and back to a Popular Front coalition in February 1936 with a cabinet of middle-class republicans backed by moderate and leftist groups, whose extreme elements the regime did not curb. The clash between left and right became open class conflict; arbitrary arrests, murders, and church burnings outraged landowners, Fascists, monarchists, and especially medievally-minded church and army leaders. A coup by the generals, who had military power at their command, was widely expected. It was also feared because Spain, though on the westward fringe of Europe, fronted on both the Atlantic, with the strategic Canary Islands off the north African coast, and the Mediterranean, with the Balearic Islands. Hostile possession of Spain's navy, air, and submarine bases would threaten Anglo-French imperial communications.

In mid-July 1936 an army uprising in Spanish Morocco spread immediately to Spain itself, where General Francisco Franco quickly took charge in what became a full-scale civil war. The rebels seized a third of Spain's territory, but the government held the rest, including industrial areas; the air force, navy, and some army units remained loyal. Thus Franco's Nationalists needed aid to bring troops, many of them Moroccan, from North Africa. After some hesitation, Mussolini sent planes, and after more hesitation, Hitler did as well, saving the revolt and ensuring a long fight against the Republicans or Loyalists of the constitutional Madrid government.

The war was above all a Spanish struggle, soon complicated by little civil wars within the main one as rivalries within coalitions became brutal, particularly on the left, for the war tended to unite the right and divide the left. Italian and German collusion with Franco was soon obvious; Russia then backed the Loyalists, and volunteers flocked to Spain from many nations to aid both sides but chiefly the left, where International Brigades were organized by the Comintern and national Communist parties.Thus statesmen feared the conflict might become a pan-European war, which none yet wanted. This prospect affected the policy of all European major powers.

Britain, torn internally by King Edward VIII's desire to wed an American divorcee, faced the divisive effect of Spain's conflict, which became a class issue, alienating the unions, who opposed government policy in Spain and thus did not co-operate in speeding rearmament. The Cabinet leaned toward Franco, partly out of anti-Communism and fear of Soviet activity in western Europe, but it opposed British involvement. It preferred Franco to a general war, thought he would win quickly, and decided a Nationalist victory would not seriously impair British interests. Defence of the empire dictated better relations with Italy and freedom from Mediterranean commitments, though its sea routes were vital and British bases there largely disarmed. London needed both a weak, friendly Spain and good relations with the winning side, for Gibraltar and Britain's crucial position in the Mediterranean were at stake. The Cabinet worried that France's new Popular Front government would aid its sister regime in Spain, widening the war dangerously and distracting from appeasement of Germany. Since it feared a potential clash between France allied with Russia by recent treaty and an Italo-German-Portuguese bloc as Portugal's conservative dictatorship backed Franco, London tried to thrust Spain aside and warned Paris against aiding the Loyalists.

France's new government under socialist Léon Blum already faced Depression, looming devaluation of the franc, strikes, demonstrations by both left and very hostile right, and cabinet divisions. Blum was sympathetic to the Loyalists, and at first he agreed to aid Madrid; then he saw that both a cabinet collapse and civil war in France could eventuate. Thus after a little initial aid, Paris merely turned a blind eye to arms smuggling and passage of International Brigades across the border. She did not want a Fascist pro-German regime to her south but feared isolation more, for Mussolini would not reconcile with her leftish regime, leaving only Britain as a potential ally. Therefore to escape an intolerable domestic and foreign dilemma, on 1 August France proposed a Non-Intervention Committee of the six states interested in the Spanish crisis. Britain fervently agreed.

Germany and Italy delayed consent until late August so as to provide substantial arms to Franco in the interim. Portugal agreed only after heavy pressure from Britain, its traditional ally. However, the Non-Intervention Committee met futilely from early September 1936 until April 1939 in deadlock from the outset. Britain honoured the non-intervention policy in full, France largely, the rest not at all, sending aid in varying degrees, though Russia did so only after Italo-German cheating was obvious. The Committee's real goals were to save Anglo-French faces and keep the war from spreading, in which it succeeded at the price of obstructing aid to the Spanish Republic. As non-intervention became farcical and Germany and Italy clearly would intervene until Franco won, Britain and France stuck with the Committee to shunt Spain to the edge of the European stage and prevent a pan-European war. Strikingly, the Committee had no ties to the League, to which Madrid had appealed and which debated without result. The Committee was a forthright device of the great powers, who had taken charge.

The least of these was the most involved. Mussolini hoped to strengthen his Mediterranean position and gain bases in the Balearics (as he did), impress Hitler, and weaken France, especially by barring its troop transit from Africa. He sent 73 000 men, who did poorly, and over 750 planes. Hitler was more cautious, hoping chiefly to prolong the war to preoccupy Britain and France and gain an Italo-German rapprochement, which occurred. In his first overt intervention outside Germany, he obtained raw materials and strategic advantage, but primarily he sent enough planes and tanks with 5000 technicians and pilots to ensure that Franco did not lose, and used Spain as a testing ground for his new weapons and tactics. Salazar sent a Portuguese Legion; Republican attacks on churches and priests brought the Vatican to Franco's side as well.

The Spanish government received much less aid and was largely dependent on Russia, which in return took most of Spain's gold reserve, over US $500 million. Moscow, where the first trials of Stalin's purge of those who might oppose him were starting, feared isolation and a pan-European war, favoured Popular Fronts, and now wanted a tie with the Western democracies against Germany. If that failed, possibly a war of Fascism – a term coming to mean any right-wing authoritarian regime – against democracies might exhaust both, allowing the Soviet Union to emerge as arbiter. Russia sent enough equipment to Spain to keep the Republic going and a thousand senior personnel who intervened against revolution to curb excesses and anarchists and to reassure the West that Spain was not Communist. This aid stiffened Madrid until October 1938 when the Munich conference about Czechoslovakia doomed Loyalist hopes of a Western–Soviet coalition, and Moscow decided to focus more exclusively on the German problem.

In the New World, Latin American states were aloof and self-absorbed except for Mexico, which helped the Republic to its limited ability. In the United States, FDR's sympathies lay with the Loyalists, but 1936 was a presidential election year and Roman Catholic pressure against the Spanish Republic was powerful, so Roosevelt ducked, backing Anglo-French efforts to prevent a pan-European war. Neutrality legislation did not yet apply to civil wars, but he banned arms shipments to both sides. However, American corporations aided Franco, supplying some oil.

The policies of the powers jelled in the first three months of the war. By October, an international conflict was raging in Spain; it had become a European affair, albeit with at least 70 000 North African troops. The sight of Moors again in Spain, as in the Middle Ages but now to defend the Catholic Church, displeased the West, giving a propaganda point to the

Loyalists. As atrocities mounted on both sides and public opinion fixed on the ideological factor which diplomats ignored, propaganda became important but not determining. Though Germany's pose as the bulwark against Communism impressed some, the Loyalists won the propaganda battle in the West – but did not survive. The Spanish war was seen as a European war by proxy, and in many other ways, for it contained something for most views. The flood of volunteers to both sides, but chiefly to the Republicans, arose from the fact that the struggle in Spain represented a crusade of freedom against tyranny, Christian civilization against atheistic Communism, law and order against barbarism, democracy against Fascist authoritarianism, and a dress rehearsal for a coming pan-European war. American correspondent Martha Gelhorn epitomized the attitude of Western liberals in saying, 'We knew, we just *knew* that Spain was the place to stop Fascism. This was it. It was one of those moments where there was no doubt.'[23] This belief was reinforced by the German incendiary bombing in April 1937 of the Basque cultural centre of Guernica, giving rise to outrage and Pablo Picasso's powerful painting of the same name.

The statesmen were more outraged by Italian submarine attacks on Mediterranean shipping. After a torpedo narrowly missed a British warship, London called a great power conference at Nyon, Switzerland, in September 1937 to deal with 'piracy' by 'unknown submarines'. Mussolini ceased the attacks before the conference met, but it established an Anglo-French naval patrol of the western Mediterranean. Chamberlain wanted a naval agreement with Italy, and Mussolini briefly behaved well in return. The war dragged on in Spain, ending only after Madrid fell on 28 March 1939. Germany and Italy had long since recognized Franco's regime, lent it sizeable sums of which little was repaid, signed secret treaties with him, persuaded him in March 1939 to adhere to the Anti-Comintern Pact, and proffered much advice which he ignored. But they gained little of substance for their pains from the new *caudillo* as he established a corporatist military-dominated *nuevo estado* (new state).

Outside Spain, Nyon was the last major episode as the war was shunted to the wings, but its effects lingered along with the war itself. Prospects of an Italian alliance with the West were destroyed, of one with Germany much improved. Fear of Communism and of Russia grew in Spain's neighbours, as did pacifism in the West, for many decided war was worse than Fascism. The Axis saw this and used it. Hitler in particular had tested Britain and France and found them weak; he decided they would not act unless attacked. Thus he was emboldened. In that sense and others, the Spanish war proved to be the curtain-raiser to the great conflict so many dreaded.

*   *   *

By the time Spain became a sideshow in late 1937, most European states were preparing for that war. Britain and France were rearming in earnest whereas Germany reached full production of troops and weapons. It prolonged military service and began planning to attack Czechoslovakia. In Russia, however, Stalin's vast purges of those who might unseat him started to destroy the military leadership, causing Western experts to discount the Red Army. The Soviet stance was defensive, wavering between confrontation and compromise with Germany. Hitler spurned Russian overtures but offered trade deals, while using the Soviet menace as an excuse for any move he cared to make.

Britain and France treated Russia distantly but tried unsuccessfully to restore relations with Italy as the Ethiopian crisis ended and the Spanish one began. Hitler's attentions, the crises, and France's Popular Front were all factors in their failure. Paris also sought to revive its influence in eastern Europe with limited success, for most states there feared Russia more than Germany. France was now well into the lean years of a small army, still in Depression, deeply divided, and overwhelmingly pacifist. With the eastern alliances in tatters, Italy alienated, Belgium neutral, and Britain resisting defensive co-ordination, it stood in fearful isolation.

Britain favoured reducing the eastern ties, which it saw as an affront to Hitler. Its Cabinet debated offering colonies to bribe him into moderation, but not Tanganyika, which he chiefly coveted, for it lay astride the Cape to Cairo air route, a consideration replacing the unbuilt railway. By 1937, London decided that Hitler should receive French mandates, which Paris rejected to avoid German airfields in west Africa. Berlin wanted all colonies returned and major concessions in Europe, but Chamberlain continued to seek compromise with a Hitler who did not exist. Knowing Britain was too weak to fight in both East Asia and Europe, Chamberlain after he became Prime Minister in May 1937, firmly set British priorities as the British Isles, sea routes to them, and finally Allied territories.

Like London, Washington tried to avoid conflict with Japan but watched its pressure on north China, border tensions with Russia, and signing of the Anti-Comintern Pact as well as growing conservative military domination of its government. Assassinations and attempted coups destroyed such power as cabinet, diet, and political parties retained, leaving only a façade of constitutionalism, which key army factions preferred to maintain, but the consequences of Japan's internal situation and external policy were not faced in the West. Roosevelt was as committed to the appeasement of Japan as Chamberlain was to that of Germany, and from the same military weakness. American opinion was indifferent and uninterested in crusades either east or west though Washington, like London, worried most about Europe since Hitler proved to be the prime actor threatening the peace.

He was laying the basis for new moves while the rearmament gap still favoured Germany. In July 1936 he pressured Austria into an agreement whereby Vienna would more closely follow Berlin's lead in foreign policy.

Austria saw this as a maximum concession, Hitler thought it only prepara-tory, as he supplanted Italy in Austria. He also courted Mussolini, who succumbed in stages, signing the Anti-Comintern Pact in September 1937. Meanwhile, Germany consolidated its grip on most east European states except Poland and Czechoslovakia. In addition, by 1937 local Nazis in Danzig, still nominally under League administration, created such tension that Poland feared war within two years. Berlin's propaganda attacks on Czechoslovakia grew, using the German minority as an excuse but rejecting Czech offers to negotiate and make concessions for, in Hitler's eyes, the German minority was not the issue. Britain urged concessions, misjudging Hitler's intent, but resisted his offers of an agreement leaving Britain its empire and Germany Europe. After London rejected the Anti-Comintern Pact, Hitler abandoned any serious thought of a British treaty. His policies became more dynamic as he committed to force and in 1937 drew up his first aggressive military plan to seize Czechoslovakia.

By that time, a new great war was widely seen as possible, even prob-able. Most expected it to come in Europe, not East Asia, for Hitler, as dicta-tor of the strongest European power, was clearly preparing his nation for war and France could no longer stop that, even if it could summon the will. The crises from 1931 through mid-1937 had considerably altered the power balance in both Europe and Asia, but they had not set off a chain reaction of aggression. From mid-1937 on, that prospect seemed all too possible, and nobody in the democracies knew what to do. In July 1937, Roosevelt, who was edging toward a larger role on the world stage, publicly declared that pressure existed 'for somebody outside of Europe to come forward with a hat and a rabbit in it. Well, . . . I haven't got a hat and I haven't got a rabbit in it.'[24] Nor had anyone else.

◆ Notes to Chapter 15

1. Hans Mommsen, 'The Failure of the Weimar Republic and the Rise of Hitler', in Michael Laffan, *The Burden of German History, 1914–45* (London, Methuen 1998), p. 127.
2. Robert H. Ferrell, *American Diplomacy in the Great Depression* (New Haven, CT, YUP), 1957) p. 141.
3. Zara Steiner, 'The League of Nations and the Quest for Security', in R. Ahmann *et al.*, eds, *The Quest for Stability: Problems of West European Security, 1918–1937* (New York, OUP, 1993) p. 59.
4. Christopher Thorne, *The Limits of Foreign Policy* (London, Hamish Hamilton, 1972), p. 420.
5. *Ibid.*, p. 7.
6. P. M. H. Bell, *France and Britain, 1900-1940* (London, Longman, 1996), p. 173.

7. Klaus Hildebrand, *The Foreign Policy of the Third Reich*, tr. Anthony Fothergill (Berkeley, CA, University of California Press, 1973), p. 123. On Nazi foreign policy, this work is highly recommended, along with Volker Berghahn, *Modern Germany*, 2nd edn (Cambridge, CUP, 1987); William Carr, *Arms, Autarky, and Aggression* (New York, Norton, 1972); and Gerhard L. Weinberg. *The Foreign Policy of Hitler's Germany* (2 vols, Chicago, University of Chicago Press, 1970, 1980). I owe a considerable debt of gratitude to Prof. Weinberg and his many works on Hitlerian policy.
8. Laurence Weschler, 'Mind-Sets', *The New Yorker*, 12 April 1999, p. 25.
9. For a detailed discussion of this concept, particularly in regard to the United States in more recent years, see Paul Kennedy, *The Rise and Fall of the Great Powers* (New York, Random House, 1987).
10. Gerhard L. Weinberg, 'German Recognition of Manchukuo', cited in Arnold Offner, *American Appeasement* (Cambridge, MA, Belknap Press, 1969), p. 165.
11. Robert O. Paxton, *French Peasant Fascism* (Oxford, OUP, 1997), p. 17.
12. Gerhard L. Weinberg, *Germany, Hitler, and World War II* (Cambridge, CUP, 1995), p. 86.
13. Thomas M. Veritch, *The European Powers and the Italo-Ethiopian War, 1935-1936* (Salisbury, NC, Documentary Publications, 1980), p. 66.
14. Anita J. Prażmowska, *Eastern Europe and the Origins of the Second World War* (London, Macmillan, 2000), p. 211.
15. *Ibid.*, p. 49.
16. Frank McDonough, *Neville Chamberlain, Appeasement, and the British Road to War* (New York, St Martin's Press, 1992), p. 26.
17. Veritch, *Italo-Ethiopian War*, p. 211.
18. For French military deficiencies, see Stephen A. Schuker, 'France and the Remilitarization of the Rhineland, 1936,' *French Historical Studies* XIV (1986), pp. 299-338.
19. James T. Emmerson, *The Rhineland Crisis* (Ames, IA, Iowa State University Press, 1977), p. 184.
20. *Ibid.*, p. 147.
21. Weinberg, *Foreign Policy of Hitler's Germany*, I, p. 262.
22. P. M. H. Bell, *The Origins of the Second World War in Europe* (London, Longman, 1986), p. 211. I owe much to this outstanding book.
23. David Clay Large, *Between Two Fires, Europe's Path in the 1930s* (New York, Norton, 1990), p. 243.
24. Robert Dallek, *Franklin D. Roosevelt and American Foreign Policy, 1932–1945* (New York, OUP, 1979), p. 144.

THE WORLD'S WAR

Peace wun't keep house with Fear;
Ef you want peace, the thing you've gut to du
Is jes' to show you're up to fightin', tu.

James Russell Lowell
The Biglow Papers, II, ii

CHAPTER

16

WAR EAST AND WEST, 1937–1941

When did the curtain rise on World War II? Opinions vary, usually according to where the viewer sits in the global theatre. Some Africans and Africanists point to October 1935; however, though the Ethiopian crisis eased Mussolini's slide toward Hitler and resistance continued until liberation, the episode was essentially self-contained, not leading to more war. The Chinese and Japanese claim July 1937. Europeans and many in their colonies chorus, 'September, 1939'. Americans, north and south (but not Canadians), in a view both parochial and global, often say December 1941. To be sure, Japan's attack on American soil united the various wars into one great conflict. But one cause of that attack was the Sino-Japanese clash which turned into an eight-year struggle. Thus World War II's opening and closing scenes were set in East Asia.

This new Great War was more global than its predecessor, affecting every inhabited continent, some acutely. Destruction was far greater, loss of life doubled, and atrocities enormous. Civilians suffered more where saturation bombing of cities occurred. In Axis- or Soviet-occupied areas, strong resistance movements embraced all ages and both sexes. Radio propaganda mattered: Berlin's and Tokyo's broadcasts tried to sap Allied troop morale while Britain's BBC aired news and aided European resistance movements. As often happens, war brought social change, including new roles for women, especially Anglo-American ones who served in the military, but not in combat. Some aspects of warfare remained traditional, though with newer weapons. But technology had made giant strides in twenty years; battles were now dominated by tanks, fleets of sturdy aeroplanes, and aircraft carriers. The manufacture of these generated an insatiable thirst for oil, rubber, steel, and strategic metals which often dictated diplomacy as well as military strategy and tactics. Along with China, oil was a key factor in Japan's attack at Pearl Harbor.

Intelligence operations assumed a greater role than before. Spies played their part, as always. Italy had a spy in Britain's Rome embassy before the war, one in the American embassy in its first years. Berlin penetrated the British embassy in Ankara, and before the war tapped both Polish telephones and lines from Prague to Paris and London, which ran through

Germany. Moscow had a network in Germany as well as spies in Britain, the United States, and Tokyo.

With armed forces spread across entire continents and oceans, communication relied on radio. What was broadcast could be heard by any who listened; hence codes and codebreakers. In World War I, cryptanalysis was in its infancy; in World War II, it matured rapidly and was vital to Allied victory. Great care was taken to conceal possession of enemy codes, so they would not be changed. These were gained by theft (with photography and rapid return), capture of code books, acquisition of code machines, replication of machines, or intricate mathematical attack, aided by the foe's human errors. Italy did well at theft, not at cryptanalysis. Germany had some modest successes, Japan almost none against Britain and the United States, who produced the dramatic achievements. In August 1939, Poland gave its pioneering work on the German Enigma code machine, copies of the machine, and a device to speed computation to Britain and France. From this base, creating an infant computer, Britain read high-level German communications with partial but growing facility by mid-1940; this intelligence was termed ULTRA. Within months, a heroic American effort (MAGIC), which replicated the Japanese code machine, enabled Washington to read Tokyo's top diplomatic code; this also provided information about Europe, for Japanese envoys in Berlin were assiduous reporters. Before American entry into the war, Anglo-American resources were partially pooled; thereafter co-operation was close, as hundreds of men and women in both countries pored over intercepts, gradually increasing the number of codes read.

In intelligence assessment, hindsight is unerring, but contemporary analysis is marred by human failures, delays, and 'noise'. Picking the right reports out of thousands of conflicting ones is not easy; rumours, misinformation, disinformation, double agents' fear of entrapment, planting stories, deception schemes, and weak analysis clutter the picture. Cryptanalysis is slow, often partial, sometimes too late, and radio silence defeats any codebreaker. Leaders fail to receive intelligence or ignore it if it does not fit their assumptions. Unlike the Anglo-Americans, Germany and Japan refused to accept that their codes were broken. But MAGIC and ULTRA were reliable, except when the foe maintained radio silence, believed, intensely protected, and fully used.

*   *   *

When World War II opened, these technological triumphs lay in the future. The initial scenes in China were those of a fairly traditional war. An accidental clash on 7 July 1937 near Peking soon escalated. Neither Chiang nor most Japanese leaders in Tokyo wanted war, but neither side was conciliatory. Japan's field commanders and General Staff insisted on massive reinforcement to solidify their grip on the region; of political necessity, Chiang drew the line. Chinese Communists, junior officers on both sides, and

Kwantung army elements in China resisted resolution. By late July fighting spread, and Japan took Peking and Tientsin (Tianjin). In August, it moved toward Shanghai, with a partial blockade of the south China coast, challenging British interests there. Prince Konoe Fumimaro's Cabinet feared Soviet military power in Asia, but army elements overcame its caution. Then and thereafter, army and navy ministers made the most of their direct access to the Emperor, telling other ministers little. The Cabinet gained German mediation, as Hitler wished to turn Japan against Britain, not China, but the two sides never pursued moderation at the same time. By late 1937, the army's aggressive elements prevailed.

Britain also tried to mediate but, lacking American co-operation, failed. It ruled out action with Moscow, whose intervention in East Asia it feared, and vainly sought co-ordination with Washington at a time of mutual Anglo-American distrust. Like France, Britain was preoccupied with Germany, Italy, and unstable Middle Eastern mandates. Neither could risk war with Japan. Lacking a Pacific fleet and a major Asian naval base,* Britain used diplomacy and bluff, avoiding confrontation, for Germany was the direct threat and Chamberlain had little interest in East Asia. To maintain global prominence and imperial pre-eminence as its power waned, Britain avoided active appeasement of Tokyo; however, it was often passive in defending a position that was no longer viable as Japan emerged against the West, marking a key phase of the end of Western predominance in Asia. Sanctions against Japan were avoided, lest they spur Germany and Italy to new action in Europe or lead to an unthinkable Asian war. But London remained officially committed to defence of the entire Empire; this was a question of prestige, of the basis of British power, and of ensuring Britain did not become 'nothing but an insignificant island in the North Sea'.[1]

What Britons saw as defence of their Empire, Asians viewed as aggressive or oppressive, while London saw the Japanese as impertinent upstarts and aggressors. Anglo-American racism and ignorance led to underestimating Japan. Washington also opposed sanctions, for Roosevelt was coping with a sharp new recession as well as domestic political battles and feared Britain's more active policy would lead to a war where the United States would carry the burden. Both countries preferred the *status quo*, stability, and peace, partly for reasons of trade, for they relied heavily on Asian raw materials. Over half of such American imports came from Asia, including 98 per cent of its rubber and 90 per cent of its tin.[2] Roosevelt, aware of acute military weakness, did not officially recognize Japanese conquests but avoided clashes; Tokyo concluded it could push the United States if it did not force a war. Like London, Washington relied on bluff and diplomacy. British and American policies were similar but separate, as the gulf remained wide.

---

* The Singapore based opened in 1938 but was not fully operational until late 1940.

Washington soon aided China modestly. As the war was undeclared, Roosevelt avoided invoking the Neutrality Acts,* whose 'cash and carry' provision would benefit Japan. American opinion favoured China, thanks to historic ties and Pearl S. Buck's novel and film, *The Good Earth*. Lacking military means to halt Japan, Roosevelt appealed to world opinion, to little effect. In October, he spoke of the need to 'quarantine aggressors'; this vague warning had no sequel, for American isolationists howled. But he began to fortify American Pacific islands and sought to enlarge the navy. Chamberlain rejected his overtures, so American policy drifted, though secret naval staff talks began in January 1938 as a small start to a growing collaboration.

The Soviet Union, which had a 3000-mile (4825-km) border with Japanese-controlled mainland territories, was relieved at the outbreak of the Sino-Japanese war. As purges destroyed the Red Army's High Command and Siberian border clashes mounted, Moscow wished to keep Japan embroiled elsewhere. Thus it began aid to China in late July 1937 and signed a non-aggression treaty in August. Partly as a result, Chiang's Kuomintang (KMT) and the Chinese Communists (CCP) reached an uneasy truce in September, nominally forming a united front against Japan.

Also in September, China appealed to the League, which duly censured Japan for violation of the 1922 Nine Power Treaty and the Kellogg–Briand Pact, but Britain and France blocked any consideration of sanctions. Thus the League merely called a conference of the Nine Power Treaty states plus Russia and others to meet in Brussels in November. Japan refused to attend, but Italy, which adhered as the conference opened to the 1936 Anti-Comintern Pact (understood in London to be as anti-British as anti-Russian), spoke for Tokyo and was obstructive. Since neither London nor Paris nor Washington offered any lead, the conference produced only hollow resolutions.

Meanwhile military disaster engulfed China. In November, Shanghai fell to the Japanese who then marched on Nanking, the KMT capital. On 12 December on the Yangtze River, they sank or seized British and American gunboats and tankers with some fatalities. The next day, they began the 'Rape of Nanking', a six-week massacre costing up to 300 000 civilian lives. World opinion hardened; indiscriminate bombing of Canton in the spring of 1938 reinforced Western hostility. FDR increased aid to China, proclaimed a 'moral embargo', and restricted export licences, but Berlin completed its switch from China to Japan, partly to pin London and Moscow down in East Asia during Europe's 1938 crises. Border incidents with Russia led Japanese army hotheads to seek an open break with Moscow, thinking it could not fight; when a large clash amounting to a small war came in mid-summer, they learned otherwise, losing badly. By

* See Chapter 15.

then, the KMT army had collapsed. Its government moved to Chungking (Chongqing) in the interior. Japan took one city after another in the autumn and proclaimed a 'New Order' for East Asia with no major role for the West. It held a vast area with 170 million people and all seaports but lacked effective control against Communist guerrillas and could not end the war.

Japan kept winning but never decisively, as Chiang traded space for time, yielding territory but resisting somewhat while awaiting American deliverance. Tokyo was trapped in the dreaded China quagmire with too much invested to withdraw but no end in sight. By 1939, Japan wanted peace and a puppet state but could not attain it. The Communists, far more nationalistic than the Nationalists, fought on. When KMT military power crumbled, CCP political influence grew. As the war continued, so did the struggle between the KMT and the CCP, to which Chiang soon gave primacy. Idle in Chungking, the KMT leadership deteriorated sharply, and Chiang became more despotic. As Chinese society was breaking up under the strain, the CCP gained strength. Though fighting never ceased, the war reached an impasse in 1939, for Japan had gained what it most wanted and did not wish to risk war with the Soviet Union and the Western democracies.

*   *   *

If 1937 in Asia was a year of high drama, in Europe it was an entr'acte with rumblings of scene-shifting behind the curtain as portents but relatively little occurring before the footlights. Some thumps and bumps heralded a shift in the power balance from the satisfied *status quo* Western powers to the revisionist states, above all Germany, which by 1937 was Europe's strongest nation. It had full employment, self-confidence, and a head start on rearmament, which now produced results as Germany spent from March 1933 to March 1939 about 150 per cent on arms of what Britain and France together spent in the same period.[3] Germany's population advantage over each was large; the masses and the generals supported Hitler, whose position was secure. As he wished, the Spanish war continued, providing diplomatic distraction and a testing ground for his new weapons. He wanted rapid rearmament to scare neighbours conveniently divided by minority problems, especially Czechoslovakia (35 per cent) and Poland (30 per cent), into major concessions or to generate *Blitzkrieg* against isolated foes, with German minorities as a pretext. But first the military build-up, which continued apace. As yet, Hitler's focus was European. He had little Asian policy until 1938 or interest in the United States, which he thought weak because of its racial mix. Thus war against it lay in the indefinite future.

Roosevelt saw the threat Hitler represented and knew force would be needed but was not yet possible. American opinion was almost unanimous in its desire to avoid war, dividing only on how to do so. While in 1937–38

FDR sought to educate Americans about Germany and Japan, partly by the Quarantine Speech, he tried to demonstrate concern for European stability while escaping any responsibility. Though Russo-American relations were scant, he and Stalin tried to use each other to block Japanese and German expansion but without any agreement.

The Soviet Union remained relatively isolated. All European states, including Italy, opposed Nazi expansion, but only Prague and Paris to a degree were willing to enlist the purge-ridden Red Army. Stalin sought security, so he pursued a dual policy to keep capitalist states divided, which meant entente with or against Germany. Thus he courted an unresponsive Germany while Litvinov pursued collective security with Britain and France, only minimally more responsive. Stalin feared Germany, Japan, a German-Western alliance against him, the West turning Germany eastward – which it never attempted – and being trapped by the West into war alone against Germany and/or Japan. Thus he wooed Germany and Britain, both of whom he distrusted.

Chamberlain reciprocated that distrust, for he was intensely anti-Bolshevik and against alliances as being apt to divide Europe and lead to war. As he struggled to maintain Britain's position, substituting prestige for power, he feared that embroilment in central Europe could risk the Empire. He shared the national aversion to the Versailles treaty, the ugly memories of World War I and fear of another, the dislike of France, and the desire of most Dominions to appease Germany and Japan. Chamberlain hoped to rip up the Versailles treaty peacefully and satisfy Hitler at the expense of the Reich's neighbours, to whom he gave little thought. A satisfied Germany could block Communism, save money on costly rearmament, and permit concentration on domestic questions. Mindful that Britain lies only 22 miles (35 km) from Europe but seriously misreading Hitler, Chamberlain proceeded with excessive faith in his own skill and increasing self-delusion and obstinacy. Though focused on Germany, he also wooed Italy.

Mussolini, a bully with a limited localized power base, in January 1937 joined Britain in a Gentleman's Agreement to preserve the Mediterranean *status quo*. Encouraged by his pose of non-alignment to gain concessions, Chamberlain courted Italy, known as 'Europe's most expensive whore'.[4] But difficulties continued over the Spanish war, culminating in the Nyon conference* and driving Mussolini steadily toward Hitler. For this he was willing to pay the price: in 1937 he indicated first to Vienna and then to Berlin that he did not intend to defend Austria, accepting the prospect of Nazi troops poised on his northern frontier.

France courted Italy earlier, but Mussolini's interest in French North Africa was obvious. Blum's Popular Front, which London disliked, had no sympathy for Fascism and pursued its own line in this respect, if not others.

* See Chapter 15.

Despite slow rearmament, France was deep in depression until late 1938 with a new financial crisis in early 1937. A divided country faced lean years militarily, the League's collapse, and the unravelling of eastern alliances. After Blum fell in mid-1937, his successor focused on domestic problems. An effort to revive the eastern alliances failed, except with Prague, for economic dependence on and fear of Germany generated paralysis. Paris followed London's lead regarding Berlin, for she saw no policy not entailing a loss of what power she possessed. France was less inclined than Britain to appeasing Hitler with concessions, but she used pretexts – including British policy – to do nothing. As she weakened vis-à-vis Germany and as Britain was deemed more vital than all other allies combined, she became more dependent.

Britain was the senior partner, it and Germany the major protagonists. By late 1937, Hitler was nearly absolute in a Reich showing economic strains. He could slow rearmament or conquer new assets; he chose conquest. On 5 November 1937 Hitler told his generals he intended to have Austria and Czechoslovakia soon and later would seek *Lebensraum*.* He would use force against Prague, which he saw as key to the ring of states supposedly encircling Germany. A visiting British cabinet minister, Lord Halifax, implied Britain would accept change in central Europe if the states concerned agreed, but Hitler had no interest in negotiations. There was little meeting of minds, particularly as he urged Britain to settle unrest in India by shooting Gandhi. Soon after, Chamberlain told his Cabinet Britain's military weakness required fewer enemies and more allies. Since he thought it 'always best and safest to count on nothing from the Americans but words',[5] and his distrust for Moscow was visceral, he tried to reduce the number of Britain's foes.

Both dominant leaders engaged in preliminary house-cleaning. Two generals who protested the risks of Hitler's plans were replaced and Hitler became commander in chief. His inept envoy in London, Joachim von Ribbentrop (christened Herr Brickendrop by the Foreign Office)[6] became Foreign Minister. Chamberlain also gained a more complaisant Foreign Secretary in Halifax, but as he was in the House of Lords, Chamberlain's control of policy grew, particularly when the Foreign Office's top official, the anti-Nazi Sir Robert Vansittart, was replaced.

*   *   *

With the stage thus set, crises came quickly. On 12 February 1938, Austria's Chancellor, Kurt von Schuschnigg, visited Hitler's mountaintop eyrie at Berchtesgaden in the Bavarian Alps. Hitler demanded Austria become a Nazified satellite. But he reneged on a promise to recognize

---

* The reliability of the memorandum of this meeting has been impugned, but mainly by those who find its contents inconvenient. Subsequent directives leave little doubt.

Austrian independence publicly, so on 9 March Schuschnigg announced a national plebiscite for 13 March on that issue. A vote for independence was likely, creating a barrier to *Anschluss,* which Hitler intended. Thus he decided to invade, giving his army one day's notice. Mussolini agreed, for he was too occupied in Spain to act even if he wished. Pressure from Berlin and Rome led Schuschnigg to cancel the plebiscite and resign, saying Austria would not resist force. Hitler followed his army to Vienna; his reception was so enthusiastic that he annexed Austria, which became a German province. Austrian Jews and socialists suffered at once.

Like the Rhineland remilitarization, the *Anschluss* was one of Hitler's weekend surprises, though not entirely unexpected. Britain had issued no warnings, and Hitler assumed it would not risk war. Chamberlain and Halifax seemed little bothered that a League member had been abruptly swallowed. France was in the midst of a cabinet crisis and lacked a government, but in any event would not act without Britain and Italy. *Pro forma* protests over the use of force came from Paris, London, and Moscow, but not Rome. On the whole, the *fait accompli* was quietly accepted.

Hitler quickly signalled his next target, saying he must protect Czechoslovakia's 3.5 million Germans. These so-called Sudeten* Germans in the mountainous Czech borderlands were a pretext, for Hitler intended to destroy Czechoslovakia. The Germanic element had largely accepted the new state until sharply impacted by its late, severe Depression. Then they flocked to the Sudeten German Party (SDP) led by a plausible Nazi puppet. On 24 April at Karlsbad (Karlovy Vary), he demanded concessions (written in Berlin) so sweeping that the state's integrity was potentially at stake. Hitler ordered him to ensure that no agreement was achieved.

Czechoslovakia possessed alliances with France and Russia, with the latter obliged to defend it if France did. However, Britain and France quickly wrote it off. Rebuffing Soviet pleas for a united front and terrified of war, they decided Czechoslovakia was not viable and tried each to ensure the other took the blame for what ensued. Acutely aware of its own weakness, France overestimated Germany's as yet minimal Westwall (Siegfried Line) forts in the Rhineland. The new Premier in April, Edouard Daladier, was irresolute whereas his Foreign Minister, Georges Bonnet, wished to appease. A frightened cabinet maintained public support of Prague but succumbed to British pressure to press for concessions. Both states misdiagnosed the problem, thinking that meeting the SDP's demands would prevent the war Hitler was determined to have.

---

* 'Sudetenland' was a term which Nazis used to imply a coherent geographic area where none existed. The German minority dwelt in a jagged horseshoe-shaped fringe of southern Silesia, Bohemia, and Moravia, of which the Sudeten mountains were the north-eastern segment.

Chamberlain wanted to get past the Czech problem and on to a settlement with Hitler. He feared German air power and a war without Dominion and American men and money. As he could not muster two fully equipped divisions to serve in France, Prague must be coerced or abandoned; Cabinet, press, and public agreed until late in the crisis. Chamberlain hoped to alter the *status quo* at Czech expense just enough to preserve most of it and Britain's position while limiting Hitlerian expansion. Thus from May to September London and Paris pressed Prague for concessions. Beneš, now President, made these, but slowly. In May a false report misled Prague to expect invasion. It mobilized its army, while London and Paris warned Hitler off. In fury, he accelerated his plans, setting a 1 October deadline for destruction of Czechoslovakia. Britain and France, however, were terrified by the apparent brush with war. In July, France told Beneš she would not fight; Britain insisted he 'invite' a nominally independent British mediator, whose role was to hasten Czech concessions and give London control of the crisis without commitment. Both intimated that if Prague resisted, it would fight alone, be destroyed, and not regain the borderlands in any eventual victory. In early September, Beneš conceded most of the Karlsbad programme, causing the SDP to use a minor incident to end negotiations.

As Hitler screamed abuse at the Czechs, Chamberlain visited him at Berchtesgaden on 15 September. Hitler demanded outright cession of the borderlands by 30 September. By saying Britain would guarantee the indefensible Czech remnant, Chamberlain persuaded his Cabinet and Paris to agree. He told the appalled Czechs to choose destruction or dismemberment. Beneš sought heavy pressure to convince his Cabinet and justify its submission, so an Anglo-French ultimatum was duly provided at 2.00 a.m. on 21 September. The next day Chamberlain bore the Czech surrender to Hitler at Godesberg on the Rhine, only to face greater ultimative demands. Chamberlain wished to accept but his Cabinet refused, led by Halifax. The Czechs mobilized on 23 September, followed on the 27th by France and on the 28th by the Royal Navy as Anglo-French opinion rejected overt bullying. War was very close as Chamberlain begged Mussolini to intercede. Since Italy could not fight, Rome offered a conference. Hitler then pulled back: he wanted a small, localized war, not a great power conflict. He had failed to isolate Prague; Britain and France (and perhaps Russia) would fight, but not Italy. His generals opposed war, and Berlin crowds were sullenly hostile to military parades. His frustration, however, guaranteed war in the future.

Mussolini stage-managed the gathering in Munich with much prompting from Berlin. It was a great power concert minus Moscow, not invited since Hitler would not come if the Soviets did. Nor were the Czechs invited, though emissaries arrived to await their fate. Unlike the British and French, the two dictators consulted ahead, and Mussolini offered proposals drafted in Berlin. Hitler gained what he demanded but not the localized war he wanted. Polish and Hungarian claims were to be satisfied, and there would be a four-power guarantee of the Czech remnant. Prague yielded to a new ultimatum, and Beneš resigned. Chamberlain returned from Munich waving an Anglo-German declaration signed by Hitler that the two countries desired never to go to war with each other. He thought he had made peace. Daladier knew better.

Germany gained much, including most Czech heavy industry and arms factories and a replica of the Maginot Line. Poland took Teschen. Without consulting Britain and France, Italy and Germany awarded Hungary a southern strip of Slovakia. Czechoslovakia became a German satellite – without a guarantee, for Hitler avoided signing it and Chamberlain insisted it operate only if three of the four powers agreed. Hitler, furious at being denied his war, said he would take the remnant in the spring. In the coming year, he took care not to be trapped in negotiations again.

Britain and France have been criticized for failing to fight for Czechoslovakia, especially as opinion in both countries hardened after Godesberg, but France's rearmament had not reached real mass production, and its fighter planes were slower than German bombers. Britain had one squadron of Hurricanes and a single Spitfire, but could not use them above 15 000 feet because of defective oxygen masks. The crucial radar net was barely begun and no network of command centres existed.[7] Britain would have had to fight without radar, Enigma, planes, or much Dominion support, which it had in 1939. It feared the Commonwealth, its proudest interwar achievement, would shatter. It gained in comparative military strength in the next year, but Chamberlain was not buying time to rearm. Though war in Europe was delayed, a price was paid elsewhere for Japan decided Britain was a paper tiger, took Canton, isolated Hongkong, and proclaimed its 'New Order'. France also paid as its eastern allies, especially oil-rich Rumania, flocked to Hitler. However, British leaders and opinion believed Hitler's promise that the 'Sudetenland' was his last territorial demand in Europe and that he wished to incorporate only Germans. They instinctively defined this as the limit of what they would accept, a fact Hitler did not understand.

The Soviet role has also been much debated. Moscow maintained throughout that it would honour its obligation. Many historians think it would have done so to some degree, despite the purges and summer battles with Japan, using a limited Rumanian offer of air and rail transit to reach Czechoslovakia.[8] It never had to say whether it would fight unilaterally if France did not, but most scholars are doubtful. Moscow pressed all summer for a united front to use this last chance to deter Hitler without war. It then decided that collective security had failed but retained the policy temporarily as a defensive measure, though exclusion from the Munich conference rankled.

*   *   *

After Munich, the British Cabinet's power balance shifted from Chamberlain to Halifax. The Cabinet pressed rearmament over

Chamberlain's objections and in February 1939 offered France full military staff talks. Public opinion reacted sharply to an organized German anti-Semitic pogrom on 10 November 1938, burning synagogues and smashing windows of Jewish-owned shops. American opinion was also affected; Roosevelt made the most of that, increasing the defence budget, boosting economic support to Britain and France, preventing a break with Mexico over its oil nationalization, and in December obtaining a hemispheric declaration at Lima, Peru, against foreign threats.

In France, Bonnet gained a German statement of friendship in December to match what Chamberlain signed at Munich, but Daladier, who detested him, became more firmly anti-Nazi. By 1939, French opinion was hardening against Germany as well.[9] But the Cabinet doubted British resolve, since London had not introduced conscription, and worried about Chamberlain's courtship of Italy. Mussolini avoided alliance with Germany until 1939 but in May signed the Pact of Steel, an Italo-German military alliance aimed at France and Britain. He did so partly in hopes of gaining Nice, Savoy, Corsica, Djibouti, and Tunis from France.

Europe's prime mover, having declared on 26 September that he had no further territorial demands, made one on 24 October 1938, claiming Danzig. Warsaw considered a compromise which did not interest Hitler, for the issue was Polish submission.[10] Talks continued into March 1939, but Poland refused to be a satellite, so Hitler ordered its conquest for 1 September. He was in a hurry to proceed before German military superiority faded, economic pressures worsened, and he aged. Thus he attained his Italian pact and vainly sought one with Japan against Britain.

On 15 March 1939, Hitler sent his army to Prague, annexed the Czech domains, made Slovakia an 'independent' German protectorate, and awarded Ruthenia to Hungary. The British Cabinet was initially passive, and Chamberlain declared that since Czechoslovakia no longer existed, neither did the guarantee. But public opinion raged, and Halifax reacted. Hitler had broken his promise, taken new territory, and incorporated non-Germans. By 17 March Chamberlain shifted; the Cabinet agreed to resist Nazi domination. It now distrusted Germany, but Chamberlain less than others. He could not accept that giving Hitler what he wished meant Nazi European hegemony, and he was so determined to prevent war that his policy did not shift appreciably. Opposition to it increased, however, and the Cabinet decided to seek allies against Germany.

This decision owed something to false reports of an imminent German attack on Rumania, and was reinforced by Hitler's ultimative seizure on 23 March of Memel, Lithuania's only major port, and more false rumours of an impending attack on Poland. Thus on 31 March a British guarantee of Polish independence was announced. France joined in and both states received Poland's cryptanalytic secrets in August. In fact, in Anglo-French staff talks, which opted for a defensive stance and a long war, the two states decided to do nothing for Poland. The guarantee was a political act to deter Hitler by threat of a two-front war. Chamberlain saw a guarantee of independence, not of Poland's boundaries, with London deciding when independence was threatened. Nonetheless, Britain's first real east European commitment was a dramatic departure from past policy.

Mussolini, who had not been told in advance of Hitler's latest seizures, grumbled, 'Every time Hitler occupies a country, he sends me a message.'[11] As the Spanish war ended, the leader of Europe's most Catholic nation chose Good Friday, 7 April 1939, to occupy Albania, an act 'like raping your own wife'.[12] This violation of the Gentleman's Agreement led to one-sided Anglo-French guarantees in April of Greece and Rumania against Italy and Germany but not Russia, and mutual defensive guarantees with Turkey against Mediterranean aggression in May after France ceded Syrian Alexandretta to improve relations. They aimed to gain bases against Italy, for neither could act significantly in eastern Europe. Yugoslavia let it be known that it would reject a guarantee if offered. Otherwise, France had revitalized its position in the east and Britain had gone, over Chamberlain's objections, in one month from no eastern commitments to several.

As Britain and France drew closer, so did Britain and the United States, for Chamberlain at last accepted that Congressional and public opinion were real barriers to action, not excuses. A silent joint strategy evolved against all three potential foes, and in April, as Britain finally announced plans for conscription, Roosevelt shifted his only fleet from the Atlantic to San Diego, California, so London could focus on the Mediterranean without worrying about promises to send a fleet to Pacific waters in a crisis. On 15 April, FDR tried to embarrass Hitler and Mussolini by asking them to guarantee not to attack 31 named European and Middle Eastern states for ten years. In a taunting speech, Hitler replied that all 31 said they did not feel threatened, and denounced his Polish non-aggression treaty and British naval agreement. As summer arrived, he renewed demands for return of Danzig and extraterritorial routes across the Polish Corridor, while also creating incidents over Poland's German minority. These were pretexts. The issue was conquest of Poland by *Blitzkrieg*.

Meanwhile, Britain and the United States remained wary of Japan, which engaged from May to September 1939 in a new small losing war with the Soviets. In June Britain also tangled with Japan at Tientsin, an extraterritorial British enclave 80 miles (130 km) from Peking, in a test of wills illustrating the dilemma of a weak global power spread too thin. Britain could not divert naval forces from the Mediterranean without repercussions regarding France, Italy, and Germany; it could not fight Japan without the United States; and it could not cede to Japanese demands without losing American support. Thus it stalled, resisting a little in its first subordination of British policy to American, until the 23 August Russo-German treaty alarmed Tokyo, ending the threat of an immediate Anglo-Japanese war. Though FDR cancelled the Japanese-American trade agreement, he and Chamberlain avoided pushing Japan toward Germany and Italy.

*   *   *

In April, Britain sought a unilateral Soviet guarantee of Poland and Rumania. Moscow's reply proposed an Anglo-French-Soviet alliance and military convention. As talks continued into August, the three powers had differing goals and rates of speed. Moscow knew from a spy in the Foreign Office that Britain aimed to scare Berlin by negotiations and prevent a Russo-German treaty but did not want a commitment. France would sign a new bilateral treaty. Stalin pursued a pact and more, but his price was Poland and a free hand in the Baltic states to bolster Leningrad's defences. Moscow demanded Red Army entry into Poland, but like other eastern states, Poland feared Germany less. This, plus Chamberlain's obstruction, doomed any agreement.

In early May, Litvinov, who was Jewish and Moscow's apostle of collective security, was replaced by Vyacheslav Molotov, who was neither. Germany, fearing a Russian treaty with the West, began courting Moscow without much response until late July. London and Paris finally agreed on a military mission to Moscow, but sent by slow merchant steamer only second rank officials with no authority to sign anything. The August talks between the Anglo-French mission and the Russians collapsed over a Soviet demand to enter Poland to fight Germany, though fear that war would bring Communist domination of Europe also underlay Chamberlain's policy. By now, Moscow was negotiating seriously with Berlin. Hitler was in a hurry, as Stalin knew, for his war must be completed before mid-October rains rendered Poland's dirt roads and grass airstrips unusable. On 21 August, he peremptorily demanded that Ribbentrop arrive in Moscow on 23 August to sign a treaty. Stalin broke off the Anglo-French talks and agreed. He dreaded embroilment in the coming war, feared a German-Japanese combination, and needed peace for domestic and military reasons. After long ambivalence, he opted for avoiding battle.

London and Paris sought Soviet military action with no reward. Ribbentrop came bearing gifts. The ten-year Nazi–Soviet non-aggression pact ensured Soviet non-belligerence. A secret protocol paid Stalin's price: a sphere comprising Finland, Bessarabia, and much of the Baltic states and Poland.* The pact meant Polish resistance would be brief with no Soviet resupply. The world was aghast, especially Japan, over this blatant violation of its Anti-Comintern Pact.

---

* After the fall of Poland, a subsequent Russo-German agreement gave the Soviets all of the Baltics and somewhat less of Poland.

In Europe, where the impact was acute, much energy was vainly devoted in the next week to preventing war. As FDR appealed for peace, an aide remarked, 'These messages will have about the same effect as a valentine sent to somebody's mother-in-law out of season.'[13] So did other efforts. Hitler misjudged Britain's will; it leaked word that it would fight over Danzig, but as it had done little at Tientsin, he thought it would cede. On 25 August, however, London signed a Polish pact covering Danzig, primarily to deter Hitler; France trailed after. Japan ended alliance talks with Germany, and Mussolini said he could not fight unless given a mountainous list of supplies; his foreign minister said, 'It's enough to kill a bull – if a bull could read it.'[14] So Hitler delayed his 26 August invasion to isolate Poland and eliminate Britain, offering disarmament, a non-aggression treaty, and a guarantee of Britain's Empire in exchange for Danzig and the Polish Corridor. As London refused, the Poles would not go to Berlin to receive ultimata, and Hitler would not be trapped in diplomacy, the scurrying came to naught. Nobody else wanted war, including the German people, but only Hitler's generals could stop him, and they did not try.

On 1 September 1939, Germany invaded Poland. Twenty-three of Europe's 27 states promptly declared neutrality, as did Japan and the United States. British and French opinion had faced the necessity of fighting, though Chamberlain and Bonnet* had not. In London, the Cabinet and the House of Commons forced Chamberlain to act, and Britain forced France, where the National Assembly was tepid. On 1 September Britain and France warned Hitler to withdraw from Poland; he did not. When Chamberlain did nothing further, he faced revolt in both Cabinet and Commons. Thus after a two-hour ultimatum, Britain declared war on 3 September; France followed.

The British Empire, with no interest in Poland, was full of disaffection, especially in Egypt, Palestine, and India, but it rallied. Ireland, nominally a Dominion, remained neutral, but the other Dominions followed Britain into war, South Africa only after a cabinet crisis. In India, the viceroy told Indians they were at war – to the fury of Congress leaders at the lack of consultation; the Muslim League co-operated, as did most Indians, but Congress, despite its anti-Nazi views, left provincial governments in protest. Britain's dependent colonies and France's Empire also had no say, but did their part, including unsung contributions by Africans and West Indians.

Hitler was briefly shaken to find himself at war with the entire British and French empires, but not for long. After all, he had planned to fight Britain and France later, anyway. He had his war, if not an entirely localized one. Others were shattered. One American official said of the final countdown to war, 'These last two days have given me the feeling of sitting in a house where someone is dying upstairs.' Some spoke of the death of a civilization or the end of the world.[15]

---

* Whom Daladier removed from the Foreign Ministry within two weeks.

It was Poland which died of *Blitzkrieg* spearheaded by tanks and air attacks. Serious resistance ceased after 18 days, and Hitler's little war ended on 1 October. Before that, on 17 September, after a truce with Japan, Moscow – still neutral – occupied its sphere, moving to the Curzon Line. Germany annexed western Poland and created of the rest the 'General Government' as a dumping ground for Poles expelled from annexed areas, and later for Europe's Jews.

*   *   *

Hitler had told his generals that Poland would be conquered to gain food and *Lebensraum*. But his ideology stressed race as well as space, and he soon launched a second war against Jews and Gypsies as well as homosexuals, those with disabilities, enemy leaders, dissidents and resistants. The primary thrust, however, was for the purity of the German blood and elimination of those deemed unclean. Earlier, he had removed German Jews from the professions, deprived them of citizenship, sent some to concentration camps, and ousted them from commercial activities, as well as sterilizing Germany's tiny black minority. In 1939, Berlin's Jews were ghettoized. With war came systematic euthanasia for Germans with physical or mental disabilities.

In Poland at first the large Jewish minority faced random, unpredictable terror. When western Europe was conquered, the army was initially in charge and fairly correct, but in Russia the SS* engaged in mass slaughter by shooting and with mobile gas vans devised for the euthanasia programme.[†] In mid-1941 or soon after, Berlin decided on a 'Final Solution' to exterminate Europe's Jews and Gypsies. The first death camp opened in December; in January 1942 a conference organized large-scale implementation, mostly in Poland. Round-ups of French Jews began; the first transports arrived at Auschwitz (Oświęcim), the most infamous killing centre, in late March 1942. Slavic populations would be reduced by mass starvation and probably mass sterilization. The peak years of the Holocaust, which killed six million Jews and a million others, were 1942–44.

This vast operation had economic and military implications, for Hitler often put his ideological imperatives ahead of military necessity. Though factories existed at some camps, millions of useful workers were killed instead of used to manufacture arms. Scarce engines and freight cars hauled Jews to Auschwitz, not supplies to the Russian front. Large numbers of SS staffed the many camps. Also, pre-war emigration and wartime extermination hampered Germany's cryptanalytic effort; moreover, most of its theoretical physicists were Jews; as internationally known scholars, they had

---

* Schutzstaffel, or protection staff, originally Hitler's bodyguard but now swollen into a vast militarized army of special selected and indoctrinated fanatics.
  † For the Nazi 1940 conquest of western Europe and 1941 invasion of the Soviet Union, see below.

fled to American universities, where they contributed to development of the atomic bomb.

*   *   *

After Warsaw fell, a lull set in, christened the Phoney War. It was punctuated by Soviet demands on Finland in October for territory and bases to protect Leningrad, 20 miles (32 km) from the border. As Helsinki refused, Moscow invaded in November, earning wide condemnation and expulsion from the League. Its purge-ridden, half-reorganized troops did badly at first against stiff resistance, but as Germany did not assist Finland, the end was not in doubt. Britain and France considered crossing Norway and Sweden to aid Finland and block winter shipment of Swedish iron ore through Norwegian waters to Germany. Knowing this, Stalin wanted peace and, after two military breakthroughs, signed a treaty on 12 March 1940 whereby Finland lost more than 10 per cent of its territory but remained independent. The Soviets and the Anglo-French had narrowly avoided war with each other, but Finland slid into Hitler's orbit from fear of Moscow.

The Finnish debâcle led to Daladier's fall and an Allied decision to mine Norwegian waters. Britain began doing so on 8 April 1940; the next day, Germany invaded Denmark and Norway. Denmark yielded in four hours, keeping its king and government but soon losing Iceland to British pre-emptive occupation. Norway fought, though Oslo and other ports were seized at once. Hitler's amphibious operation was costly in lost ships but sought to protect ore shipments, break out of the Baltic, and seize Norway before Britain did. Allied landings in several places failed. The shambles led to Chamberlain's replacement on 10 May by Winston Churchill and Allied withdrawal in June. Sweden, now at German mercy, was obliged to stretch its neutrality considerably.

Churchill's Cabinet immediately faced Hitler's 10 May Blitzkrieg against the Low Countries and France. Luxembourg surrendered at once, Holland in five days, Belgium in 18. France, which dominated Allied planning since Britain's army was so small, had a fixed view of how the war would proceed, and with its poor communications, geriatric generals, and rigid tactics, 'needed close to a "perfect war" in 1940';[16] Hitler did not follow France's script. Assuming he would drive across the Belgian plains, the French army rushed north, committing its reserve. Instead, German tanks rolled through the hilly, supposedly impassable Ardennes of south Belgium and Luxembourg. In ten days, they reached the sea, cutting the Allies off, and halted for repair, expecting the Luftwaffe (air force) to destroy the trapped armies; bad weather and the RAF prevented that, so 337 000 Allied troops were evacuated without their equipment at Dunkirk (Dunkerque).

Anglo-French distrust worsened as Britain tried to aid France without squandering scarce resources in a losing cause. FDR offered encouragement, some supplies, and little else. A German offensive on 5 June sent the

French Cabinet southward; resistance ended, and the aged Marshal Philippe Pétain, who became premier on 16 June, gained an armistice on 22 June. Meanwhile, on 10 June Italy declared war but only moved ten days later when the fighting ended. Its disorganized army gained 100 yards (91 metres) against French resistance. Italy signed a separate armistice, but Hitler blocked many of its claims in hope of deterring France's colonies from siding with Britain.

Under the German armistice, the northern two-thirds of France – with most of its coal, iron, heavy industry, and population – was occupied; Pétain's regime at Vichy could run the rest, for a cabinet in exile would be a barrier to signature of a peace treaty in the west. Hitler concealed his plans for a vast African empire and let France keep its colonies (since he lacked a navy to reach them) and its fleets (to keep them out of London's hands). Reparations were immense compared to Weimar's burden. France's youngest general, Charles de Gaulle, appealed on 18 June by radio for continued resistance. By autumn, from London, he was rallying the Free French movement, which French Equatorial Africa joined partly from fear that Germany would seek return of the Cameroons. Also in London, the number of governments in exile swelled in 1940. Their gold reserves, merchant fleets and empires were Allied assets, especially the vast resources of the Belgian Congo and the Dutch East Indies.

Hitler, who thought the war nearly won, engaged in post-war planning and called for large-scale naval construction, partly with an eye to that future African empire, primarily to use against the United States. Meanwhile, his new European empire developed *ad hoc* arrangements. Some areas were annexed outright, including all western ones lost in the Versailles treaty. Denmark and Vichy were allowed to run themselves – within limits. Elsewhere there were occupied states or dependent protectorates as well as satellites, especially in south-east Europe.

Britain stood alone, saved so far by the English Channel. Until June 1940, it focused its diplomacy on the neutrals to deprive Hitler's economy and reinforce its Atlantic blockade – though Berlin's ability to import Asian rubber through Vladivostok punctured it a bit. From June 1940 to December 1941, London pursued the diplomacy of survival. Hitler hesitated, offering peace, for defeating Britain would hand its Empire to Tokyo and Washington. Britain, with its tiny army lacking equipment, could not survive without American aid, leading to eventual domination; but domination was a lesser evil than destruction, so Churchill begged desperately for help. Since Britain did not accept peace,[17] Hitler ordered an invasion, but his naval weakness meant air superiority was essential. Thus the air Battle of Britain was fought over the summer. It was close run, but radar, ULTRA, the heroism and advanced planes of the RAF's Fighter Command, and the *Luftwaffe*'s shifts of tactics saved Britain. Raids continued until May 1941, but by mid-September it was clear that Britain could go on, and

Hitler 'postponed' invasion indefinitely. FDR had at first doubted Britain's survival and resisted Churchill's appeals. He wished to help Britain without awakening isolationist outcries, for American opinion emphatically opposed any risk of war; further, he was running for an unprecedented third term* and promising no foreign wars. By August, he thought Britain would survive.

France's fall ended American complacency but increased its fear of war. In May 1940, the army was less than a third the size of Belgium's and ill equipped,[18] the navy weak. Congress quintupled the military appropriation, planned a two ocean navy, and authorized conscription in September. Republicans were given charge of the War and Navy departments to create a bipartisan administration, and Roosevelt began joint defence planning with Canada. He also moved to block Nazi penetration of Latin America or seizure of Allied New World domains, gaining at the Havana conference a declaration against transfer of sovereignty and creation of an inter-American trusteeship until colonies could be returned to their owners. But the urgent question was whether to aid Britain and if so, how much. Churchill begged for fifty over-age American destroyers to replace British losses. Once British survival looked likely, his Republican presidential opponent co-operated, and Roosevelt decided Congressional approval was not necessary, he produced a scheme to exchange the destroyers for 99-year leases on bases in British territories from Newfoundland through the Caribbean to British Guiana. Though this was an unneutral act, American opinion approved of such a cheap bargain.

After re-election in November, Roosevelt promised as much aid as Congress would allow, agreed to military talks with London, and despite tension in the Pacific, put Europe first to ensure Britain and its strategic Empire survived. Despite the destroyers, its future was uncertain, for it was out of money to purchase supplies for cash, as required by the Neutrality Laws, and could not be given a loan because of defaults on 1917–18 debts. In November, its ambassador told the press, 'Britain's broke. It's your money we want.'[19] FDR cleverly declared on 17 December that if your neighbour's house is on fire, you lend him your garden hose, which he returns later. A senator noted that, 'lending arms was like lending chewing gum: you don't want it back',[20] but the garden hose analogy ensured popular support and Congressional approval in March 1941. The Lend-Lease Act authorized sale, transfer, exchange, or leasing of arms to any state whose defence was deemed vital to American security. Repayment later could be in kind, property, or other ways. A flood of credits was released, ensuring arms to Britain, China, and then others, while avoiding the issue of new war debts; the price demanded was an end to imperial preference and acceptance of Washington's vision of the post-war global economy.

* Now barred by constitutional amendment.

Since salvation was at stake, London complied. Roosevelt, however, knew Lend-Lease, which approached an act of war, was not enough; the question was not whether but when the United States would fully enter the conflict.

*   *   *

France's and Britain's travail had immediate repercussions in East Asia. Until then, Japan was too pinned in China to move into the relative Asian power vacuum caused by Europe's war. It wished to end the Chinese war by creating an obedient satellite but made few concessions, so negotiations failed, as did talks with Washington. Japan then set up a puppet regime at Nanking, ignored by other powers. FDR and especially Stalin armed Chiang to keep him fighting Japan rather than Chinese Communists. In Tokyo, debate on policy continued as some in the army still hoped to go north against Siberia while the navy wanted to move south through Indochina to the Dutch Indies; that required occupation of Malaya and Singapore, a naval base without a fleet, and risked war with the United States, which the army opposed.

During the Phoney War, Britain and France were cautious lest Japan seize their undefended possessions. London, whose policy was mainly oratorical and after June 1940 subordinate to Washington's, used its diplomatic and economic tools to deter invasion of South-east Asia. Tokyo and Washington also tried to deter, each seeing the other's deterrence as aggression. Neither was yet primarily interested in the other. Like London, Washington wished to save the Asian *status quo* but chose to do so just as Japan decided to alter it and was given an opening by Hitler. As FDR focused on re-election, the Battle of Britain, and the Battle of the Atlantic of supply convoys to Britain against German submarines, he stalled until summer, trying to slow Japan by diplomacy to prevent attack on the East Indies. To deter that, he held the fleet at Hawaii after spring exercises.

The spring and summer of 1940 in Europe, however, rendered French, British, and Dutch South-east Asian holdings extremely vulnerable, intensifying American concern about the Asian power balance. European events loosened the colonial grip, offering Japan an opportunity it found irresistible, for it hoped to end the China impasse by cutting two of Chiang's three supply lines from French Indochina and British Burma.* It rejected Hitler's pleas to attack Britain and sought an alliance, which he refused lest pressure on Indochina lead France's African colonies to join de Gaulle. But Japan gained an agreement with Moscow in June which protected its Soviet border.

Tokyo then demanded that London close its Burma Road supply line to Chiang, which it helplessly did for three months. Roosevelt responded in July by banning export to Japan of aviation fuel and top-grade scrap iron,

---

* It could not reach the immensely long Soviet supply line.

imposing his first economic sanctions, which soon escalated. The more Washington limited sale of strategic materials, the more vital the Dutch East Indies became to Japan, which relied on imported oil. Some generals saw seizure of South-east Asia as a way out of the China mire and believed occupation of Indochina and/or the Dutch Indies need not entail war with the United States, particularly after a fairly moderate Cabinet was replaced in July by a new Konoe Cabinet with General Tōjō Hideki, former chief of staff of the Kwantung army, as War Minister and Matsuoka Yōsuke as Foreign Minister; it was authoritarian, expansionist, and army-dominated. Matsuoka was unstable, pro-German, prone to wishful thinking, and sure Washington and Moscow would bend if he was resolute, especially after Japan joined the Axis in September. Neither did, but the Cabinet, thinking the European war over, set a pan-Asian policy, announcing the Greater East Asia Co-Prosperity Sphere, which somewhat paralleled the Monroe Doctrine but rejected existing colonies and Western trade. On 1 August 1940 it demanded bases in northern Indochina; Vichy complied in September, ending its rail link to Chiang. FDR then banned export of all steel and scrap iron; the next day Japan joined the Axis. Washington made new loans to Chiang to deter further Japanese southward moves. Still focusing on British survival, FDR improvised, hoping forceful words would be effective and wishfully thinking the Japanese would behave as Americans did. But by December 1940, Tokyo decided an eventual American war was inevitable and it should proceed into southern Indochina and the Dutch Indies.

* * *

Stalin was not privy to Tokyo's plans and so looked nervously both east and west, but especially westward. The capitalist war there had not been the long struggle he wanted, and he feared Hitler would dominate all Europe. In June 1940, he occupied the Baltic states, annexing them soon after. Of Rumania he demanded Bessarabia and northern Bukovina, the latter not in his spheres agreement with Hitler. On German advice, Rumania complied. A diplomatic effort in the Balkans produced only trade deals. Like Hitler, Stalin was gaining time, space and resources, but less space and fewer resources; he engaged in fearful co-existence while he reorganized his army. His behaviour toward Germany was impeccable to avoid any provocation; he did not even fortify the new border. Grain, oil, and ores were faithfully shipped to Germany, along with Asian rubber, but with scant return. He also sought a spheres agreement in the Balkans, which in November Hitler refused, trying vainly instead to turn Moscow toward India and war with Britain.

Moscow's stance renewed Hitler's determination to invade the Soviet Union to build Germanic peasant villages on the Russian plains. In mid-1940, he began to plan the attack and transfer troops eastward, persuaded that Russia's defeat would force Britain to cede and that, with only one land front, this would not be a two-front war. He cultivated Finland and met Franco without result, for the Spanish leader would enter the war only if he were granted North African territories which Hitler wished to keep as bases to use against the United States. On the other hand, the tripartite German–Italian–Japanese Axis pact signed in September aimed to pressure Moscow, force London to yield, and prevent American entry into the fray.

Meanwhile, Hitler arranged the Balkans to his benefit. As Rumania's neighbours sought areas lost in 1920, he awarded much to Hungary and Bulgaria in August 1940, guaranteed the rest, forced the King's abdication, and turned Rumania into a satellite. German troops soon arrived there and in Finland. As weak economically dependent states read the signs, in November Hungary, Rumania, and Slovakia joined the Axis. On 1 March 1941, Bulgaria did as well, dooming Moscow's last hope of a Balkan sphere. Yugoslavia soon followed, but a 27 March coup reversed that decision, leading to Germany's punitive invasion, against which Moscow did nothing.

Mussolini was furious about the Balkans, for Hitler had vetoed an Italian invasion of Yugoslavia. When Germany entered Rumania and took its oil fields, Mussolini vowed that in the future he would act without telling Hitler. In August 1940 he seized British Somaliland; then in September he invaded Egypt from Libya. Britain rushed troops from India and obtained Australian and New Zealand forces, leaving both Dominions almost undefended except for hollow British promises. Egypt was thus saved, and a British counterattack seized half of Libya by February 1941. British forces from Kenya liberated the Somalilands, Eritrea, and Ethiopia, ending Italy's East African Empire and enabling Haile Selassie's return. Before this torrent of disasters, however, an early success in Egypt led Mussolini to overestimate his military prowess, and in late October 1940 he attacked Greece without telling Hitler. Greece threw his troops back 30 miles (48 km) into Albania. The RAF bombed the Italian navy, hitting three battleships. When the East and North African losses were added, Mussolini's regime became precarious; Germany rescued him in Greece and North Africa at the price of his total subordination. Italy ceased to be a factor, especially as it soon ran out of oil. Hitler paid, too, in delay of his plans and dispersal of his forces.

Greece's success led Britain to send planes, shift troops from Libya, and occupy Crete in the Mediterranean. Hitler feared the RAF might bomb Rumania's oil fields from Greece so he invaded, causing Greek surrender on 21 April and British evacuation. German paratroopers took Crete in May at such great cost that they did not try to take Malta or Cyprus. Meanwhile, London had coped with an anti-British coup in Iraq in early April, suppressed in late May by Indian forces. A month later, Hitler might have intervened, but the ill-timed coup came as he awaited clear weather to invade Yugoslavia from Bulgaria, as he did on 6 April. Stalin hoped

Belgrade could resist for two months to prevent invasion of Russia until 1942, but surrender came on 17 April.

Hitler was equally occupied with North Africa. General Erwin Rommel's Afrika Korps arrived in February to rescue Italy, which was losing both battles and ships, sunk by the RAF thanks to ULTRA, as were later German supply vessels. With skilful use of fine intelligence, Rommel attacked in late March and drove Britain out of Libya except for Tobruk. But North Africa overextended German forces; in November Britain regained the lost territory in its first defeat of a German army, forcing Hitler to move troops from Russia (invaded in June, see below). Meanwhile, an Allied invasion of Syria on 8 June to shift it from Vichy to the Free French succeeded within a month, depriving Germany of a potential Middle Eastern base.

By then, Hitler was absorbed in plans to invade the Soviet Union, his primary goal, the solution to Germany's economic difficulties, and the way, he thought, to force Britain's surrender. His Balkan ventures delayed the attack from 15 May to 22 June, but Hitler expected to defeat mere Slavs, Jews, and Communists in a few weeks, freeing Japan for Pacific expansion which would distract FDR from aid to Britain. Despite numerous warnings, Stalin believed the attack would come in 1942 when his forces would be ready. He thought Berlin was bluffing or trying to intimidate him; that British warnings were a snare to entrap him in war with Germany, which opposed a two-front war; and that an ultimatum would precede action. Stalin refused to consider that he had miscalculated, fooled himself, and was fooled by a fine German deception scheme. When Hitler attacked (soon followed by Finland), Stalin assumed this was intimidation. When forced to accept that the surprise *Blitzkrieg* was a real invasion, he suffered a ten-day nervous crisis while Germany swallowed the Baltic states and eastern Poland.

The initial massive three-pronged invasion toward Leningrad, Moscow, and the Ukraine and Caucasus lacked reserves and logistic support, for Hitler expected the first blows to be decisive; he hoped to trap and destroy large segments of the Red Army, causing a general Soviet collapse. His armies swept a large area, and anti-Russian Ukrainians welcomed them, but brutal treatment soon aroused bitter opposition in occupied and unoccupied areas. In July Hitler thought he had won; he engaged in new post-war planning and spoke of a German-Japanese war against the United States. But the Soviet armies were only partly trapped; Hitler had underestimated Soviet reserves and resources. More Soviet armies kept coming, and his successes produced no knock-out blow. His forces had to refit and repair railways, for they reached the limit of their truck supply line.[21] By August, a final victory in 1941 looked unlikely so Hitler sent troops southward, gaining Ukrainian grain and the Crimea, but not Caucasian oil. Still, victory in 1942 seemed probable.

A new offensive in October neared Moscow; then it stalled, as did the northern and southern prongs. Germany had spent its offensive strength, and its troops in summer uniforms faced mud, slush, and snow. Roosevelt promised Moscow Lend-Lease in November while Britain attacked in North Africa, so Stalin gambled on intelligence that Japan would not strike, shifting troops from Siberia. He attacked on 5 December in arctic cold that froze German men and machines. As Japan brought the United States into the war at Pearl Harbor, Soviet units scored a major victory. Moscow was 'saved by three great Russian generals: General Mud, General Winter and finally General Zhukov,'[22] primarily the latter,* for the victory was the Red Army's and the winter to be expected. The front stabilized in January, but Hitler could not again mount offensives in more than one sector. The Russian front consumed men and matériel endlessly; until defeat in 1945, Germany committed half to three-fourths of its resources there, losing more than ten million men.[23] As Soviet losses were more than twice that, FDR and Churchill feared Stalin would seek a separate peace. He showed some interest in late 1942 and 1943 but not on terms Hitler would accept.

*   *   *

In Washington, Roosevelt, who at first doubted Soviet survival, edged closer to war during 1941 in both oceans, but especially the Atlantic, where bolstering Britain led to an undeclared war, though he and Hitler tried to avoid incidents. In January FDR struck a high note, enunciating the Four Freedoms (of speech and worship, from want and fear) but also initiated staff talks with Britain to co-ordinate strategy if the United States entered the war. He knew London's desperation: beyond continued bombing of English cities and defeats in Greece and Libya, it was losing the Battle of the Atlantic as sinkings were high and escort vessels scarce. At first, since American opinion opposed escorting British ships and he had promised to avoid war, his support was mostly oratorical, for he admitted privately, 'I am waiting to be pushed into this situation.'[24] But then he extended the Neutral Zone patrolled by the American navy halfway across the Atlantic, took over protection of Greenland, occupied Iceland in July, and escorted American convoys that far.

In August Roosevelt met Churchill at sea off Argentia, Newfoundland. They agreed on aid to Moscow, a new American warning to Japan about South-east Asia, and the Atlantic Charter vowing neither state would take more territory and opposing forced territorial change. This strikingly Wilsonian document called for self-determination, restored sovereignty and self-government, free trade with some loopholes, improved labour standards and social security, freedom of the seas, and disarmament.† It endorsed peace, freedom from fear and war, and a future system of general

---

* Marshal Georgi K. Zhukov.
† Britain and the Soviet Union, which soon adhered, exempted their respective empires from the clause promising self-determination.

security. Naval incidents thereafter with German raiders led to revision of the Neutrality Laws, enabling FDR to convoy British ships to Iceland and Lend-Lease supplies to Britain in American ships. Attacks on American vessels were predictable, with war resulting. By now, American conduct was so unneutral that Hitler saw little added risk in formal war.

*   *   *

As the United States approached war in the Atlantic, it did the same in the Pacific. With some racism, American leaders misjudged the danger, thinking Japan would not risk war against a power with seven or eight times its productive capacity.[25] Lacking much Pacific naval might as his Atlantic commitment grew, FDR relied on delay, diplomacy, and deterrence, seeing the British Empire as moral and a vital American interest but Japan's efforts to create its own as immoral. But his China policy evolved from trying to stop the China war to insisting Japan withdraw. The other key issue was economic, for Britain and the United States were as dependent on South-east Asia as was Japan, especially for rubber, tin, and tungsten to strengthen tank armour. Washington thought it could not manage without the area's resources, though in the end it did so for four years.

Japan needed the same resources plus either American oil or that of the Dutch East Indies. With Hitler's consent, it staked out East Asia as its sphere of supremacy. As Italy and Germany had no Asian colonies, Japan found them acceptable allies. Japan's leaders, resentful over the racial equality issue, American immigration barriers, and naval ratios, consciously led an Asian revolt against the West. In a sense, Japanese aims were limited, for Tokyo wanted nobody's unconditional surrender and did not wish to make China a colony, but it wanted all of South-east Asia and claimed supremacy in Asia and the western Pacific. These ambitions ignored realities of American power and Japanese weakness, especially in an extended conflict. Tokyo counted on German victory in Europe but forgot that Hitler's victories so far, not Japan's actions, had created its opportunities. Tokyo assumed a short war, ignoring its sure defeat in a long one, disregarding American industrial potential, and underestimating its will.

Each side misjudged and talked past the other. Both tried to scare the foe into backing down; each found that prior decisions narrowed options. Both focused on strategic resources and China. Individuals complicated matters, especially Japanese ones. Emperor Hirohito opposed war but not forcefully,* Matsuoka was sure Washington would accept Japan's Asian supremacy, and his envoy in Washington had little English and less skill. Under pressure from mid-level officers, military leaders accepted the risk of

---

* Herbert P. Bix, *Hirohito and the Making of Modern Japan* (New York, HarperCollins, 2000) dissents, arguing that Hirohito had come to favour war, in combination with the nationalist element. For example, see pp. 12, 410–20

an American war. In early 1941, Japanese talks with the Americans and Dutch failed, but Matsuoka, on a trip to Berlin and Moscow, gained a neutrality treaty with the Soviets which freed both states. Hitler urged him to attack Singapore to divert British ships from the Battle of the Atlantic, shift more American ships to the Pacific, and perhaps cause war with the United States. In that event, he promised to declare war, too, for he expected to gain the Japanese navy to use against the United States.

Roosevelt knew that only the United States could keep Chiang in the war and prevent Japan's control of Asia, where its navy came to dominate as other fleets were dispersed. In April Secretary of State Cordell Hull laid down four principles, whose import escaped the Japanese ambassador and thus Tokyo. Hull demanded territorial integrity and sovereignty for all states, non-interference therein, equal commercial opportunity, and only peaceful change in the *status quo*. When Tokyo finally noticed a repetition in November, it deemed this tantamount to surrender. By spring, the ABCD bloc (America, Britain, China, Dutch) had developed, partly in response to the exclusionary Co-Prosperity Sphere, and in June ABD powers began joint military planning, with later co-ordination of economic sanctions. Japan rightly saw this group as an effort to block its expansion. As European states had traditionally combined against the prospect of a single power dominating their continent, they and their offspring now used the same balance of power mechanism against a similar perceived threat in Asia. The European war had delayed this coalescence until Japan's moves south directly threatened the British and Dutch empires, whose assets the United States deemed a vital interest.

Though startled by Hitler's invasion of Russia, Japan decided on 2 July, after Dutch refusal to sell it more oil, to move into southern Indochina despite American warnings of an oil embargo. Tokyo now knew an attack on Anglo-French colonies meant war with Washington; oil would then be critical, for 60 per cent of Japan's needs came from the United States. Invading the Dutch Indies from Indochina might cause destruction of wells and refineries or war with the United States, which might sink Japan's few tankers. But the military oil stockpile sufficed for only 18 months of active war. As Japan debated and Matsuoka was ousted, FDR did nothing to rouse Tokyo, saying 'I simply have not got enough Navy to go round.'[26] Thanks to MAGIC which now read all messages to the Japanese embassy in Washington, he knew Tokyo's decision at once and thought it meant invasion of South-east Asia. Vichy yielded, and Japan moved south. In a crucial act, FDR froze Japanese assets, as did the British and Dutch, and embargoed oil sales to all nations except Britain and Latin American states. The former action ended all trade, and the latter started the 18-month oil clock ticking in Tokyo. The embargo was meant to be partial, but bureaucrats extended it completely. As a collision course to war was set, Hull muttered, 'Everything is going hellward.'[27]

Japanese generals saw the choice as continuation or surrender; they thought war better now than later and, in the samurai tradition, death preferable to surrender. At Hirohito's urging, Tokyo sought more negotiation but without much concession. Washington was willing to talk to gain time, strengthen Pacific defences, and focus on Europe. Meanwhile, the Japanese economy faltered owing to the trade cut-off. Talks on China failed as both sides tried to dictate terms. Washington required a free China, but Tokyo would not abandon a four-year military investment.

Through the autumn, the gulf did not narrow. With American opinion intensely anti-Japanese, FDR challenged Tokyo and Berlin overtly but for political reasons left the question of war to them. He rosily saw China as the anchor of future Asian peace and feared new appeasement in Asia would encourage Hitler dangerously. As Washington again sought withdrawal from China and Indochina as well as free trade and the Pacific *status quo*, Japan decided to invade the Dutch East Indies before 1941 ended unless Washington ceded on all points. Thus the countdown to war began. December was the latest date Japan could move before the monsoons, and the oil supply was dwindling. After Tōjō became Prime Minister in October, a policy review brought no change.

On 1 November the Japanese Cabinet decided that if Washington did not concede by 30 November, war would follow. Its embassy was told 'After that, things are automatically going to happen',[28] but no more; Roosevelt, reading the decryption, foresaw an attack somewhere soon, probably on Dutch or British colonies, but did not understand Japan's logic, though his envoy in Tokyo warned it might seek war from desperation. Japan faced economic strangulation and potential internal or imperial collapse as well as a likely military coup if the Cabinet did not act; since it erroneously expected a Russo-German deal, it seemed best to act before Moscow was free. Key leaders told each other, 'There is no alternative',[29] ruling out concession and compromise, though many instinctively knew they should avoid an American war. After four draining years in China, Japan could not win a long war of attrition. However, they thought it best to fight while Japan had a naval edge and the power and oil to do so, gambling that they could win and end the war within a year or two. They expected to destroy the American fleet, causing Washington to crumble and negotiate terms on trade and China. If that move failed, it was better to lose later than sooner, avoiding humiliation and abandonment of a decade's ideology as well as empire. Tōjō said fatalistically, 'Sometimes a man has to jump from the veranda of Kiyomizu Temple* with his eyes closed.'[30]

Talks continued through November but in vain. Washington decided to fight if only British or Dutch soil was attacked, to Churchill's intense relief. Assured that Germany and Italy would declare war, Tokyo sent forth a fleet

---

* A Shinto shrine in Kyoto.

which maintained radio silence and told its embassy in Washington nothing, defeating MAGIC. On 6 and 7 December, it transmitted a long message ending current negotiations; FDR and Hull saw the decryption at once, but decoding delays at the embassy meant the message was delivered not 20 minutes before Japan bombed the naval base at Pearl Harbor, Hawaii, as intended, but an hour after.

Early on Sunday morning, 7 December,[*] planes from the Japanese fleet achieved total surprise. Tokyo benefited from Washington and Hawaii's massive disbelief in the danger, for both expected an attack in South-east Asia and doubted Japan's capacity to hit Pearl Harbor simultaneously. In fact, it had already attacked Malaya and Thailand, proceeding onward within hours to Hongkong, the Philippines, and the American islands of Guam, Wake, and Midway. Though many ships were hit and casualties were high, Pearl Harbor, which symbolized Tokyo's revolt against the West, was a blunder. The original plan to attack the American fleet at sea would have brought greater loss, for many lives and all but two battleships[†] were salvaged, and no permanent installations were hit. Also, Japan knew the United States had the power to defeat it, but doubted its will; the attack on American soil ensured that will as Americans reacted with nearly unanimous fury.

On 8 December Britain and the United States declared war on Japan, followed by China and the Dominions, launching a war to dominate the Pacific. Hitler was away from Berlin, coping with Stalin's December offensive, but he issued 'sink on sight' orders and, upon his return, declared war on 11 December, to Anglo-American relief. Italy followed, as did Rumania, Hungary, and Bulgaria. As usual, Hitler considered only his plans, not the policies and capacities of others. He had long intended war against the United States so he was willing to accelerate its advent, for Japan would stay out of his Russian war, attack Britain, and pin the American navy down.

The various military sectors had long impacted each other, but now they united (though Russo-Japanese neutrality survived) in one global conflict pitting the Axis against an Anglo-American coalition which soon encompassed the Soviets, the French Empire, the Dominions, exile governments, and much of Latin America. The Axis powers had divergent goals, as Japan sought its Asian sphere, Italy the Mediterranean and French North Africa, and Hitler probably the world, eventually. All three saw themselves as crowded have-nots lacking resources and were relatively new to world power politics, dissatisfied with World War I's outcome, authoritarian, and expansionist. In the opposing coalition, Britain, France, and the United States were essentially defensive (though FDR a bit aggressive about it),

---

[*] 8 December Japanese time.
[†] Significantly, the aircraft carriers were at sea and thus not hit.

democratic, and non-expansionist, having completed their expansions earlier. Their vital fourth partner, the Soviet Union, had long been a world power, like Britain and France, and its entry into the war was defensive, because it was attacked, but it was neither democratic nor non-expansionist. Its primary goal was the lost lands of 1918, but it wanted much the same east European sphere as Hitler did. With such differing interests, Stalin proved a difficult if essential partner to Roosevelt and Churchill, who allowed the prickly de Gaulle little say, as they led their unwieldy coalition of large and small states in a struggle fought all across the world stage.

◆ Notes to Chapter 16

1. Admiral Lord Chatfield, First Sea Lord, 4 June 1934, as quoted in Stephen L. Endicott, *Diplomacy and Enterprise: British China Policy, 1933–7* (Vancouver, University of British Columbia Press, 1975), p. 176.
2. Jonathan Marshall, *To Have and Have Not: Southeast Asian Raw Materials and the Origin of the Pacific War* (Berkeley, University of California Press, 1995), pp. 12–13.
3. Christopher Thorne, *The Approach of War, 1938–9* (London, Macmillan, 1967), p. 25.
4. W. R. Louis, 'The Road to Singapore', in Wolfgang J. Mommsen and Lothar Kettenacker, eds, *The Fascist Challenge and the Policy of Appeasement* (London, George Allen & Unwin, 1983), p. 371.
5. Norman A. Graebner, *America as a World Power* (Wilmington, DE, Scholarly Resources, 1984), p. 40.
6. Anthony Read and David Fisher, *The Deadly Embrace: Hitler, Stalin, and the Nazi-Soviet Pact, 1939–1941* (New York, Norton, 1988), p. 20.
7. Donald Cameron Watt, *Too Serious a Business: European Armed Forces and the Approach to the Second World War* (Berkeley, University of California Press, 1975), pp. 21, 74.
8. For the text of the Rumanian offer, see Appendix C (pp. 194–201) of Jiri Hochman, *The Soviet Union and the Failure of Collective Security, 1933–1940* (Ithaca, Cornell University Press, 1984). Dov B. Lungu, *Romania and the Great Powers, 1933–1940* (Durham, NC, Duke University Press, 1989), p. 256, n. 79, doubts the authenticity of this document.
9. See William D. Irvine, 'Domestic Politics and the Fall of France in 1940', in Joel Blatt, ed., *The French Defeat of 1940: Reassessments* (Providence, RI, Berghahn, 1998), pp. 85–99.
10. Gerhard L. Weinberg, *Germany, Hitler, and World War II* (Cambridge, CUP, 1995), p. 12.

11. Barbara Jelavich, *History of the Balkans* (2 vols, Cambridge, CUP, 1983), II, p. 217, citing Galeazzo Ciano, *The Ciano Diaries, 1939–1943*, Hugh Gibson, ed. (Garden City, NY, Doubleday, 1946), p. 43.
12. Philip Morgan, *Italian Fascism, 1919–1945* (New York, St Martin's, 1995), p. 169, quoting M. Donosti, *Mussolini e l'Europa* (Rome, Leonardo, 1945), p. 166.
13. Robert Dallek, *Franklin D. Roosevelt and American Foreign Policy, 1932–1945* (New York, OUP, 1979), pp. 196–7.
14. Donald Cameron Watt, *How War Came: The Immediate Origins of the Second World War, 1938–1939* (New York, Pantheon, 1989), p. 501.
15. Dallek, *Franklin D. Roosevelt*, pp. 197–8.
16. Joel Blatt, 'Introduction,' in Blatt, ed., *The French Defeat*, p. 11.
17. Some Cabinet members had been tempted. For a detailed account of the debate, see John Lukacs, *Five Days in London: May, 1940* (New Haven, CT, YUP, 1999).
18. Weinberg, *Germany, Hitler*, p. 185.
19. Dallek, *Franklin D. Roosevelt*, p. 252.
20. Senator Robert A. Taft of Ohio. Thomas A. Bailey, *The American Pageant*, 3rd edn (Boston, D.C. Heath, 1966), p. 873.
21. Gerhard L. Weinberg, *A World at Arms: a Global History of World War II* (Cambridge, CUP, 1994), p. 270. My debt to this important work is large.
22. Read and Fisher, *The Deadly Embrace*, p. 649.
23. Geoffrey K. Roberts, *The Unholy Alliance: Stalin's Pact with Hitler* (Bloomington, IN, University of Indiana Press, 1989), p. 221.
24. Robert A. Divine, *Roosevelt and World War II* (Baltimore, Johns Hopkins University Press, 1969), p. 42.
25. Charles E. Neu, *Troubled Encounter: The United States and Japan* (New York, John Wiley, 1975), p. 188.
26. *Ibid.*, p. 181.
27. Walter LaFeber and Richard Polenberg, *The American Century* (New York, John Wiley, 1975), p. 244.
28. William Carr, *Poland to Pearl Harbor: The Making of the Second World War* (London, Edward Arnold, 1985), p. 163.
29. Robert A. Scalapino, 'Introduction', in James William Morley, ed., *The Fateful Choice: Japan's Advance into Southeast Asia, 1939–1941* (New York, Columbia University Press, 1980), p. 119.
30. David A. Titus, 'Introduction', in James William Morley, ed., *The Final Confrontation: Japan's Negotiations with the United States, 1941* (New York, Columbia University Press, 1994), xxx.

CHAPTER

17

WORLD WAR II, 1942–1945

Pearl Harbor explosively ended the opening scenes of World War II and launched a dramatic six months of Axis successes and Allied defeats, for Germany and Japan, when stalled against a major opponent in 1941, sought to win by attacking a greater foe. Confident of their superiority, each foresaw a short final campaign. Underestimating Anglo-American and Russian will to resist, neither contemplated a long war of attrition against multiplying enemies with more material and human resources. Thus they both moved briskly in early 1942.

Japan's Pacific *Blitzkrieg* of air and amphibious attack in December 1941 took American west Pacific islands, sank two British capital ships just arrived at Singapore – reducing Britain's Pacific role to insignificance, and invaded the Philippines to gain a springboard to the Dutch Indies. General Douglas MacArthur botched the Philippine defence but, as a hero was needed in dark days for the Allies, he became one before being ordered to direct the largely American defence of Australia, whose forces, with those of New Zealand, mostly remained in the Middle East.

Meanwhile, Japan invaded northern Malaya, fighting south through 200 miles (325 km) of supposedly impenetrable jungle to Singapore. Its fall on 15 February 1942 was as cataclysmic as that of France in 1940. Another emperor lacked clothes, and the implications reverberated through Asia. By then, Japan had conquered Borneo; it next seized the Dutch Indies, landed on New Guinea, and took most British Pacific islands. It gained control of Thailand in December and invaded Burma in January. Rangoon fell on 8 March, and Japan pressed north, threatening the Burma Road to China. Roosevelt sent to Chiang Joseph Stilwell, an able but acerbic Chinese-speaking general whose campaign to save the Road failed in May. Thereafter Chiang could be supplied only by a long, dangerous flight over the Himalayas. The China theatre became minor, but Chiang rejected a Japanese peace offer, trusting to eventual American victory.

Australia and India now faced invasion, and Anglo-American-Australian confidence was shaken. As yet, the United States had little military power, but it shifted ships and troops to the Pacific. It also bombed Tokyo in April and in February interned all 110 000 Japanese-Americans on its west coast, though most were loyal and many were American citizens.* Britain, pressed by the crisis and FDR, discussed with Indian leaders a 'draft declaration'[1] (never issued) for more wartime consultation and early post-war self-government with likely separation of a Muslim state. Congress rejected delay and division, and Indian nationalism swelled. The myth of Western superiority had shattered in Asia, ending imperialism's rationale. Many Asians welcomed Tokyo's creed of 'Asia for the Asians', but Japanese exploitation and assumption of superiority shifted opinion. Collaboration and resistance, often in turn, bred nationalist leaders and more nationalism.

Japan had gained its desiderata in less than six months. It now wanted a negotiated peace. As nobody obliged, it faced immediate problems.[2] The samurai mentality of military leaders stressed the heroic deed and sneered at mundane details. Thus Japan had the coveted resources of Malaya and the Dutch Indies with rings of island garrisons to protect them but not the tankers, cargo ships, convoy techniques, and escort vessels to supply the island outposts and convey the rubber, tin, and oil to Japan. In time, Allied submarines, bombing – at first from aircraft carriers, mining of Japanese waters, and blockade shattered the Japanese economy.

The other problem was what to do next. Raising the war's cost for Washington so it would quit was agreed, but nothing else. A bitter split between the army and navy produced three plans which failed. Since Rommel in North Africa was nearing the Suez Canal, a drive west into the Indian Ocean to link with him and take India was tempting, but the army held troops in Manchuria to invade Siberia if Hitler defeated Russia. So the navy moved alone but was thwarted by a British landing on Madagascar in May and naval reinforcement in the Indian Ocean.

Japan also tried a thrust south toward Australia but was halted at the battle of the nearby Coral Sea in May, the first of two great naval battles demonstrating the importance of aircraft carriers and cryptanalysis. Partial Allied success in reading the Japanese naval code eliminated surprise and led to a naval battle fought entirely in the air over vast distances. It was a very costly Japanese victory, and the advance southward ceased. The third plan was a move east in the central Pacific to destroy the American navy and take Hawaii. Cryptanalysis defeated Japanese feints and again eliminated surprise at the battle of Midway in June, a decisive American victory. The Japanese navy, which lost four carriers and air superiority, was broken and never recovered. The immediate threat to Australia ended, but Japanese forces remained on nearby New Guinea.

*   *   *

---

* Internment of enemy aliens was a normal practice of war; confining American-born or naturalized citizens was unconstitutional but popular.

Japan's ally was also winning. Italy was now a bit player, but Germany seemed triumphant on three fronts. A North African offensive in January 1942 marched across Libya, taking Tobruk in June and endangering the Allies in the Middle East. Rommel was soon 60 miles (95 km) from Alexandria. Allied reinforcements, German exhaustion, supply problems, and the British stopped him at El Alamein in July, leading to stalemate. In Russia as well Hitler hoped for decisive victory. The Russian offensive of December 1941 had regained 20 per cent of the lost areas, but then a January offensive to relieve besieged Leningrad and spring drives in the centre and south of the 1000-mile (1600-km) line failed. However, Germany's June offensive south toward the Caucasian oil took the Crimea and part of the Caucasus before Hitler shifted troops north to attack Leningrad.

Germany also seemed to be winning the Battle of the Atlantic, where Allied shipping losses exceeded new construction. Control of the seas was vital to Canadian-American supply of food and arms to Britain and Anglo-American convoys on the Arctic route to Russia as well as to counter-offensives, which required amphibious assaults at long range. German U-boat attacks on merchant ships brought Brazil and Mexico into the war and led to a major Canadian role in the Battle of the Atlantic but forced ending convoys to Russia in the dangerous all-daylight summer months of 1942, partly to prepare the North African invasion in November,* itself limited and prolonged by German submarines. Each side read the other's codes, but Britain realized this and changed codes, contributing to a gradual 1943 tipping of the balance in the Battle of the Atlantic.

In January 1942 at Tokyo's request an agreement defined Axis spheres, granting Japan from India's western coast to that of the United States. Despite this, the effort to link in 1942, and minor naval co-operation, Germany and Japan fought separate wars and rarely consulted or co-ordinated strategy. When they did, the Allies listened with interest. Neither could work with allies, for each was sure of its own superiority, and both lacked global perspective. Racial hostility was mutual, as was acute suspicion; disagreement about Russia was constant, for Hitler sought to conquer it while Japan wanted his Soviet war to end. Neither foresaw Allied ability to organize greater resources; both overestimated Japan's power. Hitler thought Washington would refuse a two-front war and focus on the Pacific, where Japan would engage it fully. Japan did not realize how much it owed to Hitler and that it, like Italy, could not win unless Germany did.

Hitler long underestimated the United States's potential and, like Japan, its will. His early successes owed much to American absence as well as to the advantage of interior lines. He was impervious to all allies, large and small, each of which tried in vain to persuade Germany to act in its interests. His

---

* See below

Russian campaigns suffered from his reluctance (occasionally overcome) to yield territory to straighten the line or avoid entrapment. But in mid-1942, victory seemed in sight, and, with his distrust of the home front, he did not seek full-scale mobilization until late in the year.

*   *   *

The opposing alliance – or alliance and a half – was very different. A Marxist state in an Allied coalition was a novelty, and the Soviet tie to the West rested on mutual suspicion, though it was Moscow's closest relationship since 1917. Stalin offered little information, receiving more, but the Anglo-Americans did not share atomic or some intelligence secrets though aware that Moscow knew of them. Co-ordination of military campaigns was only occasional, and Stalin refused to join a Supreme War Council and other Allied agencies, partly to avoid the Pacific war. He also evaded travel, which limited consultation, though Molotov sometimes replaced him. Western supplies, but never enough to satisfy Stalin, were shipped by the Arctic route, via the Persian Gulf and Iran to Russia and up the Volga River, and especially from the American west coast to Vladivostok.*

Stalin was curt and distrustful, especially of the historic British rival, and, as he assumed deception in diplomacy to be the norm, he disbelieved explanations of delays in aid and in creating a Second Front or of problems with public or legislative opinion, thinking instead that the West hoped for stalemate or Soviet defeat. In Russia, public opinion had never been a factor, and power had always been concentrated. Both its tradition and its war were entirely different from those of the West. It fought a land war without naval or amphibious problems where liberation, victory, and conquest all hinged on army drives westward, simplifying both strategy and policy.

Stalin's goals were as traditional as his war, and rested on the power balance and spheres of influence. He craved security as well as victory, demanding massive supplies, a Second Front in western Europe to relieve Nazi pressure on Soviet armies, and formal recognition of his June 1941 border, which (aside from northern Bukovina and Galicia) included only areas Russia ruled in 1914. The Second Front slipped from a small invasion in 1942 to a large one in 1943 to mid-1944. Churchill so feared a separate Soviet peace that he was willing to accept the 1941 border in early 1942, for Germany could not be defeated without Russia, but Roosevelt dissuaded him, leaving no clear policy and more Soviet distrust. With military success, Stalin's aspirations grew. He sought German dismemberment, with Russia and Poland each to get pieces, massive reparations, domination of European neighbours, Japan's exclusion from the Asian mainland, and

---

* In Russian-flagged and -crewed American ships which Japan carefully ignored to avoid war with Russia.

Russia's 1904 rights limiting China in Manchuria. FDR stalled, though he was later amenable – there being little choice – if Moscow co-operated in the post-war peace. Russia was badly hurt in the war but retained raw power and meant to use it to gain the strongest possible post-war position. Moscow foresaw a new clash and largely opted for unilateralism and ending an alliance based on wartime necessity.

The key powers in the diverse Western coalition had much more in common than with Russia and developed an alliance whose closeness was unprecedented in military history. Much has been written about its disputes, which were legion, but it functioned remarkably well, owing partly to the relationship between its two leaders. FDR and Churchill shared elite backgrounds, health problems, increasing weariness, a love of the telephone (with German intelligence listening in), ignorance of the other's country, and a lack of candidness. Still, they got on well, and both put the alliance and the common good first, even if they disagreed on the common good. The alliance functioned mainly on Washington's terms since Britain subsisted on American supply, but worked best at first, when military efforts were fairly equal, before Britain became a junior partner.

Both leaders were prima donnas, personally directing their war. Roosevelt was his own secretary of state (Hull being a political appointee) except as to Latin America, which he left to Welles. He relied on Army Chief of Staff General George Marshall, who told him unwanted truths. Churchill was close to Anthony Eden, his Foreign Secretary, and generally trusted his top military adviser. FDR avoided bureaucracy, using direct contact with other leaders and special envoys to bypass the State Department, hoping charm and geniality might dissolve disputes, especially with Stalin. Churchill embodied British defiance but was politically precarious after the May and June 1942 defeats in Burma and North Africa. He sought early deals with Moscow before British power waned further, whereas Roosevelt delayed while American might grew. Both saw the world globally, as did their chief military advisers. They learned quickly from mistakes, unlike their opponents, who tended to assume their own infallibility.

After Pearl Harbor, Churchill rushed to Washington; he and Roosevelt agreed to defeat Germany first, as that would ensure Japanese defeat, but the reverse was not true. Roosevelt gained a Combined Chiefs of Staff Committee, significantly located in Washington. This unity of Anglo-American command meant unified strategic direction. Co-ordination of strategy and logistics led to more summits to set priorities and other joint agencies to allocate shipping and war matériel. This remarkably merged Anglo-American war effort with its diverse coalition required generals with diplomatic talents. A military theatre commander was of one nationality, his top deputy often of the other. According to theatre, they might lead units from India, China, Australia, New Zealand, Holland, Mexico, Brazil,

Canada, South Africa, Allied African colonies, Belgium, the Free French, free Poles, and eventually Italy. States such as Canada contributing full divisions shared in the senior command structure. Some leaders such as Admiral Lord Louis Mountbatten in South-east Asia and General Dwight Eisenhower in North Africa and Europe were adept at inter-Allied command. MacArthur and General Sir Bernard Montgomery were decidedly not.

The knottiest problems facing the alliance were those of shipping, supply, and landing craft. Despite Stalin's disbelief, shortages delayed operations and altered strategy, for scarce landing craft could not be used simultaneously in Burma and Italy – and could not be used at all if sunk en route. Since any Second Front meant amphibious assault, command of the seas was vital but not easily gained, and production of cargo ships had to exceed sinkings but at first did not. Washington raised and equipped an army of 12 million, still segregated, which had to be deployed overseas. Troops were sent by speedy luxury liners which outran submarines, but their armour and logistic support, as well as equipment for Britain and Russia, required quantities of cargo ships. Thus early in 1942 the United States launched a crash programme of industrial production, enlisting 'Rosie the Riveter',* which eventually produced 5000 ships and an aeroplane every five minutes.[3] Even so, deployments and supply convoys were limited by lack of ships or landing craft.

The debates between Churchill and Roosevelt addressed wartime strategy and post-war policy. For the United States these were separate matters while for Britain they were entwined, as Roosevelt looked to the future without need to gain or retain his country's position but Churchill sought to preserve the past. American leaders, especially Marshall, favoured the speediest, most direct destruction of Nazi military might whereas Britain's strategy aimed at salvaging Britain's great power status and empire as well as thwarting future German and possibly Soviet threats.

Marshall sought an early Second Front in northern France, adhering to 'Germany first' despite pressures from American opinion and naval leaders for action against Japan. Churchill consistently urged a Mediterranean strategy and attack on the supposedly 'soft underbelly' of Europe through the rugged terrain of Italy and the Balkans into the continent's eastern heart. This would open British supply routes, especially to India, avoiding the long trip around Africa, reinforce the precarious Middle East with its precious oil, and prevent Soviet expansion into the Mediterranean and eastern Europe. Churchill's reluctance to invade France stemmed in part from fear of defeat and his initial need for a quick victory to reinforce his precarious political position. He was influenced too by painful memories of carnage there and

---

* Emblematic of millions of American women working – many for the first time – in war industries.

defeat at Gallipoli* during World War I as well as by the British tradition of naval war and blockade, which did not require a large army.

Anglo-American visions of the post-war world also differed. The traditionalist Churchill thought Europe would determine the world's fate as in the past and hoped to rebuild western Europe with American aid against future German aggression. He and Eden favoured a European power balance and spheres of influence. Churchill was determined to maintain the Empire, basis of Britain's power, and, though his views of the Soviets shifted with circumstances, he tended to distrust the traditional foe as a rival who might dominate Europe. He hoped to use Russia only against Germany, whereas Roosevelt, who opposed spheres and sought an open world, wanted to anchor peace on co-operation with Moscow. Trying to temper Wilsonian idealism with practicality, he arrived early at the concept of the Four Policemen – the United States, Russia, Britain, and China – who would each maintain peace in its region by quick effective use of force, as only great powers could do. The regions would not be spheres of influence but patrol beats, and the patrolmen, significantly, would be two states on Europe's fringes and two non-European ones. This scheme, which was not made public, was in 1943 enlarged to include an international organization as a debating society for small states and then perhaps more – but always dominated by the Four Policemen. FDR thought Russia wanted security in Western terms, which could be arranged in return for co-operation. He has been accused of naïveté in staking so much on Soviet co-operation, but he was less naive than appalled by the alternatives: a Cold War or a hot one.

Roosevelt, like Stalin and Churchill, expected to disarm the aggressors. He also opposed closed economic systems and sought free trade; Britain's need of Lend-Lease forced reluctant assent. Self-determination was agreed, at least for independent states, but its application in eastern Europe was never resolved, with Churchill inclined to accept Soviet domination and Roosevelt seeking improvements for appearance's sake. Though FDR did not resist economic imperialism, especially American, he sharply opposed colonies, expecting traditional imperialism to die. His pressure for Indian independence led to such Churchillian explosions that the issue had to be dropped. Then Roosevelt sought to end the French Empire, for he saw France as a source of decay, loathed and underestimated de Gaulle, and opposed return of French colonies. Churchill also disliked the imperious de Gaulle, but not with FDR's intensity. He defended the French Empire† in self-interest, because he feared ending European rule in Asia and Africa would mean instability and disorder, and to gain a strong France as a bulwark against Germany and perhaps Russia.

---

* The failed 1915 British attack on the Dardanelles at Gallipoli had led to Churchill's resignation from the Cabinet.
† Except Syria and Lebanon to whom Britain and France promised independence in 1941.

De Gaulle's Asian counterpart in some respects, including arrogance, was Chiang Kai-shek. Like Churchill, he was thrilled by Pearl Harbor, but he wanted 'Japan first' and expected more aid than he received – and quickly; its absence was an excuse not to fight, though he also had little control of warlord armies. His regime suffered from misgovernment, corruption, factional strife, colossal inflation, famine, heavy taxes, low morale, evaporating popular support, and civil war for, as in some European states, resistance movements battled for future control. Chiang withheld his best troops to use against Mao, but Washington failed to see how bitter the Chinese civil war was and sought a joint war effort as if the two elements were British or American political parties instead of deadly foes. Roosevelt and Churchill agreed that China's wartime roles were to provide air bases and tie down Japanese armies; both abrogated existing unequal treaties early in 1943, but they disagreed about China's future. Churchill's view was contemptuously racist but more realistic in the short term. Roosevelt saw China's potential and, overly optimistic about its realization, hoped China could balance Russia in Asia. American diplomats in China had no illusions, but Roosevelt tried to overlook Chinese weakness, sent supplies and 'loans', about which Chiang was extortionate, and granted him gestures affording 'face' but little else. By 1944, he accepted Chiang's weakness but stuck with him for the sake of American opinion and for lack of an alternative.

In Asia policy and strategy were entwined as both affected China's future and that of the British Empire, but Churchill left China to Roosevelt, for his interest in Asia, like that of France, was the retaining and regaining of empire. At the December 1941 meeting, a division of the world left China, Australia, the Pacific, and the Americas mainly to Washington, with Europe shared and London chiefly responsible for the Middle East, Africa, India, and South-east Asia. The two men issued a Declaration of the United Nations, which had nothing to do with the agency founded in 1945, though the name carried over; it was a promise by Allied combatants to adhere to the Atlantic Charter, commit their full resources to the war, and sign no separate peace.

In these darkest Allied days, Roosevelt and Churchill agreed to go on the offensive but not on where, with Churchill pressing against Marshall for a North African landing. The Battle of the Atlantic showed that little could be done in France in 1942, Molotov extracted a promise of 'a second front in 1942', and Churchill needed a victory to solidify his position after Tobruk's fall. Besides, Roosevelt wanted American troops in action against Germany before political and public pressure forced diversion to the Pacific, preventing American leadership in European campaigns. Thus Churchill's vision initially prevailed, and FDR in July accepted a North African invasion.

*   *   *

By then, the Allies were no longer suffering disastrous defeats but not yet achieving victories. Madagascar was still contested, Egypt stalemated, India and Australia far from secure. In Russia, German troops neared the Caucasian oil fields. But when the North African invasion occurred in November, the Americans were on the offensive in the Pacific, Germany was halted in the Caucasus, and a battle was raging for Stalingrad (Volgograd). In October at El Alamein in Egypt, Montgomery's counterattack surprised Rommel, who had lost his main intelligence source. His Afrika Korps was routed just before the North African invasion 2500 miles (4025 km) to the west. It escaped, but British pursuit over 2000 miles (3225 km) reached Tripoli in three months, continuing west to link with Allied forces moving east. This Axis defeat was irreversible: Italy lost the last of its African empire, and Hitler any hope of reaching the Middle East.

The first landing, mostly American, of the North African invasion in Morocco and Algeria on 8 November 1942 succeeded, but neither its initial composition nor American diplomacy prevented resistance by Vichy forces. Eisenhower seized upon the chance presence in Algiers of Admiral François Darlan, Vichy's key figure under Pétain, promising him control in North Africa if he ended French resistance. The 'Darlan deal' was criticized in the West but resistance in Algeria and Morocco ceased, ensuring Allied control. French West Africa joined the Allies, contributing troops, resources, and a position on Africa's bulge opposite Brazil, affording a narrow south Atlantic crossing for aeroplanes of limited range. Darlan was killed at Christmas, leaving a complex political situation.

Meanwhile, Hitler seized southern France and Tunisia, gaining the French fleet in Algeria but not that at Toulon, which scuttled itself. Hitler's swift action and Darlan's lack of authority in Tunisia enabled Germany to reinforce there, partly to prevent Italy's collapse. Allied lack of vehicles forced a slow slog over the 500 miles (800 km) from Algiers to Tunis. This struggle aided Stalin, for Hitler could not shift troops and supplies from Tunisia, but it delayed invasion of France until 1944. Conquest of Tunisia from east and west finally ended in May 1943.

By then, Hitler had attacked Stalingrad, which controlled the Volga River, an artery for essential Caucasian oil and food as well as Allied supply via Iran; he took part of it in October 1942, but in late November the Red Army moved north and south of the city, trapping the Axis forces in a pincers. A ten-week struggle ensued until the German army there surrendered on 2 February 1943. Russian survival, not victory, was assured but Soviet–Western distrust increased. The Anglo-Americans feared Stalin would quit, knowing he had offered Hitler an armistice, whereas Moscow feared the West meant to let Russia and Germany destroy each other.

This distrust influenced the Churchill–Roosevelt meeting at Casablanca in Morocco in mid-January 1943. Stalin refused to come, citing the Stalingrad battle in progress. Fighting the U-boat menace was given top priority, followed by more aid to Russia. Over Marshall's objections, the Allies would invade Sicily in the summer, further delaying France, but FDR resisted commitment to the eastern Mediterranean. Strategic bombing of Germany, begun by the RAF in 1940 and joined by the United States in 1942, would be stepped up, as would stockpiling in Britain for a 1944 invasion of France. As the Allies no longer feared defeat, Anglo-American discussions focused more on policy than on strategy, with Roosevelt taking Britain for granted, putting Soviet-American relations first, and brushing aside Churchill's efforts to serve as honest broker.

Casablanca's most controversial aspect was a declaration requiring the Axis to surrender unconditionally. The Allies, who knew of the Holocaust, felt this necessary before essential reforms in Germany and to bar a rerun of its post-World War I grievances based on the myth that it had not lost that war. Besides, after the Darlan deal, regaining the high moral ground was imperative, as was reassuring Chiang and Stalin. In part, the declaration aimed to keep Russia in the war. It stressed that peoples would not be destroyed; later statements promised no slavery or extermination, only elimination of Axis regimes. Despite much controversy, there is no evidence that the unconditional surrender demand (not entirely adhered to with Italy and Japan) prolonged the war. It did not deter German attempts to kill Hitler, Italy's armistice, or Tokyo's efforts toward a Russo-German peace. The German surrender at Stalingrad came a week after its issue.

*   *   *

Within days, Stalingrad was matched by a Pacific victory. Australians inflicted Japan's first land defeat on New Guinea in August 1942 as Americans landed on Guadalcanal in the Solomon Islands. Japan lost costly naval battles, and both sides incurred heavy casualties – though the Americans learned much – before Japan evacuated on 7 February 1943. The South-west Pacific (MacArthur) and South-east Asia (Mountbatten) theatres had complex inter-Allied structures, but the Pacific Ocean Areas Command (Admiral Chester Nimitz) was an American show with land, sea, and air forces fully unified. Seeking air and naval bases ever closer to Japan to bomb it and dominate large chunks of the western Pacific, Nimitz engaged in island-hopping, by-passing heavily fortified Japanese bases to offset complex logistics, limited forces, and supply shortages owing to the 'Germany first' strategy. Guadalcanal was this campaign's first success. By then, the Allies were winning in North Africa and at Stalingrad. Losses in the Battle of the Atlantic had peaked, and Allied economic superiority was starting to tell. Russia's industrial revival was militarily significant, for the 2500 enterprises moved eastward in late 1941 were now operational. Also, in December 1942 American physicists achieved an atomic chain reaction. Meanwhile, Italian–German friction worsened, while Berlin and Tokyo steadily disagreed. Early in 1943 Japan decided it could only hang on, hoping to exhaust the Allies or gain a naval victory. Hitler, too, was forced to a defensive war in 'Fortress Europe' and vain hopes of a lucky victory.

The Allies sought to deny him both. In Washington in May, Roosevelt agreed to invade Italy to eliminate it from the war and gain air bases to bomb Germany, and Churchill agreed to France in 1944. Moscow was being icy and making new offers to Hitler, leading FDR to oppose Churchill's plan to attack on the periphery more persistently, lest Stalin quit or conquer all of Europe. He knew he needed Russia for victory but also needed to invade France to gain leverage in Europe and prevent Soviet domination there. Hence he wanted to limit the Italian campaign and get on to France.

The first Allied European landing on Sicily in July 1943 led to rapid conquest. Hitler, knowing Mussolini was precarious, rushed troops in at the expense of the Russian front to save him, but too late. The Fascist Grand Council, the military, and the king overthrew Mussolini, who was arrested on 26 July. Marshal Pietro Badoglio, an ex-Fascist, led a new regime which dithered, neither surrendering nor controlling Italian territory. Thus Germany took key positions in August. Another Anglo-American meeting at Quebec in mid-August refought the debate over France versus the eastern Mediterranean. Roosevelt conceded Italian campaigns north of Rome, retention of the Italian monarchy and reluctant recognition of Badoglio, plus an invasion of southern France, but with absolute priority in 1944 to the northern France invasion, code-named OVERLORD.

As agreed, in early September Anglo-American troops invaded southern Italy but moved slowly, giving Hitler a chance to organize defences. Just before the landings, Badoglio signed an armistice made public on 8 September. Though allowed to keep the king and Badoglio, Italy surrendered largely unconditionally, expecting lenient treatment, which it received. The 'Badoglio deal' was criticized in Allied capitals, and Roosevelt disliked it, preferring sadly inexperienced Italian liberals, but acceded to British wishes from fear of Communism or chaos. When the Allies had gained Naples and the desired air bases, they created a military government for occupied territory. Soviet exclusion from it and the surrender negotiations arose from convenience, setting a precedent which Moscow used in eastern Europe, but Churchill and FDR assumed it would do as it pleased there in any event. Italy declared war on Germany and was recognized as a co-belligerent. Much of the Italian army evaporated, but the Allies gained the fleet and the anti-Fascist partisans.

Germany's reaction to Italy's defection was twofold. It seized most of Italy except the Allied-held south; a daring raid rescued Mussolini, who was given a puppet regime on Lake Garda in the north.* Much of Italy became

---

* There he remained until the last days of the European war, when he and his mistress fled toward Switzerland. Partisans caught and killed them, hanging them head-down from a girder.

Nazi-occupied territory for two years. As German generals used the mud and mountains well, resisting fiercely, and Allied forces were held in England for OVERLORD, the Italian campaign became a long, costly struggle.

Hitler's commitment to Italy aided Russia, where the situation fluctuated until mid-summer. He had not yet lost the Soviet war and hoped a fanatical effort of will would prevail, but troop shifts to Italy doomed that. Besides, Stalingrad affected his satellites, bringing peace feelers from Hungary and Rumania. Though his retreat from the Caucasus began, a German offensive in February and March 1943 retook most of Russia's winter gains except a 120-mile (200-km) salient bulging west at Kursk. Stalin, angry at Western delay of OVERLORD, and hoping either to leave the war or force Western invasion of France to prevent that, tried to dicker with Berlin, which refused. Instead, in July Hitler attacked the Kursk salient in history's greatest tank battle, but broke off in a week with much of his tank force lost. The battle was decisive, though Germany was not yet defeated. During the ensuing Soviet march west, sharp resistance and local victories fed Hitler's hopes, though he never regained the initiative. Soviet armies and attack equipment now were twice those of Germany, and the Red Army launched its first successful summer offensive, liberating much of the Ukraine, reaching and crossing the Dnepr River before starting a winter offensive. Stalin, without a Second Front to help him, had fought 80 per cent of the Nazi army and liberated two-thirds of his territory at great human and material cost.

*   *   *

As overtures to Germany had failed, Stalin opted for the West, agreeing to meet FDR and Churchill late in 1943 with a senior preparatory session in advance, so the three foreign ministers met in Moscow in October. Molotov accepted 'unconditional surrender' and a four-power Declaration on General Security, which the Chinese ambassador signed (representing the fourth power – or Policeman), after phrases potentially tying Soviet hands were deleted. Aimed at bringing Russia into the international community, this Declaration promised wartime co-operation and a post-war organization for all states, and implied renunciation of annexations, but the only real commitment was to 'consult'. A tripartite European Advisory Committee (EAC) was created in London, to which many German issues were referred. Molotov's sole agenda item was a Second Front; he gained a firm promise of OVERLORD. In return, Stalin privately said he would enter the Pacific war after the European one ended. Meanwhile, Roosevelt reluctantly recognized a new French Committee of National Liberation (FCNL), which de Gaulle headed. The Moscow meeting was fairly harmonious, raising Roosevelt's hopes of post-war co-operation, but harmony derived mainly from American refusal to discuss borders or Soviet expansion. Russia rejected military co-ordination or discussion of post-war economic relations. Still, it gained tacit consent to bilateral pacts with its neighbours, implying their subservience (though Communism was popular in Europe only at a distance from Russia), as well as to unilateral decisions on armistice terms for Hungary, Rumania, and Finland. No formal commitments were made, but Soviet leadership in eastern Europe was implicitly accepted.

In part, harmony was gained by minimal discussion of Poland, an issue which now loomed large. How was it possible to give Poland and other eastern states self-determination and still satisfy Stalin's territorial aims and craving for security, particularly since Russian occupation of the area was likely? Britain sought agreement on spheres of influence, which Washington opposed, though Hull knew the Four Policemen would amount to that. Clearly, Moscow would decide the fate of eastern Europe; the West sought Soviet co-operation for lack of any other viable policy. Roosevelt and Hull thought if Stalin's primary concern was power, they would gain nothing, but if his priority was security, they might manage a deal. Especially in 1943 they sought a security deal. By 1944, Roosevelt knew real co-operation was unlikely but did not revise his policy, primarily because MacArthur insisted that Russian aid was essential against Japan.

The two Polish issues were borders and regime. Moscow sought the proposed 1919 Curzon Line, slightly less than the 1941 boundary, taking Polish areas whose population was one-third Polish. Poland's exile Cabinet held to its interwar borders to avoid losing credibility with the Polish Underground. FDR knew he could not prevent Polish territorial loss but sought compensation elsewhere. This was eventually arranged in smaller but desirable German territory, in effect shoving Poland westward, and East Prussia, aside from Königsberg (Kaliningrad) and environs.

In the interim, the Moscow discussions implied consent to Soviet plans. Poland's exile government, known as the London Poles, was anti-Communist, so Moscow intended to end diplomatic relations. An opportunity arose in April 1943 when Germany revealed mass graves of thousands of captured Polish officers slaughtered by Russia in April 1940 at Katyn near Smolensk. Soviet denials were unconvincing, and the London Poles accepted Berlin's offer of an independent international investigation. Stalin promptly severed relations and took initial steps toward creating his own puppet Polish regime.

At Moscow, Stalin insisted that the Big Three meeting be in Tehran, the Iranian capital. Churchill and Roosevelt were ill but had to make the long trip to him. However, they broke their journey at Cairo. As the Chinese were coming and Russia was not a party to the Asian war, Stalin refused to send Molotov. Since Roosevelt was courting Stalin, he avoided a long meeting alone with Churchill which might look like Western collusion. A bitter clash occurred when Churchill backslid about OVERLORD, trying again for the eastern Mediterranean – which would mean delaying France until

1945, but most of the November meeting 1943 was devoted to Asian questions.

Chiang's only encounter with Roosevelt and Churchill was not a success. Thus far, the need for air bases in China to bomb Japan had given him some leverage, but island-hopping was gaining bases and Stalin's promise to enter the Pacific war also reduced China's role. Nonetheless, Chiang was imperious and demanding, changing his mind repeatedly and offending everybody. Roosevelt emerged with no illusions about his will and ability to fight but unable to find an alternative. He feared a large Chinese civil war, which would mean no Fourth Policeman and no Asian stability, but tried to keep China in the war, hoping in time it would become a great power. Meanwhile, it would have that status in the new international system and perhaps could be used against Britain, Russia, and Japan in the future. With British consent, FDR promised return of all areas lost since 1894. Along with a Cairo Declaration that Japan must cede all conquered territory and Korea would be independent 'in due course', this meant confining Japan to its home islands.

Churchill and Roosevelt then joined Stalin in Tehran, where much was settled without formal decision. Anglo-American tension over matters strategic and imperial – and future relations with Moscow – affected other issues as the Western alliance deteriorated, and Britain became a junior partner. FDR again evaded meetings with Churchill and wooed Stalin. Assuming future American influence would be non-military, as it would leave Europe within two years of the war's end, he relied on personal diplomacy to create trust, seeing this as the sole hope of real peace. As his wife noted, he was hoping 'something "big" will come out of this war: a new heaven and a new earth'. She thought that assuming great powers would be good neighbours was 'fraught with danger'.[4]

Churchill agreed with this view, doubting international politics could be reformed and seeking Anglo-American condominium and a balance of power to curb Russia. He was pessimistic about post-war relations with Moscow, and Roosevelt had doubts, too, but conceded somewhat to allay Soviet suspicions and reinforce Russian security. However, Stalin assumed that 'whoever conquers a territory imposes on it his own social system'.[5] Roosevelt's treatment of Churchill was tactless but not anti-British. He thought Britain was an ally and a great power and wanted it to be both but did not understand how hard Churchill was struggling to preserve that great power status, complaining all the while that 'the poor little English donkey' was caught between 'the Great Russian Bear' and the 'Great American Buffalo'.[6]

Stalin, who did not trust the West to remain in the war, pressed for an early invasion of France. Two were agreed, OVERLORD in the north, and ANVIL* on the Mediterranean coast; meanwhile amphibious operations

* Later renamed DRAGOON.

would continue in Italy. Stalin promised an offensive to synchronize with OVERLORD and formally pledged to enter the Pacific war after European hostilities ended. FDR agreed to his price: the Kurile islands, the southern half of Sakhalin, privileges on the Manchurian railways, a base at Port Arthur (Lüshun), and Dairen (Dalian) as a free port. There was no agreement on Germany as Churchill, who wanted barriers to Soviet expansion, fought Russo-American desires to dismember it, so the matter was sent to the EAC.

Stalin liked FDR's sketch of a future world organization better than did Churchill, who doubted peace could be based on great power co-operation or that Chiang would survive to play China's role in the Four Policemen. Roosevelt proposed an assembly as a debating society for all states, and a council of the Four plus several smaller states for non-binding advice on non-military matters. The Four Policemen would enforce peace and serve as trustees for liberated colonies.

Aside from Germany, the most painful question was Poland, as the Red Army neared its borders. The London Poles resisted Soviet territorial plans and supervision of elections, seeking guarantees the Allies could not provide. As Stalin insisted on the Curzon Line, Churchill urged that Poland be shifted west to the Oder, and agreed to impose this shift on the London Poles – without getting guarantees about their return or a free election. Roosevelt would not endorse the Curzon Line openly before the 1944 presidential election, where the Polish-American vote might matter, but though no formal decision was taken, he put the Grand Alliance before Poland, for which he could do little. In fact, delay meant acceptance as the Red Army moved west. Stalin was delighted, thinking Soviet aims in eastern Europe endorsed, including 'friendly governments' in neighbouring states with the political domination, not conquest, he desired.

At Tehran, preserving the Grand Alliance came first, and cordiality was used as glue. Future decisions were prefigured, mainly those made formally at Yalta in 1945. En route home, FDR and Churchill met again in Cairo where they delayed a projected Burma campaign, reduced island-hopping because landing craft were lacking, chose Eisenhower to command OVERLORD, and tried to lure Turkey into the war, but found President Inönü's price too high. The diverse agendas of their three meetings in Cairo and Tehran indicated how global their war was and how the tide had turned. Able German and Japanese military men delayed defeat and won some battles but could not stem Allied advances in Russia, Italy, and the Pacific, where Japan in September 1943 created a new defence perimeter, which the Americans broke. MacArthur was preparing a second prong to the American attack toward the Philippines, and Tokyo lacked the resources to defend against both. In Europe, war came home to the German people as they felt the effects of full mobilization in 1943, and Allied bombing increased, both strategic targeting of economic and military sites and terror bombing of major cities. The raids were costly but damaged the German economy, though support for the Nazi regime remained strong. Ruthless exploitation of occupied territories eased the strain until 1944, but Germany now had to focus on home defence.

*   *   *

An isolated Hitler counted on miracle weapons, but the V-1 pilotless small plane and the V-2 liquid fuel rocket launched against London in 1944, though harbingers of the future, did little damage, especially compared with greater Allied strategic bombing from February on. American industrial strength was telling; its gross national product had doubled since 1940, and it produced 40 per cent of the world's armaments.[7] This told against Japan's fading economy, now one-tenth that of the United States. In February 1944, American forces took the Marshall Islands and moved 700 miles (1125 km) closer to Japan, then 300 miles (500 km) more. Despite 'Germany first', nearly two million Americans were deployed in the Pacific and a like number in Europe as the build-up for OVERLORD continued apace. In the spring, Anglo-American deployments were roughly equal, with British forces in the Middle Eastern and South-east Asian theatres, Americans in the Pacific, and North Africa and Europe shared. Thereafter Britain's share of the total fell as more Americans streamed abroad. It was close to economic collapse and would indeed collapse at war's end without American aid. Nonetheless, Anglo-American disagreement continued. There were disputes about ANVIL and OVERLORD, colonies, the conservative Greek and Italian monarchies which Britain backed, de Gaulle, free trade versus imperial preference, post-war civil aviation, and especially policy toward Moscow. Churchill favoured early deals while FDR delayed. Disputes on Middle Eastern oil and the occupation of Germany were resolved by Britain conceding greater American access on the former and gaining its way on the latter. In the autumn, Washington accepted the British plan for German occupation zones with Berlin deep in the Soviet zone.

Through the squabbles and the build-up for OVERLORD, the Italian campaign continued, tying up 25 German divisions (and another 25 in the Balkans) but also draining Allied forces. After a January landing south of Rome, the American commander sat on the beach instead of dashing for Rome, leading Churchill to sigh, 'I had hoped that we were hurling a wild-cat onto the shore, but all we had got was a stranded whale.'[8] Break-out came in May, and on 4 June Rome fell. Victor Emmanuel III abdicated, and the Italian campaign continued, with Churchill urging invasion of Yugoslavia. The German line south of the Po valley was only broken in April 1945.

Two days after the Allies took Rome, they invaded northern France, creating the Second Front at last, though Soviet need of it had diminished.

Churchill resisted OVERLORD until mid-May even as the build-up for it in Britain continued, and persisted in resisting ANVIL. On D-Day, 6 June, Canadian, British, and American forces surged onto Normandy beaches, achieving surprise, for a successful deception plan kept the Nazis awaiting the 'main landing' elsewhere until Allied forces broke out in late July and poured eastward as German resistance collapsed. In part, Russian victories prevented shifting forces west, and the 15 August ANVIL landings on France's Mediterranean coast prevented moving other German units north. The Normandy break-out ensured eventual victory and Anglo-American control of western Europe. Meanwhile the ANVIL campaign seized the key Toulon and Marseilles ports and linked with OVERLORD in September. By then Paris had fallen to the Allies. The overextended American units paused, but Montgomery tried and failed at Arnhem to leapfrog the Dutch rivers with a dramatic aerial spearhead of paratroops. Eisenhower's policy of moving forward on a broad front then prevailed, and France was liberated by the end of 1944 as German forces withdrew to the Rhine.

Even before the Normandy invasion, de Gaulle's FCNL proclaimed itself the 'provisional government of the French Republic'. As de Gaulle seemed the sole alternative to disorder, revolution, and possibly civil war, Washington in July grudgingly recognized it as the 'temporary *de facto* authority for civil administration in France' under Eisenhower's military authority. At British insistence, the Big Three granted it *de jure* recognition as the provisional government in October, but refused admission to meetings of the EAC or the Big Three.

Soviet co-operation aided Allied military success in France. Stalin broke the 900-day siege of Leningrad and drove toward Russia's 1941 borders, with a major breakthrough in June and conquest of Rumania in August, as Hitler shifted troops west to meet the expected invasion and offered a peace Stalin no longer wanted. Having promised an offensive to synchronize with Normandy, Stalin attacked Finland on 10 June, leading to an armistice in September. A larger Soviet offensive carried the Red Army by late July to the outskirts of Warsaw, where it paused to resupply.

As west and east reinforced each other militarily and the successful Second Front ensured Soviet conquest of eastern Europe and Anglo-American of the west, inter-Allied relations did not improve. Hitler was what the alliance had in common, and as he weakened, it frayed. Stalin still feared the Anglo-Americans would combine against him, and a British proposal for a west European bloc alarmed him as a potential new *cordon sanitaire*. Since victory was assured, Stalin was in no hurry, pausing four months east of Warsaw and refusing a Big Three meeting.

Russian refusal to discuss borders with the London Poles revived that issue in July when the Red Army crossed the Curzon Line and in Lublin, the first large city west of it, Stalin created a Communist Polish Committee of National Liberation (Lublin Poles), granting it the civil administration and achieving a satellite regime to go with his desired border. Britain urged the London Poles to yield to Soviet desires, return home, and gain popular support. They did not and probably could not. Roosevelt told them to seek a deal with Stalin, saying the West would not fight for Poland but Moscow would not dare destroy Polish freedom. He knew better, but also knew that nothing could be done for Poland short of starting World War III before World War II had ended.

The impossibility of action soon became clear. When Soviet forces halted outside Warsaw in late July, Russian radio urged it to revolt. The underground Home Army, which backed the London Poles, did so at once. Stalin condemned the initially successful uprising, which lasted two months; at times prevented Western air drops by refusing landing rights at Soviet airstrips; and let German counterattacks destroy his Polish enemies, severely weakening the Polish Underground and levelling the city. Popular and official Western opinion was much affected. Military co-ordination was breaking down, and Stalin ignored protests. But American generals told Roosevelt that Russia was still needed against Japan – and his post-war plans needed it as well.

* * *

Seeking future economic and political stability, Washington sponsored two planning conferences. The first, in July 1944 at Bretton Woods, a New Hampshire resort, aimed to re-establish the world's economic order by creating currency stability and free trade. Recognizing American financial domination, the 44 delegations established gold and the dollar (at $35=1 ounce of gold) as mediums of exchange for international debts, with all currencies pegged to one or the other. To prevent currency fluctuations or competitive devaluations, avoid high tariffs, foster trade, and provide emergency loans, an International Monetary Fund was created, as was a United Nations Bank for Reconstruction and Development (World Bank) to guarantee loans of private banks for long-term projects and enable resources of rich states to help poorer ones to develop.

On the political side, a tripartite conference at Dumbarton Oaks, a Washington estate, drafted the United Nations (UN) Charter in September, with American senators of both parties involved and later endorsement by China and France. The structure was agreed: a General Assembly, a Security Council of five permanent members including France and six chosen for two-year terms, an International Court of Justice, and a Secretariat. Under the Assembly would be an Economic and Social Council, a Trusteeship Council, and the League's specialized agencies. Since the Big Three leaders were not there, decision was deferred on whether all 16 Soviet republics would have seats and whether the great power veto would be absolute, as Moscow hoped – remembering its ouster from the League – or limited to substantive matters.

Meanwhile, Roosevelt and Churchill met in Quebec in mid-September. Stalin had refused a meeting. His forces now stood at Warsaw, in Rumania, and at Slovakia's border. These facts plus his actions during the Warsaw revolt led Churchill to urge an Istrian landing to dash through the mountains to Vienna to block Soviet advances. This Roosevelt refused, but he agreed to full Anglo-American atomic collaboration, to transport British forces to Greece, and to accept the British plan for German occupation zones and division of Berlin into three sectors, without provision for Western access. As Britain had already gained Soviet consent in the EAC, he had little choice. A similar system for Austria was anticipated.

The Three had agreed in the EAC to eliminate Germany's war-making potential but had not decided how to do so. London favoured moderation, Moscow harshness; Washington was divided. At Quebec, Roosevelt and Churchill – the latter only to get post-war American economic aid – accepted American Treasury Secretary Henry Morgenthau Jr's plan for two weak rural states, with removal of all industry. This pastoralization meant permanent occupation and would impede European recovery. For that reason, and because of public outcry before the 1944 presidential election, British reluctance, and Russian demand for greater rigour and insistence on reparations from current industrial production, not just removals, the Morgenthau Plan did not last. Roosevelt backed off. As policy toward Russia affected that toward Germany, he stalled and made no decisions. Should Germany be destroyed, as Stalin wanted, or should its economic strength be used, as Churchill urged, to rebuild western Europe as a barrier to Soviet domination of the continent?

Churchill sought his own solution to the Soviet problem in Moscow in October. He made a deal with Stalin in percentage terms which in effect allocated Greece to Britain, Soviet-occupied Rumania and Bulgaria to Russia, and supposedly divided influence evenly in Yugoslavia and Hungary. This spheres agreement, carefully not called that, ratified Soviet rule in eastern Europe and implied to Stalin that the West was abandoning post-war co-operation, making him even less amenable. Churchill was trying to protect Britain's European role and the power balance as well as to salvage something, but the deal seemed cynical. What he salvaged was Greece, where Stalin honoured the agreement as Britain backed anti-Communists in a civil war. Otherwise, Stalin took eastern Europe, and recognized the Lublin Poles as the provisional government.

*   *   *

The Red Army finally took Warsaw but remained stalled outside Budapest. In the west, the advance was slowed first by Montgomery's failure at Arnhem and then by the Battle of the Bulge in December 1944 in the Belgian Ardennes. This final Nazi offensive using Hitler's last reserves aimed to protect the Ruhr, to halt and split the Allies, and either to win in the west or to gain a Western alliance – all before Russia launched a winter offensive. Radio silence achieved surprise but little advance: the Germans were soon stopped. The Ardennes offensive did not appreciably delay the Allies, who could replace their losses as Hitler could not, for he had nothing left and was now conscripting young boys as mobilization became total. The Battle of the Bulge led to rapid Soviet advances, there being little to obstruct them, but, together with the slow Italian campaign, heightened American eagerness for Russian entry into the Pacific war.

In Asia as well, the Allies met reverses. In March 1944, a Japanese offensive from northern Burma into India forced Britain into a Burma campaign and desperate resistance against encirclement. Chiang refused to mount a relief operation from the east until FDR threatened to suspend Lend-Lease deliveries; thereafter American and Stilwell-trained Chinese troops joined the fray. By June Japan was defeated but not finished. Further battles linked the Anglo-Indian and Sino-American forces in January 1945; the Burma Road* soon reopened via a new Indian route.

Washington had by then written off China except for air bases, many of which were lost in April 1944 as a Japanese offensive caused the KMT armies to collapse. In July Roosevelt insisted that Stilwell become commander of all Chinese forces, including Communist ones; Chiang demanded his recall. His successor, General Albert Wedemeyer, was known as 'Honey' to Stilwell's 'Vinegar Joe', and by tact achieved some of Stilwell's goals but not a unified command. Roosevelt also sent Patrick J. Hurley, who knew nothing of China and whom the Chinese called 'the big wind',[9] as special envoy and then ambassador. Seeking a coalition of two deadly enemies, Hurley visited Mao, greeting him with Choctaw war whoops and addressing him as Mr Moo.[10] Whether Mao wanted a coalition is unclear, though he hoped America would supply aid and curb KMT attacks on him. Hurley at first was enthusiastic but then reversed, backing the KMT over protests by the embassy and army staff, who knew the future was not to Chiang. Mao felt betrayed, and Chiang rejected any merger unless the CCP armies were subordinated to him, for he meant to destroy them before they destroyed him. Hurley remained, backed by FDR; his endorsement of Chiang meant no reform.

In the Pacific, unlike China, events accelerated. In June, simultaneously with D-Day and the Russian offensives, American forces moved 1000 miles (1600 km) from the Marshall Islands to the Marianas, penetrating Japan's Zone of Absolute National Defence and gaining bases from which new long-range B-29 aeroplanes could bomb Japan. Tōjō resigned, bringing a weaker successor. From November 1944 on, bombing was systematic if inaccurate, devastating cities whose homes were built of wood and paper

---

* American black troops helped rebuild the Road, but Chiang, who had urged a racial equality clause for the UN at Dumbarton Oaks, said they were unwelcome in China.

and strangling the Japanese economy. Kamikaze (divine wind) suicide attacks by inexperienced pilots in old planes made little difference.

The second American prong also swept past Formosa (Taiwan) toward the Philippines, Iwo Jima in the Bonin Islands, and Okinawa in the Ryukyus close to Japan. After a naval battle in the Philippine Sea which cost Japan 500 planes, MacArthur invaded Leyte island on 20 October to gain harbours and air bases, reinstating the Philippine territorial government at once. Japan sought a decisive victory at Leyte Gulf, the war's largest naval battle, but suffered disastrous defeat, losing most of its fleet. It was now cut off from South-east Asia and its forces there. Nonetheless, the Japanese army reinforced its position on Leyte and was consumed in a bitter struggle which facilitated American conquest of other Philippine islands. Leyte was largely seized by year's end; by then American forces had landed on Mindanao and were preparing to invade the main island of Luzon.

The Allies were now bombing both Axis powers at will, with German industry, military, and fuel supplies as disrupted as Japan's. The most serious of several German attempts to kill Hitler, based on hope of a continued war with Russia and a soft negotiated peace with the West, had failed in July; September brought proof of Nazi concentration camps in Belgium and Poland. Hitler refused to consider strategic retreat or surrender; will and miracle weapons would win, though the Allies were on or across German borders in both the east and the west.

Allied success brought political problems, including clashes between resistance movements and exile regimes, which sometimes lacked credibility. Governments were often upper-class and conservative, whereas resistance movements demanded social and economic change. This was so in Greece, where British troops landed in October 1944 as Germany withdrew, starting to pull out of the Balkans. When civil war erupted between rival Communist and non-Communist resistance groups, Britain rushed troops in to impose an unpopular authoritarian royal regime. After two months, it succeeded as Moscow and Washington did nothing. Churchill saw the intervention as a test of Britain's great power status and role in the Mediterranean.

He was tiring, as was an ailing Roosevelt, though neither's policies seemed much affected by reduced energy. Hull had retired; his successor played an even smaller role. In November 1944, Roosevelt was re-elected, and most Congressional isolationists were defeated. This was seen as a mandate for American participation in the UN. With the election over, Roosevelt conceded a great power veto in that organization except for procedural questions, largely gave up on the Four Policemen or a substantial role for China in the near future, and effectively wrote off Poland.

The most intractable political problem was eastern Europe, where Russia had taken Belgrade and Warsaw and by late January 1945 was in Germany 40 miles (65 km) east of Berlin. It created puppet states as it went, installing tiny unpopular Communist parties. Its actions in the Balkans and Poland raised acute Anglo-American doubts about the future of the alliance and post-war co-operation, but no new policy presented itself as the European war approached its end.

*   *   *

Despite Roosevelt's health and constitutional problems,* Stalin insisted that the next Big Three meeting be held at Yalta, a newly liberated, rather battered Crimean resort whose tsarist palaces had startlingly few bath-rooms and startlingly large quantities of bedbugs.[11] En route, Roosevelt and Churchill met briefly on Malta, where the final European offensives were planned, along with European relief efforts, redeployment to the Pacific, and the Japanese war. They thought the European war would end late in 1945 and the Pacific war a year and a half thereafter.

The Yalta conference largely ratified the Tehran decisions. Despite later controversy, it contributed little that was new and left many decisions vague. It rested on the new realities of power, including implicit European spheres. As British power and the Anglo-American tie waned, Roosevelt concentrated on Stalin, avoiding a Western front. In fact the West had little leverage. It was into Germany but still needed the Red Army, which limited disagreement. The Soviet winter offensive had rolled to the Oder; FDR and Churchill did not know it was stalling there, awaiting supplies. In the Pacific, MacArthur was stuck in the Philippines while the other prong of the American attack met greater resistance as it neared Japan. Nonetheless, many debates were bitter.

Most Polish and eastern European issues had been settled by the Red Army. Western efforts to gain concessions achieved little. A Declaration on Liberated Europe and another on Eastern Europe promised democracy and free elections but left Moscow able to impose its version of democracy – which Stalin thought he had consent to do in what he deemed the Soviet sphere. Roosevelt vainly sought alleviations in Poland's favour. Stalin's insistence on the western Neisse River as its western border led Churchill to remark, 'It would be a pity to stuff the Polish goose so full of German food that it died of indigestion.'[12] Ultimately, Moscow seized the area and expelled six million Germans. Stalin granted token London Polish delegates in an enlarged Lublin regime but no reorganization nor any international supervision of elections. To end debate about Poland, Stalin linked it to the issue of great power vetoes in the UN Security Council. He abandoned his insistence that Russia be allowed to veto discussion of matters where Russia was an interested party but retained the veto for decisions on action, and settled for two Assembly seats for the Ukraine and Byelorussia (Belarus). A

---

* Congressional bills must be signed or vetoed within 10 days, but the round trip to Yalta could not be safely made in that time.

founding conference for the UN, which would oversee trusteeships limited
to League mandates, Axis territory, and voluntary transfers, would take
place in San Francisco in late April.

Germany's future received much attention. A French occupation zone
and Berlin sector were carved out of the Anglo-American zones. All agreed
on the need to occupy, disarm, and denazify a smaller Germany and to
punish its leaders. Problems arose over dismemberment, which Moscow
wanted, and reparation in kind. Roosevelt now sought to reconstitute
Germany under tight controls in order to reconstruct Europe, while
Churchill wanted to enlist it in the power balance; both feared the eastern
zone would become a Soviet client. Conversely, Stalin feared a new *cordon
sanitaire*. He meant to strip Germany to restore Russia; thus he sought $20
milliard in reparation, half for Russia, which the others thought excessive.
Churchill wanted Germany self-supporting, and Washington was determined not to foot the bill again. Neither dismemberment, reparations nor
access to Berlin were settled, though the Cold War soon brought division.

Asian questions were discussed without awareness that the end was near.
Chiang was collapsing, and both American prongs were costing many lives.
Since the atomic bomb's power and availability were not yet known, it was
not a planning factor. So Russian aid seemed needed, and Roosevelt agreed
to Stalin's price (the Kuriles, southern Sakhalin, and major concessions in
Manchuria), promising to gain Chiang's consent, both as fourth Policeman
and as future ruler of Manchuria. However, nobody bothered to tell Chiang
the terms for some months. At Yalta, the Tehran terms were ratified; it was
not yet clear that Moscow could seize these areas, as it did. Fearing Mao
would lose a civil war, Stalin agreed to a treaty with Chiang and Soviet
support for a coalition. The *status quo* in Outer Mongolia (technically
autonomy under Chinese sovereignty) would stand until a post-war
plebiscite, which opted for independence. Korea would initially be under
Russian and American tutelage with zones divided at 38° latitude.

Roosevelt and Churchill put a brave face on the results of Yalta, neither
preparing opinion for heavy-handed Soviet imperialism in eastern Europe,
but privately Roosevelt admitted, 'it was the best I could do'.[13] To avoid
endangering any hope of great power co-operation, on which peaceful co-
existence and post-war stability – and perhaps victory in the Pacific –
depended, he briefly sought to give Yalta a chance because the alternative
was so grim. Churchill urged him to stand up to Moscow, mainly where
Britain dared not risk it or might lose the benefit of prior deals. To a degree,
Roosevelt faced up to Russian hostility and on 1 April joined Churchill in
a protest to Stalin, threatening public disclosure if Moscow did not allow
east European states more independence and choice of government, as he
went off on vacation.

He never returned; on 12 April he died of a massive cerebral haemor-
rhage. Nazi leaders exulted, seeing a new miracle of the house of

Hohenzollern. Radio Tokyo played special music for 'the passing of a great man'.[14] His successor, Harry Truman, as blunt as Roosevelt was dissembling, had limited education and little international expertise but a capacity for decision and long experience in playing poker, which proved useful in dealing with Stalin. He had been excluded from the war's conduct and was pitched suddenly into full responsibility. At first he rested on Roosevelt's advisers and policies, but his instinct to stand up to Stalin soon asserted itself.

Roosevelt had insisted that the planning sessions, founding conference, and headquarters of the UN all be in the United States to encourage American support for joining. As the San Francisco conference neared, Turkey, Egypt, and Argentina declared war on the Axis to gain a place at 'the victors' table'. As a Turkish leader explained, 'We wanted to be on the guest list, not on the menu.'[15] There were 51 original members; by the century's end, the number approached two hundred. As at Paris in 1919, private meetings of the Big Four (including China) foreign ministers decided much, though many questions had been settled earlier. The UN Charter was signed on 25 June 1945; in April 1946, the League transferred its authority to the UN and expired.

*   *   *

Military events did not wait upon meetings. On 7 March 1945, the Allies seized an intact bridge across the Rhine, then more. The Ruhr was encircled and isolated as Allied armies moved swiftly. Germans still blocked the Soviets in Hungary, and the Red Army remained at the Oder but in late March moved to gain Berlin. Eisenhower, whose orders were to pursue and destroy the Nazi armies, has been criticized for not challenging or ignoring them and racing the Soviets to Berlin. He opted, as Roosevelt and Marshall and then Truman preferred, to head for Saxony and western Czechoslovakia to end Germany's arms production and block any move into its Bavarian alpine redoubt for a final stand. Churchill was furious, wanting Montgomery to seize Berlin and hold it until paid in Soviet concessions to withdraw. Eisenhower knew the Soviets could take Berlin, that Montgomery moved slowly, that the formal agreement on zonal boundaries had been signed in November, and that the top priority was ending the German war in order to shift troops to the Pacific. He opposed taking Berlin for the Soviets and backed the view that suffering 100 000 casualties to do so would be 'a pretty stiff price to pay for a prestige objective, especially when we've got to fall back and let the other fellow take it'.[16]

Eisenhower's decision improved relations with neither Britain nor Russia. Moscow scented Western-Nazi collusion in denial of a Soviet role in the surrender of German forces in Italy. In late March 1945, Eisenhower told Stalin his plans, trying to arrange the coming juncture with Soviet troops. Stalin thought he was being tricked, told Eisenhower he would not attack Berlin until late May, and ordered an assault for 16 April. Peace feelers from top Nazis for a Western peace and continued war against Russia, all refused, heightened Soviet suspicions though American troops stopped at the Elbe River to await the Soviets. Juncture occurred on 25 April, as the UN conference opened. In Czechoslovakia the Americans stopped as well, letting the Red Army take Prague. The Soviets surrounded Berlin and fought in its streets as senior Nazis fled.

On 30 April Hitler completed his personal and political wills, naming Admiral Karl Dönitz as his successor, married his mistress, and killed himself at his underground Berlin bunker. The Berlin garrison surrendered to the Russians. Dönitz, who, like most Germans deeply feared Soviet vengeance, tried to yield to the West alone, but London and Washington refused to desert Moscow. Thus on 7 May Dönitz accepted unconditional surrender to agents of the Big Three. Military leaders were required to sign the capitulation so they could not again blame the home front for defeat. The Allies moved into their proper occupation zones, pending a peace conference which did not take place.

A similar regime developed for Austria and Vienna. Elsewhere, Russia ruled, with few exceptions. Finland managed independence by subservience to Moscow. Yugoslavia's coalition was controlled by Tito (Josip Broz), an independent-minded Marxist whose nation did not abut Russia. In Prague, Soviet pawns held the key posts. Hungary's Cabinet was ignored by Soviet occupiers, who stripped the country for reparations and food. In Rumania and Bulgaria, Russian rule was absolute. With no voice in eastern Europe, London and Washington recognized the reconstituted Lublin regime in Poland. A new *cordon sanitaire* arrived, facing west instead of east, but comprised mainly of the same states as before.

Europe was awash in misery and Displaced Persons; Britain was also miserable as its economy worsened. It and Russia suffered from the end of Lend-Lease on 8 May, as required by law; Stalin saw a hostile act therein. Photographs of liberated concentration camps had a huge impact, as did shipping shortages, which limited food supplies for a starving continent while American troops were shifted to the Pacific. Meanwhile, the Big Three met once more at Potsdam near Berlin from 17 July to 2 August. As the French were not invited, they vetoed some plans for Germany, including a central administration. Churchill arrived tired and gloomy, knowing he had lost the British election of 5 July, though ballots would not be counted for three weeks to allow the troops to vote; the election forced a five-day adjournment in mid-conference, but Churchill's and Eden's Labour successors, Clement Attlee and Ernest Bevin, were well briefed. In his diplomatic debut, Truman was blunt, crisp, and firm. Stalin wanted to consolidate his gains, not new agreements which might limit them, so he sought loopholes in all texts.

As at Yalta, certain *faits accomplis* were recognized, such as tentative acceptance of the Oder/Neisse line as the Polish–German border. Russia was awarded reparations from its own zone, which it stripped, and briefly some from the Western zones, but no total was set. Other agreements helped to ratify Europe's division into two spheres. Stalin got nothing new but was not rolled back. A Council of Foreign Ministers (including France and China) was created to prepare peace treaties and submit them to the UN. It achieved 1947 treaties with Bulgaria, Finland, Hungary, Italy, and Rumania. But little was agreed on Germany as the last Western illusions evaporated.

Much attention was given to the Asian war. Though the atomic bomb was successfully tested as the meeting opened, military advisers told Truman that Russia was needed against Japan because casualties would be high in the planned invasion of Kyushu island. Truman gave Churchill full details of the atomic test; during the hiatus, he told Stalin he had a destructive new weapon. Stalin urged him to use it and, wanting to join the war before it ended, promised to do so by 15 August. A Potsdam Declaration on 26 July demanded unconditional surrender of the Japanese military, said the Japanese people could choose their own regime (implying retention of the Emperor), limited Japan to its home islands, and promised 'prompt and utter destruction' if Tokyo did not surrender. Japan announced it would ignore this statement and closed ranks.

*　　　*　　　*

The Pacific war's end was closer than Truman realized. In the spring the military figured two more years to defeat Japan, which made Russian entry seem vital. Having underestimated Japan in 1940–41, Western experts now overestimated its persistence almost to the end, especially as resistance increased. The campaign for Iwo Jima in February and March 1945 was costly but facilitated bombing Japan. Okinawa, only 325 miles (525 km) from Japan, was more costly, requiring a three-month struggle until late June with heavy losses, especially to kamikazes. Thus Truman decided Kyushu must be invaded. Meanwhile in the Philippines, MacArthur landed on Luzon in early January, arriving at Manila's outskirts in a month. Japan burnt much of the city and defended it block by block, but by 1 March Americans possessed its ruins.

Meanwhile, China was veering toward chaos. Roosevelt had given up on Chiang, but Hurley continued to seek a coalition – on Chiang's terms, though the bypassed State Department and embassy knew that was impossible and favoured limited co-operation with Mao to avoid civil war and CCP reliance on Moscow. Roosevelt continued to back Hurley, as did Truman after him.

In South-east Asia, Japan seized the Indochinese administration from Vichy officials in March, ending their nominal authority lest they should actively support de Gaulle or the Allies should invade. A scramble for

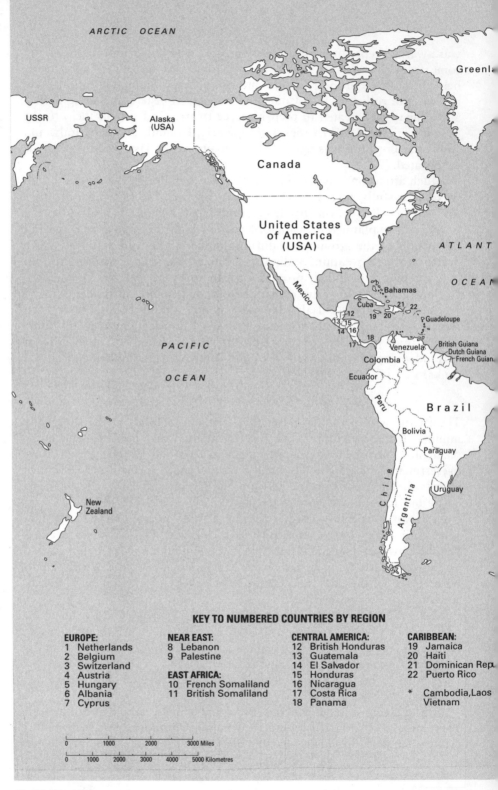

ARCTIC OCEAN

USSR

Alaska
(USA)

Canada

Greenl

United States
of America
(USA)

Mexico

PACIFIC

OCEAN

Bahamas

Cuba

21 22

19 20

Guadeloupe

British Guiana
Dutch Guiana
French Guian.

Venezuela

Colombia

Ecuador

Peru

Brazil

Bolivia

Paraguay

Chile

Argentina

Uruguay

New
Zealand

ATLANT

OCEAN

KEY TO NUMBERED COUNTRIES BY REGION

EUROPE:	NEAR EAST:	CENTRAL AMERICA:	CARIBBEAN:
1 Netherlands	8 Lebanon	12 British Honduras	19 Jamaica
2 Belgium	9 Palestine	13 Guatemala	20 Haiti
3 Switzerland		14 El Salvador	21 Dominican Repu
4 Austria	**EAST AFRICA:**	15 Honduras	22 Puerto Rico
5 Hungary	10 French Somaliland	16 Nicaragua	
6 Albania	11 British Somaliland	17 Costa Rica	* Cambodia, Laos
7 Cyprus		18 Panama	Vietnam

0	1000	2000	3000 Miles
0	1000	2000	3000	4000	5000 Kilometres

The World in 1945

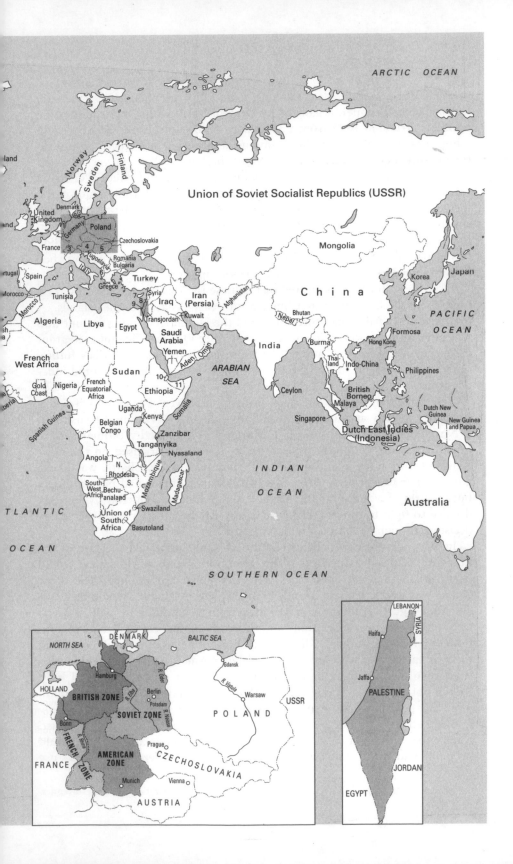

ARCTIC OCEAN

Union of Soviet Socialist Republics (USSR)

Norway
Sweden
Finland
Denmark
United Kingdom
Germany
Poland
2
France
3   4   5
Czechoslovakia
Portugal
Spain
Italy
Yugoslavia
Romania
Bulgaria
6
Turkey
Greece
7
Morocco
Tunisia
Syria
8
9
Iraq
Iran (Persia)
Kuwait
Afghanistan
Mongolia
Korea
Japan
Algeria
Libya
Egypt
Transjordan
Saudi Arabia
Yemen
Aden Oman
Nepal
Bhutan
China
PACIFIC OCEAN
Formosa
Hong Kong
French West Africa
Gold Coast
Nigeria
French Equatorial Africa
Sudan
10
11
Ethiopia
ARABIAN SEA
India
Burma
Thailand
Indo-China
Philippines
Spanish Guinea
Uganda
Kenya
Somalia
Belgian Congo
Zanzibar
Tanganyika
Nyasaland
Ceylon
British Borneo
Malaya
Singapore
Dutch East Indies (Indonesia)
Dutch New Guinea
New Guinea and Papua
Angola
N. Rhodesia
S.
Mozambique
Madagascar
South-West Africa
Bechuanaland
Swaziland
Union of South Africa
Basutoland
INDIAN OCEAN
Australia
TLANTIC OCEAN
SOUTHERN OCEAN

NORTH SEA
DENMARK
BALTIC SEA
HOLLAND
Hamburg
R. Elbe
Gdansk
R. Vistula
Warsaw
USSR
BRITISH ZONE
Berlin
Potsdam
R. Oder
R. Neisse
POLAND
Bonn
SOVIET ZONE
FRENCH ZONE
AMERICAN ZONE
Prague
CZECHOSLOVAKIA
FRANCE
Munich
Vienna
AUSTRIA

LEBANON
Haifa
SYRIA
Jaffa
PALESTINE
EGYPT
JORDAN

power ensued among local factions, especially the Viet Minh (Vietnam Independence League), organized by Ho Chi Minh with American blessing upon his arrival in 1941 from a 31-year exile. By now, however, Roosevelt, whose priorities were elsewhere, saw no alternative to France's return. In the interim, a compromise between Mountbatten and Wedemeyer allocated the south to Britain and the north to Chiang. Famine and political crisis set off a national uprising in August in which the Viet Minh took major cities, including Hanoi, proclaimed a Democratic Republic of Vietnam, and vainly sought Allied recognition. In response, British forces moved into Saigon in the south, cultivated elites, and ignored intense nationalism including hostility to all white peoples. As Ho held the north, Truman was absorbed by other matters and accepted French re-occupation.

Elsewhere, Burma was cleared of Japanese by May, and Tokyo could no longer supply its troops in China, South-east Asia, and the islands. A predominantly Australian force liberated the Dutch East Indies in June and July after futile efforts by Roosevelt to convince Queen Wilhelmina to grant independence. Though Churchill had refused to reconsider India's future, others had done so. In particular, the new Labour leaders favoured independence.

The immediate Anglo-American priority, however, was gaining Tokyo's surrender quickly at minimum cost. Plans called for invasion of Kyushu on 1 November 1945, Honshu on 1 March 1946. Casualty estimates were horrific, perhaps a million Americans; as both sides focused on the same Kyushu location for a landing and confrontation, a great battle was likely, and another near Tokyo. After loss of Okinawa, Japan had no real hope, but the army favoured fanatic defence. On 8 June an Imperial Conference decided to fight to the end. Hirohito cautiously began trying to reverse this decision, though he feared a military coup.*

In Washington, two debates continued. One concerned the fate of the Emperor. Without assurances of his retention, Japanese resistance would lengthen. In the end, assurances were not given but implied. The other debate was over use of the atomic bomb which, by chance, would be available for August. Truman, who had little time to consider, thought it was a large explosive for a small zone, and, like others, did not realize its revolutionary nature, including radiation and blast. The atomic bomb could end the war faster and without invasion, saving American lives. It could also strengthen Washington's diplomatic position vis-à-vis Moscow and keep Russia out of Japan. Though Marshall worried about moral opprobrium, most did not. Japanese atrocities, unlike those of Germany, were widely known before hostilities ended, and racial hatred had mounted. By August, some experts thought casualty estimates were excessive and the war could probably end without invasion. But when Truman ordered the bomb's use

* Bix, *Hirohito*, argues (pp. 15, 509, 521–4) that Hirohito's hesitations delayed surrender.

from Potsdam, that was not the consensus. A landing was still planned, and Japan's determination was overestimated.

On 6 August* the first atomic bomb was dropped on the industrial city of Hiroshima. A single bomb killed 50 000 to 80 000 people and wounded a like number. Despite these figures, the atomic bomb may have saved Japanese lives as well as American ones. Washington promised 'a rain of ruin from the air',[17] though only one more bomb existed. On 8 August, Russia declared war; the next day, its troops poured into Manchuria as the second bomb fell on Nagasaki. In Tokyo, impasse existed between civilians who wished to surrender and generals who did not.

On 10 August, Hirohito intervened for surrender, reserving only his imperial prerogative, and sent a message via Switzerland accepting the Potsdam Declaration. The Allied reply implied that he could remain, under an Allied supreme commander. As Japan's military situation worsened, a struggle occurred in Tokyo, culminating on 14 August in Cabinet acceptance of surrender and an attempted military coup, which narrowly failed when key leaders were loyal to the Emperor. On 15 August, the Emperor-god (soon stripped of his divinity) made his first ever broadcast to his people, announcing surrender. No troops ceased hostilities until the broadcast and confirmation by special envoys, often imperial princes, and sometimes not then.

Japanese collapse was total. American forces landed on 21 August, and formal surrender took place on an American warship in Tokyo Bay on 2 September. MacArthur alone commanded the Allied occupation, which was essentially American, despite a small area awarded to the British Commonwealth. Soviet participation was not allowed. The Americans came to reform, and briefly did, bringing demilitarization, democracy, a 1951 treaty, and an end to traditional beliefs.

The Pacific war ended suddenly, leaving more than a million Japanese troops in China, whom the United States eventually repatriated. More immediately, they were to surrender to the KMT and officially did so, but in the north the CCP took the surrender, gaining much equipment, though the United States transported KMT troops northward in a vain effort to prevent this. Sino-Soviet negotiations were in progress on the treaty foreshadowed at Yalta. After Russia occupied Manchuria, which it stripped of industry, Chiang accepted the terms and signed on 15 August. Though Moscow soon withdrew from Port Arthur and the Manchurian railways, it had regained all its 1905 losses in Asia as well as all its 1917–18 losses in Europe.

World War II ended where it began, in Asia. The United States and Britain fought to prevent Japanese domination there but now faced the prospect of Soviet domination, especially as the Chinese civil war erupted

* Dates hereafter are Western, not Tokyo time.

in earnest. In both Asia and in Europe, where armies stood at the end proved crucial. Greater Allied resources, population, and industrial strength won, as usually happens in long wars. More distinctively, World War II ended in absolute victory and absolute defeat. But Russia's victory was very costly, while that of other European Allies was Pyrrhic, amounting in some senses to defeat and resulting in a diminishing, less global role. Europe still mattered greatly, but, after hundreds of years in the spotlight, it no longer occupied centre stage.

◆ Notes to Chapter 17

1. For text, see Nicholas Mansergh, ed., *The Transfer of Power, 1942–7*, vol. 1, *The Cripps Mission* (London, HMSO, 1970), pp. 357–8.
2. For the clearest exposition of Japanese plans and problems, see Gerhard L. Weinberg, *A World at Arms: A Global History of World War II* (Cambridge, CUP, 1994), pp. 323–40, 391–4.
3. Walter LaFeber, *The Clash: US–Japan Relations throughout History* (New York, Norton, 1997), p. 228.
4. Warren F. Kimball, *Forged in War: Roosevelt, Churchill, and the Second World War* (New York, William Morrow, 1997), p. 243.
5. Milovan Djilas, *Conversations with Stalin*, tr. Michael B. Petrovich (New York, Harcourt, Brace & World, 1962), p. 114.
6. Georg Schild, *Bretton Woods and Dumbarton Oaks* (New York, St Martin's Press, 1995), p. 244.
7. David Reynolds, *The Creation of the Anglo-American Alliance* (Chapel Hill, NC, University of North Carolina Press, 1982), p. 284.
8. Gordon Wright, *The Ordeal of Total War, 1939–1945* (New York, Harper, 1968), p. 193.
9. Van Alstyne, *The United States and East Asia*, p. 160.
10. John Costello, *The Pacific War* (London, Collins, 1981), p. 524.
11. For a graphic description of the setting, see Diane Shaver Clemens, *Yalta* (New York, OUP, 1970), pp. 113–17. This book also contains a useful collection of conference documents.
12. Gaddis Smith, *American Diplomacy during the Second World War, 1941–1945* (New York, Wiley, 1965), p. 49.
13. Vojtech Mastny, *Russia's Road to the Cold War* (New York, Columbia University Press, 1979), p. 521.
14. Robert Dallek, *Franklin Delano Roosevelt and American Foreign Policy, 1932–1945* (New York, OUP, 1979), p. 528.
15. Bernard Lewis, *The Middle East: A Brief History* (New York, Scribner, 1995), p. 350.
16. Kimball, *Forged in War*, pp. 323–4.
17. Smith, *American Diplomacy*, p. 169.

EPILOGUE

A DIFFERENT WORLD

Roll on, thou ball, roll on!
Through pathless realms of
space roll on!

W. S. Gilbert, 'To the Terrestial Globe'
The Bab Ballads

Previous page: Indonesian independence slogan in Malang, Java, 1948

THE AFTERMATH

In 1945, the world stage was littered with corpses, blackened ruins, and barely breathing states. About 60 million people had been killed, half of them European, more than twice the figure of World War I. In the war and its aftermath, a similar number were permanently uprooted by dislocation, expulsion or fearful flight, again half in Europe, for this time peoples moved more often than borders, creating the largest short-term migrations in history and, along with wartime extermination, largely ending eastern Europe's minority problems and reducing those of the Indian subcontinent. The most severely war-impacted areas were Europe, Asia and the Pacific, and North Africa, the most conventionally obliterated cities Warsaw, Manila, and Minsk. Though Europe was the most devastated continent, Asian cities and rural China also suffered. At least 20 million Russians were killed, 6 million Poles (half of them Jews), 4 or 5 million Germans, under 2 million Japanese – many from starvation or disease, British and Americans (from a much larger population) each about 300 000. How many millions of Chinese died is unknown.

On top of physical and demographic devastation came financial, for World War II cost 13 times as much as World War I. Japan and Italy exhausted their resources, as did Britain, who owed $30 milliard to the United States as well as several milliard pounds to the Dominions, India, and the colonies in an era when both currencies bought much more. In Europe, few borders changed greatly, aside from Russia's reversion to approximately its 1914 frontier, but much else did. East European Jewish culture no longer existed; central Europe was awash with 30 million Displaced Persons; food, shoes, jobs, and economic activity were scarce; east and west, misery almost universal. Germany was devastated and knew it had lost this war; it paid more reparations – mostly in removals to Russia – more willingly than after World War I. Italy also knew it had lost and accepted that it was not a great power. France's efforts to revert to the past proved futile, as did Britain's; both had aged visibly and lost muscle, as all could see. The political, economic, and moral devastation of Europe, as its prestige sank globally, had sweeping power implications for the future.

Post-war Europe, 1945–52

░	Soviet-annexed territories of 1939–40, reclaimed in 1945
▓	Former Czechoslovakian and German territory annexed by USSR in 1945

0   400 miles

Post-war Europe, 1945–52

Of European combatants, only Britain and Russia were not defeated, but the price to both was great, to Britain too great to bear. Its resources were depleted, its economy a shambles, its exports 40 per cent of the pre-war level; the former second largest creditor nation was now the largest debtor. It had survived thanks to Russia, the United States, and its own Empire. Rationing became more stringent as Britain tried to revive its economy and exports, but its efforts to remain a great power were frustrated by lack of money, exhaustion, and the crumbling of empire. The new Labour government soon let go those colonies which could not be held, hoping to retain the rest, but had to abdicate Britain's world role in 1947.

Russia emerged during and after World War II as the United States had in World War I, gaining an empire – albeit a partially indirect one, but at first it was weakened by the war, as it had lost 30 per cent of its national wealth to devastation. It refused outside aid and launched new five-year plans to reconstruct. The war brought greater internal cohesion, and the advantage that neither Germany nor Japan could check its expansion at first, nor could Britain alone in the Middle East. Militarily, the Soviet air and naval forces were weak at first, and the Red Army was concentrated in eastern Europe, but in 1949 Russia became an atomic state and emerged as a superpower.

In most areas, reconstruction began at once, and a population explosion filled the demographic void. The chief exception was China where Japanese surrender set off a race between the Kuomintang and the CCP for territory and Japanese weapons which quickly slid into full-scale civil war. Mao's forces had begun to win China during the war by treating the peasants well and fighting the Japanese, which the KMT seldom did. In 1937, the CCP controlled a few thousand square miles, one million people, and an army of 80 000. By 1945, it held a quarter of China and 100 million people; its army of nearly a million soon swelled.[1] Russia and the United States, whose policies here were similar, both opposed the civil war, seeking to stabilize Chiang with a coalition government; neither had much effect. Washington sent him more aid than Moscow, which distrusted Mao since Stalin could not control him and his unorthodox peasant Communism. Truman also sent Marshall for 13 months of futile negotiations toward a coalition from late 1945 to early 1947; neither side had any interest in the other's terms. Though the KMT had a heavy numerical advantage at first in troops and weapons, it was out of touch with the population, suffered from weak leaders and troops, and was undermined by new inflation. Despite intense efforts by Washington's 'China lobby' of prominent Americans close to Chiang, American aid was gradually cut in 1948 as the CCP launched successful 'human sea' attacks. In 1949, Chiang and the KMT withdrew to Taiwan; on 1 October Mao proclaimed the People's Republic of China in Peking. Thereafter land reform and destruction of the landlord class with several million killed meant some material improvement for the masses. Britain and the United States lost their pre-war positions in China altogether; Moscow recouped with a treaty in 1950 which brought technical aid and an edgy relationship. Britain promptly granted *de facto* recognition to the new regime; the United States did not, ensuring that the KMT represented China in the UN.

*   *   *

War-torn Allied countries had lived until 1945 on hope, English-speaking ones singing:

> There'll be love and laughter and peace ever after
> Tomorrow, when the world is free.[2]

Only in Australia, New Zealand, and the Americas, however, did the post-war approach expectations. Of the major powers, the United States alone was not impoverished by World War II. As others weakened, it grew richer; its Gross National Product more than doubled between 1940 and 1945, and its institutions, international activity, and industry all grew. Despite rapid demobilization, it remained the world's strongest military power, especially in naval, air, and atomic terms. At first, it enjoyed much prestige owing to its wartime role and pronouncements such as the Atlantic Charter, and because it granted the Philippines independence on schedule in 1946, though it handed over to local oligarchs and by treaty retained economic privileges and military bases, setting a pattern of neocolonialism later used by France.

American goals, like those of Britain, were peace and 'normalcy', not territory. The United States was still a reluctant great power but gradually matured into its world role, not always gracefully, as it struggled against its own traditions, becoming a superpower and progressively taking over global responsibilities from Britain, despite a brief partial withdrawal from Europe at first and temporary disintegration of the Anglo-American alliance. As it moved into a power vacuum, creating a Pax Americana, Washington developed spheres of influence, though reluctant to admit it, in western Europe, the Pacific and Japan, the Americas, and economically in the Middle East. As it took on the responsibilities of a global power, the weight of the past together with fear of becoming a garrison state contributed to preventing that eventuality, despite an unheard-of peacetime military establishment and development of what Eisenhower termed a military-industrial-scientific complex.

To the south, Latin America's involvement in the war was comparatively minor though much greater than in World War I. Brazilian and Mexican forces served abroad in the region's first overseas combat. Other states provided bases, raw materials, and anti-submarine patrols. In return, Washington provided much Lend-Lease aid, especially to Brazil, loans for war industries, cultural missions in its first efforts at cultural diplomacy, and military instruction. Aside from hostile Argentina and also Chile, who doubted that the United States could protect their southerly exposed coast-lines, continental solidarity was complete after Pearl Harbor. To ensure that it remained so as other markets and suppliers were cut off, the United States bought excess Latin American goods it did not need and engaged in other actions to limit the war's economic impact; Latin American states vainly expected this largesse to continue after the war. Meanwhile, the war brought urbanization and some industrialization, but the area remained underdeveloped.

Briefly, Latin America swung toward more democratic regimes at the war's end, with nationalism, reform and demands for more, populism, and rising expectations, some of which led to unrest. But American contracts and loans ceased, and Washington's attention turned elsewhere. It was slow to see any Communist threat in Latin America, but as it became preoccupied with a presumed global Communist conspiracy, it opted for stability over democracy and in Latin America, as elsewhere, backed conservative anti-Communist regimes, which regained power by 1948. After perhaps too much wartime American attention, the region now saw too little as Washington focused on the Cold War with Russia, and Latin America became the only region of the world without a well-funded American aid programme. World War II had promised much change, but in the end delivered relatively little.

Canada's military role was far greater and brought with it economic growth along with more self-confidence and independence. In 1946, it established a distinct Canadian citizenship; other Dominions followed suit, ending the Commonwealth's common nationality, and by 1948 British citizenship was limited to Great Britain and its dependent colonies. The Dominions, especially Australia, grew to independence in World War II, sending diplomatic agents to each other, Washington, and sometimes elsewhere. The war demonstrated, as Australia and New Zealand recognized, that the United States was the dominant Pacific power. It provided protection but no more voice than Britain had. Some loyalty to Britain remained, particularly in New Zealand, despite disrupted economic ties and bitterness, especially in Australia,[3] about broken British promises. As they developed greater self-reliance, the two Dominions consulted toward a united front and learned to live in Asia instead of being protected from it. Australia emerged onto the world stage with its own foreign policy. So did South Africa, which prospered from the war but remained sharply divided over participation. The war brought more Afrikaner nationalism and republicanism, but greater racial problems which led soon to an official policy of *apartheid*, rigid racial segregation to perpetuate white minority rule.

* * *

Refusal to arm blacks limited South Africa's number of wartime combatants, but Indians fought in quantity in the Middle East, Africa, and South-east

Asia, and defended India itself amid industrialization, famine, mounting nationalist unrest, and growth of the Muslim League, which sought an independent Pakistan. Since Muslims had a large role in the Indian Army, its calls were heeded, especially when post-war chaos in Muslim areas proved impossible to control; at that point, the Indian National Congress reluctantly accepted partition. Because there was no agreement on any plan, Britain set a date for withdrawal to force one, but thereby destroyed its bargaining power. Hasty British efforts gave birth to India and Pakistan in August 1947 amid riots, border fights, and then an Indian-Pakistani war. A million people were killed and 15 million migrated across the new borders without ending religious minorities. India was democratic but unable to feed its soaring population. Pakistan, poor, unstable, and soon under military rule, consisted of two pieces – separated by a thousand miles (1600 km) of India – with nothing in common except religion.* Burma and Ceylon gained independence early in 1948. Burma left the Commonwealth, as did Ireland; the other three Asian states remained members as republics, as did South Africa; the monarch was now merely the president of a weaker and politically divided Commonwealth.

In Burma and to a degree in India, Japan had been an unwitting agent of revolutionary pressures. In South-east Asia, where the American role grew as European powers weakened, this factor was especially important, for wartime Japanese puppet 'independence' spawned demands for genuine self-rule which in time ended all of Europe's Asian empires. When Japan surrendered, both Ho Chi Minh in Vietnam and Sukarno in the Dutch East Indies proclaimed independence. France and the Netherlands resisted, regaining some territory and setting off bloody wars. Since Washington favoured independence for non-Communist movements and Sukarno was anti-Communist, the United States, with Australian endorsement, exercised extreme financial pressure on the Dutch to force creation of an independent Indonesia in 1949. The Marxist Ho was mistakenly viewed as a Russian puppet, so Washington backed the French war in Vietnam until France withdrew in 1954, then embarked on its own prolonged effort there.

*　　　*　　　*

When Britain decided to leave India, the Middle East became less vital to it, aside from oil states, though the Attlee government saw the region as a barrier to Soviet emergence into the Mediterranean. Except in North Africa, the Middle East had little direct involvement in the war but contributed use of its territories, resources, and facilities, and noted Anglo-French weakness. World War II had less influence than World War I, which ended the Ottoman Empire, but still hastened France's exit and later that of Britain. Early hardship was followed by prosperity generated by Allied

* In 1971, East Pakistan broke away and became Bangladesh.

needs and by rising expectations focused on an anti-colonial revolt, demands for a higher share of oil profits, and the Palestine question. In addition, Soviet-American competition developed in aid programmes; the Northern Tier (Turkey, Iraq, Iran, and Afghanistan) was subject to Soviet pressure but resisted. Oil became more important as production soared from less than 5 per cent of the 1940 world total, oil replaced coal in Western industry and homes, and automobile production grew apace after the war. In the first post-war decade, the region's states with oil generally developed; those without did not. The Middle East's war and aftermath also showed that Britain was overextended; increasingly its influence was replaced by that of the United States.

This was clear in the Persian Gulf where Western-Soviet rivalry began during the war after a joint Anglo-Russian invasion of Iran in 1941 to protect supply routes and oil and eliminate German influence. By treaty, both promised to withdraw within six months of the end of hostilities; Anglo-American forces did, but Russia did not until faced in 1946 by intense American pressure in response to Iran's appeal to the UN. Similarly, American pressure and that of the Arab League reinforced British efforts to extract France from Syria and Lebanon, finally completed in 1946. American influence soon fully replaced that of Britain in Saudi Arabia as Lend-Lease compensated for wartime loss of pilgrim traffic and temporary inability to expand American-dominated oil production; the Zionist movement also shifted its focus to New York during the war.

In Palestine, British efforts to restrict Jewish immigration to prevent an Arab explosion and retain regional Arab support clashed with the determination of Holocaust survivors to reach it and with American domestic politics, as the Democratic party in power supported them. The Arab two-thirds of the population in 1945 did not see why the Holocaust should be resolved at its expense, nor did the Arab League which agreed on the Palestine issue and on ousting Britain from the Middle East, if on little else. As illegal immigrants arrived despite British efforts at interdiction, Zionist guerrilla units engaged in violence which Britain tried to suppress, outraging American opinion, if not key Washington circles. In 1947, London informed the UN that it would withdraw in 1948. Civil war followed, particularly after the UN, with Soviet and American support, opted for partition, which Arabs opposed. As Britain withdrew in May 1948, transferring power to nobody, Israel declared independence, which Moscow and Washington recognized at once. War ensued, in which Israel gained one-third more territory and a million Arabs became refugees. In 1949 Israel was admitted to the UN on condition that the refugees could return or choose compensation.

Meanwhile, the Middle East's political centre had shifted to Cairo, which dominated the Arab League. Though Egypt was supposedly independent, Britain had of military necessity treated it humiliatingly as a recalcitrant colony during the war. Resentment erupted once the war was over, reinforced by inflation hurting the middle class and by a huge British financial debt to Egypt. Intense nationalism led to assassination of leaders who were or were thought to be pro-British. As Britain tried to avoid real independence, negotiations deadlocked. However, it was clear that here, as elsewhere, Britain's moment in the Middle East had passed.

In sub-Saharan Africa, the war's effects were less immediate but more profound, except in neutral Portugal's colonies. Both the British and the Free French, whose initial military base lay in French Equatorial Africa, relied heavily on African troops. Those from French colonies served in Ethiopia, Madagascar, North Africa, the Levant, Italy, and France. British Africans also served in Italian East Africa and Madagascar as well as India, Burma, and Indochina. They were well fed and clothed, taught to read and write, and gained technical skills and wider political horizons. In the Middle East and India they encountered anti-imperial movements and literature, which they sent home. Military service in other parts of Africa increased pan-Africanism. In Burma, they met Indians, African Indians, American blacks, and West Indians with resulting cross-fertilization of ideas. Everywhere they saw white men destroying each other and recognized that they were not invincible. The rivalry between the Free French and Vichy, which was more repressive and racist than pre-war Parisian policy, particularly impaired European prestige.

The economic contribution was also large, both financially and in goods as Africa was pressed to supply Allied needs, not its own. Colonies endured frustrating economic controls but were allowed hitherto forbidden activities, partly to save shipping, and ordered to produce sometimes startling items, especially in French West Africa where Vichy's orders reflected Nazi desires. An official there countered a demand for honey with: 'Agreed honey. Send bees.'[4] More forced labour, especially in Vichy-controlled areas, intensified resentment, as did conscription, shortages, and price inflation, though some areas, notably Zanzibar and the Belgian Congo, prospered thanks to loss of Asian competitors. On the other hand, industrialization, urbanization with accompanying shanty towns, new job opportunities as whites left, and the fact that some colonies virtually ran themselves for the war's duration led to rising political ferment along with ambitions and expectations. Afterwards Africa had larger cities, more industry, and better transportation, especially air networks, and briefly was richer than some masters.

During the war, Britain sent cheap battery-powered radios to African villages to receive British propaganda, but villagers also learned of the Atlantic Charter, the United Nations Charter, and other wartime democratic proposals. Though Churchill claimed that the Atlantic Charter's promise of 'the right of all peoples to choose the form of government in which they live' and its desire to see 'sovereign rights and self-government restored to those who have been forcibly deprived of them' did not apply to the British Empire, both Roosevelt and Attlee dissented, as did Africans. As the war served as a catalyst for nationalism, African elites in British and French colonies rejected colonialism altogether and formed or revitalized political parties by 1945. In British colonies these were territorial, not tribal; in French Africa they were inter-territorial.

The war taught Africans to listen to new leaders and to be much more nationalistic, but it did not teach Europeans to be much less imperialistic. Britain and France made wartime plans for modest reform and more expenditure but rejected progress toward independence, providing too little too late. Both knew empire was vital to their power and international status, and both intended, like other European powers in Africa, to retain what they held. But they overlooked the impact of India's fight for independence, China's peasant revolution, and Ho's struggle in Vietnam. Both foresaw no end to colonies and still recruited for their colonial services, but both were thinly represented in much of Africa and had relied on collaborators achieved by power or the illusion thereof in terms of white prestige and superiority. By 1945, the collaborators, the power, and the prestige were largely gone. Further, full suffrage and semi-responsible government in Jamaica in 1944 and UN-sponsored independence for Libya in 1951 (since the great powers could not agree on its future) contributed to rising expectations which European overlords did little to meet.

*   *   *

In part, they were preoccupied elsewhere, especially in Europe, with recovery and the deteriorating East–West relationship, which seemed far more immediate to fearful Europeans than tensions in distant colonies. Survival in extreme austerity, repairing the damage, and economic revival preoccupied most. In the east, recovery was especially slow, despite UN efforts in Allied states, because Russia stripped its satellites of their assets to aid Soviet reconstruction. Lack of Polish exports affected the west, as did the flood of refugees from Soviet-occupied areas. UN efforts, American loans, and colonial products did not suffice to counter food and coal shortages, plus loss of overseas assets, markets, and such invisible exports as financial services and shipping profits. Governments were precarious, and Communist parties growing, bolstered by Russia's victory and their own wartime Resistance efforts, particularly in France and Italy. In addition, the winter of 1946–47 was exceptionally brutal.

An exhausted Britain, which still held a large Empire, struggled until 1947 to retain its power, prestige, and world role, along with the American tie. Indeed, a young candidate for a Foreign Office career, when asked to name the most important things in the world, supposedly replied, 'Love and the Anglo-American relationship.'[5] But it was living on loans, coping with devastation and a shattered economy, as damaged in the power sense by

World War II as France had been by World War I. In February 1947, it decided to withdraw from India (including Pakistan), Ceylon, Burma, and Palestine, and informed Washington that it could not continue economic and military aid to Greece and Turkey, in effect abandoning a traditional British eastern Mediterranean sphere. In short, Britain abdicated its world role to the United States, which had already supplanted it in Australia, New Zealand, and much of the Middle East.

These factors and others contributed to the advent of a Soviet–American Cold War, which had been increasingly likely for several years as the wartime marriage of convenience frayed. Tensions usually arise in victorious coalitions as wars end, especially as divisive questions are postponed and then begin to divide, as happened regarding Germany. Roosevelt had sought post-war collaboration, and both parties made an effort in 1945–46, Washington recognizing east European regimes and seeking a comprehensive settlement, Moscow holding troops back from western borders and making some concessions. But distrust was mutual and fundamental, and the actions of each strengthened opponents of compromise in the other. Though they were now dominant, neither could halt the spread of the other's influence. Two towering actors on the world stage, they talked not to one another but past each other. Their perceptions and misperceptions were crucial, often based on ignorance of the other. Both felt insecure, and the other's actions heightened this feeling.

For Stalin, whose nation now bestrode half of Europe and much of Asia, security was territorial, especially a buffer zone against Germany. He had little comprehension of Western political processes or the role of public opinion, and no concern for appearances. His actions in eastern Europe, especially Poland, led to new hatred there and more American reluctance to accept a Soviet sphere. In 1947, he created the Communist Information Bureau (Cominform) to tighten control over east European satellites and effectively to revive the Comintern, nominally dissolved in 1943 to placate Western Allies. Stalin shared the traditional Russian suspicion of foreigners as well as the Marxist distrust of capitalist democracies, remarking in the autumn of 1945, 'I think we can tear off the veil of amity, some semblance of which the Americans are so eager to preserve.'[6] In February 1946, Stalin, who made all key decisions himself, spoke of capitalist encirclement and announced new Five Year Plans to defend Russia economically and militarily against its ring of enemies. In time, Washington's military budget and creation of new overseas bases proved to him that Truman was leading an anti-Soviet coalition which threatened to strangle Russia.

Stalin's fears were a bit previous but partially justified. The United States emerged from the war feeling threatened by Soviet domination of much of Eurasia, particularly after Soviet brutality in Poland was evident. American opinion, especially Roman Catholic organizations, turned anti-Soviet by the end of 1945. Truman, who was less inclined than Roosevelt to chalk Soviet behaviour up to insecurity and who doubted that Stalin's suspicions could be allayed, decided by early 1946 that Soviet actions endangered American security and must be resisted. Involvement, not isolation, was necessary because American security required military and economic expansion, the latter to gain raw materials, especially oil. Still, Churchill's famous speech in March 1946 declaring that an Iron Curtain had clanged down across Europe was criticized as a call for an anti-Soviet alliance by a Britain which had reverted to the historic feud and hoped to stiffen the American stance. But 'containment', which soon became the American policy, was already being discussed. Washington understood that Russia was too weak as yet for war, but feared it could exploit power vacuums, chaos, civil wars, dislocation, and decolonization in an effort to export Communism and overthrow capitalism. In this, the United States probably overreacted; Stalin was willing to expand where that entailed little risk but was less imperialist than Washington assumed and more obsessed with security. As Americans tried to create an international order compatible with their interests and way of life, creating overseas bases and a new ideology of national security in the process, Russian expansion was seen as a strategic threat, a danger to free markets and private property, an indicator of a master plan to spread south and west, and a barrier to the world Washington sought. Thus it opted for anti-Communism and containment, abandoning conciliation in favour of propaganda and covert operations. In response, Soviet distrust mounted.

*   *   *

When Britain declared in February 1947 its inability to continue aid to Greece and Turkey, Washington moved beyond rhetoric to action. Civil war raged in Greece, with Communist guerrillas receiving Yugoslav Communist support but little Russian aid. A militarily and economically weak Turkey faced Soviet demands for military bases and a new Straits regime enabling it to become a Mediterranean power. The Truman Doctrine of March 1947 not only ensured economic and military aid to both states but promised assistance to any state resisting Communist attacks. Global containment of Communism was launched.

Then in June at Harvard University, Marshall, now Secretary of State, offered the European Recovery Programme (Marshall Plan) of financial aid 'not against any country or doctrine' but 'against hunger, poverty, desperation, and chaos'.[7] American motives were several. The terrible winter had taken a social and economic toll which might lead to Communist victories in the 1948 French and Italian elections; European countries apparently soon would be unable to purchase American products and agricultural surpluses, thus retarding their recovery and American prosperity; west European collapse and Communist advances should be prevented; and Europe should be pressed toward economic integration. As Washington expected and hoped, Moscow refused to join and obliged its satellites to decline as well. Though it would have liked American aid on its own terms, it was unwilling to reveal its financial needs, as required, and objected to aspects involving continental co-operation. Stalin thought the Plan would increase American influence in Europe and threaten Soviet hegemony in the east by trying to destabilize the region. The Plan, which lasted until the end of 1951, indeed increased American influence in the west, aided European recovery, checked further Communist advances in Europe, ensured a market for American products, and provided an early impetus toward European integration as well as widening the East–West divide.

Action bred counter-action. After the three Western Allies announced currency reforms in their zones of Germany and Berlin as a step toward merger of their zonal regimes, Moscow in June 1948 cut off rail and road access to Berlin, hoping to prevent unification and perhaps to gain all of Germany easily. In response, an Anglo-American airlift, Operation Vittles, supplied Berlin's western zones with food and fuel during the 300 days of the blockade until May 1949. The emergency led to closer Anglo-French-American co-ordination of dealings with Russia, though Washington negotiated resolution of the crisis alone with Moscow.

The blockade also produced a British proposal for a military organization to parallel the Marshall Plan, to allay a sense of insecurity, and to prevent accidental war, though deliberate Soviet military aggression seemed unlikely. Thus the North Atlantic Treaty Organization (NATO) – including Italy and Portugal, and later Greece and Turkey – came into being in April 1949. As its British first secretary-general remarked, it was designed 'to keep the Americans in, the Germans down, and the Russians out'.[8] At first more symbolic than solid, it became a serious military organization after Russia's first atomic explosion later in 1949.

In 1950, the preoccupation with Europe was suddenly jarred by North Korea's invasion of South Korea. The 'temporary' Soviet and American occupation zones had bred two states, one Marxist, one capitalist, each eager to invade the other. The North did so in June with Soviet approval, arms, and air support and Chinese consent, after announcement of an American defence perimeter which seemed to exclude South Korea. Washington, which had withdrawn its troops, acted quickly. As Moscow was boycotting the UN to protest continued seating of Nationalist China, the United States achieved a resolution for the UN to resist aggression (as the League had never done) in South Korea,* then led its diverse military coalition there. Peking did not object to liberation of South Korea but warned against American invasion of the North. When that occurred, it invaded in turn. Eventual stalemate near the 38th parallel led to a 1953 armistice and continuing division. It also

---

* The UN did not act militarily against aggression again until 1991 in response to Iraq's invasion of Kuwait. The Soviet Union never again boycotted it.

produced greater stature for the new China, frozen Sino-American relations, an American containment policy in Asia against China, and a new American defence perimeter including South Korea, the Philippines, Taiwan, and Vietnam.

By then, the Cold War dominated American policy, which assumed a global Communist conspiracy. Washington moved to counter that as military budgets skyrocketed, causing inflation and deficit financing. It bolstered Taiwan, financed France in Vietnam as Ho's struggle was subsumed by the Cold War, and saw any Marxist move anywhere as a threat to its security and freedom. The Cold War ensured continuance of the division of Germany and Europe as well as of Korea and Vietnam – and in a sense of the world. Both superpowers remained in the heart of Europe in force, shattering what remained of the old power balance. The Soviet empire, like others before it, rested chiefly on coercion or the threat of it, the American bloc primarily on consent, though Washington made the decisions. As Stalin's physical and mental health deteriorated, the Cold War provided an external foe as a rationale for domestic repression; similarly it offered justification for projecting American power globally, as Washington encouraged regional alliances and created bases which Moscow found threatening. A nuclear race ensued, followed by a space race and a missile race, but the atomic bomb's sheer horror generated a balance of terror and a Cold Peace, preventing total war. Some historians suggest that it deserved the Nobel Peace Prize.

*   *   *

The Cold War much affected further developments in Europe and elsewhere, additional decolonization, American attitudes toward new and existing states, and the rehabilitation of Germany and Japan. Both the latter were occupied and subjected by the victors to large-scale trials of alleged war criminals for waging aggressive war and the new offence of crimes against humanity, with death, life imprisonment, and other sentences resulting. But restrictions were relaxed as the Cold War became established, for the United States and its allies wished to use both against the Soviet bloc. Thus West Germany and Japan enjoyed dramatic economic miracles and an economic and political revival which soon outpaced Britain, now falling out of the ranks of the great powers. In the end, the losers did not lose as the second tier victors did.

The division of Germany was not planned but emerged with and from the Cold War. Zonal boundaries meant that Russia had the agriculture, Britain the industry and the costliest zone to administer, the United States the scenery.[9] As Moscow denuded its zone, London and Washington rebuilt – along with intense German efforts – in the west. In September 1946, the three Western powers began a phased merger of their zones, culminating three years later in creation of the German Federal Republic (DBR or West Germany) as a buffer against Russia. Allied troops remained, as

Washington reluctantly committed itself to a long-term occupation to block Moscow, who responded with creation of the German Democratic Republic (DDR or East Germany).

Japan emerged a little later, thanks largely to the Korean War. Disarmed and demilitarized, it was confined to its home islands, including the Ryukyus. Its former Pacific outposts were under American trusteeship until independence, in a UN system not unlike the League's mandates. Japan's devastation was less severe than Germany's; though it had lost its trade and shipping, the early Cold War started a trade revival in 1947. Washington intended and began to make sweeping reforms, but as the Chinese civil war indicated in 1947–48 that China would not be the regional ally and relations with Moscow worsened, its focus shifted to reconstruction and stability rather than reform, though demilitarization continued. The outbreak of the Korean War in 1950 was decisive economically and politically. American spending during that war provided an economic stimulus of which Japanese industriousness took full advantage. American experts wrote in a week a Japanese constitution which blended monarchy, democracy, and pacifism and which improbably took root. Then a peace treaty in 1951, to which Russia was not a party, ended the American occupation, although bases remained, primarily in the Ryukyus. Later American efforts to rearm Japan against China and Russia were stubbornly resisted by a population now attached to pacifism.

No peace treaty could be agreed for Germany, but the Cold War greatly facilitated integration of both halves into their respective blocs. With Germany weakened and divided and France's security needs met by the American commitment to NATO, West Germany could be reintegrated into western Europe. This happened first economically as the Russo-American confrontation produced a startling Franco-German rapprochement, but because Moscow had a military edge in Europe, if not globally, West Germany was invited into NATO in 1954 and thus allowed to rearm in 1955. In response, Russia created the east bloc Warsaw Pact.

Meanwhile, western Europe had begun halting steps toward political and economic unity with the foundation of the Council of Europe in 1949 and the European Coal and Steel Community in 1951. Gradual moves toward further integration continued with American support but according to European plans. In part, Britain, France, Italy, and West Germany were seeking with limited success, despite British hesitations and de Gaulle's efforts to lead France to the past, to gain a greater voice together to replace the stature they had individually lost. East European states, including those born of World War I, had lost a good deal more, including independence officially or unofficially. For 45 years the Red Army repressed national and historic rivalries in the east; Germany's division until 1989 meant it no longer distorted Europe's power balance.

*　　　*　　　*

West European integration in part hoped to compensate for continuing global decline as empires melted away. Initially both Moscow and Washington were anti-colonial, with the latter viewing itself and Britain as 'an enlightened son and a wayward father'[10] though less wayward than other European powers. Moscow continued to support independence movements, capitalizing on anti-Western sentiment in colonies, but the Cold War led Washington to opt for stability and for strengthening European allies. However, the UN Charter contained an explicit goal of colonial emancipation; the UN, like the Commonwealth, became a forum for protest against the existing system by anti-colonial states. Its Trusteeship Council was not dominated by the great powers, for Latin American, Asian, and African states were elected and tried to speed decolonization in general though the Council was officially concerned with former Japanese and Italian colonies. This factor, along with colonial rebellion and growing European inability to counter it, meant that from 1945 to 1975 more than a quarter of the world's population achieved independence.

In 1957, Ghana led off the second round of decolonization, chiefly in Africa. In Asia, independence movements centred in geographically discrete island groups or peninsulas with separate languages and cultures; they did not much affect each other, nor were they greatly influenced by events elsewhere. But in Africa, Asian struggles (especially the decisive French defeat in Vietnam at Dienbienphu in 1954) and events in other colonies had great effect for colonies were not geographically isolated, and borders were random and recent, with languages, tribes, and cultures crossing political lines. Moreover, white settlers were largely concentrated in the extreme north and south of Africa where resistance to independence was most prolonged.

Britain intended to retain its remaining colonies, which cushioned a declining world role and masked economic inefficiency, but it proved too weak, particularly as willing collaborators disappeared and rule by force was necessary. It chalked the nationalist ferment up to a 'Communist conspiracy,' jailing 'agitators'; as earlier in Asia, future prime ministers of new nations were schooled in British prisons. France was at first equally determined to retain its Empire, but defeat in Vietnam in 1954 just as a new war of liberation began in Algeria soon decided it to grant longtime collaborators in sub-Saharan African colonies nominal independence with close economic, financial, and military ties ensuring neocolonialism for some years. Thus, most of Africa except Portuguese colonies gained independence in 1960 or soon thereafter. Within a few more years, the world's two greatest empires had been reduced to tiny outposts which the French called 'confetti'. In this, public indifference in Europe, French governmental instability, and the anti-imperial tradition of Britain's Labour Party all played a role.

The infant states were not allowed a peaceful childhood. Tribal rivalries which European overlords had suppressed now erupted, giving

Moscow and Washington a chance to compete by proxy in wars and civil wars with aid, advisers, covert operations, and troops; former colonial powers also intervened, at least to rescue Europeans and sometimes to restore order. The United States usually backed anti-Communist regimes, however dictatorial, as in Latin America, whereas the Soviet Union exploited anti-Western sentiment. New nations scrambled to avoid being squashed or becoming puppets, learning the wisdom of the African saying that 'When elephants fight, it is the grass that gets trampled.'[11] One result was creation of a Non-Aligned Movement under Indonesian, Indian, Egyptian, and Yugoslav leadership from 1955 on. It aimed to become a third force but never succeeded though a majority of the world's people soon were represented in its members, most of whom were Asian, African, or Latin American. They agreed on an end to colonialism and racial discrimination, on disarmament, economic co-operation, and UN membership, but on little else. Many were not neutral and some were not non-aligned, being clients of one side or the other, especially of Moscow.

By this time, it had become commonplace to speak of the First World, meaning the American-led bloc, the Second World of Soviet-dominated states, and the Third World of the others, though extremely impoverished states were sometimes termed Fourth World. It had also become routine to speak of a bipolar world and a north/south axis. Both these latter terms are over-simplifications. The north/south axis refers to the haves and have-nots, the rich nations of the world and the poor, usually underdeveloped ones. Though states north of the equator tended to have noticeably higher standards of living than those south of it, any Mongolian herder would have much envied the comforts of an Australian or Argentinian rancher, whereas most Spanish peasants would have thrilled at the life of South African whites. However, with notable exceptions, the comfortable middle-class industrial societies – which also held the lion's share of arable land – were in the north, while impoverished one-crop former colonies, with barely marginal peasants and urban slums ringing cities, concentrated in the south.

Similarly, the east–west divide into a bipolar world was not tidy. There were some genuinely neutral states, and both blocs frayed and had defeats in retaining allies. In the east, Yugoslavia left the Soviet bloc and became an independent Marxist state in 1948. In 1960, China split off, creating a separate secondary power centre, followed by Albania, which found Yugoslavia a useful buffer against the Warsaw Pact. In the West, most of Latin America remained, however grudgingly, in Washington's orbit, but Cuba did not. After Fidel Castro seized power there in 1959, it asserted its independence and then became an economically dependent client of Moscow. France never left the Western bloc but under de Gaulle's leadership it withdrew from NATO's military command, ousted it from France, and created its own atomic bomb to assert its independence. And intermediate centres of power, at least economically, began to emerge in China, Japan, India, Brazil, the Arab-led Organization of the Petroleum Exporting Countries (OPEC), and Israel, as well as Germany. This further diffused power, mostly out of Europe and especially into Asia and the Middle East.

*   *   *

Change and continuity marched together. Nationalism remained as powerful as ever, perhaps more so as additional national states emerged. The sovereign state continued as the basis of the international system, a fact reflected in the structure of the United Nations. But there were nearly three times as many states. More nations meant more diplomats from one to another or to the proliferating international organizations, many of them regional. Brussels developed an enormous diplomatic corps as many states sent three ambassadors to Belgium, NATO, and the European Economic Community created in 1958. At the other extreme, some new Lilliputian states sent only one envoy – to the UN, where he could meet representatives of almost all other states. Non-governmental organizations and subnational entities entered international politics as well.

Such an expansion of numbers led to a certain democratization of diplomacy in some states. More members of the middle class entered the diplomatic corps, as did women and blacks; diplomatic wives were no longer required to act as full-time unpaid embassy servants. The diplomatic ranks were further swelled by new roles as the United States, Britain, Canada, and other Western nations engaged in cultural diplomacy in terms of educational exchanges, information centres and libraries, and technical assistance, as did Russia. Language followed power as English became the universal language of diplomacy, eclipsing French almost altogether.

As the ranks of professional diplomats swelled, their roles diminished, owing to technology. Television, transistor radios, and later innovations shaped opinion and thus affected foreign policy, as did a vastly increased role for propaganda, also usually in English. Jet aeroplanes reduced an ambassador's negotiating role since foreign ministers could engage in frequent summits, whether of the two superpowers, the leading economic states, or regional groupings. The United States invented shuttle diplomacy in trying to deal with the Palestinian problem, which continued to fester in a new form, as one senior statesman after another winged from Israel's capital to Arab ones and back in search of a solution.

Technology shrank the globe, causing Western influence, culture, language, and technology to spread as Western empires receded. But technical progress and a global village had their negative aspect, for man's power to kill had multiplied a thousandfold, propaganda now inflamed opinion on a mass scale, and medical advances curbed epidemics, causing a population explosion and thus famines. Poor, hungry, and impatient nations were particularly to be found where populations soared.

Increasingly, they demanded a greater share of the world's wealth, as television brought images of the West's affluence into their consciousness. As change accelerated dramatically, their effect in the future remained unclear.

*   *   *

Though the world of 1950 and later was sharply different from that of 1930 and even more so from that of 1910, it was not entirely new. Past history, hatreds, cultural traditions, and economic patterns still affected the circumstances in which states, old and new, conducted their relations with each other. But the days when five or six individual European states decided the destiny of much of the world were now only a memory. Since the ancient Roman Empire, Europe had more often than not dominated events, thanks to a power gap and, in modern times, a technological advantage – which by the latter half of the twentieth century no longer existed. Two great wars brought the end of the Austro-Hungarian, Ottoman, Italian, German, Japanese, British, and French empires and dropped the states in question out of the first rank or in some instances removed them from the world stage altogether. Loss of empire only heightened Europe's physical, psychic, economic, financial, and demographic losses of the second great world war. It is said that 'when American and Soviet forces met on the Elbe in April 1945, a European civil war, which had begun in 1914, ended with the fate of Europe in the hands of two extra-European powers.'[12] After 1945, not Europe but the West collectively, led by the United States, continued to dominate economically thanks to continued wealth, technical preeminence, and faith in its own superiority, but these advantages increasingly faced challenges. Where power would shift next remained uncertain, but probably further from Europe.

During World War II, if not before, Europe had ceased to shape the world, as became clear afterwards, for the European state system, which had dominated for centuries – and increasingly so, no longer ruled. Europe was now a shrunken continent, especially in the power realignment generated by World War II and its aftermath. Both individually and collectively, the surviving former European great nations became greybeards, elder statesmen full of advice and possessing some influence but not much far-ranging authority. In this changed power configuration, Europe remained prominent but no longer dominant on the global stage; rather, it had become an important member of the supporting cast in the world's ongoing historical drama.[13]

◆ Notes to Chapter 18

1. 1 Michael Schaller, *The United States and China in the Twentieth Century*, 2nd edn (New York, OUP, 1990), p. 94.

2. Walter Kent and Nat Burton, 'The White Cliffs of Dover' (London, 1941, http://www.volcano.net/~jackmearl/.../wsongs/white_cliffs_of_dover.ht ml).
3. See, for example, Jill Ker Conway, *The Road from Coorain* (New York, Vintage, 1989), pp. 67–9, 183, 208.
4. Michael Crowder, 'The 1939–45 War and West Africa', in J. F. A. Ajayi and Michael Crowder, eds, *History of West Africa*, 2 vols (New York, Columbia University Press, 1973), II, p. 607.
5. Robert M. Hathaway, *Ambiguous Partnership: Britain and America, 1944–1947* (New York, Columbia University Press, 1981), p. 5.
6. Richard Overy, *Russia's War* (London, Allen Lane, 1998), p. 334.
7. Charles L. Robertson, *International Politics since World War II* (Armonk, NY, M. E. Sharpe, 1966), p. 91.
8. Alan Sharp, 'Reflections on the Remaking of Europe: 1815, 1919, 1945, post-1989', *Irish Studies in International Affairs*, VIII (1997), p. 16.
9. Gerhard L. Weinberg, *Germany, Hitler, and World War II* (Cambridge, CUP, 1995), p. 191.
10. Wm Roger Louis, *Imperialism at Bay* (Oxford, Clarendon Press, 1977), p. 19.
11. Richard Goff, Walter Moss, Janice Terry and Jiu-hwa Upshur, *The Twentieth Century: A Brief Global History*, 5th edn (Boston, McGraw Hill, 1998), p. 295.
12. Sharp, 'Reflections,' p. 17.
13. For the further history of the twentieth century, see P. M. H. Bell, *The World Since 1945: An International History* (London, Edward Arnold, 2001).

FURTHER READING

Note: Space considerations dictate exclusion of the following categories even if cited in the notes: 1) primary materials; 2) foreign language works; 3) articles; 4) memoirs, biographies, and autobiographies; 5) studies of a single independent country (with a few non-Western exceptions) unless it is at least nominally a great power; 6) works seriously deficient in accuracy, clarity, organization, or focus; 7) books on narrow topics; 8) works which are not fairly readily available.

◆ General

For a summary history of diplomacy with bibliography, see 'Diplomacy', *Encyclopaedia Britannica* (15th edn, Chicago, 1991), Macropedia, XVII, pp. 331–40. The rise of the modern state system may be traced in any basic European history text.

The best general survey of twentieth-century international history is William R. Keylor, *The Twentieth Century World: An International History* (Oxford, 2000 edn). Richard Goff, Walter Moss, Janice Terry, and Jiu-Hwa Upshur, *The Twentieth Century: A Brief Global History* (Boston, 1998 edn) provides a summary of all aspects of the century with unusual emphasis on Latin American and the non-Western world. Gordon A. Craig and Felix Gilbert, eds, *The Diplomats, 1919–1939* (2 vols, New York, 1965 edn) remains a classic. Its successor, Gordon A. Craig and Francis L. Loewenheim, eds, *The Diplomats, 1939–1979* (Princeton, 1994) is also useful. Paul Kennedy, *The Rise and Fall of the Great Powers* (New York, 1989 edn) surveys five centuries unevenly R. P. Barston, ed., *The Other Powers: Studies in the Foreign Policies of Small States* (London, 1973) remains valuable, especially for its global coverage. Frank McDonough, *The Origins of the First and Second World Wars* (Cambridge, 1997) is brief and largely European but contains good short summaries of the historical debates about both wars.

Surveys of twentieth-century Europe are numerous. Among the more recent and useful are Felix Gilbert, *The End of the European Era, 1890 to the Present* (New York, 1984 edn), Martin Kitchen, *Europe Between the Wars: A Political History* (London, 1988), and especially J. M. Roberts, *Europe, 1880–1945* (London, 1989). Paul Hayes, ed., *Themes in Modern European History, 1890–1945* (New York, 1992) contains a number of useful essays. Derek H. Aldcroft, *The European Economy, 1914–1970* (New York, 1977) provides a clear brief summary without jargon or mathematical formulae. Surveys of other continents are listed under those continents.

◆   The Coming of the First World War

The literature is vast. Two classic works, still valuable, are Luigi Albertini, *The Origins of the War of 1914*, tr. Isabella M. Massey (3 vols, London, 1952–3) and Sidney B. Fay, *The Origins of the World War* (2 vols, New York, 1966 edn). The finest short work is James Joll, *The Origins of the First World War* (London, 1984). Gordon Martel, *The Origins of the First World War* (2nd edn, London, 1996) provides a brief and good starting point. Fritz Fischer, *War of Illusions: German Policies from 1911 to 1914* (London, 1975) is controversial but important. Fischer's student, Imanuel Geiss, in *July 1914: The Outbreak of the First World War* (New York, 1967) provides an admirable summary of the July crisis. John W. Langdon, *July 1914: The Long Debate, 1918–1900* (New York, 1991) analyses the historiographic argument. Two recent works, David G. Hermann, *The Arming of Europe and the Making of the First World War* (Princeton, 1996) and David Stevenson, *Armaments and the Coming of War: Europe, 1904–1914* (Oxford, 1996) examine the role of the arms race, especially in land armaments.

Macmillan's (now Palgrave's) The Making of the Twentieth Century series offers a good set of studies of the role of individual great powers: V. R. Berghahn, *Germany and the Approach of War in 1914* (London, 1993 edn); Richard Bosworth, *Italy and the Approach of the First World War* (London, 1983); John F. V. Keiger, *France and the Origins of the First World War* (London, 1983); D. C. B. Lieven, *Russia and the Origins of the First World War* (London, 1983); Zara S. Steiner, *Britain and the Origins of the First World War* (London, 1977); Samuel R. Williamson Jr, *Austria-Hungary and the Origins of the First World War* (London, 1991).

◆The First World War

David Stevenson, *The First World War and International Politics* (Oxford, 1988) provides a clear survey of an extended era of international disequilibrium, addressing key questions. Z. A. B. Zeman's lively, readable *The Gentlemen Negotiators: A Diplomatic History of World War I* (New York, 1971) is still worthwhile. The final chapter of A. J. P. Taylor's *The Struggle for Mastery in Europe, 1848–1918* (Oxford, 1954) stresses efforts to gain and retain allies. Arno Mayer, *Political Origins of the New Diplomacy, 1917–18* (New Haven, 1959) is a controversial comparative study of the breakdown of Europe's political and ideological equilibrium. Gerd Hardach, *The First World War, 1914–1918* (Berkeley, 1977) deals with economic factors with admirable clarity. Kathleen Burk, *Britain, America and the Sinews of War, 1914–1918* (Boston, 1985) does the same on the financial side.

J. M. Bourne, *Britain and the Great War, 1914–1918* (London, 1989) is good on British military problems. David French, *British Strategy and War Aims, 1914–1916* (London, 1986) and *The Strategy of the Lloyd George Coalition, 1916–1918* (Oxford, 1995) are important works primarily devoted to diplomacy. David Stevenson, *French War Aims against Germany, 1914–1919* (Oxford, 1982) is the standard work on the subject. Hans W. Gatzke, *Germany's Drive to the West (Drang nach Westen): A Study of Germany's Western War Aims during the First World War* (Baltimore, 1950) was a pioneering study, whose conclusions are confirmed by Fritz Fischer's famous *Germany's Aims in the First World War* (New York, 1967).

Harold Nelson, *Land and Power: British and Allied Policy on Germany's Frontiers* (London, 1963) discusses inter-Allied negotiations. For German-Austrian relations and the eastern front, see Holger H. Herwig, *The First World War: Germany and Austria-Hungary, 1914–1918* (London, 1997). Ulrich Trumpener, *Germany and the Ottoman Empire, 1914–1918* (Princeton, 1968) concludes that Germany did not dominate Turkey. Frank G. Weber, *Eagles on the Crescent: Germany, Austria, and the Diplomacy of the Turkish Alliance, 1914–1918* (Ithaca, 1970) focuses more on Austro-German disagreement on Balkan and Turkish issues. The African war is addressed in a special issue of *The Journal of African History*, XIX:1 (1978) and in Byron Farwell, *The Great War in Africa, 1914–1918* (New York, 1986).

◆ The Russian Revolution

Entry level accounts include John M. Thompson, *Revolutionary Russia, 1917* (New York, 1981); Rex A. Wade, *The Russian Revolution, 1917* (Cambridge, 2000); Sheila Fitzpatrick, *Russian Revolution* (Oxford, 1982); and Edward Action, *Rethinking the Russian Revolution* (London, 1990). Richard Pipes, *The Russian Revolution* (New York, 1990) is massive, up-to-date, and anti-Bolshevik. None of these general works focus on foreign policy, but Richard K. Debo's two volumes *Revolution and Survival: The Foreign Policy of Soviet Russia, 1917–1918* (Toronto, 1979) and *Survival and Consolidation: The Foreign Policy of Soviet Russia, 1918–1921* (Buffalo, NY, 1992) provide an excellent, clear diplomatic analysis, including civil wars, Allied interventions, and Russo-German relations.

Evan Mawdsley, *The Russian Civil War* (Boston, 1987) brings clarity to a confusing subject. Until the Soviet archives are combed, John M. Thompson, *Russia, Bolshevism, and the Versailles Peace* (Princeton, 1966) remains standard, as does John W. Wheeler-Bennett, *Brest-Litovsk: The Forgotten Peace, March 1918* (New York, 1971 edn). George F. Kennan's *Russia and the West under Lenin and Stalin* (Boston, 1960) and *Soviet-American Relations,*

1917–1920 (2 vols, Princeton, 1956) are outdated in some respects and lack scepticism about American policy but are admirably clear, readable, and focused. Equally clear but based on extensive archival research is Georg Schild's solid *Between Ideology and Realpolitik: Woodrow Wilson and the Russian Revolution, 1917–1921* (Westport, 1995). David S. Fogelsong, *America's Secret War against Bolshevism: US Intervention in the Russian Civil War, 1917–1920* (Chapel Hill, 1995) stresses anti-German and especially anti-Bolshevik motives.

Georges Haupt, *Socialism and the Great War: The Collapse of the Second International* (Oxford, 1972) is useful on socialism and the coming of the war. Julius Braunthal, *History of the International*, tr. John Clark (2 vols, New York, 1967) is old, ponderous, and ideological but contains much information. A more recent study, Kevin McDermott and Jeremy Agnew, *The Comintern: A History of International Communism from Lenin to Stalin* (New York, 1996) is chiefly useful for historiography and a chapter on Asia. Tim Rees and Andrew Thorpe, eds, *International Communism and the Communist International, 1919–1943* (Manchester, 1998) is more international, containing essays with a global reach.

◆ The Peace Settlements

The essential introductory survey is Alan Sharp, *The Versailles Settlement: Peace-making in Paris, 1919* (London, 1991). On the Versailles treaty, the latest international scholarship is contained in Manfred F. Boemeke, Gerald D. Feldman, and Elisabeth Glaser, eds, *The Treaty of Versailles: A Reassessment after 75 Years* (Cambridge, 1998). Arno Mayer's early *The Politics and Diplomacy of Peacemaking* (New York, 1967) is controversial, ideological, and heavily researched. Inga Floto, *Colonel House in Paris* (Princeton, 1980) covers much ground, while Lorna S. Jaffe carefully addresses *The Decision to Disarm Germany* (Boston, 1985). Wm Roger Louis, *Great Britain and Germany's Lost Colonies, 1914–1919* (Oxford, 1967) remains the standard work. Thomas J. Knock, *To End All Wars: Woodrow Wilson and the Quest for a New World Order* (New York, 1992) deals ably with the pre-history of the League of Nations in the United States. Warren F. Kuehl's earlier *Seeking World Order: The United States and International Organization to 1920* (Nashville, 1969) continues the story. George W. Egerton, *Great Britain and the Creation of the League of Nations* (Chapel Hill, 1978) is an excellent counterpart.

On the policies of the great powers, Michael Dockrill and J. Douglas Goold, *Peace without Promise: Britain and the Peace Conferences, 1919–1923* (Hamden, 1981) is uneven, as is Antony Lentin, *Lloyd George, Woodrow Wilson, and the Guilt of Germany* (Baton Rouge, 1985). Klaus Schwabe, *Woodrow Wilson, Revolutionary Germany, and Peacemaking,*

1918–1919, tr. Robert and Rita Kimber (Chapel Hill, 1985) and Arthur Walworth, *Wilson and his Peacemakers* (New York, 1986) are much more substantial. Aside from David Stevenson's book on French war aims, listed above, little scholarly work written in English focuses on French policy. On Italy, H. James Burgwyn, *The Legend of the Mutilated Victory: Italy, the Great War, and the Paris Peace Conference, 1915–1919* (Westport, CT, 1993) provides a well-researched study. There are also specialized works addressing the diplomacy of the Four regarding Belgium, Greece, Poland, Rumania, and Yugoslavia.

Russell H. Fifield, *Woodrow Wilson and the Far East* (New York, 1952) focuses on the Shantung question in 1919, whereas Roy W. Curry, *Woodrow Wilson and Far Eastern Policy, 1913–1921* (New York, 1957) has a longer, broader reach. Both are well researched and have not been replaced. David Fromkin, *A Peace to End all Peace* (New York, 1989) deals with the Middle Eastern settlement, as does Z. N. Zeine, *The Struggle for Arab Independence: Western Diplomacy and the Rise and Fall of Feisal's Kingdom in Syria* (Beirut, 1960) in a more scholarly fashion. Paul C. Helmreich, *From Paris to Sèvres: the Partition of the Ottoman Empire at the Peace Conference of 1919–1920* (Columbus, OH, 1974) is the standard work on the treaty of Sèvres. Bülent Gökay, *A Clash of Empires: Turkey between Russian Bolshevism and British Imperialism, 1918–1923* (London, 1997) deals more with the Russo-British clash than with the peace treaties, whereas Salahi R. Sonyel, *Turkish Diplomacy, 1918–1923* (London, 1975) expresses the Turkish nationalist view. David Mitrany, *The Effect of the War in Southeastern Europe* (New Haven, 1936), despite its age, contains information not readily available elsewhere. Maria Ormos, *From Padua to the Trianon, 1918–1920*, tr. Miklos Uszkay (New York, 1990) is a solid, heavily archival study of the treaty of Trianon. Karl Stadler, *The Birth of the Austrian Republic, 1918–1921* (Leiden, 1966) covers the treaty of St Germain. The north-east European settlements are addressed in Stanley W. Page, *The Formation of the Baltic States* (Cambridge, MA, 1959).

◆ **Imperialism**

Raymond F. Betts, *Uncertain Dimensions: Western Overseas Empires in the Twentieth Century* (Minneapolis, 1985) is a useful standard work dealing primarily with non-Western areas in the interwar era. Roy F. Holland, *European Decolonization, 1918–1981* (New York, 1985) outlines long-term factors for weakening control and is especially good on World War II. Henri Grimal, *Decolonization: The British, French, Dutch and Belgian Empires, 1919–1963*, tr. Stephan De Vos (Westview, CO, 1978 edn) is a thoughtful survey by a French scholar. Philip D. Curtin, *The World and the*

West (Cambridge, 2000) offers topical essays on the responses to Western societies of Asia, Africa, and Indians of the Americas.

Literature on the British Empire is vast. Bernard Porter, *The Lion's Share: A Short History of British Imperialism, 1850–1970* (London, 1975) is lively, impressionistic, and thought-provoking. Equally thoughtful is D. A. Low, *Lion Rampant: Essays in the Study of British Imperialism* (London, 1973). Edward Grierson, *The Death of the Imperial Dream: The British Commonwealth and Empire, 1775–1969* (New York, 1972) is solid. A. J. Christopher, *The British Empire at its Zenith* (London, 1988) usefully takes up factors which are usually ignored.

Kenneth C. Wheare, *The Statute of Westminster and Dominion Status* (London, 1953 edn) is standard on the transition to the Commonwealth. Frank H. Underhill, *The British Commonwealth* (Durham, NC, 1956) provides a Canadian view. Denis Judd and Peter Slinn, *The Evolution of the Modern Commonwealth, 1902–80* (London, 1982) is brief, comprehensive, and clear. Nicholas Mansergh, *Survey of British Commonwealth Affairs: Problems of External Policy, 1931–1939* (London, 1952) is a valuable work of reference.

Nicholas Mansergh, *The Unresolved Question: The Anglo-Irish Settlement and its Undoing, 1912–72* (New Haven, CT, 1991) is heavily researched and solid. The same may be said of S. M. Burke and Salim Al-Din Quraishi, *The British Raj in India: An Historical Review* (New York, 1995), which focuses on the period from 1914 on. Stanley Wolpert, *A New History of India* (New York, 1989 edn) is also substantial. For the old Dominions, there is Philip G. Wigley, *Canada and the Transition to Commonwealth: British-Canadian Relations, 1917–1926* (Cambridge, 1977) as well as C. P. Stacey's excellent *Canada and the Age of Conflict* (2 vols, Toronto, 1977, 1981) and Amry Vandenbosch, *South Africa and the World* (Lexington, KY, 1970). On the budding policies of the antipodes, see T. B. Millar, *Australia in Peace and War: External Relations, 1788–1977* (New York, 1978) and Bernard K. Gordon, *New Zealand Becomes a Pacific Power* (Chicago, 1960).

On the French Empire, the works of Raymond F. Betts are essential, especially *Tricouleur: The French Overseas Empire* (London, 1978) and *France and Decolonization, 1900–1960* (London, 1991). Both examine both sides of the equation. Robert Aldrich, *Greater France* (New York, 1996) is also multi-faceted. Frederick Quinn, *The French Overseas Empire* (Westport, CT, 2000) is a serviceable survey. Christopher Andrew and A.S. Kanya-Forstner, *France Overseas: The Great War and the Climax of French Imperial Expansion* (London, 1981) examines Anglo-French imperial rivalries from the French side.

John T. McAlister, Jr, *Vietnam: The Origins of Revolution* (New York, 1969) examines Indochina under French rule. On the Maghrib, Richard M. Brace, *Morocco, Algeria, Tunisia* (Englewood Cliffs, NJ, 1964) is a brief, clear starting point. Samir Amin, *The Maghreb in the Modern World*, tr. Michael Perl (London, 1970) is also brief and clear with a heavy economic cast. Jamil M. Abun-Nasr, *A History of the Maghrib* (Cambridge, 1975 edn) is solid and useful, particularly as it includes material on Spanish Sahara and Libya.

Claudio Segrè, *Fourth Shore: The Italian Colonization of Libya* (Chicago, 1974) is well researched and written but primarily concerned with Italian settlement. Roger Anstey, *King Leopold's Legacy: The Congo under Belgian Rule, 1908–1960* (London, 1966) is substantial. James Duffy, *Portuguese Africa* (Cambridge, MA, 1959) is a standard work, while Gervase Clarence-Smith, *The Third Portuguese Empire, 1825–1975* (Manchester, 1985) is thorough on the interwar era. Malyn Newitt, *Portugal in Africa* (London, 1981) has a helpful chapter on the island groups. Stanley Karnow, *In Our Image: America's Empire in the Philippines* (New York, 1989) is valuable, especially on the terms arranged in the 1930s for independence. There are no readily available general studies of the Danish and Dutch empires.

◆ **Sub-Saharan Africa**

Note: Many of the works listed here contain contributions by many authors and thus tend to be uneven in quality.

The two final volumes of the UNESCO *General History of Africa* are essential: A. Adu Boahen, ed., *Africa under Colonial Domination, 1880–1935*, VII (London and Paris, 1985) and Ali A. Mazrui, ed., *Africa since 1935*, VIII (Paris, Berkeley, and Oxford 1993). L. H. Gann and Peter Duignan, *Colonialism in Africa, 1870–1960* (5 vols, Cambridge, 1969–75) is also a major work, of which II, *The History and Politics of Colonialism, 1914–1960* (1970) is particularly useful. Another multi-volume work, J. D. Fage and Roland Anthony, eds, *The Cambridge History of Africa* (8 vols, Cambridge, 1982–6) fills many holes, especially VII, A. D. Roberts, ed. (1986) covering 1905 to 1940.

Shorter works include J. D. Fage, *A History of Africa* (London, 1988 edn), which is especially strong on East Africa. Ali A. Mazrui, *Africa's International Relations: The Diplomacy of Dependence and Change* (London, 1977) is essential, as is Ali A. Mazrui and Michael Tidy, *Nationalism and New States in Africa from about 1935 to the Present* (Nairobi, 1984). Catherine Coquery-Vidrovitch, *Africa: Endurance and Change South of the Sahara*, tr. David Maisel (Berkeley, CA, 1988) analyses sociological factors, especially urban and rural movements. Imanuel Geiss, *The Pan-African Movement: A History of Pan-Africanism in America, Europe, and Africa*, tr. Ann Keep (New York, 1974) is exhaustive, able, and far-ranging. P. Olisanwuche Esedebe, *Pan-Africanism: the Idea and Movement, 1776–1991* (Washington, 1994) has a pan-Africa perspective, especially on the effect of the Ethiopian crisis.

General works primarily emphasizing the British colonies include Henry S. Wilson, *The Imperial Experience in Sub-Saharan Africa since 1870* (Minneapolis, 1977), Roland Oliver and J. D. Fage, *A Short History of Africa* (New York, 1964), and Roland Oliver and Anthony Atmore, *Africa since 1800* (Cambridge, 1972). John Chipman, *French Power in Africa* (Oxford, 1989) is useful for ideas, attitudes, and concepts. Patrick Manning, *Francophone Sub-Saharan Africa, 1880–1985* (Cambridge, 1988) is clear, brief, centred on 1900–1950, and inclusive of Belgian colonies. Jean Suret-Canale, *French Colonialism in Tropical Africa, 1900–1945*, tr. Till Gottheimer (New York, 1971) is a bitingly anti-imperial Marxist critique.

On west Africa, the second volume of J. F. A. Ajayi and Michael Crowder, eds, *History of West Africa* (2 vols, New York, 1973) is helpful on 1914–1945, especially essays by Crowder. An earlier work by the same author, *West Africa under Colonial Rule* (Evanston, IL, 1968) compares the impact of British and French rule. Alice L. Conklin, *A Mission to Civilize: The Republican Idea of Empire in France and West Africa, 1895–1930* (Stanford, CA, 1997), based on French and Senegalese archives, is valuable on Senegal and on forced labour. As a starting point, John D. Hargreaves, *West Africa: The Former French States* (Englewood Cliffs, NJ, 1967) provides a brief, thoughtful, topical, entry-level work.

Lewis H. Gann, *Central Africa: The Former British States* (Englewood Cliffs, NJ, 1971) is a clear basic starting point for the region. David Birmingham and Phyllis M. Martin, eds, *History of Central Africa* (2 vols, London, 1983) defines central Africa broadly, including French Equatorial Africa. Terence O. Ranger, ed., *Aspects of Central African History* (Evanston, IL, 1968) focuses on Africans and their emerging politics in Northern and Southern Rhodesia, Nyasaland, and the Belgian Congo. Robert I. Rotberg, *A Political History of Tropical Africa* (New York, 1965) is strongest on central and eastern Africa, aside from the Italian colonies.

Vincent Harlow, E. M. Chilver, and Alison Smith, eds, *History of East Africa*, II (Oxford, 1965) addresses the effect of colonial rule on Africans and their reactions in Uganda, Kenya, Tanganyika, and Zanzibar between the 1890s and 1945. Kenneth Ingram, *A History of East Africa* (London, 1962), based on African archives, is tedious but thorough. Stanley Diamond and Fred G. Burke, *The Transformation of East Africa: Studies in Political Anthropology* (New York, 1966) has some useful chapters, particularly on individual countries.

Bereket Habte Selassie, *Conflict and Intervention in the Horn of Africa* (New York, 1980) offers background on more recent events from an Eritrean perspective. Richard Sherman, *Eritrea: The Unfinished Revolution*

(New York, 1980) does the same on a narrower topic. Robert L. Hess, *Italian Colonialism in Somalia* (Chicago, 1966) is well researched but uncritical, having adopted the Italian viewpoint. Saadia Touval, *Somali Nationalism: International Politics and the Drive for Unity in the Horn to Africa* (Cambridge, MA, 1963) is a brief, clear, and balanced starting point. Like it, I. M. Lewis, *The Modern History of Somaliland: From Nation of State* (New York, 1965) covers an extended period and is useful. Virginia Thompson and Richard Adloff, *Djibouti and the Horn of Africa* (Stanford, CA, 1968) provides historical background to later events. Works on Ethiopia are listed with studies of the crises of the 1930s.

◆ The Middle East

Albert Hourani, *A History of the Arab Peoples* (Cambridge, MA, 1991) is a useful introduction to the culture of imperialism, European rule, and nascent nationalism. Peter Mansfield, *The Ottoman Empire and its Successors* (London, 1973) is a bare outline covering 1900–72. Malcolm E. Yapp, *The Near East since the First World War* (London, 1996 edn) is much more substantial and a clear, well-organized survey. Elie Kedourie, *Politics in the Middle East* (Oxford, 1992) provides much useful information though focused on the failure of constitutionalism. Uriel Dann, ed., *The Great Powers in the Middle East, 1919–1939* (New York, 1988) contains both broad and narrowly specialized essays. Elizabeth Monroe, *Britain's Moment in the Middle East, 1914–1971* (Baltimore, 1981) offers a classic British imperialist exposition. Jukka Nevakivi, *Britain, France and the Arab Middle East, 1914–1920* (London, 1969) is well researched, intelligent, and workmanlike. Michael J. Cohen and Martin Kolinsky, eds, *Britain and the Middle East in the 1930s* (New York, 1992) is a varied collection emphasizing Palestine. John DeNovo, *American Interests and Policies in the Middle East, 1900–1939* (Minneapolis, MN, 1963) ranges far beyond oil on a strong archival base.

Daniel Yergin, *The Prize: The Epic Quest for Oil, Money, and Power* (New York, 1991) is a lively, massive, archivally based global history of the entire history of oil. Edward W. Chester, *United States Oil Policy and Diplomacy: A Twentieth Century Overview* (Westport, CT, 1983) and Stephan J. Randall, *United States Foreign Oil Policy, 1919–1948* (Kingston, ON, 1985) are both global and tend to compensate for each other's deficiencies and omissions.

John Marlowe, *The Persian Gulf in the Twentieth Century* (New York, 1962) provides a tedious but useful pro-British survey. Briton Cooper Busch, *Britain, India, and the Arabs, 1914–1921* (Berkeley, 1971) stresses the important role of the Government of India. Alexei Vassiliev, *The History of Saudi Arabia* (London, 1998) systematically traces the transition from medieval tribe to modern kingdom with much attention to the British and American roles. These are further explored in Clive Leatherdale, *Britain and Saudi Arabia, 1925–1939* (London, 1983) and Aaron David Miller, *Search for Security: Saudi Arabian Oil and American Foreign Policy, 1939–49* (Chapel Hill, 1980), which summarizes 1900–1939. Rosemary Said Zahlan, *The Making of the Modern Gulf States* (London, 1989) covers all the smaller states competently.

On Egypt and the Sudan, two brief, clear introductory works are Peter Mansfield's flavourful, readable *The British in Egypt* (New York, 1971) and Robert O. Collins, *Egypt and the Sudan* (Englewood Cliffs, NJ, 1967). John Marlowe, *A History of Modern Egypt and Anglo-Egyptian Relations, 1800–1956* (Hamden, CT, 1965) is straightforward and more substantial. For a detailed study of interwar Egypt's struggle, see Janice J. Terry, *The Wafd, 1919–1952* (London, 1982). M. W. Daly, *Empire on the Nile: The Anglo-Egyptian Sudan* (2 vols, Cambridge, 1986, 1991) is extremely detailed.

For the non-Arab Northern Tier, Feroz Ahmad, *The Making of Modern Turkey* (London, 1993) is a good starting survey with some attention to foreign policy. George Lenczowski, *Russia and the West in Iran, 1918–1948* (Ithaca, NY, 1949) is pre-archival but useful for the general reader. Ludwig W. Adamec, *Afghanistan's Foreign Affairs to the Mid-Twentieth Century: Relations with the USSR, Germany, and Britain* (Tucson, AZ, 1974) is well researched but poorly organized. For the French mandate, Stephan H. Longrigg, *Syria and Lebanon under French Mandate* (London, 1958) is balanced and serviceable. Philip S. Khoury's excellent *Syria and the French Mandate* (Princeton, 1987) focuses on Arab national-ism and is well complemented by Peter A. Shambrook, *French Imperialism in Syria* (Reading, PA, 1998), which concentrates on French decision-making. For the Hashemite kingdoms, Phebe Marr, *The Modern History of Iraq* (Boulder, Co, 1985) delineates Iraq's struggle for independence. Mary C. Wilson, *King Abdullah, Britain, and the Making of Jordan* (Cambridge, 1987) is brief, clear, and measured. Yoav Gelber, *Jewish-Transjordan Relations, 1921–48* (London, 1997) and Joseph Nevo, *King Abdallah and Palestine* (New York, 1997) are both well researched, solid, and scant on the early years. Avi Shlaim, *Collusion across the Jordan: King Abdullah, the Zionist Movement, and the Partition of Palestine* (New York, 1988) dwells chiefly on 1945 on but contains a long useful summary of earlier years.

Introductions to the Palestine question include, Walter Laqueur, *A History of Zionism* (New York, 1972), which is fairly balanced from the Zionism viewpoint; Elie Kedourie, *In the Anglo-Arab Labyrinth: The McMahon–Husayn Correspondence and its Interpretations, 1914–1937* (Cambridge, 1976), which is the most detailed study and a defence of Britain; and Jacob C. Hurewitz, *The Struggle for Palestine,* (New York, 1950), an early but classic work of admirable clarity and balance. Two major works derived from the same archival material are Isaiah Friedman, *The Question of Palestine, 1914–1918: British-Jewish-Arab Relations* (New Brunswick, NJ, 1992 edn), which defends Britain and the Zionists, and Abdul L. Tibawi, *Anglo-Arab Relations and the Question of Palestine, 1914–1921* (London, 1978), which supports the Arab cause. Recent works of synthesis include Charles D. Smith, *Palestine and the Arab–Israeli Conflict* (New York, 1992 edn), based on English language sources only, and Tom Segev, *One Palestine, Complete: Jews and Arabs Under the British Mandate*, tr. Haim Watzman (New York, 2000), arguing that the mandate speeded Israel's creation. Bernard Wasserstein, *The British in Palestine* (London, 1978) covers 1917–1929 ably. Yehoshua M. Porath, *The Palestinian Arab National Movement* (London, 1977) is a judicious study of 1929–39. Ibrahim Abu-Lughod, ed., *The Transformation of Palestine* (Evanston, IL, 1971) is a pro-Arab collection of essays covering both pre- and post-World War II. On specialized aspects, see Kenneth W. Stein, *The Land Question in Palestine, 1917–1939* (Chapel Hill, NC, 1984), a heavily researched study from the Zionist viewpoint; Charles S. Kamen, *Little Common Ground: Arab Agriculture and Jewish Settlement in Palestine, 1920–1948* (Pittsburgh, PA, 1991) covering similar material with more balance; Anita Shapira, *Land and Power: The Zionist Resort to Force, 1881–1948* (New York, 1992), a level-headed exposition of the Jewish view; and Barbara J. Smith, *The Roots of Separatism in Palestine: British Economic Policy, 1920–1939* (Syracuse, NY, 1993), a heavily archival analysis of an important factor. The first two volumes of Neil Caplan, *Futile Diplomacy* (4 vols, London, 1983–97) deal with Arab-Jewish negotiations to the end of the mandate.

◆ East Asia

Note: Where last names are listed first for some Asian authors, the first name is given in parentheses.

Of general works, those of Akira Iriye, *The Origins of the Second World War in Asia and the Pacific* (London, 1987), covering the entire interwar period, *After Imperialism* (Cambridge, MA, 1965) dealing with 1921–31, and *Across the Pacific: An Inner History of American–East Asian Relations* (New York, 1967) tend to a Japanese viewpoint, the latter work analysing the American-Chinese-Japanese triangle. Meribeth E. Cameron, Thomas H. D. Mahoney, and George E. McReynolds, *China, Japan, and the Powers* (New York, 1960 edn) is old but good. A. Hamish Ion and Barry D. Hunt, eds, *War and Diplomacy across the Pacific, 1919–1952* (Waterloo, ON, 1988) fills gaps, as does Richard Dean Burns and Edward M. Bennett, *Diplomats in Crisis: United States–Chinese–Japanese*

Relations, 1919–1941 (Santa Barbara, CA, 1974) on individual diplomats. Ernest R. May and James C. Thomson, Jr, eds, *American–East Asian Relations* (Cambridge, MA, 1972) is historiographic. Wm Roger Louis, *British Strategy in the Far East, 1919–1939* (Oxford, 1971) focuses especially on the earlier years. John E. Dreifort, *Myopic Grandeur: The Ambivalence of French Foreign Policy toward the Far East, 1919–1945* (Kent, OH, 1991) provides a well researched study of French ineffectual weakness.

On the naval conferences, Roger Dingman, *Power in the Pacific: The Origins of Naval Arms Limitation, 1914–1922* (Chicago, 1976) is the standard work. Erik Goldstein and John Maurer, eds, *The Washington Conference, 1921–22* (London, 1995) is a multinational collection of essays. Ian Nish, *Alliance in Decline* (London, 1972) traces the ending of the Anglo-Japanese alliance. James William Morley, ed., *Japan Erupts: The London Naval Conference and the Manchurian Incident, 1928–1932* (New York, 1984) presents essays by Japanese scholars and is the first volume of Morley, ed., *Japan's Road to the Pacific War* (5 vols, New York, 1976–94).

On South-east Asia, N. J. Ryan, *A History of Malaysia and Singapore* (Kuala Lumpur, 1976) is a clear, useful survey. Donald E. Nuechterlein, *Thailand and the Struggle for Southeast Asia* (Ithaca, NY, 1965) provides a judicious summary of international politics. Maung Htin Aung, *The Stricken Peacock: Anglo-Burmese Relations, 1752–1948* (The Hague, 1965) presents the Burmese view. For states on China's periphery, Pradynmna P. Karan and William M. Jenkins, Jr, *The Himalayan Kingdoms: Bhutan, Sikkim, and Nepal* (Princeton, 1963) is weak on historical aspects. Melvyn C. Goldstein, *A History of Modern Tibet, 1913–1951* (Berkeley, 1989) is extremely detailed. George G. S. Murphy, *Soviet Mongolia: A Study of the Oldest Political Satellite* (Berkeley, 1966) is well-informed. Chong-Sik Lee, *The Politics of Korean Nationalism* (Berkeley, CA, 1963) is clear, useful, and only partially replaced by Bruce Cumings, *Korea's Place is the Sun* (New York, 1997), presenting the Korean viewpoint.

General works on Japan include Michael A. Barnhart, *Japan Prepares for Total War, 1919–1941* (Ithaca, NY, 1987) and *Japan and the World since 1868* (London, 1995). Sydney Gifford, *Japan among the Powers, 1890–1990* (New Haven, 1994) is tedious but solid. Akira Iriye, *Japan and the Wider World* (New York, 1997) is a rambling, thoughtful survey of the main themes of Japanese foreign policy. W. G. Beasley, *Japanese Imperialism, 1894–1945* (Oxford, 1987) provides helpful background and good analysis. Richard Storry, *Japan and the Decline of the West in Asia, 1894–1943* (London, 1979) is useful, as is Ian Nish's idiosyncratic, *Japanese Foreign Policy, 1869–1942* (London, 1977). For specific factors affecting Japanese policy, see Leonard A. Humphrey's solid *The Way of the Heavenly Sword: The Japanese Army in the 1920s* (Stanford, CA, 1995) and James B. Crowley, *Japan's Quest for Autonomy: National Security and Foreign Policy, 1930–1938* (Princeton, 1966), especially for the 1930 London naval conference. For Japanese-American relations, Charles E. Neu, *Troubled Encounter: The United States and Japan* (New York, 1975) is an excellent starting point, judiciously making key connections. William R. Nester's more detailed *Power across the Pacific: A Diplomatic History of American Relations with Japan* (New York, 1996) also offers a sensible survey. Malcolm D. Kennedy, *The Estrangement of Great Britain and Japan, 1917–1935* (Berkeley, 1969) explains the Japanese viewpoint but lacks a broader context. Ian Nish, ed., *Anglo-Japanese Alienation, 1919–1952* (Cambridge, 1982), contains some useful essays.

Some early general works on China are still useful. Werner Levi's clear, well-organized *Modern China's Foreign Policy* (Minneapolis, MN, 1953) is a good starting point. F. F. Liu, *A Military History of Modern China* (Princeton, 1956) has a fairly broad political application, including regarding Russia and Germany, whereas Edward L. Dreyer, *China at War, 1901–1949* (London, 1995) does not, dwelling narrowly on the many civil wars. Richard T. Phillips, *China since 1911* (New York, 1996) is a competent brief introduction. William L. Tung, *China and the Foreign Powers* (Dobbs Ferry, NY, 1970) provides a diplomatic history from the mid-nineteenth century. Zhang (Yongjin), *China in the International System, 1918–20* (New York, 1991) exhaustively presents a Chinese view of its role at the Paris peace conference in a broader context. Ch'ien (Tuan-sheng), *The Government and Politics of China, 1912–1949* (Cambridge, MA, 1961) untangles a confusing subject.

The literature on Sino-Japanese relations is large. For the pre-1931 period, see Nobuya Bamba, *Japanese Diplomacy in a Dilemma: New Light on Japan's China Policy, 1924–1929* (Vancouver, BC, 1972), which contrasts the approaches of Shidehara and Tanaka, as well as William Fitch Morton, *Tanaka Giichi and Japan's China Policy* (New York, 1980), a clear analysis of Tanaka's erratic indecision. Two uneven multi-author collections are Alvin D. Coox and Hilary Conroy, eds, *China and Japan: A Search for Balance since World War I* (Santa Barbara, CA, 1978) and Peter Duus, Ramon H. Myers, and Mark R. Peattie, eds, *The Japanese Informal Empire in China, 1895–1937* (Princeton, 1989).

As to China's relations with other powers, Edmund S. K. Fung, *The Diplomacy of Imperial Retreat: Britain's South China Policy, 1924–1931* (Hong Kong, 1991) studies the British response to Chinese nationalism in the key Yangtze region. Michael Schaller, *The United States and China in the Twentieth Century* (New York, 1990 edn) provides a brief introduction highly critical of both Chiang and American policy. Warren I. Cohen, *America's Response to China: A History of Sino-American Relations* (New York, 1990 edn) is clear, hostile to Chiang, and helpful, if rather narrowly focused. John K. Fairbank, *The United States and China*

(Cambridge, MA, 1979 edn) provides general background. Dennis L. Noble, *The Eagle and the Dragon: The United States Military in China, 1901–1937* (New York, 1990) is over-detailed on an otherwise neglected topic. William C. Kirby, *Germany and Republican China* (Stanford, CA, 1984) competently covers another neglected topic from both sides, dealing with the 1928–1938 Nanking decade. Brace A. Elleman, *Diplomacy and Deception: The Secret History of Sino-Soviet Diplomatic Relations, 1917–1927* (Armonk, NY, 1997) is a serious, rather anti-Soviet study based on records of both countries. C. Martin Wilbur and Julie Lien-ying How, *Missionaries of Revolution: Soviet Advisers and Nationalist China, 1920–1927* (Cambridge, MA, 1989) is exhaustive, heavily researched, and half documents. S. C. M. Paine, *Imperial Rivals: China, Russia, and their Disputed Frontier* (Armonk, NY, 1996) uses Russian and Chinese archives to explore the relationship to 1924 and is particularly important on Mongolia.

◆ Latin America

Relevant volumes of Leslie Bethell, ed., *The Cambridge History of Latin America* (11 vols, Cambridge, 1984–95) are helpful, though some, like other works, include little on foreign policy. Two collections which help to redress the balance are Heraldo Muñoz and Joseph Tulchin, eds, *Latin American Nations in World Politics* (Boulder, CO, 1984) and Harold Eugene Davis, John J. Finan, and F. Taylor Peck, *Latin American Diplomatic History* (Baton Rouge, LA, 1977), which provides an introductory diplomatic survey.

On specific factors, Hugh M. Hamill, ed., *Caudillos: Dictators in Spanish America* (Norman, OK, 1992) offers varied essays, many on individuals. George Philip, *Oil and Politics in Latin America: Nationalist Movements and State Companies* (Cambridge, 1982) is solid and scholarly. Alain Rouquié, *The Military and the State in Latin America*, tr. Paul E. Sigmund (Berkeley, 1978) is well written, thoughtful, and analytical, whereas George Philip, *The Military in South American Politics* (London, 1985) is theoretical but deals with military coups of 1930 and after. Frederick M. Nunn, *Yesterday's Soldiers: European Military Professionalism in South America, 1890–1940* (Lincoln, NE, 1983) addresses French and German involvement in several countries. Victor Bulmer-Thomas, ed., *Britain and Latin America* (Cambridge, 1989) focuses on post-1945 with an excellent summary of earlier years. J. F. Norman and Antonelle Gerbi, *The Japanese in South America* (New York, 1943) deals with Brazil and Peru.

A few works address specific periods generally. Bill Albert, *South America and the First World War* (Cambridge, 1988) is narrow but exhaustive on

Argentina, Brazil, Chile, and Peru. R. A. Humphrey, *Latin America and the Second World War* (2 vols, London, 1981–2) contains an able interwar summary and then a detailed narrative. Two collections of essays on the 1940s are David Rock, ed., *Latin America in the 1940s: War and Postwar Transitions* (Berkeley, CA, 1994) and Leslie Bethell and Ian Roxborough, eds, *Latin America between the Second World War and the Cold War, 1944–1948* (Cambridge, 1992) which is left wing and state by state.

On disputes between South American countries, see Bryce Wood, *The United States and Latin American Wars, 1932–1942* (New York, 1966) which summarizes all the disputes. Joe F. Wilson, *The United States, Chile, and Peru in the Tacna and Arica Plebiscite* (Washington, 1979) is narrow and less clear. Leslie B. Rout, *Politics of the Chaco Peace Conference, 1935–1939* (Austin, TX, 1970) is far superior to other works on the subject, covering the pre-war and war as well as the resolution.

The more balanced works on United States relations with Latin America tend to be the older ones. Two good introduction are Federico G. Gil, *Latin American–United States Relations* (New York, 1971) and J. Lloyd Mecham, *A Survey of United States–Latin American Relations* (Boston, 1965). Mecham's *The United States and Inter-American Security, 1889–1960* (Austin, TX, 1961) is also useful. Frank Niess, *A Hemisphere to Itself: A History of US–Latin American Relations*, tr. Harry Drost (London, 1990) contains valuable statistics but is extremely hostile to the United States, always assuming the worst motives. Joseph S. Tulchin, *The Aftermath of War: World War I and US Policy Toward Latin America* (New York, 1971) is heavily researched in American materials and helpful on oil, cables, and banks. Irwin F. Gellman, *Good Neighbor Diplomacy* (Baltimore, 1979) is a lively readable account, giving FDR unilateral credit for the policy. Donald M. Dozer, *Are We Good Neighbors?* (Gainesville, FL, 1959) takes a trilingual approach to 1930–1960. David Green, *The Containment of Latin America: A History of the Myths and Realities of the Good Neighbor Policy* (Chicago, 1971) also covers an extended time period and tries to examine Latin American viewpoints. Charles G. Fenwick, *The Organization of American States* (Washington, 1963) is exhaustive, with a good historical section.

Joseph Smith, *Unequal Giants: Diplomatic Relations between the United States and Brazil, 1889–1930* (Pittsburgh, PA, 1991) is conscientiously researched but tedious. Two older works are easier to use: Ronald M. Schneider, *Brazil, Foreign Policy of a Future World Power* (Boulder, CO, 1976) examines many factors in Brazilian policy formulation, Wayne A. Selcher, ed., *Brazil in the International System* (Boulder, CO, 1981) deals with the history of Brazilian foreign policy as well as Brazil and India as Third World middle powers. Arthur P. Whitaker, *The United States and the Southern Cone* (Cambridge, MA, 1976) surveys the region with some attention to foreign policy. Aldo César Vacs, *Discreet Partners: Argentine and the USSR since 1917* (Pittsburgh, PA, 1984) is brief and clear but limited. Guido di Tella and D. Cameron Watt, eds, *Argentina between the Great Powers* (Pittsburgh, PA, 1990) is a collection of essays on relations with Britain and the United States which argues that there was little Nazi influence in Argentina, as does Ronald C. Newton's massively researched *The 'Nazi Menace' in Argentina, 1931–1947* (Stanford, CA, 1992). Michael J. Francis, *The Limits of Hegemony: United States Relations with Argentina and Chile during World War II* (Notre Dame, IN, 1977) rests on American and German documents. William F. Stater, *Chile and the United States* (Athens, GA, 1990) is brief, clear, and balanced. Fredrick B. Pike, *Chile and the United States, 1880–1962* (Notre Dame, IN, 1963) focuses chiefly on the Chilean left. The same author's *The United States and the Andean Republics* (Cambridge, MA, 1977) scants diplomacy. Ronald Bruce St John, *The Foreign Policy of Peru* (Boulder, CO, 1992) is a useful survey covering relations with Peru's neighbours, the League of Nations, and the United States. James C. Carey, *Peru and the United States, 1900–1962* (Notre Dame, IN, 1964) stresses the role of American business.

Dana G. Munro, *The United States and the Caribbean Republics, 1921–1933* (Princeton, 1974) studies State Department policy. His earlier *Intervention and Dollar Diplomacy in the Caribbean, 1900–1921* (Princeton, 1964) is a controversial defence of American policy. H. Michael Erisman and John D. Martz, eds, *Colossus Challenged: The Struggle for Caribbean Influence* (Boulder, CO, 1982) is a useful collection. Eric Paul Roorda, *The Dictator Next Door: The Good Neighbor Policy and the Truijillo Regime in the Dominican Republic, 1930–1945* (Durham, NC, 1998) is clear and scholarly, arguing that Trujillo manipulated Washington. Brenda Gayle Plummer, *Haiti and the Great Powers, 1902–1915* (Baton Rouge, LA, 1988) carries the story to 1934 from a Haitian viewpoint, criticizing the United States. Louis A. Pérez, Jr, *Cuba and the United States* (Athens, GA, 1990) examines how Washington has influenced Cuban history, whereas his *Intervention, Revolution, and Politics in Cuba, 1913–1917* (Pittsburgh, PA, 1978) addresses the 1917 intervention and is difficult to read. Robert Freeman Smith, *The United States and Cuba* (New York, 1961) deals with economic aspects of Cuban-American relations over a long period.

John E. Findling, *Close Neighbors, Distant Friends: United States-Central American Relations* (Westport, CT, 1987) surveys five republics, excluding Panama. Walter LaFeber, *Inevitable Revolutions: The United States in Central America* (New York, 1983) is readable but scants the pre-1945 era. James Dunkerley, *Power in the Isthmus* (London, 1988) is more knowledgeable but difficult to read. Thomas M. Leonard, *Central America and the United States* (Athens, GA, 1991) surveys a long period of time competently. Jeffrey M. Paige, *Coffee and Power: Revolution and the Rise of Democracy in Central America* (Cambridge, MA, 1997) spotlights a key factor but primarily for the post-1945 years. Richard V. Salisbury, *Anti-Imperialism and International Competition in Central America, 1920–1929* (Wilmington, DE, 1989) argues that Nicaragua was the crux of the matter. Paul Coe Clark, Jr, *The United States and Somoza, 1933–1956* (Westport, CT, 1992) maintains that Somoza manipulated Washington. Michael L. Conniff, *Panama and the United States* (Athens, GA, 1992) is a survey covering the entire relationship from both sides.

There is a large literature on the Mexican revolution and on relations with the United States. On the revolution itself, Ramón Eduardo Ruíz, *The Great Rebellion: Mexico, 1905–1924* (New York, 1980) deals briefly with the global context and maintains that no social revolution occurred. Using another definition of revolution, John Mason Hart, *Revolutionary Mexico* (Berkeley, 1987) provides more global context and argues that there was a revolution. Linda B. Hall and Don M. Coerver, *Revolution on the Border: The United States and Mexico, 1910–1920* (Albuquerque, NM, 1988) is confusing but useful on specific topics. Josefina Zoraida Vázquez and Lorenzo Meyer, *The United States and Mexico* (Chicago, 1985) is brief, even-handed, and very clear, even on the Mexican revolution. Alan Knight, *United States-Mexican Relations, 1910–1940* (La Jolla, CA, 1987) stresses similarities, not differences. Linda B. Hall, *Oil, Banks, and Politics: The United States and Post-revolutionary Mexico, 1917–1924* (Austin, TX, 1995) is a careful study of key factors in the relationship. Friedrich E. Schuler, *Mexico between Hitler and Roosevelt: Mexican Foreign Relations in the Age of Lazaro Cardenas, 1934–1940* (Albuquerque, NM, 1998) is a solid study arguing that Mexico used foreign policy to domestic ends, exploiting the weakness of foreign envoys other than Daniels. Daniela Spenser, *The Impossible Triangle: Mexico, Soviet Russia, and the United States in the 1920s* (Durham, NC, 1999) is an impressive work of scholarship examining how Russia and Mexico saw each other and the American view of Mexico as Bolshevik. Alton Frye, *Mexico, Germany and the American Hemisphere, 1933–41* (New Haven, 1967) argues that Hitler had grandiose plans for the western hemisphere but was colossally ignorant of it and achieved little real penetration.

◆ **The United States**

John Milton Cooper, Jr, *Pivotal Decades: The United States, 1900–1920* (New York, 1990) presents an excellent picture of the United States early in the century. William Appleman Williams, *The Tragedy of American Diplomacy* (New York, 1962 edn), which has influenced many historians, is a Cold War era analysis of overseas economic empire as the determining force in American foreign policy. Surveys include Robert D. Schulzinger, *American Diplomacy in the Twentieth Century* (Oxford, 1984) and Michael J. Hogan, ed., *The Ambiguous Legacy: US Foreign Relations in the*

'*American Century*' (New York, 1999), a multi-author, multi-faceted broad treatment. Frank A. Ninkovich, *The Wilsonian Century: US Foreign Policy since 1900* (Chicago, 1999) dwells on the role of ideology in American policy formulation. Lloyd G. Gardner, *A Covenant with Power: America and World Order from Wilson to Reagan* (Oxford, 1984) emphasizes the domestic origins of foreign policy, whereas Norman A. Graebner, *America as a World Power: A Realist Appraisal from Wilson to Reagan* (Wilmington, DE, 1984) stresses drift, lack of policy, and lack of reality. Lloyd Ambrosius, *Woodrow Wilson and the American Diplomatic Tradition* (Cambridge, 1987) offers a useful exposition.

Warren Cohen, *Empire without Tears: America's Foreign Relations, 1921–1933* (Philadelphia, PA, 1987) maintains that the United States wanted an informal economic empire without use of force. In the same vein are Carl P. Parrini's very narrow *Heir to Empire: United States Economic Diplomacy, 1916–1923* (Pittsburgh, PA, 1969) and Joan Hoff Wilson's broader, more reliable *American Business and Foreign Policy, 1920–1933* (Boston, 1973 edn). Michael Hogan, *Informal Entente: The Private Structure of Co-operation in Anglo-American Economic Diplomacy, 1918–1928* (Chicago, 1991) is very able, well researched, and useful.

Relations with Europe in the 1920s are covered by Frank Costigliola, *Awkward Dominion: American Political, Economic, and Cultural Relations with Europe, 1919–1933* (Ithaca, NY, 1984). Relations with individual powers are addressed by Melvin P. Leffler, *The Elusive Quest: America's Pursuit of European Stability and French Security, 1919–1933* (Chapel Hill, 1979); William C. McNeil, *American Money and the Weimar Republic* (New York, 1986); John E. Moser, *Twisting the Lion's Tail* (New York, 1999); and Katherine Siegel, *Loans and Legitimacy: The Evolution of Soviet-American Relations, 1919–1933* (Lexington, KY, 1996). Warren F. Kuehl and Lynne K. Dunn, *Keeping the Covenant: American Internationalists and the League of Nations, 1920–1939* (Kent, OH, 1997) is sympathetic to the League. Studies of relations with other continents are listed under those areas.

For the Roosevelt era, Robert Dallek's lively, well-written *Franklin D. Roosevelt and American Foreign Policy* (Oxford, 1979) is important, solid, and sympathetic to FDR. Edward M. Bennett, *Franklin D. Roosevelt and the Search for Security: American-Soviet Relations, 1933–1939* (Wilmington, DE, 1985) is largely based on American archives. See also listings under Latin American and the sections dealing with 1931–45.

◆ Europe, 1918–1933

The only general survey of the period is Sally Marks, *The Illusion of Peace: International Relations in Europe, 1918–1933* (London, 1976). Hans W.

Gatzke, ed., *European Diplomacy between Two Wars, 1919–1939* (Chicago, 1972) is a fine collection of articles. Monographs on the era include Keith L. Nelson, *Victors Divided: America and the Allies in Germany, 1918–1923* (Berkeley, 1975) on the Rhineland occupation, and Carole Fink, *The Genoa Conference* (Chapel Hill, 1984), exploring the ramifications of that multi-faceted event. Jon Jacobson, *Locarno Diplomacy: Germany and the West, 1925–1929* (Princeton, 1972) examines the late 1920s largely from the German viewpoint. Robert H. Ferrell, *Peace in their Time: The Origins of the Kellogg–Briand Pact* (New York, 1952) has not been superseded.

On matters economic, Derek H. Aldcroft, *From Versailles to Wall Street, 1919–1929* (Berkeley, 1977) offers an able survey. Richard H. Meyer, *Bankers' Diplomacy: Monetary Stabilization in the Twenties* (New York, 1970) is readable for non-economists and has not been replaced. Marc Trachtenberg, *Reparation in World Politics: France and European Economic Diplomacy, 1916–1923* (New York, 1980) is heavily technical and pro-French. Bruce Kent, *The Spoils of War: The Politics, Economics, and Diplomacy of Reparations, 1918–1932* (Oxford, 1989) is entirely committed to the German view. Stephan A. Schuker, *American 'Reparations' to Germany 1919–33* (Princeton, 1988), which is much more balanced, asks who really paid. Christine A. White, *British and American Commercial Relations with Soviet Russia, 1918–1924* (Chapel Hill, 1992) is sensible and thorough, whereas Andrew J. Williams, *Trading with the Bolsheviks* (Manchester, 1992) is erratic and has gaps, particularly regarding France.

Paul W. Doerr, *British Foreign Policy, 1919–1939* (Manchester, 1998) is a substantial but rather anti-French survey. David Dilks, ed., *Retreat from Power: Studies in Britain's Foreign Policy of the Twentieth Century* (2 vols, London, 1981) contains some excellent essays. Carolyn J. Kitching, *Britain and the Problem of International Disarmament, 1919–34* (London, 1999) criticizes Britain's lack of policy. Gábor Bátonyi, *Britain and Central Europe, 1918–1933* (Oxford, 1999) traces London's gradual withdrawal from Austria, Hungary, and Czechoslovakia. Anne Orde's *Great Britain and International Security, 1920–1926* (London, 1978) and *British Policy and International Reconstruction after the First World War* (Cambridge, 1990) are essential though not always digestible. F. L. Carsten, *Britain and the Weimar Republic* (New York, 1984) demonstrates the British bias toward Germany through the British documents.

Many studies of France in the 1920s are unsatisfactory. A. Adamthwaite, *Grandeur and Misery: France's Bid for Power in Europe, 1914–1940* (London, 1995) is uneven on the early years and assumes France sought European hegemony. Stephan A. Schuker's magisterial *The End of French Predominance in Europe* (Chapel Hill, 1976) deals with much more than France and reparations, recognizing French weakness. William I. Shorrock,

From Ally to Enemy: The Empire of Fascist Italy in French Diplomacy, 1920–1940 (Kent, OH, 1988) is a balanced survey from the French side. Piotr S. Wandycz, *France and Her Eastern Allies, 1919–1925* (Minneapolis, MN, 1962) and *The Twilight of French Eastern Alliances, 1926–1936* (Princeton, 1988), both addressing ties to Poland and Czechoslovakia, are detailed and solid. P. M. H. Bell, *France and Britain, 1900–1940: Entente and Estrangement* (London, 1996) is very fine.

The literature on the Weimar Republic is large and very uneven. V. R. Berghahn, *Modern Germany* (Cambridge, 1987 edn), a brief introduction, is extremely good on Weimar and Nazi foreign policy. Helmut Heiber, *The Weimar Republic*, tr. W. E. Yuill (Oxford, 1993) misreads French policy but is otherwise very perceptive. Michael Laffan, ed., *The Burden of German History, 1919–45* (London, 1988) is a good collection of essays, including a brilliant one by Imanuel Geiss. Gerald D. Feldman, *The Great Disorder: Politics, Economics, and Society in the German Inflation, 1914–1924* (New York, 1993) is an immense and important study from a moderately pro-German viewpoint. Carl-Ludwig Holtfrerich, *The German Inflation, 1914–1923*, tr. Theo Balderston (Berlin, Walter de Gruyter, 1986) is an invaluable work sharing the same viewpoint. Hans W. Gatzke's pioneering *Stresemann and the Rearmament of Germany* (New York, 1969 edn), anchored in German archives, has not been superseded.

Alan Cassels, *Mussolini's Early Diplomacy* (Princeton, 1970) is the standard work which has not been replaced by newer studies. R. J. B. Bosworth, *Italy and the Wider World, 1860–1960* (London, 1996) contains a useful summary of foreign policy with a strong historiographic cast. H. James Burgwyn, *Italian Foreign Policy in the Interwar Period, 1918–1940* (Westport, CT, 1997) is an archivally based survey which is generally sympathetic to Italy but not to Mussolini.

Much literature on Soviet Russia is essentially biographic and thus excluded. Jon Jacobson, *When the Soviet Union Entered World Politics* (Berkeley, 1994) is an excellent synthesis reflecting the state of knowledge before the Soviet archives opened. Gabriel Gorodetsky, ed., *Soviet Foreign Policy, 1917–1991* (London, 1994) contains several worthwhile essays. Piotr S. Wandycz, *Soviet-Polish Relations, 1917–1921*(Cambridge, MA, 1969) has not yet been superseded. Aleksandr M. Nekrich, *Pariahs, Partners, Predators: German-Soviet Relations, 1922, 1941*, ed. and tr. Gregory L. Freeze (New York, 1997) rambles without orderly exposition but provides useful information about the Rapallo tie.

On Europe's northern fringes, Patrick Salmon, *Scandinavia and the Great Powers, 1890–1940* (New York, 1997) does a solid job from a British viewpoint. T. K. Derry, *A History of Scandinavia* (Minneapolis, MN, 1979) is substantial and includes Finland and Iceland. John Hiden and Patrick Salmon, *The Baltic States and Europe* (London, 1994) examines the interwar diplomacy of the Baltic republics from the British viewpoint. John

Hiden, *The Baltic States and Weimar Ostpolitik* (Cambridge, 1987) is harder to read but sensible, although it scants Lithuania.

On eastern Europe, Joseph Rothschild, *East Central Europe between the Two World Wars* (Seattle, WA, 1974) is essential, especially the brilliant introductory chapter. Raymond Pearson, *National Minorities in Eastern Europe, 1848–1945* (London, 1983) provides useful data on an important problem. Barbara Jelavich, *History of the Balkans, Twentieth Century* (Cambridge, 1983) contains a good deal of interwar material, covering Turkey, Greece and states up to Rumania. Magda Ádám, *The Little Entente and Europe (1920–1929)*, tr. Mátyás Esterházy (Budapest, 1993) is scholarly and detailed. F. Gregory Campbell, *Confrontation in Central Europe: Weimar Germany and Czechoslovakia* (Chicago, 1975) offers a Czech view of Prague's main problem. Jan Karski, *The Great Powers and Poland, 1919–1945* (Lanham, MD, 1985) is a well-researched survey. Eugene Boia, *Romania's Diplomatic Relations with Yugoslavia in the Interwar Period, 1919–1941* (New York, 1993) is detailed and useful.

◆ The Great Depression

Note: works designed primarily for economists are omitted.

The two classic works are John Kenneth Galbraith's entertaining, digestible *The Great Crash, 1929* (Boston, 1988 edn), dwelling on the American origins and background, and Charles P. Kindleberger, *The World in Depression, 1929–1939* (London, 1939), a less clear Keynsian analysis continuing the story. W. R. Garside, ed., *Capitalism in Crisis: International Responses to the Great Depression* (New York, 1993) usefully deals with various countries, chiefly Europe. Herman van der Wee, ed., *The Great Depression Revisited* (The Hague, 1972) contains useful essays, especially on the British Empire and Latin America. Mark Wheeler, ed., *The Economics of the Great Depression* (Kalamazoo, MI, 1998) has an Anglo-American focus but is helpful about the historiography of the Depression's causes and contains a splendidly clear essay by Carol E. Heim dealing briefly and usefully with Latin America and Africa.

Patricia Clavin, *The Great Depression in Europe, 1929–1939* (New York, 2000) examines economic aspects of international politics, 1919–1945. Her *The Failure of Economic Diplomacy* (New York, 1996) examines the World Economic Conference of 1933 from a British viewpoint. Carlo M. Cipolla, *Contemporary Economies* (Hassocks, nr Brighton, 1977) is uneven but clear in examining individual countries, 1920–79, and Europe in the world economy. Derek H. Aldcroft, *Studies in the Interwar European Economy* (Aldershot, Hants, 1997) is a well written series of essays, useful on the Depression and the inflations of the 1920s.

Rosemary Thorp, ed., *Latin America in the 1930s: The Role of the Periphery in World Crisis* (New York, 1984) is an important collection, some of which is readable. Other works on the crisis on the economic periphery tend to be unsatisfactory, although relevant portions of Leslie Bethell, ed., *The Cambridge History of Latin America*, cited above, and of the second volume of Nicholas Tarling, ed., *The Cambridge History of South-east Asia* (2 vols, Cambridge, 1992) are helpful. Ian Brown, ed., *The Economies of Africa and Asia in the Inter-War Depression* (London, 1989) is very selective and often narrow, whereas Angus Maddison, *Two Crises: Latin America and Asia, 1929–1938 and 1973–83* (Paris, 1985) is extremely compressed and not always clear but sometimes useful. Other available works are not recommended.

◆ The Crises of 1931–1937

Among works on the policies of individual powers in Asia in the 1930s is You-li Sun, *China and the Origins of the Pacific War, 1931–1941* (New York, 1993), a well researched analytical study examining Chinese assumptions and the question of why it fought. Stephen E. Pelz, *Race to Pearl Harbor: The Failure of the Second London Naval Conference and the Onset of World War II* (Cambridge, MA, 1974) is broader than its title implies, studying Japanese, British, and American policy, 1933–41, on the basis of the respective archives. Stephen L. Endicott, *Diplomacy and Enterprise: British China Policy, 1933–7* (Vancouver, BC, 1975) explores a narrow topic with wide implications, especially the factors in economic imperialism. Ann Trotter, *Britain and East Asia, 1933–1937* (London, 1975) is a bit broader, helpfully analytical, and witty at times. Richard J. Aldrich, *The Key to the South: Britain, the United States, and Thailand during the Approach of the Pacific War, 1929–1942* (Kuala Lumpur, 1993) is important and intelligent, stressing the division of British and American policy. Walter LaFeber, *The Clash: US–Japan Relations throughout History* (New York, 1997) is an archivally based survey which tends to be choppy, aphoristic, and gossipy. John J. Stephan, *The Russian Far East* (Stanford, CA, 1996 edn) is a solid archivally based survey, covering the entire 1914–45 period, excluding Russian-Chinese relations. John P. Fox, *Germany and the Far East Crisis, 1931–1938* (London, 1982) expounds the German view on the basis of German and British records and those of the International Military tribunals.

On the Manchurian crisis and its international implications, Christopher Thorne, *The Limits of Foreign Policy: The West, the League, and the Far Eastern Crisis of 1931–1933* (London, 1972) is a massively archival, thoughtful classic. Sadako N. Ogata, *Defiance in Manchuria: The Making of Japanese Foreign Policy, 1931–1932* (Berkeley, 1964) is another classic, focusing on the crucial role of the Kwantung army. Ian Nish, *Japan's Struggle with Internationalism: Japan, China, and the League of Nations, 1931–3* (London, 1993) is well researched but narrowly focused. Parks Coble, *Facing Japan: Chinese Politics and Japanese Imperialism, 1931–1937* (Cambridge, MA, 1991) is an important work exploring the bases of Chinese policy and reactions of Chinese opinion to Japanese pressure. George A. Lensen, *The Damned Inheritance: The Soviet Union and the Manchurian Crisis, 1924–1935* (Tallahassee, FL, 1974) is based primarily on Japanese archives but also such Soviet and Chinese documents as were then available.

Of general works on Europe in the 1930s, the outstanding study is P. M. H. Bell, *The Origins of the Second World War in Europe* (London, 1986), which impressively deals with both events and underlying forces for the entire interwar era. Andrew J. Crozier, *The Causes of the Second World War* (Oxford, 1997) is chiefly European and from a British viewpoint but not unfair to France. David E. Kaiser, *Economic Diplomacy and the Origins of the Second World War* (Princeton, 1980) covers most of the continent intelligently. David Clay Large, *Between Two Fires, Europe's Path in the 1930s* (New York, 1930) contains popular, often colourful essays of uneven quality. On a more scholarly level, both versions of Gordon Martel, ed., *'The Origins of the Second World War' Reconsidered* (Boston, 1986; New York, 1999) contain essays ranging far beyond A. J. P. Taylor's controversial book. Martin Thomas, *Britain, France and Appeasement* (Oxford, 1996) suggests that Britain blamed France for German actions. MacGregor Knox, *Common Destiny: Dictatorship, Foreign Policy, and War in Fascist Italy and Nazi Germany* (Cambridge, 2000) consists of well-written, intelligent essays. On American policy, Robert H. Ferrell, *American Diplomacy in the Great Depression* (New Haven, 1957) covers 1929–33, while Arnold A. Offner, *American Appeasement* (Cambridge, MA, 1969) deals with policy toward Germany, 1933–38. Robert A. Divine, *The Illusion of Neutrality* (Chicago, 1962) narrowly traces the history of American neutrality legislation.

Works on Britain and France in the 1930s include David Carlton, *MacDonald verses Henderson: The Foreign Policy of the Second Labour Government* (London, 1970), which is important for the Disarmament Conference. Nicholas Rostow, *Anglo-French Relations, 1934–1936* (New York, 1994 edn) stresses the role of prejudice in policy formulation and assigns partial responsibility for the advent of war to Britain and France, especially Britain. Nicole Jordan, *The Popular Front and Central Europe* (New York, 1992) deals primarily with 1934 on, stressing French weakness. Factors in that weakness are explored in two able works: Kenneth Mouré, *Managing the franc Poincaré: Economic Understanding and Political Constraint in French Monetary Policy, 1928–1936* (New York, 1991) and Eugenia Kiesling, *Arming against Hitler: France and the Limits of Military*

Planning (Lawrence, KS, 1996). On the 1931 crisis, see Edward W. Bennett's two outstanding works, *Germany and the Diplomacy of the Financial Crisis, 1931* (Cambridge, MA, 1962) and *German Rearmament and the West* (Princeton, 1979) as well as Stanley Suval, *The Anschluss Question in the Weimar Era* (Baltimore, 1974).

Nazi foreign policy has been extensively studied, often in the numerous biographies of Hitler. Two good brief introductory surveys are William Carr, *Arms, Autarky, and Aggression: A Study in German Foreign Policy, 1933–1939* (New York, 1972), which is heavily economic, and Klaus Hildebrand, *The Foreign Policy of the Third Reich*, tr. Anthony Fothergill (Berkeley, 1973), carrying the story to 1945, which argues for continuity of policy as well as Hitlerian preoccupation with Britain. For a detailed analysis, Gerhard L. Weinberg's outstanding *The Foreign Policy of Hitler's Germany* (2 vols, Chicago, 1970, 1980) is an essential monumental work of scholarship on 1933–39. As a supplement, Geoffrey Stoakes, *Hitler and the Quest for World Domination* (New York, 1986) provides a sensible discussion of Hitler's goals in the 1920s and suggests they remained consistent, if opportunistically pursued.

On the Ethiopian crisis, Alberto Sbacchi, *Legacy of Bitterness: Ethiopia and Fascist Italy, 1935–1941* (Lawrenceville, NJ, 1997) is heavily researched in many archives, including Ethiopia's, and exhaustive, examining all sides before, during, and after the war. George W. Baer, *The Coming of the Italian–Ethiopian War* (Cambridge, MA, 1967) and *Test Case: Italy, Ethiopia, and the League of Nations* (Stanford, CA, 1976) are valuable studies, the first much clearer than the second. Angelo Del Boca, *The Ethiopian War, 1935–1941*, tr. P. D. Cummins (Chicago, 1969) is a balanced account of military and social aspects and the aftermath. Thomas M. Verich, *The European Powers and the Italo-Ethiopian War, 1935–1936* (Salisbury, NC, 1980) is a purely European study. Esmonde M. Robertson, *Mussolini as Empire Builder: Europe and Africa, 1932–36* (London, 1977) is knowledgeable but indigestible. Anthony Mockler, *Haile Selassie's War* (New York, 1984) provides the Ethiopian and African angles.

J. T. Emmerson, *The Rhineland Crisis, 7 March 1936* (Ames, IA, 1977) remains the only detailed account of the diplomacy of the Rhineland crisis. Gabriel Jackson, *A Concise History of the Spanish Civil War* (London, 1974) provides a clear, moderately pro-Republican entry-level survey by an expert on the subject. Michael Alpert, *A New History of the Spanish Civil War* (New York, 1994) is sympathetic to the left (including Russia), and sound on the Anglo-French relationship, stressing Britain's refusal of involvement. George Esenwein and Adrian Shubert, *Spain at War: The Spanish Civil War in Context, 1931–1939* (New York, 1995) is primarily domestic but non-ideological and deals well with propaganda and the International Brigades.

◆ War East and West, 1937–1941

On the Sino-Japanese war, James William Morley, *The China Quagmire: Japan's Expansion on the Asian Continent, 1933–1941* (vol. 2 of *Japan's Road to the Pacific War*, cited above; New York, 1983) contains long essays by Japanese scholars. Peter Duus, Ramon H. Myers, and Mark R. Peattie, eds, *The Japanese Wartime Empire, 1931–1945* (Princeton, 1996) contains essays on China, earlier gains, and South-east Asia. Iris Chang, *The Rape of Nanjing* (New York, 1997) is rebutted on specific points by Honda (Katsuichi), *The Nanjing Massacre*, tr. Karen Sandness, ed. Frank Gibney (Armonk, NY, 1997), though it is equally critical of Japan. Bradford A. Lee, *Britain and the Sino-Japanese War, 1937–1939* (Stanford, CA, 1973) stresses the interplay between Europe and Asia and British dependence on the United States in the Pacific. John W. Garver, *Chinese-Soviet Relations, 1937–1945* (New York, 1988) is a thoughtful, scholarly analytic study chiefly from the Chinese side.

Works, mainly with a European focus, dealing generally with the approach of the 1939 war include Richard Overy with Andrew Wheatcroft, *The Road to War* (London, 1999 edn), comparing military strength of a number of powers. Donald Cameron Watt, *Too Serious a Business: European Armed Forces and the Approach to the Second World War* (Berkeley, 1975) stresses British, French, and Italian military weakness. On the diplomacy of the era, the second volume of Gerhard L. Weinberg, *The Foreign Policy of Hitler's Germany*, cited above, is essential on all the powers. British policy has received much attention. R. A. C. Parker, *Chamberlain and Appeasement* (New York, 1993) is an important analysis, defending Chamberlain in some particulars but not in general. John Charmley, *Chamberlain and the Lost Peace* (London, 1989) is the chief defence of Chamberlain. Frank McDonough, *Neville Chamberlain, Appeasement, and the British Road to War* (New York, 1992) is very hostile. On France, A. Adamthwaite, *France and the Coming of the Second World War, 1936–9* (London, 1977) stresses timidity and lack of courage, whereas Robert J. Young, *France and the Origins of the Second World War* (London, 1996) argues for ambivalence in the face of difficult choices; both reject arguments about decadence and dependence.

Anita J. Prażmowska, *Eastern Europe and the Origins of the Second World War* (London, 2000) surveys country by country. Dov B. Lungu, *Romania and the Great Powers, 1933–1940* (Durham, NC, 1989) stresses Bucharest's determination to ditch Czechoslovakia and its Little Entente obligations. On Soviet policy, Geoffrey K. Roberts, *The Soviet Union and the Origins of the Second World War* (London, 1995) argues that Moscow preferred collective security but pursued a dual policy, keeping its options open. Jiri Hochman, *The Soviet Union and the Failure of Collective*

Security, 1934–1938 (Ithaca, NY, 1984) is an anti-Soviet study of Russian overtures to Germany and is the mirror image of Jonathan Haslam, *The Soviet Union and the Struggle for Collective Security in Europe, 1933–1939* (New York, 1984), which defends Soviet policy, Haslam's *The Soviet Union and the Threat from the East, 1933–41* (Pittsburgh, PA, 1992) is important and knowledgeable but difficult to read.

On the Munich crisis, J. W. Breughel, *Czechoslovakia before Munich: The German Minority Problem and British Appeasement Policy* (Cambridge, 1973) is a major work of scholarship. Telford Taylor, *Munich: The Price of Peace* (New York, 1980) is massive but selective. Igor Lukes, *Czechoslovakia between Stalin and Hitler* (Oxford, 1996) is erratic and sarcastic but contributes material from Czech archives. Igor Lukes and Erik Goldstein, eds, *The Munich Crisis, 1938* (London, 1999) is an uneven collection of essays on various countries, including China, the Dominions, and the League of Nations.

On the coming of the 1939 European war, Keith Eubank, *The Origins of World War II* (New York, 1989 edn) stresses Hitler's determination to have a war. Sidney Aster, *1939: The Making of the Second World War* (London, 1973) defends Chamberlain and agrees that Hitler wanted war. Donald Cameron Watt, *How War Came* (New York, 1989) is massive, meaty, and flavourful. Two useful collections of essays are Wolfgang J. Mommsen and Lothar Kettenacker, eds, *The Fascist Challenge and the Policy of Appeasement* (London, 1983) and John Hiden and Thomas Lane, eds, *The Baltic and the Outbreak of the Second World War* (New York, 1992), which includes Scandinavia, Finland, and Danzig. On the Nazi–Soviet alliance, Michael Jabara Carley, *1939: The Alliance that Never Was* (Chicago, 1999) is selective and defends Moscow, faulting Britain, France, and Poland. Geoffrey K. Roberts, *The Unholy Alliance* (Bloomington, IN, 1989) is more restrained and balanced, but speculative and moderately pro-Soviet.

The literature on the intelligence aspect of World War II is growing. Two entertaining, entry-level works by Ronald Lewin are *Ultra Goes to War* (New York, 1980) and *The American Magic* (New York, 1982). Stephen Budiansky, *Battle of Wits: The Complete Story of Codebreaking in World War II* (New York, 2000) is more recent and more scholarly, stressing the limitations of intelligence. David Kahn, *The Code-breakers* (New York, 1966 edn) is a full history of cryptology. Ernest R. May, ed., *Knowing One's Enemies: Intelligence Assessment before the Two World Wars* (Princeton, 1984) is valuable for more than intelligence, especially for 1937–41. Christopher Andrew and David Dilks, eds, *The Missing Dimension: Governments and Intelligence Communities in the Twentieth Century* (Urbana, IL, 194) is a solid collection covering the entire century. On Nazi intelligence efforts, Ladislas Farago, *The Game of the Foxes* (London, 1974 edn) is popular but archivally based, dealing with espionage in Britain and

America. David Kahn, *Hitler's Spies* (New York, 1978) is more serious, heavily researched, and thorough. Richard A. Woytak, *On the Border of War and Peace: Polish Intelligence and Diplomacy in 1937–1939 and the Origins of the Ultra Secret* (Boulder, CO, 1979) details the first stage of the Allied ULTRA effort. James E. Dillard and Walter T. Hitchcock, eds, *The Intelligence Revolution and Modern Warfare* (Chicago, 1996) contains useful essays about the efforts of all sides. Richard J. Aldrich, *Intelligence and the War Against Japan* (Cambridge, 2000) is especially useful on political aspects. Chief works on the British intelligence community include: Christopher Andrew's lively *Her Majesty's Secret Service* (New York, 1987), a sweeping survey which particularly dwells on 1914–45; Wesley Wark, *The Ultimate Enemy: British Intelligence and Nazi Germany, 1933–1939* (Ithaca, NY, 1985), useful especially for the influence of intelligence on Chamberlain's policy; and F. H. Hinsley *et al.*, *British Intelligence in the Second World War* (3 vols, London, 1979–88), which is really an exhaustive five volumes.

General histories of World War II include, R. A. C. Parker, *Struggle for Survival* (Oxford, 1990 edn), which discusses key episodes and aspects. John Keegan, *The Second World War* (New York, 1990) is an able military history dealing with Europe, 1940 on, and the Pacific, December 1941 on. Martha Byrd-Hoyle, *A World in Flames* (New York, 1970) is outdated but a serviceable brief outline. Peter Calvocoressi, Guy Wint, and John Pritchard, *Total War* (New York, 1989 edn) massively deals with both military and diplomatic aspects of the European and Pacific wars separately. Gerhard L. Weinberg's equally meaty *A World at Arms: A Global History of World War II* (Cambridge, 1994) is essential, the first work based on ULTRA and MAGIC, and very thought-provoking. See also his two collections of essays, *World in the Balance* (Hanover, NH, 1981) and *Germany, Hitler, and World War II* (Cambridge, 1995), which cut through the thicket.

Michael R. Marrus, *The Holocaust in History* (Hanover, NH, 1987) is an excellent starting point for exploration of literature on the Holocaust, dealing briefly with both key issues and historiography. On the geographic fringes of the European war in the early years, Max Jacobson, *The Diplomacy of the Winter War* (Cambridge, MA, 1961) is dated but still useful for its Finnish and Swedish sources. MacGregor Knox, *Mussolini Unleashed; 1939–1941* (Cambridge, 1981) is contemptuous of Mussolini, whereas his more recent *Hitler's Italian Allies* (Cambridge, 2000) stresses Italian military weakness and lack of German support. Norman J. W. Goda, *Tomorrow the World: Hitler, Northwest Africa, and the Path Toward America* (College Station, TX, 1998) is an excellent study of Hitler's global aims covering a previously slighted aspect of the war. Martin Kolinsky, *Britain's War in the Middle East* (London, 1999) argues that Britain gained its goals there by 1943 but that dependence on the United States prevented consolidation.

On Russo-German relations, Anthony Read and David Fisher, *The Deadly Embrace: Hitler, Stalin, and the Nazi-Soviet Pact, 1939–1941* (New York, 1988) is colourful, detailed, and rather popular. Gabriel Gorodetsky, *Grand Delusion: Stalin and the German Invasion of Russia* (New Haven, 1999) is much more scholarly, using Soviet files which have since closed. Barton Whaley, *Codeword BARBAROSSA* (Cambridge, MA, 1973), intended for the general reader, focuses on the German deception plan and the importance of strategic surprise. Bernd Wegner, ed., *From Peace to War: Germany, Soviet Russia, and the World, 1939–1941* (Providence, RI, 1997) contains some very good essays.

David Reynolds, *The Creation of the Anglo-American Alliance, 1937–41* (Chapel Hill, 1982) is heavily researched and very detailed. B. J. C. McKercher, *Transition of Power: Britain's Loss of Global Preeminence to the United States, 1930–1945* (Cambridge, 1998) presents streams of facts from the British point of view. Eleanor M. Gates, *The End of the Affair* (Berkeley, 1981) is admirably solid and intelligent, as is P. M. H. Bell, *A Certain Eventuality: Britain and the Fall of France* (London, 1974). Joel Blatt, ed., *The French Defeat of 1940: Reassessments* (Providence, RI, 1997) is an unusually good set of essays.

The literature on the road to Pearl Harbor is large, including the final three volumes of James William Morley, ed., *Japan's Road to the Pacific War*, cited above, offering essays by Japanese scholars, as do Dorothy Borg and Shumpei Okamoto, *Pearl Harbor as History: Japanese-American Relations, 1931–41* (New York, 1973) which apportions blame to both sides, and Hilary Conroy and Harry Wray, eds, *Pearl Harbor Re-examined* (Honolulu, 1990), with varied interpretations. David J. Lu, *From the Marco Polo Bridge to Pearl Harbor: Japan's Entry into World War II* (Washington, 1961) is also even-handed as it traces Japanese policy. Hilary Conroy and Harry Wray, eds, *Pearl Harbor Re-examined* (Honolulu, 1990) is another collection of essays by Japanese and American scholars with assorted interpretations.

Of works dwelling chiefly with American policy, Gordon W. Prange, *At Dawn We Slept* (New York, 1981) is a massive account with a historiographic discussion. Gordon W. Prange, Donald M. Goldstein, and Katherine V. Dillon, *Pearl Harbor: The Verdict of History* (New York, 1986) addresses not events but the question of responsibility, absolving FDR of guilt but not of error and stressing the total disbelief in danger. Peter Lowe, *Great Britain and the Origins of the Pacific War* (Oxford, 1977) is tedious but informative. Antony Best, *Britain, Japan and Pearl Harbor* (New York, 1995) is also tedious but worthwhile, arguing that the war was a clash between Japanese revisionism and the *status quo* powers. David Day, *The Great Betrayal: Britain, Australia, and the Onset of the Pacific War, 1939–1942* (New York, 1989) expresses Australian bitterness about British promises made in knowledge that they could not be fulfilled.

Jonathan Marshall, *To Have and Have Not: Southeast Asian Raw Materials and the Origins of the Pacific War* (Berkeley, 1995) offers an able non-Marxist analysis of the key economic factor for Britain, the United States, and Japan. Nicholas Tarling, *Britain, Southeast Asia, and the Onset of the Pacific War* (New York, 1996) is narrower and less economic but very detailed.

◆ The Second World War, 1942–1945

For the Allied alliance, Warren F. Kimball, *The Juggler: Franklin Roosevelt as Wartime Statesman* (Princeton, 1991) offers entertaining and penetrating essays on key aspects of FDR's wartime policies. Robert H. Ferrell, *The Dying President* (Columbia, MO, 1998) criticizes those policies and, unlike Kimball, considers health a factor from early 1944 on. John L. Gaddis, *The United States and the Origins of the Cold War* (New York, 1972) is a well-written account of Russo-American relations based on American archives. Randall Bennett Woods, *A Changing of the Guard: Anglo-American Relations, 1941–1946* (Chapel Hill, 1990) stresses economic and financial matters while criticizing American policy. Robert M. Hathaway, *Ambiguous Partnership: Britain and America, 1944–1947* (New York, 1981) is an intelligent and thoughtful analysis, especially on the British collapse in 1947. Warren F. Kimball, *Forged in War: Roosevelt, Churchill, and the Second World War* (New York, 1997) is essential, heavily researched, meaty, and thoughtful. Keith Sainsbury, *Churchill and Roosevelt at War* (New York, 1994) is chatty and organized by topics. David Reynolds, Warren F. Kimball, and A. O. Chubarian, *Allies at War: The Soviet, American, and British Experiences, 1939–45* (New York, 1994) is an outstanding tri-national collection, analysing strategy, economics, home front, and foreign policy in all three countries. Ann Lane and Howard Temperley, eds, *The Rise and Fall of the Grand Alliance, 1941–1945* (New York, 1996) also includes Russia but is particularly stimulating on the Anglo-American relationship. Steven M. Miner, *Between Churchill and Stalin: The Soviet Union, Great Britain, and the Origins of the Grand Alliance* (Chapel Hill, 1988) deals narrowly with Anglo-Soviet relations, 1940–41. David Carlton, *Churchill and the Soviet Union* (Manchester, 2000) studies Churchill's shifting views in the context of domestic politics. Vojtech Mastny, *Russia's Road to the Cold War: Diplomacy, Warfare, and the Politics of Communism, 1941–1945* (New York, 1979) will remain a classic exposition of the Russian point of view until the Soviet archives are fully available and explored. Richard Overy, *Russia's War* (London, 1998) explains the Soviet viewpoint for the general reader.

Works on specialized topics, chiefly European, include G. E. Maguire's able *Anglo-American Policy towards the Free French* (New York, 1995).

Mark Harrison, ed., *The Economics of World War II: Six Great Powers in International Comparison* (Cambridge, 1998) addresses the contribution of economies to the outcome and the long-term economic impact. Diane Shaver Clemens, *Yalta* (New York, 1970) has not been superseded by more recent work. Georg Schild, *Bretton Woods and Dumbarton Oaks* (New York, 1995) provides a brief clear introduction. Robert C. Hilderbrand, *Dumbarton Oaks* (Chapel Hill, 1990) is sensible, realistic, and clear. Townsend Hoopes and Douglas Brinkley, *FDR and the Creation of the UN* (New Haven, 1997) is competent, straightforward, and systematic. Arieh J. Kochavi, *Prelude to Nuremberg: Allied War Crimes Policy and the Question of Punishment* (Chapel Hill, 1998) deals primarily with Anglo-American policy toward Germany. Charles L. Mee, Jr, *Meeting at Potsdam* (New York, 1975), based on conference transcripts, remains the main work.

On Allied relations with other continents, Wm Roger Louis, *Imperialism at Bay* (Oxford, 1977) is a classic analysis of American anti-imperial pressure on Britain during the war. Aviel Roshwald, *Estranged Bedfellows: Britain and France in the Middle East during the Second World War* (Oxford, 1990) criticizes the actions of both states in Syria and Lebanon. Ritchie Ovendale, *Britain, the United States, and the End of the Palestine Mandate, 1941–1948* (London, 1989) traces American concern for the Jewish role and British concern for relations with Arab states. John Kent, *The Internationalization of Colonialism: Britain, France, and Black Africa, 1939–1956* (Oxford, 1992) focuses on London and Paris. A special issue of *The Journal of African History*, XXVI:4 (1985) covers the war in Africa, while Prosser Gifford and Wm Roger Louis, *The Transfer of Power in Africa, Decolonization 1940–1960* (New Haven, 1982) contains useful essays on the start of a long process. Maria Emilia Paz Salinas, *Strategy, Security, and Spies: Mexico and the US as Allies in World War II* (University Park, PA, 1997) is stronger on Mexican-American relations than on the German aspect. Stephen R. Niblo, *War, Diplomacy, and Development: The United States and Mexico, 1938–1954* (Wilmington, DE, 1995) argues that Mexico co-operated partly to gain aid for economic development.

John Costello, *The Pacific War* (London, 1981), is a lively detailed survey, primarily military but useful for reference. Christopher Thorne, *Allies of a Kind: The United States, Britain, and the War against Japan, 1941–1945* (London, 1978) massively analyses Anglo-American disagreements, dwelling primarily on China, the British Empire, Australia and New Zealand, and South-east Asia. Roger J. Bell, *Unequal Allies: Australian-American Relations and the Pacific War* (Carleton, Vic, 1977) and David Day, *Reluctant Nation: Australia and the Defeat of Japan, 1942–45* (New York, 1992) cover Australia's role.

Michael Schaller, *The US Crusade in China, 1938–1945* (New York, 1979) gives more attention to Chiang's problems than most authors but primarily dwells on how the United States locked itself into a policy which led to eventual failure. Hsi-sheng Ch'i, *Nationalist China at War: Military Defeats and Political Collapse* (Ann Arbor, MI, 1982) stresses KMT militarism and lack of social programme or popular support. Paul A. Varg, *The Closing of the Door, Sino-American Relations, 1936–1946* (East Lansing, MI, 1973) is balanced, restrained, and good on conditions in wartime China. Xiaoyuan Liu, *A Partnership for Disorder: China, the United States, and their Policies for the Postwar Disposition of the Japanese Empire, 1941–1945* (New York, 1996) covers a narrow topic intelligently.

Louise Young, *Japan's Total Empire: Manchuria and the Culture of Wartime Imperialism* (Berkeley, 1998) does an excellent job on another narrow subject. Edward J. Drea, *In the Service of the Emperor: Essays on the Imperial Japanese Army* (Lincoln, NE, 1998) is especially useful on Allied intelligence on the invasion of Kyushu and the need for the atomic bomb. Richard B. Frank, *Downfall: The End of the Imperial Japanese Empire* (New York, 1999) addresses the same questions from a military viewpoint. See also the several studies of Hirohito as well as works listed in the 1937–41 section. Robert James Maddox, *Weapons for Victory: The Hiroshima Decision Fifty Years Later* (Columbia, MO, 1995) is a well-researched defence of use of the atomic bomb. J. Samuel Walker, *Prompt and Utter Destruction: Truman and the Use of Atomic Bombs against Japan* (Chapel Hill, 1997) traces the historiographic debate and judges in terms of 1945.

On South-east Asia, Evelyn Colbert, *Southeast Asia in International Politics, 1941–1956* (Ithaca, NY, 1977) provides a handy outline of all states in the region, broadly interpreted. Nicholas Tarling, *Britain, Southeast Asia, and the Onset of the Cold War, 1945–50* (Cambridge, 1998) traces the key British role in the French return to Indochina and the Dutch return to Indonesia. The best work of several on the start of a long story in Indochina is David G. Marr's exhaustive *Vietnam 1945: The Quest for Power* (Berkeley, 1995).

◆ **The Aftermath**

For a recent bibliography of works on the post-1945 era, see P. M. H. Bell, *The World since 1945: An International History* (London, 2001).

INDEX